Tehillim

PSALMS / A NEW TRANSLATION WITH A COMMENTARY ANTHOLOGIZED FROM TALMUDIC, MIDRASHIC AND RABBINIC SOURCES.

Published by

Mesorah Publications, ltd

Volume II

ספר תהלים

Commentary and Overview by
Rabbi Avrohom Chaim Feuer

Translation by
Rabbi Avrohom Chaim Feuer
in collaboration with
Rabbis Nosson Scherman *and* Meir Zlotowitz

FIVE VOLUME
PERSONAL SIZE EDITION
First Impression . . . June 1996
Second Impression . . . March 1998
Third Impression . . . April 2002
Fourth Impression . . . November 2003
Fifth Impression . . . September 2005

Published and Distributed by
MESORAH PUBLICATIONS, Ltd.
4401 Second Avenue
Brooklyn, New York 11232

Distributed in Europe by
LEHMANNS
Unit E, Viking Business Park
Rolling Mill Road
Jarrow, Tyne & Wear NE32 3DP
England

Distributed in Israel by
SIFRIATI / A. GITLER — BOOKS
6 Hayarkon Street
Bnei Brak 51127

Distributed in Australia & New Zealand by
GOLDS WORLD OF JUDAICA
3-13 William Street
Balaclava, Melbourne 3183
Victoria Australia

Distributed in South Africa by
KOLLEL BOOKSHOP
Shop 8A Norwood Hypermarket
Norwood 2196, Johannesburg, South Africa

THE ARTSCROLL TANACH SERIES
TEHILLIM / PSALMS
PERSONAL SIZE EDITION VOL. II
© Copyright 1977, 1985, 1996 by MESORAH PUBLICATIONS, Ltd.
4401 Second Avenue / Brooklyn, N.Y. 11232 / (718) 921-9000 / www.artscroll.com

ISBN
PERSONAL SIZE — FIVE VOLUME SET 0-89906-383-7

Typography by CompuScribe at ArtScroll Studios, Ltd.
4401 Second Avenue / Brooklyn, N.Y. 11232 / (718) 921-9000

Printed in the United States of America by Noble Book Press
Bound by Sefercraft Quality Bookbinders, Ltd., Brooklyn, NY

This volume is dedicated to the glowing memory of our beloved grandparents

Max Schachter

מנחם מנדל בן אשר אנשל ז"ל   יג' חשון תשכ"ג

Sarah Schachter

שרה בת שמואל צבי ע"ה   ז' אדר תשל"ג

They came to America with an unyielding determination that their Yiddishkeit would remain strong, and that their new American generations would make their forebears proud.

Hardworking and uncompromisingly dedicated to family and Torah life, exuding warmth to their children and grandchildren, they echoed David HaMelech's resolve that

אֶתְהַלֵּךְ לִפְנֵי ה' בְּאַרְצוֹת הַחַיִּים,
"I shall walk before Hashem in the lands of the living" (116:9).

Such devotion and selflessness was the foundation of today's vibrant Torah life.

תנצב"ה

Joyce and Eric Austein
Debra and Elliot Tannenbaum
Judy and Martin Braun
Aliza and Shlomie Liechtung
Mindy and David Greenberg

❧

and Families

31 מזמור לא

David composed this psalm while he was fleeing from the wrath of
Saul (Radak), who pursued him relentlessly. Although the psalm
does not specify particular episodes, the commentators find in it allusions to various instances when David was in mortal danger at Saul's
hands.

Once while playing music to soothe Saul's troubled spirit, David
was the target of a spear hurled at him by the king. It missed him only
by a hair's-breadth (Sforno). The persecution forced David to flee
from Eretz Yisrael. The prophet Gad called upon him to return to the
Land (I Samuel 22:5). Then, a divine message sent David to the
town of Ke'ila to save its inhabitants from the invading Philistines.
The townspeople treacherously betrayed David to Saul and planned
to lock him inside their fortified walls to prevent his flight. Divinely
forewarned, David escaped this trap and hid in the Desert of Ziph.
Once again his whereabouts were betrayed to Saul (I Samuel, ch. 23)
this time by the inhabitants of this wilderness (Malbim).

David's most precarious plight was when he was trapped by Saul's
army while on the סֶלַע הַמַּחְלְקוֹת, the rock of division (ibid.) again
God intervened to save him.

In each of these episodes David sought aid and refuge in God
alone. In gratitude, he dedicated this psalm to God, his Savior.

א־ב לַמְנַצֵּחַ מִזְמוֹר לְדָוִד: בְּךָ־יהוה חָסִיתִי
אַל־אֵבוֹשָׁה לְעוֹלָם בְּצִדְקָתְךָ פַלְּטֵנִי:
ג הַטֵּה אֵלַי | אָזְנְךָ מְהֵרָה הַצִּילֵנִי הֱיֵה לִי |
לְצוּר־מָעוֹז לְבֵית מְצוּדוֹת לְהוֹשִׁיעֵנִי:
ד כִּי־סַלְעִי וּמְצוּדָתִי אָתָּה וּלְמַעַן שִׁמְךָ
ה תַּנְחֵנִי וּתְנַהֲלֵנִי: תּוֹצִיאֵנִי מֵרֶשֶׁת זוּ טָמְנוּ
ו לִי כִּי־אַתָּה מָעוּזִּי: בְּיָדְךָ אַפְקִיד רוּחִי

---

2. בְּךָ ה' חָסִיתִי — *In You, HASHEM, I took refuge.*

When I was trapped in Saul's palace where he attempted to slay me, I sought no avenue of escape other than Your salvation (Sforno) for I trusted in Your word (Targum), i.e., the assurances You gave me to see me safely to the royal throne.

Later, I was forced into exile. I could have assured my safety by indefinitely remaining in a foreign sanctuary. Yet, when You sent Gad the Prophet to call me back to the Holy Land, I disregarded my personal security and hastened to return, seeking refuge only in Your merciful protection (Malbim).

אַל אֵבוֹשָׁה לְעוֹלָם — *Let me not be shamed, ever.*

By virtue of the confidence I have in Your word, spare me from humiliation and disappointment (Radak).

בְּצִדְקָתְךָ פַלְּטֵנִי — *In Your righteousness provide me escape.*

The fact that I sought refuge only in You should make me worthy of Your salvation. But if I am still undeserving, then please let me be saved by virtue of Your righteousness (Metzudas David).

3. הַטֵּה אֵלַי אָזְנְךָ מְהֵרָה הַצִּילֵנִי — *Incline to me Your ear, quickly rescue me.*

I pray that You hear my plea without delay and respond swiftly to my call, for I ask no harm from my pursuers — only that I be rescued from their murderous threat (Alshich).

הֱיֵה לִי לְצוּר מָעוֹז — *Become for me a mighty rock.*

Reinforce my steadfast resolve to act properly in all my relations with Saul. Do not let anger or frustration overwhelm me lest I be aroused to slay him (Alshich, Eretz HaChaim).

לְבֵית מְצוּדוֹת לְהוֹשִׁיעֵנִי — *A fortress to save me.*

The expression בֵּית מְצוּדוֹת [lit. *house of fortresses*] is most unusual. Alshich perceives it as an allusion to David's two-fold dilemma. He was threatened *physically* if he did not kill Saul, for the jealous king was determined to kill him, and he was endangered *spiritually* if he killed Saul, God's anointed monarch. David asks for *fortresses* to protect him against both dangers.

[While hiding from Saul, David and his band lived in *fortresses*. It was in such a stronghold that Gad the Prophet found David (I Samuel 22:4-5). David hid in a stronghold once again when he fled from Ke'ilah to the wilderness of Ziph (ibid. 23:14,19).]

Chazah David interprets בֵּית מְצוּדוֹת figuratively as a reference to the two Holy Temples which were fortresses of faith for the Jewish people, and the source of their salvation.

4. כִּי סַלְעִי וּמְצוּדָתִי אָתָּה — *For my rock and my fortress are You.*

[Cf. 18:3 and *commentary* s.v. ה' סַלְעִי וּמְצוּדָתִי.]

Here David continues his plea of the

XXXI
1-6

For the Conductor, a song unto David.
² In You HASHEM, I took refuge,
  let me not be shamed, ever.
In Your righteousness provide me escape.
³ Incline to me Your ear; quickly rescue me,
  become for me a mighty rock,
  a fortress to save me.
⁴ For my rock and my fortress are You,
  for Your Name's sake guide me and lead me.
⁵ Remove me from this net they have hidden for me
  for You are my stronghold.
⁶ In Your hand do I entrust my spirit —

---

previous verse. His reference to God as
סַלְעִי, *my rock,* corresponds to צוּר מָעוֹז,
a mighty rock, in the previous verse.
מְצוּדָתִי, *my fortress,* corresponds to
בֵּית מְצוּדוֹת, *a fortress.* [Thus, he
proclaims that he seeks refuge and
protection only in God because he
recognizes Him as the Sole source of
salvation to the exclusion of all other
defenses.] *(Ibn Ezra).*

Alshich explains that there are two
types of defenses. A soldier warding off
a frontal assault may stand with his
back against a *rock* to protect him
against attack from behind. But the
fortress, because it provides walled
protection from all four sides, is
superior to the *rock.*

תַּנְחֵנִי וּתְנַהֲלֵנִי — *Guide me and lead me.*

[In *Exodus* 15:13 we read נָחִיתָ
בְחַסְדְּךָ ... נֵהַלְתָּ בְעָזְּךָ, *You guided with
Your kindness ... You led with Your
might. Malbim* (ibid.) explains that he
who *guides* does so with the full approval of his followers (נָחִיתָ is cognate

with נֹחַ or נַחַת, *pleasant). However, the
one who leads does so even with force.*

Here David asks God to *guide* him
gently, but, if necessary, he hopes that
God will lead him forcefully to the
proper destination.]

5. תּוֹצִיאֵנִי מֵרֶשֶׁת זוּ טָמְנוּ לִי — *Remove
me from this net they have hidden for
me.*

When David composed this psalm,
he was not yet ensnared in the traps
of his foes, but the wicked people of
Ziph gloated as if he had already fallen
into their hands. Now he requests that
these enemies be shown that he is far
removed from their control *(Radak).*

6. בְּיָדְךָ אַפְקִיד רוּחִי — *In Your hand do I
entrust my spirit.*

I am not frightened by the nets they
spread to capture me because I have
entrusted my life to You for safekeeping and You will undoubtedly redeem
me *(Radak).*[1]

---

1. Often it happens that an object which is entrusted to another person, is accidentally exchanged for a different one. But with the Holy One, Blessed be He, this never happens. Does it
ever occur that upon rising in the morning one finds that God has exchanged his soul with
someone else's?

Rabbi Alexandri said: A man of flesh and blood is entrusted with a new article and he
returns it later worn and tattered. But the Holy One, Blessed be He, is not so. The laborer toils

ז פָּדִיתָה אוֹתִי יהוה אֵל אֱמֶת: שָׂנֵאתִי
הַשֹּׁמְרִים הַבְלֵי־שָׁוְא וַאֲנִי אֶל־יהוה
ח בָּטָחְתִּי: אָגִילָה וְאֶשְׂמְחָה בְּחַסְדֶּךָ אֲשֶׁר
ט רָאִיתָ אֶת־עָנְיִי יָדַעְתָּ בְּצָרוֹת נַפְשִׁי: וְלֹא
הִסְגַּרְתַּנִי בְּיַד־אוֹיֵב הֶעֱמַדְתָּ בַמֶּרְחָב
י רַגְלָי: חָנֵּנִי יהוה כִּי צַר לִי עָשְׁשָׁה בְכַעַס

פָּדִיתָה אוֹתִי ה' אֵל אֱמֶת — *You redeemed
me, HASHEM — O God of truth.*

Since the Psalmist spoke of entrusting his spirit to God, he now elaborates that He is אֱמֶת, a true and reliable guardian (*Ibn Ezra*).

Every night when we go to sleep we entrust our souls to God. Although our debt to God is great, He does not hold back the soul as payment. He is אֱמֶת, *true,* to His role as guardian of souls, and returns them in the morning (*Zohar; Ketzos HaChoshen* 4:1).

David is confident that God will redeem him from his enemies in order to be true to His promise that David would become king (*Radak, Sforno*). [See commentary of *Harav Yitzchak Zev Soloveitchik of Brisk* to *Haftorah of Chayei Sarah.*]

7. שָׂנֵאתִי הַשֹּׁמְרִים הַבְלֵי שָׁוְא — *I despise those who anticipate worthless vanities.*

I.e., those who turn to worthless idols for salvation (*Rashi*), or, those who depend on astrology or divination to determine the most propitious time for going to war.

David said: When I fled from Saul my life was in constant uncertainty. Yet, never did I turn to the seers and astrologers to clarify the future and allay my doubts. Rather, I spurned these vain and worthless soothsayers and blindly placed my faith in God, with no concern for the future (*Radak*).

[In this respect David's conduct excelled Saul's. When confronted by the Philistine army, Saul was so distraught that, in desperation, he sought out the witch of Ein Dor to communicate with the spirit of Samuel, in order to discover the future.]

The translation of הַשֹּׁמְרִים, *those who anticipate,* is based on *Rashi,* who departs from the common meaning of *watchmen. Rashi* derives this translation from וְאָבִיו שָׁמַר אֶת הַדָּבָר, *and his father* [Jacob] *anticipated the matter* [i.e., the fulfillment of Joseph's dreams] (*Genesis* 37:11).

וַאֲנִי אֶל ה' בָּטָחְתִּי — *As for me — in HASHEM do I trust!*

Midrash Shocher Tov and *Shemos Rabbah* 7:4 interpret his homiletically as the cry of the Garden of Eden which proclaims: Send me no wicked men, for *I despise those who anticipate worthless vanities.* Let the wicked descend to Gehinnom where they will be welcomed! *As for me* — I welcome only

all day and at night he falls asleep and deposits his worn and weary soul with his Maker. In the morning his soul is returned to his body refreshed as if newly created as it says, *They are renewed every morning, great is Your faithfulness* (Lamentations 3:23). Rabbi Shimon said in the name of Rabbi Semon: From the phenomenon of our renewal every morning we learn to have faith in Your future redemption [and renewal] of Israel (*Midrash Shocher Tov*).

Based on this *Midrash,* the *Talmud* (*Berachos* 5a) states: Although a Torah scholar need not recite the *Shema* at bedtime [to protect him from evil thoughts and spirits, for he is protected by the Torah thought which occupy his mind], nevertheless he should at least recite the verse: *In Your hand do I entrust my spirit, You redeemed me, HASHEM, O God of truth.*

> *You redeemed me HASHEM, O God of truth.*
> ⁷ *I despise those who anticipate worthless vanities.*
>   *As for me — in HASHEM do I trust!*
> ⁸ *I will exult and be glad at Your kindness,*
>   *in noting my affliction,*
>   *You know the troubles of my soul,*
> ⁹ *And delivered me not to the grip of the foe,*
>   *but stood my feet expansively.*
> ¹⁰ *Favor me HASHEM, for I am distressed,*
>   *dimmed in anger are my eyes, my soul*

the righteous men who declare — *in HASHEM do I trust!*.

8. אָגִילָה וְאֶשְׂמְחָה בְּחַסְדֶּךָ — *I will exult and be glad at Your kindness.*

Hirsch explains that גִּיל, *exultation*, is the vocal expression of joy. It is a far more intensive emotion that שִׂמְחָה, *gladness*, which is related to צְמִיחָה, *growth*, and connotes serenity, a feeling of continued inner maturity and blossoming. Usually a person is first overwhelmed by a wave of גִּיל, *exultation*, and later he settles down to a constant, quiet gladness [שִׂמְחָה]. [See commentary to 14:7.]

אֲשֶׁר רָאִיתָ אֶת עָנְיִי — *In noting* [lit. *that you noted*] *my affliction.*

You ordained my suffering for You determined it to be in my best interest. I accept Your concern for my welfare as a kindness over which *I will exult and be glad* (Kiflayim L'tushiah).

יָדַעְתָּ בְּצָרוֹת נַפְשִׁי — *You know the troubles of my soul.*

[You realize that my soul is plagued with sin and so You seek to cure me with the therapy of *affliction*.]

And despite the shortcomings of my troubled soul You still do not abandon me to my foes (Tzafnas Paneach).

9. וְלֹא הִסְגַּרְתַּנִי בְּיַד אוֹיֵב — *And* [You] *delivered me not to the grip of the foe.*

This is the translation according to

Rashi, Radak, and Metzudos. This refers to the people of Ziph, who betrayed David and revealed his whereabouts to Saul (Radak). However, Menachem renders *You have not closed me up* [an allusion to the incident at Ke'ila when he was locked in the fortified city].

הֶעֱמַדְתָּ בַמֶּרְחָב רַגְלָי — [But] *stood my feet expansively.*

Not only have You released me from confinement, You have even widened my stride. I enjoyed complete freedom of movement and I traveled wherever my heart desired (Ibn Ezra).

10. חָנֵּנִי ה' כִּי צַר לִי — *Favor me HASHEM, for I am distressed.*

But the freedom and mobility of the previous verse are now a thing of the past. Once again my enemies dog my footsteps and threaten to incarcerate me. Moreover, I am stricken with a debilitating disease (Ibn Ezra).

עָשְׁשָׁה בְכַעַס עֵינִי — *Dimmed in anger are my eyes.*

[Cf. 6:8, עָשְׁשָׁה מִכַּעַס עֵינִי.]

Radak translates עָשְׁשָׁה, *consumed with rot and decay.*

Metzudas Zion notes that the usage of עָשְׁשָׁה as *consumed* is derived from the noun עָשׁ which is the name of a worm which eats garments as in הֵן כֻּלָּם, כַּבֶּגֶד יִבְלוּ עָשׁ יֹאכְלֵם, *They will all be*

יא עֵינַי נַפְשִׁי וּבִטְנִי: כִּי כָלוּ בְיָגוֹן חַיַּי
וּשְׁנוֹתַי בַּאֲנָחָה כָּשַׁל בַּעֲוֹנִי כֹחִי וַעֲצָמַי
יב עָשֵׁשׁוּ: מִכָּל־צֹרְרַי הָיִיתִי חֶרְפָּה וְלִשְׁכֵנַי
מְאֹד וּפַחַד לִמְיֻדָּעָי רֹאַי בַּחוּץ נָדְדוּ
יג מִמֶּנִּי: נִשְׁכַּחְתִּי כְּמֵת מִלֵּב הָיִיתִי כִּכְלִי
יד אֹבֵד: כִּי שָׁמַעְתִּי דִבַּת רַבִּים מָגוֹר

worn out like a garment, a worm will consume them (Isaiah 50:9).

נַפְשִׁי וּבִטְנִי — My soul and my belly.

Radak explains that נֶפֶשׁ here refers to the 'spirit of desire' in man which yearns to eat and drink. Many times while fleeing Saul, David had nothing to eat or drink. The threat of starvation was so great that Achimelech of Nob was compelled to give David the sacred לֶחֶם הַפָּנִים, show-bread, in order to save David's life (I Samuel 21:7). In those difficult times not only were his eyes consumed with rot [i.e. pain], but also his soul and his belly were overcome by hunger and thirst.

11. כִּי כָלוּ בְיָגוֹן חַיַּי — For my life is spent with grief.

From the moment that I killed Goliath and the women came out to sing: Saul has slain his thousands and David his tens of thousands (I Samuel 18:7), Saul's jealousy was kindled and my life became an endless succession of agony and grief (Radak).

וּשְׁנוֹתַי בַּאֲנָחָה — And my years with sighing.

The sighs which I utter because of Saul's persecution rob my body of its vitality; as the Talmud (Berachos 58b) states: A sigh breaks half of the body (Radak).

כָּשַׁל בַּעֲוֹנִי כֹחִי — Because of my iniquity my strength has failed.

I deserve these afflictions to atone for

my sins, otherwise God would not have allowed them to befall me (Radak).

Rabbi Tanchuma bar Chiya said that four things rob a person of his strength: sin, travel, fasting, and exile. Sin, as it says: Because of my iniquity my strength has failed (Midrash Shocher Tov).

12. הָיִיתִי חֶרְפָּה — I became an insult.

[If a person wished to insult another he would call him 'David'.]

וְלִשְׁכֵנַי מְאֹד — And to my neighbors exceedingly.

My neighbors, more than anyone else, witness the humiliation and insults that I suffer at the hands of my tormentors (Ibn Ezra).

According to Radak, David's humiliation is at the hands of his neighbors, i.e. his fellow Jews, for it is they who revile and insult him.

וּפַחַד לִמְיֻדָּעָי — A fright to those who know me.

[A close friend is a מוֹדָע; as in וּמֹדָע לַבִּינָה תִקְרָא, and call understanding a close friend (Proverbs 7:4).]

רֹאַי בַּחוּץ נָדְדוּ מִמֶּנִּי — Those who see me outside flee [lit. wander] from me.

They run away from me as from the plague (Metzudas David).

According to Radak, this phrase refers to David's dear friends who are pained by his plight. נָדְדוּ means they shake and tremble, as they commiserate with the effect that this terrible situation has upon him.

and my belly.

¹¹ *For my life is spent with grief*
and my years with sighing,
Because of my iniquity my strength has failed
and my bones are consumed.

¹² *From all my tormentors have I become an insult,*
and to my neighbors exceedingly;
A fright to those who know me,
those who see me outside flee from me.

¹³ *I became as forgotten as the dead from the heart,*
I became like a lost vessel.

¹⁴ *For I have heard the connivance of the multitude,*

---

13. נִשְׁכַּחְתִּי כְּמֵת מִלֵּב — *I became as forgotten as the dead from the heart.*

My acquaintances are so afraid for me (v. 12) that they have given up hope that I will survive Saul's persecution, just as no one hopes that the dead will come back to life (Radak).

According to *Ibn Ezra* it is God who has forgotten and abandoned David.[1]

כִּכְלִי אֹבֵד — *Like a lost vessel.*

[The Psalmist likens the body to a coarse vessel of flesh and blood which houses a precious, noble spirit. As long as it protects its contents, the receptacle is important, but if the soul is corrupted, the body loses its significance. It perishes and is immediately forgotten like a useless vessel.]

Rashi notes that whenever the Scriptures refer to a lost article, they never refer to the owner as having lost his property, but in terms of the object which *becomes* lost from its owner.

Thus we find: *So you shall do with every lost thing of your brother's which gets lost from him* (Deuteronomy 22:1).

[Similarly, God never abandons any of His human creations; it is they themselves who become lost from God as we read (Psalms 1:6): וְדֶרֶךְ רְשָׁעִים תֹּאבֵד, *And the way of the wicked goes lost.*]

14. דִּבַּת רַבִּים — *The connivance of the multitude.*

The translation follows *Rashi* who renders the word דִּבַּת as *advice*, i.e., the results of a council to discuss plans to deal with a problem.

Metzudas Zion, however, renders דִּבָּה as an *evil report*, by which a person slanders his foe as in וַיָּבֵא יוֹסֵף אֶת דִּבָּתָם רָעָה אֶל אֲבִיהֶם, *and Joseph brought their evil report to their father* (Genesis 37:2).

Radak combines both versions: This

---

1. The *Talmud* (*Berachos* 58b) observes:
Rav said: The deceased are forgotten only after twelve months have elapsed from the date of death; as it says. *I became forgotten as the dead from the heart, I became like a lost vessel.* [An owner usually gives up hope and forgets about his lost vessel after twelve months; as it is taught (*Bava Metzia* 28a): Whoever finds a lost vessel or any other article must announce this publicly during the course of three festivals which cover a period of an entire year. Afterwards, he can terminate his efforts, for the owner is assumed to have given up hope of recovering his property, thereby relinquishing his ownership (*Rashi*).]

מִסָּבִיב בְּהִוָּסְדָם יַחַד עָלַי לָקַחַת נַפְשִׁי

זָמָמוּ: וַאֲנִי | עָלֶיךָ בָטַחְתִּי יהוה אָמַרְתִּי   טו

אֱלֹהַי אָתָּה: בְּיָדְךָ עִתֹּתָי הַצִּילֵנִי מִיַּד־   טז

אוֹיְבַי וּמֵרֹדְפָי: הָאִירָה פָנֶיךָ עַל־עַבְדֶּךָ   יז

הוֹשִׁיעֵנִי בְחַסְדֶּךָ: יהוה אַל־אֵבוֹשָׁה כִּי   יח

קְרָאתִיךָ יֵבֹשׁוּ רְשָׁעִים יִדְּמוּ לִשְׁאוֹל:

refers to David's enemies who first held counsel together to plot against David and then slandered David before Saul with false reports of alleged evil.

מִסָּבִיב — *Terror all around.*

The danger does not appear from one direction, it rises against me from all sides (*Radak*).

בְּהִוָּסְדָם יַחַד עָלַי — *When they consult together against me.*

Consultation is likened to the יְסוֹד, foundation, of a building because all future action is based on the original plan (*Metzudas Zion*).

15. וַאֲנִי עָלֶיךָ בָטַחְתִּי ה' — *But as for me — in You have I trusted, HASHEM.*

Although my enemies taunt me and say that You have forgotten me, my trust in You remains steadfast and I say, 'You are my God' (*Ibn Ezra*).

Only You have control over my destiny (*Radak*).

16. בְּיָדְךָ עִתֹּתָי — *In Your control [lit. hand] are my times.*

The different periods of danger which I have undergone were all pre-ordained by Your order and decree (*Rashi*).

All of the *times*, i.e., occasions, when my enemies seek to harm me are in Your hands and under Your control, and so I ask You to deliver me (*Radak*).

Ibn Ezra notes that David makes this statement in defiance of those who heed the advice of the vain and worthless astrologers (*v.* 7) who consult their

horoscopes to find a propitious time to harm him. 'As for me,' David declares, 'all of my times are in God's hands and, so, whatever time He chooses for my salvation is acceptable to me.'

Gevul Binyomin calls our attention to the *Midrash* (*Va'eschanan* 2:10) which says that different types of prayer are answered at different times. Some prayers are answered only after forty days, some after twenty, some after three, some after a full day, some after half a day. Some prayers are answered even before a person utters them.

Therefore, David says to God: You know the acceptable time for my prayer, but I do not. Therefore, I rely upon You to answer it at whatever time You deem to be the most favorable time.

הַצִּילֵנִי מִיַּד אוֹיְבַי וּמֵרֹדְפָי — *Rescue me from the control [lit. hand] of my foes and my pursuers.*

The *Vilna Gaon* says that the word מִיַּד is superfluous, as it would suffice to say מֵאוֹיְבַי, *from my foes.* The extra word יַד alludes to David whose name [דָוִד] has the numerical value of יַד, fourteen. David is symbolized by the moon which becomes full after fourteen days. Furthermore, there were fourteen generations from Abraham until David, who culminated the ascent to greatness which was begun by Abraham. Thus, David represented climax and perfection, like the full moon. After David there were fourteen generations of descent until King Zidkiyahu in whose time the Temple was destroyed, similar

XXXI
15-18

> *terror all round,*
> *When they consult together against me,*
> *   to take my life have they plotted.*
> ¹⁵ *But as for me — in You have I trusted, HASHEM.*
> *   I said, 'You are my God.'*
> ¹⁶ *In Your control are my times,*
> *   rescue me from the control of my foes*
> *   and my pursuers.*
> ¹⁷ *Shine Your face upon Your servant,*
> *   save me in Your kindness.*
> ¹⁸ *O HASHEM, let me not be shamed*
> *   after having called upon You!*
> *Let the wicked ones be shamed —*
> *   be silenced in the nether world.*

to the waning moon which vanishes after fourteen days.

The twenty-eight periods of life enumerated in *Koheles* (3:2-8) contain fourteen positive, ascendant times and fourteen negative, descendent times, corresponding to the waxing and waning of the moon. David's life too, consisted of fourteen periods of salvation and goodness, and fourteen periods of bleakness and agony. This verse contains exactly twenty-eight letters corresponding to the twenty-eight time periods (*Tehilla L'David*). [Cf. *Rabbeinu Bachya* to Genesis 38:30 quoted in *Overview,* part VIII].

17. הָאִירָה פָנֶיךָ עַל עַבְדֶּךָ — *Shine Your face upon Your servant.*

Danger and fear shroud me in gloom. Save me and light up my life *(Ibn Ezra).*

Show me Your favor by accepting my petition out of kindness, even if I am unworthy of Your grace *(Sforno).*

18. ה' אַל אֵבוֹשָׁה כִּי קְרָאתִיךָ — *O HASHEM, let me not be shamed after having called upon You.*

Tehillos Hashem cites the *Talmud* (*Bava Kama* 93a) which states that he

who is מוֹסֵר דִּין, *invokes heavenly judgment,* against his fellow is himself punished first, as in the case of Sarah who invoked heavenly judgment upon Abraham and, as a result, predeceased him. For it was taught: punishment is meted out first to the one who cries, and is more severe than for the one against whom justice is invoked.

Rashi (*Rosh Hashanah* 16b) explains that the Heavenly Court, on being invoked, declares: Let us consider whether this appellant is worthy that his neighbor be punished on his account.

David, who now invokes heavenly judgment, anticipates the negative reaction which his charges may elicit. Therefore he begs that he not be shamed by his own invocation because he demands Justice sincerely, for the sake of God, and not for his own honor, as he cries out in the next verse, *Let them be silenced — those lying lips, those which speak malicious falsehood of the righteous.*

יִדְּמוּ לִשְׁאוֹל — *[Let them] be silenced in the nether world.*

This translation follows *Rashi.*

יט תֵּאָלַמְנָה שִׂפְתֵי שָׁקֶר הַדֹּבְרוֹת עַל־צַדִּיק

כ עָתָק בְּגַאֲוָה וָבוּז: מָה רַב־טוּבְךָ אֲשֶׁר־
צָפַנְתָּ לִּירֵאֶיךָ פָּעַלְתָּ לַחֹסִים בָּךְ נֶגֶד

כא בְּנֵי אָדָם: תַּסְתִּירֵם | בְּסֵתֶר פָּנֶיךָ מֵרֻכְסֵי

כב אִישׁ תִּצְפְּנֵם בְּסֻכָּה מֵרִיב לְשֹׁנוֹת: בָּרוּךְ

However, *Radak* and *Metzudos* render
יֵרָמוּ, *Let them be cut off,* based on Jeremiah 51:16.

19. תֵּאָלַמְנָה שִׂפְתֵי שָׁקֶר — *Let them be
silenced — those lying lips.*

David said: *I have heard the connivance of the multitude* (v. 14), now I
ask that their treacherous words be
silenced (*Ibn Ezra*).

Radak explains that David was especially eager to silence the liars who accused him to Saul of boasting that he
had already become king.

הַדֹּבְרוֹת עַל צַדִּיק עָתָק — *Those which
speak malicious falsehood of the
righteous.*

These villains attempt to convince
Saul that the truly righteous David
seeks to harm him (*Rashi*).

The evil also speak against God who
is צַדִּיקוֹ שֶׁל עוֹלָם, *the Righteous Ruler of
the Universe* (*Yerushalmi, Chagigah*
2:1).

עָתָק — *Malicious falsehood.*

This translation follows *Rashi* who
renders עָתָק as something which is not
there, based on *Genesis* 12:8, וַיַּעְתֵּק
מִשָּׁם, *and he moved away from there.*

Dunash (quoted by *Rashi*) and *Radak*
translate עָתָק, *strong,* as in *Psalms* 94:4,
יְדַבְּרוּ עָתָק, *they speak strong words*
[against the righteous].

20. מָה רַב טוּבְךָ — *How abundant is
Your goodness.*

The abundance which God will
bestow upon the righteous is beyond
the power of mortal man to describe.
The Psalmist can but exclaim: *How
abundant!*

Rambam emphasizes that in this
finite, material world we cannot conceive of the infinite spiritual rewards
stored in the Hereafter. Just as the blind
man has no conception of colors nor the
deaf man an idea of sound, similarly,
our limited senses have no way of sens-
ing this spiritual bliss as long as we are
enclosed in the body which restricts our
soul. [Therefore, the Torah never
makes promises of spiritual rewards for
obeying its commands, for they are in-
describable] (*Commentary to Mishnah,
Sanhedrin* 11:1).

אֲשֶׁר צָפַנְתָּ — *Which you have treasured.*

[The verb צָפַן usually refers to a
spiritual treasure which is hidden away;
as in בְּלִבִּי צָפַנְתִּי אִמְרָתֶךָ *In my heart I
treasured Your sayings* (Psalms 19:11).
The customary word for the concealment of a material object is טָמַן: as in
וַיִּטְמְנֵהוּ בַּחוֹל, *and he hid him* (i.e., the
dead body of the Egyptian taskmaster)
in the sand (Exodus 2:12).]

This refers to the rewards stored
away for the righteous in the World to
Come. The wicked, who speak against
them with falsehood and contempt,
have no idea of the wonderful treasures
that await the righteous (*Radak*).[1]

---

1. *Chovos Halevovos* (*Shaar Habitachon* 4) writes:
There are two kinds of good deeds. Some, like the duties of the heart, are concealed; they
are known only to the Creator. Other good deeds entail physical action and are, therefore, apparent to all. For the fulfillment of external duties, the Creator bestows a reward which is visi-

19 Let them be silenced —
          those lying lips,
     Those which speak malicious falsehood of the
          righteous,
          with arrogance and contempt.
20 How abundant is Your goodness
          which You have treasured for Your reverent ones,
     That You performed for those who seek refuge in You,
          in the presence of men.
21 Protect them — when Your Presence is concealed
          — from bands of wicked men.
     Treasure them in an abode
          from the quarreling of tongues.

פָּעַלְתָּ לַחוֹסִים בָּךְ נֶגֶד בְּנֵי אָדָם — That You
performed for those who seek refuge in
You, in the presence of men.

In addition to the spiritual treasures
reserved for the future, You have often
greatly rewarded the righteous in This
World, not secretly, but openly, for all
to see (Radak).

Tosefos Yom Tov lays down this
principle: For performance of מִצְוֹת בֵּין
אָדָם לַמָּקוֹם, Mitzvos between man and
God, one receives no compensation in
This World, only in the Hereafter. But
for מִצְוֹת בֵּין אָדָם לַחֲבֵירוֹ, Mitzvos
between man and his fellow man, a
person is rewarded in This World as
well [see Rambam, Mishna Peah 1:1.]
Thus David says: For those who fear
You [i.e. who observe the commandments relating directly to You] Your
abundant treasure is reserved for the
future. But if we see God executing
great miracles in This World, for people
who seek refuge in Him it is surely by
virtue of the deeds they perform נֶגֶד

בְּנֵי אָדָם, towards their fellow man
(Shaarei Chaim).

21. תַּסְתִּירֵם בְּסֵתֶר פָּנֶיךָ — Protect them
— when Your Presence is concealed.

I know that abundant good is
treasured for the reverent ones in the
World to Come, but I ask You to
provide them with security even in This
World where Your Presence is concealed and the wicked surround the
righteous from all sides (Rashi).

מֵרֻכְסֵי אִישׁ — From bands of [wicked]
men.

Save the devout from the conspiracies of the wicked who join
together to harm them (Rashi).

[Cf. Exodus 28:28, וְיִרְכְּסוּ, and they
will join together. Rashi (ad loc.) cites
our verse to corroborate his translation.]

תִּצְפְּנֵם בְּסֻכָּה — Treasure them in an
abode [lit. booth]

Alshich notes that a סֻכָּה is a flimsy,
temporary shelter. Thus, when God

ble in This World, but for the fulfillment of internal duties, God gives recompense in the
World to Come.
    David refers to concealed rewards in the verse, How abundant is Your goodness which You
have treasured for Your reverent ones.

יְהֹוה כִּי הִפְלִיא חַסְדּוֹ לִי בְּעִיר מָצוֹר:

כג וַאֲנִי | אָמַרְתִּי בְחָפְזִי נִגְרַזְתִּי מִנֶּגֶד עֵינֶיךָ
אָכֵן שָׁמַעְתָּ קוֹל תַּחֲנוּנַי בְּשַׁוְּעִי אֵלֶיךָ:

כד אֶהֱבוּ אֶת־יְהֹוה כָּל־חֲסִידָיו אֱמוּנִים נֹצֵר

---

wishes to protect someone, even the
flimsiest of shelters is adequate to the
task.[1]

מֵרִיב לְשֹׁנוֹת — *From the quarreling of*
tongues.

[There was no reason for two
righteous men such as David and Saul
to quarrel. It was only the slanderous
tongues of quarrelsome men who fan-
ned the flames of dissension.]

The *Vilna Gaon* observes that 'each
letter of the word סֻכָּה involves one of
the four main areas of verbal pronunciation. ס, *Samech*, represents the hiss-
ing sounds controlled by the teeth. ו,
Vav, represents the sounds formed by
the lips. כ, *Kaf*, is sounded by the
tongue and the upper palate. ה, *Hey*, is a
guttural sound emanating from the
throat. All of these vocal passageways
control and modify the articulation of
the tongue. Therefore, the Sages say
that the *mitzvah* of סֻכָּה, *Tabernacles*, is
a powerful agent in controlling the inclination to speak evil. This idea is alluded to here: You HASHEM treasure
the tongue, in the letters of the סֻכָּה,
succah, in order to control the quarreling of tongues.

22. בָּרוּךְ ה' כִּי הִפְלִיא חַסְדּוֹ לִי — *Blessed*
be HASHEM, for He has been
wondrously kind to me.

David thanks God for the wondrous
kindness shown him when he was
trapped inside the walls of Ke'ila
(*Rashi*).

When he and his men were locked in
Ke'ila, David asked two questions of
God through the אוּרִים וְתֻמִּים, the
breastplate of the High priest, 'Will the
people of Ke'ila betray me to him? Will
Saul come [to attack me]?' (*I Samuel*
23:11).

The *Yerushalmi* (*Yoma 7:3*) says that
ordinarily only one question at a time
may be asked of the *Urim v'Tumim*. If
two inquiries are made, together, some
hold that one will be answered while
others say neither will be answered.
However, concludes the *Yerushalmi*,
both questions posed by David were
answered because he pleaded for extraordinary divine kindness, as it says
'HASHEM, my God please inform Your
servant' [*I Samuel 23:11*] (*Divrei Shlo-*
mo).]

בְּעִיר מָצוֹר — *In the city besieged.*

This refers to Ke'ila of which Saul
said, *God has delivered him into my*
hand for he is shut in, by entering a city
that has gates and bars [*I Samuel 23:7*]
(*Rashi*).

23. וַאֲנִי אָמַרְתִּי בְחָפְזִי — *But I said in my*
panic.

---

1. The *Midrash* relates that God once saved David's life with the most fragile of shelters. It
happened that David asked God, 'Of what value is the spider? It spins and weaves its web all
year, yet it never wears the fruit of its loom?'
  Said the Holy One, Blessed be He, 'By your life, the day will come when you yourself will
need the services of a cobweb!'
  When David and his men hid in a cave while fleeing from Saul and his armies [as a result of
a רִיב לְשֹׁנוֹת, *quarreling of tongues*] God summoned a spider to quickly weave a web over the
mouth of the cave. Saul saw the web and said to himself: 'Certainly David cannot be here for
he would have broken the fragile web upon entering.' Thus, God demonstrated to David that
no part of creation is superfluous, for David's own life had been saved by the insect he reviled.

22 *Blessed be HASHEM, for He has been*
wondrously kind to me in the city besieged.
23 *But I said in my panic, 'I am cut off from Your sight!'*
But in truth, You heard the sound of my pleas
when I cried to You.
24 *Love HASHEM, all His devout ones!*
The truthful, HASHEM safeguards!

This verse refers to the time when David was on the mountain, surrounded on all sides by Saul's men. Scripture says of that incident: וַיְהִי דָוִד נֶחְפָּז לָלֶכֶת מִפְּנֵי שָׁאוּל, *And David was hurrying to depart because of Saul* [I Samuel 23:26] (*Metzudas David*).

[See *Midrash Shocher Tov* partially quoted in footnote to *Psalms* 18:3. When Saul had him surrounded, David's plight was so hopeless that he cried out: 'It was for naught that Samuel anointed me to be king! How will his promise be fulfilled now?'

Where do we find an allusion to this statement? From the verse אֲנִי אָמַרְתִּי בְחָפְזִי כָּל הָאָדָם כֹּזֵב, *I said in my haste, 'All men are deceitful'* [Psalms 116:11].]

נִגְרַזְתִּי — *I am cut off.*

Dunash traces the root of this word to גרז which contains the same letters as גָזַר, *to cut*. Thus, the axe or hatchet which cuts down the tree is called a גַּרְזֶן. However, *Menachem* relates this word

to נְגְרַשְׁתִּי, *I am chased,* and claims that its form is unique and is not found elsewhere in Scripture (*Rashi*).

אָכֵן שָׁמַעְתָּ קוֹל תַּחֲנוּנַי בְּשַׁוְּעִי אֵלֶיךָ — *But in truth You heard the sound of my pleas when I cried to You.*

[The doubt which I cast upon Samuel's prophecy was the result of panic and confusion. In truth, O God, You heard my pleas and saved me through a messenger angel (I Samuel 23:27). See footnote to *Psalms* 18:24.]

24. אֶהֱבוּ אֶת ה' כָּל חֲסִידָיו — *Love HASHEM, all His devout ones.*

With these words the Psalmist is issuing a command (*Ibn Ezra*).

David says: when you witness all the wonders which God performed for me, it becomes incumbent upon you to intensify your love for God (*Radak*).[1]

אֱמוּנִים נֹצֵר ה' — *The truthful, HASHEM safeguards.*

[See *commentary* to *Psalms* 12:2

---

1. *Rabbi Akiva Eiger* observed:

In the portion of *Shema* (Deuteronomy 6:4) the Torah commands: וְאָהַבְתָּ אֵת ה' אֱלֹהֶיךָ, *And you shall love HASHEM, your God*. This precept is difficult to comprehend because love is an emotional response which cannot be forced by a command.

We must understand this commandment in a different light. When a person realizes that he is the object of another person's affection and concern, it is only natural and instinctive that this will evoke from his heart a reciprocal feeling of tenderness and love. Thus, we are obligated to discover the countless ways whereby God demonstrates His boundless love for us, for this will strike a responsive chord in our hearts which, in turn, will be filled naturally with adoration for God.

For this reason, the benediction immediately preceding the recital of *Shema* begins with a recounting of God's concern for us '...אַהֲבָה רַבָּה אֲהַבְתָּנוּ ה' אֱלֹהֵינוּ, *With abounding love have You loved us, HASHEM, our God ...*' This awareness prepares us to accept the exhortation *And you shall love HASHEM, your God*.

כה   יְהוָה וּמְשַׁלֵּם עַל־יֶתֶר עֹשֵׂה גַאֲוָה: חִזְקוּ
וְיַאֲמֵץ לְבַבְכֶם כָּל־הַמְיַחֲלִים לַיהוָה:

where *Malbim* explains that the אֱמוּנִים are people who adhere faithfully to everything which duty demands. Since they are truthful to God by scrupulously safeguarding His law, God safeguards them, measure for measure, with utmost care.]

וּמְשַׁלֵּם עַל יֶתֶר עֹשֵׂה גַאֲוָה — *But He pays with precision him who acts with arrogance.*

Rashi explains that the word יֶתֶר,

literally a *bowstring*, denotes precision because the arrow must be perfectly positioned on the string in order to hit the mark. A יֶתֶר is also a *measuring rope* used to make exact calculations.

Another interpretation of יֶתֶר [cognate with יוֹתֵר] is *excessive pride* [see *Isaiah* 15:7]. God punishes the proud and arrogant measure for measure. He unleashes His full power and fury against them and, thus, He appears to act with *excessive pride*.

But He pays with precision
him who acts with arrogance.
²⁵ *Be strong, and firm your hearts,*
all who wait for HASHEM.

25. חִזְקוּ וְיַאֲמֵץ לְבַבְכֶם כָּל הַמְיַחֲלִים לַה׳ —
Be strong and firm your hearts, all who
wait for HASHEM.

[David concludes by saying that the
example of his danger-filled life should
serve as an inspiration to others.]

The *Sefer Ha'Ikkarim* observes:
When a person puts all of his hope in
God, his heart is fortified with courage

and strength; as David says, קַוֵּה אֶל ה׳
חֲזַק וְיַאֲמֵץ לִבֶּךְ וְקַוֵּה אֶל ה׳, *Place confi-*
dence in HASHEM, strengthen yourself
and He will give you courage; and place
confidence in HASHEM (27:14). And
the prophet Isaiah says: וְקוֹיֵ ה׳ יַחֲלִיפוּ
כֹחַ, *Those who place confidence in*
HASHEM shall renew their strength
(Isaiah 40:31).

32 מזמור לב

*O*ne of David's greatest teachings was that of the difficult art of repentance. David was מֵקִים עוֹלָה שֶׁל תְּשׁוּבָה, he who lifted the burden of repentence (Moed Katan 16b); he demonstrated that forgiveness is accessible to all who sincerely seek it. [See Overview].

Of the many psalms addressed to this topic, this is the first. In it, David explains that there is more to repentance than simply attaining Divine forgiveness.

Rabbeinu Yonah of Gerona (Shaarei Teshuvah 1:9) summarizes the essence of this psalm:

There are many levels of repentance by which one draws closer to the Holy One, Blessed be He. Although every type of repentance brings about at least some forgiveness, the soul cannot become completely purified to the extent that the sins are regarded as never having been committed, unless the heart is cleansed and the spirit is properly conditioned; as it is written, 'Praiseworthy is the man to whom HASHEM does not account iniquity and whose spirit is without deceit' (v. 2). The soul may be compared to a garment that needs cleansing. A little washing will suffice to remove the surface dirt, but only after repeated washings will it become entirely clean. Therefore, it is written that the penitent says: Wash me thoroughly from my iniquity (51:4).

The highest level of purity and forgiveness is achieved on Yom kippur; as the Torah states: For on this day He shall atone for you to purify you from all your sins, before HASHEM shall you be purified (Leviticus 16:30).

Verse 5 of this psalm tells how Nathan the Prophet informed David that God had completely forgiven his transgression with Bath Sheba. The Zohar (Bereishis 8b) says that Nathan made this pronouncement on Yom Kippur.

The Vilna Gaon designates this psalm as the שִׁיר שֶׁל יוֹם, the Song of the Day, for Yom Kippur (Maaseh Rav 216). The Ashkenazic custom, as recorded in Siddur Avodas Yisrael, is to recite this psalm on Shabbos Shuvah, the Sabbath preceding Yom Kippur.

1. מַשְׂכִּיל — A Maskil.

Rashi quotes *Pesachim* 117a: Any psalm introduced with the word *Maskil* was said through a תּוּרְגְּמָן *Turgeman*, an orator who translated and interpreted the psalm for the benefit of the assemblage.

[מַשְׂכִּיל is derived from שֵׂכֶל, *wisdom, good sense, enlightment*. The message of this psalm is so essential that David took great care to assure that it would be accurately transmitted to the entire nation so that all would properly be enlightened.]

Ibn Ezra attributes the use of this unique superscription to the fact that verse 8 of this psalm contains the promise אַשְׂכִּילְךָ וְאוֹרְךָ, *I will enlighten you and I will instruct you.*

Meiri, in accord with his interpretation on other superscriptions, holds that a *maskil* is a musical instrument. It derives its name from its capacity to enlighten the human intellect. The chords of the *maskil* focused the mind upon what was being said. Futhermore it inspired the heart to repentance. Thus, the medium truly complemented the message.

Finally, *Midrash Shocher Tov* quotes the verse אֹרַח חַיִּים לְמַעְלָה לְמַשְׂכִּיל, *The path of life is upwards for the wise* (*Proverbs* 15:24); and explains that the מַשְׂכִּיל is he who is מִסְתַּכֵּל לְמַעְלָה, *trains his gaze only upward.*

אַשְׁרֵי — Praiseworthy.
[See *commentary* to 1:1.]

נְשׂוּי פֶּשַׁע — Whose transgression is forgiven [lit. *whose rebellious sin is lifted*].

The *Talmud* (*Yoma* 36b) classifies three main categories of transgression: פֶּשַׁע is a sin committed with the intention of rebelling against God and casting off His sovereignty. עָוֹן, too,

refers to an intentional sin, but one which results from weakness in face or desire rather than from rebelliousness. חֲטָאָה is an unintentional sin as a result of carelessness. It requires repentance and forgiveness because if more care had been exercised, the mistake would not have occurred. The *Talmud* goes on to explain God's forgiveness, which is one of His Thirteen Attributes of Mercy: נֹשֵׂא עָוֹן וָפֶּשַׁע וְחַטָּאָה, *He forgives iniquity, transgression and sin* (*Exodus* 34:7):

Moses said to the Holy One, Blessed be He, 'Sovereign of the Universe. When the children of Israel sin against You, please consider their intentional transgressions (עָוֹן וָפֶּשַׁע) as if they were merely unintentional errors (חֲטָאָה).

[God surely exercises His Attribute of Mercy towards one who sincerely repents. Therefore, our verse may be interpreted: אַשְׁרֵי נְשׂוּי פֶּשַׁע, *fortunate is he whose intentional rebellion is removed through repentance,* thus it becomes כְּסוּי חֲטָאָה, *covered over,* i.e. its severity is mercifully obscured, and it is considered חֲטָאָה, *an unintentional sin*].

Meiri holds that the intentional sin discussed here is removed only through painful affliction; as we find וְהֵם יִשְׂאוּ עֲוֹנָם, *and they will suffer for their iniquity* (*Numbers* 18:23). He goes on to explain that in these two verses David enumerates four different groups of people who will enter the Hereafter cleansed of sin, however their means of achieving this state differ greatly. The man described as נְשׂוּי פֶּשַׁע, i.e., cleansed through affliction, represents the first group. [The rest will be described as the commentary progresses.]

Bereishis Rabbah 22 translates נְשׂוּי as *lifted above,* and comments that it refers to the potential sinner and not to the sin. *Fortunate is he who is נְשׂוּי פֶּשַׁע,*

To David, A Maskil:
Praiseworthy is he whose transgression is forgiven,
whose sin is covered.
² Praiseworthy is the man to whom
HASHEM does not account iniquity,

lifted *above his sin,* [and able to overcome the evil impulse which entices him] and whose sin is not above him [more powerful than he].

כְּסוּי חֲטָאָה — *Whose sin is covered.*

Radak (v. 1) quotes his father who explains that this refers to the man who has an abundance of merits and righteous deeds to his credit, but has also committed a חֲטָאָה, a relatively minor sin. The misdeed is *covered* by his countless merits and is not visible, like a lone kernel of millet which fell into many bushelfuls of wheat.

Meiri holds that the relatively slight חֲטָאָה, sin, is covered by a proportionally mild punishment. This is the second group which enters the Hereafter in cleanliness.

The Talmud (Yoma 86b) teaches, Rav noted that the following verses seem to be in contradiction. Our verse reads: *Fortunate is he whose transgression is removed, whose sin is covered,* yet elsewhere it is written, *He who covers his transgressions will not succeed, but whoever confesses and forsakes them shall have mercy* (Proverbs 28:13). Rav explained that there is really no difficulty. The verse in Proverbs refers to a sin which is well-known to the public [so it is better that the sinner should confess publicly and shame himself rather than deny his transgression (Rashi).] Our verse refers to a sin committed privately [it is preferable not to reveal it for the sake of preserving God's honor, for, to publicize the fact that a transgression was committed, detracts from God's honor and awe (Rashi).] Rav Zutra bar Tuvia said in the name of Rav Nachman, that the

verse in Proverbs refers to a sin committed against one's fellow. [If the victim refuses to forgive the sinner, other people may be informed so that they may try to induce the victim to accept the apology of the penitent (Rashi).] Our verse, however, refers to a sin committed against God. [See *Rabbeinu Yonah, Shaarei Teshuvah;* and *Rambam, Kesef Mishneh* and *Lechem Mishneh, Hilchos Teshuvah* 2:5. See also *commentary to v. 5.*]

2. אַשְׁרֵי אָדָם — *Praiseworthy is the man.*

[Unlike Verse 1 which discusses the various sinners, the subject of this verse is אָ, *the man,* par excellence: a person who is free of sin].

לֹא יַחְשֹׁב ה׳ לוֹ עָוֹן — *To whom HASHEM does not account iniquity.*

Although he has sinned, this man has repented so sincerely that God ascribes no sin to him, having forgiven him completely (Radak).

Quoting his father, however, Radak gives a different interpretation. He derives יַחְשֹׁב from מַחֲשָׁבָה, *thought.* This verse is in praise of the righteous who has never even had a *thought of iniquity.*

Meiri identifies this as the third category of righteous people. It consists of those who never sinned in deeds but who did allow improper thoughts to enter their minds. God's reaction to these thoughts is לֹא יַחְשֹׁב לוֹ, [lit. *He gives it not a thought*] for the Talmud (Kiddushin 40a) establishes the rule that מַחֲשָׁבָה רָעָה אֵין הקב״ה מְצָרְפָהּ לְמַעֲשֶׂה *God does not consider an evil thought to be equivalent to an evil deed.*

ג עָוֹן וְאֵין בְּרוּחוֹ רְמִיָּה: כִּי־הֶחֱרַשְׁתִּי בָּלוּ
עֲצָמָי בְּשַׁאֲגָתִי כָּל־הַיּוֹם: כִּי | יוֹמָם
ד וָלַיְלָה תִּכְבַּד עָלַי יָדֶךָ נֶהְפַּךְ לְשַׁדִּי
בְּחַרְבֹנֵי קַיִץ סֶלָה: חַטָּאתִי אוֹדִיעֲךָ וַעֲוֹנִי
ה לֹא־כִסִּיתִי אָמַרְתִּי אוֹדֶה עֲלֵי פְשָׁעַי
לַיהוה וְאַתָּה נָשָׂאתָ עֲוֹן חַטָּאתִי סֶלָה:

וְאֵין בְּרוּחוֹ רְמִיָּה — *And whose spirit is
without deceit*. [lit. *and there is not in
his spirit deceit*].

Rashi and *Radak* hold that this is a
requisite quality of the man *to whom
HASHEM does not account iniquity*, i.e.,
his repentance is so completely sincere
as to assure that he will never again
repeat this transgression. [Otherwise,
his very repentance is deceitful and is
compared to *a dog who returns to (eat)
his vomit* (Proverbs 26:11).]

According to *Meiri*, this is the fourth
and final category of righteous people.
It is composed of those who have never
even contemplated deceitful acts.

3. כִּי הֶחֱרַשְׁתִּי — *When I kept silent*.

I refrained from confessing my sins
before You (*Rashi*).

בָּלוּ עֲצָמָי — *Away wasted my bones*.

This deterioration resulted from my
constant sighing and groaning as I worried about my sins and the inevitable
punishment for them (*Rashi*).

[Similarly we read אִישׁ דְּאָגָה בְלֶב
וְיַשְׁחֶנָּה, *Worry in a man's heart lets him
diminish it* (Proverbs 12:25). The
Talmud (*Sotah* 42b) recommends two
courses of dealing with worry. Either
one should attempt to forget his worries
by being optimistic, or he should relieve
his anxiety by discussing his problems
and fears with others. However, David
says that he repressed his worries,
הֶחֱרַשְׁתִּי, *I kept silent* — and suffered
silent frustration and torture. Consequently, בָּלוּ עֲצָמָי, *my bones*, [i.e., *my
very essence*] wasted away.'

בְּשַׁאֲגָתִי — *Through my anguished roar*.

According to *Rashi*, the absence of
repentance caused David to worry over
his fate and to roar in anguish, i.e., to
groan. This groaning caused his bones
to waste away. However, *Metzudas
David* says that anxiety had
deteriorated his bones and the pain
caused him to roar in anguish.

כָּל הַיּוֹם — *All day long*.

The *Talmud* (*Bava Metzia* 4b) relates
that Rabbi Elazar ben Rabbi Shimon bar
Yochai, wishing to purify himself from
the slightest trace of a certain sin actually sought pain and affliction. However,
he only welcomed the pains at night
while he slept. When dawn broke, he
addressed his suffering saying: 'My
brothers and my friends, depart so as
not to deter me from Torah study'.
Since Rabbi Elazar could exercise such
control over these pains, obviously they
were יִסּוּרִין שֶׁל אַהֲבָה, *afflictions of love*,
inflicted by God to bring the sufferer
closer to his Maker. However, David
had no such control over his pains and
they caused him to groan כָּל הַיּוֹם, *all
day long*, thus proving that they were a
harsh punishment and not *afflictions of
love* (*Kesef Mezukak*).

4. כִּי יוֹמָם וָלַיְלָה תִּכְבַּד עָלַי יָדֶךָ — *For day
and night You hand was heavily
upon me*.

Day and night I anticipate Your
dreaded punishment (*Radak*).

נֶהְפַּךְ לְשַׁדִּי — *My freshness* [lit.
moisture] *was transformed*.

and whose spirit is without deceit.

³ *When I kept silent, away wasted my bones*
through my anguished roar all day long.

⁴ *For day and night Your hand was heavily on me,*
my freshnesss was transformed
by summer dryness, Selah.

⁵ *My sin I make known to You*
my iniquity I do not hide.

I said, 'I will confess my transgressions to HASHEM'
but You had forgiven my iniquitous sin, Selah.

My flesh shriveled and my weight decreased as anxiety sapped my strength. לְשַׁד refers to the internal fat and moisture which provide vitality; as we find in *Numbers* 11:8 that the manna tasted like לְשַׁד הַשָּׁמֶן, *a cake soaked in oil* (Radak; *Dunash* quoted by *Rashi*).

However *Menachem* (quoted by *Rashi*) renders: *I was turned over to be plundered;* לְשַׁדִי being derived from שׁוֹד, *plunder.* (See 12:6, 17:9.)

בְּחַרְבֹנֵי קַיִץ — *By* [lit. *through*] *summer's dryness.*

The Sages teach that the flesh of a totally righteous person will not decay after death even if it is exposed to intense heat. In his humility and distress over his sins David bemoans his inferior state of purity, for he is sure that his fat would deteriorate if it were left in the summer heat (*Kesef Mezukak*).

[The person who thrives in God's favor flourishes like a plant nourished by abundant water (see 1:3). Not so the sinner who is parched and withered because of divine neglect.]

5. חַטָּאתִי אוֹדִיעֲךָ — *My sin I make known to You.*

This statement is in the present tense to indicate that David continuously confesses his sins and seeks forgiveness for them (*Rashi*).

Although all is apparent to God, it is still incumbent upon man to confess his sins [not because God needs the information, but so that man should recognize and take responsibility for his deeds] (*Radak*).

וַעֲוֺנִי לֹא כִסִּיתִי — *My iniquity I do not hide.*

The *Beis HaLevi* observes that David seems to contradict himself, for in *verse* 1 he said: *Praiseworthy is he whose sin is covered,* whereas here he prides himself on his courage in revealing his sin. This may be explained according to *Rashi* (*Yoma* 86b), who says that it is best not to reveal a sin of which the public has no knowledge, for every sin is a disgrace to God and detracts from the glory of the Sovereign of the Universe. However, says the *Beis HaLevi*, this is only before the sinner is punished. But if the sinner is afflicted and is publicly acknowledged to be a righteous man, it is commendable to inform the public of the reason for his suffering, lest they come to complain that God has unjustly punished a *tzaddik.* Indeed, the more he promulgates his crime and punishment, the more God's name will be sanctified for the masses will recognize that His justice shows no favor, even to the righteous. [See *commentary* to *verse* 1 and 38:18-19].

אָמַרְתִּי אוֹדֶה עֲלֵי פְשָׁעַי לַה׳ וְאַתָּה נָשָׂאתָ עֲוֺן
חַטָּאתִי סֶלָה — *I said: 'I will confess my*

ו עַל־זֹאת יִתְפַּלֵּל כָּל־חָסִיד | אֵלֶיךָ לְעֵת
מְצֹא רַק לְשֵׁטֶף מַיִם רַבִּים אֵלָיו לֹא
ז יַגִּיעוּ: אַתָּה | סֵתֶר לִי מִצַּר תִּצְּרֵנִי רָנֵּי
ח פַלֵּט תְּסוֹבְבֵנִי סֶלָה: אַשְׂכִּילְךָ | וְאוֹרְךָ

*transgressions to HASHEM', but You
had forgiven my iniquitous sin. Selah!*

Rashi and Sforno comment that this
alludes to the harsh rebuke which
Nathan the Prophet hurled against
David after he sinned concerning Bath
Sheba. The penitent David responded
with a heartfelt confession which consisted of but two words חָטָאתִי לַה׳, *I
have sinned to HASHEM* (II Samuel
12:13). [1]

6. עַל זֹאת יִתְפַּלֵּל כָּל חָסִיד אֵלֶיךָ — *For
this let every devout one pray to You.*

At every opportune time, let the penitent recite the prayer given at the conclusion of our verse (*Rashi*).

Now that it is evident to all that You
heard my prayer and removed my sin,
let every devoted man follow suit and
pray for forgiveness, if ever he should
err and sin (*Radak*).

לְעֵת מְצֹא — *At a time of accessibility.*

There are moments when God is
more accessible as the prophet said
דִּרְשׁוּ אֶת ה׳ בְּהִמָּצְאוֹ, *Seek out HASHEM
when He is found* (Isaiah 55:6) (*Ibn
Ezra*).

Or לְעֵת מְצֹאוֹ may mean when the
penitent *finds* his heart free of all dis-
turbance and preoccupation and feels
fully prepared to concentrate on sincere
repentance (*Radak; Ibn Ezra*).

In a similar statement David said,
עַל כֵּן מָצָא עַבְדְּךָ אֶת לִבּוֹ לְהִתְפַּלֵּל אֵלֶיךָ
אֵת הַתְּפִלָּה הַזֹּאת, *Therefore Your servant has found his heart ready to pray
to You this very prayer* (II Samuel 7:27)
(*Rav Yaavetz HaDoresh*).

[In accord with the commentary of
the Vilna Gaon to the preceding verse,
we may interpret לְעֵת מְצֹא as the *time*
[when You, God] find his heart to be
purified with sincere, total repentance.
This is a status for which *every man of
devotion should pray.*]

רַק לְשֵׁטֶף מַיִם רַבִּים אֵלָיו לֹא יַגִּיעוּ — *Only
that the flooding, mighty waters not
overtake him.*

David likens his many enemies to a
flood and pleads that he not fall into
their hands. Similarly, after David's sin
of counting the population of Israel he
prayed (II Samuel 24:14): *And David
said to [the prophet] Gad: 'I am sorely
distressed! Let me fall into the hand of
HASHEM, for His mercies are greater,
but let me not fall into the hands of
men'* (*Rashi*).

He should not pray that afflictions
(which are likened to the raging waters)
should not reach him at all, for without
affliction one cannot be cleansed of his
sins. Rather, he should pray that he
should not be overwhelmed by a sudden
wave of tragedy (*Metzudas David*).

1. The Vilna Gaon elaborates on this, noting that the words חָטָאתִי לַה׳ are followed by a פִּסְקָא,
a pause, i.e., an open space left after the word לָה׳. This indicates that, originally, David had
intended to continue his confession, but Nathan interrupted him. For, the confession of the
penitent should consist of at least three words חָטָאתִי עָוִיתִי פָּשַׁעְתִּי, *I have sinned* [uninten-
tionally], I have committed iniquity [intentionally], I have rebelled (Rambam, Hilchos
Teshuva 1:2). But after David said, חָטָאתִי, *I have sinned...,'* Nathan stopped him, as we read,
And Nathan said to David: 'HASHEM also has forgiven your sin, you shall not die (ibid.). Most
penitents cannot express their total remorse adequately without using these three words
because even if they believe their sin was unintentional, they must suspect that subconscious-

*6 For this let every devout one pray to You
    at a time of accessibility:
Only that the flooding, mighty waters
    not overtake him.
7 You are shelter for me.
    From distress You preserve me.
With glad song of rescue
    You envelop me, Selah!
8 I will make you wise and enlighten you
    in the proper path to travel,*

Sforno interprets: Let the devout man begin to pray לְעֵת מְצוֹא, at the very moment he finds himself starting to be afflicted. He dare not wait until it is too late and he is engulfed in an overwhelming flood of misfortunes.

According to *Radak* this is not a prayer but rather a promise to all the devout who learn the art of repentance from David. They will surely escape a torrent of punishment.

7. אַתָּה סֵתֶר לִי — *You are shelter* [lit. concealment] *for me.*

I find shelter in Your shadow from my fearsome enemies (*Rashi*).

You constantly perform concealed miracles for me, therefore I should envelop myself in endless exclamations of praise for Your kindness (*Zekan Aharon*).

מִצַּר תִּצְּרֵנִי — *From distress You preserve me.*

You protect me from tormentors, danger and illness (*Ibn Ezra*).

רָנֵּי פַלֵּט תְּסוֹבְבֵנִי סֶלָה — *With glad song of rescue You envelop me, Selah!*

Whereas I was previously surrounded by my enemies, now I will be encircled by many exclamations of joy at having escaped from them (*Radak*).

So said the Holy One, Blessed be He, to David: 'If you wish Me to safeguard you from distress (מִצַּר תִּצְּרֵנִי), then you must keep My Torah, as it says נָצְרָה כִּי הִיא חַיֶּיךָ, *safeguard it, for it is your life! (Proverbs 4:13).* If you wish Me to help you escape from the wicked, then cry out joyously before Me; as it says, *With glad song of rescue You envelop me, Selah! (Midrash Shocher Tov).*

8. אַשְׂכִּילְךָ וְאוֹרְךָ בְּדֶרֶךְ זוּ תֵלֵךְ — *I will make you wise and enlighten you in the proper path to travel* [lit. *in this way you will go*].

I have traveled down the arduous path of self-improvement and I have experienced the efficacy of prayer and penitence. Therefore I can instruct you

---

ly they might have wanted to commit the transgression. But God told Nathan to declare that He knows the heart of man knows that David's sin was truly unintentional, a mere חֲטָאָה, and nothing more. Therefore, David has no need to continue his confession. David refers to this event in saying, חַטָּאתִי אוֹדִיעֲךָ, *I acknowledged my sin to You*, *and did not* [wish to] *conceal*, i.e., I wished to continue my confession, by saying, 'My iniquity,' אָמַרְתִּי אוֹדֶה עֲלֵי פְשָׁעַי לַה׳, I said (to myself) "I will confess my rebellion to Hᴀsʜᴇᴍ." But before I could do so, Nathan informed me that *"You had already removed the iniquity* (the suspicion of premeditation) *of my sin'* [See *Avi Ezri*, by Eliezer Schach, Hilchos Teshuva 1:2).

ט בְּדֶרֶךְ־זוּ תֵלֵךְ אִיעָצֶךָ עָלֶיךָ עֵינִי: אַל־
תִּהְיוּ | כְּסוּס כְּפֶרֶד אֵין הָבִין בְּמֶתֶג־וָרֶסֶן
י עֶדְיוֹ לִבְלוֹם בַּל קְרֹב אֵלֶיךָ: רַבִּים
מַכְאוֹבִים לָרָשָׁע וְהַבּוֹטֵחַ בַּיהוה חֶסֶד
יא יְסוֹבְבֶנּוּ: שִׂמְחוּ בַיהוה וְגִילוּ צַדִּיקִים
וְהַרְנִינוּ כָּל־יִשְׁרֵי־לֵב:

on how to follow my example (Metzudas David).

אִיעָצֶךָ עָלֶיךָ עֵינִי — *I will signal you with
my eye.*

Rashi comments that אִיעָצֶךָ refers to
a signal given by winking the eye as in
קֹצֶה עֵינָיו, *he winks his eyes* (Proverbs
16:30). Thus the Psalmist promises his
followers that he will continue to guide
them by means of whatever signals are
at his disposal; he will not allow them to
grope aimlessly.

However, *Radak* and *Metzudos* relate
אִיעָצֶךָ to יָעַץ, *advice* and render: *I will
advise you of what I have witnessed
with my own eyes.*

אַל תִּהְיוּ כְּסוּס כְּפֶרֶד אֵין הָבִין — *Be not
like a horse or mule, uncomprehending.*

They cannot differentiate between a
person who is treating them well and
one who is causing them harm. When
one inserts a bit in their mouths to make
them work they clamp their jaws shut
and eagerly chew it. But when one
combs and grooms them to cleanse and
beautify them, they react angrily and
must be muzzled to prevent them from
biting (*Rashi*).

But you, whom I am instructing,
please don't imitate these dumb
creatures. Appraise well and appreciate
the afflictions which come upon you
and repent (*Radak*).

Malbim comments: The Psalmist uses
the simile of the horse and mule when
exhorting man because the flesh and
blood of man resemble that of the beast.
The principle difference between them
is that man possesses an intelligent soul
which *muzzles* and *bridles* his beastly
nature, coaxing it to do God's bidding.
If the *beastly* body is not reined, i.e.,
kept in check, it can damage the soul
just as an untamed horse can throw and
injure its rider [cf. *Malbim* to 36:7
אָדָם וּבְהֵמָה תּוֹשִׁיעַ ה'[11]].

בְּמֶתֶג וָרֶסֶן — *With muzzle and bridle.*

The translation follows *Targum*,
בְּזִמָּא וּבְפַרוּמְבְּיָא. *Rashi, Radak*, and
Metzudos follow this opinion, rendering מֶתֶג and רֶסֶן as approximately the
same type of equipment, designed to
restrain the animal's mouth in particular.

Other Scriptural references, however,
indicate that מֶתֶג is similar to a stick,
whip, or riding crop; as we find: שׁוֹט

1. The Torah warns us, *You shall not despise the Egyptian for you were a sojourner in his
land* (Deuteronomy 23:8). [Even though the Egyptians drowned your sons in the Nile,
nevertheless, you must still appreciate them for providing you with a haven in time of famine
(*Rashi*).]

Harav Yisroel Ordman of Telz noted Leo Tolstoy's comment that the above verse expresses
the pinnacle of human civilization, the highest moral level to which man can possibly aspire;
i.e. to appreciate the favor performed by a hated oppressor. To that same precept, however,
the *Midrash* cites the admonition of our verse: *Be not like a horse, or mule, uncomprehending.*

To our Sages, basic decency demands gratitude for every kindness, even that of an oppressor. To do otherwise is to sink to the level of an uncomprehending animal. What Tolstoy considered the height of morality was, to our Sages, a basic element of human behavior.

I will signal you with my eye.

⁹ *Be not like a horse or mule,*
uncomprehending;
Restrained with muzzle and bridle
when being adorned
to keep them from approaching you.
¹⁰ *Many are the agonies of the wicked —*
but he who trusts in HASHEM,
kindness surrounds him.
¹¹ *Be glad in HASHEM and rejoice, O righteous.*
Cry out in joy, all upright of heart.

לְסוּס מֶתֶג לַחֲמוֹר וְשֵׁבֶט לְגֵו כְּסִילִים, *a whip for the horse, a stick for the mule, and a rod for the back of fools (Proverbs* 26:3); *and,* וַיִּקַּח דָּוִד אֶת מֶתֶג הָאַמָּה מִיַּד פְּלִשְׁתִּים, *and David seized the ruler's staff from the hands of the Philistines (II Samuel* 8:1, *Rashi ibid.)*

Meiri and Ibn Yachya render מֶתֶג *as the sharp iron spur attached to the rider's boot which he uses to prod the mule.*

Meiri and Rambam (comm. to Mishnah Sanhedrin 11) *emphasize that herein lies the main difference between the man and the beast. The dumb beast can be aroused or restrained only by external threats or blows. Man, however can be motivated by his sense of right and propriety. He requires no outside goads or whips to spur him to mend his ways. [This echoes Talmud Berachos* 7a: *'One self-inflicted blow of rebuke inside the heart of a man is far more effective than many external beatings.']*

עֶדְיוֹ — *When being adorned [lit. 'his adornment'].*

This follows Rashi who renders עֶדְיוֹ *as his beautification [as we find* וַיִּתְנַצְּלוּ בְנֵי יִשְׂרָאֵל אֶת עֶדְיָם מֵהַר חוֹרֵב, *And the children of Israel stripped themselves of their ornaments from Mount Horeb (Exodus* 33:6).] *While one beautifies the beast by combing, grooming, and cleaning, it incorrectly suspects harm and must be muzzled (*לִבְלוֹם*) lest it bite.*

Ibn Ezra, Radak, and *Metzudos* render עֶדְיוֹ as *his mouth,* as in הַמַּשְׂבִּיעַ בַּטּוֹב עֶדְיֵךְ, *he satisfies your mouth with goodness (*103:5 cf. *Radak ibid.)*

לִבְלוֹם — *Restrained [lit. to muzzle].*

As we find תֹּלֶה אֶרֶץ עַל בְּלִימָה, *He hangs the world on nothingness (Job* 26:7), *which the Talmud (Chullin* 89a) *interprets to mean: The world endures by the virtue of he who muzzles his mouth in a quarrel [and makes himself like nothing] (Rashi, Metzudas Zion).*

בַּל קְרֹב אֵלֶיךָ — *To keep them from approaching [lit. not to approach you].*

They must be restrained lest they inflict physical damage upon you (Rashi).

Maharit interprets these words homiletically. Do not act like the dumb beasts who respond only to the whip, for your intellect is incomparably loftier than theirs; they cannot approach to your level of comprehension.'

10. רַבִּים מַכְאוֹבִים לָרָשָׁע — *Many are the agonies of the wicked.*

He who places his trust in his power and wealth rather than in God and is oblivious to his own shortcomings will be afflicted with incurable suffering (Radak).

וְהַבּוֹטֵחַ בַּה' חֶסֶד יְסוֹבְבֶנּוּ — *But he who trusts in HASHEM, kindness surrounds him.*

Contrary to the wicked who are sur-

rounded by pain, the person who trusts in God is surrounded by kindness (Radak).

[Many take note of the fact that the אֶתְנַחְתָּא, a cantillation which indicates the end of a phrase, is placed on the word בַּה׳, in HASHEM. This indicates that the verse is to be read: *many are the agonies of the wicked and he who trusts in HASHEM*, thus implying that the wicked and the righteous suffer the same lot. It would have seemed more logical for the cantillation to connect the person of faith to the blessing of kindness with which the verse concludes. The construction of the verse suggests that we read these words: 'Many are the afflictions of the wicked, and included among them is he who trusts in HASHEM.' Nothing enrages the wicked more than the sight of the righteous man whose very behavior is a denunciation of the evil of the wicked.]

Another possible reading suggested by the placement of the אֶתְנַחְתָּא sign is: *Many agonies afflict the wicked and also the one who trusts in Hashem.* If so, what is the difference between the wicked and the righteous? The trusting man does not feel the suffering as much as the wicked one because he is confident that every affliction is for his good in accordance with the Divine Will. The Chofetz Chaim explained this concept with a parable. In earlier times medicines were bitter and harsh. Later, pharmacists discovered how to cover their foul tasting drugs with a sugar coating. The potency and taste of the medicine remained the same, but never

came in contact with the taste buds. Similarly, the severity of the pains which cleanse the righteous may be equal to those which punish the wicked, but the suffering does not make the righteous melancholy for it does not affect their emotional well-being. They realize that the result of the suffering will be to cleanse them and make them worthy of the World to Come. This knowledge 'sugar-coats' the bitter medicine!

Ibn Ezra defines the בּוֹטֵחַ בַּה׳ as the man who seeks no cures from doctors. The ultimate Healer is God; His therapy is to strengthen the soul and increase in the patient's heart the sense of heavenly awe. He who trusts in God is granted relief from his maladies. [See *commentary* of *Ibn Ezra* to Exodus 21:19 וְרַפֹּא יְרַפֵּא, *and he shall surely heal*].

11. שִׂמְחוּ בַה׳ וְגִילוּ צַדִּיקִים — *Be glad in HASHEM and rejoice, O righteous.*

You who trust in Hashem rejoice in that confidence and in the goodness you have achieved as its result (Radak).

וְהַרְנִינוּ כָּל יִשְׁרֵי לֵב — *Cry out in joy, all upright of heart.*

הַרְנִינוּ literally means *make others cry out in joy*. As the righteous rejoice over their own good fortune, let them share their experiences with all men of upright hearts so that they, too, may be made happy by the knowledge of God's goodness (Radak).

[See *Malbim* to 33:1, for detailed definition of צַדִּיק and יָשָׁר as they apply to this verse].

33 מזמור לג

Malbim *introduces this psalm by saying that God controls the world in two ways. 1) Through the laws of nature which are pre-ordained and unchanging; 2) through* הַשְׁגָּחָה,Hashgachah, *His personal supervision and intervention. The manner of Hashgachah changes constantly, for it is totally dependent on the deeds of man, for better or for worse.*

The laws of nature serve to conceal the true supervision of the Creator. One who perceives only this external cloak, sees an arbitrary, capricious world without justice or mercy. The challenge of mankind is to penetrate the mist and see the internal order dictated with precision by the Almighty.

All who truly seek this revelation will be elevated. The wicked will become good and the good will become better. They will all rejoice with musical instruments, because the symmetry and coordination of all the forces in the universe resemble the harmony and precision of superbly tuned instruments playing a well orchestrated symphony.

א רַנְּנוּ צַדִּיקִים בַּיהוה לַיְשָׁרִים נָאוָה
ב תְהִלָּה: הוֹדוּ לַיהוה בְּכִנּוֹר בְּנֵבֶל עָשׂוֹר
ג זַמְּרוּ־לוֹ: שִׁירוּ־לוֹ שִׁיר חָדָשׁ הֵיטִיבוּ נַגֵּן

1. רַנְּנוּ — Sing joyfully.

Let your voices be heard! *(Ibn Ezra).*

Hirsch notes that רִנָּה, usually translated as a joyous cry, or joyous song, can also express sadness as in קוּמִי רֹנִּי בַלַּיְלָה, *Arise, cry out at night* (Lamentations 2:19). Generally רָנַן implies the articulation of powerful emotions and thoughts evoked by some external stimulus. Therefore a form of פָּצַח, *bursting forth* [of emotions], frequently appears in conjunction with רָנַן as פִּצְחוּ וְרַנְּנוּ, *burst forth and sing joyfully* (98:4), but פָּצַח never appears in conjunction with any other word.

צַדִּיקִים — O righteous.

Malbim explains: The יָשָׁר *upright, straight,* man is on a higher level than the צַדִּיק, *righteous* man, because in his mind God's control over the universe is *straight,* i.e., plain and obvious. Consequently, he sees his own path in life clearly, i.e., to follow in God's ways. Therefore, the יָשָׁר, *upright one,* never deviates. However, the צַדִּיק, *righteous one,* has not yet attained that level of stability. In his mind there still exist doubts to be resolved. In his heart, conflicting emotions and desires are still at war. Nevertheless, to his great credit, he disciplines himself rigidly and so his external deeds are in complete conformity with the divine dictates.

The previous psalm ended with the exhortation שִׂמְחוּ בַה׳ וְגִילוּ צַדִּיקִים וְהַרְנִינוּ כָּל יִשְׁרֵי לֵב, *Be glad in HASHEM and rejoice, O righteous. Cry out in joy all upright of heart.* The highest level of joy bursts forth in song. In the previous psalm only the *upright* attained that level of intense happiness. This Psalm tells that when the *righteous* study God's supervision, they too will rise to the level of רַנְּנוּ, *singing joyfully.*

[This concept resolves a difficulty raised by many commentators: Why does the Psalmist say בַה׳, *because of HASHEM,* rather than לַה׳, *to HASHEM?* The usage is intended to emphasize that they *sing joyfully* precisely *because* they have found an enhanced understanding of God.]

בַה׳ — Because of [lit. in] HASHEM.

Because of His words [the Torah] *(Targum).*

Let only HASHEM be your joy and praise, nothing else *(Radak).*

לַיְשָׁרִים נָאוָה תְהִלָּה — For the upright praise is fitting.

The *upright* can best judge God's greatness; therefore they should praise him most *(Radak).*

Malbim continues: the *upright* who always accepted God's ways, always sang His praises joyfully. Further *it is fitting to give praise* to the *upright* in recognition of their spiritual greatness.

נָאוָה — It is fitting.

From the word נָאֶה, *comely, proper.* Praise is appropriate for them because they neither pursue nor glorify mundane, material things *(Radak).*

The Sages (Sotah 9a) stress that just as the upright are perfect, their works are perfect and everlasting: Do not read the verse נָאוָה, but נָוֶה, *abode.* This teaches that the Sanctuaries built by Moses and David, the *upright* ones, were never desecrated by the enemy. We find that the gates of the Temple sank into the ground before the enemies could destroy them. [The gates were a monument to David because, he made the preparations for the construction of the Temple and because, when the Temple was consecrated, the gates

XXXIII
1-3

Sing joyfully, O righteous, because of HASHEM;
   for the upright, praise is fitting.
² Thank HASHEM with the Kinor,
   with the Neivel Ossor sing to Him.
³ Sing Him a new song,

---

opened in David's honor (*Shabbos* 30a).]

Furthermore, the Tabernacle built by Moses, was also preserved for all times, because when the Jews constructed the First Temple they hid the tent, beams, poles and sockets of Moses' Tabernacle in the caves beneath the Holy Mount.

2. בְּכִנּוֹר — *With the* Kinor.

[Although there are many opinions concerning the exact translation of 'Kinor' most commentaries agree that it is a harp.] [1]

The Psalmist refers to the use of instruments in praising God because music arouses the inner spirit of the intellect and enhances its faculties (*Radak*).

בְּנֵבֶל עָשׂוֹר — *With the* Neivel Assor.

Rashi comments that *neivel* and *assor* [lit. *ten*] are both descriptive names for the same instrument, i.e., a *neivel*-instrument which produces עָשׂוֹר, *ten* different tones. *Targum* describes it as having ten strings. *Rabbi Moshe* quoted by *Ibn Ezra* says it was a wind instrument with ten holes.

However, *Ibn Ezra* himself holds that the *neivel* and the *assor* are two separate instruments, the proof being

עֲלֵי עָשׂוֹר וַעֲלֵי נָבֶל, *On the Assor and on the Neivel* (92:4). Elsewhere, *Ibn Ezra* agrees that although the *neivel* and *assor* are not identical, still the *neivel* also had ten holes (see his *commentary* to 150:3 and *Isaiah* 5:12).

The *Talmud* (*Arachin* 13b) says that the כִּנּוֹר, *harp*, of the Temple had seven strings, in Messianic times it will have eight, and in the World to Come, ten. It derives the last fact from our verse and explains it thus: 'That which is now a seven-stringed *kinor* will then become a ten-stringed *assor*, of a beauty rivaling that of the hitherto unsurpassed *neivel*. This proves that the *neivel* and the *assor* are two different instruments. *Rashi* (*ibid.*) says that the *neivel* derives from נֶבֶל יַיִן, *a leather wine bag* (filled with air and squeezed to produce sound).

The *Midrash* on 81:3 provides a different source for this name: It is called *neivel* because its exquisite music makes all other instruments seem to be נָבֵל, *worn out, disgraced, withered.*

3. שִׁירוּ לוֹ שִׁיר חָדָשׁ — *Sing Him a new song.*

Continue to compose new songs of praise at all times (*Radak*).

Rashi (*Arachin* 13b) quotes the

---

1. In support of this translation, *Shiltei Hagibborim* (Chapter 9) cites *Berachos* 3b: A 'Kinor' was suspended over David's bed. At midnight the north wind would blow through its strings and it would play by itself. The only known instrument whose strings could be strummed by the wind is a harp.

The author goes on to say that the name כִּנּוֹר is derived from כֵּן, *straight*, (see *I Kings* 7:31), because the harpstrings are positioned with great precision. כֵּן also means *base* (*Exodus* 38:8), referring to the wide base of the harp which provides stability for this heavy instrument.

Eretz HaChaim and *Zera Yaakov* note that, kabbalistically, *kinor* symbolizes the soul. Rearranged, the letters of כִּנּוֹר can be made to form כ"ו and כ"ו: כ"ו, *twenty-six* is the numerical value of the Four-Letter Name, and נֵר, *flame*, is the soul as we find נֵר ה' נִשְׁמַת אָדָם, *a flame of* HASHEM *is the soul of man* (*Proverbs* 20:27).

ד בִּתְרוּעָה: כִּי־יָשָׁר דְּבַר־יהוה וְכָל־
ה מַעֲשֵׂהוּ בֶּאֱמוּנָה: אֹהֵב צְדָקָה וּמִשְׁפָּט
ו חֶסֶד יהוה מָלְאָה הָאָרֶץ: בִּדְבַר יהוה
ז שָׁמַיִם נַעֲשׂוּ וּבְרוּחַ פִּיו כָּל־צְבָאָם: כֹּנֵס
כַּנֵּד מֵי הַיָּם נֹתֵן בְּאוֹצָרוֹת תְּהוֹמוֹת:

Midrash which notes that throughout Scriptures the word for song is שִׁירָה in the féminine form, for in This World of misery, after every song of joy, a new tragedy is born, just as the female gives birth to one child after another. But the song of the World to Come is called שִׁיר in a masculine form because this will be the final song after which no more misfortunes will be born.

הֵיטִיבוּ נַגֵּן בִּתְרוּעָה — *Play well with sounds of deepest feeling.*

[The word *teruah* implies 'shattering', thus it is used to denote short sounds similar to the anguished sighs or tearful whimpers of people who cannot catch their breath (*Rosh Hashanah* 26b). The *Midrash* tells us that it symbolizes the person broken by affliction and pain as in תְּרֹעֵם בְּשֵׁבֶט בַּרְזֶל, *You will smash them with a rod of iron* (22:9).

In this world it is difficult to sing joyfully over the תְּרוּעָה, *shattering affliction*, but in the future, when the divine plan of history will be revealed, men will see the purpose of even the worst pains and they will make happy music (i.e., a new song) to God even out of the *teruah* blast.]

4. כִּי־יָשָׁר דְּבַר ה' — *For upright is the word of HASHEM.*

God's decrees are all upright and just, therefore, the righteous rejoice over *His every deed,* for better or for worse (*Radak*).

וְכָל מַעֲשֵׂהוּ בֶּאֱמוּנָה — *And His every deed is done with trust.*

This refers to the natural forces which God set up to guide the world. They are reliable and unchanging so that one need not live in constant fear of upheaval and disaster (*Malbim*).

5. אֹהֵב צְדָקָה וּמִשְׁפָּט — *He loves charity and justice.*

God sometimes exercises charity, and, at other times, strict justice (*Radak*).

Sforno explains that צְדָקָה, *charity,* denotes a combination of God's Attribute of Mercy and His Attribute of Justice (see *commentary* to 35:24).

חֶסֶד ה' מָלְאָה הָאָרֶץ — *The kindness of HASHEM fills the earth.*

צְדָקָה *charity,* is a limited form of mercy for it is restricted within the bounds of justice (*Sforno*). [However, חֶסֶד, *kindness,* knows no bounds, *it fills the earth.*]

God's relationship to mankind is based on the three traits enumerated in this verse. He utilizes each in the proper time and hopes that mankind will follow His example. As the Prophet says: *For I am HASHEM who performs kindness, justice, and charity on the earth, for it is these that I desire* [man to imitate] (*Jeremiah* 9:23) (*Radak*). [1]

6. בִּדְבַר ה' שָׁמַיִם נַעֲשׂוּ — *By the word of HASHEM the heavens were made.*

As we find throughout the story of

1. *Eitz Yoseif* explains this verse with the words of *Yalkut Shimoni* (*Ki Sisah*): Ilfah (a Talmudic sage) explained why God's attribute of רַב חֶסֶד, *abundant in kindness,* precedes that of אֱמֶת, *strict truth* (*Exodus* 34:6). This may be likened to a man who owed a king a great sum of money but could not pay. The king was merciful and placed the entire amount into a purse and secretly threw it into the debtor's house. Just as the debtor was beginning to rejoice over

play well with sounds of deepest feeling.
⁴ *For upright is the word of HASHEM,*
and His every deed is done with trust.
⁵ *He loves charity and justice,*
the kindness of HASHEM fills the earth.
⁶ *By the word of HASHEM the heavens were made,*
and by the breath of His mouth all their host.
⁷ *He assembles like a mound the waters of the sea,*
He places in vaults the deep waters.

Creation וַיֹּאמֶר אֱלֹהִים, *And God said* (Radak).

[The *word of God* refers to the Torah which has been transmitted to Israel. Without the constant study of Torah, the universe would cease to exist as the prophet said: *'If not for my covenant of day and night* [i.e., the constant study of Torah] *I would not have set up the order of heaven and earth' (Jeremiah* 33:25). This process of creation continues, for the word of God, in the form of Torah continues to perpetuate creation.]

וּבְרוּחַ פִּיו כָּל צְבָאָם — *And by the breath of His mouth all their host.*

From this verse the *Talmud* (Chagigah 14a) derives: 'Each word which went forth from God's mouth at Creation, brought another ministering angel into being.' [Every physical creation on earth has a spiritual force above which controls it.]

Radak finds allusions in these verses to the four basic elements of creation.

Fire is the basis of the heavens (and the luminaries). *Air* is the breath of God's mouth. *Water* is in the seas and deep waters (next verse). *Earth* is where God's kindness abounds (v. 5).

7. כֹּנֵס כַּנֵּד מֵי הַיָּם — *He assembles like a mound the waters of the sea.*

Similarly, in reference to the Splitting of the Sea, the constrained water is described as a נֵד, *mound*: נִצְּבוּ כְמוֹ נֵד, *they stood upright like a mound* [Exodus 15:8] (Rashi).

Originally, water covered the face of the entire earth. Afterwards, God gathered the waters into the seas, where He commanded that they remain. There is sufficient water in the seas and ocean to cover the entire face of the earth, but God keeps it confined as if the water were piled up in an immovable mound (Radak).

נֹתֵן בְּאוֹצָרוֹת תְּהוֹמוֹת — *He places in vaults the deep waters.*

The waters of the sea should inundate

---

his new-found fortune, the king sent his guards to demand immediate payment of the long outstanding debt. The man was left as poor as before, but at least his debt was paid. So, too, a person commits a sin for which the heavenly penalty is death. But God is kind and does not exact payment immediately. He waits until the man marries and bears children, then the Lord snatches the life of the young child to pay for the father's sin. This man has discharged his debt to heaven in a most painful manner, but he at least survives to repent and improve himself.

Our verse conveys the same message. God loves to do צְדָקָה, *charity*. Yet, there are times when a man's deeds are such that God must punish him with מִשְׁפָּט, *justice*. Nevertheless, God is compassionate. First, he showers an abundance of kindness upon him. Then, He exacts punishment by snatching away that very kindness. The sinner is disappointed, but, in truth, he is now no worse off than he was initially.

ח יִירְאוּ מֵיהוה כָּל־הָאָרֶץ מִמֶּנּוּ יָגוּרוּ כָּל־
ט יֹשְׁבֵי תֵבֵל: כִּי הוּא אָמַר וַיֶּהִי הוּא־צִוָּה
י וַיַּעֲמֹד: יהוה הֵפִיר עֲצַת־גּוֹיִם הֵנִיא
יא מַחְשְׁבוֹת עַמִּים: עֲצַת יהוה לְעוֹלָם
יב תַּעֲמֹד מַחְשְׁבוֹת לִבּוֹ לְדֹר וָדֹר: אַשְׁרֵי
הַגּוֹי אֲשֶׁר־יהוה אֱלֹהָיו הָעָם | בָּחַר

---

the dry land, but God's rules of nature keep them as if in *vaults*. The waves and the tides furiously thunder upon the shore but then subside and dare not go beyond their boundaries (*Radak*).

Rashi refers this to the waters deep beneath the earth's surface. In the subterranean world there are both sweetwater and salt-water pools, yet God stores them so that they never mix (*Bamidbar Rabbah 18:22*). *Alshich* also notes that if the tremendous reservoirs of underground water should ever erupt and shoot to the surface, they would flood the earth [*Succah* 51b.] It is God who keeps them pent up. [1]

8. יִירְאוּ מֵיהוה כָּל־הָאָרֶץ — *Fear HASHEM, all the earth.*

God in His wisdom, fashioned the world in such a way that man should never feel totally secure and complacent. Every man must be humbled by the fact that there exist forces of nature which are beyond his control. Therefore, the seas were made in such a way that it should be plain that only a miracle keeps the mighty, endless waters from overwhelming the earth. This instills fear in the hearts of man (*Alshich*).

יִירְאוּ . . . יָגוּרוּ — *Fear . . . be in dread.*

Malbim explains that יִרְאָה is fear of an external threat, while יָגֹר is a much more powerful emotion for it is a man's

inner dread when he trembles lest he be punished for his deeds (see *commentary* to 22:24). [Even animals can experience יִרְאָה, *fear*, but only יֹשְׁבֵי תֵבֵל, *the* (human) *inhabitants of the world*, can feel pangs of conscience and fear of punishment.]

9. כִּי הוּא אָמַר וַיֶּהִי — *For He spoke and it became.*

Creation came into being at His word and exactly as He commanded. This can also be interpreted as a prologue to the succeeding verses: the plans of the nations are doomed to frustration because they go counter to His will (*Radak*).

[This reflects the first of *Maimonides* Thirteen Principles of Faith: The Creator, Blessed be His Name, creates and rules all creations and He alone made, makes and will make all works.]

הוּא־צִוָּה וַיַּעֲמֹד — *He commanded and it stood firm.*

[When God created the world it spread out and expanded like the threads stretching out through the loom until God roared and the earth stood firm (*Chagigah* 12a). This is why God is called שַׁדַּי, *Shaddai* [lit. *it is enough*] because it was He who halted the expansion of the world by roaring דַּי, *enough!*

Since God is perfect and complete, everything He creates should be fully developed and complete. However, the

---

1. Rabbi Eliezer, sees here an allusion to the entire water cycle which sustains the earth. What causes נָתַן בְּאוֹצָרוֹת, [*The grain*] *to be placed in storehouses?* — the תְּהוֹמוֹת, *deep waters*, which evaporate from מֵי הַיָּם, *the sea*, and are כְּנֵס כַּנֵּד, *gathered into clouds*, like liquid in a נֹאד, *water bag, gourd.* Then they rain down as precipitation, through condensation (*Taanis 9a*).

8 *Fear HASHEM, all the earth;*
of him be in dread, all inhabitants of the world.
9 *For He spoke and it became,*
He commanded and it stood firm.
10 *HASHEM annuls the counsel of peoples,*
he balks the designs of nations.
11 *But the counsel of HASHEM stands forever,*
the designs of His heart for all generations.
12 *Praiseworthy is the people whose God is HASHEM,*
the nation He chose for His own estate.

Creator ordained that the world remain imperfect in order to provide mankind in general and Israel in particular with the task of completing and perfecting the world (*Beis HaLevi, Lech Lecha*).]

10. הֵפִיר עֲצַת גּוֹיִם ה' — *HASHEM annuls the counsel of peoples.*

Now that we understand that the command of God stands firm and invincible forever (v. 9) we realize that every effort to challenge Him is futile and will be nullified (*Ibn Ezra*).

Specifically, this refers to the coalition of all the peoples of the earth who planned to build the Tower of Babel as a challenge to God (*Genesis 11:1-4*). They came together and adopted a simple counsel. Not only the physical structure of the Tower of Babel collapsed, but also the intellectual faculties which designed it were hampered. God confused the minds of its builders and deprived them of common speech and the power to communicate with one another (*Sforno*).

הֵנִיא מַחְשְׁבוֹת עַמִּים — *He balks the designs* [lit. *thoughts*] *of nations.*

Malbim explains that הֲפָרָה, *annulment*, applies to something which has already come into existence whereas הֲנָיאָה, *foiling*, means preventing its ever taking effect.

11. עֲצַת ה' . . . מַחְשְׁבוֹת לִבּוֹ — *HASHEM's counsel . . . the designs of*

His heart.

This verse contrasts God's counsel to that of humans (v. 10). The counsel of the peoples is nullified, but HASHEM's counsel stands forever. Their designs are balked, but the designs of HASHEM endure eternally (*Ibn Ezra, Radak*).

Etz Yoseif quotes the *Vilna Gaon* who differentiates between עֵצָה, the *counsel* that one person receives from another, and מַחְשָׁבָה, *design*, which a person decides on his own. The plans of God always supercede those of man and therefore we read, רַבּוֹת מַחֲשָׁבוֹת בְּלֵב אִישׁ וַעֲצַת ה' הִיא תָקוּם, *Many are the designs in the heart of man,* [which he devises himself] *but the counsel of HASHEM will stand* (*Proverbs 19:21*).

This means that after all of man's own personal designs, God will implant in his mind His advice and counsel, and that will be the one that will eventually win out over the rest.

12. אַשְׁרֵי הַגּוֹי אֲשֶׁר ה' אֱלֹהָיו — *Praiseworthy is the people whose God is HASHEM.*

Any people which would put their faith in God would be praiseworthy, for then He would provide them with His הַשְׁגָּחָה, *supervision* (*Malbim*).

הָעָם בָּחַר לְנַחֲלָה לוֹ — *The nation He chose for His own estate.*

But Israel is even more fortunate than others. For not only has Israel made

יג לְנַחֲלָה לֹו: מִשָּׁמַיִם הִבִּיט יהוה רָאָה
יד אֶת־כָּל־בְּנֵי הָאָדָם: מִמְּכֹון־שִׁבְתֹּו
טו הִשְׁגִּיחַ אֶל כָּל־יֹשְׁבֵי הָאָרֶץ: הַיֹּצֵר יַחַד
טז לִבָּם הַמֵּבִין אֶל־כָּל־מַעֲשֵׂיהֶם: אֵין־
הַמֶּלֶךְ נֹושָׁע בְּרָב־חָיִל גִּבֹּור לֹא־יִנָּצֵל
יז בְּרָב־כֹּחַ: שֶׁקֶר הַסּוּס לִתְשׁוּעָה וּבְרֹב
יח חֵילֹו לֹא יְמַלֵּט: הִנֵּה עֵין יהוה אֶל־יְרֵאָיו

HASHEM their God, but He has also chosen them for His nation. He reveals Himself to them with miraculous Providence (Malbim).

מִשָּׁמַיִם הִבִּיט ה׳ רָאָה אֶת כָּל בְּנֵי הָאָדָם .13 — *From heaven HASHEM looks* [lit. *looked*] *down, seeing* [lit. *He saw*] *all of mankind.*

In this verse and the next the Psalmist discusses the two forms of divine supervision. Our verse, in describing God as 'looking down', implies that He is distant and relatively uninvolved in earthly affairs. This is הַשְׁגָּחָה טִבְעִית, *supervision through nature*, i.e., the law of nature by which heavenly forces exercise control over the universe within a set of fixed laws (Malbim).

מִמְּכֹון שִׁבְתֹּו הִשְׁגִּיחַ אֶל כָּל יֹשְׁבֵי הָאָרֶץ .14 — *From His dwelling-place He supervises all inhabitants of earth.*

From the more general הִבִּיט, *looks*, of the previous verse the Psalmist changes to the more intense הִשְׁגִּיחַ, *oversees*, which implies הַשְׁגָּחָה פְּרָטִית, *individual supervision*, of all inhabitants of earth. God observes each, not from the distant heavens, but rather מִמְּכֹון שִׁבְתֹּו, *from His dwelling-place*, i.e., where He sits in judgment on each individual according to his unique situation (Malbim).

Etz Yoseif notices in the initials of the words מִמְּכֹון שִׁבְתֹּו הִשְׁגִּיחַ the name מֹשֶׁה, *Moses*, and explains that it was by virtue of the Torah transmitted by Moses that God granted us the privilege of receiving His personal attention.

הַיֹּצֵר יַחַד לִבָּם הַמֵּבִין אֶל כָּל מַעֲשֵׂיהֶם .15 — *He Who fashions their hearts all together, Who understands all of their deeds.*

Because He alone fashioned their hearts, only He can truly understand them (Radak).

[Although He made them all together, each has a unique personality and must be understood according to his particular characteristics. As the Sages teach: just as no two faces are alike so are no two personalities alike (Berachos 58a).

Elsewhere God is praised: A man mints many coins with one form and they all emerge alike, but the King of Kings, the Holy One, Blessed be He, minted all of mankind with the mold of Adam, yet no man looks exactly like his neighbor (Sanhedrin 37a).]

Alshich interprets the words *their hearts all together*, as an allusion to the diverse elements which God has fused together in the human heart. Within man are both good and evil inclinations which are in perpetual conflict. Therefore, *He understands all of their deeds*, realizing man's inherent inconsistency.

אֵין הַמֶּלֶךְ נֹושָׁע בְּרָב חָיִל .16 — *A king is not saved by a great army.*

History furnishes ample proof of God's intervention on behalf of His chosen ones. By the laws of nature and logic, the mighty army should always crush the tiny one, yet many a king has

¹³ *From heaven HASHEM looks down,*
     seeing all of mankind.

¹⁴ *From His dwelling-place He oversees*
     all inhabitants of earth,

¹⁵ *He Who fashions their hearts all together,*
     Who comprehends all their deeds.

¹⁶ *A king is not saved by a great army,*
     nor is a hero rescued by great strength;

¹⁷ *A sham is the horse, for salvation;*
     despite its great strength, it provides no escape.

¹⁸ *Behold, the eye of HASHEM is on those*
     who fear Him,

---

been defeated despite the superiority of his forces. For example, King Sennacherib of Assyria conquered almost all of the inhabited world, and he arrogantly blasphemed God and besieged Jerusalem. Then, in a single night, the angel of God smote the entire Assyrian army of 185,000 men *(Radak)*.

גִּבּוֹר לֹא יִנָּצֵל בְּרָב כֹּחַ — *Nor is a hero rescued by great strength.*

Though his entire army was annihilated, the mighty Sennacherib was spared, only to be assassinated by his own sons. All his strength was of no avail. Similarly, the giant Goliath fell before the young shepherd, David. Thus, history shows that victory depends not on physical strength but on the will of God *(Radak)*.

17. שֶׁקֶר הַסּוּס לִתְשׁוּעָה — *A sham is the horse for salvation.*

The horse's might emanates from God who can deprive him of it at will *(Radak)*.

Furthermore, it is often difficult to maneuver the powerful steed and thus the rider is vulnerable to enemy attack, whereas the foot soldier exercises greater control over his own movements *(Alshich)*.

וּבְרֹב חֵילוֹ לֹא יְמַלֵּט — *Despite its great strength, it provides no escape.*

The strength of the horse provides no assurance that it will carry its rider away from danger *(Radak)*.

Often a frenzied horse will carry its rider right into the camp of the enemy instead of galloping in the direction of escape. Or the horse terrified by battle, will throw and trample its own rider. Thus, its great strength can be a curse instead of a boon *(Alshich)*.

The mighty horse may not even be able to save itself from destruction *(Ibn Ezra)*.

18. הִנֵּה עֵין ה' אֶל יְרֵאָיו — *Behold, the eye of HASHEM is on those who fear Him.*

Those who trust in their military prowess stumble, but those who place their trust in HASHEM merit His protection *(Radak)*.

The *Midrash* observes: When Israel performs according to the will of God, He looks at them with two eyes, as it says עֵינֵי ה' אֶל צַדִּיקִים, *The eyes* [plural] *of HASHEM are upon the righteous ones* (34:16); but when they do not perform according to His will, He looks only with one eye, as in our verse,

יט לַמְיַחֲלִים לְחַסְדּוֹ: לְהַצִּיל מִמָּוֶת נַפְשָׁם
כ וּלְחַיּוֹתָם בָּרָעָב: נַפְשֵׁנוּ חִכְּתָה לַיהוה
כא עֶזְרֵנוּ וּמָגִנֵּנוּ הוּא: כִּי־בוֹ יִשְׂמַח לִבֵּנוּ כִּי
כב בְשֵׁם קָדְשׁוֹ בָטָחְנוּ: יְהִי חַסְדְּךָ יהוה
עָלֵינוּ כַּאֲשֶׁר יִחַלְנוּ לָךְ:

Behold, the eye of HASHEM is on those who fear Him (Shir HaShirim Rabbah 8:12).

The commentaries explain the superiority of the *righteous* of 34:16 to *those who fear Him* of our verse. One may fear God but serve Him only half-heartedly to avoid punishment and acquire reward, as this and the next verse continue: *upon those who await His kindness, to rescue their soul from death, sustain them in famine.*

However, the *Zohar (Naso)* interprets the supervision with one eye as the

highest level of divine attention. When two eyes are watching, the right one symbolizes *mercy*, and the left one *strict justice*. But he who ascends to the highest level is supervised by but one eye, that of *mercy*. [1]

19. לְהַצִּיל מִמָּוֶת נַפְשָׁם — *To rescue from death their soul.*

In times of war (*Radak*).

וּלְחַיּוֹתָם בָּרָעָב — *And sustain them* [lit. *keep them alive*] *in famine.*

1. *Ramban*, in his commentary to *Job* (36:6) explains the verse לֹא יִגְרַע מִצַּדִּיק עֵינָיו, *He does not withdraw His eyes from the righteous.* He describes the truly devout who train all of their thoughts upon God without interruption. Commensurate with the intensity of their concentration on God, He trains His eyes on them and elevates them to a lofty sphere of existence, totally insulated from the chance happenings of life; as it says in *Psalms: the eye of HASHEM is on those who fear Him.*

upon those who await His kindness,
¹⁹ To rescue from death their soul,
and sustain them in famine.
²⁰ Our soul longed for HASHEM —
our help and our shield is He.
²¹ For in Him will our hearts be glad
for in His Holy Name we trusted.
²² May Your kindness, HASHEM, be upon us,
just as we awaited You.

By virtue of this man's confidence in God's ability to protect, God will cause him to be fed even in time of severe famine (Radak).

[In *Job* 5:20 we read בְּרָעָב פָּדְךָ מִמָּוֶת, *Through famine He redeems you from death*. *Malbim* (ibid.) explains: When the All Merciful decrees that a country is about to be destroyed by an earthquake or a similar holocaust, what does He do? He visits a devastating famine upon the land, forcing the inhabitants to flee in time to escape the catastrophic upheaval of the earth. Thus, the harsh curse of famine was truly a blessing in disguise, for it limited the extent of the later catastrophe.

Based on this we may render our verse as וּלְחַיּוֹתָם בְּרָעָב, *and sustain them*, i.e., save their lives, *through famine*.]

20. נַפְשֵׁנוּ חִכְּתָה לַה׳ — *Our soul longed* [lit. *waited*] *for HASHEM.*

Because we saw that those who fear God and await His help are answered, we too look to Him for help (Ibn Ezra).

21. כִּי בוֹ יִשְׂמַח לִבֵּנוּ — *For in Him will our hearts be glad.*

When He will save us from all the evils which threaten us, we will rejoice in the knowledge that our salvation stems from Him (Radak).

22. יְהִי חַסְדְּךָ ה׳ עָלֵינוּ כַּאֲשֶׁר יִחַלְנוּ לָךְ — *May Your kindness, HASHEM, be upon us just as we awaited You.*

[This re-emphasizes the concept that God's beneficience rests upon man in proportion to his sincere trust in God.]

34 מזמור לד

To truly appreciate this psalm we must be aware of the events which inspired it. Midrash Shocher Tov provides the essential background:

Koheles says: He made everything beautiful in its proper time (Ecclesiates 3:11). David said to the Holy One, Blessed be He: 'All that You created is beautiful, and wisdom is the most beautiful of all. However, I fail to appreciate the value of madness. What satisfacton can You derive from a lunatic walking about, ripping his clothing, chased by little children and mocked by all?'

God replied: 'David, by your life, I promise that you will some day need this madness which you now criticize. As Solomon said, He who despises something will be punished by it (Proverbs 13:13). Furthermore, David, I promise that you will even pray that I give this madness to you.'

A short time later, David, forced to escape from the wrath of Saul, fled to the land of the Philistines with nothing but the sword of Goliath, which he took from the giant after slaying him. Goliath's brothers were the bodyguards of Achish, King of the Philistine city of Gath. They recognized David and the sword of their recently slain brother. They asked the king for permission to avenge Goliath by killing David. After some hesitation, the king agreed. Upon hearing this, David prayed for help.

'What do you wish?', God asked.

'Please give me a measure of that madness which I once criticized'.

David assumed the role of a madman, acting strangely. He wrote on the city gates, 'King Achish owes me one hundred myriad [coins] and his wife owes fifty myriads.' The mother and daughter of Achish also went mad. They shouted and raved insanely inside the palace and David ranted outside. Exasperated, Achish drove David away, saying: Am I lacking in mad people that you bring this fellow to rave in my presence? (I Samuel 21:16). Then David composed this Psalm in gratitude for his madness.

א לְדָוִד בְּשַׁנּוֹתוֹ אֶת־טַעְמוֹ לִפְנֵי אֲבִימֶלֶךְ
ב וַיְגָרֲשֵׁהוּ וַיֵּלַךְ: אֲבָרֲכָה אֶת־יהוה בְּכָל־
ג עֵת תָּמִיד תְּהִלָּתוֹ בְּפִי: בַּיהוה תִּתְהַלֵּל

1. בְּשַׁנּוֹתוֹ — *When he disguised* [lit. *changed*].

When he feigned idiocy by drooling, with saliva running down his beard (*I Samuel* 21:14) (*Rashi*).

Zais Ra'anan asks why David had to ask God to send a fit of madness upon him — could he not have pretended to be berserk? He answers that David's primary request was not that he become mad, but that Achish's mother and daughter should also be seized with lunacy; for that, too, was essential for the success of his deception (see Prefatory Remarks). However, *Yaavetz Hadoresh* holds that feigned idiocy is easily detected. Hence, David asked for true madness in order to be convincing.

טַעְמוֹ — *His sanity.*

Metzudas Zion refers this to the ability to communicate ideas logically and intelligibly as in the verse, וְטַעַם זְקֵנִים יִקָּח, *He takes away the* [טַעַם] *understanding of the aged* (*Job* 12:20). [Or as in, טוּב טַעַם וָדַעַת לַמְּדֵנִי, *Good understanding and wisdom, teach me* (119:6-6)]

לִפְנֵי אֲבִימֶלֶךְ — *Before Abimelech.*

Although in *I Samuel*, this king is called Achish, perhaps he had two names (*Ibn Ezra*); or Abimelech was the generic title of all Philistine kings, and Achish was his given name. Similarly, all Egyptian kings bore the royal title Pharoah (*Rashi*). [See *Rashbam* to *Genesis* 41:10.]

Midrash Shocher Tov explains that Achish was called Abimelech because, since he released David unharmed, he resembled an earlier Philistine King Abimelech, who acted righteously towards Abraham and Isaac, sending them away from his land safely.

וַיְגָרֲשֵׁהוּ — *Who drove him out.*

Yaavetz Hadoresh explains that this, too, was a miracle because Achish should have suspected that David's madness might be only, even if genuine, temporary. Logically he should have killed David lest his sanity return making him once again a dangerous enemy.

וַיֵּלַךְ — *And he left.*

That David was able to leave Gath was another miracle, notes *Yaavetz Hadoresh*, because even after Achish released him, only Divine intervention prevented the furious, vengeful brothers of Goliath from pursuing the helpless David and killing him.

Alshich observes a different wonder here. The moment David turned his back on Achish his Divinely imposed lunacy ended, and וַיֵּלַךְ, *he left*, calmly and normally. Nevertheless, Achish allowed him to go.

Radak notes that the verses of this psalm are arranged according to the alphabet with the exception of the letter ו, *vav*, which appears in the middle of *v.* 6, and not at the beginning.

Chazah Zion explains that David now realized that just as each letter is vital, so does every situation in life, even lunacy, play an essential role in the development of God's universal scheme.

2. אֲבָרֲכָה אֶת ה׳ — *I shall bless HASHEM.*

David's harrowing experience and his miraculous escape taught him that under no circumstances should one complain against God, for all His ways are infused with kindness and mercy. Therefore, he dedicated the rest of this psalm to God's praises (*Sforno*).

To David:
   When he disguised his sanity before Abimelech
      who drove him out and he left.
   ² I shall bless HASHEM at all times,
      always shall His praise be in my mouth.
   ³ In HASHEM does my soul glory,

בְּכָל עֵת — *At all times.*

Now that I recognize that He constantly performs miracles for me, I must bless Him at all times (*Radak*).

Even in times of tragedy I realize that there is reason to bless God, for what could seem more tragic than being afflicted by lunacy, yet for me this was the ultimate blessing (*Kedushas Levi*).

[Koheles (3:2-8) lists twenty-eight different types of עִתִּים, *times*. Some are happy; some are sad. David vows to bless God in all of these diverse times, for he has come to realize that God directs the world at all times for the benefit of the wise and righteous.]

Rambam in the introduction to *Commentary on Mishnah* (Ch. 6), asks why God created so many fools who are without intellect and who live only to pursue their lusts. He answers that the world was created exclusively for those who seek God and despise material comforts. In order to facilitate their survival, God created countless common men who are afflicted with the lunacy of pursuing wealth and security. As a result, they settle and cultivate the earth, toiling incessantly and risking their lives for a pittance, while the wise man reaps the fruits of their labors. David praises this form of productive madness, too.

תָּמִיד תְּהִלָּתוֹ בְּפִי — *Always shall His praise be in my mouth.*

The blessings of God are so sweet to my tongue, that even after the words are concluded the taste of the praise lingers (*Eretz Hachaim*).[1]

3. בָּהּ תִּתְהַלֵּל נַפְשִׁי — *In HASHEM does my soul glory.*

I feel personally glorified and praised because I have so great a Patron to save and protect me (*Rashi*).

David was once described to Saul in glowing terms: *He is adept in playing an instrument, a mighty warrior, a man of war, wise in speech, handsome of form and HASHEM is with him* (I Samuel 16:18). Now David declares that the only one of those flattering descriptions which matters to him is the one which attributes all of his outstanding talents to the fact that *HASHEM is with him* (*Eretz HaChaim*).

Malbim adds that although self-glorification is repulsive, the essence of humility is to feel that one has no personal worth except for that with which God has endowed him. Thus, ego fades entirely and disappears into the splendor of God; as it says: וַיִּגְבַּהּ לִבּוֹ בְּדַרְכֵי ה', *And his heart was lifted up in the ways of HASHEM* (II Chronicles 17:6).

---

1. When a man realizes that God created everything in the world for His honor, he must desire to honor God-at all times, to sanctify Him in all his actions, and to extol, thank, and bless Him always; as it says, *I shall bless HASHEM at all times, always shall His praise be in my mouth.* Whatever he utters, to friends or strangers, must be proper so that God is sanctified through his words. He should extol the great value of serving and fearing God and praise those who do so. In this manner a person can attain heavenly merit through the meditation of his heart and the utterance of his lips, without physical exertion. This is among the main purposes for which man was created (*Shaarei Teshuva, III*:148).

ד נַפְשִׁי יִשְׁמְעוּ עֲנָוִים וְיִשְׂמָחוּ: גַּדְּלוּ

ה לַיהוה אִתִּי וּנְרוֹמְמָה שְׁמוֹ יַחְדָּו: דָּרַשְׁתִּי

   אֶת־יהוה וְעָנָנִי וּמִכָּל־מְגוּרוֹתַי הִצִּילָנִי:

ו הִבִּיטוּ אֵלָיו וְנָהָרוּ וּפְנֵיהֶם אַל־יֶחְפָּרוּ:

ז זֶה עָנִי קָרָא וַיהוה שָׁמֵעַ וּמִכָּל־צָרוֹתָיו

יִשְׁמְעוּ עֲנָוִים וְיִשְׂמָחוּ — *May humble ones hear and be glad.*

David's friends were the humble people [for he himself was the epitome of humility] and so they rejoiced upon learning of his salvation. Not so the haughty people who were David's enemies (*Radak*).

The humble are generally those who are downtrodden and beset by misfortune and tragedy. Now that they hear that David's tragedy was turned into wondrous salvation, they too may become encouraged to recognize the blessings concealed in their woes (*Kedushas Levi*).

4. גַּדְּלוּ לַה' אִתִּי — *Declare the greatness of HASHEM with me.*

David now addresses his sympathizers, the humble ones (*v.*3), and asks them to join him in lauding God (*Radak*).

וּנְרוֹמְמָה שְׁמוֹ יַחְדָּו — *And let us exalt His Name together.*

I.e., when I return safely to *Eretz Yisrael,* from the land of the Philistines (*Sforno*).

Alshich says that David's call to join him in exalting God alludes to the obligation upon one who is miraculously saved from danger to recite בִּרְכַּת הַגּוֹמֵל, *the Blessing of Thanksgiving.* The *Talmud* (*Berachos* 54b) derives this duty from the verse וִירוֹמְמוּהוּ בִּקְהַל עָם, *They will exalt Him in the congregation of the nation* (107:32).

Malbim differentiates between the words גָּדוֹל and רָם. גָּדוֹל describes one who is elevated, or great, yet who remains accessible and within human reach. רָם, however, denotes one exalted beyond the human sphere. The gentile cannot conceive of a deity who descends to supervise the lowly affairs of men. To him, God is רָם, *exalted,* as it says, *Exalted above all of the peoples is HASHEM, His glory is upon the heavens* (113:4). Israel, however, knows that although the true essence of Hashem's Being is beyond human comprehension, He is intimately involved in shaping human affairs. Thus, God may well be described as גָּדוֹל, *great,* as we find ה' בְּצִיּוֹן גָּדוֹל וְרָם הוּא עַל כָּל הָעַמִּים *HASHEM is great in Zion, and exalted above all of the nations* (99:2).

Continuing this theme, David challenges those who deny God's *greatness* [i.e., His accessiblity to humans and His concern with earthly affairs], for God involves Himself even with madmen, as He did to effect David's rescue from Achish. Therefore, David proclaims, גַּדְּלוּ לַה' אִתִּי, *declare the greatness of HASHEM with me.*

David continues his address, saying: For my part, I am prepared to agree with you that God, in His true essence, is indeed totally removed from us. His Name, i.e., His real identity and Being, is רָם, *exalted.* Therefore I invite you to join me וּנְרוֹמְמָה שְׁמוֹ יַחְדָּו, *And let us exalt His Name* [His true Being] *together.*[1]

1. Three who eat together are obligated to respond and recite the Grace after Meals in unison. From where is this derived? Rav Assi said: From the verse, *Declare the greatness of HASHEM with me and let us exalt His Name together.*

may humble ones hear and be glad.
⁴ *Declare the greatness of HASHEM with me,*
and let us exalt His Name together.
⁵ *I sought out HASHEM and He answered me,*
and from all my terrors He delivered me
⁶ *They look to Him and become radiant,*
and their faces were not shamed.
⁷ *This poor man called and HASHEM hears—*

---

5. 'ה אֶת דָּרַשְׁתִּי — *I sought out HASHEM.*

When I was in the hands of Achish I pleaded with God to save me from that danger and all similar threats (*Radak*).

הִצִּילָנִי מְגוּרוֹתַי וּמִכָּל — *And from all my terrors He delivered me.*

Not only from Achish but also from Saul who threw a spear at me a number of times and later sent men to my house to kill me (*Radak*).

מְגוּרוֹתַי describes fear as in *Numbers* 22:3, מוֹאָב וַיָּגָר, *And Moab was terrified* (*Rashi*).

[Indeed, Moab's fear of Israel was unfounded, for God delivered them from destruction in the merit of David who was destined to descend from Moab via Ruth.]

6. אֵלָיו הִבִּיטוּ — *They look to Him.*

I.e., all those who were motivated to turn to God because of their woes (*Rashi*).

Although the verb is in past tense, *Radak* interprets it as a reference to the future, describing what will happen to those who *will* look to God.

וְנָהָרוּ — *And become radiant.*

Similarly we find נְהָרָה עָלָיו תּוֹפַע וְאַל, *let the radiance not shine upon it* (*Job* 3:4).

Radak and *Ibn Ezra* suggest that the

word is related to נָהָר, *river.* Until they looked to God they were paralyzed with fear, but now they are infused with new courage, surging ahead confidently like a mighty river.

Hirsch combines both definitions explaining that נְהָרָה is a *stream of light* flowing from its source [light travels in waves which resemble a river]. He notes that the word נֵר, *candle, lamp,* is derived from נוּר or נְהָרָה.

יֶחְפָּרוּ אַל וּפְנֵיהֶם — *And their faces were not shamed.* [See *commentary* to 35:4.]

A person whose request is refused is humiliated, but these were answered and therefore, not put to shame (*Metzudas David*).

7. קָרָא עָנִי זֶה — *This poor man called.*

David humbly described himself as a helpless pauper, wanting for the mercies of God (*Radak*).

God's concern for David may be illustrated with a parable: There was a king who was extremely fond of a certain pauper. Once, the poor man made a modest feast to celebrate with his sons. Suddenly, the king himself entered and protested against his exclusion from the banquet. The pauper excused himself, explaining that he was ashamed to invite the great king to so meager a repast. The king declared to his dear friend,

---

Rav Chanan bar Abba said: From where do we know that he who answers Amen should not raise his voice above that of the one who recited the blessing? From the verse, *Declare the greatness of* HASHEM *with me and let us exalt His Name together* [with the same volume] (*Berachos* 45b).

ח הוֹשִׁיעַוּ: חָנֶה מַלְאַךְ־יהוה סָבִיב לִירֵאָיו
ט וַיְחַלְּצֵם: טַעֲמוּ וּרְאוּ כִּי־טוֹב יהוה אַשְׁרֵי
י הַגֶּבֶר יֶחֱסֶה־בּוֹ: יְראוּ אֶת־יהוה קְדֹשָׁיו

'You have no cause for shame. I swear that your simple fare is far more dear to me than the most lavish banquets of the noblemen.' [Similarly, God prefers the prayers of the humble people who pray with genuine sincerity] (Aggadas Bereishis). [See also Rashi, Numbers 29:35.]

וַה' שָׁמֵעַ — And HASHEM hears.

It does not say that Hashem heard (in the past tense), but hears (in the present tense). This emphasizes that at the very moment that the poor man calls, before his prayer is even ended, God hears and responds; as in Isaiah 65:24, עוֹד הֵם מְדַבְּרִים וַאֲנִי אֶשְׁמָע, While they still speak, I will hear (Rav Chaim Vital).

8. חָנֶה מַלְאַךְ ה' סָבִיב לִירֵאָיו — The angel of HASHEM encamps around His reverent ones.

David refers to the fact that he was surrounded by the men of Achish and yet God sent His angel to release him (Ibn Ezra).

Similarly we find that Daniel [a descendant of David] was thrown into the den of lions but emerged unscathed, for Hashem dispatched His angel to muzzle the lions' mouths (Radak).

וַיְחַלְּצֵם — And he releases them.

I.e., the angel of God removes the righteous from the menace of the surrounding foe (Ibn Ezra, Radak, Metzudas David).

Malbim translates he armed them with weapons [as in חָלוּץ לַמִּלְחָמָה, armed for war (Numbers 32:29).] He explains this entire verse as an allusion to yet another kindness which God bestowed upon David. After he fled from Achish, David was alone and defenseless. He hid in the cave of Adullam and immediately he was joined by four hundred God-fearing and well-armed men (I Sam. 22:1-2).[1]

9. טַעֲמוּ — Taste.

Utilize your intellect and fully understand this (Radak). [See commentary to v. 1.]

וּרְאוּ — And see.

Comprehend this concept intellectually and examine it empirically with your eyes (Radak).

Taste with your senses and see with your intellect (Sforno).

כִּי טוֹב ה' — That HASHEM is good.

According to Yalkut Shimoni every time one tastes of the delicacies of the physical world it is an opportunity to experience the wonders of the spiritual force which created it:

1. The Rabbis taught: Beloved are the people of Israel, for the Holy One, Blessed be He, has surrounded them with Mitzvos: Tefillin (phylacteries) on their heads and arms; Tzitzis (fringes) on their garments, and Mezuzos on their doorposts. Anyone who is encircled by all these mitzvos is assured that he is protected against sin; as it says:— The angel of HASHEM encamps around His reverent ones and he releases them (Menachos 43b).

A person should be very scrupulous about the mitzvah of Mezuzah. Every time he enters and exits and notices the Unity of the Holy One, Blessed be He, he is reminded of His love, and he awakens from his 'slumber' and erring ways in the transitory existence of This World. Then he will know that nothing exists forever and for all eternity except the knowledge of the Eternal Savior. Realizing this, he will immediately return to his good sense and follow the straight path. The Sages said: Whosoever is surrounded by Tefillin, Tzitzis and Mezuzah is assured of protection from sin for he has many reminders, and these are the very 'angels' which save him from sin; as it says: The angel of HASHEM encamps around His reverent ones, and he releases them (Rambam, Hilchos Mezuzah 6:13).

and from all his troubles He saved him.

⁸ *The angel of HASHEM encamps around His*
reverent ones.
and he releases them.

⁹ *Taste and see that HASHEM is good —*
praiseworthy is the man who takes
refuge in Him.

¹⁰ *Fear HASHEM, you — his holy ones,*

Said the Holy One, Blessed be He, 'If you eat of the fruit of the earth or the trees, make a blessing first, otherwise, you are considered as stealing the fruits from their Maker. But if you first bless properly and then eat, it is as if you crowned their maker as King as it says, *Taste — and see that HASHEM is good.'*[11]

אַשְׁרֵי הַגֶּבֶר יֶחֱסֶה בּוֹ — *Praiseworthy is the man who takes refuge in Him.*

After comprehending and experiencing God's goodness, one can appreciate the good fortune of the one who places his trust in God (*Radak*).

[Only after a person *tastes* and *sees* the generosity of God in providing for all, can he appreciate His kindness. And if God is so generous even to those who have not asked for His assistance, how much more magnanimous must He be to those who actually *take refuge in Him.*]

10. יִרְאוּ אֶת ה׳ — *Fear HASHEM..*

This is a command: *stand in fear before God* (*Rashi*).

Fear of God falls into two categories. One is יִרְאַת הָעוֹנֶשׁ, *fear of punishment.* This is an inferior dimension of fear, for it is entirely motivated by self-concern. It has in it a מַחְסוֹר, *a deficiency.* The more desirable form of fear expresses itself in יִרְאַת הָרוֹמְמוּת, a sense of awe and reverence for God's greatness and perfection, i.e., יִרְאַת ה׳, *Fear of the Name.* The person who rises to this level of God-fearing, is a קָדוֹשׁ, *holy one.* Because his fear is perfect, he will experience no deficiencies in his life. This is the sense of our verse: Fear HASHEM in such a lofty manner that you can be considered holy; then you will lack nothing (*Zekan Aharon*).

קְדוֹשָׁיו — *His holy ones.*

These are people who restrain themselves from indulging their lusts,

1. The *Yerushalmi* (*Kiddushin* 4:12) relates: In the Hereafter a person will be brought to judgment for every species of plant which his eye saw but which he failed to eat. Rabbi Eleazer was scrupulous about fulfilling this dictate and, therefore, he would frugally save in order to buy at least one fruit from every species at least once a year [so that he could bless God for creating such a wide variety of species in This World (*Korban Hoeida, Pnei Moshe*)].

Similarly, we find that Rabbi Judah the Prince mourned when a thousand recipes for figs were partially forgotten (*Nedarim* 50b). Why? Because each recipe brought out a different flavor in the food and exhibited the incredible abundance with which God blessed this world (*Rav Gifter*).

[The difference between a great *tzaddik* and an ordinary man was once described thus: The average person sees and apple and his appetite is whetted. He wants to eat the succulent fruit but remembers that it is forbidden to eat unless a blessing is recited — so he recites a blessing in order to *taste.* However, the *tzaddik* observes an apple and is filled with admiration for the Master of Creation who fashioned so marvelous a fruit. He desires to pronounce the blessing for fruits, but it is not permissible to do so if one does not eat. So he *tastes* the apple in order to be permitted to recite the blessing.]

יא כִּי־אֵין מַחְסוֹר לִירֵאָיו: כְּפִירִים רָשׁוּ
וְרָעֵבוּ וְדֹרְשֵׁי יהוה לֹא־יַחְסְרוּ כָל־טוֹב:
יב לְכוּ־בָנִים שִׁמְעוּ־לִי יִרְאַת יהוה

---

as we find that the Torah refers to the *Nazir*, who abstains from wine, as קָדשׁ, holy [*Numbers* 6:5] (*Radak*).

Reishis Chochmah (*Shaar Hakedushah*, 1) explains: Although the holy person is not divorced from normal life, he goes to great lengths to isolate himself from the areas of life which have the potential for sin. Because he is a יְרֵא ה׳, *one who fears HASHEM*, he avoids sin strenuously and erects safeguards to separate himself from the possiblity of evil. Therefore he is called קָדוֹשׁ, holy, [lit. *one who abstains and separates*.]

Malbim contrasts the gentile concept of the saint with the Jewish ideal of sanctity. To them holiness implies a monastic existence, that excludes joy. The underlying motivation of such a course is a wish to run from the dangers and challenges of life. But those who seek God through Torah are totally involved in all aspects of life, for by experiencing every phase of life in accord with the commands of the Torah one meets the living God.

כִּי אֵין מַחְסוֹר לִירֵאָיו — *For there is no deprivation for His reverent ones.*

David addresses the people who have consecrated themselves to Hashem, saying that they need fear Hashem alone and nothing else, for He will provide all of their needs. David was moved to make this pronouncement after he was lost among the hostile Philistines with not a friend in the land to offer him food or lodging. Nevertheless, because

he feared only God, David lacked nothing (*Radak*).

11. כְּפִירִים — *Young lions.*

Some render this as כּוֹפְרִים, *unbelievers*, but the proper reading is *young lions*. It describes those who exert themselves excessively [like ferocious beasts] to acquire their sustenance. Some say that Achish's men starved David after they captured him yet God sustained him miraculously as He did Elijah who lived in a desolate cave and subsisted on the food brought him by the ravens (*Ibn Ezra*).

רָשׁוּ וְרָעֵבוּ — *May want and hunger.*

Rabbeinu Bachya in *Kad Hakemach* (*Middas HaBitachon*) observes:

God provides for all of the weak creatures such as the embryo inside its mother's womb or the chick inside the unhatched egg. God sustains the bird in the sky and the fish in the sea — He even nourishes the tiny ant. But God may well deprive mighty creatures of their food; as we read concerning the strongest of animals, *Young lions may want and hunger*. [He does this to demonstrate that it is not might or skill which assures man of his sustenance, only the will of God.]

וְדֹרְשֵׁי ה׳ לֹא יַחְסְרוּ כָל טוֹב — *But those who seek HASHEM will not lack any good.*

[The Psalmist speaks from personal experience, as he said earlier (v. 5), דָּרַשְׁתִּי אֶת ה׳ וְעָנָנִי, *I sought out HASHEM and He answered me*.] [1]

---

1. The *Shaloh Hakadosh* observes: It does not say, *Those who seek out HASHEM possess all good things*, but that they *will not lack any good*. They feel no lack because they are happy without unnecessary baubles which selfish people pursue. This may be compared to a man who pitied his neighbor who had no medicines. The neighbor laughed at him, since the absence of medicine was a blessing, because it was an indication of good health rather than sickness. [Cf. *Avos* 4:1, *Who is rich? He who rejoices in his lot.*]

Similarly, an ordinary person observing the home of a Torah scholar bereft of luxuries may

XXXIV   *for there is no deprivation for His reverent ones.*

11-12   11 *Young lions may want and hunger,*

      but those who seek HASHEM will not lack

      any good.

    12 *Go, O sons, heed me,*

      the fear of HASHEM will I teach you.

12. לְכוּ — *Go*

[If the Psalmist wanted people to come and listen, he should have said בֹּאוּ, *come,* rather than לְכוּ, *go.*]

Radak answers that sometimes לְכוּ denotes encouragement to accomplish a goal and does not actually mean an exhortation to walk away.

Chazah Zion takes the word לְכוּ literally: Go forth and travel to the yeshivas to pursue your Torah studies in order to fulfill the Rabbinic dictum, 'Exile yourself to a place of Torah'(*Avos* 4:14).

However, if you do not educate yourselves in accordance with my advice, you will not *go* through life without stumbling as the Psalmist says (82:5): *They do not know, nor do they understand, they walk on in darkness* (*Lachmei Todah*).

This verse speaks of לִמּוּד, *learning,* and so, most appropriately it begins with the letter ל, *lamed,* which literally means *learning.* For this very reason, *lamed* is the tallest of all the letters, to show that the study of how to fear God is the loftiest of all pursuits (*Sefer Chassidim*).

בָּנִים — *O sons.*

Although he is addressing adults, David calls them *sons,* for they are mere novices in the discipline of heavenly fear, and so they resemble children. [Furthermore, all students of a teacher are considered as his sons (cf. *II Kings* 2:3)] (*Ibn Yachya*).

Or, he does not mean that they are his sons, rather they are God's sons by virtue of the fear of heaven they attempt to acquire, as the *Talmud* (*Bava Basra* 10a) says: When Israel does the will of God they are called sons, but when they do not do the will of God they are called slaves! (*Shaarei HaYashar*).

Malbim adds: In other religions, the study of theology and fear of God is reserved for advanced priests. The Jewish ideal strives to inculcate the fear of God into the children at the earliest possible age when they are still impressionable בָּנִים, *sons.*

This is especially true in regard to the sin of slander (v. 14). If a father does not train his son to guard his tongue in his early youth, the hapless child will develop vicious speech habits which will cripple him for a lifetime (*Siach Yitzchak*).

שִׁמְעוּ לִי — *Heed me.*

If you hearken to my teachings you will be לִי, *unto me,* i.e., my devoted disciples who accompany me both in This World and the Hereafter [where I will share with you all new revelations of divine wisdom which are granted to me] (*Chazah Zion*).

יִרְאַת ה' אֲלַמֶּדְכֶם — *The fear of HASHEM will I teach you.*

The masses fear sin only because they dread אֱלֹהִים, *the Dispenser of Strict Justice,* who punishes for transgressions. They fail to realize that the act of

be concerned about the latter's welfare. The scholar, however, rejoices because he is not sick with a desire for luxurious trappings. He does not miss the luxuries which ordinary men attain only with sweat and toil. Hence, David rightly says: *Those who seek HASHEM will not lack any good* (*Lev Eliyahu* Vol. I).

יג אֲלַמֶּדְכֶם: מִי־הָאִישׁ הֶחָפֵץ חַיִּים אֹהֵב

יד יָמִים לִרְאוֹת טוֹב: נְצֹר לְשׁוֹנְךָ מֵרָע

טו וּשְׂפָתֶיךָ מִדַּבֵּר מִרְמָה: סוּר מֵרָע וַעֲשֵׂה־

sin in itself is harmful to both body and soul. I will teach you that ה', *HASHEM, the Dispenser of Mercy*, is the author of the prohibition against sin because in His boundless Mercy He is concerned for our welfare. You will learn to fear sin because HASHEM has determined it to be harmful, just as a kind father orders his son away from the thorns (*Eitz Yosef*).

13. [Now David turns to a matter very close to his heart because it was the cause of much suffering for him and for others. Evil men constantly slandered him to Saul and kept the flames of the king's jealousy burning. While David fled to Achish, Doeg the Edomite was hastening to tell Saul of David's visit to Nob, the city where he was hospitably received by the priests who thought he was still one of Saul's favorites. Doeg distorted the facts and convinced Saul that the priests were conspiring with David in rebellion against the throne. Thus misled, the angry Saul had the in-

habitants of the city executed as rebels.

The *Yerushalmi* (*Peah* 1:1) teaches that David's generation was generally God-fearing, but its people fell in battle because they were lax with their tongues. The *Talmud* (*Shabbos* 56a) cites an opinion that even David was *once* guilty of accepting a slanderous report. Therefore, David expounds upon the evils of לָשׁוֹן הָרָע, *evil speech*.]

מִי־הָאִישׁ הֶחָפֵץ חַיִּים — *Which man desires life?*

The eternal life of the World to Come (*Sforno*).

[In truth, the man who guards his tongue is assuring himself life and longevity in This World as well. The *Baal Shem Tov* said that every man is alloted only a certain amount of words for his entire lifetime. Once he has used up his quota, he must depart from this world.] [1]

אֹהֵב יָמִים — *Who loves days.*

I.e., the fleeting *days* of This World which are insignificant in comparison

1. The *Talmud* (*Avodah Zarah* 19b) relates:

Rabbi Alexandri went about shouting like a peddler hawking his wares, 'Who wants life, who wants life!'

Everyone crowded around him and pleaded 'Give us life.' He quoted our verse: *Which man desires life, who loves days of seeing good? Guard your tongue from evil, and your lips from speaking deceitfully.*

Perhaps a person will say, 'Now that I have avoided evil I can rest and sleep,' therefore, the following verse says, *Turn away from evil and do good*; there is no *good* but Torah study, as it says, *I have given you a good lesson, do not forsake my Torah* (*Proverbs* 4:2).

What was the novelty of Rav Alexandri's message? Surely his listeners were familiar with the verse from *Psalms*! Indeed, they knew the verse, but they considered it to be a homiletical formula intended for exalted scholars and pious saints. Rabbi Alexandri meant to demonstrate that David's words should be taken quite literally — by zealously protecting the purity of his speech, one does indeed assure himself of earthly reward (*Rav Eliyahu Meir Bloch, Shiurei Daas*).

[In spreading his message as if he were a peddler, Rabbi Alexandri may have intended to portray the contrast between himself and a slanderer. The Torah portrays the slanderer as a רָכִיל, *peddler*, (*Leviticus* 19:16), because he goes from house to house bartering tales and offering malicious talk like a peddler selling his wares. Rabbi Alexandri wished to show that the same character trait could be used for good. As Solomon said, *Death and life are in the power of the tongue* (*Proverbs* 18:21). The gossip peddles death, Rabbi Alexandri peddled life.]

13 *Which man desires life,*
who loves days of seeing good?
14 *Guard your tongue from evil,*
and your lips from speaking deceitfully.
15 *Turn from evil and do good,*

with the eternity of the World to Come (*Sforno*).

Again, stresses the *Malbim*, we see that the lessons of fearing God are meant for those who love the fullness of life, not for those who shun it.

[This alludes to the fact that the man who does not guard his tongue is actually shortening the days of his life (as if he does not love his days), for the *Talmud (Arachin 15b)* states: לָשׁוֹן הָרָע, *evil speech*, kills three people: the speaker, the listener, and the subject.]

לִרְאוֹת טוֹב — *Of seeing good.*

[This alludes to the fact that those who slander will lose even the merit of the good deeds which they performed, as *Chovos Halevavos* says in *Shaar Hakniah* 7:

On the day of reckoning many people will find unearned merits inscribed in their ledgers. They will say, 'We have not performed these good deeds.'

They will be told, 'These are the good deeds of people who spoke against you.' The people whose merits were taken away will be told, 'You forfeited your good deeds when you spoke against others.'

Similarly, some will find offenses in their ledgers that they never committed. They will be told, 'These are the offenses committed by the people you have spoken against.']

14. נְצֹר לְשׁוֹנְךָ מֵרָע — *Guard your tongue from evil.*

Radak observes that in these two verses David discusses three categories of sin; sins of thought, of speech, and of deed. The first category, transgressions of the evil tongue, includes not only slander, but also false testimony, curs-

ing parents, judges, kings, and certainly, God Himself.

The *Midrash (Vayikra Rabbah 33:1)* relates: Rabbi Shimon ben Gamliel told Tavi, his servant, 'Go to the marketplace and buy some good food.' Tavi went to the market and returned with a tongue. Afterward, Rabbi Shimon said to Tavi, 'Go to the marketplace and buy some bad food.' Tavi again returned with a tongue.

'What is this?' asked Rabbi Shimon. 'When I told you to buy food that is good you bought tongue, and when I told you to buy food that is bad, you also bought tongue?'

Tavi replied, 'From a tongue can come good and bad. When a tongue is good, there is nothing better. But when a tongue is bad, there is nothing worse.'

וּשְׂפָתֶיךָ מִדַּבֵּר מִרְמָה — *And your lips from speaking deceitfully.*

Deceit is the second category of sin which includes the evil thoughts which the deceptive man contrives while his mouth speaks words of friendship (*Radak*).

Not only outright slander is forbidden, but there are instances when it is forbidden even to speak in praise of another man (*Arachin* 15b), for laudatory description can easily lay the groundwork for a listing of the admired man's flaws as well. To slyly recount someone's virtues as an excuse for discussing his vices is true מִרְמָה, *deceit* (*Chazah David*).

15. סוּר מֵרָע — *Turn from evil.*

This is a warning against the third area of sin, the performance of evil actions (*Radak*).

Indeed, the Psalmist warns that it is

טז טוֹב בַּקֵּשׁ שָׁלוֹם וְרָדְפֵהוּ: עֵינֵי יְהוָה אֶל־
יז צַדִּיקִים וְאָזְנָיו אֶל־שַׁוְעָתָם: פְּנֵי יְהוָה
יח בְּעֹשֵׂי רָע לְהַכְרִית מֵאֶרֶץ זִכְרָם: צָעֲקוּ
יט וַיהוָה שָׁמֵעַ וּמִכָּל־צָרוֹתָם הִצִּילָם: קָרוֹב
יְהוָה לְנִשְׁבְּרֵי־לֵב וְאֶת־דַּכְּאֵי־רוּחַ

insufficient to merely refrain from offensive actions. One must *turn away* from evil and shun everything that can lead to it. One should erect safeguards to prevent himself from sinning (*Avos* 1:1), thereby abstaining from any act that may eventually result in evil, even if that particular act happens to be permissible.

Furthermore, one must remember that the performance of good begins only after abstinence from evil; one may never do evil to accomplish good. The ends do not justify the means. Never should one delude himself into thinking that his good deeds will make amends for his evil ones, as long as he has not repented from evil (*Hirsch*).

וְעָשֵׂה טוֹב — *And do good.*

This is an exhortation to perform the positive commandments (*Radak*).

[In regard to evil speech, merely to *turn from evil* by refraining from slander is considered a positive accomplishment. The *Vilna Gaon* in *Iggeres HaGra* cites the *Midrash* which says: For every second that a person remains silent, he will merit a reward of a magnitude that is even beyond the comprehension of the celestial angels.

However, *Hirsch* cautions that although we are obligated to make every personal sacrifice for the sake of peace, disregarding personal interest, advantage, and honor in the name of harmonious accord — nevertheless we may not abandon our duties to God even if they arouse the hostility and opposition of the entire world. We cannot *seek peace* at the expense of the principle of סוּר מֵרָע וַעֲשֵׂה טוֹב, *turn from evil and do good.*

בַּקֵּשׁ שָׁלוֹם — *Seek peace.*

Where you live (*Rashi*).

One who spreads slander creates conflicts and quarrels. The holy *Ari* promises that one who does not slander others will merit, measure for measure, that others will not speak about him. Thus his life will be peaceful.

וְרָדְפֵהוּ — *And pursue it.*

Elsewhere, too! (*Rashi*).

The *Talmud* (*Berachos* 6b) states: Rav Chelbo said in the name of Rav Huna, Whoever knows that his friend is accustomed to greet him, should make an effort to greet that friend with a blessing of 'Shalom' first (in order to enhance their friendship) as it says, *Seek peace (shalom) and pursue it.*[1]

16. עֵינֵי ה' אֶל צַדִּיקִים — *The eyes of HASHEM are toward the righteous.*

This is the reward of the God-fearing man described above: God constantly takes note of him and protects him (*Radak*).

1. Hillel said: Be among the disciples of Aaron; love peace and pursue peace, love people and draw them close to Torah (*Avos* 1:12).

This dictum is elaborated upon in *Avos D'Rabbi Nathan* (12:3):

When Aaron would happen to meet a wicked man on the street he would greet him warmly. On the morrow when the wicked man had an urge to sin, he would restrain himself saying, 'How can I do this? I won't be able to look my dear friend, Aaron, in the eye the next time he greets me!' So Aaron's 'Shalom' restrained this man from sin.

seek peace and pursue it.

¹⁶ The eyes of HASHEM are toward the righteous,
and His ears to their cry.

¹⁷ The face of HASHEM is against evildoers,
to excise from earth their memory.

¹⁸ They cried out and HASHEM hears
and from all their troubles He rescues them.

¹⁹ HASHEM is close to the brokenhearted;
and those crushed in spirit, He saves.

The People of Israel determine the intensity and intimacy of God's relationship with His nation. When they choose to neglect God, He neglects them in return. But when they search Him out, He eagerly responds in like fashion, as Daniel prayed, *My God, turn Your ear and hear, open Your eyes and see (Daniel 9:18).* Thus, in our verse, too, the eyes of God are upon His righteous ones when they cry out to Him, thereby demonstrating their closeness to Him (*Kedushas Levi*).

וְאָזְנָיו אֶל שַׁוְעָתָם — *And His ears, to their cry.*

If some mishap were to befall the *tzaddik*, God would immediately hear his cry (*Radak*).

Alshich asks: If God's eyes carefully supervise and protect every step of the righteous, how can any mishap befall them? He answers: God loves to hear the prayers of the righteous. He sometimes allows a mishap to occur in order to increase their prayers, and thereby carry their souls to otherwise unattainable heights.

17. פְּנֵי ה׳ — *The face of HASHEM.*

Rashi comments that this usage always describes a countenance of anger as God says of the man who sacrifices

his son to Molech, וְשַׂמְתִּי אֲנִי אֶת פָּנַי בָּאִישׁ הַהוּא, *Then I will set my face (of anger) against that man (Leviticus 20:5).*

לְהַכְרִית מֵאֶרֶץ זִכְרָם — *To excise from earth their memory.*

[The *Talmud (Sanhedrin* 110b) cites a number of opinions as to how the wicked are uprooted from the world. Not only are their bodies destroyed, so are their souls. Not only do *they* vanish, their young children are also cut off. And, although the remembrance of their sins endures, God makes every effort to blot out any trace of their good deeds. He quickly repays them in This World for every good deed, so that He can eradicate all their merits for entry in the World to Come.]

18. צָעֲקוּ — *They cried out.*

The righteous ones (*Rashi*), and the repentant sinners (*Ibn Ezra*).

וַה׳ שָׁמֵעַ — *And HASHEM hears.*

Even if words cannot express their anguish and their cry remains stifled in their hearts, Hashem still hears (*Sfas Emes*). [See also v. 7.]

19. קָרוֹב ה׳ לְנִשְׁבְּרֵי לֵב — *HASHEM is close to the brokenhearted.*

The singular form נִשְׁבָּר לֵב would have been sufficient to describe the

When Aaron heard that two men were quarreling, he would go and sit next to one, saying: 'I just saw that other fellow beating his breast and tearing his clothes in anguish and remorse, crying out that he is at fault in your quarrel.' Aaron did not leave until the man was appeased. He repeated this procedure with the other party, too. Later, when these two men chanced to meet, they hugged and kissed each other in total reconciliation.

כ יוֹשִׁיעַ: רַבּוֹת רָעוֹת צַדִּיק וּמִכֻּלָּם יַצִּילֶנּוּ

כא יְהוָה: שֹׁמֵר כָּל־עַצְמוֹתָיו אַחַת מֵהֵנָּה לֹא

כב נִשְׁבָּרָה: תְּמוֹתֵת רָשָׁע רָעָה וְשֹׂנְאֵי צַדִּיק

כג יֶאְשָׁמוּ: פּוֹדֶה יהוה נֶפֶשׁ עֲבָדָיו וְלֹא

יֶאְשְׁמוּ כָּל־הַחֹסִים בּוֹ:

broken heart. The plural form emphasizes that one break is not enough; the truly contrite heart should be broken into many pieces. The more shattered the heart, the closer is God (*Turei Zahav*).

Rabbi Alexandri said: To use broken dishes and utensils is a disgrace even for the most simple of men. Nevertheless, God prefers to use broken vessels in His service, as it says, *HASHEM is close to the heartbroken*; and, *The sacrifices of God are a broken spirit, a broken and crushed heart, God will not despise* [51:19] (*Midrash, Vayikra Rabbah* 7:2).

20. רַבּוֹת רָעוֹת צַדִּיק — *Many are the mishaps of the righteous man.*

Grammatically the word צַדִּיק, *righteous man*, should have been preceded by the prepositional prefix לְ, *to*, or *of*. By omitting it, the Psalmist alludes to an additional lesson: רַבּוֹת רָעוֹת, *from many mishaps* — צַדִּיק, there emerges a righteous man i.e., greatness is a product of challenges and the effort to surmount them (*Sfas Emes*).

וּמִכֻּלָּם יַצִּילֶנּוּ ה' — *But from them all HASHEM rescues him.*

Radak observes that God constantly tests the *tzaddik* with many a difficult נִסָּיוֹן, *trial*, in order to elevate him and to

demonstrate to others the loyalty of the *tzaddik* so that they will be inspired by his example. However, God will rescue the *tzaddik* from any real danger and will not allow him to stumble.

21. שֹׁמֵר כָּל־עַצְמוֹתָיו אַחַת מֵהֵנָּה לֹא נִשְׁבָּרָה — *He guards all his bones, even one of them was not broken.*

The term *bones* is used to describe the entire body because the skeletal structure is the body's mainstay (*Radak*).

The *tzaddik* has scrupulously observed all of God's 613 commands which correspond to the 248 organs and 365 sinews, ligaments and tendons; a total of six hundred thirteen. Hashem reciprocates and watches over all 613 parts of his body (*Tehillos Hashem*).[1]

22. תְּמוֹתֵת רָשָׁע רָעָה — *The death blow of the wicked is evil.*

תְּמוֹתֵת is the same as תָּמִית, *will slay*. The evil of the wicked man will kill him (*Rashi*).

The *tzaddik* is rescued from רַבּוֹת רָעוֹת, *many evils* (v. 20), but even one רָעָה, *evil*, is sufficient to undo the wicked man. As Solomon said (*Proverbs* 24:16) *The tzaddik falls seven times and rises up again, but the wicked are ensnared in [one] evil* (*Siach Yitzchak*).

The very evil which he plots against

---

1. *Sefer HaBris* (Part I, Essay 11, Chapter 10) states that the entire body disintegrates after death with the exception of one indestructible bone at the top of the spinal column. This bone, called *Luz* or *Nasqui*, can be neither shattered by hammers nor consumed by fires (*Midrash, Vayikra Rabbah*). When God resurrects the dead, this surviving bone will be used as the starting point for the restoration of the rest of the body. The Psalmist alludes to this phenomenon saying, *He safeguards all of his* (the skeleton's) *bones*, i.e., even after the skeleton turns to dust. This will be so because נִשְׁבָּרָה לֹא מֵהֵנָּה אַחַת, *one of them* [i.e., the *Luz*] *was never broken*. However, this is not the case with the wicked who are totally corrupted. They shall not be resurrected for even their *Luz* bone rots in the dust, לְהַכְרִית מֵאֶרֶץ זִכְרָם, *to excise from earth their memory* (v. 17).

20 *Many are the mishaps of the righteous man,*
but from them all HASHEM rescues him.
21 *He guards all his bones,*
even one of them was not broken.
22 *The death blow of the wicked is evil,*
and the haters of the righteous
will be condemned.
23 *HASHEM redeems the soul of His servants,*
and all who take refuge in Him
will not be condemned.

the righteous will lash back and kill him instead, as in *Psalms 7:17: He falls into the very trap which he set* (Radak).

Based on verses 21-22, *Rabbeinu Yonah* (*Shaarei Teshuvah* 4:13) expounds on two forms of Divine punishment: The afflictions which God brings upon the wicked are יִסּוּרֵי נָקָם, *afflictions of revenge*, so to speak, which have the purpose of destroying those who are unworthy of mercy. When they are punished, the afflictions merited for even a *single* sin are enough to destroy them, for the entire punishment is brought upon them at once as we read, תְּמוֹתֵת רָשָׁע רָעָה, *The death blow of the wicked is evil* (in the singular form). Their other transgressions remain unatoned for and continue to blemish their souls.

The righteous, however, have earned the privilege of being punished by gradual, bearable degrees. Thus, all of their transgressions are eventually atoned for. The Sages (*Avodah Zarah* 4a) liken this to a lender's policy with

his borrowers. From his antagonists whom he does not trust, he demands prompt and total payment. From his friends, he is satisfied with partial payments within their means.

יֶאְשָׁמוּ — *Will be condemned.*

This translation follows the *Targum* (יִתְחַיְּבוּן). *Radak* and *Metzudas David* render *they will be made desolate*, deriving the word from שִׁמָּמוֹן, *desolation*. Similarly, we find עֶרְרֵי הַצֹּאן נֶאְשָׁמוּ, *the flocks of sheep were devastated* (Joel 1:18).

23. פֹּדֶה ה' נֶפֶשׁ עֲבָדָיו — *HASHEM redeems the soul of His servants.*

The misfortune which was originally prepared for the righteous is diverted from its path and directed towards the wicked instead, as Solomon said (*Proverbs* 11:8): צַדִּיק מִצָּרָה נֶחֱלָץ וַיָּבֹא רָשָׁע תַּחְתָּיו, *The righteous man is released from trouble and the wicked man comes in his stead* (Eitz Yoseif).

Mordechai was redeemed from the gallows and Haman hung in his place.

When Adam ate from the Tree of Knowledge, all his organs derived pleasure from this sin, and were condemned. Only the *Luz* refused to absorb any part of this forbidden fruit and remained immortal.

After the three generous Sabbath meals, the body is surfeited and derives no physical pleasure from the *Melaveh Malkah* eaten after the Sabbath ends. Only the *Luz* is nourished by this meal exclusively, for it is eaten only for the sake of enriching the immortal spirit. The *Melaveh Malkah* is call *the feast of King David*, for David, King of Israel lives on and endures! It is he who will restore the immortality of Adam for he will bring the Messianic era which will be followed by the resurrection of the dead (whose formation is based on the *Luz* bone) for all eternity.

Chananyah, Mishael, and Azariyah emerged from the furnace alive, while their executioners were burned instead (*Vilna Gaon*).

Sforno interprets: Hashem redeems His servants from sin, i.e., He guides their footsteps away from temptation and error.

וְלֹא יֶאְשְׁמוּ כָּל הַחֹסִים בּוֹ — *All who take refuge in Him will not be condemned.*

Targum and *Ibn Ezra* translate יֶאְשְׁמוּ here as they do in the previous verse,

will be condemned.

Rashi paraphrases: Those who ask God to rescue them from sin will never have cause to regret their actions and cry out in remorse, 'אָשַׁמְנוּ, *We are guilty!'*

[David sought refuge in God while in the grip of his Philistine enemies. The Philistines found him guilty and sought to condemn him for the death of Goliath, but God redeemed the righteous David and set him free.]

D avid concluded the preceding psalm with the hopeful declaration
of his belief that פּוֹדֶה ה' נֶפֶשׁ עֲבָדָיו, HASHEM redeems the soul of
His servants. Now, he requests that this Divine attribute be put into
practice, and he pleads with God to redeem him from the menace of
his many enemies (Tehillas Hashem).

Radak comments that David composed this psalm while fleeing
from Saul. According to Sforno, these verses record David's pleas as
he fled from his rebellious son, Absalom.

א לְדָוִד ׀ רִיבָה יהוה אֶת־יְרִיבַי לְחַם אֶת־
ב לֹחֲמָי: הַחֲזֵק מָגֵן וְצִנָּה וְקוּמָה בְּעֶזְרָתִי:
ג וְהָרֵק חֲנִית וּסְגֹר לִקְרַאת רֹדְפָי אֱמֹר
ד לְנַפְשִׁי יְשֻׁעָתֵךְ אָנִי: יֵבֹשׁוּ וְיִכָּלְמוּ

1. רִיבָה ה׳ — *Fight, HASHEM.*

Radak explains this term as a command. *Midrash Shocher Tov* elaborates on its implications:

Is it conceivable that a flesh and blood servant should order his master, 'Go out and fight my enemies for me?' Yet we find that the Holy One ‚Blessed be He, said to David, 'You immerse yourself in Torah study and I will fight your wars.' This is what Moses meant in the verse, עַל כֵּן יֵאָמַר בְּסֵפֶר מִלְחֲמֹת ה׳, *Therefore it shall be said in the Book of HASHEM's wars* (Numbers 21:14). Hashem said: 'If you are [immersed] *in the Book* [of Torah study], then מִלְחֲמֹת ה׳ [your wars will become] *the wars of HASHEM* [and I, HASHEM, will fight them for you].'

יְרִיבַי ... לֹחֲמָי — *My adversaries* [lit. *those who fight me*] ... *my attackers* [lit. *those who declare war on me.*]

David emphasizes that the quarrel is only one-sided. He does not say that *he* fights *them*, rather *they* fight *him*, but he does not reciprocate their hostility (*Hirsch*).

According to *Yaavetz Hadoresh*, the word יְרִיבַי describes David's main adversaries, such as Saul or Absalom. Had the feud been limited only to these individuals, it would have been a mere רִיב, *quarrel*. But now that many others joined forces with the principal antagonists, the limited *quarrel* turned into a מִלְחָמָה, *war*. David refers to these outside interlopers as לֹחֲמָי, literally *those who declare war against me.*

Midrash Chachamim suggests that the difference between these words may be understood in light of the fact that

every war which flares up on earth is evidence of a tremendous spiritual struggle between celestial forces representing each side. David asks that Hashem first vanquish his adversaries above, יְרִיבַי, and consequently this will spell the doom of those who make actual war below, לֹחֲמָי, his *attackers.*

2. הַחֲזֵק — *Take hold.*

Grasp it tightly, with חֹזֶק, *strength* (*Radak*).

מָגֵן וְצִנָּה — *Shield and armor.*

[These two words, which appear to be synonymous, warrant deeper scrutiny. On the verses כַּצִּנָּה רָצוֹן תַּעְטְרֶנּוּ, *You will surround him with Your favor like a shield* (5:13), *Rashi* describes the צִנָּה as a shield which protects from only three sides. However, on the verse צִנָּה וְסֹחֵרָה אֲמִתּוֹ, *Like encircling armor is His truth* (91:4) *Rashi* explains that צִנָּה surrounds the wearer from almost four sides. Similarly, we read כִּי שֶׁמֶשׁ וּמָגֵן ה׳, *for HASHEM is a sun and a shield* (*ibid.*) on which the *Midrash* comments: A מָגֵן is a shield which protects from only three sides. From where do we know that Hashem guards even from the fourth side? From the verse כַּצִּנָּה רָצוֹן תַּעְטְרֶנּוּ. This indicates that a צִנָּה is indeed a four-sided protective armor.

Interestingly, *Targum* always renders מָגֵן as תְּרִיסָא. Also, whenever צִנָּה is mentioned alone the *Targum* translates it as תְּרִיסָא. But, when the words מָגֵן וְצִנָּה come together, as in this verse, the *Targum* for צִנָּה changes to עֲגִיל, *a round encircling armament.* This leads us to conclude that when the word צִנָּה is used alone it is the same as מָגֵן (i.e., a three-sided shield), and thus it should be translated as *shield.* But when it appears in conjunction with מָגֵן it indicates greater protection than a shield and should be translated as *armor.* The *Targum* of תְּרִיסָא וַעֲגִילִין is צִנָּה וְסֹחֵרָה and, according to *Rashi* (*ibid.*), the second word is

To David: Fight, HASHEM, my adversaries,
battle my attackers.
² Take hold of shield and armor,
and rise up in my defense.
³ Draw the spear,
and barricade before my pursuers;
Say to my soul,
'Your salvation am I.'
⁴ May they be shamed and disgraced,

---

an adjective, and so the phrase is translated *encircling armor.* Perhaps the word צִנָּה has some relationship to צִנְעָה, *privacy, secrecy, enclosure.*]

וְקוּמָה בְּעֶזְרָתִי — *And rise up in my defense* [lit. *help.*]

Since I do not rely on my own shield and armor, only Yours, it is proper that You should defend me (*Ibn Ezra*).

Paamonei Zahav offers a general explanation of this psalm which records David's repeated requests for the destruction of his enemies. Elsewhere, David preached a different message, as we find יִתַּמּוּ חַטָּאִים מִן הָאָרֶץ, *Let sins cease to be on earth* (104:35), which the *Talmud (Berachos* 10a) interprets as meaning 'let *sins* cease but not the *sinners*,' i.e., do not pray for the death of the people who sin; rather pray that they should repent and consequently sin will cease. However, the wicked discussed here are so corrupt that the paths of repentance are sealed before them. Their hearts are consumed with hatred as is evidenced by the fact that such they hate without any reason. Such fierce, bitter animosity can never be cured. Similarly we find in the *Talmud (Gittin* 7a) that the righteous Mar Ukava was gratuitously threatened and cursed by violent men and Rabbi Elazar advised him to pray morning and evening for their destruction.

3. וְהָרֵק — *Draw.*

[This comes from רִיק, *empty.* When a spear or sword is drawn, its sheath or scabbard is emptied of it, as we find אָרִיק חַרְבִּי, *I draw my sword* (Exodus 15:9).]

It also means *to arm* as in וַיָּרֶק אֶת חֲנִיכָיו, *And he armed his trained men* (Genesis 14:14).

חֲנִית — *The spear.*

Here David alludes to the spear which Saul threw at his head, narrowly missing him [*I Samuel* 18:11] (*Chazah Zion*), and also to the spear which was lying by the head of the sleeping Saul which David did not use to kill him [*I Samuel* 26:7-9] (*Zera Yaakov*). [Because David did not defend himself against the spears of Saul out of fear that he might harm God's anointed, he calls upon God Himself to do him justice.]

אֱמֹר לְנַפְשִׁי יְשֻׁעָתֵךְ אָנִי — *Say to my soul, 'Your salvation, am I.'*

Inject strength, fortitude and courage into my heart so that it should not fear the enemy (*Radak*).

4. [*Malbim* traces the various levels of humiliation documented in this verse.]

יֵבֹשׁוּ — *Be shamed.*

This an inner, self-generated shame.

יִכָּלְמוּ — *Be disgraced.*

This embarrassment is more severe and is inflicted by others.

מְבַקְשֵׁי נַפְשִׁי יִסֹּגוּ אָחוֹר וְיַחְפְּרוּ חֹשְׁבֵי

ה רָעָתִי: יִהְיוּ כְּמֹץ לִפְנֵי־רוּחַ וּמַלְאַךְ יהוה

ו דּוֹחֶה: יְהִי־דַרְכָּם חֹשֶׁךְ וַחֲלַקְלַקֹּת

ז וּמַלְאַךְ יהוה רֹדְפָם: כִּי־חִנָּם טָמְנוּ־לִי

ח שַׁחַת רִשְׁתָּם חִנָּם חָפְרוּ לְנַפְשִׁי: תְּבוֹאֵהוּ

שׁוֹאָה לֹא־יֵדָע וְרִשְׁתּוֹ אֲשֶׁר־טָמַן תִּלְכְּדוֹ

יִסֹּגוּ אָחוֹר — *Retreat* [lit. *fall back*].

This is more intense than shame, but it is a turnabout which comes from the person's own realization of his defects.

וְיַחְפְּרוּ — *Be humiliated.*

This is the most intense embarrassment which is caused by others.

The word is related to the root חפר, *to dig,* and suggests that the victim is so humiliated that he desires to bury himself. [In the Yiddish idiom this intense humiliation is called 'tzu bagrubben a mentsch lebedigerheit,' to bury a person alive.]

5. יִהְיוּ כְּמֹץ לִפְנֵי רוּחַ — *May they be like chaff before the wind.*

[Compare with 1:4: לֹא כֵן הָרְשָׁעִים, כִּי אִם כַּמֹּץ אֲשֶׁר תִּדְּפֶנּוּ רוּחַ, *Not so the wicked, they are like the chaff which the wind drives away.*]

Tanchuma (Bamidbar 4) compares the Children of Israel, who are well nourished with *mitzvos,* to the nutritious grain heaped in abundant piles, whereas the empty, meaningless lifestyle of heathens makes them similar to worthless chaff.

וּמַלְאַךְ ה' דּוֹחֶה — *With the angel of HASHEM driving them on.*

Sometimes the flight of the blown chaff is aborted by an obstacle in its path, but these wicked men will be relentlessly pursued by angels who will give them no respite *(Radak).*

Maharam Markado suggests that this refers to the angel who drove Saul away from David when he was trapped on the סֶלַע הַמַּחְלְקֹת, *mountain of division* [*I Samuel* 23:27-28].

6. חֹשֶׁךְ וַחֲלַקְלַקֹּת — *Dark and exceedingly slippery.*

Ibn Ezra notes that חָלָק alone means *smooth, slippery,* but here part of the root is repeated as חֲלַקְלַק to give it increased emphasis.

Rashi explains that when both of these difficulties come together, they spell disaster. The wicked stumble on the slippery spots. Had it been light, they could avoid the danger, but because it is dark they cannot see where they are going.[1]

Rabbeinu Yonah (Shaarei Teshuvah 3:192) says: It is written וּפֶה חָלָק יַעֲשֶׂה מִדְחֶה, *A smooth* [i.e., false] *mouth causes stumbling (Proverbs* 26:28). A smooth mouth is likened to a slippery road. Just as a slippery road causes a person to stumble, so a smooth mouth, i.e., insincere flattery, causes one to falter. Regarding this, David said: יַכְרֵת ה' כָּל שִׂפְתֵי חֲלָקוֹת, *May HASHEM cut off all smooth lips* (12:4).

---

1. The wicked represent darkness as it says: *And their deeds are in the darkness (Isaiah* 29:14). Therefore God punishes them in the darkness of night. The angels arrived to overturn Sodom at night. The first-born of Egypt were smitten at midnight. Sennacherib's army was destroyed at midnight. Belshazzar was slain at night. Haman's downfall began when the King Ahaserus could not sleep at night. So, too, in the future the wicked will be covered by darkness, but the righteous will be bathed in light; as it says *(Proverbs* 4:18), *And the path of the righteous is like a shining light (Yalkut Shimoni).*

those who seek my life;

Let them retreat and be humiliated,
those who plot my harm.

⁵ *May they be like chaff before the wind,*
with the angel of HASHEM driving them on.

⁶ *May their way be dark and exceedingly slippery,*
with the angel of HASHEM pursuing them.

⁷ *For without cause,*
they hid me in a pit with their net;

Without cause
they dug to kill me.

⁸ *May darkness come upon him, unaware,*
and his own net which he concealed —
may it ensnare him. In darkness may he fall.

וּמַלְאַךְ ה' רֹדְפָם — *With the angel of HASHEM pursuing them.*

This completes the catastrophe. A person walking on slippery ground in the dark can at least walk very cautiously and slowly and thereby avoid falling, but now that they are pursued by the angels they must run recklessly and slip (*Radak*).

7. טָמְנוּ לִי שַׁחַת רִשְׁתָּם — *They hid for me a pit [with] their net.*

They prepare a deep pit which destroys all who fall into it, and camouflage it by covering it with a net [see *comm.* to 7:16]. They try every possible trick and deception in order to kill me (*Radak*).

Sforno suggests that this refers to Achitophel's advice to Absalom. He urged Absalom to pursue and trap David in order to destroy him on the first night of his flight (*II Samuel* 17:2).

8. תְּבוֹאֵהוּ — *May [it] come upon him.*

David now changes from the plural form to the singular, because he addresses each enemy individually or because he refers to Saul, the one principal enemy (*Radak*).

Sforno holds that this refers to Achitophel who was confident that Absalom would follow his advice to pursue David, until he was suddenly thrust into *darkness* by the unexpected counsel of Chushai who successfully convinced Absalom to cautiously restrain himself.

שׁוֹאָה — *Darkness.*

Rashi and *Metzudos* translate here שׁוֹאָה as *darkness.* However, *Rashi* renders יוֹם שֹׁאָה וּמְשׁוֹאָה [*Zephaniah* 1:15] as *a day of desolation* [from שִׁמָּמוֹן, *utter desolation.*]

Radak translates שׁוֹאָה as *turmoil and confusion.* In *Ezekiel* 38:9, *Radak* renders this word as *a roaring, sudden, tidal wave.* Both in *Ezekiel* and *Zephaniah*, the *Targum* of this word is אִתְרְלוֹשָׁא or אִתְרְגוּשְׁתָּא, from רְגַשׁ, *agitation* or *turbulence.* According to *Ibn Ezra*, the devastation which befalls each enemy will be so staggering that all who hear will be מִשְׁתָּאֶה, *amazed,* dumb-struck.

וְרִשְׁתּוֹ אֲשֶׁר טָמַן תִּלְכְּדוֹ — *And his own net which he concealed — may it ensnare him.*

ט בְּשׁוּאָה יִפָּל־בָּהּ: וְנַפְשִׁי תָּגִיל בַּיהוה

י תָּשִׂישׂ בִּישׁוּעָתוֹ: כָּל עַצְמֹתַי | תֹּאמַרְנָה

יהוה מִי כָמוֹךָ מַצִּיל עָנִי מֵחָזָק מִמֶּנּוּ

יא וְעָנִי וְאֶבְיוֹן מִגֹּזְלוֹ: יְקוּמוּן עֵדֵי חָמָס

יב אֲשֶׁר לֹא־יָדַעְתִּי יִשְׁאָלוּנִי: יְשַׁלְּמוּנִי רָעָה

Achitophel sought to ensnare David
with his counsel, but precisely because
his counsel was rejected he was so dejected that he hung himself (Sforno).

9. [Now David describes how he will
react to the downfall of his enemies.]

תָּגִיל ... תָּשִׂישׂ — Exult ... rejoice.

Malbim explains that גִּילָה is inner
joy, whereas שָׂשׂוֹן describes the external
manifestations of gladness.

10. כָּל עַצְמֹתַי תֹּאמַרְנָה — All my limbs
[lit. bones] will say.

Radak comments that David chose
the bones to symbolize the entire body
because they are its mainstay. The ecstatic shaking and swaying of the body
during the recital of prayers, is itself an
eloquent expression of praise. Also,
when one studies the wonders of the
human anatomy, he is moved to laud
the Creator who fashioned the organs
with such wisdom.

The halachic implications of this
verse are recorded in Berachos [4:3]:
The daily prayers contain eighteen
benedictions corresponding to the eighteen vertebrae in the spine. During
prayer one must bow down and bend
them all, as it says, All of my limbs will
say ...

The Midrash [Vayikra Rabbah 30:14]
relates the Four Species of Sukkos to
the four major organs:

—The Lulav (palm-branch) resembles
the spine.

—The Hadas (myrtle leaf) resembles
the human eye.

—The Aravah (willow leaf) resembles
the mouth.

—The Esrog (citron) resembles the
heart.

David said: 'These four major organs
are fundamental to the rest of the body
and soul, I therefore select them to
praise God; All my limbs will say ...

The Pesikta cites numerous verses
from Psalms which demonstrate that
David praised God with every single
organ of his body. This alludes to the
Talmudic dictum, that here are 248
organs corresponding to the 248
positive commandments. Thus, the performance of each commandment, in effect, involves its organ, as it were, in the
praise of God.

Tehillas Hashem adds that the organs
representing the respective commandments are destined to proclaim the
praises of their possessors who so
lavishly embellished them with spiritual
finery.

הי מִי כָמוֹךָ — HASHEM, who is like You?

All of my limbs were endangered by
my enemies and my debilitating sickness
(Malbim), only You, Hashem, could
provide salvation against such odds
(Metzudas David).

מַצִּיל עָנִי מֵחָזָק מִמֶּנּוּ — Deliverer of the
poor from one mightier than he.

God protects Israel in its exile among
the nations where it resembles a lamb
among seventy hungry wolves. How
could Israel survive if not for Hashem
Who delivers it every moment? (Pesikta 9:2)

וְעָנִי וְאֶבְיוֹן מִגֹּזְלוֹ — Of the poor and
needy from him who robs him.

The Pesikta (ibid.) homiletically

⁹ *Then my soul will exult in* HASHEM,
rejoice in His salvation.
¹⁰ *All my limbs will say,*
'HASHEM, *who is like You?*
Deliverer of the poor from one mightier than he,
of the poor and needy from him who robs him.'
¹¹ *Extortive witnesses rise up;*
what I know not, they demand.
¹² *They repay me evil for good,*

---

refers this to the יֵצֶר הַטּוֹב, *Good Inclination*, which is impoverished of good deeds. It is overpowered by the יֵצֶר הָרַע, *Evil Inclination*. The *Good Inclination* must toil long and hard before it can accomplish even one mitzvah, but then the temptation to sin deprives it of all it had earned. Is there any robber more dangerous than this?

11. יָקוּמוּן עֵדֵי חָמָס — *Extortive witnesses rise up.*

[The *Targum* renders חָמָס as חֲטוֹפִין, *those who seize by force*. The word usually describes someone who will go to any lengths, even violence, to extract a desired object from its owner.]

Radak comments that among David's many enemies was a group which sought to extort money from him. Though there is no record of such people in the Book of *Samuel*, this is implied by our verse.

Sforno says that this alludes to Absalom, who would stand at the gates of Jerusalem and greet all who came to David to seek justice. Absalom would tell them: *Your cause is just, however, the king will never listen to you. If only I could be the judge over the land, then I* would deal righteously with all (II *Samuel* 15:2). [Thus he bore false testimony against his father in order to extort and usurp the throne.]

The *Tosefta (Bava Kamma* 7:3) states: There are seven categories of thieves, the worst of which is the גּוֹנֵב דַּעַת הַבְּרִיּוֹת, *one who tricks others by means of misrepresentation*. Thus Absalom was called a thief for he stole the hearts of all Israel [by falsely slandering David and misrepresenting himself.]

What was the result of Absalom's treachery? Absalom deceived three hearts by means of deceit, the heart of his father, of the Sanhedrin, and of all Israel. Therefore, he died with three javelins piercing his heart (*Sotah* 9b).

12. יְשַׁלְּמוּנִי רָעָה תַּחַת טוֹבָה — *They repay me evil for good.*

David had acted kindly towards them, but they betrayed his friendship (*Radak*).

According to *Sforno*, this refers to the elders of the Sanhedrin, who were David's friends, but who later joined Absalom and concurred in Absalom's plot to kill David immediately.[1]

---

1. *Yerushalmi (Sotah* 1:8) relates how Absalom lured the elders to his cause. Prior to his revolt, Absalom told his father that he wished to go to Hebron to offer up special sacrifices. Absalom slyly requested of his father, 'Assign two elders to accompany me so that I may be guided by their counsel.'

David acceded and asked, 'Which elders shall I command to accompany you? I will write their names on this letter with my order!'

Absalom cunningly replied, 'Leave the spaces blank and I will insert the names of

יג תַּחַת טוֹבָה שְׁכוֹל לְנַפְשִׁי: וַאֲנִי | בַּחֲלוֹתָם
לְבוּשִׁי שָׂק עִנֵּיתִי בַצּוֹם נַפְשִׁי וּתְפִלָּתִי
יד עַל־חֵיקִי תָשׁוּב: כְּרֵעַ־כְּאָח לִי
הִתְהַלָּכְתִּי כַּאֲבֶל־אֵם קֹדֵר שַׁחוֹתִי:
טו וּבְצַלְעִי שָׂמְחוּ וְנֶאֱסָפוּ נֶאֶסְפוּ עָלַי נֵכִים

שְׁכוֹל לְנַפְשִׁי — *Death for my soul.*

These men stop at nothing, not only will they take my money, they will even take my soul (*Radak*).

Since שְׁכוֹל usually refers to the death of children in the lifetime of their parents (see *Genesis* 42:36), support is lent to *Sforno's* commentary. The treacherous elders, who misguided Absalom, eventually caused David to be שְׁכוֹל, *bereft*, of his son Absalom who was killed as a result of his rebellion.

13. וַאֲנִי בַּחֲלוֹתָם לְבוּשִׁי שָׂק עִנֵּיתִי בַצּוֹם נַפְשִׁי — *But as for me, when they were ill my clothing was sackcloth, I afflicted myself* [lit. *my soul*] *with fasting.*

[These men rejoiced over his tragedies, but David acted nobly toward them. Although earlier in the psalm we find David requesting the destruction of his enemies, that was only after he was convinced that there was no hope for them to repent. Here, however, he discusses his initial, compassionate reaction to their evil. His foes were great scholars, but they did not work on the refinement of their characters. Absalom pandered to their pride and ambition and enmeshed them in his plot.]

The *Talmud* (*Berachos* 12b) states that whoever refrains from praying for divine mercy on behalf of his friend and does not do so is called a sinner ... And if the friend is a Torah scholar, then he who prays should become sick with misery over the scholar's plight ... As David said (in reference to Doeg and Achitophel, who were Torah scholars): *When they were ill, my clothing was sackcloth, I afflicted myself with fasting.*

From this verse *Midrash Hane'elam* learns that one should pray for the spiritual recovery of the wicked whose souls are sick. By no means should he pray for their destruction, however; for if God had removed the idol-worshiper, Terach, from the world, there never would have been an Abraham, or the twelve tribes, or David, or Messiah. The Torah would not have been given and all of the righteous, the devout, and the prophets would never have arrived on this world.

וּתְפִלָּתִי עַל חֵיקִי תָשׁוּב — *As for my prayer, upon my own bosom let it return.*

My profuse supplications wre motivated by concern for my own safety. My paranoid enemies, however, claim that my sole desire was to influence God to harm them. It that be true, may the suffering which I allegedly wished them descend upon me (*Rashi; Radak*).

whomever I wish!' Absalom then approached pair after pair of the heads of Sanhedrin in every city of the realm and convinced them that the king had no respect for them, as evidenced by the fact that he wrote them a strict order without even according them the honor of referring to them by name! Absalom, however, esteemed them so highly that he chose them as his elite honor guard. In this treacherous manner, Absalom gathered not just two, but two-hundred elders for this entourage. All who witnessed this grand processsion exclaimed with joy: 'Observe how truly dignified Prince Absalom is! Surely he is worthy of the throne!'

death for my soul.

¹³ But as for me, when they were ill,
        my clothing was sackcloth
        and I afflicted myself with fasting.
    As for my prayer,
        upon my own bosom let it return.
¹⁴ As if for a companion, as if for my own brother,
        I went about;
    As if in mourning for a mother
        I bleakly bent over.
¹⁵ But when I limped they rejoiced and gathered,
        against me gathered the lame — I know not why.

---

14. בְּרֵעַ כְּאָח לִי — *As if for a companion, as if for my own brother.*

I mourned for my enemies as if they were dear friends or brothers — as if I were personally affected, because the closer a tragedy strikes, the more one must be concerned, not only for the victim, but for himself. As the *Talmud* states (*Shabbos* 106a): Rabbi Yochanan said, If one of the brothers dies, all the rest should worry [fear death (*Rashi*).] If one member of a group dies, all of the others should worry (*Eretz HaChaim*).

כַּאֲבֶל אֵם — *As if in mourning for a mother.*

David uses the example of the mother because a person grieves more over the loss of his mother than of his father. For, he is conceived in her womb, nursed at her breast, raised and nurtured at her side until he is grown. Even in later life she is always ready to provide for her son's needs, his food, and his drink (*Radak*).

When a father dies, the blow is softened by the inheritance he leaves behind, which provides at least partial consolation, not so the departure of the mother, who usually leaves over nothing (*Meiri*).

קֹדֵר — *Bleakly* [lit. *black, dark.*]

Because of his pain and anguish, the face of the mourner loses its glow, and seems darker. Also, the mourner wears dark clothing (*Radak*).

15. שָׂמְחוּ וְנֶאֱסָפוּ — *They rejoiced and gathered.*

When they heard of my mishap they gathered to savor the details and rejoice over them (*Radak*).

וְנֶאֶסְפוּ עָלַי נֵכִים — *Against me gathered the lame.*

The translation follows *Rashi*. *Radak*, however, translates this as *lowly people* who are beaten and mistreated because of their miserable state. [Thus נָכֶה, is related to מַכָּה, *blow*.]

I went to visit these wretched people when they were bedridden. Now they reciprocate by gathering around my bed to applaud my pains (*Ibn Ezra*).

These cripples have their own problems about which to be concerned, yet when they see me disabled, they forget their own woes and rejoice over mine (*Meiri*).

וְלֹא יָדָעְתִּי — *I know not why* [lit. *I did not know.*]

I cannot understand why they desire

טז וְלֹא יָדַעְתִּי קָרְעוּ וְלֹא־דָמּוּ: בְּחַנְפֵי לַעֲגֵי

יז מָעוֹג חָרֹק עָלַי שִׁנֵּימוֹ: אֲדֹנָי כַּמָּה תִרְאֶה הָשִׁיבָה נַפְשִׁי מִשֹּׁאֵיהֶם מִכְּפִירִים

יח יְחִידָתִי: אוֹדְךָ בְּקָהָל רָב בְּעַם עָצוּם

יט אֲהַלְלֶךָּ: אַל־יִשְׂמְחוּ־לִי אֹיְבַי שֶׁקֶר שֹׂנְאַי

כ חִנָּם יִקְרְצוּ־עָיִן: כִּי לֹא שָׁלוֹם יְדַבֵּרוּ וְעַל

my injury for I never did them any harm (Radak).

קָרְעוּ — They tore.

Rashi, following Sanhedrin 107a, interprets this as referring to David's flesh which was being torn.[1]

Radak observes: When one howls in laughter he opens his mouth so wide it seems to be tearing apart. Radak adds an explanation from his father: When one commits a terrible wrong which cannot be righted, it resembles a gash that can never be mended.

וְלֹא דָמּוּ — And they would not be silenced.

Rashi cites the Talmud's homiletical explanation deriving דָמּוּ from דָם, blood. Thus, despite the tearing of David's flesh, his blood did not drip (Rashi).

16. בְּחַנְפֵי לַעֲגֵי — Because of flattery and mockery.

David's enemies fawned upon his adversaries, particularly Saul. David laments: They flatter my enemies and mock me. (Rashi; Metzudas David).

What is the difference between the לֵץ, one who ridicules (Psalms 1:1) and the חוֹנֵף, the flatterer? What is good, the mocker calls bad. What is bad, the flatterer calls good (Tzidkas HaTzaddik).

מָעוֹג — A meal [lit. a cake.]

Although מָעוֹג means cake, it is used to describe eating in general. Thus, these men fawn upon Saul in order to get free meals from him.

Radak renders מָעוֹג as worthless talk in which they engage.

חָרֹק עָלַי שִׁנֵּימוֹ — They grind their teeth at me.

This term describes the gleeful grinding of the teeth by one who gains revenge over his enemy, as in וַיַּחַרְקוּ שֵׁן, they grind [their] teeth (Lamentations 2:16) (Radak; Metzudas Zion).

17. כַּמָּה תִרְאֶה — How much can You bear? [lit. look on].

How much patience do You have that You are able to restrain Yourself after seeing all this? (Rashi).

מִשֹּׁאֵיהֶם — From their darkness.

[See comm. to v. 8.]

1. David said to the Holy One, Blessed be He: 'It is well-known and revealed to you that even if my enemies would tear my flesh, my blood would not drip to the earth.' [The sin born of lust is symbolized by surging, racing blood. Now, as he repented his sin, David froze his passions and his blood.]

Furthermore, David said, that even when his enemies engaged in the study of complex laws of leprosy and ritual purity, they would turn to him and say derisively, 'What is the form of the death penalty of David the adulterer?' [Even though leprosy is a heavenly inflicted punishment for slander and evil tale-bearing, their study of those laws does not deter them for one moment from viciously slandering my name (Maharsha).]

David answered that the adulterer dies by חֶנֶק, choking, but at least he still can hope for a share in the World to Come. However, he who disgraces another man in public forfeits his portion in the World to Come.

They tore at me
> *and would not be silenced.*

¹⁶ *Because of flattery and mockery offered for a meal,*
> *they grind their teeth at me.*

¹⁷ *My Lord,*
> *how much can You bear?*

Return my life from their darkness;
> *from the young lions, my soul.*

¹⁸ *I will thank You in a great congregation,*
> *before a mighty throng I will praise You.*

¹⁹ *Let them not rejoice over me, my foes,*
> *for false cause;*

Or those who hate me baselessly,
> *let them not wink their eyes.*

²⁰ *For it is not peace that they speak,*

מִכְּפִירִים — *From young lions.*

I.e., save my life from the foes who are as ferocious, powerful, and hungry as young lions (*Radak; Metzudas Zion*).

יְחִידָתִי — *My soul* [lit. *my only one.*]

This is a description of the soul (*Radak*). [See comm. to *Psalms* 22:21.]

18. אוֹדְךָ בְּקָהָל רָב — *I will thank You in a great congregation.*

David vowed (*Ibn Ezra*) to give thanks before all of Israel after God will save him from his enemies (*Radak*). [Compare 103:31-32.]

בְּעַם עָצוּם — *Before a mighty throng.*

This denotes a tremendous number of people. David vowed that his gratitude to God would be expressed openly (*Metzudas Zion*).

19. אֹיְבַי שֶׁקֶר — *My foes for false cause.*

They hate me because of the very lies which they fabricated about me. They attribute to me crimes so outlandish that they would never even enter my mind (*Rashi*).

יִקְרְצוּ עָיִן — [*Let them not*] *wink their eyes.*

The adverb אַל, *not,* at the beginning of the verse refers to this final phrase as well (*Rashi; Metzudas David*).

The expression קְרִיצַת עַיִן describes the opening and closing of the eyelid in a suggestive manner in order to silently mock someone (*Radak*).

20. כִּי לֹא שָׁלוֹם יְדַבֵּרוּ — *For it is not peace that they speak.*

This refers to Absalom who promised to bring everyone peace, but whose true intention was to massacre all those who favored David (*Sforno*).

[At birth, David gave this son the name אַבְשָׁלוֹם, literally, *father of peace.* David recognized fully the violent nature of this son. However, he hoped to channel Absalom's violence in a beneficial direction by making him a great military leader who would subdue the nations in the Name of God, and thus bring about universal peace. Unfortunately, Absalom did not share his father's peaceful intentions.]

Chazah David suggests that these words describe the enemies of David who harped on the fact that he was a descendant of Ruth the Moabite. They

רַגְעֵי־אֶרֶץ דִּבְרֵי מִרְמוֹת יַחֲשֹׁבוּן:
וַיַּרְחִיבוּ עָלַי פִּיהֶם אָמְרוּ הֶאָח | הֶאָח כא
רָאִיתָה עֵינֵנוּ: רָאִיתָה יהוה אַל־תֶּחֱרַשׁ כב
אֲדֹנָי אַל־תִּרְחַק מִמֶּנִּי: הָעִירָה וְהָקִיצָה כג
לְמִשְׁפָּטִי אֱלֹהַי וַאדֹנָי לְרִיבִי: שָׁפְטֵנִי כד
כְצִדְקְךָ יהוה אֱלֹהָי וְאַל־יִשְׂמְחוּ־לִי: אַל־ כה
יֹאמְרוּ בְלִבָּם הֶאָח נַפְשֵׁנוּ אַל־יֹאמְרוּ

refused to accept the correct halachic ruling that all restrictions mentioned in the Torah against Moab apply only to male converts and their offspring, and not to female converts. Therefore, in their false righteousness they were most scrupulous in practicing against David the Biblical prohibition concerning Moab, לֹא תִדְרֹשׁ שְׁלֹמָם וְטֹבָתָם כָּל יָמֶיךָ לְעוֹלָם, *You shall not seek their peace or their well-being all of your days, forever* (Deuteronomy 23:7) and so they never extended the greeting of שָׁלוֹם, *peace*, to David.

רַגְעֵי אֶרֶץ — *The broken people of the earth.*

This refers to David's followers whom Absalom hoped to break when he was victorious over them (Sforno).

However, according to Radak, this phrase is translated, 'those who rest peacefully in the earth,' the word רַגְעֵי being related to מַרְגּוֹעַ, *rest*.

The Targum similarly elaborates: They deceitfully scheme to say false things about the righteous men who have come to their eternal rest in the Hereafter.

Alshich explains that, in particular, they cast aspersion on the words of Samuel, [then 'at rest' because he was no longer living], who announced that David was God's chosen king and that the monarchy had been taken away from Saul.

דִּבְרֵי מִרְמוֹת יַחֲשֹׁבוּן — *They scheme*

deceitfully [lit. *they think deceitful things.*]

Chazah David, continues his trend of thought in this verse: By their false claims that Ruth was unfit to enter the congregation of Israel, they falsely slandered my holy forebears, Boaz, Oved, and Jesse (who now rest peacefully in the earth), claiming that Boaz transgressed the prohibition of the Torah, 'No Ammonite or Moabite shall enter the congregation of HASHEM' [Deuteronomy 23:4], and thus, Oved and Jesse were born of an illicit relation.

21. וַיַּרְחִיבוּ עָלַי פִּיהֶם — *They broadly opened their mouths against me.*

They opened their mouths with laughter and scorn when they saw me miserably wandering in exile from place to place (Radak). [Perhaps this alludes to Shimi ben Gera who 'opened his mouth' to curse David as he fled from Absalom.]

הֶאָח הֶאָח — *Aha! Aha!*

This is the exclamation of joy which they utter when they witness the realization of their hearts' desire (Rashi).

22. רָאִיתָה ה׳ — *You have seen, HASHEM.*

This is in response to their claim, *Our own eyes have seen!* (Ibn Ezra).

אַל־תֶּחֱרַשׁ — *Do not be mute.*

You have seen their joy; do not be

> and against the broken people of the earth
> they scheme deceitfully.

²¹ They broadly opened their mouths
against me.

They say,
'Aha! Aha! Our own eyes have seen!'

²² You have seen, HASHEM, do not be mute;
my Lord do not stand far from me.

²³ Arouse Yourself and awaken for my judgment,
my God and my Lord, for my cause.

²⁴ Judge me according to Your righteousness,
HASHEM, my God,
and let them not rejoice over me.

²⁵ Let them not say in their hearts,
'Rejoice our souls!'

Let them not say,

---

mute from exacting vengeance from them on my account *(Metzudas David).*

23. הָעִירָה וְהָקִיצָה — *Arouse Yourself and awaken.*

[In the Sabbath prayer נְשָׁמַת כָּל חַי we find God described as הַמְּעוֹרֵר יְשָׁנִים וְהַמֵּקִיץ נִרְדָּמִים, *He arouses sleepers and awakens slumberers.* This indicates that the implication of *to arouse* is not as forceful an act as *to awaken.* The word מֵקִיץ is derived from the word קַץ, *end.* In the context of our verse, it literally means to put an end to deep slumber. See *Malbim* on *Habakuk* 2:19.]

Rashi holds that David is invoking divine assistance to arouse the Heavenly Tribunal of angels to mete out justice against his enemies.

Sforno comments: Arouse Your *Attribute of Mercy* to hear my prayer sympathetically. Awaken Your *Attribute of Justice* to vigorously support my cause.

מִשְׁפָּטִי ... רִיבִי — *My judgment ... my cause.*

Malbim here (and in *Isaiah* 3:13) explains that רִיב describes the preliminary arguments of a court case, when each side advocates its cause; while מִשְׁפָּט refers to the cross-examination and deliberation of the judges which lead to their final decision.

אֱלֹהַי וַאדֹנָי — *My God and my Lord.*

Radak translates these words literally, *my Judge and my Master.*

I come to You for judgment for You are the only judge whom I acknowledge. I ask You to defend my cause because You are my master, and ordinarily a master desires that his servant be dealt with equitably.

24. שָׁפְטֵנִי כְצִדְקְךָ ה' אֱלֹהָי — *Judge me according to Your righteousness HASHEM, my God.*

When מִדַּת הָרַחֲמִים, *the Attribute of Mercy,* expressed in the Name ה', and the מִדַּת הַדִּין, *the Attribute of Justice,* expressed in the name אֱלֹהִים, are joined together, the result is צֶדֶק, *righteousness (Sforno).*

כו בְּלַעֲנוּהוּ: יֵבֹשׁוּ וְיַחְפְּרוּ | יַחְדָּו שְׂמֵחֵי
רָעָתִי יִלְבְּשׁוּ־בֹשֶׁת וּכְלִמָּה הַמַּגְדִּילִים
כז עָלָי: יָרֹנּוּ וְיִשְׂמְחוּ חֲפֵצֵי צִדְקִי וְיֹאמְרוּ
תָמִיד יִגְדַּל יהוה הֶחָפֵץ שְׁלוֹם עַבְדּוֹ:
כח וּלְשׁוֹנִי תֶּהְגֶּה צִדְקֶךָ כָּל־הַיּוֹם תְּהִלָּתֶךָ:

26. יִלְבְּשׁוּ בֹשֶׁת וּכְלִמָּה — *May they be clothed in shame and disgrace.*

After they leave this world, the wicked are clothed in garments fashioned from their own wicked deeds. They are covered with the spiritual refuse and putrefaction which disgrace them (*Rav Yeibi*).

הַמַּגְדִּילִים עָלָי — *Those who are glad over my misfortune* [lit. *over me.*]

This describes Shimi ben Gera who rose up to curse David as he fled from Absalom, thus magnifying his own im-

portance as he degraded David (*Sforno*).

27. יִגְדַּל ה׳ — *Be glorified, HASHEM!* [lit. *May HASHEM be great!*]

May the *Attribute of Mercy* overwhelm the *Attribute of Justice* [in favor of David] (*Sforno*).

28. וּלְשׁוֹנִי תֶּהְגֶּה צִדְקֶךָ — *Then my tongue will express Your righteousness.*

Midrash shocher Tov comments: When do the people of Israel rejoice? Only when they see their king im-

'We have swallowed him.'

²⁶ May they be shamed and humiliated together,
    those who are glad over my misfortune;
May they be clothed in shame and disgrace,
    those who glorify themselves against me.
²⁷ May they sing in joy and be glad,
    those who want my vindication;
Let them always say, 'Be glorified, HASHEM!
    He who wants the peace of His servant!'
²⁸ Then my tongue will express Your righteousness;
    all the day, Your praise.

mersed in Torah study! The preceding verse says, *May they sing in joy and be glad, those who want my vindication.* When? *When my tongue will express Your righteousness* [by uttering words of Torah.] Similarly we read, יְרֵאֶיךָ יִרְאוּנִי וְיִשְׂמָחוּ, *Those who fear You, see me and are glad* [119:74]. When? When they see me engaged in Torah study!

[*Rambam*·(*Hilchos Melachim* 3:3) emphasizes that the king's obligation to engage in Torah study surpasses that of all other Jews, for his heart is the collective heart of all Israel and requires greater righteousness. The *Midrash* relates that when the nation observed David rising in the middle of the night to delight in Torah study, they were all aroused to follow his example (See *Overview* Part IV).

The theme of this psalm is that the enemies of David are truly enemies of God. They hate David because he represents Hashem. The proof of this is that all those who love and fear God, love His chosen king. Only through David can Israel realize the goal of יִגְדַּל ה', *HASHEM be glorified!*]

This Psalm portrays the stark contrast between those who defy
God and those who serve Him. According to **Radak**, the villain of
the Psalm is the יֵצֶר הָרָע, the Evil Inclination, which succeeds in convincing the wicked that there is no supreme Master over the affairs of
this world. The Psalmist diametrically opposes such a heresy. David
proudly calls himself עֶבֶד ה', the servant of HASHEM, a vassal totally
submissive to God's will.

Mesillas Yesharim (Chap. 24) describes the devoted servant of
Hashem who lives in awe of His Divine Majesty: he constantly fears
lest some trace of the Evil Inclination might have intruded into his actions and rendered them inconsonant with the grandeur of the Blessed One's honor and the glory of His Name. Fear of sin is an essential
element of his being and no circumstance in life can shake him from
his incessant trembling before God.

Such a man is happy and fortunate as Solomon said, Praiseworthy
is the man who fears always (Proverbs 28:14). King David exulted in
his possession of the trait of unshakeable fear, saying, '[Even while]
Princes pursued me for naught, my heart feared [only] at Your word'
(119:161).

א־ב לַמְנַצֵּחַ | לְעֶבֶד־יהוה לְדָוִד: נְאֻם־פֶּשַׁע
לָרָשָׁע בְּקֶרֶב לִבִּי אֵין־פַּחַד אֱלֹהִים לְנֶגֶד

1. לְעֶבֶד ה׳ — *For the servant of HASHEM.*

[See commentary to 18:1].

Anyone who successfully withstands his evil inclination merits a song of exultation, but this is especially true of a person of lofty spiritual stature. The *Talmud* (*Succah* 52a) teaches: כָּל הַגָּדוֹל מֵחֲבֵירוֹ יִצְרוֹ גָדוֹל הֵימֶנוּ, *The greater the person, the greater his inclination* [for evil]. Therefore, David's spiritual struggle was far more intense than that of an ordinary person. His ultimate victory, too, was sweeter, and the resultant song of gratitude was all the more heartfelt (*Alshich*).

That David assumed the title עֶבֶד ה׳, *servant of HASHEM*, should not be considered boastful, for there is not a word in all of *Tehillim* that David uttered of his own accord. The Psalmist was enveloped by a holy spirit and his every word is an expression of the thoughts of God Himself (*Tehillas Hashem*).

Midrash Shocher Tov identifies the villain of this Psalm, not as the Evil Inclination, but as Goliath, who symbolizes all of David's human enemies. God wages war for Israel and emerges triumphant. Nevertheless, He ascribes all victories to His nation. Israel in turn refuses to accept the honor and attributes all success to God.

We find that after David slew Goliath, the daughters of Israel were divinely inspired to sing, *Saul has slain his thousands, and David his tens of thousands* (I Samuel 18:7). But David, in this Psalm, refuses to accept the honor, in effect saying to God, 'You are the cause of this victory and so I shall attribute it to Your name!' Therefore David dedicated this Psalm לַמְנַצֵּחַ, literally: *to He who causes victory* [from נִצָּחוֹן, *victory*] (see *commentary* to 4:1).

Victory for whom? לְעֶבֶד ה׳ לְדָוִד, *for the servant of HASHEM, for David.*

2. נְאֻם פֶּשַׁע לָרָשָׁע — *The words of transgression to the wicked.*

פֶּשַׁע, *transgression*, is the Evil Inclination within man (*Metzudas Zion*).

Malbim interprets the Psalm as an attempt to refute the efficacy of doing good. [We will present his comments during the course of the Psalm as they appear.] Two arguments are offered to justify performance of the commandments: 1 — They are a response to the wish of God. Like a servant obeying his master, it is not for us to decide whether or not the deed will benefit us personally, for we are beholden to carry out His command. 2 — The commandments were formulated by God in His infinite wisdom to benefit us. Like a patient following his doctor's orders, we obey for our own sake, entirely apart from a desire to serve God. The evil inclination seeks to negate both arguments. (See also *Shiurei Daas of Telshe*, vol. I, p. 117).

Midrash Shocher Tov relates this verse to the encounter of David and Goliath (see I Samuel Chapter 17):

When David saw the giant warrior armed with every type of weapon, he thought, 'Who can overcome such a man?' But when he heard Goliath blaspheming God, he said, 'Now I can vanquish him for he has no fear of HASHEM!' As it says in our verse: *There is no dread of God before his eyes.* From this we learn that God does not punish the wicked until they remove all fear of God from their hearts. The *Talmud* (*Sotah* 42b) teaches: Why was he called גָּלְיָת? Because he stood בְּגִלּוּי פָּנִים, *brazenly*, before God. He approached the camp of Israel with

XXXVI
1-2

For the Conductor, for the servant of HASHEM,
for David.

² The words of transgression to the wicked
are in my heart;
There is no dread of God
before his eyes.

his blasphemy and taunts every morning and evening. Why? In order to prevent Israel from reciting the Shema [by which they accept the yoke of God's rule.] So he did for forty days, corresponding to the forty days during which Moses was at Sinai being taught the Torah which Goliath mocked.

Sforno attributes this evil speech to Achitophel who cunningly persuaded Absalom to violate his father's concubines (II Samuel 16:21). Achitophel personifies פֶּשַׁע, the seductive Evil Inclination, Absalom is the רָשָׁע, the *wicked* person who commits the sin. Achitophel's baseness proved that although he was a Torah scholar *there is no dread of God before his eyes.* [See Psalm 5 for a full description of Achitophel's insincerity.]

בְּקֶרֶב לִבִּי — *[Are] in my heart*

The Psalmist says: I imagine the Evil Inclination arguing this point to the victim whom it seduces to sin *(Rashi; Ibn Ezra).*

[Or this may refer not to the imaginative heart of the Psalmist, but to the corrupted heart of the wicked man. One chamber of the heart receives blood from the body. It symbolizes the evil in-

clination which fills man with passions and lust. A second chamber pumps oxygen-filled blood, symbolizing the good impulse which cleanses man of his vices. Therefore, the heart is often called לֵבָב, (the double ב, *Beis,* alluding to the two functions of this organ). Our verse quotes the evil-doer as speaking of לִבִּי, *my heart,* in the singular. This implies that wickedness dominates his entire heart.] [1]

אֵין פַּחַד אֱלֹהִים לְנֶגֶד עֵינָיו — *There is no dread of God before his eyes.*

The Evil Impulse coaxes: 'Do whatever your heart desires and pay no attention to threats of a future *Gehinnom* which no one has ever seen. Disregard any threat that is not visible to the human eye' *(Alshich).*

Furthermore, the Evil Inclination argues: 'If you feel that one should do the mitzvos because the King has so commanded, then why doesn't He display His power of punishment against those who disobey Him?' *(Malbim).*

According to *Rabbeinu Yonah of Gerona (Shaarei Teshuva,* Gate III: 169) this verse describes the עוֹזְבֵי ה', *the class of those who foresake God.* These men fancy themselves to be observers of

---

1. Rabbi Yose HaGallili said: The good inclination completely rules the righteous as David said וְלִבִּי חָלַל בְּקִרְבִּי, *my heart is dead within me* (109:22). [The section of the heart usually reserved for the evil impulse has been deadened within me for I have overcome it completely *(Rashi).*] However, the wicked are ruled entirely by their evil inclination, as David says, *There is no dread of God before his eyes.*

Good and evil reign jointly over the average person because he vacillates, sometimes acting nobly and sometimes wickedly. Rava declared, 'I am an example of such an ordinary person.'

To this Abaye responded, 'If this is so, the master [Rava] has left no hope for any other person.' [If even *you* are considered as merely ordinary then there is no one who can be considered completely righteous *(Rashi)*] *(Berachos* 61b).

ג עֵינָיו: כִּי־הֶחֱלִיק אֵלָיו בְּעֵינָיו לִמְצֹא
ד עֲוֹנוֹ לִשְׂנֹא: דִּבְרֵי־פִיו אָוֶן וּמִרְמָה חָדַל
ה לְהַשְׂכִּיל לְהֵיטִיב: אָוֶן | יַחְשֹׁב עַל־
מִשְׁכָּבוֹ יִתְיַצֵּב עַל־דֶּרֶךְ לֹא־טוֹב רָע לֹא

the mitzvos, however all of their actions are performed automatically and routinely without any inner conviction. Fear of heaven does not weigh heavily upon them. Therefore, when the evil inclination attempts to entice these weak men, they succumb immediately and transgress. So far removed are they from contemplation of the truth that they do not even sigh or worry over their sin. They give it no second thought. Of them, the Psalmist said, 'There is no dread of God before his eyes.'

3. בְּעֵינָיו אֵלָיו הֶחֱלִיק כִּי — *For it smoothed the way before him.*

With smooth words and facile talk, the rebellious spirit makes sin seem attractive to the wicked (Rashi; Radak).

The eye is the Evil Inclination's source of strength, as the Talmud (Sotah 8a) teaches: We have a tradition that the evil inclination can induce a person to sin only when the object of desire is visible to his eye. This was how the snake, the symbol of evil, coaxed Eve into the first sin: And when the woman saw that the tree was good for food and that it was desirable to the eyes ... she took of its fruit and did eat [Genesis 3:6] (Tehillah L'David). [See Overview, Vol. I, Part I.]

Sforno notes that initially Absalom hesitated to publicly violate his father's concubines. However, Achitophel cunningly made the abominable deed seem like the logical course of action. He counseled: And all of Israel shall hear that you are repulsive to your father, then all the hands of those who joined you shall be strengthened [i.e., the more repulsive the deed, the more powerful its effect] (II Samuel 16:21).

לִשְׂנֹא עֲוֹנוֹ לִמְצֹא — *Causing him to find his iniquity, to hate him.*

[The Evil Inclination is man's worst enemy]. He lures man to sin so that God should discover the wrongdoing and hate the sinner for it (Rashi).

Midrash Shocher Tov describes the spirit which drives the wicked: They search with their eyes and ponder in their hearts to find sins which God will find hateful so that they can then commit them out of spite.

According to *Malbim:*

Now the spirit of *Transgression* addresses itself to those who perform commandments and avoid sins because they feel that God's commands are fashioned to benefit man. The Evil Inclination counters by presenting sin in a favorable light, and challenges the observant to find what there is in his iniquity to be hateful.

Radak offers another explanation: The wicked indulge their desires to such an unbridled extent that, in time, even they find iniquity to be hateful.

4. וּמִרְמָה אָוֶן פִיו דִּבְרֵי — *The words of his mouth — evil and deceit.*

Achitophel's evil words were both contrary to the Torah and treacherously deceitful to Absalom. Achitophel's true intention was to create an irreparable rift between father and son, for if they were ever to become reconciled, Achitophel would have been blamed by both for having advised Absalom to rebel (Sforno).

לְהֵיטִיב לְהַשְׂכִּיל חָדַל — *He has ceased contemplating to do good.*

³ For it smoothed the way before him,
      causing him to find his iniquity, to hate him.
⁴ The words of his mouth — evil and deceit —
     he has ceased contemplating to do good.
⁵ Evil does he devise on his bed.
     He stations himself on a path of no good —
     evil he does not disdain.

The wicked person does not allow himself to draw a moral lesson from any incident lest it influence him to mend his ways (Rashi).

Although he does not utilize his mental gifts for the pursuit of goodness, nevertheless, his intellectual faculties work for evil, as the Prophet says, *They are wise to do evil, but to do good they have no understanding* [Jeremiah 4:22] (Otzar Nechmad).

Having come under the influence of פֶּשַׁע, *transgression*, this person ceased לְהַשְׂכִּיל, *to contemplate*, God's awesome sovereignty. Therefore, he fails to realize that it is incumbent upon him, as God's servant, to do His will. Furthermore, he fails to realize that whatever God commands us to do is לְהֵיטִיב, *for doing good*, i.e., for our own benefit (Malbim).

5. אָוֶן יַחְשֹׁב עַל מִשְׁכָּבוֹ — *Evil does he devise on his bed.*

When a person lays awake in bed, his mind is not distracted. That is the best time to think and scheme (Radak).

Man can intuitively recognize the sovereignty of God, both through his intellect and through his natural inclinations toward good. However, the wicked man strives to corrupt his innocence. One method of doing so is by developing the habit of seeking to find the benefits of evil rather than those of good (Malbim).

יִתְיַצֵּב עַל דֶּרֶךְ לֹא טוֹב — *He stations himself on a path of no good.*

At night he schemes on his bed and in the morning he arises to execute his plans (Ibn Ezra).

His wrongdoing is not intermittent. He is מִתְיַצֵּב, *he stands firm and permanent* on that road (Alshich).

Malbim continues his above interpretation by citing a second means by which the wicked person corrupts himself. He perverts his instinct for good by acting immorally. Thus he combines evil thoughts with evil deeds, thereby corrupting himself.

Why does the Psalmist say *no good*, instead of describing *evil* in a direct manner as *bad*? One reason is in order not to repeat himself since the word רַע, *bad*, begins the next phrase. Secondly, some bad things have a good side as well, but this man's way is completely corrupt without any redeeming virtue. Thirdly, Scripture often indicates that people should attempt to avoid using foul or derogatory expressions — 'not good' is preferable to 'bad'. [See *Pesachim* 3a; also *Genesis* 7:8; *Deuteronomy* 23:11; *I Samuel* 20:26] (Radak).

The Psalmist reveals the psychology of the villain. He will never admit to himself that his way is evil; instead he will rationalize that his course is merely לֹא טוֹב, *not* (so) *good* (Yoseif Tehillos).

רָע לֹא יִמְאָס — *Evil he does not disdain.*

[How can a person objectively appraise his way to determine whether it is good or not? By gauging the extent of his hatred for evil. The truly pure heart will despise it, as it says, אֹהֲבֵי ה׳ שִׂנְאוּ רָע, *Those who love HASHEM, hate evil* (97:10). One who finds himself to

ו יִמְאָס: יהוה בְּהַשָּׁמַיִם חַסְדֶּךָ אֱמוּנָתְךָ
ז עַד־שְׁחָקִים: צִדְקָתְךָ | כְּהַרְרֵי־אֵל
מִשְׁפָּטֶיךָ תְּהוֹם רַבָּה אָדָם וּבְהֵמָה

be sympathetic or apologetic towards evil has a clear indication that his own lifestyle is not far removed from sin.]

6. ה' בְּהַשָּׁמַיִם חַסְדֶּךָ עַד שְׁחָקִים — *HASHEM, to the heavens has Your kindness gone, Your faithfulness till the upper heights.*

I, *the servant of HASHEM,* recognize that Your kindness is all encompassing and streams forth faithfully from שָׁמַיִם *the heavens (Ibn Ezra).*

But, if this kindness is not always apparent, it is the fault of the wicked who force You to remove Your goodness from the lower world of man and to place Your faithfulness in the שְׁחָקִים, *upper heights (Rashi).*

Radak defines אֱמוּנָה, *faithfulness,* with reference to God and His constant provision of the necessities required for the preservation of each general species of life. [*Sefer HaChinuch,* Mitzvah 548, cites a divine assurance that no living species will ever become extinct.]

חֶסֶד, *kindness,* refers to His mercy in making the sustenance of each creature accessible with a minimum of effort. Furthermore, the more essential a substance is to survival, the more abundant its supply. Because water is a more urgent necessity than solid food, it is found in greater quantities and does not require preparation. Air, the most basic essential for supporting life, is the most abundant of all resources.

Malbim explains: There are two heavens. The material one including the planetary forces is called שָׁמַיִם. The spiritual heaven which controls the miraculous, supernatural course of events is known as שְׁחָקִים. The constant and reliable course of natural events is denoted as אֱמוּנָה, *faithfulness,* while God's supernatural deeds are called

חֶסֶד, *kindness.* Most people associate חֶסֶד, God's supernatural *kindness,* exclusively with שְׁחָקִים, *the spiritual heaven;* and אֱמוּנָה, *the natural course of events,* with שָׁמַיִם, *the lower heaven.* This belief, however, is a manifestation of פֶּשַׁע, *Transgression,* referred to in verse 2, for it claims that one may do as he pleases because God's intervention is not visible in the natural world. This view is false, however, because even our daily, natural existence is but a series of hidden miracles (see *Ramban* to *Exodus* 13:16).

Furthermore, every deed on earth, for good or evil, elicits a spiritual reaction although it may not be apparent to human beings. The Psalmist indicates all of this by juxtaposing אֱמוּנָה, *natural faithfulness,* with שְׁחָקִים, *spiritual heavens;* and חֶסֶד, *supernatural kindness,* with שָׁמַיִם, *the natural order of the heavens.*

7. צִדְקָתְךָ כְּהַרְרֵי אֵל — *Your righteousness is like the mighty mountains.*

Radak notes that Scripture customarily emphasizes the great size of an object or a geographic area by appending to it the word לָאֵל, *to God,* or an equivalent. Thus, the Assyrian capital, *Nineveh,* is described as עִיר גְּדוֹלָה לֵאלֹהִים, *a great city unto God (Jonah* 3:3; see also *Genesis* 10:9).

Radak goes on to explain how this verse is a continuation of the previous one. Although God's *kindness* and *faithfulness* both encompass the entire world, when the time of judgment arrives, the Almighty differentiates between the righteous and the wicked. Upon the righteous He bestows charities as great as the *mighty mountains* while the wicked descend to the lowest depths of *the vast deep waters.*

6 HASHEM, to the heavens has Your kindness gone —
Your faithfulness till the upper heights.
7 Your righteousness is like the mighty mountains —
Your judgments are like the vast deep waters.
Man and beast You save, HASHEM.

The abundance of good is compared to a lofty mountain peak because there, one is safe from those evil forces which seek to snatch away the rewards which he has earned in his lifetime.

Ibn Ezra observes: Just as the highest peaks are inaccessible to man, so too is full comprehension of God's goodness beyond human reach.

Midrash Shocher Tov adds: Just as the mountains are countless, so are God's charities infinite.

Rashi concludes: But if we find that God's charities are far removed from us like the remote, mighty mountains, it is because the evil men drive Him away from earth. However, when God acts charitably towards someone, He raises and fortifies him like the mighty mountain.

מִשְׁפָּטֶיךָ תְּהוֹם רַבָּה — *Your judgments are like the vast deep waters.*

The punishment of the wicked is likened to the deep, because there is no escape from its grip *(Radak).* [1]

The Psalmist notes that God's control of nature takes two forms. Sometimes we witness *revealed miracles* which are as evident as *the mighty mountains.* Most of the time, however, we must maintain our faith in God's control of nature which is as hidden as *the vast deep waters.* The reason for this will soon be explained *(Malbim).*

אָדָם וּבְהֵמָה תּוֹשִׁיעַ ה' — *Man and beast You save, HASHEM.*

However, there are times when instead of exercising His Attribute of Justice towards the wicked, God allows them to share in the good things of This World. Let it be known that this resembles the kindness which God bestows upon the beast who also does not recognize Him. For the rebellious heretic or the foolish skeptic is nothing more than a beast disguised in the form of a man *(Radak).*

Malbim continues: Every man has within himself both *man* and *beast*. His body is like that of the animal, whereas his human soul embodies the spirit of God. If he were only a soul, he would be like an angel, fit to witness God's glorious revelation all day long. But since his soul is concealed in a body, God's presence has been hidden from him as well. The challenge facing man is to discover God's judgment and control even in *the vast deep waters* [i.e., the murkiness of this material world] and

---

1. The *Talmud (Arachin* 8b) comments: *Your righteousness is like the mighty mountains,* this describes נִגְעֵי אָדָם, *the leprous spots which appear on the human body.* [For it can be determined within one week whether they are clean or unclean *(Rashi).*]

Your judgments are like the vast, deep waters refers to the leprous signs appearing in a house [for their accurate identification and classification may require as much as three weeks *(Tosfos ibid.).*]

This statement is puzzling, for the leprosy of the body would seem to be less of a charity and more of a punishment than those which merely afflict the house. *Harav Chaim Shmulewitz* explains that to be in doubt is itself equivalent to torture. It is better to suffer the restrictions of leprosy of the body after only one week, than to remain in doubt over the status of a house for three weeks.

ח תּוֹשִׁיעַ | יְהֹוָה: מַה־יָּקָר חַסְדְּךָ אֱלֹהִים
ט וּבְנֵי אָדָם בְּצֵל כְּנָפֶיךָ יֶחֱסָיוּן: יִרְוְיֻן
י מִדֶּשֶׁן בֵּיתֶךָ וְנַחַל עֲדָנֶיךָ תַשְׁקֵם: כִּי־
   עִמְּךָ מְקוֹר חַיִּים בְּאוֹרְךָ נִרְאֶה־אוֹר:

thus come to discover the soul of God buried deep within himself. [1]

8. אֱלֹהִים חַסְדְּךָ יָקָר מַה — *How precious is Your kindness, O God!*

In this world, God may sometimes shower His goodness on the righteous *man* and on unworthy *beastly* men alike (v. 7), but in the reward reserved for the World to Come evil people will not share. The word מַה [lit. *how much*] is used to emphasize that precious good which endures forever. Of it the Prophet says, *No eye has ever seen it except for You, O God!* (Isaiah 64:3). For this reason the Almighty is referred to here as אֱלֹהִים, the Name which denotes the strict *Attribute of Justice*, for in the Hereafter there will be no undeserved kindness for the wicked (*Radak*).

וּבְנֵי אָדָם — *The sons of man.*

Those who enjoy the bliss of the Hereafter are the true *sons of man*, i.e. human beings as they were meant to be, not *beasts* disguised in human form! (*Radak*).

The אָדָם, *man*, who has raised his soul above the בְּהֵמָה, *beast* part of his nature (v. 7), sees the חֶסֶד, *kindness* of Divine Providence. He realizes (v. 6) that God benignly watches over man more than over anything else in the universe, and shelters him in *the shadow of His wings* (*Malbim*).

בְּצֵל כְּנָפֶיךָ יֶחֱסָיוּן — *In the shadow of Your wings take refuge.*

Rabbi Avun said: Come and consider how great is the power of the righteous

and those who perform acts of kindness. They do not find their shelter in the shadow of the dawn nor in the shadow of the wings of the earth, nor in the shadow of the sun, nor in the shadow of the wings of the *holy beasts*, or the *cherubs* or the *fiery angels*. Under whose wings do they find shelter? — Under the shadow of He at Whose word the world came to be, as it says, *How precious are those who perform Your kindness, O God! These sons of man will take refuge in the shadow of Your wings* (Midrash Ruth Rabbah 5:4). [2]

9. יִרְוְיֻן — *They will be sated.*

The translation follows *Metzudas Zion* who relates this word to רָוָה, *satisfy, overflow.*

Ibn Ezra identifies יִרְוְיֻן, derived from the root רוֹב, *many, much,* meaning, *they will have a great abundance.*

מִדֶּשֶׁן בֵּיתֶךָ — *From the abundance of Your house.*

These men will contemplate the ways of God in the solitude of their homes and this divine service will enrich their souls immensely (*Ibn Ezra*).

Malbim explains that the man who recognizes God's kindness on earth deserves to rise above the laws of nature. His bread will come not from the grain grown by nature, but from God's spiritual abundance. Similarly, his water will come from a higher, celestial source; it will quench the thirst of his soul, not merely that of his parched

---

1. The Talmud (*Chullin* 5b) interprets this homiletically as referring to the righteous who devote themselves wholeheartedly to God's service: This describes people who have unbridled intellectual power [like אָדָם, Adam, the first man (*Rashi*)], yet humble themselves, like the בְּהֵמָה, *beast* [which is humble and obedient to its master (*Rashi*).]

⁸ *How precious is Your kindness, O God!*
The sons of man, in the shadow of Your wings
take refuge.
⁹ *They will be sated*
from the abundance of Your house;
And from the stream of Your delights
give them to drink.
¹⁰ *For with You is the source of life —*
by Your light shall we see light.

---

throat. Thus this righteous man is no longer subject to the limitations of this earth; rather he *takes refuge under God's wing* (v. 8).

According to *Radak*, however, this spiritual enrichment will be experienced only in the World to Come, which is the world of souls without bodies where the righteous men are like angels. The Scriptures refer to the future world of the spirit by a variety of names: *House of HASHEM*, *Sanctuary of HASHEM*, *Mountain of HASHEM*. [*See commentary* to 24:3 and 27:4; *Rambam, Hilchos Teshuva* 8:4.]

וְנַחַל עֲדָנֶיךָ תַשְׁקֵם — *And from the stream of Your delights give them to drink.*

The true knowledge of God will provide incessant delight for the devout in the Hereafter, like a stream which flows endlessly (*Ibn Ezra*).

The phrase *You will give them to drink* is a simile meaning that You will assist them to come to understand Your ways (*Radak*).

[However, only in proportion to one's thirst for God in This World will he be satiated with the waters of true wisdom in the Hereafter. One who yearns only for worldly gain, will never be able to quench his thirst, for, like a man drinking salt water, he grows thirstier with every swallow. See 42:2 where the yearning to comprehend God's ways is described in terms of thirst rather than hunger.]

10. כִּי עִמְּךָ מְקוֹר חַיִּים — *For with You is the source of life.*

The source of life refers to the existence of the soul which derives its vitality from above (*Ibn Ezra*).

The man who has perceived the true meaning of existence, sees that nature itself can breed no meaningful life. That can emanate only from the Divine Source above, just as all temporal light must stream from the celestial source of illumination (*Malbim*).

Literally, מְקוֹר means *a fountainhead,* or the *source of a flowing spring,* for the life of the soul flows on eternally into the Hereafter. It is life not followed by

---

2. In his work on the precepts of performing acts of kindness, the *Chafetz Chaim* explains the above *Midrash*:

When the heavenly tribunal conducts a trial, there are many angels of mercy among the Sanhedrin. They comprise the majority and stand at the right side of the Divine throne seeking merit for the person standing in judgment, and are called נְדִיבִים, *generous ones,* according to *Sha'arei Orah*. Nevertheless, they too, act in accord with strict justice; they do not plead for totally undeserved mercy. However, when HASHEM sits alone in judgment, His pure mercy and kindness hold sway. Hence the Psalmist says, (118:9): טוֹב לַחֲסוֹת בַּה׳ מִבְּטֹחַ בִּנְדִיבִים. *It is better to seek refuge in HASHEM than to trust in generous ones,* i.e., even the generous angels.

However only those who have themselves performed acts of kindness in This World will be judged exclusively by God's kindness and find shelter under his wings *Ahavas Chesed,* 2:4).

יא מְשֹׁךְ חַסְדְּךָ לְיֹדְעֶיךָ וְצִדְקָתְךָ לְיִשְׁרֵי־
יב לֵב: אַל־תְּבוֹאֵנִי רֶגֶל גַּאֲוָה וְיַד־רְשָׁעִים
יג אַל־תְּנִדֵנִי: שָׁם נָפְלוּ פֹּעֲלֵי אָוֶן דֹּחוּ וְלֹא־
יָכְלוּ קוּם:

death; light never extinguished by darkness (Radak).

בְּאוֹרְךָ נִרְאֶה אוֹר — By Your light shall we see light.

When You afflict us with Your strict Attribute of Justice we shall perceive a light which will illuminate our minds to comprehend the purpose of the suffering. In the merit of our acceptance of this light, the inner illumination of the Torah will be revealed to us and we *will be filled with the abundance of Your house* (Alshich).[1]

According to *Sforno*, this is a prayer: May Israel understand Absalom's rebellion in the light of God so that Achitophel will not succeed in *blinding the eyes of the wise* (Exodus 23:8) to stray after his counsel.

11. מְשֹׁךְ חַסְדְּךָ — Extend Your kindness i.e., endlessly (Sforno).

Radak translates: turn Your kindness towards us as in עַל כֵּן מְשַׁכְתִּיךְ חָסֶד, *Therefore I have turned kindness towards you* (Jeremiah 31:2).

Keep directing Your spiritual kindness towards those who make good use of it and utilize every manifestation of Your kindness in order to *know You* better and to see that You control all of nature (Malbim).

לְיֹדְעֶיךָ — To those who know You.

Be kind to them in This World so that

they may be free to pursue knowledge and mitzvos without interference. Or this may refer to the World to Come, לְיֹדְעֶיךָ being those who strived to know God with all their strength and ability in This World. Through God's kindness they will realize their passionate wish in the Hereafter (Radak).

וְצִדְקָתְךָ לְיִשְׁרֵי לֵב — And Your charity to the upright of heart.

The upright of heart are not as great as יֹדְעֶיךָ, those who know You. While the former perform the commandments, their deeds are in the nature of carrying on the tradition received from their forebears. They lack the clear conception of God which can be achieved only through intensive, intellectual effort (Radak; Ibn Ezra).

12. אַל־תְּבוֹאֵנִי רֶגֶל גַּאֲוָה — Bring me not the foot of the arrogant.

When God metes out the reward of the righteous in the Hereafter, may these haughty, wicked men not share in the good fortune of deserving people (Rashi).

Radak translates אַל־תְּבוֹאֵנִי, *let them not overtake me*. David prays that his enemies not be enabled to disturb the contemplation and service of God, which he pursued in solitude.

Sforno agrees with this translation, but interprets these words as referring

1. Rabbi Chaim of Volozhin (*Ruach Chaim, Avos* 6:1), interprets this as a description of the special quality of Torah study. Through seeking the light of Torah one merits the perception of even more Torah light. This may be likened to the man who enters the king's treasury which is aglow with the glitter of dazzling jewels. The most wonderful thing revealed by their light, however, is not the jewels themselves, but a door leading to an even more splendid treasure chamber. And so the visitor goes deeper and deeper in into the innermost rooms of the palace until arriving at the king's throne room, he sees an indescribable splendor. So, too, each truth of Torah leads to deeper revelations until one comes to perceive the presence of God Himself.

11 *Extend Your kindness to those who know You,*
and Your charity to the upright of heart.
12 *Bring me not the foot of the arrogant,*
and let the hand of the wicked not move me.
13 *There they fell, the practitioners of evil,*
thrust down and unable to rise.

to the arrogant and ambitious Achitophel who advised Absalom not to allow the fleeing king to slip out of his grasp. Achitophel said, *'Let me now choose twelve thousand men and I will arise and pursue David this very night. And I will overtake him while he is weary and weakhanded and I will make him afraid, and all the people who are with him shall flee and I will smite the king alone'* (II Samuel 17:1-2).

According to *Malbim*, גֵּאֲוָה, *arrogance*, refers not to the enemy from outside but rather to the enemy within. The most potent weapon utilized by פֶּשַׁע, *the spirit of transgression*, to trap the unwary is the trait of pride. Arrogance blinds man, preventing him from recognizing God's accomplishments, because in his erroneous pride, he considers His achievements to be his own.

[Many commentaries note that the רָאשֵׁי תֵּיבוֹת, *initials*, of the words אַל תְּבוֹאֵנִי רֶגֶל גַּאֲוָה, form the word *esrog*. This alludes to the fact that, according to the *Midrash*, the esrog is shaped like a human heart. Just as the esrog must be perfect and unblemished, so must people strive to cleanse their

hearts of all flaws, of which the most serious is the ugly blemish of pride.] [1]

וְיַד רְשָׁעִים אַל תְּנִדֵנִי — *And let the hand of the wicked not move me.*

Rashi comments: In the future, the righteous will inherit a double portion — their own and that forfeited by the wicked as a result of their sins. So said the Prophet, לָכֵן בְּאַרְצָם מִשְׁנֶה יִירָשׁוּ, *Therefore in their land they shall inherit a double portion* (Isaiah 61:7). The Psalmist now prays that the wicked will not be allowed to move away the righteous by reclaiming the portion which had originally been intended for them, but which they forfeited.

Do not let the wicked force me to move from the solitary retreat where I serve God (*Radak*).

Do not let Achitophel force me to flee from my position when he attempts to overtake me (*Sforno*).

13. שָׁם נָפְלוּ פֹּעֲלֵי אָוֶן — *There they fell, the practitioners of evil.*

[נָפְלוּ, *they fell*, is written in past tense because the wicked have already fallen into ruin in This World. However, they will not recognize or admit their failure

1. The *Midrash* (*Bereishis Rabbah* 15:7) relates this verse to Adam. After he sinned, Adam realized that he was naked. He tried to gather leaves from the trees to cover himself and Eve, but one tree after another said, 'This is the thief who deceived his Creator! Take no leaves from me!' As it says, *Bring me not the foot of the arrogant* — this refers to Adam who lacked humility in his conduct toward God. *And let the hand of the wicked not move me* — Adam shall remove no leaves from my tree! Only the fig-tree allowed him to take its leaves, because it was the forbidden fruit [according to one version in the *Midrash*]. Adam's experience is likened to that of the prince who seduced one of the palace maids. When the king, his father, banished him, he vainly sought refuge with the other maids, but all shut their doors in his face. Only the maid servant who had caused his disgrace would allow him in. (Cf. *Tosafos Sanhedrin* 70b s.v. בה נתקנו).

until they arrive in the world of truth, the World to Come.]

Radak notes that prophets often refer to events foretold for the future as if they had already occurred.

דֹחוּ וְלֹא יָכְלוּ קוּם — *Thrust down and unable to rise.*

[Similarly, David said: *Therefore the wicked shall not stand up in judgment nor shall the sinners arise in the assembly of the righteous* (1:5).]

The wicked begin with the free-willed ability to choose between right and wrong, as it says *the practitioners of evil will fall* [into sin of their own choice]. But once they become ac-customed to vice, habit forces them to err and they are without hope of escape. When they lock themselves into a vise-like pattern of sin, *they will be thrust down and unable to rise up (Reishis Da'as).*

Sforno concludes his commentary on this Psalm: Absalom rejected the counsel of Achitophel and accepted that of Chushai HaArki. Achitophel was thrust down into such disgrace that he hung himself and from this ig-nominious death, he was *unable to rise up.* [This alludes to the opinion of the *Mishnah (Sanhedrin* 11:1) that Achitophel forfeited his portion in the Hereafter and will not rise up to share in the bliss of the World to Come.]

37 מזמור לז

This is a sequel to Psalm 36. There, David described the forces of evil which strive to convince mankind that there is no God Who masters our destinies. The wicked point to their own success as forceful evidence that there is no Supreme Being concerned with the enforcement of the principles of righteousness and justice. Seeking to counteract this argument, the Psalmist concluded Psalm 36 by pleading with God to frustrate His adversaries and reward His faithful.

This psalm records the response to David's plea. God sternly admonishes the righteous not to be impressed with the prosperity of sinners, for it is empty and transient (Meiri, Meir Tehillos). Radak (v. 40) explains that this theme is repeated frequently in this rather lengthy Psalm because most people feel an overpowering temptation to imitate the successful ways of the wicked; therefore their faith requires constant reinforcement.

א לְדָוִד | אַל־תִּתְחַר בַּמְּרֵעִים אַל־תְּקַנֵּא
ב בְּעֹשֵׂי עַוְלָה: כִּי כֶחָצִיר מְהֵרָה יִמָּלוּ
ג וּכְיֶרֶק דֶּשֶׁא יִבּוֹלוּן: בְּטַח בַּיהוה וַעֲשֵׂה־

1. לְדָוִד — *To David.*

Whenever the superscription of a psalm is merely לְדָוִד, *to David* then it is neither a song nor a prayer. It is the רוּחַ הַקֹּדֶשׁ, *the holy spirit,* speaking through David (*Zohar, Parshas Vayechi*).

Ostensibly, the message of this psalm seems geared to the unintelligent masses, who must be cautioned to avoid the company of the wicked lest they be adversely influenced by their success. However, this assumption is false. Even the greatest people may be unduly impressed by the prosperity of sinners. Therefore, the psalm is dedicated *To David* in order to emphasize that even a person of David's stature must take care not to be impressed by evildoers (*Alshich*).

אַל־תִּתְחַר — *Do not compete* [see *Proverbs* 24:19].

Do not attempt to compete with the success of the wicked, or to imitate their corruption in order to achieve prosperity like theirs. Similarly we read אֵיךְ תְּתַחֲרֶה אֶת הַסּוּסִים, *How do you compete with the horses?* (*Jeremiah* 12:5) (*Rashi; Radak; Ibn Ezra; Metzudos*).

The *Talmud* (*Berachos* 7b) adds a further interpretation: Do not quarrel with the evil men.

[This warning applies only when they enjoy extraordinary success. That indicates that for the moment it is God's will that they should be rewarded and that the righteous should be punished. To abstain from attacking them at such a time is not a display of cowardice, but a humble submission to God's will.]

Ibn Ezra and *Meiri*, offer yet another translation of אַל־תִּתְחַר in consonance with the above theme. They derive the word from חֲרוֹן anger. Thus, 'Do not be

angered by the success of the evil!'

Sforno comments that David composed the psalm while inspired with a prophetic vision of the tragedy which was destined to split the Jewish nation. David foresaw the rebellion of Jeraboam ben Nabat who would take away the Ten Tribes of Israel, while only the tribes of Judah and Benjamin remained loyal to Rechavom, son of Solomon. David cautions Rechavom not to quarrel with the rebels. A civil war pitting Jew against Jew is to be avoided at all costs. David assures Rechavom that the success of the rebels will be short-lived provided that he concentrates his efforts on repentance.

[*Sforno* relates every verse of the psalm to an event in the long struggle between the kingdoms of Judah and Israel. However his entire commentary is beyond the scope of this work.]

בַּמְּרֵעִים — *The evil men.*

These are villains who are not satisfied with doing evil, but seek to subvert others as well. [They are not merely רַע, *evil,* they are מֵרֵעַ, (i.e., the transitive *Hiph'il* form), *they make others evil,* by enticing them to imitate their ways.] (*Nora Tehillos*).

אַל־תְּקַנֵּא — *Be not envious.*

Similarly Solomon says, אַל יְקַנֵּא לִבְּךָ בַּחַטָּאִים, *Do not let your heart be envious of the sinners* (*Proverbs* 23:17). What then should you envy? כִּי אִם בְּיִרְאַת ה' כָּל הַיּוֹם, *Only the fear of HASHEM, all day long* (*Midrash Shocher Tov*). [Envy is basic to human nature. We cannot demand that a person should obliterate it from his character, we can only sublimate his envy, directing it towards loftier aspirations. Thus, the Sages (*Bava Basra* 22a) praise envy of superior Torah know-

XXXVII
1-3

To David: Do not compete with the evil men;
be not envious of evildoers.
² For like grass will they be swiftly cut,
and like green vegetation will they wither.
³ Trust in HASHEM and do good,

ledge for it serves to spur further Torah study.][1]

בְּעֹשֵׂי עַוְלָה — *Of evildoers.*

These men sin, but do not influence others. Nevertheless, the Psalmist warns us not to envy their success (*Nora Tehillos*).

2. כֶחָצִיר — *Like grass.*

The חָצִיר is a species of grass which dries out and withers sooner than others (*Malbim*).

The wicked thrive as easily as grass, which sprouts wherever there is some soil. But do not fret. Though they proliferate quickly they fail to develop deep, hardy roots and so they will fade away as quickly as they have grown (*Hirsch*).

וּכְיֶרֶק דֶּשֶׁא — *And like green vegetation.*

Grass consists of two parts, the roots and the blades. Animals usually eat the blades and leave the root intact. Similarly, the green sprout will shrivel and dry, but the root remains intact to send forth new blades of grass. The flourishing wicked are likened to the sprouts which thrive only temporarily. (*Radak*).

יִבּוֹלוּן — *Will they wither.*

The 'soil' from which the Jewish soul sprouts is heaven, and even when it is on earth, the soul is still connected to its celestial roots. But sin can sever the shoot from its roots; such is the lot of the wicked. You may ask, 'If they have been severed from the roots of life, how can they still live and thrive?' The answer is that they resemble the blade of grass which, because of its accumulated moisture, remains green even after it is cut. Similarly, the wicked man, although cut off from his heavenly source, can still thrive on the handful of merits which he once stored away. But as those merits 'dry up', he will surely wither to death (*Alshich*).

The מְרֵעִים who subvert others will meet their dismal fate at the hands of others. They are like the חָצִיר which is cut down by an outside hand. Also, their end comes swiftly, in one stroke. The עֹשֵׂי עַוְלָה who sin only privately, wither away by themselves; slowly and gradually (*Ibn Yachya*).

3. בְּטַח בַּה' וַעֲשֵׂה טוֹב — *Trust in HASHEM and do good.*

Unlike the evil ones whose roots lie in

1. *Midrash Shocher Tov* continues: Said the Holy One, Blessed be He: Employ envy for My sake! For, without envy no man would bother to take himself a wife or to build himself a home. If Abraham had not been envious (i.e., zealous) on My behalf he would not have spread My Name all over heaven and earth. Once he met Malchizekek [Shem, the son of Noah] and asked him, 'By virtue of which merit did you survive the great Flood?' Malchizedek replied, 'By virtue of the charity and kindness which we practiced towards the helpless animals in the Ark! We did not close our eyes all night as we hurried to provide food for every single animal, beast, and bird. One time only were we late and, instantly, father Noah was bitten [by a lion.]'

Upon hearing this, Abraham said to himself, 'If these men survived by virtue of the kindness they displayed to lowly animals, how much greater would my salvation be if I would act charitably towards all men, who are created in God's Own image'? Immediately, Abraham established an inn to provide food, drink, and company for travelers. Therefore, Solomon observed: *And I saw that all labor and all skillful enterprise spring from man's rivalry with his neighbor (Koheles* 4:4).

the earth, sink your own roots in HASHEM, the source of all good (Hirsch).

The עֹשֵׂי עַוְלָה, *evildoers* (v. 1) are the victims of their own lack of trust. Do not copy this — counteract it by strengthening your trust and resolving to *do good* (Ibn Yachya).

Trust in HASHEM, thereby you will avoid evil and *do good.* Do not say to yourself, 'If I do not rob and steal or if I give my money to charity — how will I make a living and survive?' (Rashi). [1]

According to *Radak* and *Ibn Ezra*, however, this stich should be understood in the reverse order: learn to trust in God by doing good. *Do good*, and in the merit of your good deeds, you can *trust in HASHEM* to reward and protect you.

Divrei Shlomo comments that it is not enough to think or say that you trust God. Genuine trust must lead to action! If you are willing to take a risk or make a sacrifice as a result of trust, then you know that your convictions are strong and sincere. Thus, *Trust in HASHEM* [so firmly that] *you will do good.*

Ramban derives many fundamentals of faith from this verse. Like *Rashi*, he emphasizes that faith is the prime cause of all good deeds. One should be confident that if he is determined to perform *mitzvos*, God will help him *do good.*

Ramban continues that *trust* is mentioned *before* *do good* in order to emphasize that even a sinner who has not yet done any good has the right to trust in the mercy of God Who assists even those who are unworthy of reward. Whether you are righteous or wicked, *trust in HASHEM.* Then, after God has responded favorably to your

trust, you should show your appreciation by doing good (*Ha'Emunah V'ha'Betachon* ch. 1).

שְׁכָן אֶרֶץ — [*That you may*] *dwell in the land.*

Your reward for doing good will be to *dwell in the land*, in endless tranquility (Rashi).

Ramban continues: Once you have decided to dedicate yourself to doing good, you may wish to withdraw from mundane pursuits and to abandon your occupation. Such a course of action is not desirable for the average person, since he will probably fear the lack of a source of livelihood. Therefore do not be excessively enthusiastic; instead, *dwell in the land* i.e., cultivate and exploit it to earn a living.

The *Talmud* (*Berachos* 35b) states that only a select handful of men like the saintly Rabbi Shimon bar Yochai can abandon all worldly pursuits in favor of exclusive Torah study [for they were not concerned with their bodies, only with their souls]. Others must always engage in an occupation [despite their spiritual aspirations].[2]

וּרְעֵה אֱמוּנָה — *And be nurtured* [lit. *pastured*] *by faith.*

This translation follows *Rashi* who derives רְעֵה from מִרְעֶה, *pasture, grazing land.* Thus: [As a reward for trusting in HASHEM and doing good], you will eat and be nourished plentifully.

You will resemble sheep who graze in lush pastures, never worrying about the future. They have complete faith that just as there is grass today, so will there be grass tomorrow (Malbim).

Not only will your body be

---

1. The *Talmud* (*Sotah* 48b) asks: 'Who are the אַנְשֵׁי אֱמוּנָה, *men of faith?*

Rabbi Yitzchak says: They are the people who sincerely believe in the Holy One, Blessed be He, [and therefore freely spend money to enhance a mitzvah, for charity, or for Sabbath and festival expenses (*Rashi*)].

As Rabbi Eliezer HaGadol taught: Whoever has bread in his basket today, yet asks, 'What will I eat tomorrow?', is among the קְטַנֵּי אֱמוּנָה, *people of meager faith.*

nourished, but even your אֱמוּנָה, *faith*, will grow stronger and stronger (*Tanya*).

Radak relates רֹעֵה to the רוֹעֶה, *shepherd* who takes the animals out to the pasture. He explains: Do not content yourself with personal good deeds. Go out and be a shepherd, a guide, a teacher to others. This is the most desirable service you can render to God! By being a shepherd, who teaches others good, you counteract the influence of the מְרֵעִים (v. 1) who teach others to do evil (*Ibn Yachya*).

Ramban translates רֹעֵה as guard (for a shepherd who guards the sheep) and comments: 'Now that you, the average man, are destined to be שְׁכָן אֶרֶץ, i.e., one who cultivates the earth, you may be bitter that you are condemned to an empty life of material pursuit. This is not so! A great spiritual challenge confronts those who earn a living. רֹעֵה אֱמוּנָה, *guard your faithfulness!* Take care to deal with honesty and integrity. Each day that you pass this test will be well spent in a profound state of spiritual accomplishment!'

Ramban also suggests that רֹעֵה is related to רֵעַ, *friend, companion.* Always put yourself in the company of faith and wisdom, for that is the key to coming close to God.

Rabbeinu Bachya concludes: This verse begins with בְּטַח, *trust*, and ends with אֱמוּנָה, *faith*, in order to teach that *faith* is merely one aspect of the broader concept called *trust* and is subordinate to it. *Faith* is a simple intellectual concept, a belief that God can control every aspect of life. *Trust* involves translating this lofty concept of faith into action. Therefore, *Ramban* lays down the postulate כָּל הַבּוֹטֵחַ מַאֲמִין אֲבָל לֹא כָּל הַמַאֲמִין בּוֹטֵחַ, *Everyone who trusts has faith, but not everyone who has faith, trusts.*

4. וְהִתְעַנַּג עַל ה' — *Take delight in HASHEM*

If you are nourished only by faith, you will take delight exclusively in HASHEM (*Nora Tehillos*). In His service you will find the fulfillment of every delightful wish for which you ever yearned (*Radak*).

You may demand these [spiritual] delights from HASHEM for you are like a worker who has the right to request his pay (*Ibn Ezra*).

But the main delight is reserved for the World to Come (*Ibn Yachya*).

The *Talmud* (*Shabbos* 18b) states: Whoever makes the Sabbath delightful is granted all of his heart's desires as it says, *Take delight in HASHEM that He*

---

2. *Chovos Halevavos* relates the following tale: Once a saintly man traveled to a distant land to seek out a livelihood. He arrived at a city whose inhabitants were all idol-worshipers. He fiercely rebuked them, 'Fools! Why do you worship helpless images of wood and stone? Join me and worship the living, all powerful God who feeds and supports all of mankind!'

The pagans retorted, 'Your actions contradict your own words! If indeed your God supports all men at all times in all places, why then did you yourself put your life into jeopardy to travel so very far in order to seek your fortune? Stay home and let your God provide for you there!'

Upon hearing this rebuke, the pious man immediately resolved never again to leave his land in order to search for sustenance.

Based on this parable, *Tehillas Hashem* notes that even if one engages in earning a living he has the opportunity to demonstrate this trust in HASHEM by being שְׁכָן אֶרֶץ *dwelling in* (his own) *land* [i.e., *limiting the extent of his pursuit of a livelihood.*]

ה עַל־יהוה וְיִתֶּן־לְךָ מִשְׁאֲלֹת לִבֶּךָ׃ גּוֹל
עַל־יהוה דַּרְכֶּךָ וּבְטַח עָלָיו וְהוּא יַעֲשֶׂה׃
ו וְהוֹצִיא כָאוֹר צִדְקֶךָ וּמִשְׁפָּטֶךָ כַּצָּהֳרָיִם׃
ז דּוֹם | לַיהוה וְהִתְחוֹלֵל לוֹ אַל־תִּתְחַר
ח בְּמַצְלִיחַ דַּרְכּוֹ בְּאִישׁ עֹשֶׂה מְזִמּוֹת׃ הֶרֶף

will grant you the desires of your heart.
The Sabbath is a day of delight as we
read, וְקָרָאתָ לַשַּׁבָּת עֹנֶג, *And you shall call
the Sabbath a delight (Jeremiah 58:13).*

[If you take delight in HASHEM then
you will not envy the material success
of the wicked. It is not easy to attain
such spiritual contentment during the
work week, but on the Sabbath even the
humblest Jew is like a king and capable
of perceiving the futility of envy for
material benefit.]

וְיִתֶּן לְךָ מִשְׁאֲלֹת לִבֶּךָ — *That He may
grant you the desires of your heart.*

When God sees that you take delight
only in Him, He will surely fulfill your
every request, because whatever you
desire will be put to His service *(Divrei
Shlomo).*

5. גּוֹל עַל ה׳ דַּרְכֶּךָ — *Cast* [lit. *roll*] *your
way upon HASHEM.*

Shift your burdens from yourself and
put them on God. Trust Him to attend
to your every need *(Rashi, Radak).*

The use of the singular form דַּרְכֶּךָ,
your way, conveys a message. The
righteous man knows with a certainty
that the only route to good fortune is by
way of Hashem. But the evildoer who
has no faith in God must toil incessantly
to care for himself. He tries not one, but
many different ways to search for his
road to success *(Malbim).*

[If you are determined to follow in
the way of Hashem, be prepared to exert
yourself to clear away all obstacles in
your path. Roll them to the side, as the
prophet said, סֹלּוּ סֹלּוּ פַּנּוּ דָרֶךְ הָרִימוּ
מִכְשׁוֹל מִדֶּרֶךְ עַמִּי, *Raise up, raise up,
prepare the way, lift up the stumbling*

*block out of the way, My nation (Isaiah
57:14).]*

וּבְטַח עָלָיו וְהוּא יַעֲשֶׂה — *Rely on Him and
He will act.*

As we read, הַשְׁלֵךְ עַל ה׳ יְהָבְךָ וְהוּא
יְכַלְכְּלֶךָ, *Cast upon HASHEM your burden and He will provide for you* [55:23]
(Ibn Ezra)

[Now that the righteous man is assured that his every wish will be fulfilled, there is no reason for him to
imitate or envy the wicked.]

6. וְהוֹצִיא כָאוֹר צִדְקֶךָ — *And He will
reveal* [lit. *He will bring forth*] *your
righteousness like a light.*

Your righteousness will be displayed
to the entire world as clearly as a bright
light *(Radak).*

Evildoers resort to the lowest of tricks
in order to foil the righteous. With
vicious slander they cast aspersions on
the honesty of righteous people and the
purity of their motives. But David assures good men that ultimately they will
be cleared of all false accusations
(Hirsch).

The righteous are not ashamed of
their actions, but the evildoers must
perform all of their deeds in darkness
lest they be caught and disgraced
(Malbim).

וּמִשְׁפָּטֶךָ כַּצָּהֳרָיִם — *And your judgments
like high noon.*

The righteous man fears no tribunal.
He has nothing to hide from the inquiry
of a court. Not so the evildoer who
trembles before the glaring, revealing
light of justice *(Malbim).*

[The plural form מִשְׁפָּטֶךָ (lit.

that He may grant you the desires of your heart.
⁵ Cast your way upon HASHEM,
    rely on Him and He will act.
⁶ And He will reveal your righteousness like a light,
    and your judgments like high noon.
⁷ Be mute before HASHEM
    and wait with longing for Him.
Do not compete with him who prospers,
    with the man who executes malicious plans.

---

judgments) appears in the authoritative Rodelheim edition of the *Psalms*. However, *Hirsch* uses the singular מִשְׁפָּטֶךָ based on older editions of *Psalms*.]

7. דּוֹם לַה׳ — *Be mute before HASHEM.*

This translation follows the *Targum, Menachem,* and *Dunash* who relate this to וַיִּדֹּם אַהֲרֹן, *And Aaron was silent* (*Leviticus* 10:3).

The realization that your fate comes only from God should end all doubts, and silence all protests (*Hirsch*).

However, *Rashi, Radak,* and *Metzudos* render דּוֹם as *wait, tarry* as in דֹּמּוּ עַד הַגִּיעֵנוּ אֲלֵיכֶם, *Wait until we reach you* (*I Samuel* 14:9). [Do not be overwhelmed by present events, wait patiently for future developments which will make God's providence clearly evident.] [1]

וְהִתְחוֹלֵל לוֹ — *And wait with longing for Him.*

This is derived from תּוֹחֶלֶת, *waiting, longing.* [See *Proverbs* 13:12] (*Ibn Ezra, Radak, Metzudos*).

Similarly it says: טוֹב וְיָחִיל וְדוּמָם לִתְשׁוּעַת ה׳, *It is good to wait in silence for the salvation of HASHEM* (*Lamentations* 3:26). If God brings afflictions upon you, accept them with hope (*Yalkut Shimoni*).

Some relate this word to חִיל *pain* as in חִיל כַּיּוֹלֵדָה *a pain like a woman in labor* (48:7). Thus: prepare to suffer pain and torments for His sake (*Radak*).

And even be ready to endure חֳלִי, *sickness* if that is God's wish (*Tehillos Hashem*).

Or הִתְחוֹלֵל may be related to חָלָל *corpse* i.e. prepare to give up your life, to become a corpse, for His sake. Similarly we read הֵן יִקְטְלֵנִי לוֹ אֲיַחֵל *Though they slay me, for Him I* [am prepared to] *become a* (חָלָל) *corpse* (*Tanchuma Hayashan, Devarim* 4).

אַל תִּתְחַר בְּמַצְלִיחַ דַּרְכּוֹ — *Do not compete with him who prospers*

[Never seek to emulate the seemingly successful ways of the wicked. Though your attempts at righteousness result in failure and misfortune, never stop hoping for eventual salvation by Hashem.]

---

1. The *Talmud* (*Gittin* 7a) interprets דּוֹם homiletically as a reference to דִּמְדּוּמֵי חַמָּה, *the dim light of the sun* i.e. early morning and late afternoon which are times of prayer. The *Talmud* relates that the Babylonian Exilarch, Mar Ukva, was harassed by rebels who flouted his authority and insulted him. He had the authority to turn these rebels over to the Babylonian government for punishment but he was reluctant to do so. He sought the advice of Rabbi Elazar who responded דּוֹם לַה׳, *pray to HASHEM, in the early morning and late afternoon,* וְהִתְחוֹלֵל לוֹ, and He will topple your enemies before you like so many חֲלָלִים, *corpses!*

מֵאַף וַעֲזֹב חֵמָה אַל־תִּתְחַר אַךְ־לְהָרֵעַ:
ט כִּי־מְרֵעִים יִכָּרֵתוּן וְקֹוֵי יהוה הֵמָּה
י יִירְשׁוּ־אָרֶץ: וְעוֹד מְעַט וְאֵין רָשָׁע
יא וְהִתְבּוֹנַנְתָּ עַל־מְקוֹמוֹ וְאֵינֶנּוּ: וַעֲנָוִים
יב יִירְשׁוּ־אָרֶץ וְהִתְעַנְּגוּ עַל־רֹב שָׁלוֹם: זֹמֵם
יג רָשָׁע לַצַּדִּיק וְחֹרֵק עָלָיו שִׁנָּיו: אֲדֹנָי
יד יִשְׂחַק־לוֹ כִּי־רָאָה כִּי־יָבֹא יוֹמוֹ: חֶרֶב |

8. הֶרֶף — *Give up.*

This is synonymous with הֶרֶף, *let loose*, (Rashi); and is related to רָפֶה, *weak* (Metzudas Zion).

מֵאַף — *From anger.*

Desist from evil so as to prevent God's anger from pouring down on you (Rashi).

Subdue your own frustration and anger despite your failure to realize your ambitions (Radak).

Resist the temptation to join the company of the prosperous man who angers God (Metzudas David).

וַעֲזֹב חֵמָה — *And forsake wrath.*

Calm yourself. Do not let the prosperity of the wicked upset you (Ibn Ezra).

Not only must you subdue your אַף, *external rage*, but even your חֵמָה, *inner rage*, [see comm. 6:2], should be controlled (Malbim).

אַךְ תִּתְחַר אַךְ־לְהָרֵעַ — *Do not compete; it will bring but harm.*

Think carefully before you join the wicked; you may lose more than you gain. Remember, pure faith in Hashem is more precious than any other possession. Better to be a pauper with trust than a wealthy man without it (Malbim).

Perhaps you wish to associate with the wicked in order to bring them back to Hashem. Nevertheless, do not become intimate with them. The dangers of doing so are great, but the potential benefits are extremely doubtful (Alshich).

9. כִּי מְרֵעִים יִכָּרֵתוּן — *For the evil men shall be cut off.*

Don't be taken in by their success, for it is short-lived (Radak).

וְקֹוֵי ה' הֵמָּה יִירְשׁוּאָרֶץ — *But those who hope to HASHEM shall inherit the earth.*

After the wicked are swept away, the righteous shall arise to take over their possessions, as it says (Job 27:17): יָכִין, *He* [the wicked one] *prepares, but the righteous one dons* [his clothing] (Radak).

10. וְעוֹד מְעַט — *Just a little longer.*

Pay no heed to the present. In but a short while all will change and the evil will vanish (Rashi).

וְאֵין רָשָׁע — *And there will be no wicked.*

He will die and leave This World (Eretz Hachaim).

וְהִתְבּוֹנַנְתָּ עַל מְקוֹמוֹ וְאֵינֶנּוּ — *You will contemplate his place and he will be gone.*

His place will be left permanently vacant. Even his immediate heirs will not inherit his position (Otzar Nechmad).

If you consider it you will realize that not only has the evildoer left This World, but he has forfeited his place in the World to Come. And who will receive that portion? The righteous! As it says in the very next verse, *but the humble shall inherit the earth* (Eretz HaChaim).

⁸ *Give up anger and forsake wrath.*
  Do not compete; it will bring but harm.
⁹ *For the evil men shall be cut off,*
  but those who hope to HASHEM shall inherit the earth.
¹⁰ *Just a little longer and there will be no wicked,*
  you will contemplate his place and he will be gone.
¹¹ *But the humble shall inherit the earth*
  and delight in abundant peace.
¹² *The wicked man plots against the righteous*
  and gnashes his teeth at him.
¹³ *But my Lord laughs at him*
  for He sees that his day approaches.

---

11. וַעֲנָוִים יִירְשׁוּ אָרֶץ — *But the humble shall inherit the earth.*

Those who had previously been downtrodden and humbled by the wicked (*Radak*).

וְהִתְעַנְּגוּ עַל רֹב שָׁלוֹם — *And they shall delight in abundant peace.*

The haughty never enjoy the delight known as 'peace of mind.' In their excessive pride they imagine that they never have enough; that they deserve more and more. But the humble are delighted with what they have and consider it to be שָׁלֵם, *complete*, i.e., enough (*Yalkut Eliezer*).

Rav said: For four reasons the property of the wealthy householders suddenly disappears. They pay their laborers only with great reluctance. They don't pay their laborers at all. They shirk all communal responsibility. They are haughty. And haughtiness is as bad as all of those sins combined. However, the humble are different, as it says: *but the humble shall inherit the land and they shall delight in abundant peace* (*Succah* 29b).

12. וְזֹמֵם רָשָׁע לַצַּדִּיק — *The wicked man plots against the righteous.*

Do not be overawed by the wicked even when they hatch seemingly fool-proof plots against the righteous (*Malbim*).

וְחֹרֵק עָלָיו שִׁנָּיו — *And gnashes his teeth at him.*

[Even when they gnash their teeth in gleeful anticipation of the downfall of the *tzaddik*, pay no heed. See 35:16 and 112:10.]

This alludes to the encounter of the two estranged brothers, Esau and Jacob. The Sages teach that when Esau fell on Jacob's neck, ostensibly to kiss him, he tried to inflict a mortal wound by biting. However, God turned Jacob's neck to marble, and Esau blunted his own teeth. Thus, the wicked Esau plotted to bite the righteous Jacob, but ground his own teeth instead (*Tehillas Hashem*).

13. אֲדֹנָי יִשְׂחַק לוֹ — [*But*] *my Lord laughs at him.*

The Lord to whom the future is revealed, already foresees the futility of the evildoer's schemes. God laughs at the very outset, for the plots will never succeed (*Ibn Ezra, Radak*).

Or יִשְׂחַק may mean *to show* פָּנִים שׂוֹחֲקוֹת, *a smiling contenance*. Don't be

פָּתְחוּ רְשָׁעִים וְדָרְכוּ קַשְׁתָּם לְהַפִּיל עָנִי

וְאֶבְיוֹן לִטְבוֹחַ יִשְׁרֵי־דָרֶךְ: חַרְבָּם תָּבוֹא טו

בְלִבָּם וְקַשְּׁתוֹתָם תִּשָּׁבַרְנָה: טוֹב־מְעַט טז

לַצַּדִּיק מֵהֲמוֹן רְשָׁעִים רַבִּים: כִּי זְרוֹעוֹת יז

רְשָׁעִים תִּשָּׁבַרְנָה וְסוֹמֵךְ צַדִּיקִים יהוה:

יוֹדֵעַ יהוה יְמֵי תְמִימִם וְנַחֲלָתָם לְעוֹלָם יח

---

dismayed if God seems to treat the wicked person benevolently. Rest assured that God has prepared his present success to be the cause of his eventual downfall (Malbim).

כִּי יָבֹא יוֹמוֹ — *That his day approaches.*

Though the wicked one plots against the righteous, God knows that his plan will never come to fruition, because the day of his own doom draws near (Radak).

14. חֶרֶב פָּתְחוּ רְשָׁעִים — *The wicked drew* [lit. *opened*] *a sword.*

When it is sheathed, the sword appears to be locked into its cover; when it is drawn, it is *opened* and released (Radak, Ibn Ezra).

Or פָּתְחוּ may be rendered *they sharpened* as in חֶרֶב פְּתוּחָה לְטֶבַח מְרוּטָה, *the sword is sharpened, polished for the slaughter* (Ezekiel 21:33).

This implies that the wicked initiated hostilities without prior provocation (Rashi).[1]

15. חַרְבָּם תָּבוֹא בְלִבָּם — *Their sword will pierce their own heart.*

Instead of succeeding in their designs against the righteous, the wicked would

die of their own devices. Then it will be evident why God laughed at them (v. 13) when He foresaw their doom (Malbim).

The degraded one says in his heart, 'There is no God' (14:1). God responds: 'Since the degenerate rebelled against me in his heart, I will punish him measure for measure by aiming for his heart.' As it says, *Their sword will pierce their own heart* (Midrash Shocher Tov).

16. טוֹב מְעַט לַצַּדִּיק — *Better a few with the righteous* [lit. *The little which the righteous one has is good*].

The handful of men who rally to the call of the *tzaddik,* are superior to the wicked masses (Rashi).

Radak renders מְעַט literally as a *small amount,* i.e., the *tzaddik* is content even with meagre resources.

He understands that excessive wealth is often detrimental to one's faith and character because wealth can lead a man to forget that God is the ultimate source of all blessing. Therefore, he prefers to have little, because in that way he remains conscious of his dependence on God (Tehillos Hashem).

---

1. Various *Midrashim* trace violence back to the provocation of the wicked. Rabbi Yehoshua of Sichnin in the name of Rabbi Levi said: It is written, *The wicked drew a sword, and bent their bows,* this refers to Cain. *To bring down the poor and needy, to slaughter those of up-right path,* this describes his brother, Abel. *Their sword will pierce their own heart,* this is Cain's punishment of exile and wandering over the earth (Bereishis Rabbah 22:9).

Another Midrash (Bereishis Rabbah 42:1) expounds that the wicked instigated the world's first large-scale war: *The wicked drew a sword,* this refers to King Amraphel and his allies. *To bring down the poor and needy,* this is Lot. *To slaughter those of upright path,* this is Abraham. *Their sword will pierce their own heart,* this describes their ultimate defeat at the hands of Abraham.

¹⁴ *The wicked drew a sword*
and bent their bow
To bring down the poor and the needy,
to slaughter those of upright path.
¹⁵ *Their sword will pierce their own heart,*
and their bows be broken.
¹⁶ *Better a few with the righteous*
than a multitude of many wicked.
¹⁷ *For the arms of the wicked will be broken,*
but the support of the righteous ones is HASHEM.
¹⁸ *HASHEM is aware of the days of the perfect,*
their inheritance will endure forever.

מֵהֲמוֹן — *Than a multitude* [lit. *more than the many*].

הָמוֹן refers to a vast army, derived from הָמָה, *to make noise*, describing the clamor of the mob (*Hirsch*).

Amraphel and his allies started the first major world war in order to capture and antagonize Abraham [see footnote v. 14.] He threatened Abraham with a הָמוֹן, *a multitude*, but the handful of men who accompanied Abraham surpassed the mighty armies of the wicked and destroyed them (*Rashi*).

According to *Radak*, הָמוֹן refers to מָמוֹן, *money*. Abundant wealth will never satisfy the wicked who incessantly crave for more, as Solomon said, *The righteous man eats to satisfy his soul, but the belly of the wicked shall always feel want* (*Proverbs* 13:25).

רְשָׁעִים רַבִּים — *Many wicked.*

In this verse the righteous are referred to in the singular form as צַדִּיק, *righteous one*, whereas the wicked ones are described in the plural. Herein lies

the secret strength of the righteous. Although they are few, they unite together as one powerful unit. But the wicked ones can never agree on anything. Each one selfishly seeks to preserve his own personal interests. So, despite their vast numbers, they remain a weak, fragmented force (*Maharam Markado*).

17. כִּי זְרוֹעוֹת רְשָׁעִים תִּשָּׁבַרְנָה — *For the arms of the wicked will be broken.*

Just as their bows will be broken (v. 15) so will their arms, for the bows can kill only because of the strong arms which string and bend them (*Ibn Ezra*).

They will not have the strength to harm the righteous (*Radak*).

18. יוֹדֵעַ ה' יְמֵי תְמִימִם — *HASHEM is aware of the days of the perfect.*

God is concerned with their daily good deeds (*Rashi*), and providentially lengthens their lives (*Radak*).

The *Midrash* (*Bereishis Rabbah* 58:1) comments, 'Just as the righteous are

Finally, *Midrash Tanchuma* (*Lech Lecha* 7) applies these words to the life of David himself. In *II Samuel* Chapter 10, the Scriptures relate how David sent two emissaries to console Chanun ben Nachash, King of Ammon, after the death of his father. But the King opened hostilities by treating the emissaries in a most degrading fashion. He shaved off half of their beards and ripped their garments in two. The Ammonite King then hired Aram to join him in battle against Israel. Said the Holy One, Blessed be He, 'Wicked one, you started the fight with a sword, your own sword shall pierce your heart!' Thereupon, David's generals, Yoav and Avishai arose and slew them all.

יט תִּהְיֶה: לֹא־יֵבֹשׁוּ בְּעֵת רָעָה וּבִימֵי רְעָבוֹן
כ יִשְׂבָּעוּ: כִּי רְשָׁעִים | יֹאבֵדוּ וְאֹיְבֵי יהוה
כא כִּיקַר כָּרִים כָּלוּ בֶעָשָׁן כָּלוּ: לֹוֶה רָשָׁע

perfect and complete, so are their days perfect and complete.' [This can be understood in two ways. One, that the lifetime allotted to the righteous is in units of complete years. They will die on a birthday so that their years will literally be 'complete.' However, only a select few are so perfectly righteous that they can be placed in this category.

A second interpretation is that the above statement applies not to God, but to the philosophy of all devout people. To them, every day presents a unique opportunity for accomplishment, and they exploit this opportunity fully. Thus, the devout end their lives with their special mission accomplished perfectly.]

Every commandment perfects the limb which performed it. Every sin distorts the organ which was used for the spiritual perversion. Thus, *the arms of the wicked will be broken* (v. 17), whereas the days and the bodies of the righteous will achieve spiritual perfection (*Ahavas Shalom*).

וְנַחֲלָתָם לְעוֹלָם תִּהְיֶה — *Their inheritance will endure forever.*

Their God-given reward is eternal. [Since they never wasted an opportunity to accomplish good, every act they did was of enduring significance.]

19. לֹא יֵבֹשׁוּ בְּעֵת רָעָה — *They will not be shamed in times of calamity.*

I.e., in times of plague, war, or attack by beasts (*Radak*).

[A calamity which descends upon a community points an accusing finger at the inhabitants and their improper ways. Thus, those who are afflicted are shamed. But the perfectly innocent will remain unscathed, for their ways are above reproach.]

20. כִּי רְשָׁעִים יֹאבֵדוּ — *For the wicked will perish.*

The downfall of the wicked is imperative so that the perfect will never be shamed by calamity (v. 19) at their hands (*Radak*).

וְאֹיְבֵי ה' — *And the foes of HASHEM.*

Wicked people are generally those who have been overcome by their lusts. Since they lost self-control, their measure-for-measure punishment is יֹאבֵדוּ, literally, *they become lost*. But, like any lost article which can be sought and recovered, they can repent and return. However, *the foes of HASHEM* are those who wish to obliterate God's presence from their lives. Therefore, they themselves will be made to vanish forever (*Tehillos Hashem*).

כִּיקַר כָּרִים — *Like a light flashing on pastures.*

This follows *Rashi* who relates יְקַר to יְקָרוֹת, *bright light* (*Zechariah* 14:16) and כָּר נִרְחָב to בַּר, *broad pasture* (*Isaiah* 30:23). The first rays of the morning sun spread out all across the broad horizon, dazzling the beholder by their contrast to the darkness they displace. But the spectacle is soon over. Similarly, the spectacular success of the wicked does not endure.

Rashi, Radak, Ibn Ezra, and *Metzudos* also suggest a different translation. כָּרִים means *sheep,* and יְקַר, *glory,* is its rich flesh and fat. The sheep which is being fattened for the slaughter glories in its growing weight and size not realizing that it is precisely this fattening which is the prelude to its doom. So too, the prosperity of the wicked is the first step towards their destruction.

Chovos Halevavos (Shaar Avodas HaElohim, Ch. 6) observes: He who

19 *They will not be shamed in times of calamity,*
  in days of famine they will be satisfied.
20 *For the wicked will perish,*
And the foes of HASHEM —
  like a light flashing on pastures;
  consumed, like smoke they are consumed.
21 *The wicked one borrows but repays not,*

denies the existence of God and fails to recognize His abundant kindness suffers a complete decline in his personal status. No longer is he considered to be an intelligent human being. Rather, he sinks to the level of the dumb animals as it says, *And the foes of HASHEM are like the fattened sheep.*[1]

כָּלוּ בֶעָשָׁן כָּלוּ — *Consumed, like smoke they are consumed.*

David said: 'Accord to the wicked the honor reserved for the fattened sheep.' The sheep are slaughtered and hung high above the fire to be smoked (*Yalkut Shimoni*).

Other materials leave behind some residue after burning in the form of ashes, but if fat is burned [such as the fat of the sheep mentioned here], it is completely consumed by the flames. The same is true of the wicked who will perish and leave behind no remnant (*Hirsch*).

21. לוֶה רָשָׁע וְלֹא יְשַׁלֵּם — *The wicked one borrows, but repays not* [lit. *and he will not repay*].

Having lost all their possessions, the wicked will be forced to borrow money

even though they have no means of repayment (*Rashbam*).

It does not say וְלֹא מְשַׁלֵּם, *and he does not pay,* i.e., later when the debt becomes due. Rather it says וְלֹא יְשַׁלֵּם, *and he 'will' not pay,* i.e., when he first borrowed the money he had no intention of ever repaying (*Yalkut Shimoni*).

Rambam (*Hilchos Malveh* 1:3) derives a halachic principle from this verse: It is forbidden to borrow money with the intention of squandering it for no worthwhile purpose. For if the money is wasted then no assets will be available from which the creditor can extract payment. The debtor who acts so carelessly and inconsiderately is called רָשָׁע, *wicked*, as it says, *The wicked man borrows and he will not repay.* Furthermore, the Sages warned, וִיהִי מָמוֹן חֲבֵרְךָ חָבִיב עָלֶיךָ כְּשֶׁלָּךְ, *Let the money of your friend be as dear to you as your own.* (*Avos* 2:17).

Hirsch elaborates on the deeper message contained in these words: Whatever gain we receive on earth is a loan granted by God in order to help us advance the common welfare in accordance with His will. The greater the

---

1. To what may this be likened? To the farmer who owned a piglet, a donkey and its foal. He fed the piglet all it wanted. But to the foal and the donkey he gave measured portions. Said the foal to its mother, 'What a fool our master is. We toil and sweat for him and he gives us only limited rations, yet the piglet does nothing and he gives it all it wants!'
   The donkey replied, 'Do not be upset, the day will come and your will see that the pig was pampered for its doom not for its good.'
   Sure enough, when the holiday season arrived, they dragged the fat pig away to its slaughter. The master then put barley into the feedbag of the foal who shook its head and refused to eat, [thinking that it, too, was being fattened for the kill.] But the wise mother reassured it, 'Have no fear little one! It is not the feeding which marks the creature for slaughter, but idleness from productive work' (*Midrash Esther Rabbah* 7:1).

כב וְלֹא יְשַׁלֵּם וְצַדִּיק חוֹנֵן וְנוֹתֵן: כִּי מְבֹרָכָיו
כג יִירְשׁוּ אָרֶץ וּמְקֻלָּלָיו יִכָּרֵתוּ: מֵיְהוָה
כד מִצְעֲדֵי־גֶבֶר כּוֹנָנוּ וְדַרְכּוֹ יֶחְפָּץ: כִּי־יִפֹּל
כה לֹא־יוּטָל כִּי־יְהוָה סוֹמֵךְ יָדוֹ: נַעַר | הָיִיתִי

'loan' granted an individual, the greater his obligation to give something in return. The wicked person who accumulates largesse for himself with no concern for the needs of others, becomes more and more indebted to the shared inventory of common good. The righteous person, however, does all in his power to benefit others, and for this — the world is indebted to him. The classic example is that of Rabbi Chanina ben Dosa of whom a heavenly voice proclaimed every day: 'All the world is sustained by virtue of My son, Chanina, but My son, Chanina, contents himself with but one measure of carob fruit from one Sabbath eve to the next' (Berachos 17b).

This is the meaning of the Mishnah (Avos 3:16): 'The store [this world] is open, and the proprietor [God] issues [materials and resources] on credit. The ledger is open and the hand [of God] records. Whoever wishes to come and borrow is welcome to do so, but the collectors [angels of punishment and death] constantly make their rounds and extract payment from the debtors, both and without their knowledge.'

וְצַדִּיק חוֹנֵן וְנוֹתֵן — While the righteous one graciously gives [lit. shows kindness and gives].

God, who is the Righteous One of the world kindly repays the lender the money which the wicked borrower refuses to return (Rashi).

Therefore the Mishnah (Avos 2:9) says: He who takes a loan from a man is as if he took a loan from God, for God guarantees repayment (Bertenoro ibid.).

The righteous man is continuously benevolent. Even after the wicked man defaults on his debts frequently, the righteous man still gives him loans. Nor does he wait to be asked; for on his own he goes to the wicked and offers him the loan, as it says while the righteous one graciously gives (Midrash Halttamari).

The righteous one first shows kindness by making the loan. Later, he has mercy on the debtor and gives the loan money away, by canceling the debt (Yalkut Shimoni).

22. כִּי מְבֹרָכָיו יִירְשׁוּ אָרֶץ — For those blessed by Him shall inherit the earth.

Because they give generously of their wealth, righteous people will be blessed by God and they will inherit more resources with which to do even more good. Their good fortune will be permanent, just as an inheritance remains permanently in a family (Radak, Rashi).

וּמְקֻלָּלָיו יִכָּרֵתוּ — While those cursed by Him will be excised.

Their wealth will not endure and they will be cut off from this world and the next (Radak).

23. מֵיְהוָה מִצְעֲדֵי גֶבֶר כּוֹנָנוּ — By HASHEM, the footsteps of a strong man are made firm.

The word גֶבֶר derives from גְבוּרָה, strength: this is the man whose faith is strong (Rashi) by virtue of his heroic accomplishments in Torah study (Metzudas David).

Or, the righteous man firmly rejects the influence of the wicked with his good deeds (Radak).

וְדַרְכּוֹ יֶחְפָּץ — His way shall He approve.

When the tzaddik meets with success, it proves to him that God is pleased with his way (Radak).

while the righteous one graciously gives.

²² *For those blessed by Him shall inherit the earth,*
while those cursed by Him will be excised.

²³ *By HASHEM, the footsteps of a strong man are firm;*
his way shall He approve.

²⁴ *Should he fall, he will not be cast off,*
for HASHEM supports his hand.

²⁵ *I have been a youth and also aged,*

[God often limits the choice of ordinary people who are called אָדָם and אִישׁ (see *Jeremiah* 10:23) because they are under the sway of the Evil Inclination and their preferences and choices are therefore suspect. Not so the גֶּבֶר, *strong man*, who controls his evil impulse. Because he chooses only good, God approves his way and assists him thereon. This is as we read, מִי זֶה הָאִישׁ יְרֵא ה' יוֹרֶנּוּ בְּדֶרֶךְ יִבְחָר, *Who is this, the man fearful of HASHEM? He will show him the way he should choose* (25:12).]

24. כִּי יִפֹּל לֹא יוּטָל — *Should he fall he will not be cast off.*

Radak comments that even if God should cause the righteous man to fall into poverty and misfortune, He will not cast him away or reject him entirely. His misfortune is a rebuke which emanates from Hashem's love and concern. This is the main difference between the righteous and the wicked. When the wicked fall, they are completely *excised* (v. 22), never to arise. But of the righteous it is written, שֶׁבַע יִפּוֹל צַדִּיק וָקָם, *The righteous one shall fall seven times yet [still] arise* (*Proverbs* 24:16).

כִּי ה' סוֹמֵךְ יָדוֹ — *For HASHEM supports his hand.*

[Even as he falls, God is already supporting him, for the purpose of the decline is eventually to raise the righteous person even higher. Similarly we read סוֹמֵךְ ה' לְכָל הַנֹּפְלִים, *HASHEM*

supports all those who fall (145:14).]

25. נַעַר הָיִיתִי גַּם זָקַנְתִּי — *I have been a youth and also aged.*

Ibn Ezra and *Radak* attribute this statement to the Psalmist who declares, 'After experiencing all phases of life, from beginning to end, I am equipped to make the following observation.'

However, the *Talmud* (*Yevamos* 16b, quoted by *Rashi*) maintains that such a sweeping observation can be made only by one who can evaluate all of human history, not just one short lifetime. Although God Himself exists forever, we cannot attribute this verse to Him, for the word 'aged' cannot be used in reference to the Eternal. Rather this observation was made by Mitatron, the chief of all angels who is called שַׂר הָעוֹלָם, *Officer of the World.*

The *Midrash* (*Tanchuma Mikeitz* 6) follows this opinion: *The Officer of the World* said, 'I have been a youth, from the time of Adam, *and also aged*, until the days of the Messiah. Yet never did I see that God should forsake the world by leaving it devoid of righteous men. In every generation He raises up *tzaddikim.*

Tehillas Hashem lends support to those who attribute these words to David. The Sages say that Adam, David and Messiah share the same mission as if they were the same person [see *Overview*, Part 8. Thus, the youth of David started when, as Adam, he was 930 years old, making him *a youth and also aged* at one and the same time.

גַּם־זָקַנְתִּי וְלֹא־רָאִיתִי צַדִּיק נֶעֱזָב וְזַרְעוֹ
מְבַקֶּשׁ־לָחֶם: כָּל־הַיּוֹם חוֹנֵן וּמַלְוֶה
וְזַרְעוֹ לִבְרָכָה: סוּר מֵרָע וַעֲשֵׂה־טוֹב
וּשְׁכֹן לְעוֹלָם: כִּי יְהוָה | אֹהֵב מִשְׁפָּט

כו
כז
כח

וְלֹא רָאִיתִי צַדִּיק נֶעֱזָב — *But I have not
seen a righteous man forsaken.*

To be *forsaken* means to lack the
barest essentials of life i.e., food and
clothing (Radak; *Tanchuma Vayeitze*
3). We find that Jacob asked God to
always provide him with these two
staples (Genesis 28:20). God responded
by pledging: כִּי לֹא אֶעֱזָבְךָ *For I will not
forsake you* (Genesis 28:15).

A righteous man may suffer misfortune, but God will surely have mercy on
his children (*Malbim*).

The *Midrash* (*Tanchuma Mikeitz* 6)
comments: Before God brings a famine
upon the world He prepares a means of
proper sustenance for the righteous. For
instance, before God brought a drought
upon the land of Israel in fulfillment of
Elijah's prophecy, He prepared a cave
where the prophet could hide from
Ahab, and ravens to bring him his daily
meals.

וְזַרְעוֹ מְבַקֶּשׁ לָחֶם — *Nor his children* [lit.
seed] begging for bread.

Rabbi Yosi said: We have a tradition
that a scholar will not become impoverished. His students asked him,
'But is it not a fact that many of them
are impoverished?'

He replied, 'Even if they should fall
into poverty we are assured that they
will never sink to such utter destitution
as to be forced to go begging from door

to door' (*Shabbos* 151a).

Midrash Tanchuma (*Vayeitze* ibid.)
interprets these words homiletically:
Even if it happened that the children of
the *tzaddik* had to go begging, yet never
did I see their righteous father, נֶעֱזָב, *forsaken*, of his unshakeable faith in the
Holy One, Blessed be He.[1]

As *Anaf Yosef* explains, I have never
seen a righteous man *consider himself
forsaken* even if his children must beg
for bread. Whatever his lot in life, he
trusts that God brings it upon him for a
constructive and merciful purpose.

Hirsch observes that the verse does
not say that no righteous man would
ever be reduced to poverty; were that
the case, it would equate poverty with
wickedness — a patent falsehood.
Rather, the verse says that no righteous
person will be completely forsaken even
if he must beg alms for his sustenance.
Since Jews are obligated to help one
another, it is no disgrace for one to require the help of another.

26. כָּל הַיּוֹם — *All the days.*

This means at all times, as in אוֹתְךָ
קִוִּיתִי כָּל הַיּוֹם, *You I hoped all the
days* (25:5). Even in times of financial
difficulty, the righteous man shared his
meagre resources to the best of his
ability (Radak). [See comm. 41:2, s.v.
בְּיוֹם רָעָה.]

---

1. The *Midrash* (*Koheles Rabbah* 2:17) relates that Rabbi Meir was a scribe who earned three
selahs a week. He spent one *selah* on food and drink, another on clothing, and the third he
gave away for the support of scholars.

[Noticing that he never had any money], his disciples asked him: 'What are you doing to
provide for your children?'

He answered: 'If they are righteous, then it will be as David said, I have not seen the
righteous man forsaken, not his children begging for bread [i.e., God will provide for them].
However, if they are not righteous, then why should I leave my possessions to the enemies of
God!'

But I have not seen a righteous man forsaken,
nor his children begging for bread.
²⁶ *All the days he graciously lends,*
and his children are a blessing.
²⁷ *Turn from evil and do good,*
that you may dwell forever.
²⁸ *For HASHEM loves justice*

Since this generous man wishes to benefit others, even if he depletes his own wealth for charitable purposes *all the days*, he will nevertheless be blessed with enough to leave over for his offspring.

חוֹנֵן וּמַלְוֶה — *He graciously lends* [lit. *he shows kindness and lends*].

The verse implies that kindness and lending are called for in addition to generosity. It is not enough merely to give a donation to the poor. The benefactor should display *kindness* by encouraging him as well. As the *Talmud* (*Bava Basra* 9b) says, 'He who gives a penny to the poor man is blessed with six blessings, but he who comforts him with kind words is blessed with eleven.' Also, a loan is preferable to an outright gift, for it will help set the fallen man back on his feet with dignity (*Dorash Moshe*).

וְזַרְעוֹ לִבְרָכָה — *And his children are a blessing.*

The children learn to emulate the charitable deeds of their righteous father and become a blessing to all who deal with them. We find that Hashem said to Abraham וֶהְיֵה בְּרָכָה, *and you shall be a blessing* (Genesis 12:2), i.e., you will share your blessings with others through charity and kindness.

Also, the children will have numerous well-wishers who will say, 'May you be blessed by God in the merit of your fine father' (*Radak*).

The *Talmud* (*Nedarim* 82b) echoes these words, emphasizing that the poor home of an honest father is a palace. The Sages taught that Torah will go forth from the children of the poor (*Hirsch*).

[The Psalmist concludes that not only will the children of the righteous not be forsaken (v. 25), but they will thrive despite their lack of wealth.][1]

27. סוּר מֵרָע וַעֲשֵׂה טוֹב — *Turn from evil and do good.*

[See 34:15]. Avoid transgressing the negative commandments, and pursue the positive commandments (*Ibn Ezra*).

Now that the success of the righteous has been clearly demonstrated, follow in their ways and turn away from the wicked paths of ruin and failure (*Radak*).

וּשְׁכֹן לְעוֹלָם — *That you may dwell forever.*

You will abide in perpetual security without fear or loss (*Radak*).

28. כִּי ה' אֹהֵב מִשְׁפָּט — *For HASHEM loves justice.*

You may dwell securely (v. 27)

---

1. The *Chasam Sofer* devoted virtually every waking moment to his yeshiva, attending to the affairs of his rabbinate and responding to the countless halachic inquiries which were addressed to him from all over the world. A disturbed relative once complained that he neglected the training of his children. The *Chasam Sofer* replied, 'About that I need not be concerned, for David has a promise to those who give away all of their time for the benefit of others. *All the days he graciously lends* [his precious time and effort to worthy causes. For this God repays him]; *and his children are a blessing.*

וְלֹא־יַעֲזֹב אֶת־חֲסִידָיו לְעוֹלָם נִשְׁמָרוּ
וְזֶרַע רְשָׁעִים נִכְרָת: צַדִּיקִים יִירְשׁוּ־אָרֶץ כט
וְיִשְׁכְּנוּ לָעַד עָלֶיהָ: פִּי־צַדִּיק יֶהְגֶּה ל
חָכְמָה וּלְשׁוֹנוֹ תְּדַבֵּר מִשְׁפָּט: תּוֹרַת לא
אֱלֹהָיו בְּלִבּוֹ לֹא תִמְעַד אֲשֻׁרָיו: צוֹפֶה לב
רָשָׁע לַצַּדִּיק וּמְבַקֵּשׁ לַהֲמִיתוֹ: יְהוָה לֹא־ לג
יַעַזְבֶנּוּ בְיָדוֹ וְלֹא יַרְשִׁיעֶנּוּ בְּהִשָּׁפְטוֹ: קַוֵּה לד

without fear of unexpected upheaval,
because God acts according to fixed
rules of justice and propriety which insure uninterrupted tranquility for the
deserving ones (Malbim).

וְלֹא יַעֲזֹב אֶת חֲסִידָיו — *And does not forsake His devout ones.*

חֲסִידוּת, devotion, surpasses מִשְׁפָּט,
justice, because it denotes kindness
which goes beyond the letter of the law.
After a person accustoms himself to
adhere to the strict dictates of truth and
justice, he will develop a desire to go
beyond the boundaries of strict justice
by acting kindly even toward those who
are undeserving according to the strict
standard of justice (Radak).

לְעוֹלָם נִשְׁמָרוּ — *Eternally they will be
protected.*

It is written, רַגְלֵי חֲסִידָיו יִשְׁמֹר, *He
guards the feet of His devoted ones* [i.e.
from sin] (I Samuel 2:9). It is really necessary to guard the devoted? This can
be understood with the folk-saying, 'To
the fenced-in area you add more fence
and to the breached wall you add more
breaches'. Similarly it says: *His devout
ones, eternally they will be guarded*
(Tanchuma, Vayeshev 14).

וְזֶרַע רְשָׁעִים נִכְרָת — *But the children of
the wicked will be excised.*

Not only are the wicked themselves
destroyed, but even their seed is uprooted (Radak).

29. צַדִּיקִים יִירְשׁוּ אָרֶץ — *The righteous
will inherit the earth.*

They will inherit the estates of the
wicked who have been excised
(Malbim).

וְיִשְׁכְּנוּ לָעַד עָלֶיהָ — *And dwell forever
upon it.*

The *Midrash* (Bereishis Rabbah
19:17) comments that after the wicked
drive the שְׁכִינָה, *God's Presence*, from
the world with their repulsive deeds, the
righteous will merit that His Presence
return to dwell in their midst by virtue
of their goodness.

30. פִּי צַדִּיק יֶהְגֶּה חָכְמָה — *The mouth of
the righteous man utters wisdom.*

Rashi here follows his opinion [see
comm. to 1:2] that יֶהְגֶּה does not refer to
verbal articulation, but to the thoughts
of the heart. [Although the word פִּי,
mouth, is used here in conjunction with
יֶהְגֶּה, Malbim to 39:4 explains that the
הִגָּיוֹן is a thought which is on the verge
of being expressed i.e. 'on the tip of the
tongue' therefore it is considered as if it
is in the mouth.]

Not only does the righteous man do
kindness by lending out his material
wealth (v. 26), but he is even eager to
share his intellectual abundance by instructing others (Ibn Ezra; Radak).

וּלְשׁוֹנוֹ תְּדַבֵּר מִשְׁפָּט — *And his tongue
speaks justice.*

Not only does the righteous man
speak intelligently on purely theological
topics, but he is just in settling affairs
between man and his fellow man
(Radak).

and does not forsake His devout ones —
Eternally they will be protected,
but the children of the wicked will be excised.
²⁹ The righteous will inherit the earth
and dwell forever upon it.
³⁰ The mouth of the righteous man utters wisdom,
and his tongue speaks justice.
³¹ The Torah of his God is in his heart;
his footsteps do not falter.
³² The wicked one watches for the righteous
and seeks to execute him.
³³ But HASHEM will not forsake him to his power,
nor let him be condemned in his judgment.

---

32. תוֹרַת אֱלֹהָיו בְּלִבּוֹ — *The Torah of his God is in his heart.*

What he expresses with his mouth is truly what he feels in his heart, for he is no hypocrite (*Radak*).

[He is not like Doeg and Achitophel whose Torah was *only from the lips outward,* (*Sanhedrin* 106b), i.e., insincere eloquence, while their hearts were full of treachery and pride (see 5:7, 10).]

לֹא תִמְעַד אֲשֻׁרָיו — *His footsteps do not falter.*

[Therefore the sincere scholar will not suffer a tragic downfall like those of Doeg and Achitophel.]

32. צוֹפֶה רָשָׁע לַצַּדִּיק — *The wicked one watches for the righteous.*

When he realizes that the tzaddik enjoys success while he is a failure, jealousy and hatred spur him to plot against the life of his righteous rival. If he cannot kill him, he will watch for an opportunity to libel the *tzaddik* to the authorities so that they should execute him (*Ibn Ezra; Radak*).

וּמְבַקֵּשׁ לַהֲמִיתוֹ — *And seeks to execute.*

The *Talmud* (*Sukkah* 52a) identifies the רָשָׁע of this verse as wickedness par

excellence, i.e., the Evil Inclination who is man's deadliest enemy. The Evil Inclination renews its powerful attack on man every day and tries to kill him as it says. *The wicked one watches for the righteous and seeks to execute him.* Were it not for God's assistance, no man could survive the onslaught, as it says, *But HASHEM will not forsake him to his power.*

33. ה' לֹא יַעַזְבֶנּוּ בְיָדוֹ — *But HASHEM will not forsake him to his power.*

God will foil the plot of the wicked. He will not abandon the *tzaddik* to the custody of the authorities before whom he has been slandered (*Radak*).

Olelos Yehudah interprets this in reference to the Evil Inclination: 'Even when you have made a habit of sin and are addicted to its enticement, still God will deliver you from its grip [if you sincerely desire to be released.]

וְלֹא יַרְשִׁיעֶנּוּ בְּהִשָּׁפְטוֹ — *Nor let him be condemned in his judgment.*

Ramban (*Deuteronomy* 19:19) explains that if a legitimate Jewish court executes a condemned criminal, that constitutes the most convincing proof of his guilt. God would never allow

אֶל־יהוה ׀ וּשְׁמֹר דַּרְכּוֹ וִירוֹמִמְךָ לָרֶשֶׁת

לה אֶרֶץ בְּהִכָּרֵת רְשָׁעִים תִּרְאֶה: רָאִיתִי

רָשָׁע עָרִיץ וּמִתְעָרֶה כְּאֶזְרָח רַעֲנָן:

לו וַיַּעֲבֹר וְהִנֵּה אֵינֶנּוּ וָאֲבַקְשֵׁהוּ וְלֹא נִמְצָא:

לז שְׁמָר־תָּם וּרְאֵה יָשָׁר כִּי־אַחֲרִית לְאִישׁ

שָׁלוֹם: וּפֹשְׁעִים נִשְׁמְדוּ יַחְדָּו אַחֲרִית

לח רְשָׁעִים נִכְרָתָה: וּתְשׁוּעַת צַדִּיקִים

לט מֵיהוה מָעוּזָּם בְּעֵת צָרָה: וַיַּעְזְרֵם יהוה

מ וַיְפַלְּטֵם יְפַלְּטֵם מֵרְשָׁעִים וְיוֹשִׁיעֵם כִּי־

חָסוּ בוֹ:

righteous judges to be duped by false witnesses into shedding innocent blood, because He promised that His spirit will reside in every court to guide it towards the truth. Secondly, God would never abandon a guiltless man to the wicked who seek to condemn him falsely, as it says, *But HASHEM will not forsake him to his power, nor let him be condemned in his judgment.*

34. קַוֵּה אֶל ה' וּשְׁמֹר דַּרְכּוֹ — *Hope to HASHEM and safeguard His way.*

[If you will do what is expected of you by safeguarding God's way, He will reciprocate by helping you realize your hopes. But if you don't fulfill God's wishes, what can you hope for?]

וִירוֹמִמְךָ לָרֶשֶׁת אֶרֶץ בְּהִכָּרֵת רְשָׁעִים תִּרְאֶה — *Then He will raise you high to inherit the earth. Upon excision of the wicked, you will see it.*

This verse refers to Noah whose hopes were directed towards God because He [God] safeguarded his way. God raised him high above the flood waters while the wicked drowned. When the waters subsided, Noah emerged from the Ark to inherit the earth (*Tanchuma, Berachah* 6).

35. רָאִיתִי רָשָׁע עָרִיץ — *I saw a ruthless wicked man.*

I observed a wicked man who intimidated everyone with his might (*Radak*).

וּמִתְעָרֶה — *Well-rooted.*

The translation follows *Rashi* who relates it to עָרוֹת עַל יְאוֹר, *roots by the river* (Isaiah 19:7). *Radak* renders this word as *well-watered, thriving.*

כְּאֶזְרָח רַעֲנָן — *Like a native evergreen.*

The sturdy, well-watered tree is called *native* because it is outstanding and noticeable to all by virtue of its unique beauty. It resembles the native citizen of a settlement who is well-known to all (*Radak*).

The well-established citizen who enjoys the security of having a powerful family backing him in all phases of community life resembles the flourishing tree with many spreading branches. But the גֵּר, *stranger*, is isolated and alone like a גַּרְגִּיר, *fragment; splinter*, which is cut off from the tree (*Ibn Ezra*).

The powerful villain is reinforced by a solid financial status (*Rashi*).

36. וַיַּעֲבֹר וְהִנֵּה אֵינֶנּוּ — *Yet he vanished*

³⁴ *Hope to HASHEM and safeguard His way,*
then He will raise you high to inherit the earth.
Upon excision of the wicked,
you will see it.
³⁵ *I saw a ruthless wicked man,*
well-rooted like a native evergreen.
³⁶ *Yet he vanished, and behold! he was no more;*
then I sought him, but he was not found.
³⁷ *Safeguard the perfect and watch the upright,*
for there is a destiny for the man of peace.
³⁸ *The sinners shall be destroyed together,*
the destiny of the wicked is to be excised.
³⁹ *But the salvation of the righteous is from HASHEM,*
their might in time of distress.
⁴⁰ *HASHEM helped them*
and caused them to escape,
He will cause them to escape from the wicked
and He will save them,
for they took refuge in Him.

[lit. *he passed*] *and behold! he was no more.*

He disappeared without prior warning (*Metzudos David*).

His body departed from this world (*Malbim*).

וַאֲבַקְשֵׁהוּ וְלֹא נִמְצָא — *Then I sought him, but he was not found.*

No trace of him remains. His residence has disappeared; even his children have vanished (*Radak*).

His body departed from this world but his soul did not pass on to the World to Come. It has been cut off so it is nowhere to be found (*Malbim*).

[Similarly we read, אֲנִי רָאִיתִי אֱוִיל מַשְׁרִישׁ וָאֶקּוֹב נָוֵהוּ פִתְאֹם, *I have seen the foolish man taking root, but suddenly I beheld his habitation cursed* (Job 5:3).]

37. שְׁמָר תָּם וּרְאֵה יָשָׁר — *Safeguard the perfect and watch the upright.*

Pay heed to their enviable life-style so that you may be inspired to emulate them, and not the wicked (*Rashi*).

כִּי אַחֲרִית לְאִישׁ שָׁלוֹם — *For there is a destiny* [lit. *aftermath*] *for the man of peace.*

Although his beginning is unimpressive [i.e., downtrodden and oppressed], he is destined to enjoy a great reward after his sojourn in This World has ended (*Rashi*).

38. וּפֹשְׁעִים נִשְׁמְדוּ יַחְדָּו — *The sinners shall be destroyed together.*

When they die, both their bodies and their souls will be destroyed and nothing will remain (*Malbim*).

אַחֲרִית רְשָׁעִים נִכְרָתָה — *The destiny of the wicked is to be excised.*

Thus will any temptation to emulate their ways cease, for they will no longer

exist. Any temptation to copy them may be momentarily successful in this world, yet the result of their labors is doomed to failure (Malbim).

39. וּתְשׁוּעַת צַדִּיקִים מֵה׳ — *But the salvation of the righteous is from HASHEM.*

They will enjoy an everlasting salvation in the presence of Hashem in the eternal Hereafter (Malbim).

מָעוּזָם בְּעֵת צָרָה — *Their might in time of distress.*

Even though the bulk of their reward is reserved for the future, the righteous can still hope for God to deliver them from the perils of this world (Malbim).

40. וַיַּעְזְרֵם ה׳ וַיְפַלְּטֵם — *HASHEM helped them and caused them to escape.*

We have seen Him do this for many righteous people in the past (Ibn Ezra).

יְפַלְּטֵם מֵרְשָׁעִים וְיוֹשִׁיעֵם — He will cause them to escape from the wicked and He will save them.

There is no doubt that He will continue to do so in the future (Ibn Ezra).

These words and this theme are continually repeated in this psalm, in order to fortify the faith of the righteous, so that they should not succumb to the lure of the success of the wicked. Since most people are envious of the fruits of evil, the Psalmist concludes with this final exhortation to uphold one's faith in God's ultimate salvation (Radak).

38 מזמור לח

The series of four psalms concluding with Psalm 41 (the final psalm of the First Book) deals with one theme — the illness with which David was afflicted as a result of his sins. Rather than viewing his sickness as a purely negative experience, David sought to learn from it and share with posterity the lessons and insights which he gained from his suffering.

According to many commentators this psalm also contains a deeper message, as it expresses the feelings of the entire nation of Israel which suffers from the ravages of the long, dark exile. It concludes with a hopeful plea for swift redemption.

מִזְמוֹר לְדָוִד לְהַזְכִּיר: יְהוָה אַל־בְּקֶצְפְּךָ ‎א־ב
תוֹכִיחֵנִי וּבַחֲמָתְךָ תְיַסְּרֵנִי: כִּי־חִצֶּיךָ ‎ג
נִחֲתוּ בִי וַתִּנְחַת עָלַי יָדֶךָ: אֵין־מְתֹם ‎ד
בִּבְשָׂרִי מִפְּנֵי זַעְמֶךָ אֵין־שָׁלוֹם בַּעֲצָמַי

---

1. מִזְמוֹר לְדָוִד לְהַזְכִּיר — *A song unto David; For Remembrance.*

Rashi comments that David had all of Israel in mind when he composed this psalm. He intended it as a reminder to God to pay heed to the misfortunes of His nation in times of distress.

Radak and *Metzudas David*, however, maintain that David intended the psalm for the suffering individual. Therefore, he added the superscription, *For remembrance*, in order to encourage and remind every afflicted man to pray to God using these very words of supplication. *Radak* also suggests that לְהַזְכִּיר might be directed to the accompanist to indicate a special musical embellishment.

Malbim interprets this Psalm as David's response to the sickness which afflicted him after his sin concerning Bath Sheba. He intended its tragic theme to serve as a constant reminder of his sins.

Alshich adds that for anyone other than David, the superscription of so tragic a work would have been קִינָה, *a lament*. But David could see with perfect clarity the purifying effect of pain which atones for sin. Therefore, he entitled this psalm מִזְמוֹר, *a song* [full of hope and joy] לְהַזְכִּיר, *to remind* all men to accept misfortune as gratefully as they accept the good.

2. הי אַל־בְּקֶצְפְּךָ תוֹכִיחֵנִי — *HASHEM, in Your wrath rebuke me not.*

[In 6:2 David prayed, הי אַל בְּאַפְּךָ תוֹכִיחֵנִי, *HASHEM, rebuke me not in Your wrath*.] *Malbim* says that אַף and קֶצֶף are synonymous terms for *wrath*. Both terms represent anger openly dis-

played, while חֵמָה refers to anger kept hidden in the heart. Thus: 'although You rebuke me, let Your words of rebuke be soft, not harsh utterances of wrath'.

וּבַחֲמָתְךָ תְיַסְּרֵנִי — *Nor in Your rage chasten me.*

The translation follows *Radak* and *Metzudos* who comment that the word אַל, 'do not', in the first half of the verse modifies the second half as well. [Thus we have a repetition of the second half of 6:2 which reads וְאַל בַּחֲמָתְךָ תְיַסְּרֵנִי].

Malbim however, observes that אַל is intentionally deleted in the second half of the verse, for this statement means something very different from that of 6:2. Here, after his sin, David readily accepted the fact that he must suffer. But suffering can come in one of two ways. The wrathful words of God's תוֹכֵחָה, *rebuke*, may shroud the soul in melancholy bitterness (בְּקֶצְפְּךָ תוֹכִיחֵנִי). Or it may be only the body which is afflicted with physical יִסוּרִים, *chastisement*, (בַּחֲמָתְךָ תְיַסְּרֵנִי) for the sake of atonement. David feels that he possesses the strength to overcome either of these afflictions when applied separately, but he pleads that he is incapable of withstanding both at once. *HASHEM, rebuke me not in Your wrath*, while simultaneously *chastening me in Your rage*, i.e., I cannot endure the chastisement of both physical pain and mental anguish together.

3. חִצֶּיךָ — *Your arrows.*

Radak to our verse comments that heaven-sent ailments are like arrows of God [in that they go unerringly to fulfill

A song unto David. For Remembrance.
² HASHEM, in Your wrath, rebuke me not,
   nor in Your rage chasten me.
³ For Your arrows were shot into me,
   and down upon me is Your hand.
⁴ There is no perfection in my flesh
   because of Your wrath,
No peace in my bones

God's objective]. In *Habakuk* 3:11 he explains that lightning is the arrow of God. The wicked are struck down by it, while the righteous make use of its light.

The angels of fury which do God's bidding by punishing the guilty with swift accuracy are called His *arrows* (*Alshich*).

The first *arrow* with which You pierced my heart was the frightful prophecy of Nathan which followed the incident with Bath Sheba: *Therefore the sword shall not depart from your house ... Behold, I will raise up evil against you from out of your own house* (II Sam. 12:10-11) (*Sforno*).

נִחֲתוּ בִי — *Were shot into me.*

Literally נָחַת means to step down on the bow in order to bend and string it. This is the main preparation for the shooting of the arrows [cf. *commentary* to 18:35] (*Rashi*).

וַתִּנְחַת עָלַי יָדֶךָ — *And down upon me is Your hand.*

תִּנְחַת is derived from נָחָה, *to come down to rest* (*Rashi*).

The Psalmist laments that he feels the hand of Hashem weighing down upon him heavily through the many ailments

with which he was punished (*Metzudas David*).

Nathan's prophecy of doom was uttered, and immediately took effect. *Your hand came down upon me*, and *HASHEM struck the child that Uriah's wife bore to David* [II Samuel 12:15] (*Sforno*).

4. אֵין מְתֹם בִּבְשָׂרִי — *There is no perfection in my flesh.*

Radak explains that מְתֹם is derived from the root תָּמַם, *complete, perfect*; thus the מ at the beginning of this word is a prefix rather than a root letter. The Psalmist laments, 'There is no perfection in my body for every organ is afflicted.'

However, *Radak* quotes his father, *Rav Yosef Kimchi*, who maintains that מְתֹם is related to מתה (and the opening מ is indeed part of the root which means *people, persons* as in מְתֵי מִסְפָּר, *few in* [numbers of] *people* (105:12). [See also 17:14, 26:4]. Thus David means to say that his flesh has been so mutilated by sickness that it has lost its human form and he no longer resembles other people.[1]

מִפְּנֵי זַעְמֶךָ — *Because of Your wrath.*

Because of Your righteous anger

---

1. Before Adam sinned, his flesh was the essence of perfection — a radiant garment of spiritual splendor described as כָּתְנוֹת אוֹר, *robes of light* (not עוֹר *skin*). But Adam's transgression aroused God's זַעַם, *wrath* which reduced his flesh to mere בָּשָׂר, *flesh*, which inherently lacks מְתֹם, *perfection*. The *Talmud* (*Sotah* 5a) states that the letters of בָּשָׂר form an acrostic which alludes to בּוּשָׁה, *shame*, שְׁרוֹחָה, *decay*, רִמָּה, *wormy rot* (*Tehillos Hashem*). [See also *Overview* to *Bircas Hamazon*, ArtScroll Edition, p. 19.]

ה מִפְּנֵי חַטָּאתִי: כִּי עֲוֹנֹתַי עָבְרוּ רֹאשִׁי

ו כְּמַשָּׂא כָבֵד יִכְבְּדוּ מִמֶּנִּי: הִבְאִישׁוּ נָמַקּוּ

ז חַבּוּרֹתָי מִפְּנֵי אִוַּלְתִּי: נַעֲוֵיתִי שַׁחֹתִי עַד־

ח מְאֹד כָּל־הַיּוֹם קֹדֵר הִלָּכְתִּי: כִּי־כְסָלַי

ט מָלְאוּ נִקְלֶה וְאֵין מְתֹם בִּבְשָׂרִי: נְפוּגֹתִי

---

which was provoked by my sins
(Radak, Malbim).

אֵין שָׁלוֹם בַּעֲצָמַי מִפְּנֵי חַטָּאתִי — [There is]
no peace in my bones because of my sin.

[After David sinned, his realization
of the enormity of his error was more
than mere intellectual conception. He
was physically ill, particularly in the
limb which performed the sin. שָׁלוֹם also
means whole (שָׁלֵם). David bewailed the
fact that every transgression leaves an
indelible imprint on the perpetrator as is
taught in Maseches Kallah Rabbasi
Chapter 3: Every sin a person commits
is engraved and recorded on his bones.
David moans that his every bone has
been carved out with a chisel of guilt
and he remains eternally scarred. Similarly the prophet warns וַתְּהִי עֲוֹנֹתָם
עַל עַצְמוֹתָם, And their iniquities
remained on their bones (Ezekiel
32:27)].

5. כִּי עֲוֹנֹתַי עָבְרוּ רֹאשִׁי — For my
iniquities have inundated me [lit. gone
over my head].

David compares his sins to swirling
sea waters which rose above his head
and threatened to drown him (Radak).

[רֹאשִׁי, my head, symbolizes the intellectual capacity which provides the
ability to control passions. Unfortunately, my lustful flesh, overcame my
better judgment.]

כְּמַשָּׂא כָבֵד יִכְבְּדוּ מִמֶּנִּי — Like a
heavy load they are burdensome ...

I do not possess sufficient mitzvos
and merits with which to bolster my
soul which staggers under a massive
burden of guilt (Radak).

[I have lost all self-control, because
my innate tendency to sin far outweighs
my capacity for self-discipline].

The Sages say that King Menashe of
Judah sinned for many years, but finally repented. He was so ashamed of his
iniquitous past that he dared not raise
his face towards the sky. He wore a
heavy copper helmet which forced his
face to be turned earthward. Similarly
the Psalmist says that the burden of his
sin is so crushing that it forces him to
bow his head in shame (Tehillos Hashem).[1]

6. הִבְאִישׁוּ נָמַקּוּ חַבּוּרֹתָי — Putrid and
rotted are my sores.

חַבּוּרָה sometimes refers to a bruise
caused by the blood which collects under the skin. Here it means a pus-filled
blister. Eventually the blister will burst
and the pus will ooze out (Radak).

מִפְּנֵי אִוַּלְתִּי — Because of my folly.

My foolishness led me to the sins
which caused my affliction. As the
Talmud (Sotah 3a) says: A person does
not sin unless he is overwhelmed by a
spirit of foolishness (Migdal David).

---

1. Rabbi Yehudah the Prince expounded: Great is the power of repentance, for, should the
slightest thought of it flicker in a man's heart, immediately it rises before the heavenly throne.
This is true no matter how guilty the penitent. David said, 'For my iniquities have inundated
me'. Ezra also said, 'For our iniquities have multiplied far above our heads and our guilt has
increased greatly, up to the heavens' (Ezra 9:6). But the Holy One, Blessed be He, responded,
'Fear not! Even if your sins should reach until the very foot of my heavenly throne, I will
forgive you if you repent (Pesikta Rabbasi 45:9).

XXXVIII
5-9

because of my sin.

⁵ *For my iniquities have inundated me;*
like a heavy load, they are burdensome
beyond me.

⁶ *Putrid and rotted are my sores,*
because of my folly.

⁷ *I am bent and bowed exceedingly,*
all day long in bleakness I go.

⁸ *For my self awareness is full of futility,*
and there is no perfection in my flesh.

⁹ *I am faint and crushed exceedingly.*

---

7. נַעֲוֵיתִי — *I am bent.*

As in וְהִתְעַוְּתוּ אַנְשֵׁי הֶחָיִל, *And the powerful men will be bent* [*Ecclesiastes* 12:13] (*Metzudas Zion*).

שַׁחֹתִי — *And bowed* [down]. By the burden of my sickness (*Radak*).

כָּל הַיּוֹם קֹדֵר הִלָּכְתִּי — *All day long in bleakness* [lit. *in blackness*] *I go.*

My facial characteristics have drastically changed. My countenance is so dark that it seems as if I have been exposed to the blazing sun all day (*Ibn Ezra*).

[Black clouds of sorrow and anxiety darken my brow and sink me into melancholy.]

8. כְּסָלַי — *My self awareness* [lit. *my flanks*].

The Translation follows *Rashi* who interprets the word as a reference to inner thoughts because the כְּסָלִים, *flanks*, are near the כְּלָיוֹת, *kidneys*, which are often considered the center of counsel and reflection (*Ibn Yachya*).[See commentary to 7:10.]

Literally, however, כְּסָלִים refer to the lower spine near the kidneys as in *Leviticus* 3:4 (*Metzudas Zion*), a delicate area which is susceptible to illness (*Radak*).

Or, David refers to his mind as כְּסָל

because when he sinned he acted like a כְּסִיל, *fool*, [as mentioned in verse 6 David cites the reason for sin as *commentary* ibid.).]

Yeibi.

מָלְאוּ נִקְלֶה — *Is full of futility.*

I have no illusions of grandeur. I am fully aware that I am, קַל *insignificant, worthless* (*Rashi*).

[I sinned because my mind was קַל, *lighthearted, frivolous* and thus easily overcome by my passions which *are like a heavy load, beyond my strength* (see *commmmentary* ibid)].

Literally נִקְלֶה, *inflamed* derives from קָלוּי, *roasted* (*Metzudos*). My kidneys are inflamed as a result of my sickness (*Targum, Rav Yosef Kimchi*).

וְאֵין מְתֹם בִּבְשָׂרִי — *And there is no perfection in my flesh.*

These words are a repetition of verse 4, for the distraught man weeps incessantly in his anguish and recounts his woes over and over again (*Radak*).

9. נְמוּגוֹתִי — *I am faint.*

My internal organs have lost their strength (*Malbim*), as we read concerning Jacob:

וַיָּפָג לִבּוֹ, *And his heart became faint* (*Genesis.* 45:26) (*Rashi, Radak, Ibn Ezra, Metzudas Zion*).

וְנִדְכֵּיתִי עַד־מְאֹד שָׁאַגְתִּי מִנַּהֲמַת לִבִּי:
אֲדֹנָי נֶגְדְּךָ כָל־תַּאֲוָתִי וְאַנְחָתִי מִמְּךָ לֹא־
נִסְתָּרָה: לִבִּי סְחַרְחַר עֲזָבַנִי כֹחִי וְאוֹר־
עֵינַי גַּם־הֵם אֵין אִתִּי: אֹהֲבַי | וְרֵעַי מִנֶּגֶד
נִגְעִי יַעֲמֹדוּ וּקְרוֹבַי מֵרָחֹק עָמָדוּ:

וְנִדְכֵּיתִי — *And [I am] crushed.*

All of my limbs are broken and splintered (Malbim).

שָׁאַגְתִּי מִנַּהֲמַת לִבִּי — *I roar because of the groaning of my heart.*

The feeble invalid, *faint and crushed,* feels his strength ebbing as he slips toward death. Then he marshals his last traces of vitality for a final effort, like the final flicker of a dying candle. Although his heart groans (נוהם) from infirmity, he still has strength for one last שָׁאֲנָה, joyous, triumphant *roar,* a demonstration of his faith that although his body may perish his soul will live on (Malbim).

10. אֲדֹנָי נֶגְדְּךָ כָל־תַּאֲוָתִי — *My Lord, before You is all of my yearning.*

These are the words of the heart's final cry: 'My Lord, as I stand ready to return my soul to You, my bodily needs and desires fade into insignificance' (Malbim).

For now I have but one wish, and that is to stand נֶגְדְּךָ, *before You* (Meiri).

Some people are inspired to serve God only after they observe others who are diligent in the performance of commandments. David declares, however, that the attainments of others do not move him. He is motivated exclusively by a pure yearning for God (Rabbeinu Yonah, Avos 4:21).

וְאַנְחָתִי מִמְּךָ לֹא נִסְתָּרָה — *My sighing is not concealed from You.*

To You it makes no difference whether or not I openly express my innermost feelings, for all is revealed to You (Radak).

The only reason for me to sigh over leaving this material world is the fear that I have not adequately prepared my soul to stand before You in the Hereafter (Meiri).

I only hope and pray that מִמְּךָ לֹא נִסְתָּרָה, *It* [my soul] *should not be concealed from You* and Your presence in the Hereafter (Tehillos Yisroel).

Rabbeinu Yonah in *Shaarei Teshuva* (1:12-14) cites יָגוֹן, *sorrow,* as the third principle of repentance. The sinner must be saddened by the enormous evil of disobedience to his Creator. He must sigh in bitterness and despair as King David said: 'My Lord, before You is all of my yearning, my sighing is not concealed from You. You know that my sole desire is to serve You. I groan only because of my sins and inadequacies in Your service.'

11. לִבִּי סְחַרְחַר — *My heart is engulfed.*

Misery and woe encircle me from all sides (Rashi).

Or *my heart goes around in circles,* as we find the *Targum* of סָבִיב, *around,* to be סְחוֹר. The tranquil man can concentrate and think clearly. Not so the troubled man whose thoughts dart here and there in an endless, confusing circle (Radak).

My mind goes around in circles searching and probing for my sins (Alshich).

עֲזָבַנִי כֹחִי — *My strength has forsaken me.*

The Torah is the strength of Israel. Because I forsook the Torah, the Torah abandoned me and left me helpless

I roar because of the groaning of my heart.

¹⁰ *My Lord, before You is all my yearning,*
my sighing is not concealed from You.

¹¹ *My heart is engulfed,*
my strength has forsaken me,

The light of my eyes —
that, too, has left me.

¹² *My friends and companions stand aloof from*
my affliction,
and my close ones stand at a distance.

(*Maharam Markado*). [See *Targum* to 29:11 where עֹז, *strength*, is translated אוֹרַיְיתָא, *Torah*.]

וְאוֹר עֵינַי גַּם הֵם אֵין אִתִּי — *The light of my eyes — that, too, has left me'.*

It is no coincidence that my heart is in turmoil and that my eyes have failed me. The Torah warns וְלֹא תָתוּרוּ אַחֲרֵי לְבַבְכֶם וְאַחֲרֵי עֵינֵיכֶם, *And you shall not stray after your heart and after your eyes* (Numbers 15:39). The heart and the eye are two agents that seek out sin (*Rashi, ibid.*). The heart is mentioned first, for the eyes follow the desires of the heart [and perceive what the heart wants them to perceive] (*Sifri ibid.*). Now that sickness has removed lust and craving from my heart, my eyes no longer search out evil (*Tehillos Hashem*).

אֹהֲבַי וְרֵעַי מִנֶּגֶד נִגְעִי יַעֲמֹדוּ — *My friends and my companions stand aloof from my affliction.* **12.**

Those who pretend to be my friends when it is beneficial for them, desert me in my time of need. They stand at a distance refusing to step closer to offer assistance (*Rashi*).

Many sick unfortunates find themselves forsaken by their former friends. Sympathy and compassion, give way to estrangement as people tire of observ-

ing another's misery. As Solomon said: כָּל אֲחֵי רָשׁ שְׂנֵאֻהוּ אַף כִּי מְרֵעֵהוּ רָחֲקוּ מִמֶּנּוּ, *All the brethren of the poor despise him, how much more so his companions who go far away from him* (Proverbs 19:7). Nothing strengthens the soul of the ill as much as a visit by a friend, but my 'friends' refuse to come near (*Radak*).

Instead of encouraging me, they convey to me their own conviction that I will not survive. Even when they visit me, they slowly draw away from my bedside, not wishing to be near a doomed man (*Malbim*), and because they cannot bear the stench of my festering sores (*Ibn Ezra*).

וּקְרוֹבַי מֵרָחֹק עָמָדוּ — *And my close ones stand at a distance.*

The קָרוֹב, *close one,* may be a friend, neighbor, or a blood relative (*Radak*).

The *Vilna Gaon* offers a homiletical interpretation: After the sick man discovers that his family, friends, wealth, and influence are of no avail, he realizes that only one hope remains — the merit of his *mitzvos*. He had imagined such merits to be stored away for the Hereafter, and inaccessible in his time of need, but behold — they alone now stand by his bedside. Thus: My truly close ones whom I thought were far away — only they stood up for me (*Sheiris Yisroel*).

יג וַיְנַקְשׁוּ| מְבַקְשֵׁי נַפְשִׁי וְדֹרְשֵׁי רָעָתִי

יד דִּבְּרוּ הַוּוֹת וּמִרְמוֹת כָּל־הַיּוֹם יֶהְגּוּ: וַאֲנִי

כְחֵרֵשׁ לֹא אֶשְׁמָע וּכְאִלֵּם לֹא יִפְתַּח־פִּיו:

טו וָאֱהִי כְּאִישׁ אֲשֶׁר לֹא־שֹׁמֵעַ וְאֵין בְּפִיו

טז תּוֹכָחוֹת: כִּי־לְךָ יְהוָה הוֹחָלְתִּי אַתָּה

יז תַעֲנֶה אֲדֹנָי אֱלֹהָי: כִּי־אָמַרְתִּי פֶּן־

13. וַיְנַקְשׁוּ מְבַקְשֵׁי נַפְשִׁי — *They lay snares, the seekers of my life.*

While my former friends shun me, my enemies have not been idle. With their slanderous accusations they lay traps to destroy my soul (*Radak*).

Now that there is no one left at my bedside to protect me, my enemies draw near to assure my swift demise by poisoning or stabbing me (*Malbim*).

דִּבְּרוּ הַוּוֹת וּמִרְמוֹת...יֶהְגּוּ — *They speak treacheries ... and contemplate deceit.*

[See commentary to 5:10].

Sforno explains: They incessantly taunt me with their treacherous words of self-righteous deceit. *Midrash Shocher Tov* (Psalm 3) records the solemn moral dissertations which they delivered to David: 'He who stole the lamb [Bath Sheba], and killed the shepherd [Uriah], has no salvation in God.'

They spread lies about me in order to gain public support for their campaign against me (*Malbim*).

14. וַאֲנִי כְחֵרֵשׁ לֹא אֶשְׁמָע — *But I, like a deaf man, [I] do* [lit. will] *not hear.*

As they plot my death while standing at my bedside I pretend not to hear. (*Malbim*).

I make myself oblivious to the treacherous lies they spread regarding me (*Radak*).

[David was eager to pay attention to his critics when their charges contained some truth, as he said בַּקָּמִים עָלַי מְרֵעִים תִּשְׁמַעְנָה אָזְנָי, *When evil ones rise up against me my ears hear* (92:12). From such criticism, he could learn to repent. But to their slanders, he turned a deaf ear.]

Rashi interprets these words as referring to the nation of Israel as a whole which hears insults, yet remains silent.[1]

וּכְאִלֵּם לֹא יִפְתַּח פִּיו — *Like a mute who opens not his mouth.*

I do not respond to their false accusations in order to justify myself (*Radak*).

[From this verse the Talmud (*Chagi-*

1. *Pesikta Rabbasi* (41:6) quotes the following request which Abraham made of God after showing his willingness to successfully withstand his most difficult test and was prepared to sacrifice his beloved son Isaac to God. [See *Bereishis II*, Artscroll ed., Ch. 22 and *Overview*]:

'Sovereign of the Universe! It is clearly revealed before You that when You commanded me to sacrifice my son Isaac I had strong arguments to counter Your command; arguments which You would have had to accept. I could have asked: Yesterday, You promised me, — "*In Isaac shall your seed be called*" (*Genesis* 21:12), but today You tell me to slaughter that very same Isaac? But I held my tongue; *I was like a deaf man, I did not hear, like a speechless man who opens not his mouth.* Therefore, in this merit I request that when the offspring of Isaac stand before You in judgment on this day (of *Rosh Hashana*) every year, even if many prosecuting angels accuse them, please do not hearken to their accusations but answer the prayers of my offspring!'

13 *They lay snares,*
the seekers of my life;
Those who seek my harm speak treacheries,
all day long they contemplate deceit.
14 *But I, like a deaf man I do not hear,*
like a mute who opens not his mouth.
15 *I became like a man who cannot understand*
and in whose mouth there are no rebuttals.
16 *Because for You, HASHEM, I waited,*
You will answer, my Lord, my God.
17 *For I thought, 'Perhaps they will be glad about me,*

---

gah 2b) derives a principle: Wherever
Scripture mentions a חֵרֵשׁ it refers to
someone who is deaf but can speak. An
אִלֵּם is a mute who can hear. In
Talmudic Hebrew, however, the word
חֵרֵשׁ describes a deaf-mute]

15. וָאֱהִי כְּאִישׁ אֲשֶׁר לֹא שֹׁמֵעַ — *I became
like a man who cannot understand.*

[At first, I only pretended not to hear
their insults, but after a while I became
so oblivious to their false accusations
that I actually did not even hear their
remarks.]

From this we can deduce the intensity
of David's devotion to God. And the
very essence of his humility is clearly
reflected in those words. His sole concern is for the honor of his Creator, so
he has no regard for his own dignity.
Therefore, he is oblivious of insults
hurled at him. David demonstrated this
level of intense devotion when Shimi
ben Gera cursed him maliciously and
yet he (David) paid no attention
(*Reishis Chochma, Shaar HaAhava, II*).

וְאֵין בְּפִיו תּוֹכָחוֹת — *And in whose mouth
there are no rebuttals.*

[I was offended by their insults and I
composed rebuttals in my mind, but I
restrained myself. Eventually, however,
I stopped thinking of rebuttals because I
no longer heard their words].

16. כִּי לְךָ ה׳ הוֹחָלְתִּי — *Because for You,
HASHEM, I waited.*

I pay no heed to their threats for I
have complete confidence ·in Your
ability to save me (*Rashi*).

אַתָּה תַעֲנֶה אֲדֹנָי אֱלֹהָי — *You will answer
my Lord, my God.*

I do not respond to their insults
because I wait for You to take up my
cause and to answer them far more ef-
fectively than I can (*Radak*).

I await Your response, for You are ה׳,
HASHEM, the Dispenser of Mercy. Yet
I will regard it as a kindness even if *You
will answer for me my Lord, my God*
[i.e., as אֱלֹהִים, the Dispenser of Strict
Justice] (*Eretz HaChaim*).

17. כִּי אָמַרְתִּי פֶּן יִשְׂמְחוּ לִי — *For I
thought* [lit. *I said*] *'Perhaps they will be
glad about me'.*

I fervently await Your aid lest I succumb to my illness, thus giving my
enemies cause for rejoicing (*Radak*).

We, the people of Israel, never dared
answer our tormentors audaciously. We
feared that we were unworthy of Your
aid and that our failure to prevail would
cause our oppressors to rejoice even
more (*Rashi*).

[This brief comment provides us with
an insight into the so-called golus→
[exile-] *mentality* of the Jew who has so

יח יִשְׂמְחוּ־לִי בְּמוֹט רַגְלִי עָלַי הִגְדִּילוּ: כִּי־

יט אֲנִי לְצֶלַע נָכוֹן וּמַכְאוֹבִי נֶגְדִּי תָמִיד: כִּי־

כ עֲוֺנִי אַגִּיד אֶדְאַג מֵחַטָּאתִי: וְאֹיְבַי חַיִּים

כא עָצֵמוּ וְרַבּוּ שֹׂנְאַי שָׁקֶר: וּמְשַׁלְּמֵי רָעָה

תַּחַת טוֹבָה יִשְׂטְנוּנִי תַּחַת °רְדוֹפִי־טוֹב:

°רָדְפִי ק׳

often been despised for his cowardly submission to his gentile masters. *Rashi* proclaims that the Jew never was *intimidated* by the gentile. His lack of response was not an admission that he was at a loss for a reply. The Jew was silent only because he feared that his spiritual shortcomings would cause God to punish him with continued subjugation. *Rashi's* commentary on the subsequent verses will serve to amplify and clarify this concept.]

בְּמוֹט רַגְלִי עָלַי הִגְדִּילוּ — *At the faltering of my foot they will gloat over me.*

Having already witnessed that they reacted with joy to my slightest faltering, I can imagine their haughty response should I collapse completely (*Radak*).

18. כִּי אֲנִי לְצֶלַע נָכוֹן — *For I am set always to limp.*

This translation follows *Radak* who renders צֶלַע as *limp*. Because I am always limping in pain I cannot stop thinking of my sickness and my imminent death.

According to *Rashi* it would be best to render צֶלַע as *collapse*. Israel again

explains why it is silent before diatribes. Although we always hope for the best, we are prepared for the worst; for *collapse and devastation*.

צֶלַע also means *rib* and has a special connotation in reference to the wife whom God has pre-ordained for each man. As we read: וַיִּבֶן ה׳ אֱלֹהִים אֶת הַצֵּלָע אֲשֶׁר לָקַח מִן הָאָדָם לְאִשָּׁה, *And HASHEM, God, fashioned the rib which He took from Adam into a woman* (Genesis 2:22).[1]

19. כִּי עֲוֺנִי אַגִּיד אֶדְאַג מֵחַטָּאתִי — *Because of my iniquity, I think* [lit. *tell*], *I fret about my sin.*

Therefore I fear the specter of death (*Radak*). All of Israel fears suffering and degradation at the hands of the enemies. (*Rashi*).

Rabbeinu Jonah in *Shaarei Teshuva* (1:16) sets down the fifth principle of repentance as דְּאָגָה, *Worry*. The third principle, יָגוֹן, *Sorrow*, pertains to the past [see *commentary v.* 10], whereas דְּאָגָה, *Worry*, applies to the future. The sinner should worry over the punishments which are in store for him. He should also worry lest he has not

1. According to the Talmud (*Sanhedrin* 107a) David here shares with us a fact which puts his entire relationship with Bath Sheba in a different perspective. It was pre-ordained during the Six Days of Creation that David the son of Jesse should wed Bath Sheba the daughter of Eliam. כִּי אֲנִי לְצֶלַע נָכוֹן, *For I am prepared* [i.e., predestined] *for this rib* [i.e., his wife]. However, he was too hasty in uniting with her. Therefore the road to wed Bath Sheba was strewn with misfortune and pain וּמַכְאוֹבִי נֶגְדִּי תָמִיד, *and my pain is continually before me'*.

[This is a key verse in this psalm, which seeks to demonstrate how David never forgot his sins and sings here for the purpose of לְהַזְכִּיר, *For remembrance*. David keeps his sin in mind at all times, and his enemies do not let him forget it either. Even as he fled from Absalom, we read, וַיְקַלֵּל ... וְשִׁמְעִי הֹלֵךְ בְּצֵלַע הָהָר, *And Shimi went along the mountain-side* [lit. *the ribs of the mountain*] ... *and cursed* [David] (II Sam. 16:13). Midrash Shocher Tov comments: He came to taunt him and remind him of the incident of *the rib* (i.e., Bath Sheba.]

*at the faltering of my foot they will gloat
over me!'*

18 *For I am set always to limp,
and my pain is always before me.*

19 *Because of my iniquity, I think,
I fret about my sin.*

20 *But my foes abound with life,
and great are those who hate me without cause.*

21 *Those who repay evil for good
harass me for my pursuit of good.*

---

repented completely, and has been deficient in his suffering, bitterness, fasting, and weeping, as David said, *'Because my heart tells me of my iniquity, I worry about my sin.'*

20. וְאֹיְבַי חַיִּים עָצֵמוּ — *But my foes abound with life.* I decline steadily yet they constantly thrive and flourish (*Radak, Rashi*).

Another reason why I dare not oppose my oppressors is because they now enjoy abundant success, and the *Talmud* cautions against quarreling with the wicked during a period of their good fortune [cf. *commentary* to 37:1] (*Maharam Markado*).

The words of the Psalmist describing the degradation of Israel in the face of the success of her enemies echoes the words of the prophet, הָיוּ צָרֶיהָ לְרֹאשׁ, *Her tormentors have become leaders* (*Lamentations* 1:5), which the *Midrash* (*ibid.*) explains, Whosoever comes to torment Israel [being utilized by God as His agent to punish] becomes a great [world] leader (*Shaarei Chaim*).

וְרַבּוּ שֹׂנְאַי שָׁקֶר — *And great are those who hate me without cause.*

They have waxed mighty and prosperous as a result of their שָׁקֶר, *lie* (*Rashi*), while I have sunk into poverty (*Radak*).

21. וּמְשַׁלְּמֵי רָעָה תַּחַת טוֹבָה — *Those who repay evil for good.*

These enemies should love me because of the many kindnesses I have shown them, but instead they repay my benevolence with evil (*Radak*).

יִשְׂטְנוּנִי — *They harass me.*

They bear a malicious grudge against me as we read וַיִּשְׂטֹם עֵשָׂו אֶת יַעֲקֹב, *And Esau carried malice against Jacob* (*Genesis* 27:41) (*Metzudas Zion*).

תַּחַת רָדְפִי טוֹב — *For of my pursuit of goodness.*

Their hatred is motivated by envy. They see that I am dedicated to the pursuit of perfection while they are involved only in their quest for yet more evil. The קְרִי, *reading*, of the word is רָדְפִי, *my pursuit*, whereas the כְּתִיב, *spelling*, is רְדוּפִי, *my exclusive pursuit* (*Radak*). [This is to emphasize that I am alone, in my single-minded quest for goodness, *it is pursued by me alone*].

These vicious people are masters of perversion. Just as they repay kindness with treachery, so do they misinterpret my good as being evil. My many good deeds performed should have changed their low opinion of me. Instead, they claim that my righteousness is a deceitful masquerade, an effort to conceal my crimes (*Alshich*).

כב אַל־תַּעַזְבֵנִי יהוה אֱלֹהַי אַל־תִּרְחַק

כג מִמֶּנִּי: חוּשָׁה לְעֶזְרָתִי אֲדֹנָי תְּשׁוּעָתִי:

Israel declares: Because we stubbornly cling to the Holy One, Blessed be He,
and His commandments the nations
eternally hate us! (Rashi).

22. אַל־תַּעַזְבֵנִי ה׳ — Forsake me not,
HASHEM.

They hope that I am eternally forlorn
and abandoned. Do not let their wish
come true (Radak).

אֱלֹהַי אַל תִּרְחַק מִמֶּנִּי — My God, be not
far from me. As I lay on my sickbed, my
close ones stand far away (ע. 12) but

You will take their place and stand at
my side (Ibn Ezra).

23. חוּשָׁה לְעֶזְרָתִי — Hasten to my
assistance. These words are an appropriate ending for this psalm which is
dedicated to the lonely exile of Israel
which drags on interminably. In this exile we continue to suffer from constant
slander and insults hurled at us personally and at our religious convictions.
Moreover, we are constrained to witness
the tremendous success and prosperity
of our enemies who repay our kindness

XXXVIII
22-23

²² Forsake me not, HASHEM,
my God, be not far from me.
²³ Hasten to my assistance,
O my Lord, my Salvation.

with evil. How fitting then that the Psalmist should conclude with an anguished plea that God hasten our redemption from this bitter exile (Me-iri).

And how can we cause the redemption to come about swiftly? The *Talmud (Sanhedrin* 98a based on Isaiah 60:22) says: זְכוּ אַחִישֶׁנָּה, *If they are worthy, I shall hasten it.* Therefore the Psalmist beseeches God to seek out our merits so that we may witness our speedy salvation *(Chazah Zion).*

אֲדֹנָי תְּשׁוּעָתִי — *O my Lord, my Salvation.*

Tehillas Hashem differentiates between עֶזְ, *assistance,* which is temporary and תְּשׁוּעָה, *salvation,* which is a permanent solution to an oppressing problem. When God dispatches an *agent* to alleviate distress, the assistance is as short-lived as is the agent. However, says the Psalmist, if אֲדֹנָי, *my Lord,* Himself will intervene, then He will bring about my permanent תְּשׁוּעָה, *salvation.*

39 מזמור לט

This psalm, dedicated לידותן, to Yedusun, conveys the dismal mood of the crushed man (or nation) shrouded in the gloom of failure and defeat. Rashi cites the Midrash (Shir HaShirim Rabbah 4:3) which derives ידותן from the word רָת, decree. Every psalm introduced with the word ידותן refers to רָתוֹת וְדִינִים, the [evil] decrees and [oppressive] laws which the enemy imposes upon the individual or the community of Israel. The persecuted man who witnesses his life's work going up in smoke, embarks upon an agonizing expedition of self-examination, searching for meaning in a life which appears to have been robbed of all purpose.

א-ב   לַמְנַצֵּחַ °לִידִיתוּן מִזְמוֹר לְדָוִד: אָמַרְתִּי

א-ג   °לִידוּתוּן ק׳   אֶשְׁמְרָה דְרָכַי מֵחֲטוֹא בִלְשׁוֹנִי אֶשְׁמְרָה־

ג   לְפִי מַחְסוֹם בְּעֹד רָשָׁע לְנֶגְדִּי: נֶאֱלַמְתִּי

1. לִידִיתוּן — *To Yedusun.*

[See Prefatory Remarks]. *Radak* explains that David composed this psalm and gave it to Yedusun, the Temple singer, to chant.

[David divided the Levite families into twenty-four watches to serve as singers in the Temple on a rotating weekly basis. Of these, six families were headed by the six sons of Yedusun, and they in turn, *were under the charge of their father, Yedusun, who prophesied with a Kinnor to give thanks and to praise HASHEM. (I Chronicles 25:3)*].

Rashi adds that there was also a musical instrument called a *Yedusun* which was used by the Levites in the Temple.

2. אָמַרְתִּי אֶשְׁמְרָה דְרָכַי מֵחֲטוֹא בִלְשׁוֹנִי — *I said: 'I will guard my ways from sinning with my tongue'* [cf. comm. 38:14.]

I made up my mind that no matter how intense my afflictions are, I will take care not to impugn God's ways with skeptical thoughts or with irreverent words (*Rashi*).

Binah L'Ittim notes that this is the basis for the words of the *Chovos Halevovos* who stresses that if a person seeks self-discipline he should begin by controlling his tongue. This mastery should reach the point where the heaviest bodily organs can be more easily moved than the tongue. The tongue is the key to the treasury of self-control in all areas of life.

[Silence is the initial reaction of the good man persecuted by what he perceives as harsh, unjust, דָתוֹת, decrees.

He struggles to accept his divinely ordained lot. This resembles Job's initial reaction to his afflictions: *Despite all this Job did not sin, and he uttered not a base word against God (Job* 1:22)].

Radak and *Sforno* are of the opinion that this psalm describes David's reaction to a severe illness, specifically a plague of leprosy. [Leprosy is the punishment for the person who has spoken slanderously.]

אֶשְׁמְרָה לְפִי מַחְסוֹם — *I will guard my mouth with a muzzle.*

I will take such diligent care not to make an improper utterance that my mouth will seem to have a מַחְסוֹם, muzzle, on it (*Metzudas David*).

People wracked with sickness and fever usually scream out deliriously, but I guard my tongue at all times (*Ibn Ezra*).

Malbim differentiates between לָשׁוֹן, tongue, and פֶּה, mouth. Tongue, the internal organ of speech, symbolizes the expression of deeply felt intellectual concepts. On the other hand *mouth*, the external aspect of vocalization (from the lips outward), symbolizes words spoken without prior thought. David stresses that not only will he refrain from questioning God's ways intellectually, (with his internal לָשׁוֹן), but he also will take care to make no utterance (with his external פֶּה) which might be interpreted as displaying dissatisfaction with God's actions.[1]

בְּעֹד רָשָׁע לְנֶגְדִּי — *Even while the wicked one stands before me.*

Even at the height of my distress,

---

1. *Midrash Shocher Tov* illustrates the importance of the tongue with a parable: Once the King of Persia was on the verge of death. His physicians told him that his only chance for a cure was to drink the milk of a lioness. One of his physicians volunteered to undertake the task of obtaining such milk. He took ten goats with him and entered the den of a nursing lioness. On the first day he stood far off and threw one goat to her. The next day he edged up

For the director, for Yedusun,
a song unto David.
² I said: 'I will guard my ways
from sinning with my tongue,
I will guard my mouth with a muzzle
even while the wicked one stands before me.'
³ I became mute with stillness,

while my oppressors still torment me, I remain silent (Rashi). [In this interpretation the wicked one is the direct cause of the Psalmist's suffering.]

Other commentator's interpret that the wicked one is not the cause of the pain, but that he has come to visit an ailing righteous person. 'At *that* time,' the Psalmist says, 'I take special care not to let the slightest groan of agony escape my lips lest this cause the wicked to rejoice over the afflictions of the righteous' (Radak, Metzudas David).

[According to these commentaries, בְּעֹד would be rendered only while, for the patient can allow himself to groan only when he is *not* in the presence of evildoers.]

Rav Yitzchak Chajes draws our attention to the incident of Shimi ben Gera who cursed David to his face. Nevertheless, the king refused to exercise his royal prerogative to have him killed. In his last will and testament, however, David *did* instruct Solomon to have Shimi punished. This teaches that one must especially muzzle his tongue while the wicked man stands before him, because then he is apt to speak from uncontrolled anger, thus harming himself and adding unnecessary fuel to the flames of dissension and dispute.

3. נֶאֱלַמְתִּי דוּמִיָּה — *I became mute with stillness.*

I kept silent for so long that I began

somewhat closer and threw her another goat. So he continued until he became familiar enough to play with her and she let him take her milk. On the way home to the palace, he fell asleep and dreamt that his organs were debating over which had played the most important role in his success. The physician's legs insisted that without them the milk could not be transported. His hands argued that they had milked the lioness. His eyes said that they had shown the way. His heart declared that it thought of the idea. Suddenly, his tongue spoke up and said: 'If not for me, where would you be?'

All of the organs laughed. 'How dare you compare yourself to us, you lowly tongue, locked away in the darkness of the mouth and not even possessing a hard bone like the rest of us?' The tongue warned them, 'On this very day I shall prove that I am sovereign over you all!'

The physician awoke and *proceeded* to the palace. As he handed the milk to the grateful king, his tongue said, 'Here is the milk of a dog.' The king was furious and commanded that this physician be hung.

All of the physician's organs wept and wailed until the tongue addressed them: 'If I save you all, will you admit that I am king?'

They all agreed. The tongue began to scream, 'Take me back to the king!' In the presence of the king the tongue complained, 'Why do you give orders to have me killed, is this my reward for serving you! Why don't you at least try to drink the milk, maybe it will work. Not only that, don't you know that a לָבִיא, *lioness*, is also called a כָּלְבִיא, the same word used for a female dog?' They tested the milk and found it to be genuine and healing. Whereupon all the organs proclaimed the tongue as their sovereign.

Therefore David said, 'I will guard my ways from sinning with my tongue.'

ד דוּמִיָּה הֶחֱשֵׁיתִי מִטּוֹב וּכְאֵבִי נֶעְכָּר: חַם־
לִבִּי | בְּקִרְבִּי בַּהֲגִיגִי תִבְעַר־אֵשׁ דִּבַּרְתִּי
ה בִּלְשׁוֹנִי: הוֹדִיעֵנִי יהוה | קִצִּי וּמִדַּת יָמַי

to seem like an אִלֵּם, *one who has lost
his power of speech* (Radak).

הֶחֱשֵׁיתִי — *I kept still.*

Malbim makes this differentiation
between דְּמָמָה and הֶחֱשֵׁיתִי: דּוּמִיָּה
describes the silence of one who has
stopped speaking. חָשָׁה refers to the
silence of the person who has never
spoken.

מִטּוֹב — *From the good.*

I.e., the greatest good possible, which
is Torah study. The pain which the
wicked foes inflicted upon me were so
fearful that they disturbed my concentration on Torah study and this
made the situation unbearable (Rashi).

In a homiletical sense, the *Talmud
(Berachos* 5a) derives from our verse
that whoever has the opportunity to
engage in Torah study but does not do
so, will be afflicted with distressing
maladies. Thus, הֶחֱשֵׁיתִי מִטּוֹב, *I was
silenced* [i.e. prevented from studying]
from the good [Torah]. Therefore, וּכְאֵבִי
נֶעְכָּר, *my pain was intensified.*

וּכְאֵבִי נֶעְכָּר — *And my pain was intensified.*

According to *Rashi*, without the opportunity to concentrate on Torah, the
pain becomes so unbearable that David
is compelled to break his silence.

Radak, however, holds that David is
saying that despite all of his intolerable
pains he still remained mute. He even
refrained from saying something good
about God [הֶחֱשֵׁיתִי מִטּוֹב] for fear lest he
might attempt to qualify his praise with
a critical comment.

4. חַם לִבִּי בְּקִרְבִּי — *My heart grew hot
within me.*

[At this point a change occurs. As a
result of terrible illness (Radak) and the

frustration of remaining mute
(*Malbim*), the man who previously suffered in silence moves slowly toward
speech. This resembles the example of
Job, who accepted everything with
heroic patience at first. Later, however,
his calm vanished, although his outward silence endured. *Despite all this,
Job did not sin with his lips* (Job 2:10),
but he did sin with complaints against
God in his heart (Rashi).]

בַּהֲגִיגִי — *In my contemplations.*

Malbim defines הִגָּיוֹן as the mid-point
between thought and speech, i.e. an idea
on the verge of expression.

Sforno also says that הִגָּיוֹן is more
than mere thought, rather it refers to the
words which a person articulates
privately. [See comm. *Psalms* 1:2 and
37:30].

תִבְעַר אֵשׁ — *A fire blazed.*

This idea demands urgent expression,
just as a blazing fire requires immediate
attention (Rashi).

My illness gives rise to a burning
temperature which resembles a roaring
fire (Radak).

דִּבַּרְתִּי בִּלְשׁוֹנִי — *Then I spoke out openly* [lit.
with my tongue].

I gave in to my burning desire for
self-expression and allowed myself to
ask the following question (Rashi).

My very breath was fiery as I finally
spoke out (Radak).

5. הוֹדִיעֵנִי ה׳ קִצִּי — *Let me know,
HASHEM, my end.*

How long will I continue to be in distress? When will my suffering come to
an end? (Rashi).

When Israel was suffering in exile,
the people refused to be consoled, saying, 'If You HASHEM will inform us

I was silent from the good;
and my pain was intensified.
⁴ *My heart grew hot within me,*
in my contemplations a fire blazed,
then I spoke out openly.
⁵ *Let me know, O HASHEM, my end,*
and the measure of my days, what is it?

when the misery will come to an end we will be consoled.' This may be likened to the father who told his son, 'You will receive ten lashes'. Each lash included an element of relief to the son for he knew that each blow was bringing him closer to the conclusion of his punishment *(Midrash Shocher Tov).*

Similarly, Job asked, מַה כֹּחִי כִּי אֲיַחֵל וּמַה קִצִי כִּי אַאֲרִיךְ נַפְשִׁי, *What is my strength that I should hope, and what is my end that I should prolong my soul's*

existence? *(Job 6:11).* Job said: 'If I can still expect to live a normal lifetime, then I can patiently endure my grave illness, reinforced by the hope of recovery and better times to come. But if my days are few and there is no hope of recovery, then I ask that my end come swiftly for I cannot bear the excruciating pain' *(Radak).*[1]

וּמִדַּת יָמַי מַה הִיא — *And the measure of my days, what is it?*

1. The *Talmud (Shabbos* 30a) relates: David requested of the Holy One, Blessed be He, *'Let me know HASHEM, my end.'* God replied, 'I have already established a rule that no creature of flesh and blood shall know his end.' But David persisted, asking *'the measure of my days, what is it?'* [i.e. in what season of the year — when the days are of short measure or long? *(Maharsha)*]. Again God replied, 'I have already established a rule that no man will be informed of the measure of his days.' Finally David pleaded, *'Let me know when I will be deficient* [i.e., *dead].'* God answered, 'Your life will come to an end on the Sabbath day'. David asked, 'Let me die on the day after the Sabbath [so that there will be ample time to make funeral preparations and proper eulogies *(Rashi)*]. God denied this request saying, 'By then, the reign of your son Solomon will have commenced, and one kingdom may not encroach on another one by even as little as a hair's-breadth.' David then asked to die on the day before the Sabbath, and God refused this too, saying, *'One day in your courtyard is worth more than one thousand* (84:11). One day of Torah study is worth more than a thousand burnt-offerings which your son Solomon will offer up in the Temple courtyard'.

From then on, David dedicated every Sabbath exclusively to the study of Torah. When the Sabbath on which he was destined to die arrived, the Angel of Death could not take his soul for he was protected by virtue of his incessant Torah study. So the Angel of Death went down into the garden behind the royal palace and made a tremendous crashing noise among the trees. David went out to determine the cause of the commotion [and continued to study Torah orally even as he walked]. However, a step suddenly broke under his foot and, startled, he momentarily stopped learning. At that moment, the Angel of Death claimed his soul!'

[What motivated David to inquire after his final day? Every man has a unique mission to accomplish on this earth. God gives him the talent, resources and opportunity to fulfill a specific quota of good deeds in an allotted time. The expression קֵץ, *end,* refers to the conclusion of that period. Most people lose sight of theirmission and stray from the path leading to their pre-ordained goal. ('The day is short, the work is great, and the laborers are lazy' [*Avos* 2:15]). Therefore, David pleaded, 'Let me know the extent of my capabilities, and what is expected of me, and how much time I have to realize the quota. Thus, I will constantly be goaded onward.' Furthermore, the nature of man is that while he is alive he cannot envision himself as ever being dead. He considers death as reserved for others. Therefore, David sought to be made aware of the fact that his life is indeed limited by a קֵץ,*end.*]

ו מַה־הִיא אֶדְעָה מֶה־חָדֵל אָנִי: הִנֵּה
טְפָחוֹת | נָתַתָּה יָמַי וְחֶלְדִּי כְאַיִן נֶגְדֶּךָ
ז אַךְ־כָּל־הֶבֶל כָּל־אָדָם נִצָּב סֶלָה: אַךְ־
בְּצֶלֶם | יִתְהַלֶּךְ־אִישׁ אַךְ־הֶבֶל יֶהֱמָיוּן

[Note that David does not ask to know מִסְפַּר יָמַי, *the number of my days*, rather he seeks to be informed of *the measure of my days*, i.e. how is my accomplishment measured according to what is expected of me at my קֵץ, *end?*

Another point: Most people measure themselves by their years, for a year represents a sizeable amount of time worthy of reckoning, whereas a month or a week and certainly a day, is of small significance and of little consequence. Not so the righteous. They cherish each *day* as a short but precious opportunity which must be measured and appraised. David asked about his *days* similar to Abraham of whom Scripture says, *And Abraham was old, well on in days* (Genesis 24:1)].

אֶדְעָה מֶה־חָדֵל אָנִי — *Then I will realize how deficient I am.*

[חָדֵל literally means *to cease, to be missing*. In the context of this verse it means that David wants to know how his accomplishment measures up to final expectations so that he will realize his deficiencies and how far he is from his ultimate goal].

Ibn Ezra, Metzudas Zion, and *Malbim* identify חָדֵל as synonymous with חֶלֶד, *a lifetime,* (v. 6) with the letters transposed. Thus, they render 'So that I may know how long I will remain in this life.'

6. טְפָחוֹת נָתַתָּה יָמַי — [Like] *hand-breadths have You made my days.*

My days are so few that they can be measured with one of the smallest of measures: the טֶפַח, *handbreadth* (Rashi).

The righteous man is acutely aware of the fleeting nature of life which vanishes before his very eyes. He feels how every breath he breathes brings him closer and closer to his last one, and how every step he takes, every small טֶפַח, *handbreadth*, of space which he traverses brings him nearer to the grave (Yaavetz Hadoresh).

וְחֶלְדִּי — *My lifetime.*

The translation follows *Radak* and *Metzudos* who render this word as synonymous with חֶלֶד (v. 5) which also refers to the termination of a lifetime.

However, according to *Rashi*, חֶלֶד is a metaphor for old age which is likened to חֲלוּדָה, *turning rusty* [cf. comm. to מֶחְלָד (17:14).]

[Life is futile because it is no more than a prolonged process of 'rusting out.' From the moment man is born, he is already deteriorating and headed toward the grave.]

כְאַיִן נֶגְדֶּךָ — *Is as naught before You.*

The fleeting moments of our lives cannot compare to Your eternal, infinite existence (Radak)[1]

אַךְ כָּל הֶבֶל — *All is total* [lit. *nothing but*] *futility.*

Human existence is the sum total of all futile, worthless pursuits, as Solo-

1. *Ohel Yaakov* explains this phrase with a parable. A rich man refused to make a loan to a beggar. Even though he was sure that the honest pauper would eventually pay him back, he was equally certain that the manner of repayment would be unsuitable. The rich man argued that the beggar would reimburse him one penny at a time at intervals, and so, by the time the second penny was paid, the first would surely be gone and thus the full sum would never be

Then I will realize

how deficient I am.

⁶ *Like handbreadths have You made my days,*

and my lifetime is as naught before You.

All is total futility —

all human existence, Selah.

⁷ *In total darkness does man make his way,*

mon taught in his wisdom, הֲבֵל הֲבָלִים
אָמַר קֹהֶלֶת הֲבֵל הֲבָלִים הַכֹּל הָבֶל
'Futility of futilities! — Said Koheles — Futility of futilities! All is futile!' (Koheles 1:2) (Radak).

However, Metzudos David renders this particular usage of הֶבֶל as pain, sorrow, as we find כִּי בַהֶבֶל בָּא וּבַחֹשֶׁךְ יֵלֵךְ For he [man] arrives [is born] in pain and departs [to the grave] in darkness (Koheles 6:4).

כָּל אָדָם נִצָּב — All human existence [lit. All men stand erect.]

[Not only when man is merely עוֹמֵד, standing (casually), is his existence precarious, but even when he reinforces his position in life by being נִצָּב, standing erect and firm, all his efforts are still futile.]

[At this point the persecuted man is overwhelmed by his tragedy, and questions the value of life itself. Since all is futile it is indeed better not to have been born. Again, this resembles Job who was finally compelled by his sufferings to hurl blasphemous complains against the heavenly design of life. And Job replied and said: 'If only the day of my birth had been lost, and also the night on which they announced, "A man has been conceived" (Job 3:1-2).]

7. אַךְ בְּצֶלֶם יִתְהַלֶּךְ אִישׁ — In total darkness does man make his way.

He lives out his life בְּצַלְמוֹת, under the shadow of death, constantly fearing the sudden, unknown death which may be lurking just around the corner (Dunash quoted by Rashi, Radak, Metzudos).

[Job too, spurned human existence, considering it worthy only of dark misery. הַיּוֹם הַהוּא יְהִי חֹשֶׁךְ, Let that day [of my birth] always be dark (ibid 3:3) יִגְאָלֻהוּ חֹשֶׁךְ וְצַלְמָוֶת despicable with darkness and the shadow of death (ibid 3:4).

Ibn Ezra renders צֶלֶם in its more common translation, 'image'. Man's image is his situation and fortune which is in constant flux (similar to the shape of a flowing body of water which never remains quite the same). This incessant change is reflected in the צֶלֶם, image, of the heavenly bodies; the stars and astrological formations which are divinely endowed with the power to affect the future [under God's supervision] and are in perpetual motion.

Thus, when God wishes to change man's fortune, He effects His wish by the agency of the heavenly bodies; in turn, man becomes their 'image'.

[This concept may be broadened, for as Nefesh HaChaim and others expound, God can be the צֶלֶם, image, or צֵל, shadow, of man, as it were. If a person molds himself into a model of kindness, God will follow suit and treat

amassed intact again! Similarly, man considers his life to be long and significant, thinking he possesses many years. But this is not so. For the past is gone, and the future may never come. All man really possesses is the one moment of the present in which he is living now, and even that fleeting second, *is as naught before You.*

ח יִצְבֹּר וְלֹא־יֵדַע מִי־אֹסְפָם: וְעַתָּה מַה־
ט קִּוִּיתִי אֲדֹנָי תּוֹחַלְתִּי לְךָ הִיא: מִכָּל־
פְּשָׁעַי הַצִּילֵנִי חֶרְפַּת נָבָל אַל־תְּשִׂימֵנִי:
י נֶאֱלַמְתִּי לֹא אֶפְתַּח־פִּי כִּי אַתָּה עָשִׂיתָ:
יא הָסֵר מֵעָלַי נִגְעֶךָ מִתִּגְרַת יָדְךָ אֲנִי כָלִיתִי:

him kindly, in turn. Thus man can shape God's manifestation in creation.][1]

אַךְ הֶבֶל יֶהֱמָיוּן — *Total futility does he lustfully pursue.*

[Man, the crown of creation, endowed with the unlimited opportunity to control the shape of God's revelation on earth, squanders his assets in the pursuit of petty lusts. Not only is it highly doubtful that he will attain his desires, but even if he does eventually succeed in realizing some of his fond wishes, he will discover that they were empty and futile (הֶבֶל), completely unworthy of his great efforts.]

Rashi and *Radak* both derive the word יֶהֱמָיוּן from the verb הֶמְיָה, *yearning, lusting.* However, *Ibn Ezra* and *Metzudos* relate it to the noun הָמוֹן, *mass.* The Psalmist laments, 'man amasses great fortunes which prove to be futile'.

יִצְבֹּר וְלֹא יֵדַע מִי אֹסְפָם — *He amasses* [lit. *makes heaps*] *riches, yet knows not who will harvest them.*

Throughout the harvest season the farmer toils to make countless צְבוּרִים, *piles* of his crops, yet he has no assurance that he will live to gather this bounty into his house (*Rashi*).

Slowly but surely bit by bit, man painstakingly amasses his treasures, yet he has no idea where they will go after his death (*Radak*).

The *Talmud* (*Bava Basra* 11a) relates that it was for this reason that King Monabaz donated to charity all his own treasures accumulated by himself and his many ancestors. He explained, 'They gathered treasures which cannot be protected from the hands of plunderers, but I gather mitzvos (spiritual treasures) stored away in heaven, safe from any foreign hand!' (*Shaarei Chaim*).

8. [Having concluded his vivid portrayal of the worthlessness of material pursuits, the Psalmist commences to outline the true mission of life.]

וְעַתָּה — *And now.*

Only now, after my terrible illness which convinced me of the frailty of man (*Radak*), and after having thoroughly analyzed the futility of wealth (*Rashi*).

מַה קִּוִּיתִי אֲדֹנָי — *For what do I hope, my Lord.*

To whom can I turn for salvation from my raging fever since all medical efforts have proven utterly futile? (*Radak*). [What can I wish for in this world that is of meaningful, enduring value?]

תּוֹחַלְתִּי לְךָ הִיא — [*What is*] *my expectation of you.*

The translation follows *Rashi* who interprets this phrase as the conclusion

---

1. When a Torah lesson is taught in the name of its deceased author, his lips move along, even in the grave. Furthermore, whoever transmits a Torah lesson in the name of its author should keep a mental image of the teacher before his eyes [thus the lesson will be taught with greater clarity and faithfulness to the source], as it says, *Only with the image* [of the teacher before him], *does man* [the disciple] *make his way* (*Yerushalmi, Shekalim* 2:5).

XXXIX   *total futility does he lustfully pursue,*

8-11   *He amasses riches,*

yet he knows not who will harvest them.

⁸ *And now, for what do I hope, my Lord?*

What is my expectation of You?

⁹ *From all my transgressions rescue me;*

a disgrace before the degenerate do not make me!

¹⁰ *I was mute, I opened not my mouth,*

because You did it.

¹¹ *Remove from me Your plague;*

by the hostility of Your hand am I devastated.

---

of the question begun earlier.

Radak, however, takes this as the answer to the question: My expectation is [only] to You!

[To know You and to imitate Your ways is the only opportunity in life really worth striving for. Only from this pursuit can I expect to derive genuine satisfaction, as it says, *HASHEM is good to those who hope for Him, to the soul which seeks Him out* (Lamentations 3:25).]

9. מִכָּל פְּשָׁעַי הַצִּילֵנִי — *From all my transgressions rescue me.*

[But before I can know You intimately, O God, I must first remove the barriers which separate me from You. I am a captive, chained to my old, sinful ways and far removed from Your presence. Please rescue me from that way of life. I now abandon the blasphemies of Job and I recognize that all of my persecutions were well deserved results of my sins].

חֶרְפַּת נָבָל אַל תְּשִׂימֵנִי — *A disgrace before the degenerate do not make me.*

[נָבָל literally means *worn out,* for the faith which the heretic once possessed has been worn away by the tribulations of life which have stripped him of his appreciation of God's justice (cf. *comm.* 14:1). When Job's wife severely criticized him for accepting God's wrath

with perfectly innocent faith, and encouraged him to curse God, Job reprimanded her harshly, saying: כְּדַבֵּר אַחַת הַנְּבָלוֹת תְּדַבְּרִי, *like the speech of one of the degenerates do you speak* (Job 2:10).]

The man of faith knows that all of his sufferings are justified. He does not ask to be released from his pain, for he recognizes their value. He requests only that the wicked ones be punished also, so that they should not disgrace the righteous by saying, 'We must be right, for God punishes only you'. Heathen nations suffer in this world as a result of God's response to this request (*Rashi*).

10. נֶאֱלַמְתִּי לֹא אֶפְתַּח פִּי — *I was mute, I opened not my mouth.*

There was no one at whom to scream or to blame for my suffering, for I recognized that all my afflictions came from You as a result of my sins (*Radak*).

11. הָסֵר מֵעָלַי נִגְעֶךָ — *Remove from me Your plague.*

This refers to the plague of leprosy which afflicted David (*Sforno*) [and to which he also referred in 38:12 (*Radak*)].

[Now that I recognize my sins, there is no reason to prolong my agony for I have learned my lesson.]

מִתִּגְרַת יָדְךָ אֲנִי כָלִיתִי — *By the hostility of Your hand am I devastated.*

בְּתוֹכָחוֹת עַל־עָוֹן | יִסַּרְתָּ אִישׁ וַתֶּמֶס   יב
כָּעָשׁ חֲמוּדוֹ אַךְ הֶבֶל כָּל־אָדָם סֶלָה:
שִׁמְעָה תְפִלָּתִי | יהוה וְשַׁוְעָתִי | הַאֲזִינָה   יג
אֶל־דִּמְעָתִי אַל־תֶּחֱרַשׁ כִּי גֵר אָנֹכִי עִמָּךְ
תּוֹשָׁב כְּכָל־אֲבוֹתָי: הָשַׁע מִמֶּנִּי וְאַבְלִיגָה   יד
בְּטֶרֶם אֵלֵךְ וְאֵינֶנִּי:

This translation follows *Rashi, Radak,* and *Metzudos* who relate תְגָרַת to תְּגָר, *hostility* or *war* as in וְאַל תִּתְגָּר בָּם מִלְחָמָה *Do not arouse hostilities of war against them* (Deuteronomy 2:9).

Rashi also quotes *Menachem* who renders תְּגָרַת as *fear,* as in וַיָּגָר מוֹאָב *And Moab was frightened* (Numbers 22:3).

12. בְּתוֹכָחוֹת עַל עָוֹן יִסַּרְתָּ אִישׁ — *With rebukes for iniquity have You chastened man.*

You warned us not to sin and threatened us with harsh rebukes. You have lived up to Your words by punishing us for iniquity (*Rashi*).

The plagues which You send upon us are like 'translators' who interpret Your displeasure into afflictions which convey to us the message that You are angered by our deeds (*Radak*).

וַתֶּמֶס כָּעָשׁ — *You rot like a moth.*

The עָשׁ is the moth [or the worm] which eats clothing and causes it to rot (*Metzudas Zion*).

חֲמוּדוֹ — *His precious* [flesh].

A person's flesh is precious to him (*Rashi*).

You wasted away the precious fat of his flesh and the power of his torso, just

as the עָשׁ, *moth,* swiftly devours a garment (*Radak*).

אַךְ הֶבֶל כָּל אָדָם סֶלָה — *Total futility is all mankind, Selah!*

If man holds his own flesh so precious and dear although it decays and putrifies so easily and swiftly, what better proof could there be of human futility and worthlessness (*Radak*).[1]

13. אֶל דִּמְעָתִי אַל תֶּחֱרַשׁ — *To my tears, be not mute.*

I shed tears not because of my pain but because of my inability to serve You with Torah study and prayer (*Sforno*).

The combination of prayers and tears is like a liquid medicine prescribed by an expert physician (*Ibn Ezra*).

The *Talmud* (*Bava Metzia* 59a) says: Since the day that the Temple was destroyed all of the gates of prayer are locked, however, the gates of tears are not locked as it says, *To my tears, be not mute.* [This proves that tears enter into heaven under all circumstances, because the only request which the Psalmist made was that they be heard and acted upon (*Rashi*).]

[*Hirsch* calls a tear 'the sweat of the soul.' Indeed, a tear of repentance is an overflow of feeling which demonstrates that he who weeps has overcome his

---

1. Rav Aharon 'Artchik' Bakst zt''l, one of the great leaders of pre-World War II Lithuanian Jewry, would bang his fist on the table in the course of a *Mussar Shmuess* (a discourse on ethics) shouting, 'What is superior, a man or a table? Certainly a table! If you don't wash this table for a month it won't start to smell foul, but don't wash a man for a month and he will be infested with lice and stench'.

XXXIX 12 *With rebukes for iniquity have You chastened man,*
12-14   *You rot like a moth his precious flesh,*
      Total futility is all mankind, Selah.
   13 *Hear my prayer, HASHEM;*
      to my outcry, lend an ear;
      to my tears, be not mute;
   For an alien am I with You,
      a settler like all my forefathers.
   14 *Release me that I may regain my strength,*
      before I depart and I am no more.

normal, calm nature and is exerting himself to be more receptive to change and renewal. If man opens the gates of his heart in order to welcome God, certainly God reciprocates by opening all the gates of heaven before his tears.

The question has been asked: If the gates of tears are never locked why did God have to make them in the first place? The *Gerrer Rebbe* said that although sincere tears always gain admission above, the gates are sealed shut in the face of false tears. We might also add that although these gates are not locked, nevertheless they are closed and can be opened only as far as the forceful flow of tears will push them!]

כִּי גֵר אָנֹכִי עִמָּךְ — *For an alien am I with You.*

Man wanders the earth like a stranger who strays about in a foreign land. He travels from place to place constantly, lacking permanence. The Psalmist adds the word עִמָּךְ, *with You,* to stress that only in the hands of God lies the decision whether an individual will remain settled peacefully in one place or if he will be exiled and disturbed. Similarly, David himself said, (I Chronicles 29:15) *For we are aliens before You and settlers like all of our forefathers (I Chronicles 29:15) (Radak).*

David is alluding to his ancestress,

Ruth the Moabitess, who was a גִּיּוֹרֶת, *convert (Rabbi Menachem Azariah of Pano.).*

תּוֹשָׁב כְּכָל אֲבוֹתַי — *A settler like all my forefathers.*

Despite the temporary nature of his stay on earth, man deludes himself into thinking that he is a settler because he follows in the footsteps of his forefathers, but they, too, were only transitory migrants in comparison with God's eternal existence (Metzudos).

If a person considers himself to be an alien in עוֹלָם הַזֶּה, *This World,* then he will join his forefathers, the Patriarchs, Abraham, Isaac and Jacob, and be permanently settled in the bliss of עוֹלָם הַבָּא, *the World to Come (Toldos Aharon).*

14. הָשַׁע מִמֶּנִּי — *Release me.*

The translation follows *Rashi, Ibn Ezra,* and *Radak.* However, *Metzudos* and *Malbim* render 'turn away from me.'

וְאַבְלִיגָה — *So that I may regain my strength.*

And thus be able to serve You as an able-bodied servant who can fulfill Your will (Radak).

בְּטֶרֶם אֵלֵךְ — *Before I depart.*

To the grave (Radak).

[495]   Tehillim

וְאֵינֶנִּי — *And I am no more.*

When I leave This World for the World to Come I will no longer have the opportunity to serve You, for that is the place of reward, not of good deeds (*Radak*).[1]

---

1. As his holy life was ebbing away, the *Vilna Gaon* called his disciples to his bedside. He held up his *tzitzis* and said: 'Behold the tremendous opportunities of This World. For a scant few *kopecks* one can purchase *tzitzis* which will afford him with thousands upon thousands of *mitzvos* as he wears them constantly. But in the Hereafter, even if a person should desire to give away a fortune he no longer has the privilege to add the smallest *mitzvah* to his account!' Then the saintly *Gaon* burst into tears at the thought that he would soon have no more opportunities to serve God.

The preceding Psalms described David in the throes of his debilitating malady. This Psalm is the joyous Song he composed when he returned to full health (Radak; Sforno). It is not an ordinary composition; but rather a very special שִׁיר חָדָשׁ, a new song (v. 4), for it describes David's unflagging faith which he renewed and refreshed (v. 2).

The first twelve verses of this Psalm would indicate that David was at the height of bliss when he uttered these words. [The ecstasy and the eloquence justify the description 'a new song' used in v. 4.] But, if we read beyong v. 12, we see that the song was written when the Psalmist was beset by many dangers and sorely in need of deliverance. In the midst of these woes David finds strength and inspiration in the many previous occasions when God rescued him. Thereby HASHEM demonstrated to David that He is the real מְנַצֵּחַ, one who grants victory, by endowing man with spiritual fortitude with which to withstand all earthly tribulations. This illustrates the unique power of David to extract rapturous joy from the depths of adversity (Hirsch).

Rashi and the Midrash emphasize another important dimension of this psalm, which addresses itself to all of Israel. In the Egyptian bondage, the nation was crippled by harsh slavery. Only by virture of their intense, enduring faith were the Israelites liberated and given the opportunity to sing a new song at the sea.

In addition, this Psalm alludes to the future Messianic redemption which will be the result of Israel's extraordinary faith and which will stimulate unprecedented waves of fresh song and jubilation.

לַמְנַצֵּחַ לְדָוִד מִזְמוֹר: קַוֹּה קִוִּיתִי יהוה א־ב

וַיֵּט אֵלַי וַיִּשְׁמַע שַׁוְעָתִי: וַיַּעֲלֵנִי | מִבּוֹר ג

שָׁאוֹן מִטִּיט הַיָּוֵן וַיָּקֶם עַל־סֶלַע רַגְלַי

כּוֹנֵן אֲשֻׁרָי: וַיִּתֵּן בְּפִי | שִׁיר חָדָשׁ תְּהִלָּה ד

---

1. לַמְנַצֵּחַ לְדָוִד מִזְמוֹר — *For the Conductor, unto David, a song.*

The superscription, מִזְמוֹר לְדָוִד, *a song unto David*, always implies that David utilized the medium of song as a means to elevate himself sufficiently to attain the rapture of God's presence. The heading לְדָוִד מִזְמוֹר, however, indicates that first he was inspired by God's spirit which came לְדָוִד, *to David*, whereupon he composed the מִזְמוֹר, *song* to express the soaring emotion engendered by that inspiration. (Cf. *commentary* to 3:1).

2. קַוֹּה קִוִּיתִי ה׳ — *I have hoped and hoped for HASHEM.*

Israel does not possess sufficient merit to warrant redemption. Only because of their unswerving faith in God's redemption are they deserving of God's help, as the Prophet declares וְאָמַר בַּיּוֹם הַהוּא הִנֵּה אֱלֹהֵינוּ זֶה קִוִּינוּ לוֹ וְיוֹשִׁיעֵנוּ זֶה ה׳ קִוִּינוּ לוֹ נָגִילָה וְנִשְׂמְחָה בִּישׁוּעָתוֹ, *And he shall say on that day, 'Behold this is our God, we hoped for Him and He saved us this is HASHEM, we hoped for Him, we shall rejoice and be glad in His salvation* (Isaiah 25:9).

Similarly, it says טוֹב ה׳ לְקוָּו, *Hashem is good to those who hope for Him* [Lamentations 3:25] (*Midrash Shocher Tov*.)

If your hopes have not been realized, hope and hope again! In Egypt, the Israelites in bondage cried out again and again, *and God heard their cries* [Exodus 2:24] (*Shemos Rabbah* 23:12).

More than the results of his faith in God, David sought the inspiration of the hope itself. The means meant more to him than the end. Thus he says, 'It is for their ability to *hope* [קַוֹּה] to

HASHEM that *I* (truly) *hope* [קִוִּיתִי] (*Tehillos Hashem*).

וַיֵּט אֵלַי וַיִּשְׁמַע שַׁוְעָתִי — *So He inclined to me and heard my cry.*

Sometimes God does not 'bend down to hear', meaning that He, in His infinite wisdom, chooses not to interfere with the normal course of events in order to effect salvation (*Malbim*).

3. מִבּוֹר שָׁאוֹן — *For the pit of turbulent waters.*

The translation of שָׁאוֹן as a reference to *turbulent waters* follows *Rashi*. However, *Metzudas Zion* renders מִבּוֹר שָׁאוֹן, *from a dark pit.*

David describes his illness as a watery grave which threatened to swallow him alive (*Radak*).

God rescued Israel from the בּוֹר, *pit*, of Egyptian bondage, and from the שָׁאוֹן, *turbulent waters*, of the Sea of Reeds (*Rashi*).

מִטִּיט הַיָּוֵן — *Out of the filthy mire.*

יָוֵן is synonymous with רֶפֶשׁ, *filth*. It refers to the mud of the seabed which Israel crossed at the Sea of Reeds [and which God miraculously hardened for them] (*Rashi*).

Shemos Rabbah (*ibid.*) explains that this describes the muck and clay which the Israelite slaves used in manufacturing their daily quota of bricks.

Radak interprets יָוֵן as a collection of many types of mud, both solid and watery [cf. *Mikvaos* 9:2]. Here the word is used as a metaphor for a variety of ailments which afflicted David.

Malbim maintains that טיט הַיָּוֵן is *quicksand* from which there is no escape as it sucks the victim downward.

For the Conductor, unto David, a song.
² I have hoped and hoped for HASHEM,
so He inclined to me, and heard my cry.
³ He raised me from the pit of turbulent waters.
out of the filthy mire;
He set my feet upon a rock,
He firmed my steps.
⁴ He put in my mouth a new song,

[This corresponds to the *Talmud* (*Eruvin* 19a) which notes that טיט הַיָּוַן is one of the seven Scriptural expressions used for describing Gehinnom (purgatory). Thus, the word *quicksand* is used to imply that there is no escape from the consequences of sin.]

וַיָּקֶם עַל סֶלַע רַגְלַי — *He set my feet upon a rock.*

This salvation refers to the threat of בּוֹר שָׁאוֹן, *the turbulent, watery pit.* The man drowning therein desperately clutches for something solid, i.e., a rock, to which he can cling. (*Be'er Avraham*).

Rashi explains: God endowed Israel with wealth: the booty taken in Egypt and the spoils taken at the Sea.

[וַיָּקֶם alludes to יְקוּם, *substance*. Elsewhere we read: וְאֵת כָּל הַיְקוּם אֲשֶׁר בְּרַגְלֵיהֶם, *And all the substance at their feet* (*Deut.* 11:6), which the *Talmud* (*Sanhedrin* 110a) explains as the wealth and substance which give someone the ability to stand on his own feet without relying on others for support].

God completely restored my health and my strong constitution (*Sforno*).

When Saul seemed to have me in his grasp, God miraculously saved me at the סֶלַע הַמַּחְלְקוֹת, *the Rock of Division* (cf. *commentary* to 18:3) (*Alshich*).

Just as all of the winds in the world cannot overturn a great rock, so is it impossible to overthrow the kingdom of David for all times, because God Himself promised David an eternal monarchy (*Nir L'David*).

[According to *Yalkut Shimoni* (*Tehillim* 736), סֶלַע refers to the Temple as we find in *Jeremiah* 33:16. David exults that he was uplifted by the opportunity to prepare for its construction. The Temple's central point was the Holy Ark situated in the Holy of Holies on top of a סֶלַע, *rock*, — the אֶבֶן שְׁתִיָּה, the rock from which the world was created (*Yoma* 53b)].

כּוֹנֵן אֲשֻׁרָי — *He firmed my steps.*

This corresponds to the victim who is completely immobilized in the טיט הַיָּוֵן, *the filthy mud* (quicksand), and who lacks solid ground on which to steady himself (*Be'er Avraham*).

My ailment left no scars or infirmities upon my body. God healed me completely without leaving any trace of my illness (*Sforno*).

4. וַיִּתֵּן בְּפִי שִׁיר חָדָשׁ — *He put in my mouth a new song.*

Radak notes that David is not content to thank God merely for His salvation. He perceives that even the inspiration to sing was a divine gift [cf. *commentary* to v. 1]. Indeed, it is incumbent upon man to create an original hymn of praise to God in recognition of every new miracle from which he benefits.

Malbim adds that when God saves through natural means, it is sufficient to express gratitude by means of an existing song of praise. But when the Creator effects salvation through a

לֵאלֹהֵינוּ יִרְאוּ רַבִּים וְיִירָאוּ וְיִבְטְחוּ
ה בַּיהוָה: אַשְׁרֵי־הַגֶּבֶר אֲשֶׁר־שָׂם יהוה
מִבְטַחוֹ וְלֹא־פָנָה אֶל־רְהָבִים וְשָׂטֵי כָזָב:
ו רַבּוֹת עָשִׂיתָ | אַתָּה | יהוה | אֱלֹהַי

miraculous phenomenon, a *new song* is called for.[1]

A *new song* is particularly appropriate here because David was on the threshold of death and God endowed him with new life (*Tehillas Hashem; Norah Tehillos*).

Rashi explains that שִׁיר חָדָשׁ also alludes to שִׁירַת הַיָּם, *the Song at the Sea*, composed by the newly redeemed nation of Israel.

תְּהִלָּה לֵאלֹהֵינוּ — *A hymn to our God.*

David refers to Him as *our God* because he is calling upon everyone, the entire congregation, to join him in this song of praise (*Radak*).

Let them not only praise HASHEM, i.e. His manifestation of Mercy, but even God, i.e., His manifestation of strict Justice (*Pa'amonei Zahav*).

יִרְאוּ רַבִּים וְיִירָאוּ — *Multitudes shall see and be awed.*

Because the verse speaks of Israel as *seeing* and *fearing*, the *Midrash* interprets it as an allusion to the rescue of Israel at the Sea from destruction at the hands of the Egyptians as we find in *Exodus* 14:31, *And Israel saw the great hand which HASHEM used against the Egyptians, and the nation feared HASHEM, and they believed in HASHEM and in Moses His servant* (*Midrash Shocher Tov*).

Only the revealed miracle brings men to fear God's might. When He merely

manipulates nature, however, in a concealed manner not really discernible to unthinking people, His greatness is not appreciated (*Malbim*).

David's life serves as a lesson even for non-believers. All will learn to fear sin when they witness His former afflictions and the extent to which God helped him (*Radak*).

Midrash Shocher Tov echoes this theme: 'Whoever wishes to repent should study David's life, as the Prophet says, *Behold, I have placed him* [David] *as a testimony for the nations* (*Jeremiah* 55:4).

[According to *Maharam Markado* David's *new song* (v. 4) begins with the words of this verse. However, *Ibn Ezra* (v. 6) maintains that this verse is an introduction to the song, which begins with the next verse.]

5. אַשְׁרֵי הַגֶּבֶר — *Praises to the man.*

[For the explanation of אַשְׁרֵי, see commentary to 1:1.]

[The גֶּבֶר is more than just an ordinary man. He is a גִּבּוֹר, *a mighty warrior*, who is self-sufficient and does not need the assistance of others. If such a secure person denies his own powers and his faith rests solely on God, he is surely praiseworthy.]

אֲשֶׁר שָׂם ה' מִבְטַחוֹ — *Who made HASHEM his trust.*

Similarly we find בָּרוּךְ הַגֶּבֶר אֲשֶׁר יִבְטַח בַּה' וְהָיָה ה' מִבְטַחוֹ, *Blessed is the*

---

1. The *Midrash* teaches that all Scriptural songs are called שִׁירָה in the feminine gender, because each victory of Israel gives birth to fresh sorrows and persecutions. However, the song of victory in the future is שִׁיר, in the masculine gender, for then our salvation will be complete and there will be no further sorrows. Therefore, wherever Scriptures refer to the composition which is חָדָשׁ, new — i.e. an allusion to the song of the future — it is called שִׁיר (see 33:3, 96:1, 98:1, 149:1, *Isaiah* 42:10).

a hymn to our God,
Multitudes shall see and be awed,
and they shall trust in HASHEM.
⁵ *Praises to the man*
who made HASHEM his trust,
And turned not to the arrogant,
and to strayers after falsehood.
⁶ *Much have You done — You HASHEM, my God,*

man who trusts in HASHEM, and makes HASHEM his trust (Jeremiah 17:7).

Some people, while trusting that God is the ultimate source of success, nevertheless turn to other forces as the vehicles to achieve that success. They put their efforts into commerce or professions in order to gain the divinely ordained prosperity. Therefore, although they *trust in HASHEM* they do not *make HASHEM their* [lit. *his*] *trust* i.e. the sole medium through which their trust is manifested. But the true believer turns to no force but HASHEM Himself even in his efforts to attain material fortune. He is the person who does *make HASHEM his trust* (Malbim).

רְהָבִים — *The arrogant.*

The word רָהַב is related to רָחָב *wide, extended,* and to רַב, *much, great.* [The arrogant have an over-inflated ego] (Hirsch).

As in יִרְהֲבוּ הַנַּעַר בַּזָּקֵן *'The youth will act arrogantly against the elder'* [Isaiah 3:5] (Rashi).

He who trusts in HASHEM asks for no assistance from mighty warriors who are excessively reliant on their own strength (Radak). Arrogant men make commitments which far surpass their ability to fulfill (Malbim).

וְשָׂטֵי כָזָב –*And strayers after falsehood.* שָׂטֵי is derived from שׂוּט, *to turn away treacherously. It refers to deceptive sorcerers* (Radak) *and to pagan idolators* (Rashi).

According to *Hirsch,* it describes the arrogant men of might. At first glance, they inspire trust. However, when their help is needed they are of no avail. They disappoint those who rely on them, as they turn away fickly.

Whereas the boastful man cannot live up to his promises, the man of כָזָב does indeed achieve results. However, he lacks the ability and the consistency to maintain these results permanently [cf. *commentary* to 4:3]. Consequently, he is כָזָב, *he disappoints,* those who depend on him (Malbim).[1]

6. רַבּוֹת עָשִׂיתָ אַתָּה ה' אֱלֹהַי — *Much have You done — You HASHEM, my God.*

---

1. The *Midrash* (*Bereishis Rabbah* 89:8) seems to contradict itself. First it presents Joseph as the perfect example of the man of sincere faith: *'Praises to the man who made HASHEM his trust'*; this describes Joseph! The *Midrash* continues: *'And turned not to the arrogant'*; this refers to the sin of Joseph in turning to Pharaoh's שַׂר הַמַּשְׁקִים, *butler,* for assistance in being released from prison. For this lack of trust in God, Joseph was punished with two additional years of imprisonment.

The *Beis HaLevi* (*Parshas Mikeitz*) reconciles these two statements. For the ordinary person it would not be a breach of faith to hope for the intervention of an influential officer, as this is the customary procedure. But when one attains Joseph's plateau of faith, he is expected to turn to none but God for all assistance. Therefore, precisely because Joseph was the paragon of faith, it was improper for him to depend on a human being for his rescue from prison.

נִפְלְאֹתֶיךָ וּמַחְשְׁבֹתֶיךָ אֵלֵינוּ אֵין | עֲרֹךְ
ז אֵלֶיךָ אַגִּידָה וַאֲדַבֵּרָה עָצְמוּ מִסַּפֵּר: זֶבַח
וּמִנְחָה| לֹא־חָפַצְתָּ אָזְנַיִם כָּרִיתָ לִי עוֹלָה

You HASHEM, are not like human
rulers and leaders whose performance
varies with the size of their audience.
Such leaders seek popularity and public
good-will, and therefore will do much
for the multitudes, but little for the few.
You HASHEM are different. You have
done many things for me alone, for You
are truly my God; concerned with my
welfare, though I am but an individual
(Alshich).

נִפְלְאֹתֶיךָ וּמַחְשְׁבֹתֶיךָ אֵלֵינוּ — Your
wonders and Your thoughts are for [lit.
to] us.

The נִפְלָאוֹת are the actual wonders
which God put into action and the
מַחְשָׁבוֹת are the divine thoughts which
precede the execution of these miracles.
Of course, to describe God as thinking
prior to action is an anthropomor-
phism, for He has no need to consider
and plan as do humans. As is common,
Scripture merely speaks of God in
human terms (Radak).

Alshich delves more deeply into this
thought: The Psalmist uses the word
אֵלֵינוּ [lit. to us] in order to emphasize
that the interval between God's thought
and the implementation of His wish is
only to us – i.e. as we, with our limited
human intellect, perceive events to occur. Unable to grasp God's true nature,
we imagine Him to be subject to the
limitations of time and to other impedi-
ments preventing the execution of His
decree. As for God Himself, however,
thought and deed are simultaneous.
Furthermore, to God, both natural e-
vents and miracles are the same. He
controls both with equal authority and
ease. Only אֵלֵינוּ, to us, do certain events
appear to be 'natural' phenomena while
others are supernatural miracles.

Rashi renders אֵלֵינוּ as for us, and

adds: For our sake You created this
world and for our sake You split the
Sea. Furthermore, Your thoughts were
occupied with long term plans for our
welfare. You saw that the inhabitants of
Canaan had exercised a scorched-earth
policy when they learned of Israel's imminent conquest. They felled their trees
and devastated their land. Therefore
You detained us in the desert for forty
years, so that the Canaanites would
have ample time to forget us and our
threat and so be aroused to develop their
land again. Thus we eventually conquered a productive country.

The Midrash (Bereishis Rabba 65:8)
amplifies this theme and stresses that
God's concern for the ultimate success
of Israel is the guiding force behind all
events in history, even those which
originally seemed to be detrimental. For
example, Isaac became blind only so
that Jacob should later be able to take
the blessings which Isaac had intended
for Esau. [All dark spots in history are
for the sake of future light.]

The Talmud (Yevamos 77a) relates
how God planned David's birth many
years before he was born. The Torah
prohibits the Ammonite and the
Moabite from entering the Congregation of God, but the restriction applies
only to males, not to females. This is
because God foresaw that David was
destined to descend from Ruth the
Moabite and that Rechavam, King of
Judah, grandson of David and
progenitor of the Davidean line, was to
be born from Solomon's wife, Na'amah
the Ammonite.

David sang You released my bonds
(117:16). He said, 'Soverign of the
Universe, two prohibitions restricted me
and You released them, i.e. the Moabite
and Ammonite, Ruth and Na'amah.

> Your wonders and Your thought are for us,
> none can compare to You.
> Can I relate or speak of them?
> They are too mighty to recount.
> ⁷ Neither sacrifice nor offering did You desire,
> but receptive ears You opened for me;

This is the meaning of the verse, *Many things You Yourself have done HASHEM, my God* (singular), *Your wondrous works and Your thoughts are for us* (plural).

David did not say *for me*, he said *for us*: Rechavam was sitting in David's lap and the grandfather told his young grandson 'These verses [permitting the females] were said for the benefit of us both.'

אֵין עֲרֹךְ אֵלֶיךָ — *None can compare with You.*

No king or savior can match Your deeds (*Rashi*). Similarly we find: *There is none like You among the gods, my Lord, and there is nothing to match Your deeds* (86:8).

Or, עֲרֹךְ can mean *to account.* No one can adequately attribute אֵלֶיךָ, *to You* all of Your miracles because they are innumerable (*Radak*).

Or, עֲרֹךְ can be rendered *value:* To the human who beholds Your wonders these are deeds of significance. But, *to You* they are of no special 'value', for You control the natural and the supernatural with equal facility (*Malbim*).

אַגִּידָה וַאֲדַבְּרָה עָצְמוּ מִסַּפֵּר — *Can I relate or speak of them? They are too mighty to recount.*

The *Talmud* (*Berachos* 33b) cautions us not to attempt to recite all of God's praises, for we are limited in what we can express, but the praises of God are infinite (*Alshich*).

7. זֶבַח וּמִנְחָה לֹא חָפַצְתָּ — *Neither sacrifice nor offering did You desire.*

זֶבַח refers to the שְׁלָמִים i.e. the animal brought as a *peace-sacrifice.* מִנְחָה refers to the *meal-offering* of fine flour mixed with oil (*Radak*).

Although Your benign attention is permanently riveted upon us, You have no desire for repayment of any sort, not even in the form of sacrifices, because Your sole concern is for our welfare. (*Ibn Ezra; Malbim*).

HASHEM said: On the day when the Torah was given at Sinai I demonstrated no desire for offerings, as the Prophet says, *For I spoke not to Your fathers, nor commanded them on the day that I brought them out of the land of Egypt, concerning burnt-offerings or sacrifices. But this I commanded them, saying, 'Heed My voice and I will be Your God and You will be My people* (*Jeremiah* 7:22-23).

Furthermore, when I spoke of sacrifices in the Scriptures, I mentioned the subject only in voluntary terms: *When any man of you shall bring an offering unto HASHEM* [of his own free will] (*Leviticus* 1:2), but I did not impose them upon you as an obligatory burden. Even the תָּמִיד, *daily* sacrifices and the מוּסָפִין, *additional* sacrifices of the Sabbath and festivals, although obligatory, are merely to cause satisfaction and pleasure to Me and they are a relatively insignificant obligation upon Israel. (*Rashi*).[1]

אָזְנַיִם כָּרִיתָ לִּי — *But receptive ears You opened* [lit. 'You dug'] *for me.*

Ears which were attuned to God were a major factor in the success of the

1. *Radak* provides an introduction to the institution of sacrifice:
   God's primary concern was that Israel should obey Him. In the Ten Commandments,

ח וַחֲטָאָה לֹא שָׁאָלְתָּ: אָז אָמַרְתִּי הִנֵּה־
ט בָאתִי בִּמְגִלַּת־סֵפֶר כָּתוּב עָלָי: לַעֲשׂוֹת־

House of David and the lack of such attentive ears brought about the downfall of David's predecessor, King Saul. Samuel the Prophet chastised Saul, the disobedient King who sought to appease God's wrath with sacrifices, הַחֵפֶץ לַה' בְּעֹלוֹת וּזְבָחִים כִּשְׁמֹעַ בְּקוֹל ה', הִנֵּה שְׁמֹעַ מִזֶּבַח טוֹב לְהַקְשִׁיב מֵחֵלֶב אֵילִים, *Does HASHEM desire offerings and sacrifices as much as He desires the hearkening to the voice of HASHEM? Behold, to heed is better than to sacrifice, to listen attentively surpasses [offering of] the fat of rams' [I Samuel 15:22] (Radak; Ibn Ezra; Alshich).*

This also alludes to the fact that David's ears were receptive to the rebuke and admonition of the prophet Nathan. God appreciated David's sincere repentance and confession far more than any sacrifice (Sforno).

The *Zohar* notes that David achieved the highest level of atonement when his ears heard the curses of Shimi ben Gera and he accepted his insulting words with the utmost humility and contrition. David could have easily silenced the vile Shimi by allowing his eager bodyguards to slay him as they considered themselves duty-bound to do. Yet he displayed enormous restraint and listened attentively. David attributes to his Maker this ability to listen humbly, for God created him with a nature so receptive to rebuke (Chazah Zion).

עֹלָה וַחֲטָאָה לֹא שָׁאָלְתָּ — *Burnt- and sin-offerings You did not request.*

The עֹלָה, *burnt offering,* atones for

הִרְהוּרֵי חֵטְא, *sinful thoughts,* and for neglecting the performance of מִצְוֹת עֲשֵׂה, *positive commandments.* The חַטָאת, *sin-offering,* atones for the commission of unintentional sins provided the sins are so severe that the transgressor would be liable to the penalty of כָּרֵת, *extirpation,* had he commited them intentionally. God would prefer that we transgress no sins at all and hence render needless the entire institution of atonement sacrifices. (Radak).

But if one is not careful, he will first neglect a seemingly 'small' mitzvah or contemplate just one sinful thought, for which he should bring an עֹלָה. This negligence will eventually bring him to more serious infractions for which he must sacrifice a חַטָאת hence the wording of the verse עֹלָה חַטָאָה (Chazah Zion).

8. אָז אָמַרְתִּי הִנֵּה בָאתִי — *Then I said, 'Behold I have come.'*

David speaks on behalf of the collective Israel, saying: *Then,* at the time of מַתַּן תּוֹרָה, *the Giving of the Torah,* we came to You with the tradition of Your divine covenant, and declared, נַעֲשֶׂה וְנִשְׁמָע, *We shall do and we shall listen* [Exodus 24:7] (Rashi, Ibn Ezra). [We fully understood at the very outset of our relationship that Your only wish was that we should obey Your commandments faithfully.]

Then, when You healed my illness, I fully comprehended Your preference for obedience rather than sacrifices (Radak).

therefore, there is no mention of service through sacrifice. Only after Israel strayed did God enjoin animal sacrifices, in order to help them onto the road to repentance.

Then He required individual sinners to bring private sacrifices and He obligated the entire congregation to offer up two תָּמִיד, *continual,* sacrifices every day. The purpose of the communal sacrifices was because, after Israel sank to a lower moral level, it became inevitable that in the course of each day there would be many incidents of inadvertent sins. The communal sacrifices atone for all those unrecognized sins [and demonstrate that unless they elevate themselves, Israel will be inextricably mired in sin.]

Burnt-offerings and sin-offerings
You did not request.
8 Then I said, Behold I have come!'
In the Scroll of the Book is written of me.

בִּמְגִלַּת סֵפֶר כָּתוּב עָלָי — *In the scroll of the Book it is written about me.*

Our declaration of נַעֲשֶׂה וְנִשְׁמָע is recorded for all time in *the Book* — i.e. the Torah Scroll — as an eternal testimony to Israel's unwavering faith (*Rashi*).

Or: Now that I have completely recovered from my illness, I scrupulously observe every commandment of the Torah, recorded on *the scroll of the book.* This form of dedicated service surpasses all sacrifices (*Radak*).

Ibn Ezra suggests: When David was wracked with pain and sickness he vowed to compose a *new song* to God if he survived (*v.* 4). To make his vow more binding he had his solemn oath recorded on a scroll.

Now, as he sings his *new song* he is fulfilling that obligation which he inscribed in the scroll.

Malbim identifies *the scroll of the*
book as the heart of the Jew [of which Scripture says: '*Write it upon the tablet of your heart*' (Proverbs 3:3, 7:3, Jeremiah 17:1)] which has a natural inclination to perform in a moral and righteous manner. Even if God had never demanded of His people any display of appreciation or sacrifice (*v.* 7), the heart of the nation would nevertheless feel that it must do something to cause Him great satisfaction (*v.* 9).

Sforno observes that David is referring to the special Torah Scroll which the king must write for himself. The *Talmud (Sanhedrin* 21b) says that this *Sefer Torah* was fashioned like an amulet which could conveniently be hung upon the king's right hand so that it would accompany him wherever he went. Thus the king might continually study the word of HASHEM wherever he went and thereby come to fear Him.[1]

1. The commentaries (*Sanhedrin ibid.*) question how a complete Sefer Torah could be made small and light enough to dangle conveniently from the King's arm at all times. Another problem is that the dangling of a Sefer Torah is specifically forbidden by the *halachah* because it is disrespectful. For these reasons, *Rashash (ibid.)* ventures that the king carried a small scroll which contained only a brief synopsis of the 613 commandments. The *Arukh* quotes *Rav Nachshon Gaon* who is of the opinion that this scroll contained only the Ten Commandments which consist of 613 letters. These opinions lend themselves well to *Sforno* who renders our verse as referring to the King's special Sefer Torah described as *the scroll* (synopsis, abridgement, cf. *Gittin* 60a) *of a book* (of the entire Sefer Torah) *written* (especially) *for me* (cf. *Sanhedrin* 21b: The king must write a Sefer Torah specifically for his own sake).

Further support for the interpretation that our verse refers to the Sefer Torah may be derived from the fact that this psalm is dedicated to a *new song*. In Deuteronomy 31:19 the obligation to write a Sefer Torah is couched in similar terms *And now write for yourselves this 'song'* (cf. *Rambam Hilchos Sefer Torah* 7:1).

These words also allude to David personally. The *Talmud (Yevamos* 77a) mentions that when David was anointed he thought that he had only recently come to God's attention (cf. footnote v. 6). David descended from the elder daughter of Lot, the mother of Moab. The daughters of Lot were saved from the holocaust of Sodom only because God wished to assure that David would emanate from their line.

In describing these daughters the Torah uses an extra word *your two daughters* הַנִּמְצָאֹת

מ

רְצוֹנְךָ אֱלֹהַי חָפָצְתִּי וְתוֹרָתְךָ בְּתוֹךְ מֵעָי:
י בִּשַּׂרְתִּי צֶדֶק בְּקָהָל רָב הִנֵּה שְׂפָתַי לֹא

9. לַעֲשׂוֹת רְצוֹנְךָ אֱלֹהַי חָפָצְתִּי — To fulfill Your will, my God, have I desired.

My natural inclination, my genuine desire, is to serve You of my own volition and to bring You pleasure (Malbim).

[This concept that it is a Jew's ingrained desire to fulfill God's will is given halachic application by Rambam (Hilchos Geirushin 2:20): 'In a situation where it is incumbent upon a husband to give his wife a bill of divorce, the Jewish court may resort to the exercise of force in order to compel the husband to discharge his obligation. Although in all cases a bill of divorce must be given with the free will and consent of the husband, the coercive method does not detract from the husband's willingness. For, despite his apparent refusal to comply with the law, the husband truly wishes to live like an Israelite and desires to perform the mitzvos and refrain from transgressions. It is merely the perversity of his evil inclination which has overwhelmed the uncooperative husband at this time. The chastisement applied by the court will serve to weaken the grip of his evil in-

clination and when he cries out [while being coerced] 'I consent' then his true self has come to the fore and the Bill of Divorce is considered as one given willingly.]

וְתוֹרָתְךָ בְּתוֹךְ מֵעָי — And Your Torah is in my innards.

It is constantly on my mind and it never slips from my attention (Radak).

My will is so inextricably bound up with Yours that I need not search through a scroll of parchment and ink to discover Your wish. I need only scrutinize my own innermost parts, my heart and mind and conscience, and they will inform me of the the Torah's commands (Malbim).

Even that which enters into מֵעָי [lit. my intestines] is controlled by Torah legislation. I am careful not to eat forbidden foods or untithed produce (Rashi).

He who desires to gain Torah knowledge must make this his exclusive pursuit. To the extent that he yearns for other pleasures, his desire and capacity for Torah is diminished. In Rabbinic lore, the Torah scholar is described as

that are found, this extra word corresponds with the verse מָצָאתִי דָּוִד עַבְדִּי בְּשֶׁמֶן קָדְשִׁי מְשַׁחְתִּיו, *I have found My servant David, with My holy oil I anointed him* (89:21).

When David realized this he exclaimed: *Then* [at first] *I said, 'Behold I have come!'* [only recently to God's attention. But I now realize that] *In the scroll of the book [i.e., the Torah]* it is [already] *written about me.*

Yalkut Shimoni (Bereishis 41) traces David's roots, to an even earlier book. It is written, *This is the Book of the generations of Adam* (Genesis 5:1). God showed Adam all future generations. He showed the soul of David to Adam, saying 'He is inscribed to live for only three hours.'

Said Adam, 'Sovereign of the Universe, how many years have been alloted to me?'

'One thousand', was the reply.

'Does the heavenly order allow a man to make a gift of his years?'

'Yes', answered God.

'If so, I give seventy of my years to this soul of David!' Adam then took a scroll of parchment and recorded his gift as a binding transaction. He signed his name to it with the signatures of God and the angel Mitatron as witnesses.

Therefore, David sang, 'Behold I have come! [To the world for seventy years, because] *In the scroll of the book [of the generations of Adam] it is written about me.'* [See Chapter I of *Overview* to Vol. 1.]

⁹ To fulfill Your will, my God, have I desired
and Your Torah is in my innards.
¹⁰ I proclaimed Your righteousness
in a vast assembly.
Behold my lips I do not restrain;

one who מִלָּא כְרֵיסוֹ, has filled up his innards [with knowledge]. The Midrash
(quoted in Tosafos Kesubos 104a s.v.
לֹא וְהֵנָתִי) warns, Before you pray that
Torah should enter into your innards,
pray first that delicacies should not
enter into your innards [and distract
you]' (Chomas Anoch).

The Sages warn us: Do not say, 'I do
not relish eating pork.' Instead say, 'I
would enjoy eating pork, but what shall
I do, my Creator has prohibited it'
(Rashi, Leviticus 20:26). Harav Gifter
explains that every God-fearing Jew actually loathes swine meat and finds it
repulsive. Does this revulsion run
counter to the above dictate of the
Sages? No! What the Sages are saying is
this. Do not say that pork is abhorrent
to you for health reasons or because of
gastronomic preferences. Say rather
that if you were permitted to, you
would enjoy this delicacy. Why then do
you not eat pork? Only because you are
a subject of your Creator! However,
now that He has forbidden this food it is
indeed repulsive and loathsome, for its
consumption represents a rebellion
against the revered Master.

[Based on this we can explain this
verse: To fulfill Your will, HASHEM, is

my desire. Your will controls my tastes
and appetites, my likes and dislikes to
the point where Your Torah is in my innards and influences my gastronomic
preferences.]

10. בְּשַׂרְתִּי צֶדֶק בְּקָהָל רָב – I proclaimed
[lit. heralded (Your) righteousness to a
vast assembly.

Not only do I fulfill Your commands
which are recorded on the scroll of the
book, but I also feel obliged to publicly
announce the many acts of kindness
that You have performed for my benefit
so that the masses will be inspired to
trust You. I call myself a מְבַשֵּׂר, a herald
of news because I always hasten to inform the public of every new kindness
which You bestow (Radak).[1]

Speaking for the entire nation, the
Psalmist says: We, the children of
Israel, announced Your kindness by
singing the Song of the Sea, the Song of
Miriam's Well and the Song of Deborah
(Rashi).

הִנֵּה שְׂפָתַי לֹא אֶכְלָא – Behold, my lips I
do not restrain

I take advantage of every opportunity
to glorify Your Name in order to attract
the masses towards Your service
(Sforno).

1. The Talmud (Eruvin 63a) relates that as long as David's teacher, Iyra Hayairi was alive,
David himself would not teach a Torah lesson nor issue a halachic decision for this would be
disrespectful to his master as David said, 'In my heart I hid Your sayings so that I should not
sin towards You' (119:11). But after the passing of his teacher, David opened up the wellsprings of his wisdom as he said, 'I proclaimed righteousness [I taught new lessons of Torah]
in the vast assembly' [before multitudes of students].

Similarly, Yalkut Shimoni 408 asks, 'What type of בְּשׂוֹרָה, good news did they need to hear
in the days of David? Were not the years of his reign a semblance of the future reign of the
Messiah when all will be blissful and tranquil? Rather the news which David announced was
Torah news, for he lectured and expounded before the people such original novellae as had
never before been heard.'

יא אֶכְלָא יהוה אַתָּה יָדָעְתָּ: צִדְקָתְךָ לֹא־
כִסִּיתִי בְּתוֹךְ לִבִּי אֱמוּנָתְךָ וּתְשׁוּעָתְךָ
אָמַרְתִּי לֹא־כִחַדְתִּי חַסְדְּךָ וַאֲמִתְּךָ לְקָהָל
יב רָב: אַתָּה יהוה לֹא־תִכְלָא רַחֲמֶיךָ מִמֶּנִּי
יג חַסְדְּךָ וַאֲמִתְּךָ תָּמִיד יִצְּרוּנִי: כִּי אָפְפוּ־
עָלַי | רָעוֹת עַד־אֵין מִסְפָּר הִשִּׂיגוּנִי
עֲוֹנֹתַי וְלֹא־יָכֹלְתִּי לִרְאוֹת עָצְמוּ
יד מִשַּׂעֲרוֹת רֹאשִׁי וְלִבִּי עֲזָבָנִי: רְצֵה יהוה

11. צִדְקָתְךָ לֹא כִסִּיתִי בְּתוֹךְ לִבִּי — *Your righteousness I have not concealed within my heart.*

I do not allow myself to forget it for a moment and I always make it known to others (Radak).

Your righteousness is so evident to all that no man can keep it a secret within his heart as we find, צִדְקָתְךָ כְּהַרְרֵי אֵל, *Your righteousness is like the mighty mountains* [Psalms 36:7] (Chazah Zion).

אֱמוּנָתְךָ וּתְשׁוּעָתְךָ אָמַרְתִּי לֹא כִחַדְתִּי חַסְדְּךָ וַאֲמִתְּךָ לְקָהָל רָב — *Of Your faithfulness and salvation have I spoken; I have not withheld Your kindness and Your truth from* [lit. *to*] *vast assemblies.*

[This verse seems to be a repetition of v. 10, but David adds a new thought. He stresses that he seized every opportunity to expound on the essential topic of faith. Even when the assembly was convened to hear a lecture on a different subject, he would not refrain from directing discussion towards of faith. (See Rambam, Berachos 9:5.)

12. אַתָּה ה׳ — *You HASHEM.*

You, Yourself, not Your agent or messenger (Tehillos Hashem).

לֹא תִכְלָא רַחֲמֶיךָ מִמֶּנִּי — *Withold not Your mercy from me.*

David reasoned that since I *do not hold back my lips* [from announcing Your righteousness] (v. 10), therefore I

deserve that You, too, should not withhold Your compassion from me (Norah Tehillos).

Furthermore, the Talmud (Shabbos 151b) states: Whoever has compassion for others will be treated with compassion by God. Therefore David asks to be inspired with a sense of compassion for his fellow man so that he will merit God's compassion (Ohel Yaakov).

חַסְדְּךָ וַאֲמִתְּךָ תָּמִיד יִצְּרוּנִי — [May] *Your kindness and Your truth always protect me*

I am protected by the fact that *I have not refrained from telling of Your kindness and Your truth to vast assemblies* [v.11] (Ibn Ezra).

13. אָפְפוּ — *Encircled.*

[See commentary to 18:5.]

רָעוֹת עַד אֵין מִסְפָּר — *Evils without number.*

The course of normal, everyday living is strewn with countless pitfalls and potential causes of injury. Yet, somehow man navigates each day unscathed. This is due to his merits which insulate him from lurking danger. But sin can remove the protective shield of merit. When that occurs he is immediately beset by the *evils without number* which had always encircled him, but had been hitherto held at bay (Radak).

11-13   ¹¹ Your righteousness I have not concealed
                within my heart,
        Of Your faithfulness and Your salvation
                have I spoken;
        I have not withheld Your kindness and Your truth
                from the vast assembly.
        ¹² You, HASHEM—withhold not Your mercy from me;
                may Your kindness and Your truth
                always protect me.
        ¹³ For evils without number encircled me,
                my sins had overtaken me, and I could not see;
        They were more than the hairs on my head
                and my heart failed me.

הִשִּׂיגוּנִי עֲוֺנֹתַי — My sins had overtaken me.

I am beset by innumerable evils because my wicked past has finally overtaken me (Radak).

Not only the sin is called עָוֺן, but its punishment as well, as Cain said, גָּדוֹל עֲוֺנִי מִנְּשׂוֺא, My punishment is greater than I can bear [Genesis 4:13] (Ibn Ezra).

וְלֺא יָכֺלְתִּי לִרְאוֺת — And I could not see.

Midrash Shmuel explains that if a person is beset with pain and affliction he should take note of the specific organ which is affected to determine whether he has sinned with that particular limb. Ordinarily such scrutiny will reveal the source of the pain, because God punishes measure for measure. Here the Psalmist bemoans the fact that he is overwhelmed by such an onslaught of pain in all of his limbs that he cannot possibly scrutinize each one minutely to discover each particular shortcoming Dorash Moshe).

עָצְמוּ מִשַּׂעֲרוֺת רֺאשׁי—They were more than the hairs of my head.

The Talmud (Succah 51a) states that the righteous refrain from sin because they realize the gravity of transgression. To them the evil inclination which attempts to persuade them to transgress appears to be a great mountain, i.e., a formidable force to be reckoned with. The wicked, however, take sin lightly and consider it to be a minor, trivial matter. They visualize the evil inclination as a flimsy hair with which they need not bother to contend.

Therefore, the Psalmist who laments his many sins attributes them to his failure to treat the specter of sin with due seriousness. Now these individual sins which he once considered to be more worthy of note than the hairs of my head, have become too numerous to count (Dorash Moshe).

וְלִבִּי עֲזָבָנִי — And my heart failed [lit. forsaken] me.

I have been deprived of my peace of mind, hence I can no longer properly concentrate on my Torah studies (Sforno).

טו לְהַצִּילֵנִי יהוה לְעֶזְרָתִי חוּשָׁה: יֵבֹשׁוּ
וְיַחְפְּרוּ| יַחַד מְבַקְשֵׁי נַפְשִׁי לִסְפּוֹתָהּ
טז יִסֹּגוּ אָחוֹר וְיִכָּלְמוּ חֲפֵצֵי רָעָתִי: יָשֹׁמּוּ
עַל־עֵקֶב בָּשְׁתָּם הָאֹמְרִים לִי הֶאָח| הֶאָח:
יז יָשִׂישׂוּ וְיִשְׂמְחוּ| בְּךָ כָּל־מְבַקְשֶׁיךָ יֹאמְרוּ
תָמִיד יִגְדַּל יהוה אֹהֲבֵי תְּשׁוּעָתֶךָ: וַאֲנִי|
יח עָנִי וְאֶבְיוֹן אֲדֹנָי יַחֲשָׁב־לִי עֶזְרָתִי
וּמְפַלְטִי אַתָּה אֱלֹהַי אַל־תְּאַחַר:

14. רְצֵה ה׳ לְהַצִּילֵנִי — *Will it, HASHEM, to rescue me.*

Spare me from illness and injury (*Radak*), from my enemies (*Alshich*), and from the evil inclination which blinds me (*Rav Yeibi*).

ה׳ לְעֶזְרָתִי חוּשָׁה — *HASHEM, to my assistance hasten.*

Help me to comprehend the words of Your Torah (*Sforno*).

15. מְבַקְשֵׁי נַפְשִׁי — *Those who seek my life* [lit. *soul*].

This refers to the evil inclination which wishes to destroy my holy spirit (*Alshich*).

Or: these are the shameless enemies who pursue me openly. Let them be put to shame openly (*Malbim*).

לִסְפּוֹתָהּ — *To put an end to it* [i.e., they seek to put an end to my life].

To make it cease to exist, as in עַד, until the entire generation תֹּם כָּל הַדּוֹר, *until the entire generation ceases to be* (Deuteronomy 2:14) which *Onkelos* renders עַד דְּסָף כָּל דָּרָא (*Rashi*).

חֲפֵצֵי רָעָתִי — *Those who wish me evil.*

These are my hidden enemies who as yet have not dared to show their true wickedness. I pray that יִסֹּגוּ אָחוֹר, *let them fall* (be held) *back,* so that they should never be able to attack me (*Malbim*).

16. יָשֹׁמּוּ — *Let them be astounded.*

The translation follows *Rashi.* However, *Radak* and *Metzudas Zion* render *desolate,* from שִׁמָּמוֹן, *desolation.*

עַל עֵקֶב בָּשְׁתָּם — *By their deserved shame* [lit. *on the heel of their shame.*]

The shame which stuns and bewilders them should come as no surprise. It follows on the heels of their wicked ways, and they receive only what they justly deserve, measure for measure (*Rashi*).

Radak maintains that the word עֵקֶב itself may be translated as *reward,* as we read וְהָיָה עֵקֶב תִּשְׁמְעוּן, *And it shall come to pass as a reward if you listen* (Deut. 7:12).

הֶאָח הֶאָח — *Aha! Aha!*

These are the exclamations of my enemies who gloat with merriment over my misfortune (*Sforno*).

Similarly, we read וַיַּרְחִיבוּ עָלַי פִּיהֶם אָמְרוּ הֶאָח הֶאָח רָאֲתָה עֵינֵנוּ, *They opened their mouths wide against me, they said, 'Aha! Aha! Our eyes have seen!'* [35:21] (*Malbim*).

17. יָשִׂישׂוּ וְיִשְׂמְחוּ בְּךָ כָּל מְבַקְשֶׁיךָ — *Let them rejoice and be glad in You, all who seek You.*

It was only to accomplish this that I took the pains to *proclaim Your right-eousness in the vast assembly* [v. 10] (*Ibn Ezra*).

Those who seek worldly fortunes are

¹⁴ *Will it, HASHEM, to rescue me;*
    HASHEM, to my assistance, hasten.
¹⁵ *Let them be put to shame and disgrace,*
    those who seek my life, to put an end to it.
Let them fall back and be humiliated,
    those who wish me evil.
¹⁶ *Let them be astounded by their deserved shame,*
    those who say to me 'Aha! Aha!'
¹⁷ *Let them rejoice and be glad in You,*
    all who seek You.
Let the always say, 'HASHEM be magnified!'
    those who love Your salvation.
¹⁸ *As for me, I am poor and needy.*
My Lord think of me, You are my assistance
    and He who causes my escape.
My God — do not delay.

---

worried until they actually find the object of their search. Not so the man who seeks God. His quest is not merely a means to an end, it is an end in itself, and so even while he still seeks he is glad *(Malbim)*.

יֹאמְרוּ תָמִיד יִגְדַּל ה' אֹהֲבֵי תְשׁוּעָתֶךָ — *Let them always say 'HASHEM be magnified!' — those who love your salvation.*

May ה', *the Attribute of Mercy*, be greater than the *Attribute of Strict Justice (Sforno)*.

Those who truly love HASHEM do not mind the advent of misfortune, for it provides them with an opportunity to seek out God's mercy and to witness His salvation; an event which inevitably adds to God's prestige and magnifies His Name *(Malbim)*.

Rabbeinu Bachya to Numbers 14:17 (see also 70:5 and 35:27) comments: The potency of God's benevolence in this world depends on Israel. If they are faithful in obeying His commands, they give Him the power, so to speak, to

shower an abundance of good upon them. Conversely, when Israel sins, they weaken God's power to be magnanimous. After Israel flagrantly disobeyed God by ignoring His words and believing the spies who slandered Eretz Yisrael, God disassociated Himself from them. Therefore Moses exerted himself to induce God to increase His influence in this world saying, *And now, may the strength of my Lord be magnified*. This was also David's intention when he prayed, *May all those who desire Your salvation continually say, 'HASHEM be magnified'.*.

18. וַאֲנִי עָנִי וְאֶבְיוֹן — *As for me, I am poor and needy.*

Throughout the Book of *Psalms*, the expression *poor and needy* refers to the nation of Israel *(Rashi)*.

אֲדֹנָי יַחֲשָׁב לִי — *My Lord think of me.*

Let Him be cognizant of me, to be aware of my poverty *(Rashi)*.

Also, יַחֲשָׁב can be translated *reckon,*

account i.e., 'May my Lord reckon my poverty as an atonement for my sins'. Or, יַחֲשָׁב may be related to חָשׁוּב, *worthy, important* i.e., 'May I be considered worthy in the eyes of my Lord' (Radak).

עֶזְרָתִי וּמְפַלְטִי אַתָּה אֱלֹהַי אַל תְּאַחַר — *You are my assistance and He who causes*

my escape. My God — do not delay.

David said: 'Sovereign of the Universe! Pay attention to my poverty and need and hasten to my assistance, because You alone are my helper and rescuer. Eventually it is You who must redeem me; sooner or later, today or tomorrow! So why tarry? Do it now! (*Midrash Shocher Tov*).

With this chapter David closes the series of psalms in which he expresses gratitude to God for having healed him. He dedicates this work to the Lord 'Who cares wisely for the sick'.

A human physician confines his diagnosis to physical symptoms. God alone has the understanding to detect the deeper spiritual deficiency which saps the sinner's vitality. Sickness is inflicted upon a person to make him aware of God's displeasure with his moral shortcomings.

Rabbeinu Yonah (Shaarei Teshuvah 2:3, 4:1) sets forth this principle: 'Just as the body is susceptible to sickness, so is the soul. The illness afflicting the soul stems from its evil traits and its sins. God heals the soul through the ailments of the body as David said, HASHEM, show me favor, heal my soul for I have sinned against You (41:5).

David was particularly upset because his illness prevented him from realizing the great ambition of his life — the construction of the Temple (see comm. to v. 11).

God cured the ailing king, allowing him the privilege of preparing the plans and materials for Solomon's construction of the Temple. This was the pinnacle of David's career, therefore, this psalm comes as the climax and conclusion of the First Book of Psalms, his first compilation of God's praises.

[A close study of Psalm 30 is invaluable to the full appreciation of this psalm, since both works discuss David's return to health which allowed him to prepare for the construction of the Temple.]

א-ב לַמְנַצֵּחַ מִזְמוֹר לְדָוִד: אַשְׁרֵי מַשְׂכִּיל אֶל־
ג דָּל בְּיוֹם רָעָה יְמַלְּטֵהוּ יהוה: יהוה|
°יַאֲשֶׁר ק' יִשְׁמְרֵהוּ וִיחַיֵּהוּ °יֻאַשַּׁר בָּאָרֶץ וְאַל־
ד תִּתְּנֵהוּ בְּנֶפֶשׁ אֹיְבָיו: יהוה יִסְעָדֶנּוּ עַל־

2. מַשְׂכִּיל אֶל דָּל — *He who cares wisely* [lit. *acts wisely*] *for the sick.*

The verse praises one who shows wise concern by visiting the sick. The word דָּל, to refer to a patient, is used similarly in the verse מַדּוּעַ אַתָּה כָּכָה דָּל בֶּן הַמֶּלֶךְ, *Why are you so sickly, O son of the king?* (II Samuel 13:4). דָּל literally means *lean*. It is used to describe the sick man who is usually thin and wasted away (*Rashi*).

[David, the bed-ridden patient who cannot stand, is called דָּל. Therefore in 30:2, when praising God for curing him, he used the words כִּי דִלִּיתָנִי, *for You have elevated me from the lowly status of the* דָּל (cf. *comm. v.* 1 *ibid.* and *Ibn Ezra v.* 2 *ibid.*).]

In the context of this verse, מַשְׂכִּיל refers to one who closely observes the condition of a sick man to have an understanding of his needs (*Radak; Ibn Ezra*).

[דָּל, also means *impoverished*. The theme of this verse is not limited to caring for the sick. It covers the broad spectrum of philanthropic activities for those in need.]

Rambam lists seven levels in the performance of charity, the very best way being to offer the poor man a loan so that he can help himself and save his dignity. The מַשְׂכִּיל, by planning his benevolence with intelligence and understanding, will see to it that his charity is provided in the fashion best suited to the circumstances (*Dorash Moshe*).

In this sense, מַשְׂכִּיל can also mean *to teach intelligence* i.e. to help the poor man understand the reason for his poverty or to comfort the sick man with an explanation of the causes of his ailment (*Ibn Ezra*).

The poor man can be made aware that his poverty is in punishment for a shortcoming such as treating food disrespectfully, or neglecting to wash his hands before meals (*Yoseif Tehillos*).

Furthermore, the considerate person will try to make the patient understand that the affliction of poverty is for his good because it serves to purge him of his sins and saves him from worse punishments (*Tehillos Hashem*).[1]

Malbim translates מַשְׂכִּיל אֶל דָּל, as 'he who learns from the poor (or sick)'. This means that the intelligent person will notice the miraculous care which God provides for the pauper who has no tangible means of support, yet survives through God's mercy and constant intervention.

בְּיוֹם רָעָה יְמַלְּטֵהוּ ה' — *On the day of disaster HASHEM will surely cause him to flee.*

1. Fortunate is the man who withstands his personal test, for there is no creature whom God does not test. God tests the rich man to see if his hands will open generously to the poor. He tests the poor man to see if he will bear his afflictions patiently without complaining against God's ways. If the rich man succeeds in his examination he will enjoy the fruits of wealth in This World and its principle will be conserved for his enjoyment in the Hereafter. Furthermore, he will be saved from the terrible fury of Gehinnom, as it says, *Praiseworthy is he who cares wisely for the poor, on the day of disaster HASHEM will surely cause him to flee.* But if the rich man fails his test, his wealth will vanish, while the possessions of the pauper who bears his poverty with patience, will double (*Midrash Shemos Rabbah* 31:3).

For the Conductor, a song unto David.
² Praiseworthy is he
who cares wisely for the sick,
On the day of disaster
HASHEM will surely cause him to flee.
³ HASHEM will preserve him
and keep him alive.
He will be made praiseworthy on earth,
and He will not present him to the will of his foes.
⁴ HASHEM will fortify him on his bed of misery;

This can be interpreted as a declarative statement in reference to the sick patient, emphasizing that when the illness reaches a crisis point, only God can provide a cure and all the ministrations of the physicians are futile (*Radak*). Or it can be understood as a prayer and a word of comfort which the visitor offers at the bedside of the invalid, fortifying the sick man's confidence with the assurance that God's aid is close at hand (*Radak* quoting his father).

Sforno interprets it as a promise of future reward to the person who attends to the sick and poor.

[Reb Shrage Feivel Mendelowitz זצ״ל would encourage his students to make sacrifices for charity not only when they prospered, but even more so when foundering in dire financial straits. He based this on his unique interpretation of this verse, *Praiseworthy is he who cares wisely for the poor*, בְּיוֹם רָעָה, *on the day of his* [i.e., the philanthropist's] *personal financial disaster*. In reward, God will surely deliver the generous benefactor from evil.]

3. ישמרהו ויחַיֵּהוּ ה' — *HASHEM will preserve and keep him alive.*

According to *Rashi* and *Sforno*, this refers to the life of the benefactor who is promised life and security as his reward for nursing another.

Since a poor man is considered as if he were dead (*Nedarim* 65a), one who assists him back to financial health and 'life' is repaid (measure for measure) with life (*Yoseif Tehillos*).[1]

וְאַשֵּׁר בָּאָרֶץ — *He will be made praiseworthy on earth.*

God will provide the pauper with sustenance in his own locality and he will not be forced to wander to distant lands to earn his livelihood (*Malbim*). [See *comm.* to 37:3.]

He will have the good fortune to outlive his contemporaries and so his enemies will never have the pleasure of seeing him die (*Ibn Ezra*).

4. יסעדנו ה' — *HASHEM will fortify him.*

The *Talmud* (*Shabbos* 12b) derives from this verse that God supplies the invalid with strength and nutrition.

1. Not only will the philanthropist's life be preserved, it will also be prolonged. The *Talmud* (*Bava Basra* 11a) tells the story of Binyamin HaTzaddik who single-handedly supported a mother and her seven sons in the years of famine. Once, when he was sick and on the verge of death, the ministering angels came before God to plead his cause. 'Sovereign of the Universe, did You not say that whoever preserves even one Jewish life is as if he preserved the entire world? Shall this man who kept alive a mother and seven sons die so young?' Immediately his death sentence was torn to pieces and twenty-two years were added to his life.

ה עֶרֶשׂ דְּוָי כָּל־מִשְׁכָּבוֹ הָפַכְתָּ בְחָלְיוֹ: אֲנִי־
אָמַרְתִּי יהוה חָנֵּנִי רְפָאָה נַפְשִׁי כִּי־
ו חָטָאתִי לָךְ: אוֹיְבַי יֹאמְרוּ רַע לִי מָתַי
ז יָמוּת וְאָבַד שְׁמוֹ: וְאִם־בָּא לִרְאוֹת שָׁוְא
יְדַבֵּר לִבּוֹ יִקְבָּץ־אָוֶן לוֹ יֵצֵא לַחוּץ יְדַבֵּר:
ח יַחַד עָלַי יִתְלַחֲשׁוּ כָּל־שֹׂנְאָי עָלַי | יַחְשְׁבוּ

Consequently, we know that the שְׁכִינָה, *Divine Presence*, rests at the head of every sick man. Therefore, the visitor should not sit on the sick man's bed [for in doing so he would be acting irreverently towards the *Shechinah* which rests on the bed].

עַל עֶרֶשׂ דְּוָי — *On his bed of misery.*

This refers specifically to the seventh day of the illness when the patient is especially miserable (*Rashi* from *Midrash Shocher Tov*). According to *Tanchuma*, the crisis point is the fourth day.

כָּל־מִשְׁכָּבוֹ הָפַכְתָּ בְחָלְיוֹ — *All his restfulness has been upset by his illness.*

This follows *Rashi* and *Radak* who interprets חָלְיוֹ as the severe stage of *his illness*, and מִשְׁכָּבוֹ as *his restfulness*.

Radak offers another interpretation: Despite the severity of the illness, You have given him the power to turn from side to side on his bed.

Malbim notes that the invalid usually soils his bedding and so it must frequently be changed and *turned over*. God sees to it that the patient is attended to and that this vital service is performed.

5. אֲנִי אָמַרְתִּי ה' חָנֵּנִי — *As for me, I said: 'O HASHEM show me favor.'*

Until now the well-meaning visitor has been speaking. Now begin the words of the sick man who seeks help only from God (*Radak*).

The forsaken patient laments: 'As for me personally, no one ever came to visit me with helpful intentions. All I can do is call to HASHEM for help' (*Rashi*).

רְפָאָה נַפְשִׁי כִּי חָטָאתִי לָךְ — *Heal my soul for I have sinned against You.*

He does not ask for his body to be healed, for he realizes that his ailment stems from his sins which are a malady of the soul. If his soul can be cured by receiving divine forgiveness, then the recovery of the body is inevitable (*Radak*).

The soul which has become desecrated by sin has lost its sensitivity to all things sacred and divine. The possessor of this soul loses his awareness of God's presence and is deadened to all experiences of the spirit (*Reishis Chochmah*).

6. אוֹיְבַי יֹאמְרוּ רַע לִי — *My foes, however, speak evil of me.*

The wise, caring person (v. 1) blessed me and cared for my needs, but my foes only await my doom (*Radak*).

Midrash Shocher Tov raises a basic question: Did David really have foes? Is it not written: וְכָל יִשְׂרָאֵל וִיהוּדָה אֹהֵב אֶת דָּוִד, *And all of Israel and Judah loved David* (I Samuel 18:16). Who then were his enemies? Only those who wished to cheat and rob, but were prevented from doing so by David — it was they who hated him!

Alshich observes that when God makes the righteous suffer as an atonement for the sins of their generation, their ordeal is not only a shield for their contemporaries whose sins were responsible for these afflictions. It is also a benefit to the righteous for they become instrumental in atoning for so many others. However, this is true only

all his restfulness has been upset by his illness.

⁵ *As for me, I said: 'O HASHEM, show me favor!*
Heal my soul for I have sinned against You!'

⁶ *My foes speak evil of me:*
'When will he die and his name perish?'

⁷ *And if one comes to see,*
insincerely does he speak.

He desires to gather himself malicious information;
upon going out he reveals it.

⁸ *United against me, all my enemies whisper,*

---

when the sinners admit their guilt and recognize the great kindness the *tzaddik* does by suffering for them. David laments that his personal suffering will not accomplish this because his wicked contemporaries attribute the evil to his sins, rather than to theirs. Therefore they do not appreciate his sacrifice on their behalf. Furthermore, they would prefer to see him dead.

מָתַי יָמוּת וְאָבַד שְׁמוֹ — *'When will he die and his name perish?'*

When my enemies hear me crying out, *'Show me favor'*, they rejoice over my agony and anxiously look forward to the day when I will perish (*Rashi*).

The Brisker Rav cites numerous verses from *Psalms* to prove that the establishment of the Temple in Jerusalem and the perpetuation of the Davidic dynasty are interdependent. David's enemies rejoice over his illness which prevents the construction of the Temple for they know that in the absence of the Temple, David's name and royal line will sink into oblivion. (See *Pref. Remarks* and *comm. v.* 11).

7. וְאִם בָּא לִרְאוֹת — *And if one comes to see.*

I.e., if one of my enemies comes to visit me in my illness (*Radak*).

He does not come to visit me or care for my needs, he comes merely to

observe my misery and gloat over my agony (*Alshich*).

שָׁוְא יְדַבֵּר — *Insincerely does he speak* [lit. *He speaks in vain*].

With his lips he speaks of his concern for my well-being, but in his heart he seeks only my injury (*Radak*).

לִבּוֹ יִקְבָּץ אָוֶן לוֹ — *He* [lit. *his heart*] *desires to gather himself malicious* [*information*].

While he speaks sympathetically to me in my sick room, his mind absorbs everything detrimental about me, which he will use against me later (*Rashi; Radak*).

יֵצֵא לַחוּץ יְדַבֵּר — *Upon going out, he reveals it* [lit. *he goes outside and speaks*].

He has filled himself with so many vicious thoughts that he can hardly wait to run outside and blurt out his venom to anyone who will listen (*Alshich*).

This enemy has come as an agent for all of my foes. His mission is to appraise my condition, whether I am about to die or not. Should I appear to be recovering, the spy will call together my enemies to plot my assassination (*Malbim*).

8. יַחַד עָלַי יִתְלַחֲשׁוּ כָּל שֹׂנְאָי — *United against me, all of my enemies whisper.*

This verse continues the thought of the previous one. After my malicious

ט רָעָה לִי: דְּבַר־בְּלִיַּעַל יָצוּק בּוֹ וַאֲשֶׁר
שָׁכַב לֹא־יוֹסִיף לָקוּם: גַּם־אִישׁ שְׁלוֹמִי |
אֲשֶׁר־בָּטַחְתִּי בוֹ אוֹכֵל לַחְמִי הִגְדִּיל עָלַי
יא עָקֵב: וְאַתָּה יְהוָה חָנֵּנִי וַהֲקִימֵנִי

---

visitor leaves, he assembles my enemies to hear his evil report (*Radak*).

Alshich, however, comments that this verse begins a new thought. It discusses a group of vicious visitors who observe all the evil they can and then, while yet in the sickroom, eagerly whisper their evil impressions among themselves, speaking softly so that the patient should not hear.

9. דְּבַר־בְּלִיַּעַל יָצוּק בּוֹ — *The result of his lawlessness is poured over him.*

This is what they think and say about me. They claim that my illness is a result of my crimes and sins (*Rashi*).

בְּלִיַּעַל is a contraction of בְּלִי עוֹל, *without a yoke* [of fear of heaven] (*Metzudas Zion*).

Yaavetz HaDoresh calls attention to the fact that David tried, sentenced, and executed the evil Naval who is described as בֶּן בְּלִיַּעַל, *a lawless person* (*I Samuel 25:17*). David's enemies now accuse him of murdering Naval unjustly. They interpret His illness as a sign from heaven, proving that he, David, is the true בְּלִיַּעַל, *lawless person*, and Naval was his innocent victim.

According to *Midrash Shocher Tov*, בְּלִיַּעַל may be understood as עַל בְּלִי, *with nothing upon him.* David's enemies claimed that he was not really ill. He feigned sickness in order to test the reactions of his visitors and discover who were his foes.

Finally, *Malbim* maintains that these words contain the secret of the assass-

ination plot. They plan to use דְּבַר בְּלִיַּעַל, *an evil thing* [poison] which they will יָצוּק בּוֹ, *pour into him.*

וַאֲשֶׁר שָׁכַב לֹא יוֹסִיף לָקוּם — '*And now that he lies ill may he rise no more.*'

May the poison serum accomplish its lethal work, without the interference of any antidote (*Malbim*).

May David not have the power to stand up to transmit the Temple scroll [see *comm.* to v. 11] (*Brisker Rav*).

10. גַּם אִישׁ שְׁלוֹמִי אֲשֶׁר בָּטַחְתִּי בוֹ — *Even my ally* [lit. *man of my peace*] *in whom I trusted.*

The invalid laments that in his hour of distress not only do his enemies attack him, but even his trusted friends betray him (*Radak*).

I cannot trust my most faithful servants to reveal to me the plot of my enemies, for all have abandoned my cause (*Malbim*).

אוֹכֵל לַחְמִי — *Who ate my bread.*

[Even more painful is the ingratitude of the person upon whom I have lavished so much kindness. Now he bites the hand which fed him].

My most trusted servant, the attendant who tastes my food before I eat it, even he cannot be trusted to warn me of the poison put into my meal (*Malbim*).[1]

הִגְדִּיל עָלַי עָקֵב — *Develops* [lit. *makes large*] *an ambush against me.*

This translation of עָקֵב follows

---

1. Rabbi Yochanan said: At first David referred to Achitophel as his master, for he had learned Torah from him. Later, after Achitophel began to sin and fall, David referred to him merely as his colleague. Finally, when Achitophel lost all of his status, David called him *my disciple*, as we learn from the verse *Even my ally, in whom I trusted* [Achitophel] *and who ate my bread*, [who partook of my Torah knowledge (*Rashi*)] even [this student] *develops an ambush against me* (*Sanhedrin 106b*).

against me they devise my harm.

⁹ *'The result of his lawlessness is poured over him —
and now that he lies ill, may he rise no more!'*

¹⁰ *Even my ally in whom I trusted, who ate my bread —
develops an ambush against me.*

¹¹ *But as for You, HASHEM, show me favor
and raise me up —
then I shall repay them.*

Rashi who bases his opinion on the verse in *Joshua* 8:13: וְאֵת עֲקֵבוֹ מִיָּם לָעִיר, *And his ambush was from the west of the city. Radak*, however, renders this phrase literally: *He raised his heel high above me* to trample me.

According to *Ibn Ezra* David bemoans the fact that his friends did not visit him at all in his sickness. Rather, they turned their heels away from his house and in their pride they held themselves aloof from him.

11. וְאַתָּה ה' חָנֵּנִי וַהֲקִימֵנִי — *But as for You HASHEM, show me favor and raise me up.*

They claim that I will not arise from my illness (v. 9), therefore I ask that You refute their claims by raising me up (*Radak*).

[With these words David expresses the true cause of his distress, God's unwillingness to permit him to construct the Temple. The following *Midrashim* elaborate on this theme.]

The Holy One, Blessed be He, transmitted to Moses the מְגִילַת בֵּית הַמִּקְדָּשׁ, *Scroll of the Beis Hamikdash,* [which described the Temple in detail and revealed its many secrets].

Moses received the scroll while standing. He stood up and gave it over to Joshua who was standing. [Because of the great holiness of the document, both parties engaged in its transmission were required to stand, as a sign of reverence and awe.] Joshua stood up and gave it to the elders as they stood.

The elders gave it to the prophets as they stood. The prophets [specifically Samuel] gave it to David as he stood. But when David fell sick he could not stand up to transmit it. He prayed, *But as for You, HASHEM, show me favor and raise me up* in order that I may transmit it to them in its entirety [וַאֲשַׁלְּמָה לָהֶם is derived from לְהַשְׁלִים, *to complete.*]

God heard his plea, *And King David stood up on his feet* (*I Chronicles* 28:2). At that time he transmitted the scroll to Solomon (*Midrash Samuel* Ch. 15; *Aggadas Bereishis* ch. 38; *Yalkut Shimoni, Chronicles,* 1081).

וַאֲשַׁלְּמָה לָהֶם — *Then I shall repay them. Radak* observes that David threatened to repay their evil measure for measure. He awaits the moment of their sickness when he will hurt them by showing no concern for their misery.

Many commentators are troubled by this uncharacteristic and inappropriate vengefulness. However, *Sforno* explains, that as king, David was required to act in this unforgiving fashion. The *Talmud* (*Yoma* 22b) severely criticizes David's predecessor, King Saul, for being unconcerned over the preservation of his honor, as Scripture testifies, *And they degraded him and brought him no gifts, but he made himself mute* (*I Samuel* 10:27). [This was one of the reasons why Saul was eventually removed from the throne, for a king's dignity is not his personal concern, but

יב וָאֶשְׁלְמָה לָהֶם: בְּזֹאת יָדַעְתִּי כִּי־חָפַצְתָּ
יג בִּי כִּי לֹא־יָרִיעַ אֹיְבִי עָלָי: וַאֲנִי בְּתֻמִּי
יד תָּמַכְתָּ בִּי וַתַּצִּיבֵנִי לְפָנֶיךָ לְעוֹלָם: בָּרוּךְ
יְהֹוָה | אֱלֹהֵי יִשְׂרָאֵל מֵהָעוֹלָם וְעַד־
הָעוֹלָם אָמֵן | וְאָמֵן:

a reflection of the national honor.]

Radak quotes *Rav Saadya Gaon* who interprets David's vow to repay his enemies in a merciful light. Indeed David vows to reciprocate their animosity — but not with vengeance. He pledges to pay them with kindness and charity [which will change their malicious attitude toward him]. This was typical of David's generous spirit.

This view is supported by *Midrash Shocher Tov*: God asked David, 'With what do you wish Me to repay them, with evil?' 'Heaven forbid' David replied. 'Is it not true that *when they* (my enemies) *made sick my clothing was sackcloth?* (35:13). Despite the fact that when I was sick they prayed that I perish, I fervently pleaded for their recovery. Furthermore, *I afflicted myself with fasting (ibid.).* And lest someone suspect that I was insincere and really prayed for their injury, then *As for my prayer, upon my own bosom let it return (ibid.),* and let that harm come upon me.' Therefore, David prayed here, *HASHEM show me favor and raise me up* [for if I fall they will interpret this as a sign that I did not pray on their behalf].

Finally, *Shaarei Chaim* suggests the following interpretation of David's request. As we have commented on the verse: *Many are the pains of the wicked* (32:10), the most intense and annoying pain is experienced by the wicked man who sees the success of *one who trusts in HASHEM (ibid.).*

Similarly, David asks here, *HASHEM show me favor and raise me up,* and this display of my good fortune will

frustrate my enemy so greatly that in this fashion *I shall repay them.*

12. בְּזֹאת יָדַעְתִּי כִּי חָפַצְתָּ בִּי — *By this shall I know that You are pleased with me.*

When You will lift me from my sick-bed and will not allow my enemies to triumph over me (*Rashi*).

Midrash Shocher Tov continues (see v. 11): God said to David, 'Since you do not desire revenge against your enemies, your generosity of spirit is a sign *by which I know that you are pleased with Me* and that you truly desire to follow in My merciful ways.

כִּי לֹא יָרִיעַ אֹיְבִי עָלָי — *That You will not let my foe applaud* [lit. shout triumphantly] *over me.*

You will not allow him to rejoice while he casts derision against me with arrogant words of scorn (*Radak*).

Sforno explains: Although David did not win every battle in his long military career, he was never defeated so decisively that his enemies could blow their trumpets triumphantly to applaud his defeat.

13. וַאֲנִי בְּתֻמִּי תָּמַכְתָּ בִּי — *Because of my integrity You have supported me.*

After You found my integrity and faith to be flawless *You supported me* to help me rise from my sick-bed (*Radak*).

I fulfilled the dictates of the Torah which is perfect (19:8) and I asked יְהִי לִבִּי תָמִים בְּחֻקֶּיךָ, *Let my heart be perfect in fulfilling Your statutes* [119:80] (*Midrash Shocher Tov*).

[Similarly, David said וַאֲנִי בְּתֻמִּי אֵלֵךְ, *As for me, I go in my perfect*

12 By this shall I know that You are pleased with me;
that You will not let my foe applaud over me.
13 Because of my integrity You have supported me,
and let me stand erect before You forever.
14 Blessed be HASHEM, the God of Israel,
from This World to the World to Come,
Amen and Amen!

---

innocence, redeem me and show me favor (26:11).]

The man who studies religion philosophically admits to faith only because it appeals to his personal logic and mentality. Therefore his 'faith' is a mere delusion, for essentially he worships only his own intellect! It stands to reason that since he believes only in himself, he must help himself. But the perfectly innocent believer who trusts in God with simple, unquestioning faith, certainly deserves divine support, for God alone is the pillar of his existence (Shaarei Chaim).

וַתַּצִּיבֵנִי לְפָנֶיךָ לְעוֹלָם — And let me stand erect before You forever.

לְעוֹלָם, forever, refers to the full term of a normal human lifetime. The sick man asks to live out all of his days fortified with divine support (Radak).

You gave me the strength to stand erect while transmitting the scroll of the Beis HaMikdash (Brisker Rav).

[The word לְעוֹלָם alludes to the Temple. The Noda B'Yehuda (II Orach Chaim 87) cites many sources to prove that whenever Scripture uses the phrase חֻקַּת עוֹלָם it should not be translated as An eternal statute but rather as, A

statute for the Eternal House, meaning the Temple.]

14. בָּרוּךְ ה' אֱלֹהֵי יִשְׂרָאֵל — Blessed be HASHEM, the God of Israel.

The invalid vows to bless God in these terms when he arises from his sickbed (Rashi).

With this verse David concludes the first of the five Books of Psalms. Therefore he offers thanks to the Lord for providing him with the inspiration and strength to accomplish this great undertaking (Metzudas David; Ibn Yachya, Yaavetz Hadoresh).

Furthermore, David prays that all of the praises and blessings which he included in this Book should reverberate from the lips of all Israel from now until the Hereafter (Malbim).

מֵהָעוֹלָם וְעַד הָעוֹלָם — From This World to the World to Come.

From the beginning of time until the very end of time (Radak).

Hashem, who is only God of Israel in This World is destined to be acknowledged and blessed by all mankind in the World to Come (Zera Yaakov).[1]

אָמֵן וְאָמֵן — Amen and Amen!

[אָמֵן is derived from the word אֱמוּנָה,

---

1. Rashi (Berachos 63a, s.v. וַיְבָרְכוּ שֵׁם כְּבוֹדְךָ) quotes the Tosefta which explains: This phrase is a proclamation that This World is merely a פְּרוֹזְדוֹר, corridor, leading to the טְרַקְלִין, main chamber, which is the World to Come. Therefore, practice and accustom yourself to recite God's praises in this temporary world so that you will be prepared to praise Him eternally in the permanent world which has no end! [The entirety of our brief earthly sojourn is no more than a preparation for the meaningful life of the Hereafter. The perfection of our existence there depends on the quality of our preparations here.]

Rabbi Chaim of Volozhin, in a gloss to Nefesh haChaim 1:6, explains that the Temple is the point where the two worlds meet. Since the Divine Presence dwells there, this world of matter

faith. By saying *Amen*, one declares, 'I firmly believe all of the aforementioned to be true.']

From the repetitive *Amen* of our verse, Rabbi Yehuda derives: Whoever answers *Amen* in This World will be privileged to answer *Amen* in the World to Come! *(Midrash Tanchuma).*

[Similarly, the *Talmud (Berachos* 4b) promises, Whoever recites תְּהִלָּה לְדָוִד, *the Hymn of David,* three times a day in This World will certainly merit a place in the World to Come. For the Hereafter is an endless hymn dedicated to our Maker, and the *Psalms of David* are the text of that eternal hymn.]

and the future world of the spirit blend there and become one. For that reason one of the benedictions recited during the service in the First Temple concluded with the words בָּרוּךְ ה' אֱלֹהֵי יִשְׂרָאֵל עַד הָעוֹלָם, *Blessed be* HASHEM, *the God of Israel until* [the End of] *the World* [singular]. This alluded to the above-mentioned fusion of both worlds in the Temple.

Second Book / ספר שני

מזמור מב 42

Ten men contributed songs to the Book of Psalms: Adam,
Malchizedek, Abraham, Moses, Heiman, Yedusun, Assaf and the
three sons of Korach (Rashi, Psalms 1:1). The entire First Book of
Tehillim (Psalms 1-41) is attributed to David. The Second Book of
Tehillim begins with a series of eight psalms (42:49) ascribed to the
sons of Korach. In the Third Book of Tehillim, another four psalms
(84, 885, 887, 88) appear in their name. The sons of Korach were As-
sir, Elkanah and Aviassaf (Exodus 6:24).

Rashi (v. 1) states that Korach's sons initially joined their father's
infamous mutiny against Moses and Aaron. In the midst of the
rebellion, however, they realized their folly and repented. When the
earth opened its mouth to swallow the entire assembly of Korach and
to transport them to Gehinnom, God miraculously provided a place
of refuge for Korach's three sons. They landed on an elevated niche
within the earth, high above the flames of purgatory. It was on that
precarious ledge that they composed these psalms.

When they ascended to the earth's surface, a holy spirit descended
upon them and they prophesied concerning the exiles of Israel, the
destruction of the Temple, and the advent of the Davidic monarchy.

Centuries later the descendants of Korach's sons still retained the
divine inspiration created by this miraculous deliverance. Korach's
descendants were the staunchest advocates of that very work of
Moses which Korach had planned to destroy by his mutiny. (Hirsch).

According to the Vilna Gaon, this psalm is the Song of the Day for
the second day of the Sukkos festival (Maaseh Rav 234). [The
שִׂמְחַת בֵּית הַשּׁוֹאֵבָה, The Festival of the Water Drawing, began on this
day in the Temple. The eighth verse refers specifically to this
celebration; many other references to water-springs and Temple
celebrations are found throughout the psalm.]

לַמְנַצֵּחַ מַשְׂכִּיל לִבְנֵי־קֹרַח: כְּאַיָּל תַּעֲרֹג
עַל־אֲפִיקֵי־מָיִם כֵּן נַפְשִׁי תַעֲרֹג אֵלֶיךָ

1. לַמְנַצֵּחַ מַשְׂכִּיל — *For the conductor, a Maskil* [see *comm.* to 32:1].

This psalm is of such universal significance that it is dedicated as a מַשְׂכִּיל *instruction*, for all to hear (Hirsch).

לִבְנֵי קֹרַח — *By the sons of Korach* [See Prefatory Remarks].

The Prophet Samuel was a descendant of Korach. Samuel's grandson was Heiman ben Yoel (I *Chronicles* 6:18) and he had fourteen sons, who were the Levites chosen by David to be the nucleus of the Temple choir and orchestra (I *Chronicles* 25:4-6). Ibn Ezra, suggests that they are the *sons of Korach* mentioned throughout the Book of *Psalms*. [See 88:1: — *A song with music ... for the sons of Korach, A Maskil unto Heiman Haezrachi.*]

Radak cites Ibn Ezra's opinion and asks why these Levites should identify themselves with the evil Korach when they could trace their genealogy to their illustrious ancestor Samuel the prophet? *Meiri* explains that despite his tragic quarrel with Moses, Korach had been the most distinguished of all the Levites; therefore it was a great honor to be his descendant.

If we assume that these *sons of Korach* were indeed David's contemporaries, it is very possible that they were not the *composers* of these psalms, but merely the *performers*. Perhaps David himself wrote them and gave them to the *sons of Korach* for inclusion in the Temple service. Some say that David created these psalms while he was a forlorn fugitive in the land of the Philistines [see Prefatory Remarks to Psalm 34]. Others say that he foretold future exiles of the entire Jewish nation. (Radak).

In reference to the opinion that בְּנֵי קֹרַח are the actual *sons of Korach* who lived at the time of Moses, Ibn Yachya

explains that when David was composing the *Book of Tehillim* he found manuscripts from centuries earlier including the works of the *sons of Korach*. David chose the most appropriate psalms and rewrote them in his own universal style.

Radak raises a question concerning the joint authorship of these psalms: How is it possible that these three men were inspired to say the same words at the same time? *Ibn Yachya* explains that when David found old manuscripts, the individual authors of the respective psalms were not recorded, so David attributed the psalms to Korach's sons as a group. *Midrash Shocher Tov* reveals that when Korach's sons were snatched at the last moment from the flames of Gehinnom, they repented simultaneously with equal fervor and sincerity. Thus united, their hearts were inspired with identical prophecies and psalms.

2. כְּאַיָּל תַּעֲרֹג — *As the hart entreats.*

Rashi notes the grammatical inconsistency in these words: אַיָּל is the male *hart*, but the verb תַּעֲרֹג is feminine.

This intentional discrepancy alludes to the longing cries of both the אַיָּל (male) *hart* and the אַיָּלָה (female) *hind*.

The Rabbis said that the hart is the kindest and most devout of all animals. When the other beasts and animals are thirsty, they gather around the hart, prodding him to supplicate Heaven. The hart then digs a hole in the earth, inserts his horns, and screams in anguish. The Holy One, Blessed be He, takes pity on him and sends water from the תְּהוֹם *the watery deep* [see verse 8].

The hind possesses an anatomical peculiarity. Its womb and birth canal are too small to allow for the birth of its young. During labor the helpless hind cries out in agony. The Holy One, Blessed be He, has mercy on her; he dispatches a snake to bite her in the area of

For the Conductor,
  a Maskil by the sons of Korach.
² As the hart entreats by the springs of water,
  so does my soul entreat You, O God.

her womb. This sudden stab of pain causes a muscle spasm which opens her womb so that the fawn can emerge safely.

Hirsch observes that the female gender is used to indicate that the hart's thirst has caused him to become extremely weak.

Rashi points out that the verb ערג refers specifically to the unique cry of the hart. The Hebrew language has specific words to describe the sounds peculiar to individual animals; examples include: נהם *roar* [lion], שוקק *growl* [bear], געה *low* [cattle], and צפצוף *chirp* [bird].

Hirsch notes that ערג is used in reference to animals in general in the verse גַּם בַּהֲמוֹת שָׂדֶה תַּעֲרוֹג אֵלֶיךָ כִּי יָבְשׁוּ אֲפִיקֵי מָיִם, *Also, the animals of the field entreat You, for the springs of water have gone dry (Joel 1:20)*. Here too, ערג is the cry of the animal thirsting for water.

Tzofnas Pa'aneach explains that although all creatures long for water, the hart becomes more parched than the others because it dwells in the arid wilderness.

עַל אֲפִיקֵי מָיִם — *By* [lit. *on*] *the springs of water.*

This refers to the springs of water which the thirsty hart digs out with his horns (*Rashi*).

The root of this word is פוק, *to emerge, to come forth*, which describes the water gushing forth from the ground (*Hirsch*).

The hart often swallows snakes whose poison causes an intense heat within its stomach. Therefore, it seeks out a spring of water in a desperate attempt to cool off. Some say that the harts are relentlessly pursued by packs of dogs. The pitiful deer run until they find a deep stream of water. They cry out and plunge into the cool water, which refreshes them and provides concealment from the dogs (*Radak*).

The poisonous snakes which the hart reputedly swallows symbolize the venomous hatred of the gentiles which Israel is forced to 'swallow' and endure in the exile (*Maharam Markado*).

כֵּן נַפְשִׁי תַעֲרֹג אֵלֶיךָ אֱלֹהִים — *So does my soul entreat You, O God.*

[The sons of Korach were singularly qualified to express such feelings. When they descended toward Gehinnom, they were as alienated from God as man can possibly be. They were truly exiled to the most arid, barren wilderness.]

This psalm echoes the cries of Israel in exile and in captivity. Their yearning for freedom is not prompted by a desire to exercise political power or to take revenge on their enemies. Their sole desire is to refresh themselves in the pure waters of God's Torah (*Mahari Yaavetz Hadoresh*).

At that same time the soul of Israel will be released from its shackles and will soar heavenward like a gushing geyser (*Hirsch*).

Although the hart is very thirsty, it unselfishly seeks enough water to quench the thirst of the other animals, as well. Similarly, the exiles of Israel do not seek redemption solely for their own sake. They yearn to bring all of mankind close to God in order to satisfy the universal thirst for the divine (*Alshich*).

ג אֱלֹהִים: צָמְאָה נַפְשִׁי | לֵאלֹהִים לְאֵל חָי
ד מָתַי אָבוֹא וְאֵרָאֶה פְּנֵי אֱלֹהִים: הָיְתָה־לִּי
דִמְעָתִי לֶחֶם יוֹמָם וָלַיְלָה בֶּאֱמֹר אֵלַי
ה כָּל־הַיּוֹם אַיֵּה אֱלֹהֶיךָ: אֵלֶּה אֶזְכְּרָה |
וְאֶשְׁפְּכָה עָלַי | נַפְשִׁי כִּי אֶעֱבֹר | בַּסָּךְ

3. צָמְאָה נַפְשִׁי לֵאלֹהִים — *My soul thirsts for God.*

Israel's craving is described as *thirst* rather than as *hunger*, because water is more essential than food for the maintenance of life. A man can live without food for a few days, but he cannot survive without water. And the soul's thirst for God is even more intense than the body's craving for water (Radak).

The perception of God achieved through Torah study is likened to drinking water. As the prophet says: הוֹי כָּל צָמֵא לְכוּ לַמַּיִם, *Ho, every one who thirsts, go to water* (Isaiah 55:1).

The congregation of Israel called out these words during the Babylonian Exile (Rashi).

For what do I thirst? Not for food and not for drink — only to see Your face, O God! (Midrash Shocher Tov).

I yearn to return to the level of sanctity which I attained at Sinai, when God Himself testified that I [Israel] merited the title אֱלֹהִים: *I said you are* אֱלֹהִים, *angels* [lit. *'gods'*] [82:6] (Pesikta Rabbasi 1:2).

I yearn to see You exercise Your Divine Attribute of Justice (symbolized by Your Name אֱלֹהִים) against the gentiles on the final day of reckoning (Pesikta Rabbosi).

לְאֵל חָי — *For the living God.*

Our soul craves contact with the *Living God* as opposed to the lifeless idols of the surrounding peoples (Radak; Hirsch).

Hashem Himself is the source of Israel's vitality, as Scripture testifies: וְאַתֶּם הַדְּבֵקִים בַּה׳ אֱלֹהֵיכֶם חַיִּים כֻּלְּכֶם הַיּוֹם *But you who cleave unto Hashem your God, are alive all of your today* (Deut. 4:4). The yearning for God is as strong as the lust for life itself (Malbim).

מָתַי אָבוֹא — *When shall I arrive?*

When shall I ascend to Jerusalem as a pilgrim celebrating the three annual festivals close to God? The Psalmist prophetically foretells the three nations destined to disrupt the Temple service: Babylon, Greece, and Rome. In all three instances, Israel will cry out for salvation and God will respond affirmatively (Rashi).

וְאֵרָאֶה פְּנֵי אֱלֹהִים — *And appear before God* [lit. *and be seen before the face of God*].

At the time of the festival, Israel comes to 'see' God's presence in the Beis Hamikdash and to 'be seen' by God. Hashem reciprocates the intensity of a person's desire to see God in the extent to which He grants that individual His הַשְׁגָּחָה, *Providence* (Nora Tehillos).

Maharam Almosnino translates thus: *and cause the face of God to be seen through me.* The יָשָׁר *upright man*, is a reflection of God's image. All who gaze at this man will glimpse the perfection of the Almighty.

Scripture attests to the fact that certain people are a reflection of God: רָאִיתִי פָנֶיךָ כִּרְאֹת פְּנֵי אֱלֹהִים *I have seen your face as if it were the face of God* (Genesis 33:10).

4. הָיְתָה לִּי דִמְעָתִי לֶחֶם — *For me, my tears were sustenance* [lit. *My tear was bread for me*].

From here we learn that weeping satisfies a person's hunger so that he no

³ *My soul thirsts for God, the living God.*
    When shall I come and appear before God?
⁴ *For me my tears were sustenance*
    day and night,
As they taunt me all day long,
    'Where is your God?'
⁵ *These do I recall and pour out my soul within me,*
    how I passed with the throng,

longer desires to eat. Similarly, when Chana cried bitterly because of her barreness, וַתִּבְכֶּה וְלֹא תֹאכַל, *She cried and did not eat* [I Samuel 1:7] (*Rashi*).

Israel's desire for God is so all-encompassing that we yearn for no other nourishment (*Hirsch*).

Two of Israel's most significant spiritual acts are likened to bread. The Temple sacrifices are termed קָרְבָּנִי לַחְמִי, *My sacrifice, My bread* (Num. 28:2) and Torah study is compared to the staff of life, לְכוּ לַחֲמוּ בְלַחְמִי, *Go forth and partake of my bread* (Proverbs 9:5). In exile Israel is deprived of three prime sources of spiritual nourishment. Then the desolate nation has nothing but bitter tears to satisfy its hunger for God (*Malbim*).

In 80:6 we read הֶאֱכַלְתָּם לֶחֶם דִּמְעָה וַתַּשְׁקֵמוֹ בִּדְמָעוֹת שָׁלִישׁ, *You fed them the bread of tears, You had them drink — the tears of a third.* Rashi quotes two interpretations. The first: this describes the seventy years of the Babylonian exile, which lasted only one-third of the duration of the Jews' 210 year bondage in Egypt. According to the second explanation (based on *Midrash Shocher Tov*), the verse refers to the exile imposed by the Romans, who were descendants of Esau. Three tears came to Esau's eyes (when he realized that Jacob had received Isaac's blessings). One teardrop fell from each eye, but the שָׁלִישׁ, *the third one,* remained unshed. The congregation of Israel exclaimed, 'Sovereign of the Universe, because

Esau cried but three tears Your pity was aroused and You gave him a pleasant existence and mastery over the entire world. When You recognize the humiliation of Your sons, who cry incessantly [as attested by this verse: *My tears are my sustenance by day and by night*], You will certainly be overwhelmed with pity for their terrible plight.

בְּאֱמֹר אֵלַי כָּל הַיּוֹם — *As they taunt me all day long* [lit. *when it is said to me all the day*]

The foe taunts me incessantly throughout the long period of exile (*Radak*).

אַיֵּה אֱלֹהֶיךָ — *Where is your God?*

If He is truly the Almighty God and if you sincerely serve Him, then why does He allow you to languish in the misery of exile? (*Radak*).

5. אֵלֶּה אֶזְכְּרָה — *These do I recall.*

The Psalmist speaks for all the exiles, even though many of them were born on foreign soil and didn't personally witness the splendor of the main pilgrimage to the Holy Temple. This is because those exiles became the repository of their forefathers' experiences in the Land of Israel (*Radak*).

וְאֶשְׁפְּכָה עָלַי נַפְשִׁי — *And pour out my soul within me* [lit. *And I pour my soul over me*].

Anguish causes my heart, the sanctuary of my soul, to melt like soft wax (*S'forno*).

אֶדַּדֵּם עַד־בֵּית אֱלֹהִים בְּקוֹל־רִנָּה וְתוֹדָה
הָמוֹן חוֹגֵג: מַה־תִּשְׁתּוֹחֲחִי | נַפְשִׁי וַתֶּהֱמִי
עָלָי הוֹחִלִי לֵאלֹהִים כִּי־עוֹד אוֹדֶנּוּ

Israel laments, 'I am in exile because my body rebelled against God and refused to do His bidding. Therefore I now pour out my soul in order to permeate my body with a new spirit of sanctity and obedience to God.' (Tehillas Hashem).

כִּי אֶעֱבֹר בַּסָּךְ — How I passed with the throng.

The word סָךְ, has several meanings: It has been translated as a partition, referring to separate groups of pilgrims (see Hirsch below). סָךְ also means a sum, a total, again referring to vast numbers of people on their pilgrimage route. It is also related to סֻכָּה and סָכָךְ, a covering and refers to the covered wagons in which people traveled to Jerusalem (Rashi).

Hirsch elaborates on Rashi's first translation rendering the words כִּי אֶעֱבֹר בַּסָּךְ as How I passed over all partitions. Israel remembers the pinnacle of its ancient glory, when the whole nation assembled for its pilgrim festivals in God's Holy Sanctuary in Jerusalem. Unified by this mandatory pilgrimage, Jews from all walks of life paid homage to God and to His Torah. Their unity transcended all barriers of social status, wealth, ability, and occupation which usually divide citizens. Thus the festival pilgrimages created a cohesive Jewish community which literally passed over all partitions.

אֶדַּדֵּם — Walking gingerly with them.

A mother's efforts to help her baby take his halting first steps are described as מִדְּדָה. The same term is used to describe the assistance given a new-born calf or foal to attempt its first wobbly paces (Rashi).

Menachem contends that this is a cognate of יְדִיד, dear friend, and indicates the bonds of friendship which united the pilgrims.

Dunash relates אֶדַּדֵּם to דְּמָמָה, silence, as in דֹּם לַה' be mute before HASHEM (37:7). The throngs kept silent until they neared the Temple Mount. Then, they suddenly burst into ecstatic song.

הָמוֹן חוֹגֵג — A celebrating multitude.

According to Sforno, this describes those who returned from the Babylonian exile to witness the newly-rebuilt Beis Hamikdash, which was vastly inferior to the grandeur of the First Temple. The הָמוֹן, the multitude, i.e. the younger people who were born in exile after the destruction of the First Beis Hamikdash, were unaware of the differences between the two Temples, so they were חוֹגֵג, celebrating joyously at the time of the Second Temple's inauguration. But the few elders who remembered the splendor of the original Temple wept (Ezra 3:13; see comm. to 30:1).

The pilgrims came to offer the קָרְבָּן חֲגִיגָה, the Sacrifice of Festival Celebration, in the Temple (Radak).

The word חוֹגֵג is related to מָחוֹג, a circle. It refers to dancing in circles and celebration, as in Eating and drinking and חוֹגְגִים, dancing [I Sam. 30:16] (Metzudas David, Malbim, Radak).

1. The congregation of Israel laments before the Holy One, Blessed be He:
In the past, I ascended to Jerusalem on well-paved roads, but now I travel on a neglected path of thorns, as the prophet says, Behold, I will hedge your way with thorns' (Hosea 2:8). In the past, great trees were סוֹכֵךְ, shading, the roads to the Holy City, but now the path is barren and open to the blazing sun. In the past, I went in the shadow of God's protection, but now I

XLII
6

Walking gingerly with them up to
the House of God
With joyous song and thanks
a celebrating multitude.
⁶ *Why are you downcast, my soul,*
and why do you yearn for me? Anticipate God!
For I shall yet thank Him

6. תִּשְׁתּוֹחֲחִי — *Downcast* [lit. *Bowed down, bent over*] (*Metzudas Zion*).

This is a cognate of שָׁחָה, as in כִּי שָׁחָה לֶעָפָר נַפְשֵׁנוּ, *For our souls are cast down to the dust* (44:26). Here it is in the passive form, as the Psalmist inquires of his soul, 'What is the outside force which has cast you into despair?' (*Rashi*).

When my soul was stricken with grief because of its estrangement from its homeland, I sought to console it, asking, 'Why are you so downcast? Wait for God's imminent salvation!' (*Radak*).

Rashi to v. 3 notes that in this psalm and the next, the query מַה תִּשְׁתּוֹחֲחִי appears three times (42:6, 42:12, and 43:5), corresponding to the three nations which were to subjugate Israel and make the Jews *downcast*. Babylon, Greece, and Rome would put a halt to the Temple service, but each time the Jewish people will cry out to God and be redeemed.

וַתֶּהֱמִי עָלָי — *And* [*why do*] *you yearn for me* [see comm. of Rashi and Radak to 39:7].

Some say that the Psalmist is chastising his own soul for its selfishness. You cry and yearn all day for your own welfare and salvation, but never consider the glory of God, which is sunk in disgrace because His nation suffers in exile! Stop thinking only about yourself! הוֹחִילִי לֵאלֹהִים, *wait for God* and be concerned about His redemption from ignominy (*Shevet M'Yisroel*).[1]

הוֹחִילִי לֵאלֹהִים — *Anticipate God!* Wait hopefully for God's ultimate redemption (*Rashi*).

Do not yearn only for ה' *the Attribute of Mercy*, but wait also for אֱלֹהִים, *the Attribute of Strict Justice*. You will, *thank Him for the salvation which comes from His Presence* through the afflictions which He sends to cleanse you (*Tehillas Hashem*).

am at the mercy of the gentile government. Alas! These things do I recall!

'In the past, I arose early and ascended with a basket of בִּכּוּרִים, *first fruits*, on my head and with God's praise on my lips. But now these same roads are desolate and still. I ascend in dead silence and I descend in dead silence. Alas! These things do I recall!

'In the past, I went up with *loud rejoicing and thanksgiving*, but now I ascend and descend in tears. In the past, I traveled with throngs and multitudes of people. But now I walk alone. Alas! These things do I recall!' (*Midrash Eichah Rabbasi* 1:52).

1. [In his rapturous Sabbath poem לְכָה דוֹדִי, *L'cha Dodi*, Rabbi Shlomo HaLevi Alkavetz paraphrases the words of this verse in the stanza:

לֹא תֵבוֹשִׁי וְלֹא תִכָּלְמִי מַה תִּשְׁתּוֹחֲחִי וּמַה תֶּהֱמִי בָּךְ יֶחֱסוּ עֲנִיֵּי עַמִּי וְנִבְנְתָה עִיר עַל תִּלָּהּ, *You shall not be put to shame, nor shall you be disgraced! Why are you downcast, and why do you moan in yearning? The poor of my people find protection with You, and the city shall be rebuilt upon its ruins!*]

ז יְשׁוּעֹת פָּנָיו: אֱלֹהַי עָלַי נַפְשִׁי תִשְׁתּוֹחָח
עַל־כֵּן אֶזְכָּרְךָ מֵאֶרֶץ יַרְדֵּן וְחֶרְמוֹנִים
ח מֵהַר מִצְעָר: תְּהוֹם־אֶל־תְּהוֹם קוֹרֵא
לְקוֹל צִנּוֹרֶיךָ כָּל־מִשְׁבָּרֶיךָ וְגַלֶּיךָ עָלַי

יְשׁוּעֹת פָּנָיו — [For] salvations of His
Presence [lit. countenance; face.]

At the end of this psalm, we find a
variation of this phrase יְשׁוּעֹת פָּנַי, [lit-
erally the salvation (which comes from)
'my' countenance]. This implies that
there are two possible causes of redemption. If Israel is worthy, then the salvation comes from my [Israel's]
Presence. But if the Jewish Nation is
not worthy, then it must rely on God in
His mercy to send the salvations which
come from His Presence (Otzar
Nechmad).

7. אֱלֹהַי עָלַי נַפְשִׁי תִשְׁתּוֹחָח — O my God,
within me my soul is downcast.

The congregation of Israel said, 'I am
filled with envy when I see the gentile
nations dwelling in tranquility although
they anger You with their wicked deeds.
They remain undisturbed while my soul
is poured out in tragedy and misfortune' (Midrash Shocher Tov).

The Talmud (Kesubos 110b) states:
Whoever lives outside of Eretz Yisrael is
like a man who has no אֱלוֹהַ, God [i.e.,
in exile one does not enjoy God's direct
supervision and interest.] Therefore I
yearn to return to Eretz Yisrael so that I
can again address You as אֱלֹהַי, my God!
As long as I cannot do so, my soul is
downcast (Chazah Zion).

עַל כֵּן אֶזְכָּרְךָ מֵאֶרֶץ יַרְדֵּן — Because I
remember you — from the land of
Jordan [i.e., I am downcast because I
remember how kind You were to us
when we came from across the Jordan].

[When I witness Your generosity
towards the gentiles] I remember that
we, the Children of Israel also angered

You with our misdeeds when we were
on the eastern banks of the Jordan. Nevertheless, You mercifully overlooked
these offenses and miraculously split
the Jordan so that we could cross into
the Land of Israel. [Why do You now
treat us with such severity and un-
bending strictness?] (Rashi).

I remember how the pilgrims would
gather from the distant communities
located on the other side of the Jordan
and on the peaks of Hermon to ascend
to Jerusalem for the festival (Radak).

וְחֶרְמוֹנִים — And Hermon's peaks
(Targum).

The people of Sidom called Hermon,
Sirion, and the Amorites called it Senir
(Deut. 3:9). [This is the snow-capped
mountain range in northern Eretz
Yisroel which is located on the present
day border with Lebanon and Syria (see
Song of Songs 4:8).]

מֵהַר מִצְעָר — From Mount Mitzor.

This describes Mount Sinai, which is
low and young (צָעִיר) in comparison
with other mountains (Targum; Rashi).

[The Talmud (Sotah 5a) elaborates:
God prefers the lowly, for He passed
over the high mountains and set His
Holy Presence to rest only on Mount
Sinai. Nevertheless, Mount Sinai did
not become proud. (See also Bamidbar
Rabbah 13:4). Furthermore, Sinai was
responsible for making Israel young
(צָעִיר) again, as the Midrash (Shir
HaShirim Rabbah 8:1) says: Scriptures
refer to Mount Sinai as בֵּית אִמִּי, My
mother's house (Song of Songs 3:4)
because it was there that Israel became
purified like a new-born child.]

for salvations of His Presence.

⁷ O my God, within me my soul is downcast,
    because I remember You —
From the land of Jordan and Hermon's peaks,
    from Mount Mitzor.
⁸ Watery deep to watery deep
    calls out to the roar of Your torrents,
All Your breakers and Your waves
    have swept over me.

Although we angered You at Sinai with the construction of the Golden Calf, You forgave our sins and accompanied us. Why then do you forsake us now that we are in exile? (Rashi).

8. תְּהוֹם אֶל תְּהוֹם קוֹרֵא — Watery deep to watery deep calls out.

One deep misfortune calls out to the next [which follows in rapid succession] (Rashi).

Before I have a chance to extricate myself from one problem, another problem develops (Metzudas David).

The Psalmist often likens tragedies to streams of water, as we read: וְנַחֲלֵי בְלִיַּעַל יְבַעֲתוּנִי, And torrents of Godless men frighten me (Psalms 18:5). These are the anguished feelings of the Psalmist as he pours out his soul over the plight of Israel in exile (Radak).

The Targum renders:, 'The upper [celestial] waters call to the lower [terrestrial] waters.'

[This alludes to the water cycle which governs all of human existence. Precipitation gathers and falls to earth as rain, which is absorbed into the earth. Later this moisture evaporates and rises upward again. On the Festival of Sukkos a water libation (נִיסוּךְ הַמַּיִם) symbolizing the upper celestial waters is poured from a spout in the side of the Temple altar and descends to the depths of the Temple Mount, to mingle with the lower terrestrial waters. This demonstrates that these two water sources are inextricably intertwined. The Talmud (Taanis 25b) bases the ritual on our verse (Maharsha, ibid.)

לְקוֹל צִנּוֹרֶיךָ — To the roar of Your torrents [lit. To the sound of Your water canals.]

[A צִנּוֹר is a duct, pipe, or gutter which channels a flow of water in a certain direction. Rashi renders it in old French as 'canals.']

Punishments rain down on me as from a flowing pipeline (Rashi). This torrent of punishment resembles rainwater which descends with great force and with a loud noise from gutters on the roofs. Also, the rainclouds with precipitation gushing down from them resemble water channels. The abundance of my woes, too may be likened to the gushing rain descending from these clouds (Radak).

כָּל מִשְׁבָּרֶיךָ — All Your breakers.

These are the towering waves which at first rise high above the surface and then smash down into foam and spray (Rashi).

[This refers figuratively to the violent catastrophes which shatter Israel in its exile.]

וְגַלֶּיךָ — Your waves.

[These are the calm waves which roll in smoothly like a גַּלְגַּל, wheel. Their flow is not tempestuous, but constant. This refers to the incessant discrimination which hounds Israel.]

ט עָבָרוּ: יוֹמָם | יְצַוֶּה יהוה | חַסְדּוֹ וּבַלַּיְלָה
י שִׁירֹה עִמִּי תְּפִלָּה לְאֵל חַיָּי: אוֹמְרָה לְאֵל
סַלְעִי לָמָה שְׁכַחְתָּנִי לָמָּה־קֹדֵר אֵלֵךְ
יא בְּלַחַץ אוֹיֵב: בְּרֶצַח | בְּעַצְמוֹתַי חֵרְפוּנִי

[The outpourings from the heart of King David struck responsive chords in every Jew in distress. The prophet Jonah, for example, drew on significant portions of the idioms and phrases from *Psalms* in his prayer to God from the belly of the fish. See specifically *Jonah* 2:5: *Your breakers and Your waves all swept over me.*

9. חַסְדּוֹ ה' יְצַוֶּה יוֹמָם — *Let dawn Arrive! — May HASHEM command His loving-kindness.*

Let the dawn of redemption shine forth and let God bestow His mercy upon us! (*Rashi*).

The Psalmist heartens the exiled and persecuted Nation of Israel by foretelling its bright future (*Radak*).

These words also refer to the pilgrims during the time of the Temple. As the masses marched all day towards Jerusalem, God provided for their needs. When they encamped at night, each one would sing of the Divine God's חֶסֶד, *lovingkindness*, which he had experienced during the day.[1]

וּבַלַּיְלָה — *But by night.*

Although we pray for the *dawn* of redemption, we pray that even while we are still submerged in the *night* of exile, may God allow His Presence to rest upon us (*Rashi*).

שִׁירֹה עִמִּי — *May His resting place be with me.*

Rashi bases this translation upon the מְסוֹרֶת הַגְּדוֹלָה, *the Great Tradition,* which, among the lists of homonyms, cites the word שִׁירֹה, as in our verse, with the word שִׁירוֹ (I *Kings* 5:12 where it definitely means *his song*). Thus, *it is clear that* שִׁירֹה does *not refer to song;* another meaning must, therefore, be sought. We find that the *Targum* of וַיִּחַן שָׁם יִשְׂרָאֵל, *'And Israel camped there,'* (*Exodus* 19:2) is שְׁרָא יִשְׂרָאֵל. Therefore, in our verse, שִׁירֹה can be interpreted as a noun meaning *place of rest.*

Rashi also quotes the *Midrash* which renders שִׁירֹה as *song.* Israel says to the Holy One Blessed be He: 'We recall what You did for us in Egypt; You commanded us to fulfill just one *mitzvah* on the day before Passover, [By day *Hashem commands His loving-*

1. The *Talmud* (*Avodah Zarah* 3b) derives a number of lessons from this verse:
1) By day God Himself engages in acts of *lovingkindness,* i.e. He sustains the world and provides it with food, and teaches Torah to the young. By night He listens to the 'Songs' of the sacred heavenly angels. 2) The devoted scholar who studies Torah deep into the night and *Sings with Me,* i.e. with God, enveloped in an aura of *loving-kindness* throughout the day. 3) One who engages in Torah study in this world, which resembles night, will be enveloped in *loving-kindness* in the Hereafter, which resembles the light of day.
[The earlier two statements may be explained in light of the *Zohar* quoted here by the *Minchas Shai.* 'During the day, God created those angels appointed to perform acts of loving-kindness. At night, He created the angels appointed to sing songs. Men worthy of hearing this celestial song will be enlightened in Torah and will understand the secrets of the past and of the future.' Thus, he who learns Torah deep into the night and in the darkness of this world is blessed with special intellectual illuminations, granted by God's great loving-kindness.]

⁹ Let dawn arrive!
  — May HASHEM command His lovingkindness,
But by night, may His resting place be with me;
  a prayer to the God of my life!
¹⁰ I will say to God:
  'My Rock — Why have You forgotten me?
Why must I walk in gloom
  because of the foe's oppression?'
¹¹ Like a sword in my bones
  are the taunts of my tormentors

kindness]. We fulfilled the mitzvah [of the sacrifice of the lamb], and You redeemed us that very night. Therefore we sang Hallel. Now [during our exile] we fulfill not one, but many commandments — yet You do not redeem us!"

Radak, however, renders שִׁירָה as His song. Thus the Psalmist proclaims that even in the dark night of exile, we sing to God concerning the many acts of loving-kindness which He performed for our forefathers and which He continues to perform for us in exile [although He has not yet redeemed us].

תְּפִלָּה לְאֵל חַיָּי — A prayer to the God of my life!

We pray to the God Who has guarded our lives (Targum) to keep us alive until the advent of the Redeemer, so that we may witness His salvation (Radak).

10. אוֹמְרָה לְאֵל — I will say unto God.

When I address A prayer to the God of my life (v. 9) this is what I will say to Him (Metzudas David).

סַלְעִי — My Rock.

You were my Rock and my tower of might in the past; why do You now abandon me? (Radak, Sforno).

לָמָה שְׁכַחְתָּנִי — Why have You forgotten me?

Why is this exile so very long? It must be that You have forgotten me! (Ibn Ezra).

לָמָה קֹדֵר אֵלֵךְ — Why must I go about in gloom

I am like a mourner who wears dark clothes [and a gloomy expression] (Ibn Ezra).

11. בְּרֶצַח בְּעַצְמוֹתַי חֵרְפוּנִי צֹרְרָי — Like a sword [lit. as a murder weapon] in my bones are the taunts [lit. they have taunted or insulted me] of my tormentors.

The taunts they hurl at me fall like a knife jabbed into my body (Rashi).

When they blaspheme You, O God, and mockingly ask 'Where are You?' I myself am wounded to the core. The עַצְמוֹת 'bones, skeletons' are the body's foundation and epitomize man's essence. רֶצַח is a noun denoting a murder weapon (Radak).

Ibn Yachya interprets the opening words of this verse as a reference to the annihilation of the Torah leaders of Israel who are its עַצְמוֹת, skeleton and support. In the preceding verse, the Psalmist declares, I will say unto God 'My rock! Why have You forgotten me?' That question will be posed when the gentiles murder Israel's Torah leaders.

צוֹרְרַי בְּאָמְרָם אֵלַי כָּל־הַיּוֹם אַיֵּה
יב אֱלֹהֶיךָ: מַה־תִּשְׁתּוֹחֲחִי | נַפְשִׁי וּמַה־
תֶּהֱמִי עָלָי הוֹחִילִי לֵאלֹהִים כִּי־עוֹד
אוֹדֶנּוּ יְשׁוּעֹת פָּנַי וֵאלֹהָי:

בְּאָמְרָם אֵלַי כָּל הַיּוֹם אַיֵּה אֱלֹהֶיךָ — *When
they revile me* [lit. *say to me*] *all day
long: 'Where is your God?'*

[The second part of this verse corresponds to the latter half of the previous
verse. After the slaughter of the Torah
leaders who guide Israel towards God,
the gentiles will cruelly taunt us with
the challenge, *'Where is your God?'* It is
that vicious taunt which stirs my soul to
ask God, *'Why must I go about in
blackness because of the oppression of
the foe?'* (v. 10).]

12. מַה תִּשְׁתּוֹחֲחִי נַפְשִׁי — *Why are you
downcast, my soul?*

[Again the Psalmist comforts his soul,
which is the collective soul of all Israel,
with promises of future good fortune.]

יְשׁוּעֹת — *My salvation* [lit. *'the salvations'*].

פָּנַי — *'My countenance'.*

Since God's Presence still illuminates
my countenance, whom should I fear
and what should I mourn?

The salvation will take place when I
turn *my countenance* towards God, i.e.,

and return to Him with sincere repentance (S'forno).

Radak notes that פָּנַי may be
translated *in my lifetime*, as in the verse
עַל פְּנֵי תֶּרַח אָבִיו, *In the lifetime of
Terach his father* (Gen. 11:28). I still
wait for God to demonstrate this
ultimate salvation in my own lifetime.'

In verse 6 the Psalmist uses the word
פָּנָיו, *His countenance*, whereas here he
uses פָּנַי, *my countenance*. This alludes
to the two tragedies of the long exile.
The first and foremost tragedy is
spiritual: the concealment of פָּנָיו *His*
(God's) *countenance*. Thus, the main
salvation will be the restoration of
God's Presence to the world. Therefore,
in verse 6 יְשׁוּעֹת, *salvations*, is spelled
out in full, to emphasize the primary
significance of the return of God's
Presence. The second tragedy of the exile is the physical catastrophe which
befell Israel. Although Jewish suffering
is a terrible misfortune, the man of faith
realizes that this tragedy is dwarfed by
Israel's even greater spiritual devastation. Therefore, Israel's physical salvation, פָּנַי, *my countenance*, is written
חָסֵר, *incomplete* (יְשֻׁעֹת) to allude to its

When they revile me all day long:
       'Where is your God?'
¹² *Why are you downcast, my soul,*
       and why do you yearn for me?
Anticipate God!
       For I shall yet thank Him — my salvation
       the light of my countenance and my God.

secondary importance *Kehilas Ephraim*).

Hirsch explains the variant readings with profound insight. Often man deludes himself into thinking that God's imperatives are in contradiction to his personal aspirations for a successful life. Man views פָּנָיו, i.e., God's purpose for creation, as incompatible with פְּנֵי, i.e., his own personal goals, although man may subordinate his own desires to Hashem's Will with painful resignation. Israel will ultimately realize that there has never been any conflict between man's own genuine goals and the goals established by God. When

Israel fully understands that Hashem is אֱלֹהַי, *My God*, Whose sole interest is Israel's welfare, then they will see clearly that the direction of *His face* and *my face* are one.

וֵאלֹהָי — *And my God.*

The agony of the exile was greatest when the gentiles taunted us, *'Where is your God?' (v. 11).* The climax of redemption will arrive when Hashem reveals Himself as our God and the nations see it *(Radak; Ibn Ezra).*[1]

This moment will occur when He will accept my repentance and my prayer *(Sforno)*

1. On the twentieth of Tammuz, 1941, the Nazis ordered the Jewish inhabitants of Telshe, Lithuania, to dig their own graves. As they stood in the open pits, the Rav and Rosh Yeshiva of Telshe, HaGaon Rav Avrohom Yitzchak Bloch זצ״ל, led the martyrs of his community in their final declaration of eternal faith, the Shema. *'Hear O Israel, Hashem is our God, Hashem is One!'*

The nazi beasts gleefully taunted the Rav, *'Where is your God now?'*

The Rav replied courageously *'Not only is He my God, He is also your God, and the day will come when you too will realize it!'*

This psalm is a direct continuation of the preceding one (Radak v.
5). Once again the Psalmist expresses his deep yearning for
redemption from the agony of exile.

The devout Jew who mourns the destruction of the Temple and the
long exile of our people arises at midnight to recite Tikkun Chatzos, a
collection of psalms and prayers which reflect the intensity of our
grief.

Tikkun Chatzos is divided into two sections. The first half, Tikkun
Rachel, is a dirge of sorrow and despair, echoing the bitter tears of
Mother Rachel who weeps for her exiled sons [See Pref. Remarks to
Psalms 79 and 137.]

The second section, Tikkun Yaakov and Leah, reveals a ray of
hope for Israel's future (Siddur Otzar HaTefillos). The Patriarch
Yaakov was never separated from his first wife, Leah; even in death
the couple did not part, for their remains were interred, side by side,
in the Cave of Machpelah.

This symbolizes the inseparable ties which link Israel to God. Even
the apparent death of the nation, its exile from its homeland, has not
severed the bond of love which unites Israel with the Almighty.

Therefore, Tikkun Yaakov and Leah begins with Psalms 42 and 43
which tell of Israel's thirst for God, a thirst which goes undiminished
and unquenched throughout the endless years of exile. Israel awaits
with hope the day when it will publicly be wed to its Eternal Partner
in the Holy Temple.

א שָׁפְטֵנִי אֱלֹהִים | וְרִיבָה רִיבִי מִגּוֹי לֹא־

ב חָסִיד מֵאִישׁ־מִרְמָה וְעַוְלָה תְפַלְּטֵנִי: כִּי־

אַתָּה | אֱלֹהֵי מָעוּזִּי לָמָה זְנַחְתָּנִי לָמָּה־

ג קֹדֵר אֶתְהַלֵּךְ בְּלַחַץ אוֹיֵב: שְׁלַח־אוֹרְךָ

וַאֲמִתְּךָ הֵמָּה יַנְחוּנִי יְבִיאוּנִי אֶל־הַר־

1. שָׁפְטֵנִי — *Avenge me* [lit. 'judge me'].

Judge me rigorously [without mercy] (*Targum*); [then you will become convinced that I am superior to my oppressors] and you will avenge the terrible injustices I have suffered at the hands of my enemies (*Rashi; Radak*).

וְרִיבָה רִיבִי — *And champion my cause* [lit. 'and fight my fight'].

I ask this of You because I lack the strength to defend myself (*Radak*).

מִגּוֹי לֹא חָסִיד — *Against a people without kindness.*

The Psalmist alludes to people like Ishmael who grew up among Abraham and Isaac, but did not learn from them (*Rashi*). [See *Ramban* to *Genesis 16:6* for an explanation of why the sons of Ishmael (the Arab nations) treat the descendants of Abraham with extraordinary cruelty.].

The Psalmist does not describe these men merely as 'wicked', because they are worse than wicked. They are, in fact, deceitful hypocrites who try to appear kind, although they are actually cruel (*Sforno*).

The hypocrites are the most dangerous villains. On his deathbed, King Yannai warned his wife, 'Beware of the צְבוּעִים, '*the camouflaged ones*' whose inner motives are as heinous as those of Zimri [who was so brazen that he committed adultery in front of Moses and the elders], but who hypocritically behave as though they merit the reward due to the righteous Pinchas [who courageously slew Zimri and his companion, thereby stopping the Heavenly

plague that had taken the lives of twenty-four thousand Jews (*Numbers* 25:1-15)] (*Tehillos Hashem*).

We find such hypocrisy in Nebuchadnezzar, who destroyed the First Temple. Daily, a heavenly voice would exhort the Babylonian king to destroy the Temple of the Jews, for they had angered God. God even called Nebuchadnezzar עַבְדִּי, *my servant*, because he fulfilled God's mission. But, in truth, Nebuchadnezzar was not at all concerned with doing God's will. His actual motive was a secret hatred for Israel (*Alshich*).

The Romans, who destroyed the Second Temple, were also masters of deception, which was part of their spiritual legacy from their ancestor, Esau. Esau deceived his father, Isaac, by asking him questions about minute points of Jewish law, in order to create the false impression that he was scrupulously observant and extremely pious, when he was, in fact, a depraved evildoer. The *Talmud* (*Avoda Zara* 3a) relates that in the future, the Romans will also try to fool God by claiming that every material advantage which they introduced to the world was done only for the benefit of Israel (*Eretz HaChaim*).

Hirsch explains that although the nations pay lip service to the concept of humane ethics [and although they do practice a measure of charity among themselves], they do not consider the '*alien*' Jewish people worthy of common decency. When the nations recognize an opportunity to take advantage of Israel's powerlessness, their underlying

XLIII
1-3

> A venge me, O God, and champion my cause
>   against a people without kindness,
> Help me to escape
>   from a man of deceit and iniquity.
> ² For You are the God of my might,
>   why have You abandoned me?
> Why must I walk in gloom
>   because of the foe's oppression?
> ³ Dispatch Your light and Your truth —
>   they will guide me,

tendencies toward violence and depravity are exposed, and they treat us with the utmost inhumanity.

מֵאִישׁ מִרְמָה וְעַוְלָה — *From a man of deceit and iniquity.*

Although the Psalmist is speaking of a multitude of fraudulent gentiles, he refers to them in the singular i.e., מֵאִישׁ, because they are all alike. Another explanation is that he is alluding to the one man who rules over all gentiles; the king (*Ibn Ezra*).

2. אֱלֹהֵי מָעוּזִּי — *The God of my might.*

In the past, when I was at the height of my glory, You defended me with your *might.* Why do You abandon me now, when I am in exile? (*Radak; Sforno*).

My forefathers called you their *might* only after You redeemed them; after the miracle at the Sea of Reeds, they sang זֶה וְזִמְרָת עָזִּי, *my might and my song is HASHEM* (Exod. 15:2). But I call You my *might* even though You have not yet redeemed me! (*Midrash Shocher Tov*).

The Jews who left Egypt were fully cognizant of God's power even before the Splitting of the Sea; they knew of it by tradition and had seen it during the Ten Plagues. However, when their redemption was completed following the crossing of the sea, they recognized God as their own Savior and, for the

first time, called Him *my might.* The Psalmist, however, uses that description even while he is in exile. This is not to imply that he is superior to his illustrious ancestors. Rather it is because our forefathers imbued their progeny with a legacy of faith in God's salvation that later generations can call Him *my might* even though they had never witnessed His acts of salvation (*Tehillas Hashem*).

לָמָּה קֹדֵר אֶתְהַלֵּךְ בְּלַחַץ אוֹיֵב — *Why must I walk in gloom because of the foe's oppression?*

You were not oblivious to the misery of our forefathers in Egypt, for Scripture states, וְגַם רָאִיתִי אֶת הַלַּחַץ, *and also I have seen the oppression* (Exodus 3:9). Why then do you allow me to sink into oppression at the hands of my present foe? (*Midrash Shocher Tov*).

3. אוֹרְךָ — *Your light.*

Send the King Messiah, who is likened to light, as we read in (132:17), עָרַכְתִּי נֵר לִמְשִׁיחִי, *I prepared a candle for my Messiah* (*Rashi; Sforno*).

Restore the light of prophecy to Israel, as we pray daily: אוֹר חָדָשׁ עַל צִיּוֹן תָּאִיר וְנִזְכֶּה כֻלָּנוּ מְהֵרָה לְאוֹרוֹ, *shine a new light upon Zion and may we all speedily merit to see its light* (*Rashbam*).

The plea for light refers to the

קָדְשְׁךָ וְאֶל־מִשְׁכְּנוֹתֶיךָ: וְאָבוֹאָה | אֶל־ ד
מִזְבַּח אֱלֹהִים אֶל־אֵל שִׂמְחַת גִּילִי וְאוֹדְךָ
בְכִנּוֹר אֱלֹהִים אֱלֹהָי: מַה־תִּשְׁתּוֹחֲחִי | ה
נַפְשִׁי וּמַה־תֶּהֱמִי עָלָי הוֹחִילִי לֵאלֹהִים
כִּי־עוֹד אוֹדֶנּוּ יְשׁוּעֹת פָּנַי וֵאלֹהָי:

---

previous lament, *'Why must I go about
in gloom?' (v. 2) (Ibn Ezra; Radak).*

וַאֲמִתְּךָ — *And Your truth.*

Send Elijah the Prophet [to herald the
advent of Messiah], for he is a
trustworthy messenger *(Rashi).*[1]

Because I am in the clutches of *the
man of deceit and iniquity,* I ask you to
rescue me with your truth *(Ibn Ezra).*

Rabbi Yonasan Eyebeschuvetz, in a
final note to his work *Kreisi U'pleisi* on
Yoreh Deah, notes that according to
tradition, if the Messiah is to come at
the pre-ordained time, Elijah will
precede his arrival by three days in
order to announce him. If Israel is especially virtuous, however, they will
merit that the Messiah and Elijah will
both arrive simultaneously, without any
prior announcement. The Psalmist
prays for this swift redemption: *'Send
forth your light (Messiah) and your
truth (Elijah), send them together
without delay!' (Tosafos Yom Tov).*

הַר קָדְשְׁךָ — *The mount of Your Sanctuary.*

This is Mount Moriah, upon which
the Temple was built *(Ibn Ezra).*

This alludes to the actual Sanctuary
constructed on earth *(Nir L'David).*

---

1. [Compare *I Kings* 17:24. After Elijah resuscitated the dead son of the widow of Tzorfas,
she exclaimed, עַתָּה זֶה יָדַעְתִּי כִּי אִישׁ אֱלֹהִים אָתָּה וּדְבַר ה' בְּפִיךָ אֱמֶת, *Now I know that you are a
man of God and that the word of God in Your mouth is true.* The *Zohar* (*Shemos* 197a) says
that the revived boy was the prophet יוֹנָה בֶּן אֲמִתַּי, *Jonah the son of Amittai.* Furthermore, says
the *Zohar,* Amittai was the prophet Elijah, who was Jonah's 'second' father and who attained
a new title of honor as a man of אֱמֶת, *truth,* for accomplishing the wonder of bringing Jonah
back to life.]
Elijah is a symbol of truth because he will be the final arbiter of an halachic questions
(Sforno). [In describing unresolved questions, the *Talmud* frequently uses the contraction
תיקו, an acrostic for תִּשְׁבִּי יְתָרֵץ קֻשְׁיוֹת וְאִיבַּעְיוֹת, *The Tishbite (Elijah) will solve all questions
and dilemmas.*]

XLIII
4-5
They will bring me to the mount of Your Sanctuary
and to Your dwellings.
⁴ *That I may come to the altar of God,*
to God the gladness of my joy,
And praise You on the Kinor,
O God, My God.
⁵ *Why are you downcast, my soul,*
and why do you yearn for me?
Anticipate God! for I shall yet thank Him,
my salvation, the light of my countenance
and my God.

מִשְׁכְּנוֹתֶיךָ — *Your dwellings.*

These are the courtyards which are destined to be built in the Third Temple (*Ibn Ezra*).

This refers to the spiritual Temple, which must be restored in heaven before its corresponding earthly edifice can be rebuilt (*Nir L'David*).

4. וְאָבוֹאָה אֶל מִזְבַּח אֱלֹהִים — *That I may come to the altar of God.*

At that time I will have the opportunity to offer sacrifices to God as in days of yore (*Radak*).

The previous altar was constructed by men, but the future altar will descend miraculously from heaven. [See *Sukkah* 41a, *Rashi* and *Tosafos ibid.* s.v. אֵי נָמֵי]. Thus the *altar* will truly be of God (*Alshich*).

שִׂמְחַת גִּילִי — *The gladness of my joy* (*Radak; Hirsch*).

Although the future redemption will be filled with signs of rejoicing, I will remember that God is the sole true source of my joy (*Hirsch*).

אֱלֹהִים אֱלֹהָי — *O God, my God.*

Although You are אֱלֹהִים, *God*, Whose majesty and power extend over the entire universe, nevertheless, to me You have a special role as אֱלֹהָי, *my* [personal] *God* (*Be'er Avraham*).

In the future *the people who are not kind* (v. 1) will come to recognize my special relationship with God (*Ibn Ezra*).

5. מַה תִּשְׁתּוֹחֲחִי נַפְשִׁי — *Why are You downcast, my soul?*

The Psalmist now repeats a refrain from the preceding psalm (vs. 6,12), because the two psalms have the same theme. [See *commentary ibid.*] (*Radak*).

This psalm, the third composition of the sons of Korach, is a memoir dedicated to their beloved country, Eretz Yisrael. They describe vividly the Divine assistance which allowed Israel to conquer the land, and they lament the Divine displeasure which caused Israel to lose it.

Arvei Nachal (Parshas Shelach) outlines the strategy for a permanent conquest of the Holy Land. God fashioned the earth in general and Eretz Yisrael in particular in accordance with His universal blueprint, the Torah. The spiritual essence of every square inch of soil is related to Torah laws. Through Torah study and the performance of its laws, Israel seizes the spiritual cone of each 'objective,' and thereby the conquest of the external physical terrain as a matter of course.

The sons of Korach depict the early triumphs of our people as they entered the Promised Land — invincible, and armed with Torah Laws. They mourn the bitter defeat which our people suffered when they abandoned these divine weapons. Nevertheless, these inspired singers are filled with hope, for even in the exile, the Jewish people have displayed undaunted loyalty to Torah by sacrificing their lives for the sanctification of God's Name. Surely this merit will unlock the gates of redemption.

לַמְנַצֵּחַ לִבְנֵי־קֹרַח מַשְׂכִּיל: אֱלֹהִים | א-ב
בְּאָזְנֵינוּ שָׁמַעְנוּ אֲבוֹתֵינוּ סִפְּרוּ־לָנוּ
פֹּעַל־פָּעַלְתָּ בִּימֵיהֶם בִּימֵי קֶדֶם: אַתָּה ג
יָדְךָ גּוֹיִם הוֹרַשְׁתָּ וַתִּטָּעֵם תָּרַע לְאֻמִּים

2. שָׁמַעְנוּ בְּאָזְנֵינוּ — *With our ears we have heard.*

Korach's sons had no need to hear about these miracles with their ears for they had been present when the wonders occurred. They witnessed the Splitting of the Sea and of the Jordan River, they were sustained by God for forty years in the Wilderness, and they participated in Joshua's miraculous conquest of Canaan. Therefore, the sons of Korach must be speaking for later generations of Jews who did not experience these miracles, but learned about them from their fathers (*Rashi*).

אֲבוֹתֵינוּ סִפְּרוּ לָנוּ — *Our fathers have recounted to us.*

[Although the Jews who witnessed the miracles could not personally recount them to their descendants born centuries later, the Psalmist implies that the transmission of this tradition remained broken.]

This tradition was transmitted from father to son through the generations, until it reached the generation which went into exile (*Radak*).

Because our forefathers were righteous, their testimony is reliable. Furthermore, since a father loves his child, he teaches him nothing but the truth (*Ibn Ezra*).

When the Jews were redeemed from Egypt Moses said to them: 'You are not being saved because of your personal merit; rather, God is granting you this salvation in order that you recount these wonders to your children.' In this way, God would be glorified, for Israel would recount His praises among the nations.

The sons of Korach retorted, 'Of what benefit is the account of ancient wonders to those who are now exiled among the nations? The exiles will benefit only when You actually perform similar miracles for them!' (*Midrash Shocher Tov*).

בִּימֵיהֶם בִּימֵי קֶדֶם — *In their days, in days of old.*

This seems to be redundant, for events which occurred *in their days* obviously took place *in days of old.* By this apparent repetition, the Psalmist alludes to a major principle in the interpretation of Jewish history: Events which occurred early in the life of the nation have lasting significance. The events of Israel's formative years foreshadow the nation's future. The beginning of Jewish history is seen as the spiritual seed from which future generations germinated [cf. *Ramban, Genesis* 2:3]. Therefore, the Psalmist emphasizes that those were not ordinary times; they were יְמֵי קֶדֶם, *days of old* [קֶדֶם] also means *prior,* i.e., those days were the prelude to the future!

We can expect the miraculous events of that period to be repeated later in our history. The double expression, פֹּעַל פָּעַלְתָּ, *the deeds which You performed* [lit. *the performance which You performed*], suggests, therefore, that God's performance [of miracles such as those about to be recounted] will be repeated. (*Ohel Yaakov*).[1]

3. אַתָּה יָדְךָ — *With Your own hand* [lit. *You Your hand ...*].

The word יָדְךָ should be interpreted as if it included the prefix בְּ: בְּיָדְךָ, *with Your hand* (*Ibn Ezra, Radak*).

Israel's military might is not credited with driving the Canaanites from the

For the Conductor, by the sons of Korach
          a Maskil.
² God, with our ears we have heard,
     our fathers have recounted to us,
The deeds which You performed in their days,
     in days of old.
³ You, with Your own hand, drove out peoples,
     and emplanted them.

Land. The *hand* of God alone was responsible for this feat (*Radak*).

גּוֹיִם הוֹרַשְׁתָּ — *You drove out peoples.*

This translation follows the *Targum*, *Radak*, and *Metzudos* who relate הוֹרַשְׁתָּ to גֵּרַשְׁתָּ, *You chased out*. However *Rashbam* contends that גּוֹיִם refers to the Twelve Tribes, of Jacob, whom God promised: גּוֹי וּקְהַל גּוֹיִם יִהְיֶה מִמֶּךָּ, *A people, and a congregation of peoples shall come forth from you* (*Genesis* 35:11). Thus, הוֹרַשְׁתָּ is cognate with יְרֻשָּׁה, *inheritance, estate*, meaning: *You bequeathed this land as an estate for the Tribes.*

וַתִּטָּעֵם — *And You emplanted them.*

Them refers to our fathers; as *Targum* renders this verse: *You drove out the peoples of Canaan and es-*

tablished the House of Israel in their stead.

The establishment of the Children of Israel in the Holy Land is compared to planting, to indicate that God has granted the Jews perpetual possession of the Land. Just as the tree is permanently rooted in its soil, the Jews are eternally bound to the Promised Land. Other verses which refer to the 'planting' of the Jews in *Eretz Yisrael* include תְּבִאֵמוֹ וְתִטָּעֵמוֹ בְּהַר נַחֲלָתְךָ, *You shall bring them and You shall plant them in the mountain which is Your estate* (*Exodus* 15:17), and וּנְטַעְתִּים עַל אַדְמָתָם וְלֹא יִנָּתְשׁוּ עוֹד מֵעַל אַדְמָתָם, *I will plant them on their land, and never again will they be uprooted from their land* (*Amos* 9:15).

This metaphor further alludes to the

---

1. *Alshich* notes that these few words contain the key which will unlock Israel's chains of exile. Before Israel can return to its land it must defend itself against the nations which challenge its claim to *Eretz Yisrael*. These nations cry לִסְטִים אַתֶּם, *You are bandits.* [They accuse Israel of having illegally driven out the Land's rightful owners.] *Rashi* begins his commentary to *Genesis* (1:1) by quoting Rav Yitzchak, who explains that the Torah — which is essentially a book of laws, not history — begins with the narrative of Creation in order to provide Israel with a reply to the charge of banditry.

'The entire universe belongs to God, He created it and He granted it to whomever was fit in His eyes. It was His desire to give it to them and it was His desire to take it back from them, ceding it to us!'

The Sages teach us that the universe was created through עֲשָׂרָה מַאֲמָרוֹת, *Ten Utterances.* In *Avos* 5, the *Mishnah* lists many other series of ten. *Maharal* and others find a relationship between them. The ten plagues, which God brought upon Egypt, correspond to these 'Ten Utterances.' Since the plagues totally defied the laws of nature, they proved dramatically that the forces of nature are subject solely to the will of God, Who created them. By demonstrating God's total mastery of even the minutest detail of nature, the plagues renewed the lesson of the Ten Utterances: that God is the Creator and Master of the universe. Thus, Israel's claim to *Eretz Yisrael* was reinforced, for if God the Creator did not give up his mastery of the world, then He could determine to whom its territories should be assigned.

ד וַתְּשַׁלְּחֵם: כִּי לֹא בְחַרְבָּם יָרְשׁוּ אֶרֶץ
וּזְרוֹעָם לֹא-הוֹשִׁיעָה לָמוֹ כִּי-יְמִינְךָ
ה וּזְרוֹעֲךָ וְאוֹר פָּנֶיךָ כִּי רְצִיתָם: אַתָּה-הוּא
ו מַלְכִּי אֱלֹהִים צַוֵּה יְשׁוּעוֹת יַעֲקֹב: בְּךָ

higher degree of holiness present in the Land. When a Jew returns to *Eretz Yisrael*, his soul draws renewed strength as if it had experienced a new birth. In this sense, it resembles a tree that was transplanted to more fertile soil (*Dorash Moshe*).

תֵּרַע לְאֻמִּים — *You afflicted* [lit. *did bad to*] *the nations.*

This translation follows *Rashi* and *Metzudas David*, who relate תֵּרַע to רַע, *evil*. *Targum* and *Rashbam* render תֵּרַע, *to break*, [as in תֵּרֹעֵם בְּשֵׁבֶט בַּרְזֶל, *smash them with a rod of iron* (2:9)].

Malbim notes that this verse records two forms of Divine action against the gentile inhabitants of *Eretz Israel*, for the nations which were to be displayed by Israel fell into two distinct categories.

The גוים are the native *people*, unified by purely physical factors, such as geographic proximity and ethnic similarity. A גוי is a physical and territorial rather than an ideological entity. The גוים must be displaced from *Eretz Yisrael* because God has reserved that territory for the Jewish people. Therefore, *You drove out the people and planted Israel in their place.*

The second group of gentiles are the לְאֻמִּים, *nations*, united by an ideological and spiritual bond. They actively deny

God's sovereignty and scoff at Him.

Such people must be removed from *Eretz Yisrael* not only to clear the territory for Jewish habitation but also to eliminate the spiritual threat which the scoffers pose to the sacred chosen people. Because the לְאֻמִּים are willfully רַע, *evil*, You brought misfortune (תֵּרַע) *upon the nations and banished them* — to demonstrate clearly the futility of their beliefs [cf. *comm.* of *Malbim*, to 2:1].

וּזְרוֹעָם לֹא הוֹשִׁיעָה לָמוֹ — *Nor did their own arm help them.*

Malbim here develops a major principle of Torah *Hashkafa*. The זְרוֹעַ refers to the upper arm, which moves the forearm and hand. The upper arm is the source of the hand's strength.

Scripture refers to this relationship between the upper arm and the hand to symbolize God's actions on behalf of Israel. When the children of Israel are righteous enough to merit Divine intervention they are described as the זְרוֹעַ, *(upper arm)* and God's actions are described as 'יַד ה, the hand of HASHEM, which derives its strength from Israel's worthiness.

When the children of Israel fail to merit Divine intervention, God's deeds are described as 'זְרוֹעַ ה, *the upper arm*

---

1. The Rabbis said: Sichon, King of the Emorites, was as indestructable as a fortified town. When Sichon sat on a high wall, his feet would reach the ground! How did the Holy One, Blessed be He, vanquish him? He took Sichon's guardian angel, bound him, and gave him to Moses. Why? God foresaw that none of Sichon's descendants, would be God-fearing; therefore, He completely eradicated Sichon and his posterity.

How did the Emorites die? Rabbi Levi said: God sent two poisonous flying insects to assault each Emorite. The insects attacked the Emorites in the eye, and they died. If not for this Divine assistance, Israel could never have overcome them. Even Moses was so awed by their might that Hashem reassured him '*Do not fear them*' (Deuteronomy 7:18). King David referred to this when he said, '*For not by their sword did they possess the land.*' (Tanchuma, D'varim 8).

You afflicted nations and banished them.

⁴ *For not by their sword did they possess the land,*
 nor did their own arm help them,

But by Your right hand, Your arm, and the light
 of Your countenance —
 for You favored them.

⁵ *Only You are my King, O God —*
 command the salvation of Jacob!

---

of HASHEM, which derives its strength not from Israel's worthiness but from God's own mercy.

The Psalmist states that when the Jews entered the Holy Land their victories were not a result of their own virtues, but of Divine kindness. Scripture attests לֹא בְצִדְקָתְךָ וּבְיֹשֶׁר לְבָבְךָ אַתָּה בָא לָרֶשֶׁת אֶת אַרְצָם, *Not because of your righteousness or because of the uprightness of your heart are you coming to possess their land* (Deuteronomy 9:5).

The Psalmist echoes this theme: *Their own upper arm did not bring them salvation*, i.e. they did not fully deserve God's help. *Rather it was ... Your upper arm*, i.e God's mercy was the sole source of their salvation.

יְמִינְךָ — [But by] *Your right hand.*

You battled against the pagans of the land and annihilated them (S'forno).

[We find battle ascribed to the right hand in the verse, יְמִינְךָ ה' נֶאְדָּרִי בַּכֹּחַ יְמִינְךָ ה' תִּרְעַץ אוֹיֵב, *Your right hand HASHEM is mighty in strength, Your right hand, HASHEM, shatters the foes* (Exodus 15:6)].

וּזְרוֹעֲךָ — [And] *Your arm.*

You destroyed them with Your right hand. Moreover, the mere threat of Your might terrified them, as we read: תִּפֹּל עֲלֵיהֶם אֵימָתָה וָפַחַד בִּגְדֹל זְרוֹעֲךָ יִדְּמוּ כָּאָבֶן, *Fear and dread will fall upon them, the greatness of Your arm will make them as still as stone* (Exodus 15:16) (Sforno).

וְאוֹר פָּנֶיךָ — *And the light of Your countenance.*

This refers to God's *Attribute of Mercy* (Sforno).

The miracles which You enacted for them were not נִסִּים נִסְתָּרִים (hidden miracles), cloaked by the laws of nature. Rather, they were openly revealed wonders which publicly demonstrated Your presence in Israel (Malbim).

Thus God fulfilled the promise He had made to Moses and to all of Israel, וַיֹּאמַר פָּנַי יֵלֵכוּ וַהֲנִחֹתִי לָךְ, *And He said, My presence will go before you and I will lead you* (Exodus 33:14) (Alshich).

כִּי רְצִיתָם — *For You favored them.*

As long as they engaged in Torah study, they found favor in Your eyes (Targum).

[Israel's conquest of Canaan was not merely a military campaign. It was a spiritual crusade to cleanse the land of pagan influence and to replace paganism with a spirit of Godliness. Therefore, when Israel abandoned the diligent pursuit of Torah study, God immediately turned His sword against them and their leader, Joshua (cf. Joshua 5:13; Megillah 3a).]

5. אַתָּה הוּא מַלְכִּי אֱלֹהִים — *Only You are my King, O God.*

You, Who performed wonders for my ancestors, have remained my sovereign and God to this very day (S'forno). Therefore, please repeat the miracles which You performed in the past (Radak).

ז צָרֵינוּ נְנַגֵּחַ בְּשִׁמְךָ נָבוּס קָמֵינוּ: כִּי לֹא

ח בְקַשְׁתִּי אֶבְטָח וְחַרְבִּי לֹא תוֹשִׁיעֵנִי: כִּי

ט הוֹשַׁעְתָּנוּ מִצָּרֵינוּ וּמְשַׂנְאֵינוּ הֱבִישׁוֹתָ:

בֵּאלֹהִים הִלַּלְנוּ כָל-הַיּוֹם וְשִׁמְךָ | לְעוֹלָם

Dorash Moshe adds: When You exhibited Your wonders in Egypt, You were not yet Israel's King, for Israel did not fully submit to Your sovereignty until they accepted the commands of Your Torah at Sinai. If my ancestors were worthy of Your kindness even before You became their King, how much more do I deserve Your kindness today, for I am totally subjugated to Your rule and You alone are *My King, O God.*

צַוֵּה יְשׁוּעוֹת יַעֲקֹב — *Command the salvations of Jacob*

The name of Jacob is associated with salvation because he blessed his descendants and prayed for their redemptions, saying: הַמַּלְאָךְ הַגֹּאֵל אֹתִי מִכָּל רָע יְבָרֵךְ אֶת הַנְּעָרִים, *The angel who redeemed me from all evil should bless the young men* (Genesis 48:16) (*Ibn Ezra*).

6. בְּךָ צָרֵינוּ נְנַגֵּחַ — *Through You we shall gore our foes.*

This translation follows *Ibn Ezra* and *Radak.* The Targum renders בְּךָ as *by Your word.* בְּךָ is composed of the letters ב and כ, which have the combined numerical value of twenty-two. This sum alludes to the twenty-two letters of the Torah, which is the *word* of God (*Zerah Yaakov*). [צָר is usually translated as *tormentor,* but in the context of this Psalm, it means *foe.*]

Radak notes that Israel's triumph over the enemy is described as *goring* in the verse, בָּהֶם עַמִּים יְנַגַּח, *With them He gores nations* (Deuteronomy 33:17).

We have begged for a supernatural Divine intervention by *Your right hand* (v. 4) so that we would not be required to wage war. But, if we are not worthy

of miracles and if we must engage in battle, then please be with us and help us to gore our adversaries (*Malbim*).

בְּשִׁמְךָ — *By Your Name.*

This refers to the power of the Torah, which is composed of many different combinations of the letters of God's real name (*Yosef Tehillos*). [See *Ramban,* Introduction to *Commentary on Torah*].

Even if we do not merit Your direct intervention in our battles, then at least aid us by sending an angel who can wage war בְּשִׁמְךָ, *in Your Name* (*Malbim*).

נָבוּס קָמֵינוּ — *Shall we trample our opponents.*

The word נָבוּס means *to wallow, to trample,* as in the phrase מִתְבּוֹסֶסֶת בְּדָמָיִךְ, *Wallowing in your blood* (Ezekiel 16:6) (*Rashi*).

[The Psalmist requests divine assistance even after the battle is won and the enemy subdued, for the threat of insurrection always looms over the occupying army which must crush all pockets of enemy resistance.]

7. כִּי לֹא בְקַשְׁתִּי אֶבְטָח — *For I do not trust in my bow.*

[The commentaries cite the sudden transition from plural to singular in this verse.]

Radak explains that the Psalmist now prefers to speak of the entire nation as one person. According to *Ibn Ezra,* these are the words spoken by each archer and swordsman in the Israelites' army. Each individual soldier declares, 'I do not expect to be saved by my own power, but by Hashem's might' (*Radak*).

⁶ *Through You shall we gore our foes;*
by Your Name trample our opponents.
⁷ *For I do not trust in my bow,*
nor does my sword save me.
⁸ *For You saved us from our foes,*
and our haters You shamed.
⁹ *In God we glory all the day,*
and Your Name forever thank, Selah!

וְחַרְבִּי לֹא תוֹשִׁיעֵנִי — *Nor does my sword save me.*

What then does save me? My prayers! The Psalmist speaks here of *the salvation of Jacob* (v. 5). Jacob said that he conquered his enemies בְּחַרְבִּי וּבְקַשְׁתִּי, *With my sword and with my bow*' (*Genesis* 48:22), which the *Targum* (ibid.) renders *With my prayers and with my supplication.* Jacob's weapon could not have been an actual sword, for that implement had been taken away from him and given exclusively to the bloody hands of Esau, as it says, עַל חַרְבְּךָ תִחְיֶה, *And you [Esau] shall live by your sword* (*Genesis* 27:40). [See Alshich and Malbim.]

8. כִּי הוֹשַׁעְתָּנוּ מִצָּרֵינוּ — *For You saved us from our foes.*

We know that we need not rely on our own weapons for salvation (v. 8) not only because *we have heard with our ears* — i.e. from our forefathers — that You alone wage our wars (v. 2), but also because we personally witnessed Your intervention when You saved us from our tormentors (Ibn Ezra, Radak).

וּמְשַׂנְאֵינוּ הֱבִישׁוֹתָ — *And our haters, You shamed.*

You literally saved us *from our tormentors,* for You forced them to help us against their own will. Since Hashem forced *our haters* to foil their own plans, they were terribly humiliated (Tehillos Hashem).

9. בֵּאלֹהִים הִלַּלְנוּ — *In God we glory.*

We compose hymns of praise to You, and our souls glory in the fact that You are our King (Ibn Ezra).

We praise ourselves in the presence of our enemies by declaring that we place our full confidence in our God, who will save us from their hands (Radak).

We tell the gentiles that for our sake God will relate to them as אֱלֹהִים, *the Dispenser of Strict Justice* and will punish them according to the letter of the law (Chazah Zion).

כָּל הַיּוֹם — *All the day.*

This really means *all of the days,* as in 25:5, אוֹתְךָ קִוִּיתִי כָּל הַיּוֹם, *I have hoped for You all the days* (Radak).

וְשִׁמְךָ לְעוֹלָם נוֹדֶה — *And Your name forever thank.*

Although the exile seems to drag on endlessly, this has not discouraged us nor caused us to forget Your name (Radak).

You punish our enemies with the name אֱלֹהִים, *Elohim*__ (Which denotes the attribute of Divine judgment), but You relate to us with שִׁמְךָ, *Your (true) Name,* ה, *HASHEM,* which denotes the attribute of Divine mercy (Chazah Zion).

10. [Having concluded his review of Israel's glorious past, the Psalmist laments the bitter exile which the nation now endures.]

י נוֹדֶה סֶּלָה: אַף־זָנַחְתָּ וַתַּכְלִימֵנוּ וְלֹא־

יא תֵצֵא בְּצִבְאוֹתֵינוּ: תְּשִׁיבֵנוּ אָחוֹר מִנִּי־צָר

יב וּמְשַׂנְאֵינוּ שָׁסוּ לָמוֹ: תִּתְּנֵנוּ כְּצֹאן מַאֲכָל

יג וּבַגּוֹיִם זֵרִיתָנוּ: תִּמְכֹּר־עַמְּךָ בְלֹא־הוֹן

יד וְלֹא־רִבִּיתָ בִּמְחִירֵיהֶם: תְּשִׂימֵנוּ חֶרְפָּה

אַף זָנַחְתָּ וַתַּכְלִימֵנוּ — *Though You abandon and disgrace us.*

Nevertheless, we will always continue *to give thanks to Your name forever* (v. 9) (Radak).

[The Psalmist introduces his description of the exile by reaffirming the staunch faith which has sustained Israel even in its darkest hours.]

Other commentators translate זָנַחְתָּ וַתַּכְלִימֵנוּ in the past tense, to signify, ''You have not redeemed us as You have our forefathers; on the contrary, You have abandoned and disgraced us. In the past *You saved us* i.e., our forefathers] *from our tormentors*; (v. 8) therefore, *In God we gloried all of the days* (v. 9). Now our enemies taunt us, 'Where is the God in whom you gloried? He has abandoned you!' In the past, *You shamed our enemies* (v. 8), but now *You disgrace us* when the enemies see that we are cast away (Ibn Ezra; Radak).

וְלֹא תֵצֵא בְּצִבְאוֹתֵינוּ — *And go not forth with our armies.*

Your Holy Spirit does not rest upon our troops (Targum).

[See 60:12 and comm. (ibid.) הֲלֹא אַתָּה אֱלֹהִים זְנַחְתָּנוּ וְלֹא תֵצֵא אֱלֹהִים בְּצִבְאוֹתֵנוּ.]

11. תְּשִׁיבֵנוּ אָחוֹר — *Caused us to retreat* [lit. *to turn back*].

You make us turn the back of our necks to them [when we fled] (Targum).

Not only did You fail to redeem us, but also You caused terror to melt our

hearts and our resolve. Therefore we lacked the courage to make a stand against the foe (Ibn Ezra).

12. תִּתְּנֵנוּ כְּצֹאן מַאֲכָל — *You delivered us like sheep for devouring.*

In exile, the murder of a Jew by a gentile was considered no more of a crime than killing a sheep (Hirsch).

Alshich points to the irony of our downfall: when we are in God's favor the prophet declares, וְאַתֵּן צֹאנִי צֹאן מַרְעִיתִי אָדָם אַתֶּם אֲנִי אֱלֹהֵיכֶם נְאֻם אֲדֹנָי ה׳, *And you my sheep, the sheep of my pasture, you are men, and I am your God says the Lord, HASHEM/Elohim* (Ezekiel 34:31).

In our relationship with God we are described as His tender *sheep,* but in comparison to all other nations, only the people of Israel are worthy of being called *men.* The barbaric atrocities of the gentiles cause them to be considered wild beasts, whereas Israel represents the epitome of civilization.

When Israel is in exile, however, the gentiles consider themselves the flower of mankind and view the Jews as outcasts of society. Moreover, we are deemed even more lowly than the animals, for *they delivered the corpse of Your servant to be consumed by the birds of the sky* (79:2), i.e. they treat us like foul, putrid carrion.

וּבַגּוֹיִם זֵרִיתָנוּ — *And among the nations scattered us.*

Those of us who were not slaughtered and devoured by the enemy were dispersed among the nations (Ibn Ezra).

¹⁰ *Though You abandon and disgrace us,*
and go not forth with our armies.
¹¹ *You caused us to retreat from the foe,*
and our haters to plunder for themselves.
¹² *You delivered us like sheep for devouring,*
and among the nations scattered us.
¹³ *You sold Your nation for no fortune,*
and did not increase their price.
¹⁴ *You made us a disgrace to our neighbors,*

In particular, we were scattered throughout the one hundred and twenty-seven provinces of the empire of Persia/Media (*Alshich*).

Because gentile law regarded us as no better than animals (sheep), we were constantly forced to search for new shelter, causing us to become increasingly dispersed. Our population in each country dwindled, and we became a weak, barely visible minority (*Hirsch*).

13. תִּמְכֹּר עַמְּךָ בְלֹא הוֹן — *You sold Your nation for no fortune.*

As the Prophet said, חִנָּם נִמְכַּרְתֶּם, *You were sold for nothing* (Isaiah 52:3). The men who sells his possessions usually does not expect to recover them. Similarly, You sold us into such a lengthy exile that it seems as if You will never take us back (*Radak*).

This sale was a great disgrace for us, for if an owner values his goods, he places a high price on them. Conversely, if he gives them away, he proves that he deems them worthless (*Nora Tehillos*).

When a master purchases a slave for a considerable sum, he treats the slave well in order to protect his investment. Since our captors acquired us at no cost, however, they have no concern for our welfare, and treat us with wanton cruelty (*Malbim*).

Even when our enemies are in a position to sell us, they regard us as so utterly devoid of value that they charge

nothing for our people. When Haman wanted to compensate Ahaseuros by paying 10,000 talents of silver for permission to annihilate the Jewish nation, Ahaseuros refused payment for he was content to get rid of the Jews at no royal expense. He said to Haman, '*The silver is given to you and the nation too, to do with it as you see fit*' (Esther 3:11) (*Alshich*).

וְלֹא רִבִּיתָ בִּמְחִירֵיהֶם *And did not increase* [*through*] *their price.*

I.e., You, Hashem, made no profit from the sale of Israel to the nations. It is not unusual for a person to give a present without taking anything in return. But in such cases it is customary for the donor to praise his gift so that the beneficiary will appreciate it. But You, Hashem, remained silent concerning Israel's true worth; You did not inform the gentiles that their conquest of our nation greatly increased their own assets. (*Baalei Bris Avrohom*).

14. תְּשִׂימֵנוּ חֶרְפָּה לִשְׁכֵנֵינוּ — *You made us a disgrace to our neighbors.*

[Cf. 79:4, הָיִינוּ חֶרְפָּה לִשְׁכֵנֵינוּ לַעַג וָקֶלֶס לִסְבִיבוֹתֵינוּ.]

Malbim comments that these tragic verses describe the progressive deterioration of our status in society. At the beginning of our exile, we had slave-masters who were eager to keep us, although they treated us harshly. In time, our dishonor was such that no

טו לִשְׁכֵנֵינוּ לַעַג וָקֶלֶס לִסְבִיבוֹתֵינוּ: תְּשִׂימֵנוּ

טז מָשָׁל בַּגּוֹיִם מְנוֹד־רֹאשׁ בַּלְאֻמִּים: כָּל־

הַיּוֹם כְּלִמָּתִי נֶגְדִּי וּבֹשֶׁת פָּנַי כִּסָּתְנִי:

יז מִקּוֹל מְחָרֵף וּמְגַדֵּף מִפְּנֵי אוֹיֵב וּמִתְנַקֵּם:

יח כָּל־זֹאת בָּאַתְנוּ וְלֹא שְׁכַחֲנוּךָ וְלֹא־

יט שִׁקַּרְנוּ בִּבְרִיתֶךָ: לֹא־נָסוֹג אָחוֹר לִבֵּנוּ

כ וַתֵּט אֲשֻׁרֵינוּ מִנִּי אָרְחֶךָ: כִּי דִכִּיתָנוּ

---

one would come near us, as it says: וְהִתְמַכַּרְתֶּם שָׁם לְאֹיְבֶיךָ לַעֲבָדִים וְלִשְׁפָחוֹת וְאֵין קֹנֶה, *And you will attempt to sell yourselves to your foes for slaves and maidservants, and no one will buy you* (Deuteronomy 28:68).

[Since no one wanted to live in our proximity, isolated ghettos were established.]

לַעַג וָקֶלֶס לִסְבִיבוֹתֵינוּ — *The mockery and scorn of those around us.*

Malbim adds: As the duration of the exile lengthens, the circle of anti-semitism continues to expand. At first, only our immediate neighbors despised us and confined us to ghettos. Eventually this senseless hatred spread until all of our gentile compatriots found it repulsive to breathe the same air and to tread the same soil as the Jews. We were unanimously scorned and forcibly expelled from the entire land.

15. תְּשִׂימֵנוּ מָשָׁל בַּגּוֹיִם — *You made us a byword among the peoples.*

Among the gentiles, the word 'Jew' became a byword used to describe anything base and despicable (*Hirsch*).

After having expelled us so cruelly, the gentile nations could have purged all hatred of Israel from their memories, but this did not occur. Although our bodies were cast out, our name remained a permanent part of the gentiles' everyday vocabulary (*Malbim*).

מְנוֹד רֹאשׁ בַּלְאֻמִּים — *A cause for the nations to shake their heads.*

They shake their heads at us in derision, as we read: כָּל רֹאַי יַלְעִגוּ לִי *the voice of* כָּל רֹאַי יַלְעִגוּ לִי יַפְטִירוּ בְשָׂפָה יָנִיעוּ רֹאשׁ *All those who see me deride me, they open their mouths, they wag their heads* [22:8] (*Radak*).

When the nations discuss the welfare of their citizens, they reject the idea that the Jew deserves kindness or consideration. Throughout their deliberations, they *shake their heads* in negation and opposition, denying the Jew favor or advantage (*Hirsch*).

16. כְּלִמָּתִי נֶגְדִּי — *My humiliation is before me.*

Malbim explains that when a person is humiliated by others this is known as כְּלִימָה. The next verse ascribes this humiliation to קוֹל מְחָרֵף *the voice of the reviler* (of Israel) and the *blasphemer* (of God)

וּבֹשֶׁת פָּנַי כִּסָּתְנִי — *My shamefacedness covers me.*

Malbim continues: בֹּשֶׁת is the feeling of shame which arises from within man when he recognizes how disgracefully he has conducted himself.

[When the exiled Jews suffer כְּלִימָה, *humiliation* at the hands of others, they begin to feel *ashamed* for they recognize that their own sins and misconduct caused the exile.]

17. מִקּוֹל מְחָרֵף וּמְגַדֵּף — *At the voice of blasphemer and reviler.*

> the mockery and scorn of those around us.
> ¹⁵ You made us a byword among the peoples,
>   a cause for the nations to shake their heads.
> ¹⁶ All day long my humiliation
>   is before me
> And my shamefacedness covers me
> ¹⁷ at the voice of reviler and blasphemer,
>   before enemy and avenger.
> ¹⁸ All this came upon us
>   yet we did not forget You;
> nor have we falsified Your covenant.
> ¹⁹ Our heart has not drawn back,
>   nor our footsteps strayed from Your path.

They degrade us intentionally, viciously and publicly, with loud, audible voices (Ibn Ezra).

וּמִתְנַקֵּם — And avenger.

They seek to take revenge, as if we had actually harmed them first (Radak).

18. [We now enter the third portion of this Psalm. After completing his description of Israel's suffering and humiliation in the exile, the Psalmist declares that Israel remained undaunted. Their undying faith in their eventual redemption and restoration invested them with the courage to withstand the calamities of the exile.]

כָּל זֹאת בָּאַתְנוּ וְלֹא שְׁכַחֲנוּךָ — All this came upon us yet we did not forget You.

Despite our suffering we never forgot that we must praise and thank You for everything (Metzudas David).

וְלֹא שִׁקַּרְנוּ בִּבְרִיתֶךָ — Nor have we falsified Your covenant.

Even when under duress, we did not desert our faith and convert (S'forno).

Although we were persecuted and threatened, we never neglected to perform the Bris Milah, nor did we cease to observe the covenant of the Sabbath (Malbim).

Alshich interprets: Nor have we falsified Your covenant by claiming that, in exile, the Torah is no longer valid or binding. God had promised וְאַף, And yet despite all this, when they are in the land of their foes, I will not despise them nor will I reject them, to destroy them, nullify My covenant with them. (Leviticus 26:44). When Israel suffers tremendously in exile and God's presence is nowhere to be seen, it would be natural for Israel to question the truth of the assurances contained in the Divine Covenant — yet we have never done so.

19. לֹא נָסוֹג אָחוֹר לִבֵּנוּ — Our heart has not drawn [lit. stepped] back .

Our hearts have not retreated from a position of firm faith (Radak).

20. כִּי דִכִּיתָנוּ — Even when You crushed us.

Rashi translates כִּי as כַּאֲשֶׁר, when.

בִּמְקוֹם תַּנִּים — In the place of Tanim.

[The word Tanim refers to a wild creature which lives in a place unfit for human habitation, but the exact identity

בִּמְקוֹם תַּנִּים וַתְּכַס עָלֵינוּ בְצַלְמָוֶת: אִם־

כא שָׁכַחְנוּ שֵׁם אֱלֹהֵינוּ וַנִּפְרֹשׂ כַּפֵּינוּ לְאֵל

כב זָר: הֲלֹא אֱלֹהִים יַחֲקָר־זֹאת כִּי־הוּא יֹדֵעַ

כג תַּעֲלֻמוֹת לֵב: כִּי־עָלֶיךָ הֹרַגְנוּ כָל־הַיּוֹם

of this creature is unknown. The word usually means reptile or fish, and in modern Hebrew, תַּן means *jackal*. Since we lack the specific guidance of Talmudic sources, the word has been left untranslated. (See comm. to *Eichah* 4:3 Artscroll edition).]

Ibn Ezra interprets the word as if the מ at the end of תַּנִּים was substituted with a נ, to create תַּנִּין, *sea giant*. This implies, we have been thrust down to the very depths of the sea, where the dangerous sea giants roam; and this dark, murky place surely resembles צַלְמָוֶת *the shadow of death*.

Ibn Ezra and *Radak* also offer an alternate interpretation for the original spelling of תַּנִּים, explaining that this is a vicious beast of the wilderness. This is an allusion to the Babylonians, who tormented their Jewish captives mercilessly.

וַתְּכַס עָלֵינוּ בְצַלְמָוֶת — *And shrouded us with the shadow of death.*

The gentiles sought to wrest us from our faith by their death threats (*Malbim*).

21. אִם שָׁכַחְנוּ שֵׁם אֱלֹהֵינוּ — *Have we forgotten the Name of our God.*
... Then God Himself would investigate and discover it (*Rashi*). Ac-

tually, any such inquiry would reveal that the thought of betraying God never even entered our minds (*Radak, Sforno*), as it says *All this came upon us, yet we did not forget You* (v. 18) (*Ibn Ezra*).

The four commentators cited above construe this verse as a denial of any wrongdoing. However, *Alshich* interprets the verse as both a confession of betrayal and an apology. The Psalmist explains that the only cause of betrayal was torture worse than death, as we read, *Because You crushed us in the place of the [cruel] Tanim* (v. 20).

The *Midrash* echoes this concept: Rabbi Chanina bar Abba said, 'If someone would tell me to give up my life for the sanctification of God's name, I would do it, provided that he kill me instantly. But I could not endure the דּוֹר שֶׁל שְׁמַד, *the generation of persecution*. Then, the enemies took iron balls and heated them until they became white-hot. They placed these balls under the armpits of their pitiable victims and squeezed the life out of them. They took sharp splinters of reed and stuck them under their victims' fingernails, until they squeezed the life out of them.[1]

וַנִּפְרֹשׂ כַּפֵּינוּ לְאֵל זָר — *And extended our hands* [lit. palm] *to a strange God?*

1. We find a similar idea in the *Talmud* (*Kesubos* 33b): The self-sacrifice of Chananya, Mishael and Azaryah is regarded as a classic example of martyrdom. They refused to bow down to the statue of Nebuchadnezzar, even though this refusal condemned them to be thrown into a raging inferno. The Talmud states, however, if the Babylonians had that beaten and tortured them incessantly, they would have yielded and bowed down to the statue.'
Rabbeinu Tam (ibid. Tosafos s.v. אלמלא) maintains that they would have bowed down rather than submit to torture only because Nebuchadnezzar's statue was not a true idol, but a glorification of the king.
[See conclusion of footnote on v. 23].

²⁰ *Even when You crushed us in the place of* Tanim
and shrouded us in the shadow of death.
²¹ *Have we forgotten the Name of our God*
and extended our hands to a strange god?
²² *Would God not have discovered this?*
for He knows the secrets of the heart.
²³ *Because for Your sake we are killed all day long*

Even when they forced us to worship
their idols under pain of death, we did
not succumb, and we gave up our lives
as it says, *For Your sake we are slain all
the time* (v. 23) (*Radak*).

22. הֲלֹא אֱלֹהִים יַחֲקָר זֹאת — *Would not
God have discovered this?* [lit. *searched
this out*].

[This is a continuation of the
rhetorical question posed in the
previous verse.] If we had forsaken
God, if even the vaguest thought of
apostasy had momentarily entered our
minds, then, *Would God not have discovered this?*

Furthermore, the most compelling
proof of our unquestioning faith is that
we never *extended our hands to strange
gods* and that we gladly died for God's
sake. Only the man whose faith is firm
can surrender his life without reserva-
tion or regret (*Radak*).

כִּי הוּא יֹדֵעַ תַּעֲלֻמוֹת לֵב — *For He knows
the secrets of the heart.*

[*Tosafos* (*Shabbos* 12b s.v. שאין
מלאכי השרת) holds that the ministering
angels are aware of the thoughts of
man's heart. *Maharitz Chayos* (*ibid.*)
however, cites a number of Scriptural
passages which indicate that only God
is capable of this all-pervasive
knowledge, as in 7:10, *O searcher of
hearts and minds, O righteous God.* (Cf.
citations in *Gilyon Rabbi Akiva Eiger*
and *S'fas Emes, ibid.*)

The solution may be that angels
know man's conscious thoughts but
only God understands *the secrets of the*

heart, i.e. the sub-conscious complexities of the human mind.

23. כִּי עָלֶיךָ הֹרַגְנוּ כָל הַיּוֹם — *Because for
Your sake we are slain all day long.*

[In every generation, the Jew has
proudly surrendered his life to sanctify
God's name. *Meshech Chochmah
(Parshas Vayeira* 22:14) explains that
martyrdom became ingrained in the
Jewish character when the Patriarch
Isaac readily encouraged his father,
Abraham, to sacrifice him in accordance
with God's command. (See *Overview* to
Breishis II Artscroll ed.)

Therefore, in the preceding verse, the
Psalmist calls upon God to acknowledge
Israel's undying loyalty to Him, *for He
knows the secrets of the heart.*]

Rashba asks how it is possible to be
slain all the time, since a person can
only die once. He comments that this
verse actually refers to the Mitzvah of
reciting the Shema every day. When the
Jew declares, וְאָהַבְתָּ אֵת ה' אֱלֹהֶיךָ בְּכָל
לְבָבְךָ וּבְכָל נַפְשֶׁךָ, *And you shall love
HASHEM your God with all your heart
and all your soul* (*Deuteronomy* 6:5), he
should firmly resolve that he is
prepared to give up his life if necessary,
for the love of God's name. This sincere
commitment is considered equivalent to
actual martyrdom, and Jews who maintain this determination are credited with
being *slain all the time* for God's sake.

Divrei Shlomo adds: The conclusion
of this verse confirms *Rashba's* interpretation, for it says נֶחְשַׁבְנוּ [lit. *We
are thought to be*] כְּצֹאן טִבְחָה as *sheep
prepared for slaughter,* i.e., with our

כד נֶחְשַׁבְנוּ כְּצֹאן טִבְחָה: עוּרָה | לָמָּה תִישַׁן |

כה אֲדֹנָי הָקִיצָה אַל־תִּזְנַח לָנֶצַח: לָמָּה־פָנֶיךָ

כו תַסְתִּיר תִּשְׁכַּח עָנְיֵנוּ וְלַחֲצֵנוּ: כִּי שָׁחָה

כז לֶעָפָר נַפְשֵׁנוּ דָּבְקָה לָאָרֶץ בִּטְנֵנוּ: קוּמָה

עֶזְרָתָה לָּנוּ וּפְדֵנוּ לְמַעַן חַסְדֶּךָ:

thoughts alone we are considered sacrifices for God's glory.[1]

נֶחְשַׁבְנוּ כְּצֹאן טִבְחָה — *We are considered as sheep [prepared] for slaughter* (*Targum*).

As animals prepared for slaughter, the righteous submit to their executioners (*Midrash Koheles* 3:18).

Although we are superior to our executioners in every way, we act like helpless animals and deliver ourselves for slaughter, to sanctify Your Name (*Ibn Ezra*).

[The Jew surrenders not because he is cowardly or weak, but because he is convinced that his death is the will of God. With true heroism, he submits to the Divine decree.]

Sacrificing one's life is not the only form of martyrdom. The *Talmud* (*Gittin* 57b) cites numerous ways in which Jews give of themselves כָּל הַיּוֹם, *all day*

long. For example, 1) Jews willingly circumcize their sons, despite the danger involved. 2) The Sages speak in praise of Torah scholars who endure such hardship in the pursuit of their studies that they may say figuratively of themselves that they commit suicide for the sake of Torah knowledge.

Sefer Chassidim adds: If a Jew is embarrassed by those who ridicule him *when he fulfills God's mitzvos,* it is considered a sacrifice of his blood for God's name, because the blood rushes to his face when he blushes in shame and disappears as he pales.

24. עוּרָה — *Awaken!*

עוּרָה should not be understood literally, as *Awaken!,* for the *Talmud* (*Sotah* 48a) emphasizes that God never sleeps. As stated in 121:4: *Behold the Guardian of Israel does not sleep, nor does He slumber.*

1. *Dorash Moshe* elaborates on this theme by citing the Talmud's description (*Berachos* 61b) of the heroic death of Rabbi Akiva. As the Romans tore at his flesh with iron combs, Rabbi Akiva calmly recited the Shema. His disciples were amazed by his fortitude, but Rabbi Akiva attempted to minimize his heroic accomplishment. He explained, *All of the days of my life* I recited the credo *And you shall love HASHEM your God with all your heart and all your soul,* but I was grieved that I was never given the opportunity to fulfill this commitment. Now that the opportunity has finally arrived should I not fulfill it (joyously)'?

The *Shaloh Hakodosh* reveals the profundity of Rabbi Akiva's statement. When reciting the words, *With all your soul,* one should imagine the excruciating pain experienced when dying and try to feel the torment of an agonizing execution. If one conditions himself in such a manner all the days of his life, then when he is actually confronted with the need to submit to a violent death for God's sake, he will be so accustomed to the pain that it will hardly affect him.

Therefore, Rabbi Akiva said, 'Since I was מִצְטַעֵר, *pained,* all my days over this verse, the actual torture does not disturb my joy now.'

The *Maharam* of Rottenburg (*Responsa* 517) emphasizes this idea and promises that once a person unconditionally resolves to surrender his life to sanctify God's name, he will feel no pain despite any torture the enemy may inflict on him.

[Consequently, Jewish law does not differentiate between brief and prolonged torture, in regard to the obligation to sanctify God's name. See conclusion of footnote to v. 21.]

we are considered as sheep for slaughter.

²⁴ *Awaken, why do You seem to sleep, O my Lord?*
Arouse Yourself, forsake not forever!

²⁵ *Why do You conceal Your face*
ignore our affliction and oppression?

²⁶ *For prostrated to the dust is our soul,*
clinging to the earth is our belly.

²⁷ *Arise — assist us!*
And redeem us by virtue of Your kindness!

Certainly, God's supervision of the world never ceases; however when He shows no reaction to the cruel persecution of the Jews, *it appears to mankind as if God 'slumbers.'*

The *Talmud (ibid.)* relates that in the Second Beis Hamikdash, there was a group of Levite singers known as the מְעוֹרְרִין *the Awakers.* They would stand on the courtyard stage and chant the verse *Awaken! Why do You [seem to] sleep my Lord?'* Yochanan, the High Priest, abolished this practice [because by interpreting the verse literally, the singers were blasphemously reproaching Hashem].

Maharsha (ibid.) stresses that even the figurative meaning of this verse applies only to the time when the Temple is destroyed and Israel is dispersed, but not to Yochanan's time, when the Temple still stood.

לָמָה תִישַׁן אֲדֹנָי — *Why do You seem to sleep, my Lord?*

We have no doubt that God is fully awake and that He is aware of all events. However, our gentile enemies taunt, 'Downtrodden Jew, where is your Saviour? Is He asleep?' (*Ibn Ezra*).

Minchas Shai notes that this verse is punctuated by a פְּסִיק, *line of interruption,* which separates לָמָה תִישַׁן *Why do You sleep from* אֲדֹנָי, *my Lord.*

This division indicates that God, being incorporeal, is not subject to physical needs, even though the Torah describes Him anthropomorphically.

הָקִיצָה — *Arouse Yourself!*

This form of awakening is more vigorous than that implied by the word עוּרָה (*Malbim*).

25. לָמָה פָנֶיךָ תַסְתִּיר — *Why do You conceal Your face?*

Vilna Gaon explains that הֶסְתֵּר פָּנִים concealment of the Divine Presence, constitutes a double punishment. We are imperiled physically because God no longer protects us; even worse, we are endangered spiritually, because God tests us by camouflaging his Providence so that preordained events appear to be mere accidents. This can mislead men to believing that God has abandoned the world to natural forces and that He no longer reigns as Master of the Universe (*Zera Yaakov*). [See *Overview* to *Megillas Esther,* ArtScroll ed.]

תִּשְׁכַּח עָנְיֵנוּ וְלַחֲצֵנוּ — [And] *ignore* [lit. *forget] our affliction and oppression.*

[The Psalmist declares that if God had not cared for us in the past, then His present indifference would be less painful. But we are well-aware that God once bestowed His full affection on us and that our shameful conduct has made Him want to forget His special relationship with us.]

26. כִּי שָׁחָה לֶעָפָר נַפְשֵׁנוּ — *For prostrated to the dust is our soul.*

The long saga of Israel's woes nears its end. Like a dying man gasping for

his last breath, Israel groans, 'I stand at the brink of death; I am about to return to the dust from whence I came!' (*Radak*).

Alshich observes that these words allude to the cause of Israel's severe degradation. Man is composed of lowly matter and a lofty spirit; life's mission is to harness this matter and discipline it to serve the purposes of the spirit. Thus the *dust* can rise to the level of the *soul*. But the children of Israel failed to subordinate the material to the spiritual; instead they used their intellect and *soul* to satisfy the mundane desires of their *dust*. God is not to blame for Israel's decline; the nation buried itself.

דָּבְקָה לָאָרֶץ בִּטְנֵנוּ — *Our belly is pressed to the earth.*

This description also underscores Israel's acute degradation. When a person trips, he usually tries to break his fall, so that he hits the ground supported by his hands and feet. In this position he looks no worse than an animal, which goes about on all fours.

But when the children of Israel stumble, the land on their faces with nothing to shield them from the impact of the

fall. They 'bite the dust' and lie flat on their bellies, in a position even lower than an animal's. They appear to have no 'hands', i.e., no means of self-support (*Midrash Shmuel*).

27. קוּמָה עֶזְרָתָה לָּנוּ — *Arise! Come to our assistance!*

Once Israel has descended to the lowest point, the nation immediately begins to ascend. As the Psalmist said, 'our soul is bowed down to the dust ... Arise!' (*Shemos Rabbah* 1:9).

Alshich adds that it is not uncommon for a fallen man to rise, for, once he has reached the bottom, his situation can only approve. However, under normal circumstances his ascent is gradual. Therefore the Psalmist pleads on behalf of Israel, 'Arise swiftly, O God, and grant Israel a meteoric rise'.

וּפְדֵנוּ לְמַעַן חַסְדֶּךָ — *And redeem us by virtue of Your kindness.*

When Israel is restored to its former glory with supernatural swiftness, the world will recognize that you no longer conceal Your presence from the Jewish people. This will demonstrate that Israel is Your chosen nation, the beneficiary of *'Your kindness'* (*Alshich*).

מזמור מה 45

This is a song of praise for the Sages of the Sanhedrin of Moses, composed prophetically by the sons of Korach (Targum).

Korach, supported by two hundred fifty leaders of the Congregation of Israel, challenged the Divine authority of Moses and slandered him with vicious accusations of selfishness and falsehood (Numbers 16:2). The sons of Korach repented and sought to undo their father's treachery by portraying Moses and all authentic Torah scholars in the light of truth, emphasizing their boundless generosity and scrupulous honesty.

Indeed, the salvation of Korach's sons, who originally collaborated with their rebellious father, was a direct result of their respect for Moses. While they were sitting with their father, Moses passed by. Korach's sons were in a quandary. They pondered: If we stand to honor Moses, we will disgrace our father; but if we sit, we will breach the Torah's command to rise in the presence of a Sage. Finally they decided that it was preferable to honor the scholar, Moses, despite the affront to their father. At that moment, the spark of sincere repentance began to flicker in their hearts (Yalkut Shimoni 752).

The Torah scholar resembles the שׁוֹשַׁנָּה, rose, a delicate flower surrounded by thorns, which seem ready to pierce the rose's fragile petals. Actually, these brambles protect the rose by discouraging the hands which try to pluck it. Similarly, those who originally oppose the Sages (who represent God) will ultimately recognize the Sages' truly splendid virtues and become their guardians and supporters.

The Midrash and commentaries relate this psalm to several individuals described in Scripture. At first Abraham was universally ostracized for his teachings, but he was later acclaimed as the leading citizen of the world. At first David was vilified and pursued, but he was finally accepted as ruler and king. At first Messiah will be challenged, but he will ultimately become the universal sovereign. Alshich and Malbim interpret this psalm as a description of the coarse body, which at first hinders the development of the soul, but is eventually trained to assist it.

Alshich and Hirsch also explain this psalm as a wedding song celebrating the marriage of a bride and groom, who begin marriage with two very different and sometimes conflicting personalities, but who ultimately blend together in perfect sublime harmony. In light of these interpretations, the Psalm's title, שִׁיר יְדִידֹת, A song of endearment, is highly appropriate.

לַמְנַצֵּחַ עַל־שֹׁשַׁנִּים לִבְנֵי־קֹרַח מַשְׂכִּיל
שִׁיר יְדִידֹת: רָחַשׁ לִבִּי | דָּבָר טוֹב אֹמֵר

1. עַל שֹׁשַׁנִּים — *Upon Shoshanim* [lit. *the roses.*]

[See Artscroll Songs 2:1 for a complete discussion of why שׁוֹשַׁנָּה is translated *rose*, rather than *lily*.]

Radak and *Malbim* identify the *Shoshanim* as the musical instrument which accompanied this psalm. Its name is derived from its rose-like shape (*Metzudas Zion*).

According to *Rashi*, this psalm was composed in honor of the Torah scholars who are tender as the rose, beautiful as the rose and saturated with good deeds as the fresh, moist rose. Just as the rose contains many exquisite petals, so is the Torah sage composed of a variety of a scholarly attainments (*Ohel Yaakov*).

[שֹׁשַׁנִּים may also be read שֶׁשּׁוֹנִים, *who study and review*, alluding to the scholars who are constantly immersed in their lessons in order to fulfill the commandment וְשִׁנַּנְתָּם, *And you shall teach them diligently* (Deuteronomy 6:7). See comm. v.6 חִצֶּיךָ שְׁנוּנִים.]

[*Targum* renders שֹׁשַׁנִּים as *Sanhedrin* as he does in 69:1 and 80:1, the only other instances where this title is used. However, *Rashi* (Psalms 60:1) identifies this name with Israel, which resembles a rose surrounded by menacing thorns and which needs a prayer for protection.]

Radak and *Ibn Ezra* (v. 2) maintain that this song was dedicated to Messiah. *Ibn Ezra* adds that it may refer to David himself; for the names of Messiah and David are one, as seen in the verse, *And David, My Servant, will be a* [Messianic] *prince for them forever* (Ezekiel 37:25).

Nora Tehillos notes that this psalm was placed after the previous one, which vividly describes the agony of Israel in exile, to foretell Israel's glorious redemption at the time of the Messiah.

לִבְנֵי קֹרַח — *For the sons of Korach.*

Just as the rose is encircled by thorns, so were the sons of Korach surrounded by their father and his followers. Just as the custom is to burn and destroy the thorns, so were Korach and his company obliterated, but his sons, who were like roses, were plucked out of the inferno and saved (*Midrash*; *Alshich*).

The sons of Korach were actually swallowed by the earth together with their father and his cohorts. They said of themselves, *Our soul is bowed to the dust, our belly is pressed to the earth* (44:26). *But at the last moment they cried out, 'Arise! Come to our assistance!* (44:27).

The Holy One, Blessed be He, responded, 'It all depends on you! Just as the rose which wishes to flourish turns itself towards the sky, so must you train your hearts towards heaven in sincere repentance. When Israel repents I will redeem them, as the prophet declares, *I will be as the dew for Israel, if they flourish like the rose,* [which lifts its head heavenward]' (Hoshea 14:6). Therefore this Psalm of Korach's son's is entitled, *Upon the roses.* (*Midrash Shocher Tov*).

מַשְׂכִּיל — *Maskil* [lit. *for enlightenment* see comm. 32:1.]

The sons of Korach were *enlightened* in that they recognized that Moses was in the rights, therefore, they repented and sang (*Tehillos Hashem*).

שִׁיר יְדִידֹת — *A song of endearment* [lit. *friendships.*]

[The term here is not the singular יְדִידוּת, *friendship* but the plural יְדִידֹת, which alludes to a number of friends

XLV
1-2

For the Conductor, upon Shoshanim,
for the sons of Korach, a Maskil,
a song of endearment.
² My heart is astir with a good theme;

(feminine) or *endearments.* The commentaries suggest that this *endearment* takes several forms.]

This is a song of love [for the Torah scholars], a song of praise for them, a song intended to endear the scholars to all men and to make their Torah appreciated by all (*Rashi*).

The song arouses Israel's love for their Father in heaven, and His love for them (*Sforno*).

The song describes God's love for His ordained Messiah (*Radak*).

The psalm is prefaced with three special [musical] terms לַמְנַצֵּחַ, מַשְׂכִּיל, שִׁיר corresponding to the three sons of Korach. All were יְדִידֹת, *friends,* of God. Furthermore, Moses, Aaron and all of the great scholars who were *friends* of God came to hear the songs which the sons of Korach composed (*Midrash Shocher Tov*).

2. רָחַשׁ לִבִּי דָּבָר טוֹב — *My heart is astir with a good theme.*

This is the preface to the song of endearment. The Psalmist declares that his heart was stirred to create a fine composition in praise of the Torah scholar (*Rashi*). [Torah is described as טוֹב, as in *Psalms* 119:72, *Proverbs* 3:14, 4:2, and *Avos* 6:3].

רָחַשׁ — *Astir* [lit. stirred, moved.]

Hirsch notes that this is the only place in Scriptures where רחשׁ is employed as a verb rather than as a noun meaning a creeping reptile.

Meiri defines this as a slight quivering motion which is almost imperceptible. The creeping reptile is called רֶחֶשׁ

because of its peculiar motion [cf. *Leviticus* 11:20-21 and 22:5, where the *Targum* of שֶׁרֶץ is רַחֵשׁ]. In the language of the Talmud, we find that the faint murmuring of the lips is termed רֹחֲשֵׁי מַרְחֲשָׁן שִׂפְוָותֵיהּ (*Sanhedrin* 90b). Here it means, *My heart was stirred to compose this song by a spirit of prophecy.*

Sforno renders רָחַשׁ as *proliferate,* thus: My heart gives birth to many good thoughts.

Midrash Shocher Tov observes that when the sons of Korach were swallowed in the earth, they were dumb — struck by the awesome sight of the fires of Gehinnom leaping from below. Although their tongues were mute, their hearts were *stirred* to repentance and God graciously accepted this minimal silent confession of guilt, and saved them. Furthermore, the Psalmist uses the singular form לִבִּי, *my heart,* to emphasize that the three sons were simultaneously aroused and developed identical thoughts at the same time and their hearts were as one.

Hirsch notes the contrast between the ordinary poet and the inspired Psalmist. Authors typically seek out pretty words and polished phrases, assuming that once they discover the proper words, the right thoughts will follow automatically. Not so the Psalmist, whose hymns well up from the depths of his heart. His main concern is the sincerity and truth of his inner thought. The words needed for outward expression are but secondary vehicles of communication. Therefore, the first thing that happens is: *My heart is astir.* Afterwards: *my tongue is the pen.*

אָנִי מַעֲשַׂי לְמֶלֶךְ לְשׁוֹנִי עֵט | סוֹפֵר

ג מָהִיר: יָפְיָפִיתָ מִבְּנֵי אָדָם הוּצַק חֵן
בְּשִׂפְתוֹתֶיךָ עַל־כֵּן בֵּרַכְךָ אֱלֹהִים

ד לְעוֹלָם: חֲגוֹר־חַרְבְּךָ עַל־יָרֵךְ גִּבּוֹר הוֹדְךָ

אֹמֵר אָנִי מַעֲשַׂי לְמֶלֶךְ — *I say: 'My works befit a king.'*

I declare that the song which I composed is fit for a king i.e., for a Torah scholar – who is called a king, *(Proverbs 8:15) (Rashi).* [See *Gittin* 62a: Who are the true kings? The Rabbis!]

This song befits the King Messiah *(Radak).*

לְשׁוֹנִי עֵט סוֹפֵר מָהִיר — *My tongue is the pen of a skillful sofer.*

Rashi quotes *Rabbi Moshe Ha-Darshan* who translates מָהִיר as בָּקִי, *well-versed, adept.* This concurs with the Targum.

Radak relates מָהִיר to מַהֵר, *swift, nimble,* suggesting that this scribe writes without delay or hesitation. He takes pains to insure brevity and conciseness *(Sforno).*

The Psalmist conveys his message in the most succinct form to fulfill the dictum *(Pesachim* 3b): One should always teach his students in the shortest way possible *(Imrei Shefer).*

According to an ancient adage, the tongue is the pen of the heart *(Ahavas Olam).* [Only when the heart is free of ambivalence and indecision can the tongue articulate its sentiments without hesitation.]

A person should remember that whatever his tongue utters here [in this world] is immediately inscribed in the record book in heaven. Thus the tongue truly functions simultaneously as a 'pen' *(Alshich).*

3. יָפְיָפִיתָ מִבְּנֵי אָדָם — *You are beautiful beyond other men.*

You [the Torah scholar] are fairer than the ordinary men who are immersed in temporal, material pursuits *(Rashi).* [1]

Your extraordinary beauty is twofold (hence the compounded form of יָפְיָפִיתָ — יָפָה): Both your outer appearance and the words which flow from within you are attractive *(Radak).*

This refers to the all-inclusive excellence of Messiah, of whom the prophet says: *(Isaiah 52:13) Behold My servant shall be enlightened, he shall be exalted and lifted up and he shall be very high (Ibn Yachya).*

Kedushas Levi renders these words literally, 'You have become beautiful from the sons of man,' intimating that the king should always bear in mind that his majesty is derived from his subjects, for if they had not accepted his rule, he would have nothing. [Therefore the king should be humble. The Torah scholar also derives the most beautiful and significant part of his learning from his students, as the Talmud *(Taanis* 7a) notes, 'From my students I learned most of all!']

1. [However, once the scholar begins to seek material benefits, he no longer appears attractive. The *Talmud (Sanhedrin* 52B) states: 'How does a *Talmid Chacham* (Torah Scholar) appear in the eyes of the *Am Haaretz* (unlearned man)? At first, he resembles a precious, golden vase. Once he starts to talk freely to the *Am Haaretz*, the Sage seems like a mere silver vase. And when the *Talmid Chacham* derives some benefit from the *Am Haaretz*, the ignorant man loses respect for the Sage and regards him as a cheap earthenware jug, which breaks easily and cannot be repaired.' (This refers to the scholars and leaders who joined Korach's revolt. They were scholars, at first, but once they accepted favors and gifts from the wealthy Korach, they lost all respect for them. Finally, he pressured them to join his evil conspiracy — *Rashi,ibid.*).]

I say: 'My works befit a king,
        my tongue is the pen of a skillful scribe.'
³ *You are beautiful beyond other men,*
        charm is poured upon your lips,
Accordingly God has blessed you
        for eternity.
⁴ *Gird your sword upon your thigh,*

הוּצַק חֵן בְּשִׂפְתוֹתֶיךָ — *Charm is poured upon your lips.*

The spirit of prophecy is placed upon your lips (*Targum*).

The Torah scholar is the most attractive of all men because God endowed him with the ability to issue truthful and authoritative halachic decisions (*Rashi*).

[The Torah scholar is exhorted to share his knowledge orally. The *Talmud* (*Eruvin* 54a) advises, Scholar, open your mouth and recite! Open your mouth and study, that your knowledge will be retained and your life will be lengthened, as it says, *Torah is life for those who spread it by their mouths* (*Proverbs* 4:22).]

עַל כֵּן בֵּרַכְךָ אֱלֹהִים לְעוֹלָם — *Accordingly God has blessed you for eternity.*

The Kingdom of Messiah shall endure forever (*Meiri*). He shall be eternally endowed with the greatest of blessings: he will find favor in the eyes of all men (*Radak*).

4. חֲגוֹר חַרְבְּךָ עַל יָרֵךְ גִּבּוֹר — *Gird your sword upon your thigh, O mighty one.*

Radak notes that sometimes the sword is girded on the מָתְנַיִם, *loins* [above the thigh; see *Exodus* 28:42] as in *II Samuel*: 20:8 [see *Rashi, ibid.*], and sometimes, as in this verse, it is fastened on the יָרֵךְ, *thigh*.

Rashi explains this phrase as an allegory describing מִלְחַמְתָּהּ שֶׁל תּוֹרָה, *the battle of Torah study.*[1]

---

1. [In many instances we find that intensive Torah study is compared to deft swordsmanship.]

See *Song of Songs* 3:8 Artscroll edition כֻּלָּם אֲחֻזֵי חֶרֶב מְלֻמְּדֵי מִלְחָמָה, *All of them gripping the sword of tradition, skilled in the battle (of Torah)*. Compare this with *Chagigah* 14a: *Mighty Man* refers to a master of tradition; *Man of War* refers to one who can dispute in the intellectual 'warfare' of Torah (i.e., he is a mentally agile debater who knows how to deal with the argumentation essential to the study of Torah).

Specifically, the girding of the mental sword denotes preparation to render a judgment or halachic decision. The *Talmud*, (*Sanhedrin* 36a) notes the words David used in bidding the members of the Sanhedrin to ready themselves for Judgment: *And David said to his men: Let every one of you men gird his sword. And every man girded his sword, and David also girded his sword* (*I Samuel* 25:13).

The *Talmud* (*Sanhedrin* 7a) emphasizes the extreme caution which the magistrate must exercise when approaching a ruling: *The judge should always imagine a sword poised on his thigh* [or, at his throat, (*Rambam, Sanhedrin* 23:8)] and the fires of Gehinnom roaring beneath him.

Rav Yosef Yitzchak interprets the girding of the sword on the loins as a simile describing self-control and restraint. The Psalmist teaches that the greatest victory is not won by the man who conquers others with his unsheathed sword, but by the man who refrains from drawing his sword. This form of self-mastery is a real triumph; it truly bespeaks *a majesty and a splendor.*

ה וַהֲדָרְךָ: וַהֲדָרְךָ | צְלַח רְכַב עַל־דְּבַר־
אֱמֶת וְעַנְוָה־צֶדֶק וְתוֹרְךָ נוֹרָאוֹת יְמִינֶךָ:

הוֹדְךָ וַהֲדָרְךָ — *Your majesty and your splendor.*

Your Torah knowledge is your praise (*Rashi*); Specifically, the knowledge which you amassed for yourself is *your majesty* and that which you teach to others is *your splendor* (*Sforno*). [The above explanation complements the commentary of *Malbim* on *Psalms* 104:1 which defines הוֹד as private and personal *majesty*, and הָדָר as external *splendor* displayed to the public eye.]

[On the Sabbath a person may not carry objects in the public domain, but he is permitted to wear garments and adornments. The *Talmud* (*Shabbos* 63a) debates whether or not the girded sword is classified as an adornment (which would permit one to wear it on the Sabbath). One opinion maintains that a sword can be considered an adornment on the basis of this verse, which describes the sword as a *majesty* and *splendor*. An opposing view refutes this by citing the verse in *Isaiah* (2:4), *And they shall beat their swords into plowshares and their spears into pruning hooks.* If, the argument goes, the sword is an adornment, then why should it be destroyed in the future? The *sword* in our verse is a metaphor to denote Torah knowledge.]

In consonance with his opinion that this psalm describes Messiah, *Radak* understands the *sword* as a real weapon. Although the prophets always portray the Messianic era as a time of universal peace, this tranquility will be achieved only after the terrible war of Gog and Magog [see *Prefatory Remarks, Psalms* 2]. During this cataclysmic confrontation, the Messiah's martial skills will be his *splendor*.

[See *Psalms* 21:6 הוֹד וְהָדָר תְּשַׁוֶּה עָלָיו *majesty and splendor You conferred*

upon him which *Midrash Shocher Tov* interprets as a reference to Messiah who is endowed with *two* forms of excellence: beauty and strength. Also, see above *v.3*, describing Messiah as possessing a two-fold excellence: יְפָיְפִיתָ.

5. וַהֲדָרְךָ — *And [this is] your splendor.*

Your most prominent attribute is not the military prowess depicted in the previous verse but the intellectual achievements described here (*Malbim*).

Radak understands *verses 4 and 5* to mean: After You (Messiah) achieve Your splendid triumph over the enemies, as described in the preceding verse, do not subjugate them (*ride over them*) with pride and haughtiness. Rather be guided always by truth and sincere humility.

צְלַח — *Gain success.*

Radak renders this as *go over, trample,* referring to the conquest of the enemy. [See *Radak* on *II Samuel* 19:18: וְצָלְחוּ הַיַּרְדֵּן לִפְנֵי הַמֶּלֶךְ, *And they passed over the Jordan before the king.*]

[Concerning Solomon, the son of David, it is written וַיַּצְלַח, *And he succeeded* (I Chronicles 29:23). According to the *Talmud* (*Sanhedrin* 93b) David, too is described as מַצְלִיחַ, *successful* (see gloss ibid.]

רְכַב עַל דְּבַר אֱמֶת — *And ride [high] on truthfulness.*

Rashi explains that the Torah scholar will issue true and honest decisions, unaffected by external factors. This is also a distinctive feature of the Messiah, as Scripture says: *And the spirit of Hashem will rest upon him, the spirit of wisdom and understanding, the spirit of counsel and might, the spirit of knowledge.... and he shall not judge after the sight of his eyes nor decide*

O mighty one — your majesty and your splendor.
⁵ *And this is your splendor: gain success,*
ride high on truthfulness and righteous humility.
May it guide you to awesome deeds
with your right hand.

---

after the hearing of his ears (Isaiah 11:2,3)

True faith and sincere belief in Hashem are hallmarks of the Messiah as Isaiah (11:5) says: *And righteousness shall be the girdle of his loins and faith the girdle of his body (Ibn Yachya; Norah Tehillos).*

Targum interprets: [Messiah] will ride on a unique royal steed.

וְעַנְוָה צֶדֶק — *And right and humility.*

This alludes to the excellent characteristics of the Messiah (Isaiah 11:4): *And with righteousness he will judge the poor, and decide with equity for the humble of the earth (Ibn Yachya).*

[*Rambam, Hilchos Melachim* 2:6 describes humility as the hallmark of the Jewish King: Although the Torah accorded the King great honor, nevertheless he must feel himself small and insignificant...He must deal compassionately with both the lowly and the great ... concern himself with the dignity of all ... speak softly to the people ... and act with extreme humility ... and untiring patience ... as a shepherd who tends to his flock.]

[In reference to the scholar, the Sages say: עֲנָוָה סְיָג לְחָכְמָה, *Humility is the safeguard of knowledge (Kallah Rabbassi* 3). Also, we find that the dimensions of the golden Ark of the Sanctuary, the repository of the Torah were given in fractions, whereas the dimensions of the other sacred vessels were given in whole numbers. *Baal Haturim (Exodus 25:10)* emphasizes that this teaches the Torah scholar humility: 'Never consider yourself whole and complete but rather a mere fraction of what you should be!']

וְתוֹרְךָ נוֹרָאוֹת יְמִינֶךָ — *May it guide you to awesome deeds with your right hand.*

Addressing the scholar, the Psalmist continues to speak of Torah study in militaristic terms: 'Your dedication to Torah and to truth will guide you to such an amazing strategy that your right hand will succeed in performing awesome deeds' [i.e., you will be endowed with an unerring perception of the true and fitting halachic decision.] Continuing his symbolism of war, the Psalmist refers to the scholars accomplishments as if he were a mighty warrior holding a weapon in his right hand (*Rashi*).

Norah Tehillos comments that Messiah will be endowed with an unerring genius for 'sniffing out' the truth, as it says: *And he shall smell with the fear of HASHEM (Isaiah 11:3).* According to *Rashi (ibid.),* the Messiah will be able to detect a person's innocence or guilt merely by observing his face.[1]

---

1. The Talmud (*Sanhedrin 93b*) relates: Bar Kuziva reigned two-and-one-half years. He declared to the Sages, 'I am the Messiah!' They said to him 'It is written of the Messiah that he has the ability to smell the truth and render judgment accordingly. Let us see whether you possess this power!' When the Sages proved that Bar Kuziva lacked this ability and that he was a false messiah, they executed him. [See *Ravad's* gloss on *Rambam, Hilchos Melachim* 11:3]

ו חִצֶּיךָ שְׁנוּנִים עַמִּים תַּחְתֶּיךָ יִפְּלוּ בְּלֵב
ז אוֹיְבֵי הַמֶּלֶךְ: כִּסְאֲךָ אֱלֹהִים עוֹלָם וָעֶד
ח שֵׁבֶט מִישֹׁר שֵׁבֶט מַלְכוּתֶךָ: אָהַבְתָּ צֶּדֶק
וַתִּשְׂנָא רֶשַׁע עַל־כֵּן | מְשָׁחֲךָ אֱלֹהִים
ט אֱלֹהֶיךָ שֶׁמֶן שָׂשׂוֹן מֵחֲבֵרֶךָ: מֹר־וַאֲהָלוֹת

6. חִצֶּיךָ שְׁנוּנִים ... בְּלֵב — *Your arrows ... sharpened ... in the heart.*

First, the metaphor of the *sword* is employed (v. 4); now the Psalmist uses the metaphor of *arrows* (Ibn Ezra).

Our translation follows *Rashi* who instructs us to read the first and last phrases of this verse as one continuous statement viewing the middle phrase עַמִּים תַּחְתֶּיךָ יִפְּלוּ as a parenthetical interruption (מִקְרָא מְסוֹרָס). Thus *Your arrows are sharpened i the heart of the foes of the king; nations fall beneath you.* Ibn Ezra maintains that יִפְּלוּ, *they fall*, refers to the *arrows*. Thus *Your arrows are sharpened...they fall into the heart of the foes of the king.*

Rashi continues to explain that the Psalmist elsewhere likens *arrows* to students, as we read, כְּחִצִּים בְּיַד גִּבּוֹר כֵּן בְּנֵי הַנְּעוּרִים , *As arrows in the hand of the warrior, so are the children of one's youth* (127:4). Furthermore, the Torah scholars who are engaged in heated discussion and dispute are considered temporary *foes* as the Psalmist (*Psalms 127:5*) concludes: לֹא יֵבֹשׁוּ כִּי יְדַבְּרוּ אֶת אוֹיְבִים בַּשָּׁעַר *They shall not be put to shame rather they shall speak with their enemies in the gate.* [See Talmud, *Kiddushin* 30a] for elaboration on this theme. There the Sages exhort the scholars, וְשִׁנַּנְתָּם 'Let the words of Torah be sharp and clear in your mouth! If someone asks you a question, do not hesitate or stammer; rather, respond immediately with clarity!']

עַמִּים תַּחְתֶּיךָ יִפְּלוּ — *Nations fall beneath you.*

In the merit of Torah study, the gen-

tile nations are vanquished by Israel (*Rashi*).

As the *Talmud* (*Gittin* 57b) says: when the voice of Jacob is raised [in Torah study], the hands of Esau are subdued (*Tehillos Hashem*).

The clarity and sharpness of Israel's Torah teachings will overwhelm the erring gentile nations to the point that they will feel compelled to admit that the truth is with the Jews (*Sforno*).

Abarbanel writes that Jerusalem is now in the hands of the Ishmaelites (Arabs), but that Edom is destined to capture the city. The Ishmaelites will not tolerate this and will gather to battle the Edomites. The redemption of Israel [and the downfall of all our enemies who slay each other] will result from this war (*Rav Vidal HaTzorfati*).

בְּלֵב אוֹיְבֵי הַמֶּלֶךְ — *In the heart of the foes of the king.*

[The initial downfall of Israel's foes does not take place on the field of battle. Our enemies defeat themselves by surrendering to the destructive passions of their hearts.]

7. כִּסְאֲךָ אֱלֹהִים — *Your throne, O judge.*

According to *Rashi*, אֱלֹהִים refers to the scholar in his role as judge. Even a mortal man of flesh and blood can merit this divine title if he sincerely seeks to administer God's justice on earth, as we read concerning Moses רְאֵה נְתַתִּיךָ אֱלֹהִים לְפַרְעֹה, *Behold I have placed you as judge* [lit. *master*] *over Pharaoh* (*Exodus 7:1*). [See also *ibid.* 21:6; 22:7.]

Ibn Ezra [cited in *Radak*] is of the opinion that אֱלֹהִים refers to God. He

⁶ *Your arrows are sharpened,*
nations fall beneath you,
in the heart of the foes of the king.
⁷ *Your throne, O judge,*
is forever and ever,
The scepter of equity
is the scepter of your kingdom.
⁸ *You love righteousness*
and hate wickedness,
Accordingly has God, your God, anointed you
with oil of joy above your peers.

renders: *Your throne [O King] is the throne of* אֱלֹהִים, *God, as it is written* וַיֵּשֶׁב שְׁלֹמֹה עַל כִּסֵּא ה׳, *And Solomon sat on the throne of HASHEM* (I Chronicles 29:23).

Rav Saadia Gaon (quoted by *Ibn Ezra* and *Radak*) translates: *Your throne [O King] is prepared and established by God.*

שֵׁבֶט מִישֹׁר שֵׁבֶט מַלְכוּתֶךָ — *The scepter of equity is the scepter of your kingdom.*

...Therefore your throne is *forever and ever* (*Rashi*), because things Divine do not deteriorate with the passage of time [and truth and Divinity are synonymous] (*Malbim*).

8. אָהַבְתָּ צֶּדֶק וַתִּשְׂנָא רֶשַׁע עַל כֵּן מְשָׁחֲךָ — *You love righteousness and hate wickedness accordingly has ... God anointed you.*

[Other monarchs gain their thrones as a result of savage power struggles in which all law, order, and decency are callously discarded. The unpopular king who rules only by brute force oppresses and tyrannizes his subjects,

plunging them into misery. Not so the king of David's line. His throne is divinely established by virtue of the king's equity and righteousness. Therefore his enthusiastic subjects welcome his anointment as a cause for national gladness.]

אֱלֹהִים אֱלֹהֶיךָ — *God, your God.*

Although אֱלֹהִים, *God*, is Master of the entire universe, He watches over you [His Chosen King] with special providential care, which makes Him אֱלֹהֶיךָ, *your* [personal] *God* (*Meiri*).

שֶׁמֶן שָׂשׂוֹן — *Oil of joy.*

Most subjects despise those who have the authority to rule over them, but your anointment was greeted with joy (*Otzar Nechmad*).[1]

Ahavas Olam raises a halachic question: If we interpret this Psalm as referring to Messiah, then this verse teaches us that the future Messiah will actually be anointed with sacred oil. This seems to run counter to the Talmudic dictum, 'A King who is the son of a King is not anointed — because the monarchy is his

1. *Yalkut Shimoni (Samuel 124)* relates that the oil itself rejoiced when anointing David. When Samuel attempted to pour the oil on the heads of each of David's seven brothers, instead of flowing downward, the oil recoiled back up to the horn. But before Samuel even had a chance to pour the oil on David, the oil spurted forth from the horn on its own and anointed David. It turned into pearls and precious gems on his head, for God had observed David's righteousness and deemed him eminently worthy of monarchy.

by inheritance ... unless his rule is disputed' (Horios 11b: Rambam, Hilchos Melachim 1:12). Since Messiah is a direct scion of the House of David and inherits the throne as his rightful estate, why will he be anointed?

The answer is that God wishes to demonstrate to the entire world that Messiah reigns on his own merit and that even if he were *not* heir to the throne, he would be fit to rule. This is the message of our verse: *You, Messiah, personally love righteousness and hate wickedness; therefore God has personally anointed you with a special anointment.*

[Minchas Chinuch (107) explains that when the ten tribes rebelled against Rechavam, the son of Solomon, he lost sovereignty over them. In order for Solomon or his heirs to regain royal status over the ten tribes, a new anointment is needed. Therefore, Messiah will require a new anointment if he wishes to reign over all of Israel, including the ten tribes.]

מֵחֲבֵרֶךָ — *Above your peers.*

Ibn Ezra comments that if this psalm is dedicated to David himself, then חֲבֵרֶךָ would refer only to Saul. [Samuel warned Saul that his monarchy would be taken away by God saying: *And He will give it to your friend who is worthier than you* (I Samuel 15:28).] If, however, the psalm refers to Messiah, then חֲבֵרֶךָ would refer to Messiah's peers, the other devout sages of his generation

Radak maintains that חֲבֵרֶךָ is plural, despite the fact that the customary י before the ך (the required spelling in the plural) is deleted.

9. מֹר — *Myrrh.*

Rav Hai Gaon identifies this as the fragrant sap of a tree, called *luvni* in Arabic (*Radak*).[See *Ramban* on *Exodus* 30:23.]

[This also alludes to the Torah scholar, as we read (*Song of Songs* 5:13) שִׂפְתוֹתָיו שׁוֹשַׁנִּים נֹטְפוֹת מוֹר עֹבֵר, *His* [the Torah scholar's (*Targum*)] *lips are roses, they drip flowing myrrh.*

The *Talmud* (*Shabbos* 88b) comments: 'With every word which the Holy One, Blessed be He, spoke, the whole world became filled with the fragrance of spice.' For God's words spiritually purify and refresh the soul, just as fragrant spices revive the body (*Alshich*).]

וַאֲהָלוֹת — *Aloes.*

Aloes are plants of the lily family. Rav Adda explained in the name of Rav Yehuda that it is called *ahalos* because it comes to us by way of אֹהָלִים [*ohalim*], *tents* [i.e., it is imported by Bedouin tent-dwellers (*Matonos Kehunah*)]. However, the Rabbis say that it was called *ahalos* because it spreads in the tent [i.e., when used as incense in the Holy Service, its smoke spread in the אֹהֶל מוֹעֵד, *Tent of Meeting'* (*Radak*)]. It was with this fragrance that the Jews perfumed themselves during their forty years in the desert. [See *Midrash* and *ArtScroll* commentary to *Song of Songs* 4:14.]

קְצִיעוֹת — [*And*] *cassia.*

This is an exceptionally fragrant spice whose odor pervades the air. We find that one of Job's unusually beautiful daughters was called קְצִיעָה (*Job* 42:14) because her fragrance spread out like that of the cassia [*Bava Basra* 16b] (*Alshich*).

Rashi, Radak, and *Alshich* identify קְצִיעוֹת as the name of one of the spices, but *Ibn Ezra* disagrees. He argues that the absence of a ו, *vov* before this word indicates that it is not preceded by the article *and*; he takes this as evidence that the word is not connected with the two previous words (מֹר וַאֲהָלוֹת). *Ibn Ezra* interprets that the word is an adjec-

⁹ *Myrrh, aloes, and cassia*
are all your garments —
Finer than ivory palaces
will be Mine that will gladden you.

tive (related to קָצַע *cut*) which modifies כָּל בִּגְדוֹתֶיךָ. His translation is: *well cut and tailored are all your garments.*

כָּל בִּגְדֹתֶיךָ — *Are all your garments.*

All your garments are permeated with a pleasant fragrance (Rashi).

It is imperative that the Torah scholar wear only fresh, clean clothing (*Ibn Yachya*). [The Talmud (*Shabbos* 114a) says that a Torah sage who wears stained garments deserves to die. *Rav Yaakov Emden* comments that if the scholar ignores visible stains on his garments, he cannot be concerned about an unseen character flaw on his soul!]

Radak and *Meiri* interpret the *garments* as a metaphor for a person's character traits. This usage is seen throughout Scripture, as in *Ecclesiastes 9:8, At all times let your garments be white.* Refined character and good deeds weave an intangible 'garment' which surrounds the soul with glory (*Alshich*). [The poetic figure of fragrances and spices is used because the sense of smell is considered the most spiritual of the senses (see *Berachos* 43b).]

Rashi concludes his commentary with the observation that allegorically, this word may be read בְּגִידוֹתֶיךָ, *your treacheries*, suggesting that even your sins and transgressions, which betray God and emit a foul stench, are atoned

for [through repentance], permitting your former fragrance to return.

מִן הֵיכְלֵי שֵׁן — *Finer than* [lit. *from*] *ivory palaces.*

The palaces which are prepared to gladden you in the Garden of Eden surpass the finest ivory palaces on earth (Rashi).

According to *Otzar Nechmad*, מִן is rendered literally as *from* and the *ivory palaces* refer to the paradise of Eden itself. The Psalmist informs us that the fragrances mentioned above come *from* Eden, as *Baal HaMaor* testifies: *Myrrh* and *aloes* are native only to Eden. The wind tears leaves and branches from these trees and casts them into the River Pishon which flows out of Eden. Arabs later gather these leaves from the river and enjoy their heavenly fragrance.[1]

Meiri identifies the *ivory palaces* as the upper heavens. From there God sends man the inspiration to cloak his soul in good deeds and splendid character traits.

מִנִּי שִׂמְּחוּךָ — *Will be Mine that will gladden you.*

Rashi renders מִנִּי as an abbreviated form of מִמֶּנִּי, *from Me.* The figurative palaces with which I [God] will reward you in the World to Come, will be far superior to even the most lavish ivory trappings of this world.

---

1. The Talmud (*Bava Metza* 114b) tells of the Sage, Rabbah bar Avuha whose dire economic straits hampered his advancement in Torah study. In order to alleviate his poverty, Elijah once took Rabbah to the Garden of Eden where he told Rabbah to remove his mantle and fill it with the wonderfully fragrant leaves of the Garden. As Rabbah was leaving Eden with his precious load, a heavenly voice proclaimed, 'Woe! Who had devoured and squandered his eternal reward as wantonly as Rabbah bar Avuha' [i.e., these leaves were reserved for the righteous in the Hereafter.] Upon hearing this, Rabbah promptly threw the leaves back into the Garden. Nevertheless, his cloak had absorbed such an extraordinary fragrance from the leaves that he sold it for 12,000 dinars and divided the profits among his sons-in-law.

י שְׁמְחֻךְ: בְּנוֹת מְלָכִים בְּיִקְּרוֹתֶיךָ נִצְּבָה
יא שֵׁגַל לִימִינְךָ בְּכֶתֶם אוֹפִיר: שִׁמְעִי־בַת
וּרְאִי וְהַטִּי אָזְנֵךְ וְשִׁכְחִי עַמֵּךְ וּבֵית
יב אָבִיךְ: וְיִתְאָו הַמֶּלֶךְ יָפְיֵךְ כִּי־הוּא אֲדֹנַיִךְ

However, *Radak* and *Meiri* translate מְנִי as an emphatic form of the word מִן, *from* (see *Judges* 5:14, מְנִי אֶפְרַיִם...מְנִי מָכִיר): *The fragrance of your garments comes from the ivory palaces, from the very same palaces which gladden you.*

10. בְּנוֹת מְלָכִים בְּיִקְּרוֹתֶיךָ — *Daughters of kings visit you.*

This translation follows *Rashi*, who derives this word, from בִּקּוּר, *visit*. Princesses from all over the world come to attend to you and, to join your royal retinue.

The *Midrash* (*Bereishis Rabbah* 45:1) relates that both Pharoah [the father of Hagar] and Avimelech gave their daughters to the Patriarch Abraham, saying, 'Far better that they should be servants in the house of Abraham than noble princesses elsewhere.'

However, *Ibn Ezra*, *Radak*, and *Menachem* (quoted in *Rashi*) relate יָקָר to בְּיִקְּרוֹתֶיךָ, *precious, dear*. Thus: *Among your dearly beloved wives are the daughters of kings*, who are deeply honored to present their daughters to you.

Targum seems to incorporate both translations, rendering: They come to *visit* [בִּיקוּר] you and to give you *honor* [יְקָר].

נִצְּבָה — *Erect stands.* [See commentary to 2:2, s.v. יִתְיַצְּבוּ.]

שֵׁגַל לִימִינְךָ — *The queen at your right.*

The *daughters of kings* are the foreign princesses who only enter the king's presence when they receive a special summons [i.e., although they have converted according to the prescribed halachic ritual, they are nevertheless mere concubines]. However, the שֵׁגַל is the Jewish queen, the king's con-

stant consort. Only she is bedecked in the most splendid crown jewels from Ophir (*Radak*).

Targum renders this allegorically: *the scroll of the Torah is in your right hand* [referring to the halachah that the king must carry a *Sefer Torah* with him at all times (*Deuteronomy* 17:19), attached to his right arm like a jeweled ornament (*Sanhedrin* 21b; see *footnote* to 16:8).]

בְּכֶתֶם אוֹפִיר — *In the golden jewelry of Ophir* (*Rashi*).

[The land of Ophir is reknowned for the quality and abundance of its gold, as seen in *I Kings* 9:28; 22:49 and in *I Chronicles* 29:4.]

11. שִׁמְעִי בַת — *Hear, O maiden* [lit. *daughter*.]

Radak says that *daughter* refers to the *daughters of kings* in the previous verse. Listen to my words of discipline.

Ibn Ezra suggests that if this psalm is for David, then *daughter* means his שֵׁגַל, *queen*; If this psalm is for Messiah, then the *daughter* is the entire congregation of Israel described elsewhere (*Lamentations* 2:6) as בַּת יְהוּדָה, *the daughter of Judah* (see *Targum* and *Rashi*).

וּרְאִי — *See.*

'Understand my words once you have heard them.' Intellectual perception is often referred to as רְאִיָּה *vision* (*Radak*).

From these words we arrive at an essential credo of Torah faith: man's idea of what is right does not necessarily concur with God's. *Every way of man is straight in his own eyes* (*Proverbs* 21:2). *There is a way which appears straight before a man yet its end is the ways of death* (*Proverbs* 14:12).

Since man's eyes are easily misled

XLV
10-12

10 *Daughters of kings visit you,*
erect stands the queen at your right
in the golden jewelry of Ophir.
11 *Hear, O maiden, see and incline your ear,*
forget your people and your father's house—
12 *Then the King will desire your beauty,*
for He is your Master — submit to Him.

[see *Overview, Tehillim I*], the Jew must first listen to the Oral Tradition handed down from Sinai, which will provide him with the basis of truth, i.e., *Hear, O daughter!* Only then will he be able to use his eyes properly to interpret visual data — וּרְאִי, *And see!* (*Ohel Yaakov; Beis HaLevi, Parshas Ki Sisa*)

וְהַטִּי אָזְנֵךְ — *And incline your ear.*

Beis HaLevi (*Parshas Ki Sisa*) continues that the Jew should first blindly accept the tradition which he receives (*hears*) from his parents and teachers. *Hear* refers to the development of this unquestioning faith in the complete truth of God's word. After his faith is firmly established, a Jew may apply his individual intelligence to Torah study and try to comprehend the logic and wisdom of each commandment; this process is suggested by the word וּרְאִי, *see*. Nevertheless, the scholar should never delude himself into thinking that his limited mind can totally grasp (*see*) the complete meaning of every *mitzvah*. Even after he studies Torah independently, he should still base his faith on what he hears and receives — וְהַטִּי אָזְנֵךְ, *And* [continue to] *incline your ear.*

וְשִׁכְחִי עַמֵּךְ — *Forget your people.*

This refers to the Samaritans, who dwell in your midst (because they ostensibly converted to Judaism and joined the Chosen People) and among whom you grew up(*Rashi*). [The Samaritans, who are known as כּוּתִים, *Kuthim*, rejected the Oral Tradition of Torah Law, and accepted only the

written tradition of תּוֹרָה שֶׁבִּכְתָב. Thus they failed to follow the prescribed path of placing שְׁמָעִי, *hear*, before רְאִי, *see*. Their detrimental influence must be shunned.]

Metzudas David interprets this entire verse in reference to the Messiah. The Psalmist exhorts all of the nations (*the daughters*) to listen to the commands of Messiah and to *forget* the wicked conspiracy of *the nations* of Gog and Magog, who plan to battle God's chosen king.

וּבֵית אָבִיךְ — *And your father's house.*

Forsake the idols worshiped by your forefathers. [Specifically, this indicates Terach, father of Abraham, who followed the pagan gods of Chaldea.]

Similarly we find that the pious Levites who refused to join the rest of Israel in the idolatrous service of the Golden Calf are praised: *Who said of his father and of his mother: 'I have not seen him', neither did he acknowledge his brethren, nor knew his own children* (*Deuteronomy* 33:9). Their loyalty and devotion to God transcends all personal considerations and relationships (*Olelos Ephraim*).

12. וְיִתְאָו הַמֶּלֶךְ יָפְיֵךְ — *Then the King will desire your beauty.*

If you follow the instructions set down in the previous verse, then the King [God] will yearn for the perfection of your deeds (*Rashi*).

כִּי הוּא אֲדֹנַיִךְ וְהִשְׁתַּחֲוִי לוֹ — *For He is your Master — submit to Him* [lit. *and you should prostrate yourself.*]

יג וְהִשְׁתַּחֲוִי־לוֹ: וּבַת־צֹר | בְּמִנְחָה פָּנַיִךְ
יד יְחַלּוּ עֲשִׁירֵי עָם: כָּל־כְּבוּדָּה בַת־מֶלֶךְ
טו פְּנִימָה מִמִּשְׁבְּצוֹת זָהָב לְבוּשָׁהּ: לִרְקָמוֹת
    תּוּבַל לַמֶּלֶךְ בְּתוּלוֹת אַחֲרֶיהָ רֵעוֹתֶיהָ

Metzudas Zion, explaining these words in reference to Messiah, renders: If you, (the nations) follow his commands, then Messiah will reciprocate by acting as your guardian and dedicated protector. Then you may submit yourselves [*prostrate yourself*] to him without any fear or reservations, for he will take you under his wings.

13. וּבַת צֹר — *As for the daughter of Tyre.*

Tyre is the [prosperous] city which is very close to the Land of Israel. Its inhabitants always bring presents to each of the wives of the King [of Israel] (*Radak*).

[Indeed, Tyre symbolizes Israel's arch-enemy, Edom. The Sages teach that Israel and Edom will never share equal stature, for the balance of power will shift in favor of only one nation at a time. 'If one is filled with abundance, the other must be desolate' (*Pesachim* 42b; *Rashi* on *Megillah* 6a). In the Messianic era, Israel will gain eternal superiority and Tyre will humbly come to Jerusalem to pay tribute.]

בְּמִנְחָה פָּנַיִךְ יְחַלּוּ — *With homage will they seek Your presence.*

Our translation follows *Rashi*. The scholar need not seek the financial aid of the wealthy, [symbolized by Tyre] because [if he is truly worthy] the rich will [deem it a privilege to] support him, and they will seek him out in order to offer him their gifts (*Sforno*).

Radak punctuates the verse differently: וּבַת צֹר בְּמִנְחָה, *And the daughter of Tyre — with homage /* פָּנַיִךְ יְחַלּוּ עֲשִׁירֵי עָם, *The rich of the nation seek your presence*, i.e., Not only the people of Tyre, but also the wealthy men of every

nation will bring gifts to the daughters of the kings (who are married to the Jewish Monarch).

14. כָּל־כְּבוּדָּה בַת מֶלֶךְ פְּנִימָה — *The complete glory of the princess is within.*

Those courtiers who are part of the royal retinue are the epitome of dignity, nobility and glory. They shun ostentation and seek privacy (*Rashi*).

[Throughout Rabbinic literature, the Sages cite this verse as a description of the chastity and modesty of the Jewish woman, who is no less a princess than the king's daughter. The glory of the Jewish wife and mother is to hold court in the inner chambers of her own home, which is her palace and royal domain.

Rambam (*Hilchos Ishus* 13:11) writes: Every woman should go out to visit her parents or to console the mourners or to rejoice at weddings or to perform acts of kindness for her friends, for a wife is not to be imprisoned in her home, as if it were a dungeon … But it is a disgrace for a woman always to go into public places and main streets and a husband should restrain his wife from acting thus … For the essence of a wife's beauty is to be enthroned in the corner of her home, as it says, *The complete glory of the princess is within*.]

מִמִּשְׁבְּצוֹת זָהָב לְבוּשָׁהּ — *Surpassing golden settings is her raiment.*

מִשְׁבְּצוֹת are the settings for precious gem (*Metzudas Zion*). [In particular, they were used in the garments of the High Priest, as in *Exodus* 28:11,13 et al. *Rashi* (ibid. 28:20) explains that the מִשְׁבֶּצֶת, *setting*, is expertly designed to perfectly cover the gem — neither too little nor too much. Similarly the rami-

¹³ *As for the daughter of Tyre,*
with homage will they seek your presence,
those richest of the nation.
¹⁴ *The complete glory of the princess is within;*
surpassing golden settings is her raiment.
¹⁵ *In embroidered apparel*
she is brought to the king,
The virgins in her train are her companions,

---

ment of the modest Jewish woman, who resembles a precious jewel, is carefully tailored and measured to cover her properly.][1]

Because the courtiers acted with privacy and modesty, they merit garments which are even more exquisite than those of the High Priest, which are adorned with golden settings (*Rashi*).

15. לְרְקָמוֹת תּוּבַל לַמֶּלֶךְ — *In* [lit. *to*] *embroidered apparel she is brought to the king.*

While wearing beautifully stitched garments they will bring gifts to the Master of the Earth, as the prophet (*Isaiah* 66:20) says: *And they shall bring all of your brothers out of all the nations — an offering to HASHEM* (*Rashi*). [Perhaps the usage of the relatively uncommon verb תּוּבַל in our verse alludes to the fact that one of the distant nations which will come to God at that time is תּוּבַל, as mentioned in the previous verse in *Isaiah* (66:19)].

According to *Targum*, this refers to the priests who bring offerings to God in the Temple while wearing embroidered clothes [מַעֲשֵׂה רֹקֵם, see *Exodus* 28:39].

Radak, Ibn Ezra, and *Malbim* render תּוּבַל literally as *she is brought* i.e., the *daughter of the king* [referred to in the previous verse] is taken into the presence of the king. *Malbim* also translates לְרְקָמוֹת literally as *to embroider,* i.e. she is brought to an embroidered (wedding) canopy.

בְּתוּלוֹת אַחֲרֶיהָ רֵעוֹתֶיהָ — *The virgins in her train* [lit. *behind her*] *are her companions.*

According to *Rashi,* the *maidens* are the *companions* of the daughter of the king. This alludes to the future, when the gentiles will follow in the train of Israel [they will suddenly relinquish their age-old animosity and become our bosom companions], as the prophet (*Zechariah* 8:23) foretells: *In those days it shall come to pass that ten men out of all the languages of the nations shall take hold and shall seize the skirt of he who is a Jew, saying, 'We will go with you for we have heard that God is with you.'* [Perhaps because the gentiles will undergo a complete change of attitude towards Israel and renew their friendship, they are described as pure, untouched *maidens.*]

---

1. There was a pious woman named Kimchis who had seven sons, each of whom served in the office of High Priest. The Sages asked her, 'By virtue of which good deeds did you merit such honor?'

She replied, 'Not even the walls of my home ever saw a hair of my head uncovered. Neither did they ever see as much as the hem of my undergarments!'

In reference to Kimchis, the Sages recited this verse; *The complete glory of the princess is within* [because she acts with extraordinary modesty, she merits sons who are High Priests] *whose raiment is set with gold* (*Yerushalmi,* Yoma 1:4).

מה טז מוּבָאוֹת לָךְ: תּוּבַלְנָה בִּשְׂמָחֹת וָגִיל
יז תְּבֹאֶינָה בְּהֵיכַל מֶלֶךְ: תַּחַת אֲבֹתֶיךָ יִהְיוּ
בָנֶיךָ תְּשִׁיתֵמוֹ לְשָׂרִים בְּכָל-הָאָרֶץ:
יח אַזְכִּירָה שִׁמְךָ בְּכָל-דֹּר וָדֹר עַל-כֵּן עַמִּים
יְהוֹדוּךָ לְעֹלָם וָעֶד:

Radak (v.16) explains the metaphor of the בְּתוּלוֹת: just as maidens have no intimate knowledge of men before they marry, so do the nations remain completely ignorant of God and Torah until they heed the commands of Messiah and accept the dictates of the Torah, either by converting to the religion of Israel or by fulfilling the seven Noachide laws.

Metzudas David, differentiates between the maidens who are maidservants, who walk behind the princess, and the companions, who walk at her side.

מוּבָאוֹת לָךְ — Are led [lit. brought] to You.

The entire retinue is brought before the presence of God (Rashi) or before the Messiah (Metzudas David).

16. תּוּבַלְנָה בִּשְׂמָחֹת וָגִיל — They are brought with gladness and joy.

They all come voluntarily, without coercion (Ibn Ezra).

The nations gather eagerly around the Messiah to follow his orders and teachings (Radak).

תְּבֹאֶינָה בְּהֵיכַל מֶלֶךְ — They enter the palace of the King.

[They will be welcomed into the inner chambers.]

17. תַּחַת אֲבֹתֶיךָ יִהְיוּ בָנֶיךָ — Succeeding your fathers will be your sons.

According to Rashi, this statement [which appears to be a blessing] was addressed to all of Israel.

[An unbroken tradition of Torah study transmitted from father to son is a special blessing in regard to Torah scholarship. The Talmud (Bava Metziah 85a) teaches, 'Whoever is himself a scholar, has a son who is a scholar, and a grandson who is a scholar is guaranteed by God Himself that Torah will never depart from his descendants, ... for the Torah always returns to its established dwelling place.']

Radak, however, interprets it as a declaration concerning Messiah, who inherits his throne from his forebears, who possessed it for generation after generation. Similarly, Messiah will transmit the monarchy to his progeny, who will continue to rule for uninterrupted generations. Thus, of each reigning member of this royal family we can say, Succeeding your fathers will be your sons.

The Midrash (Shir Hashirim Rabbah 1:6) observes that this blessing was especially apparent in Solomon, who took the place of his father in every way: A king, son of a king. A scholar, son of a scholar. A righteous man, son of a righteous man. David reigned forty years, and Solomon reigned forty years. David laid the Temple foundations; Solomon built the Temple above them. David authored books; so did Solomon. David composed songs; so did Solomon. David built an altar; so did Solomon. David brought up the Ark; so did Solomon.

are led to you.
¹⁶ *They are brought with gladness and joy,*
they enter the palace of the King.
¹⁷ *Succeeding your fathers*
will be your sons.
You will appoint them
as leaders throughout the land.
¹⁸ *I will commemorate Your Name*
through all generations,
Therefore the nations will acknowledge You
forever and ever.

תְּשִׁיתֵמוֹ לְשָׂרִים בְּכָל הָאָרֶץ — *You will appoint them as leaders throughout the land.*

This statement is addressed to God: You will place the scions of Messiah in positions of authority everywhere (*Metzudas David*).

This is a blessing: May your sons develop the competence which will enable them to assist you in ruling the land for the benefit of your subjects (*Hirsch*).

18. אַזְכִּירָה שִׁמְךָ בְּכָל דֹּר וָדֹר — *I will commemorate Your Name through all generations.*

Rashi maintains that the Psalmist is referring to God. *Radak* is of the opinion that the verse is speaking of Messiah. In every generation we make constant mention of his name and await his arrival with longing.

Chazah Zion notes the use of the poetic feminine form אַזְכִּירָה rather than the proper masculine אַזְכִּיר. He explains that the extra letter ה alludes to the Four-Letter Name which represents God's Attribute of Mercy. Thus: In all generations, at all times, both good and

bad, I will make the name of Hashem memorable, reminding myself and others that even when God punishes harshly, He has my best interests in mind and is motivated solely by His *Attribute of Mercy*.

Yaavetz HaDoresh observes that these words allude to the Sages' view that God exiled Israel and scattered them among the nations so that the Jews should promulgate His name in the farthest reaches of the globe and produce sincere converts (*Pesachim* 87b).

עַל כֵּן עַמִּים יְהוֹדֻךָ לְעוֹלָם וָעֶד — *Therefore the nations will acknowledge You forever and ever.*

Because I praise Your name incessantly even in this generation, all nations will be prepared to acknowledge You when Your full glory is ultimately revealed (*Sforno*).

Radak concludes that since Israel yearned for Messiah in every generation, therefore all nations will eventually acknowledge his [universal, absolute] sovereignty, which will be unprecedented in the annals of history.

This psalm was composed by the sons of Korach who became inspired by a spirit of prophecy when their father disappeared before their eyes (נֶעְלַם=עֲלָמוֹת, hidden). Korach's sons were saved; therefore, they recited this song' (Targum).

Hashem delivered Korach's sons from the earth which opened and threatened to swallow them with their father. This event taught Korach's sons that Divine salvation is never distant from those who deserve it, no matter how hopeless their plight may appear.

During their moment of inspiration, Korach's sons foresaw occasions in which Israel was destined to be endangered by armies and cataclysms which would threaten to tear the earth asunder. One such occasion occurred when the mighty Sennacherib and his hordes convulsed the entire globe and uprooted all of the nations (Rashbam). Another will occur during the War of Gog and Magog, when the peoples of the earth will gather to devastate Jerusalem (Yaavetz HaDoresh). In each case, God will foil the enemy's plots and miraculously rescue His Chosen People from danger.

This song is titled עֲלָמוֹת (which alludes to עוֹלָמוֹת many worlds), to indicate that God's salvation is expressed constantly, throughout the world (Dorash Moshe). Furthermore, we are obliged to trust God's guidance, which controls every aspect of life, although His deeds are נֶעְלָמוֹת, hidden and concealed (Divrei Shlomo).

א לַמְנַצֵּחַ לִבְנֵי־קֹרַח עַל־עֲלָמוֹת שִׁיר:
ב אֱלֹהִים לָנוּ מַחֲסֶה וָעֹז עֶזְרָה בְצָרוֹת
ג נִמְצָא מְאֹד: עַל־כֵּן לֹא־נִירָא בְּהָמִיר
ד אָרֶץ וּבְמוֹט הָרִים בְּלֵב יַמִּים: יֶהֱמוּ
יֶחְמְרוּ מֵימָיו יִרְעֲשׁוּ־הָרִים בְּגַאֲוָתוֹ

---

1. עֲלָמוֹת — *Alammos*

This is a musical instrument used in the Temple, as we read in *I Chronicles* 15:20 (*Rashi, Radak*).

Alshich explains that this is a song which expresses Israel's powerful love for God. Israel is referred to as עֲלָמוֹת, as we read עַל כֵּן עֲלָמוֹת אֲהֵבוּךָ, *Therefore do young maidens love You* (*Song of Songs* 1:3). [The *Midrash* (ibid.) comments: *The maidens* (i.e., Israel) *love You with youthful energy* (עֲלָמוֹת) *and vigor. . .*]

Meiri [in keeping with his theory that the names of instruments reflect their special musical characteristics (see *commentary* to 5:1 and 22:1)] explains that this instrument had the unique ability to arouse an extraordinary joy, found only in עֲלָמוֹת, *young men* or *maidens*.

[We may also interpret עֲלָמוֹת as עַל מָוֶת, *even unto death*, which alludes to Israel's irrepressible love for God, which remains steadfast even in the face of persecution and martyrdom. (See *commentary* to 9:1 and 48:15).]

2. אֱלֹהִים לָנוּ מַחֲסֶה וָעֹז — *God is for us refuge and strength*

Hashem not only defends us but also strengthens us during battle. He is our *refuge* when He protects us from the enemy's onslaught. Then He is our *strength* when we counter-attack and destroy the foe.

עֶזְרָה — *Help*

The Psalmist here refers to God as *refuge, strength,* and *help*. These three designations allude to the three sons of Korach who received Divine assistance (*Chazah Zion*).

בְצָרוֹת — *In distress* [lit. *distresses*]

This refers to the distress of חֶבְלֵי מָשִׁיחַ, *the travails of the* [advent of] *Messiah* (*Radak*).

The plural form of this word affords us a glimpse of God's *help*, for even if He must punish someone He does not bring distress upon him all at once. Instead He makes the punishment bearable by dividing it into a number of smaller, less overwhelming צָרוֹת, *distresses* (*Tehillas Hashem*).

נִמְצָא מְאֹד — *Very accessible* [lit. *'much to be found'*]

Our translation follows *Radak* who interprets מְאֹד, *much,* as the description of the עֶזְרָה, *help,* which God gives. Since He saves tiny, weak Israel from the threat posed by many mighty nations, God's help is indeed great (*much*).

According to *Metzudas Zion*, these words describe God Himself who is always available and present to lend assistance in difficult times.

Sforno maintains that נִמְצָא מְאֹד [*much to be found*] describes our צָרוֹת, which are extremely frequent because we so often incur God's wrath by choosing to do evil.

3. עַל כֵּן לֹא נִירָא — *So we shall not be afraid*

Since we have witnessed God's merciful salvation in the past, we do not fear the future, no matter how menacing it seems (*Sforno*).

בְּהָמִיר אָרֶץ — *At earth's transformation.*

The prophet (*Isaiah* 51:6) warns of that cataclysmic day [and simultaneously offers hope to those whom God

For the Conducter, for the sons of Korach,
  on the Alammos, a song.
² God is for us refuge and strength,
  a very accessible help in distress,
³ So we shall not be afraid at earth's transformation,
  and at mountains' collapse in the heart of the sea.
⁴ Its waters will rage and be muddied,
  mountains will roar in His glory, Selah.

favors]: *For the heavens shall vanish like smoke and the earth shall wear out like a garment and they that dwell therein shall die in like manner; but my salvation shall be forever [for the righteous] and My righteousness shall not be withdrawn.*

The sons of Korach witnessed a terrible transformation of the earth; they were swallowed in the ground, yet were saved from doom by being suspended in the air. Therefore, they could assure Israel that similar miracles would occur in the future (*Rashi*).

According to *Ibn Ezra*, the Psalmist assures us that God Himself promised that no threatening global transformation will occur, because He has permanently established the boundaries of the earth and has decreed that the seas will never again cover the land mass. Thus *we have no fear that the earth will be transformed.*[1]

Indeed, *Radak* renders בְּהָמִיר אָרֶץ not as an upheaval of natural forces but political and military turmoil which will turn the entire globe into a battlefield, as the prophet warns: *Many tumultuous disorders come upon the inhabitants of the earth. They are shattered — nation against nation, city against city for God confused them with all manners of distress* (*II Chronicles* 15:6).

וּבְמוֹט הָרִים בְּלֵב יַמִּים — *And at mountains' collapse in the heart of the sea*

This is metaphorical; *mountains* refers to the well-established kings who will be swept into the maelstrom [i.e., *the heart of the sea*] of the global war of Gog and Magog (*Sforno*).

Chazah Zion interprets the verse as a figurative description of the re-establishment of Jewish sovereignty. According to this view, we have no fear because there *will* indeed be a transformation, for the land will change from Arab rule to Jewish rule. The land will become transformed from desolate desert to fertile reconstructed territory. Then the *mountains*, i.e., the distinguished, righteous men, will uproot themselves from the exile and travel over *the heart of the sea* to make their way to the Holy Land.

4. יֶחְמְרוּ מֵימָיו — *Its waters...muddied.*

This refers to the waters' turbulence, which stirs up mud and slime from the sea floor [as in *Isaiah* 57:20] (*Rashi*).

1. *Ibn Ezra* makes use of this verse to negate a theory that was popular among the scientists of his day. Astronomers claimed that the orbit of the sun fluctuates a number of degrees in the sky. Therefore, they predicted, the sun would assume a new position which would have a disastrous effect on the earth's climate. Seas would evaporate into dry land and deserts would be flooded!

Nevertheless, *Ibn Ezra* points to our verse which assures mankind that it need have no fear, for God has promised to interfere with this cataclysmic course of nature, preventing a global catastrophe.

ה סֶלָה: נָהָר פְּלָגָיו יְשַׂמְּחוּ עִיר־אֱלֹהִים
ו קְדֹשׁ מִשְׁכְּנֵי עֶלְיוֹן: אֱלֹהִים בְּקִרְבָּהּ בַּל־
ז תִּמּוֹט יַעְזְרֶהָ אֱלֹהִים לִפְנוֹת בֹּקֶר: הָמוּ
גוֹיִם מָטוּ מַמְלָכוֹת נָתַן בְּקוֹלוֹ תָּמוּג

Thus יֶחְמְרוּ is derived from חֵמָר, *slime*, [see *Genesis* 14:10] (*Radak*).

Radak also suggests that חָמָר can mean *heaps*, *piles*, as in חֳמָרִם חֳמָרִם *piles upon piles* (*Exodus* 8:10). Here the raging sea waters are seen as piling up in towering waves.

Metaphorically, the armies of Gog and Magog will surge forward like a raging sea, only to be defeated and covered with slime and rubble (*Sforno*).

יֶרְעֲשׁוּ הָרִים — *Mountains will roar*.

The mighty nations who joined Gog and Magog now roar in the anguish of defeat (*Sforno*).

בְּגַאֲוָתוֹ — *In His glory* [lit. *pride*].

This defeat of the wicked will come about when God will display His glorious might, as described in verse 2 (*Rashi*).

5. נָהָר — *The river*.

Rashi comments that this river flows from the Garden of Eden. *Ibn Ezra* identifies it as *Gichon*, which is the river of Jerusalem.

[*Rashi* notes in *Berachos* 10b that, although the Sages refer to the waters of Jerusalem (*II Chronicles* 32:4) as *Gichon*, that stream is not the same as the large river flowing out of Eden (*Genesis* 2:13). The river mentioned in *Genesis* does not lie in *Eretz Yisrael*. The *Gichon* of *Chronicles* is the שִׁלוֹחַ, the *Siloam Pool*, near Jerusalem, which is also called *Gichon* in *I Kings* 1:33 (see *Targum, ibid.*).]

פְּלָגָיו יְשַׂמְּחוּ עִיר אֱלֹהִים — *Its streams will gladden the City of God*.

As opposed to all the *waters* which *rage and grow murky*, one *river* will continue to flow tranquilly out of Jerusalem, the *City of God*. [This city will be unaffected by the surrounding turmoil.] The prophet [*Zechariah* 14:8] foretells, *And it shall come to pass on that day that living waters shall go out of Jerusalem half of them toward the eastern sea and half of them toward the western sea*. [That is, the Divine influence emanating from Jerusalem shall bring peace to both halves of the turbulent world, east and west] (*Radak*).

Tne main current of Torah knowledge flows into the world from the *Beis HaMikdash*, the Divine fountainhead. From there the *river* branches out into *streams* of intellectual enlightenment which flows into every *Beis HaMidrash* [House of Study] throughout the entire world. As the prophet proclaims [*Isaiah* 2:3], כִּי מִצִּיּוֹן תֵּצֵא תוֹרָה *For out of Zion, Torah comes forth* (*Sforno*).

The prophet exhorts us to utilize these *waters*, saying [*Isaiah* 12:3], וּשְׁאַבְתֶּם מַיִם בְּשָׂשׂוֹן מִמַּעַיְנֵי הַיְשׁוּעָה *And you shall draw up water with rejoicing from the wellsprings of Salvation* (*Radak*).[1]

קְדֹשׁ מִשְׁכְּנֵי עֶלְיוֹן — *Sanctified dwelling place of the Most High*.

Although the *entire* land of Israel is God's dwelling place, the holiest place of all [where His spirit rests with the

1. *Targum* renders the verse in *Isaiah*, וּתְקַבְּלוּן אוּלְפַן חֲדַת בְּחֶדְוָא מִבְּחִירֵי צַדִּיקַיָּא, *And you shall receive a new lesson, joyously, from select righteous men. Rambam* (*Guide* 1:30) explains that the *Targum* translates in this fashion because water is a metaphor for wisdom, which will then flow abundantly from the Sages, who are *the eyes of the congregation*. The word מִמַּעַיְנֵי, *from the wellsprings*, should be read מֵעֵינֵי, *from the eyes*. This will bring the true יְשׁוּעָה, *salvation*.

⁵ *The river — its streams will gladden*
the City of God,
sanctified dwelling place of the Most High.
⁶ *God is within it, it shall not falter,*
God will help it at the break of dawn.
⁷ *Nations roar, kingdoms totter,*
He raised His voice and the earth will dissolve.

greatest intensity] is Jerusalem (*Radak*); and the Holy Temple (*Sforno*).

6. אֱלֹהִים בְּקִרְבָּהּ בַּל תִּמּוֹט — *God is within it, it shall not falter.*

Although other mountains collapse and fall (v. 3), Mount Zion in Jerusalem will remain standing (*Ibn Ezra*).

This alludes to a statement in *Avos d'Rabbi Nassan:* Ten wondrous things occurred to our forefathers in Jerusalem ... Never did a building collapse [as a result of an earthquake] (*HaChaim Yoducha*).

יַעְזְרֶהָ אֱלֹהִים לִפְנוֹת בֹּקֶר — *God will help it at the break of* [lit. *facing*] *dawn.*

Targum renders: God will assist us in the merit of Abraham, who prayed for [assistance] at the break of dawn [see *Genesis* 19:27].

Radak notes the special symbolism of the word *dawn.* He explains that a battle will rage around Jerusalem, *I will gather all of the nations against Jerusalem to do battle, and the city shall be taken and the houses plundered* (*Zechariah* 14:2). That period [of defeat] will be known as עֶרֶב, *night.*

However, the ensuing era of victory will be called אוֹר, *light,* as the prophet (*ibid. v.* 7) foretells, וְהָיָה לְעֵת עֶרֶב יִהְיֶה אוֹר, *And it shall come to pass that at the time of night there will come a light.*

Tehillos Hashem interprets these

words as a reference to the miraculous destruction of the host of Sennacherib, King of Assyria [see prefatory remarks]: *And it came to pass that night that the angel of Hashem went out and smote in the Assyrian camp one hundred and eighty-five thousand, and when they arose early in the dawn, behold, they were all dead corpses* (II *Kings* 19:35).

7. הָמוּ גוֹיִם מָטוּ מַמְלָכוֹת — *Nations roar, kingdoms totter.*

The nations which gather around Jerusalem begin roaring and boasting of their might, but eventually they will totter in defeat (*Sforno*).

נָתַן בְּקוֹלוֹ — *He raised His voice* [lit. *He gave with His voice*].

This refers to the great shofar which will be sounded at the time of the future redemption (*Chazah Zion*).

According to *Targum,* this alludes to the voice of God which thundered at Sinai, causing all of the nations to tremble and to roar in fear. [See *Zevachim* 116a. See also *commentary* to 29.11.] *Alshich* notes that his tremendous voice was heard לִפְנוֹת בֹּקֶר, *at the break of dawn* (v.6).[See *Exodus* 19:16.]

תָּמוּג אָרֶץ — *The earth will dissolve* [or: *melt.*]

This translation follows *Menachem,*

As *Shem Tov Falaquera* explains, true salvation is the liberation of the mind from the shackles of falseness and fantasy, which imagine that lust and gratification are meaningful and valuable. At the present time, a student can experience the bliss of having a personal *Messiah* if he allows his teacher (*Rebbe*) to teach him how to release his mind from its prison of personal desires. We still await the advent of the universal Messiah, who will grant this intellectual redemption to all men.

ח אָרֶץ: יהוה צְבָאוֹת עִמָּנוּ מִשְׂגָּב לָנוּ
ט אֱלֹהֵי יַעֲקֹב סֶלָה: לְכוּ־חֲזוּ מִפְעֲלוֹת
י יהוה אֲשֶׁר־שָׂם שַׁמּוֹת בָּאָרֶץ: מַשְׁבִּית

who relates this to נָמֹגוּ כֹּל יֹשְׁבֵי כְנָעַן, *All the inhabitants of Canaan melted* (Exodus 15:15). Dunash, however, defines הֶהָמוֹג as a term for *motion*, as in תָּמוֹג נָמֹוג, *The multitude moves* [I Samuel 14:16]; he translates this verse as *the earth moves* (Rashi).

Sforno draws our attention to the words of the prophet (*Zechariah* 14:12) which foretell disaster of consumption and melting: *And this will be the plague with which Hashem will smite all the peoples that have gathered against Jerusalem; their flesh shall melt while they stand upon their feet, and their eyes shall melt away in their sockets and their tongues shall melt away in their mouth.*

8. צְבָאוֹת עִמָּנוּ 'ה — *HASHEM of Legions is with us.*

When the nations totter and melt, and Israel stands firm, everyone will recognize that *HASHEM of Legions is with us* — but not with them (Ibn Ezra).

It will then be evident that God relates to us with His name HASHEM, i.e., *the Divine Attribute of Mercy* (Alshich).

Shaarei Hayashar observes that the gentile nations are supervised and controlled by a host of angels in heaven; only Israel is supervised directly by God. Thus, Hashem, who is master of legions of angels [which control the gentiles] is personally involved only *with us.*

מִשְׂגָּב לָנוּ — *A stronghold for us.*

The numerical value of לָנוּ equals eighty-six, which is the value of אֱלֹהִים. Thus, the verse esoterically signifies that HASHEM, *the Divine Attribute of Mercy*, is a *stronghold* to subdue His

Aspect of אֱלֹהִים, *the Dispenser of Strict Justice* (Yoseif Tehillos).

אֱלֹהֵי יַעֲקֹב — *The God of Jacob.*

More than any other patriarch, Jacob suffered a life filled with trials and afflictions; he survived only because God acted as his stronghold. Therefore it is most appropriate that when God is termed מִשְׂגָּב, *stronghold*, His name is associated with our father Jacob (Norah Tehillos). [Similarly we read (20:2) יְשַׂגֶּבְךָ שֵׁם אֱלֹהֵי יַעֲקֹב, *May the name of Jacob's God make you impregnable (see commentary there).*

[Simple mercy is extended only to men of meager faith. One who truly trusts in God realizes that strict judgment is the truest form of mercy, for it cleanses man of his shortcomings and propels him to higher levels of faith.]

Jacob was a man of complete faith who aspired to the level of וְהָיָה ה' לִי לֵאלֹהִים, *And HASHEM will be to me as God*, (Genesis 28:21); i.e., he asked that 'ה, *the Divine Attribute of Mercy*, should become for him אֱלֹהִים, *the Dispenser of Divine Justice* (Sforno). To Jacob, the names 'ה and אֱלֹהִים were as one, for he understood that God's justice is mercy. Therefore, whenever Jacob's name is mentioned, both names of God are used together, as we read above (20:2) שֵׁם אֱלֹהֵי יַעֲקֹב ... יַעַנְךָ ה' and here again ... צְבָאוֹת עִמָּנוּ 'ה אֱלֹהֵי יַעֲקֹב.]

סֶלָה — *Selah!*

Many translate סֶלָה as *forever* [see commentary to 3:3]. The verse ends with אֱלֹהֵי יַעֲקֹב סֶלָה *Yaakov — forever*, because Jacob has indeed been immortalized. His face is etched into the throne of God Himself and will remain engraved there forever (Ibn Yachya).

8 *HASHEM of Legions is with us,*
a stronghold for us is the God of Jacob, Selah.
9 *Go and see the works of HASHEM,*
Who has wrought devastation in the land.

9. לְכוּ חֲזוּ — *Go [and] see*

Sforno says that the Psalmist addresses his exhortation to the people of Jerusalem who will survive after the War of Gog and Magog. [Since Jerusalem will be left unscathed, they must *go* (לְכוּ) into the land of Israel which surrounds the city to witness the devastation.]

Hirsch defines חֲזוּ as the vision of the mind and soul, which perceive the full spiritual import of God's deeds and do not remain content with a superficial glance. [Thus the usage of לְכוּ *go* is justified because it suggests that in order to truly perceive the inner truth of God's works, one must make the effort to *go* and delve into the depths of events.]

In 66:5 we read לְכוּ וּרְאוּ מִפְעֲלוֹת אֱלֹהִים, *Go and see the accomplishments of God.* It is relatively easy to perceive God in the role of אֱלֹהִים, *the Dispenser of Divine Justice,* for we often see men suffering for their sins. In that verse, therefore, the Psalmist uses the word רְאוּ, *see.* But here he encourages us to recognize the Creator as 'ה *The Dispenser of Mercy,* even while He is inflicting punishment on the land. To perceive that such harsh punishments are truly motivated by Hashem's merciful concern for His erring creations is most difficult and requires the concentrated internal perception of חֲזוּ, *Behold'.*]

מִפְעֲלוֹת ה' — *The works of HASHEM.*[1]

Whatever wonders you may witness, be assured that they were wrought by none other than Hashem (*Radak*).

It may be difficult to attribute the awesome devastation to God, since He is the Creator Who desires the perpetuation of His creatures rather than their destruction. Although He is a God of peace who generally shuns violence, these devastating accomplishments are His, for He alone knows what is best for His world (*Kiflayim L'Sushiya*).

אֲשֶׁר שָׂם שַׁמּוֹת בָּאָרֶץ — *Who has wrought* [lit. *placed*] *devastation in the land.*

Many mighty armies will crowd around besieged Jerusalem, yet the handful of Jewish inhabitants will utterly destroy them. Let it be known that this is the act of God, as it says, *The remainder of the people shall not be cut off from the city. Then shall Hashem go forth and fight against those nations, as*

---

1. *Minchas Shai* confides that he finds this phrase one of the most difficult challenges in all of his studies of Scripture. The problem is whether God's name here should read 'ה or אֱלֹהִים.

In 66:5 we find a very similar passage לְכוּ וּרְאוּ מִפְעֲלוֹת אֱלֹהִים. There is no question that אֱלֹהִים is the proper version there. Here however, the traditional manuscripts read 'ה, and thus is the name rendered in *Targum* and in many *Midrashim.* However, there is overwhelming evidence from other old manuscripts, *Midrashim, Zohar,* grammatical works, lexicons, and Masoretic texts that the proper version here should be אֱלֹהִים.

In conclusion, *Minchas Shai* leaves it to the great scholars to render a final, authoritative decision, based upon the sources.

מִלְחָמוֹת עַד־קְצֵה הָאָרֶץ קֶשֶׁת יְשַׁבֵּר
וְקִצֵּץ חֲנִית עֲגָלוֹת יִשְׂרֹף בָּאֵשׁ: הַרְפּוּ יא
וּדְעוּ כִּי־אָנֹכִי אֱלֹהִים אָרוּם בַּגּוֹיִם אָרוּם
בָּאָרֶץ: יהוה צְבָאוֹת עִמָּנוּ מִשְׂגָּב־לָנוּ יב
אֱלֹהֵי יַעֲקֹב סֶלָה:

---

*when He fights on the day of battle
[Zechariah 14:2-3] (Radak).*[1]

10. מַשְׁבִּית מִלְחָמוֹת עַד קְצֵה הָאָרֶץ — *He
makes cessation of wars to the end of
the earth.*

The conclusion of the wars of Gog
and Magog will mark the end of warfare
for all time. When the nations finally
come to realize that everything is in the
hands of Hashem, they will subjugate
themselves to His service [and refrain
from all hostilities which are in defiance
of His will]. Thus will the words of the
prophet be fulfilled: *And HASHEM will
be king over all of the earth, on that day
HASHEM will be one and His Name one*
[Zechariah 14:9] (Radak).

קֶשֶׁת יְשַׁבֵּר וְקִצֵּץ חֲנִית — *The bow will He
break, [and] sever the spear.*

As the prophet forewarned Gog [Eze-
kiel 39:3]: *I will strike the bow out of
your left hand and cause the arrows to
fall out of your right hand* (Radak).

[When all nations realize that their
arms are useless against God — as will
be demonstrated by the annihilation of
the all-powerful Gog and Magog — they
will destroy their own weapons, as the
Prophet envisions: *And they shall beat*

*their swords into plowshares and their
spears into pruning-hooks (Isaiah 2:4)].*

עֲגָלוֹת יִשְׂרֹף בָּאֵשׁ — *And wagons consume in [the] fire.*

Scripture states: *I will rain down
upon him (Gog) fire and brimstone, and
upon his bands and upon the many nations who are with him [Ezekiel 38:22]
(Radak).*

[Similarly the prophet predicts (ibid.
39:9-10): *And they that dwell in the
cities of Israel shall go forth and set fire
to the weapons [of Gog] and burn them,
both shield and armor, bow and arrows,
and the clubs and the javelins and they
shall make fires with them for seven
years. They will take no wood out of the
field nor cut down any out of the
forests, for they shall make fire with the
weapons.*

11. הַרְפּוּ — *Desist!*

Desist from your assault on Jerusalem (Rashi).

These are the final words of warning
which God addresses to the nations
before *breaking their bow and spear*
(Ibn Ezra).

Sforno notes that God always attempts to warn the wicked to change

---

1. The *Talmud (Berachos 7a)* interprets this verse homiletically (rendering שְׁמוֹת as שֵׁמוֹת,
names) and teaches that the name by which a person is called is not arbitrary, but a result of
Divine inspiration. A name describes a person's true nature and affords us a glimpse into his
future accomplishments. This we learn from a homiletical reading of our verse. Instead of
שַׁמּוֹת, *devastation*, read שֵׁמוֹת, *names*. Thus, *Go out and behold the accomplishments of
HASHEM, for He has placed names* (שֵׁמוֹת) *in the land.*

For example, the name רוּת, *Ruth* foretells that she would merit to have as her descendant
David [her great-grandson], who would sate [רִוָּהוּ=sate] his Creator with songs and
praises.

¹⁰ *He makes cessation of wars*
to the end of the earth,
The bow will He break, sever the spear,
and wagons consume in fire.
¹¹ *Desist! Know that I am God,*
I shall be exalted among the nations,
exalted upon the earth.
¹² *HASHEM of Legions is with us,*
a stronghold for us is the God of Jacob, Selah.

their evil ways, יַעֲזֹב רָשָׁע דַּרְכּוֹ וְאִישׁ אָוֶן מַחְשְׁבֹתָיו, *Let the wicked forsake his way, and the man of iniquity, his plans* (Isaiah 55:7).

Shir HaShirim Rabbah (5:3) interprets הֶרֶף homiletically, relating it to הֶרֶף עַיִן, *the batting of an eyelash.* This implies: Desist from evil immediately and repent instantly, within the brief moment required for the batting of an eyelash.

וּדְעוּ כִּי אָנֹכִי אֱלֹהִים — *[And] know that I am God.*

Know that all efforts against My will are futile, for only *I* possess the power to elevate men and to crush them (Radak).

אָרוּם בַּגּוֹיִם אָרוּם בָּאָרֶץ — *I shall be exalted among the nations, exalted upon the earth.*

The Prophet (Isaiah 26:5) describes the decline of God's estate, Judea and Jerusalem, in double terms, יַשְׁפִּילָהּ יַשְׁפִּילָהּ עַד אֶרֶץ יַגִּיעֶנָּה עַד עָפָר, *He lays it low, laying it low even to the ground, bringing it even to the dust.* Correspondingly to this, the future elevation of God's kingdom is depicted in double terms. First God will utterly destroy the sovereignty of the nations: *I shall be ex-*

alted among the nations. Then, He will assume total mastery over the world: [*And HASHEM will be King over all of the earth* [Zechariah 14:19]; *I shall be exalted among the nations, exalted upon the earth.*] (Chazah Zion).

12. ה' צְבָאוֹת עִמָּנוּ — *HASHEM of Legions is with us.*

This verse repeats verse 8 to emphasize that when the eagerly awaited salvation finally arrives we will never desist from extolling God, as the Psalmist exclaims (41:14), *Blessed is HASHEM, God of Israel, from this world to the next — Amen and Amen'* (Maharam Markado).

מִשְׂגָּב לָנוּ אֱלֹהֵי יַעֲקֹב סֶלָה — *A stronghold for us is the God of Jacob, Selah.*

All nations are destined to recognize God's sovereignty, but their comprehension will be weak and unclear. Israel, however, will enjoy a vivid perception of incomparable clarity. This is because the Gentiles never sought out God previously, whereas the twelve tribes of Israel received a tradition from Jacob to search incessantly for the divine. Their quest endures סֶלָה, *forever* (Ibn Yachya).

T his Psalm is a sequel to the preceding one which describes the
defeat of all the nations who unite against God and His Chosen
People (Radak). After the earth returns to order and tranquility, the
nations will recognize God's universal mastery and will seek His
presence in Jerusalem (Malbim).

Another theme is woven into the fabric of the text: the ability of
the shofar blast to inspire mankind and to arouse God's mercy. The
shofar blast described here refers to the horn of redemption which the
Messiah is destined to blow. However, the Rabbis teach us that it also
alludes to the shofar blown every Rosh Hashanah, which symbolizes
the individual soul's redemption from its sins. Rav Saadiah Gaon
enumerates ten reasons for the sounding of the shofar on Rosh
Hashanah. (Most of these reasons are included in the Commentary to
this Psalm). On Rosh Hashanah, this Psalm is recited seven times
prior to the sounding of the shofar. The Name אֱלֹהִים, which refers to
God's manifestation as the Dispenser of Strict Justice appears here
seven times. Thus the Name אֱלֹהִים is recited a total of forty-nine
times.

The Sages teach that there are forty-nine levels of spiritual impurity before the lowest depth from which no redemption is possible.
Correspondingly, there are forty-nine ascending levels of sanctity
which man can attain. The forty-nine times which the Name is recited
allude to the power of these verses to transform the forty-nine possible levels of spiritual uncleanliness into forty-nine corresponding
levels of sanctity and purity. When Israel is inspired to purify and
perfect itself with such intensity, surely God's strict justice will be
changed to His Attribute of Mercy (Matteh Ephraim, Elef HaMagen
585:5).

לַמְנַצֵּחַ לִבְנֵי־קֹרַח מִזְמוֹר: כָּל־הָעַמִּים
תִּקְעוּ־כָף הָרִיעוּ לֵאלֹהִים בְּקוֹל רִנָּה:
כִּי־יהוה עֶלְיוֹן נוֹרָא מֶלֶךְ גָּדוֹל עַל־כָּל־

1. לַמְנַצֵּחַ — *For the Conductor.*

Most commentators agree that this psalm is dedicated to the era of the Messiah. However, *Ibn Ezra* quotes *Rabbi Moshe*, who ascribes this chapter to the exile of Babylon [reflecting Israel's yearning for redemption and return to Jerusalem]. *Ibn Ezra* cites another opinion which links this psalm to a great event in David's life, the carrying of the Ark of God up to Jerusalem.

מִזְמוֹר — *A song.*

[Although this was first composed by Korach's sons, David adopted the Psalm as his own and endowed it with universal dimensions. The *Yalkut* asserts that David's harp was related to the Messianic Shofar and the future redemption: Rabbi Chanina said, Every part of the ram which Abraham sacrificed instead of his son Isaac on Mount Moriah was used for a good purpose. Its sinews were fashioned into harpstrings for David. Its hide became the belt which girded Elijah's loins. Its left horn was sounded on Mount Sinai. Its right horn will be sounded by the Holy One, Blessed be He, at the time of the future redemption.]

2. כָּל־הָעַמִּים — *All [you] nations.*

This is an exhortation. The Psalmist addresses the survivors of the war of Gog and Magog [which are described vividly in Psalm 46] (*Sforno*).

If the psalm is dedicated to David himself, then the nations are those which were conquered and ruled by this king of Israel (*Ibn Ezra*).

תִּקְעוּ כָף — *Join hands.*

This translation follows *Rashi*, who interprets this as a call to assimilate for the purpose of praising God [see commentary. to v. 6, בְּקוֹל שׁוֹפָר]. The ex-

pression כָף תָּקַע is used in this sense in *Proverbs* (6:1, 17:18, 22:26). Thus, All you nations join hands in an alliance to collectively *call out to God!*

However, *Radak, Meiri,* and *Sforno* render תִּקְעוּ כָף as *clap your hands for joy,* as in כַף יִמְחֲאוּ, *they clap hands* (98:8).

Chazah Zion notes that the numerical value of כָף is one hundred. On Rosh Hashanah, *all of the nations* pass before God in judgment (*Rosh Hashanah* 16a; see 33:15), and at that time we are commanded: תִּקְעוּ, *blow* (on the shofar) כָף, *one hundred blasts.*

הָרִיעוּ לֵאלֹהִים — *Call out to God.*

[This may also be translated as *sound blasts of the horn,* i.e., *sound a* תְּרוּעָה, *broken note].*

Malbim observes that it is customary to sound the trumpets during a royal coronation ceremony. This is what the nations will do when they appoint God as their sovereign.

[Similarly, *Rav Saadiah Gaon* lists ten reasons for blowing the shofar on Rosh Hashanah. His first explanation is that since Rosh Hashanah corresponds to the first day of man's (Adam's) creation, humanity is obliged to coronate God as king with fanfare on this day, as David says, בַּחֲצֹצְרוֹת וְקוֹל שׁוֹפָר הָרִיעוּ לִפְנֵי הַמֶּלֶךְ ה׳, *With trumpets and the sound of the horn blast forth before the king, HASHEM* (98:6)].

Chazah Zion renders הָרִיעוּ as *break yourselves,* referring to the words of the prophet (*Isaiah* 24:19) who depicts the future downfall of the nations as רֹעָה הִתְרֹעֲעָה הָאָרֶץ, *Broken and shattered is the land.* With the sound of the broken Teruah-blast of Rosh Hashanah, the heart of the sinner is broken and so is God's wrath. [This corresponds to *Rav*

For the Conductor,
by the sons of Korach, a song.
² All you nations, join hands!
Call out to God with a cry of joy.
³ For HASHEM is Most High, awesome,
a great king 'over all of the earth.

Saadiah Gaon's seventh reason for blowing the shofar].

בְּקוֹל רִנָּה — With a cry of joy.

[Why should the nations rejoice after their downfall?] *Radak* explains that the nations will rejoice in the realization that their downfall was instrumental in helping Creation attain its purpose. Once they realize that Hashem is the only God and Israel is His chosen nation, they will know that their defeat was necessary to bring about the revelation of these historic truths.

Tehillos Hashem emphasizes that the nations are commanded to rejoice even לֵאלהִים, *to God* in his Aspect as Strict Judge, i.e., they must rejoice even after He has harshly, but justly, punished them with defeat.[1]

3. כִּי ה' עֶלְיוֹן נוֹרָא — *For HASHEM is Most High, awesome.*

This is the cry of joy which the nations are urged to shout out (*Ibn Ezra*).

He is *Most High* because He controls everyone; He is *awesome* because He performs wonders that cause the nations to fear Him (*Radak*).

Malbim explains that these two descriptions refute the two main arguments of the heretics. Some heretics deny God's reality entirely and attribute

the entire Creation to the activities of celestial bodies and cosmic forces. In the future, everyone will realize that God is *Most High*, i.e., the prime Cause and first Source of Creation.

Other idolators admit God's role as Creator, but claim that God later abandoned this world to the influences of the blind forces of nature, no longer caring about the earth's lowly creatures [see *Rambam, Hilchos Avodah Zarah* 1:1]. They claim that God no longer cares enough to punish or reward; they contend, therefore, that there is no need to fear Him. This heresy will also be abandoned in the future, when everyone witnesses the *awesome* punishments which God inflicts upon those who defy Him. These public punishments will serve as a warning to all.

[*Rav Saadiah Gaon's* second reason for sounding the shofar is that before a king punishes his subjects for neglecting his decrees,he gives them a final warning. Rosh Hashanah initiates the Ten Days of Repentance, culminating in the final judgment of Yom Kippur. The shofar blast represents Hashem's last warning to His people].

מֶלֶךְ גָּדוֹל עַל כָּל הָאָרֶץ — *A great king over all of the earth.*

Shaarei Chaim's explanation seems to

---

1. *Alshich* introduces a deep concept:
Man lives by the grace of heaven, which constantly sends energy and sustenance to earth. This sustenance may come from the hand of God, or it may come through His appointed celestial angels. Before the defeat of Gog and Magog, the nations were not subjugated, but were far removed from God, (who turned them over to the jurisdiction of the angels). After their defeat they will lose their physical freedom, but gain Godliness by becoming the vassals of Israel. For Israel's bountiful sustenance, provided by Hashem Himself, will overflow to encompass the nations as well. Thus, they will experience for the first time the ecstasy of being sustained by God, therefore, they rejoice!

ד הָאָרֶץ: יַדְבֵּר עַמִּים תַּחְתֵּינוּ וּלְאֻמִּים
ה תַּחַת רַגְלֵינוּ: יִבְחַר־לָנוּ אֶת־נַחֲלָתֵנוּ אֶת
ו גְּאוֹן יַעֲקֹב אֲשֶׁר־אָהֵב סֶלָה: עָלָה

lead directly from the *Malbim's* interpretation (cited above):

In 99:2 we read הֹ בְּצִיּוֹן גָּדוֹל וְרָם הוּא עַל כָּל הָעַמִּים, *HASHEM is great in Zion, and He is high above all the nations*. Something גָּדוֹל, *great*, resembles a tower, which rises to the sky, but is based on earth. Thus does the Jewish people (*Zion*) view God: He is *great* and lofty, yet He is also involved with the world. The word רָם, *high above*, refers to an elevated object which is completely divorced from the earth, such as a soaring bird. Thus do the gentile nations conceive of God: He is deemed aloof and remote!

In then future, however, the nations will recognize that God is indeed involved in our earthly affairs. Therefore He is described as מֶלֶךְ גָּדוֹל עַל כָּל הָאָרֶץ, *A great king over all of the earth*.

4. יַדְבֵּר עַמִּים תַּחְתֵּינוּ — *He plagues the nations in our stead.*

This translation generally follows *Targum* and particularly *Rashi*, who relates יַדְבֵּר to דֶּבֶר, *pestilence, plague*. God vents His wrath on the nations; and thus His anger abates and Israel escapes unscathed. Similarly, God tells Israel נָתַתִּי כָפְרְךָ מִצְרַיִם, *I have made Egypt your ransom'* (Isaiah 43:3).

However, the other major commentators render יַדְבֵּר as יִנְהַג, *He will lead*, indicating that God will lead the nations from the ends of the earth to Jerusalem, to bring them under Israel's rule.

Hirsch interprets יַדְבֵּר as *to gather together* [see I Kings 5:23].

וּלְאֻמִּים תַּחַת רַגְלֵינוּ — *And kingdoms beneath our feet.*

The translation of לְאֻמִּים as *Kingdoms* (see Genesis 25:23 וּלְאֹם מִלְאֹם יֶאֱמָץ) follows *Tehillos Hashem* who

emphasizes that the wicked nobles who control the hierachy of *kingdoms* will suffer much more than the simple peasants who are described above as עַמִּים, *nations*, meaning *followers*. Because the nobles conspired to tyrannize and oppress Israel, they are condemned to be crushed *beneath our feet*. The common folk who did not initiate any persecutions but merely followed their cruel leaders, will now be led (יַדְבֵּר) under the guidance and rule of Israel.

Sforno believes that this Jewish domination will be entirely beneficial to the nations. They will be *under* our intelligent guidance and will follow the path of *our feet*, as the prophet foretells: *You will be named the priests of HASHEM, men shall call you the ministers of our God* (Isaiah 61:6).

[In the Messianic era, even if the nations seek to repent and convert to Judaism, they will remain under the authority of Israel. For the *halacha* stipulates, converts are not accepted during the days of Messiah (*Yevamos* 24b), because they are assumed to be insincere and attracted only by Israel's rise to power. Converts can join our nation as equals only if they enter our ranks when we are downtrodden and despised. Those who are willing to take part in our misery can later share the fruits of our glory.]

5. יִבְחַר־לָנוּ אֶת נַחֲלָתֵנוּ — *He will choose for us our heritage.*

In the days of Messiah, Hashem will return us to our estate, the Holy Land, and to the Temple, which is the pride of Jacob (*Radak*).

Sforno stresses that despite the Jew's complete domination of the nations, Israel will not harm them nor drive

⁴ *He plagues the nations in our stead,*
and kingdoms beneath our feet.
⁵ *He will choose for us our heritage,*
the pride of Jacob which He loved, Selah.

them from their lands. Rather, Israel will choose to dwell only in its rightful ancestral estate, the Holy Land, which is hospitable only to Jewish inhabitants, as it says, *And your enemies who dwell therein shall be made desolate* (*Leviticus* 26:32).

Ibn Ezra (v.1) notes that there are those who maintain that this Psalm was an accompaniment for the Ark as it was carried to its permanent quarters. It is evident that the exact location of Mount Moriah, the site of the future Temple, was not yet known, for they said, *He will [yet] choose for us our estate.* [Thus, they walked blindly, waiting for God to guide their steps, just as Abraham had journeyed to sacrifice Isaac on Mount Moriah without advance knowledge of his destination.]

אֶת גְּאוֹן יַעֲקֹב — *The pride of Jacob.*

This is the Holy Temple, where God's spirit resides in splendor. The Jewish nation views the fact that God dwells in its midst with great גָּאוֹן, *pride,* and sees the Divine Presence as its most remarkable advantage over other nations (*Radak*).[1]

[See *Leviticus* 26:19 and *Rashi* ibid.; and *Ezekiel* 24:21 אֶת מִקְדְּשִׁי גְאוֹן עֻזְּכֶם, *My Temple, your mighty pride*].

Why does the Psalmist here refer to all of Israel as *Jacob*? *Ibn Yachya* ex-

plains that the third Patriarch is singled out because only his face is 'etched into God's celestial Throne' as representative of Israel and mankind.

Rav Shlomo Atiya notes that Jacob demonstrated a very special reverence for the Temple. It was he who was completely overwhelmed by the magnificence of God's Presence on Mount Moriah, exclaiming *How very awesome is this place* (*Genesis* 28:17). He vowed to erect a monument on the site and to serve God there. The Almighty reciprocated and took special pride in Jacob from that time onward.

[We even find that God takes the name of Jacob as His own and calls Himself גָּאוֹן יַעֲקֹב (*Amos* 8:7, *Radak* ibid.)]

Alshich comments that the first two Temples, which were temporary, were identified with Abraham and Isaac respectively. However, the third and final *Beis Hamikdash*, which will endure eternally, is ascribed to the merit of Jacob, who also lives forever [Our forefather Jacob never (really) died. (*Taanis* 5b; see *Ramban Genesis* 49:33)]. The immortal *Jacob* is the one *whom He* [God] *loved* [סֶלָה] *forever* [see *commentary* to 3:3].

[*Rav Saadiah Gaon's* fifth reason for sounding the shofar is to remind us of the *Beis HaMikdash,* which lies in

---

1. After the destruction of the *Beis Hamikdash*, God transferred His abode from the Holy Temple to the study hall. The *Talmud* (*Berachos* 8a) states: Since the day of the destruction, God has no interest in This World other that the four cubits of *halachah.* The houses of study became the main גָּאוֹן, *pride,* of God and Israel. Perhaps this is why the title given the heads of the Torah academies in Babylon was גָּאוֹן, *Gaon* [lit. *pride*].

Meiri (introduction to *Avos*) suggests a different reason. The heads of these *yeshivos* had to be completely fluent in all sixty tractates of the Talmud — by heart! The numerical value of גָּאוֹן is sixty, an allusion to this prodigious accomplishment. [There are various traditions regarding the number of tractates in the Talmud. See *Z'man Nakat* by *Rabbi David Cohen* (chapter 2), for a complete discussion.

ז אֱלֹהִים בִּתְרוּעָה יהוה בְּקוֹל שׁוֹפָר:
ח זַמְּרוּ אֱלֹהִים זַמֵּרוּ זַמְּרוּ לְמַלְכֵּנוּ זַמֵּרוּ:

ruins. The gentile marauders blew their horns and trumpets in battle as they vanquished Israel and destroyed the Temple. The sound of the shofar should arouse us to beseech God to rebuild the *Beis HaMikdash*, which is our pride.]

אֲשֶׁר אָהֵב — *Which He loved.*

Jerusalem is the city which God chose for His abode (see *I Kings* 11:13) and Zion is His desire, as it says (87:2) *God loves the gates of Zion* (Radak).

6. עָלָה אֱלֹהִים בִּתְרוּעָה — *God ascended with the blast.*

Sforno paraphrases: When אֱלֹהִים, *the Dispenser of Strict Justice*, rises up and executes His judgement against Gog and Magog, the horn of victory will sound a triumphant blast.

Radak continues: That victory will fulfill the prophecy *I shall be exalted amongst the nations* (46:1) and then God will be recognized as *Most High and awesome.*

According to *Pirkei d'Rabbi Eliezer* (Chapter 46), these words allude to the transmission of the Second Tablets at Sinai. The original Tablets were destroyed because of the Golden Calf, which was made as a result of confusion concerning the precise time of Moses' ascent and descent from the mount. When Moses went up the second time, the days were clearly marked off and recorded by the daily blast of the shofar. At that time, the faith of the people rose high above the threat of idolatry; therefore, *God ascended with the blast.* For this reason, the custom is to sound the shofar publicly from the first of Elul, the day of Moses' third ascent (*Tur Orach Chaim* 581).

[*Rav Saadiah Gaon's* third reason for sounding the shofar on Rosh Hashanah is to recall the blasts sounded at Sinai].

Ibn Ezra and *Radak* interpret this

with reference to the Holy Ark, which was concealed in the depths of Mount Moriah as the era of the First Temple drew to a close. In the future, when the great horn of redemption is blown, this Ark will *ascend* from its concealment. The Ark is called אֱלֹהִים because God's spirit rests upon it between the cherubs. Similarly, we read (*Numbers* 10:35) *And when the Ark began to journey forth Moses said, 'Arise HASHEM'* Then, too, the Ark arose to the sound of trumpets (*Yaavetz haDoresh*).

Many *Midrashim* suggest that the Psalmist is alluding to the blast of the shofar on Rosh Hashanah. Specifically the תְּרוּעָה, *teruah*, is the broken blast which symbolizes the harsh, shattering punishments of אֱלֹהִים, *the Dispenser of strict Justice.* When the Jew hears the sound of the *teruah*, he realizes that he deserves shattering punishment for his sins and is inspired to repent. Having felt remorse for his sins, he is forgiven and the verdict of אֱלֹהִים is nullified. Thus, *God* (אֱלֹהִים) *ascends and departs because of the Teruah blast.*

Also, it is taught that the sound of *tekiah* corresponds to Abraham; *shevarim*, to Isaac; and *teruah*, to Jacob and David, because the lives of both were marked by shattering tragedies, which they overcame with their complete faith (*Elef HaMagen* 585:4)].

The *Midrash* says: *Praiseworthy is the nation which knows the Teruah blast* (89:16). This is the nation of Israel which knows how to appease its Maker with the *teruah* blast, whereupon He arises from His Throne of Strict Judgement and sits down on His Throne of Mercy where He converts harsh justice to compassion (*Vayikra Rabba* 29).

ה׳ בְּקוֹל שׁוֹפָר — *HASHEM, with the sound of the shofar*

Sforno observes that this is the long

⁶ God ascended with the blast,
HASHEM, with the sound of the shofar.
⁷ Make music for God, make music,
make music for our King, make music.

awaited blast signalling the ingathering of exiles, 'And it shall come to pass on that day that a great horn shall be blown; and they shall come — those who were lost in the land of Assyria, and those who were dispersed in the land of Egypt — and they shall prostrate themselves before HASHEM in the holy mountain, Jerusalem. (Isaiah 27:13).

[The ninth reason for the sounding of the shofar offered by *Rav Saadiah Gaon* reflects this verse. He stresses that when one hears the shofar on Rosh Hashanah, he should pray for the day of the קִבּוּץ גָּלוּיוֹת, *the Ingathering of the Exiles.*]

Alshich, pursuing the theme of Rosh Hashanah, explains that after the broken *teruah* blast, אֱלֹהִים, God's strict justice is tempered with the Name 'ה, HASHEM.

Hirsch identifies the *sound of the shofar* as the unbroken sound of the *tekiah* blast. This symbolizes God's unwavering, unending love for Israel. In his commentary to *Leviticus* 23:24, *Hirsch* explains that תָּקַע means *to bring something forcefully into something else, to ram, to thrust into.* The term is also used for the handshake, which symbolically binds the parties to a transaction, as one party thrust his hand into the hand of the second party. With reference to a wind instrument, the *tekiah* is a sustained unbroken note which attracts and keeps one's attention.

Ramban relates the word, שׁוֹפָר to שֶׁפֶר, beauty. The blast of the shofar arouses Israel to repent and beautify its ways so that it may serve as an example of rectitude for all nations.

7. זַמְּרוּ אֱלֹהִים זַמֵּרוּ — *Make music for God, make music.*

Radak (v. 8) explains that this is not an exhortation to play music, but a command to compose new, fresh melodies.

[Throughout the *Book of Psalms* מִזְמוֹר is translated as *song*. However, as explained in the *commentary* to 30:1, the root word זמר, is more accurately translated as *the instrumental accompaniment* to lyrics, which are called שִׁירָה. Since the previous verse speaks of a musical instrument, the shofar, the word זמר is best rendered *make music*.]

This opinion is supported by *Alkabetz (Divrei Shlomo)* and by *Hirsch* who refers us to his *commentary* to *Genesis* 43:11 [German and Hebrew editions, deleted in English], where he explains that זמר is *not* the chanted word, but the melody, the tune arising from the soul.

Hirsch notes that זֶמֶר is related to זְמוֹרָה, *vine, branch.* Inside the branch, the sap gathers long before the fruit emerges. When a sufficient amount of this nutritious liquid accumulates, the tree is ready to burst forth with fruit.

So, too, with song. All feelings and emotions are gathered into the strains of the wordless melody. When these feelings reach a crescendo, they overflow into original words of praise. The well-chosen, inspired word of שִׁירָה is thus the fruit of the זְמְרָה.

Chazah Zion perceives זְמְרָה as a cognate of זְמִירָה, *pruning.*

Through ecstatic song, a person can remove or *prune* God's strict judgment [see *Overview*, Vol. I.]

זַמְּרוּ לְמַלְכֵּנוּ זַמֵּרוּ — *Make music for our King, make music!*

This repetition indicates that one melody inspires the next (*Divrei Shlomo*).

Yaavetz Hadoresh notes that the

כִּי מֶלֶךְ כָּל־הָאָרֶץ אֱלֹהִים זַמְּרוּ מַשְׂכִּיל:
מָלַךְ אֱלֹהִים עַל־גּוֹיִם אֱלֹהִים יָשַׁב | עַל־
כִּסֵּא קָדְשׁוֹ: נְדִיבֵי עַמִּים | נֶאֶסְפוּ עַם

---

word זַמְּרוּ is repeated five times in these
two verses, alluding to the Five Books of
Moses. The Torah was enshrined in the
Ark which David was escorting to
Jerusalem.

[This procession was accompanied by
an unprecedented outburst of music
and song. *And David and all of the
House of Israel played before HASHEM
with all manner of instruments made of
cypress wood and with harps and flutes
and with timbels and with rattles, and
with cymbals ... So David and all of the
House of Israel brought up the Ark of
HASHEM* [בִּתְרוּעָה וּבְקוֹל שׁוֹפָר] *with
shouting and with the sound of the
shofar* (II Samuel 6:5,15).]

8. כִּי מֶלֶךְ כָּל־הָאָרֶץ אֱלֹהִים — *For God is
King of all the earth.*

Although God is Master of the entire
universe, and has at His disposal the
legions of heavenly minstrels, in His
humility He desires to hear the music of
man *(Otzar Nechmad)*.

*HASHEM will be acknowledged as
king over the entire earth* (Zechariah
14:9). At that time the shofar blast will
herald universal peace. But today the
shofar is used as an instrument of war.
Then Joshua said to the people, *'Blow
(the shofar) for HASHEM has given you
the city.'*

[The *Talmud* (Berachos 56b) states
that the same dream may be interpreted
as a good or as a bad omen. The
prophecy of the dream is determined by
the interpreter. Thus if one sees a shofar
in his dream he may interpret it as a call
to battle or as a herald of peace.]

זַמְּרוּ מַשְׂכִּיל — *Make music, O enlightened one.*

Even the ordinary people are exhorted to *clap hands* and *shout out to
God a cry of joy* (v. 2), for these simple
forms of merriment are within their
ability. However, the composition of
music is a complex art reserved for the
מַשְׂכִּיל, *enlightened man* of superior intelligence (Radak).

Otzar Nechmad draws our attention
to a grammatical inconsistency. The
singular form מַשְׂכִּיל, *enlightened one,*
follows the plural verb זַמְּרוּ. This implies that although many intelligent
men are urged to compose, each should
pursue the task individually, for each
man's comprehension of God's glory is
unique.

Rav Yeibi notes that the appellation
enlightened one reflects our Sages' statement (Sanhedrin 91b): Whoever recites
songs (to God) in this world will be given
the privilege of reciting songs in the
World to Come. That is, only the מַשְׂכִּיל,
who is discerning enough in this world
to praise God, will be able to *make
music* in the future.

According to *Rav Yoseif Kimchi*
(quoted by his son, *Radak*) and *Meiri*,
מַשְׂכִּיל, is not a description of the composer but of the composition [rendering:
make enlightened music.] This is not a
mere folk tune, but a work of the highest
excellence which wins the listener's attention and stimulates him to use his
mental facilities to recognize the do-
minion of God.

9. מָלַךְ אֱלֹהִים עַל גּוֹיִם — *God reigns over
the peoples.*

Until now, God ruled only over
Israel; henceforth, He shall reign over

XLVII
8-10

⁸ *For God is King of all the earth,*
     make music, O enlightened one!
⁹ *God reigns over the peoples,*
     God sits upon His holy throne.
¹⁰ *The nobles of the nations gathered,*

all peoples [see Zechariah 14:9]
(Radak).

אֱלֹהִים יָשַׁב עַל כִּסֵּא קָדְשׁוֹ — *God sits upon His holy throne* [lit. *throne of His holiness*.]

Hostility to God will no longer exist. He will be welcomed everywhere in the world, for *He reigns over all peoples.* Nevertheless, He will choose to rest His Holy Presence only in the sacred Temple of Israel (*Sforno*). [כִּי בָחַר ה' בְּצִיּוֹן, *for God has chosen Zion, desired it as His dwelling place* (132:13).]

Eretz HaChaim comments that God's name and His throne will be incomplete, until the Messianic era, when God's enemies (particularly Amalek) will be vanquished. [See *Exodus* 17:16, *Rashi ibid.*] Only then will *God sit upon His holy throne.*

Shevet MiYisroel views this as an allusion to the *Midrash* (*Bereishis Rabbah* 82:9), which states: When God judges Israel He does it hastily, while standing [as it were], so that their examination will be brief and superficial and their verdict lenient. When judging the nations, however, He sits, in order to conduct a lengthy and exacting investigation of their deeds. Then He adopts the role of a prosecutor and accuses them.

Thus, the Psalmist foretells that אֱלֹהִים rules the gentiles *He will sit down* [for lengthy review] *upon His holy throne* [of judgment].

[Rav Saadiah Gaon's eighth reason for the sounding of the Shofar is to bring to mind the awesomeness of the Final Judgment, as the prophet says, *For the great day of HASHEM is near, it is near and swiftly draws close* ... יוֹם שׁוֹפָר, *A day of the shofar (sound) and the shout* (Zephaniah 1:14,16).]

10. נְדִיבֵי עַמִּים — *The nobles of the nations.*

Radak and *Ibn Ezra* identify these as the great nobles of the gentile nations. *Sforno* describes them as the outstanding philanthropists. According to *Rashi* the נְדִיבִים are the non-Jews who nobly submitted to slaughter and martyrdom in order to sanctify God's Name.

[Abraham is considered the paragon of נְדִיבוּת, *martyrdom,* nobility, self-sacrifice. Israel, more than any other nation, is called בַּת נָדִיב, *daughter of nobility* (Songs 7:2). This designation applies especially when Israel is prepared to sacrifice the comforts of home in order to make the arduous festival pilgrimage to Jerusalem (*Chagigah* 3a). At these times the Jews resemble Abraham, who gave up everything in order to follow God to the land of Canaan. The noble gentiles who gather in Israel are following in the footsteps of Abraham and deserve to be called נְדִיבִים.[1]]

Rav Saadiah Gaon's sixth reason for

---

1. The *Midrash* (*Devarim Rabbah* 2:24) relates that when the Sages, Rabbi Eliezer, Rabbi Yehoshua, and Rabban Gamliel were in Rome, the Senate decreed, 'Thirty days hence no Jew may exist anywhere in the entire world '.

There was one God-fearing senator, the councillor of the Emperor, who revealed this plot to

the sounding of the shofar is to remind us of *Akeidas Yitzchak*, when Abraham's son Isaac was prepared to give up his life for God. So should every Jew be ready to sacrifice himself for God.]

Rabbeinu Yonah (Sha'arei Teshuvah III: 168) identifies the נְדִיבֵי עַמִּים as the tribal heads of Israel, for the twelve tribes of Israel are called עַמִּים, *nations* (see *Deuteronomy* 33:19). When the entire congregation gathers to serve God, they are deemed stalwart followers of Abraham, who sanctified God. Anyone who deserts the congregation desecrates the Divine Service which it represents; therefore he is classed among those who despise God's Name.

נֶאֱסָפוּ — *Gathered.*

They congregate in the Holy Land (*Sforno*) in order to accept the complete sovereignty of God (*Otzar Nechmad*).

עַם אֱלֹהֵי אַבְרָהָם — *The nations of the God of Abraham.*

These martyrs are identified as the nation of *Abraham's* God because Abraham was the first man to sacrifice his entire being for the sake of God, by becoming the first convert [for Abraham incurred the wrath of Nimrod, who threw him into a blazing furnace] (*Rashi*).

[These martyrs are presumably converts to Judaism, and Abraham was the first to proselytize. Scripture considers these proselytes creations of Abraham, referring to them as *the souls he made in Haran* (*Genesis* 12:5).The very name Abraham is a contraction of אַב הֲמוֹן גּוֹיִם, *Father of a multitude of nations* [*Gen.* 17:4]. For this reason, the *halachah* stipulates that the proselyte may refer to the patriarchs as *his* forefathers and that he is considered the

the Rabbis. They were terribly distraught, but the senator encouraged them, saying confidently, 'Fear not! The God of the Jews will save them within these thirty days!'

After twenty-five days elapsed, the senator told his wife of the planned genocide. She exclaimed,'Woe, there are only five days left to nullify this decree!' This righteous woman convinced her husband to commit suicide, so that the Senate would adjourn for thirty days of mourning; thus the evil decree would expire unfulfilled.

When the Sages consoled the senator's widow, they were very upset that he had martyred himself without having had the spiritual benefits of circumcision and conversion. The widow

the nation of the God of Abraham,
For God's are the shields of the earth —
He is exceedingly exalted.

descendant of our father Abraham
(*Rambam, Hilchos Biccurim* 4:3).]

כִּי לֵאלֹהִים מָגִנֵּי אֶרֶץ — *For God's are the shields of the earth.*

[After the world witnesses God's
might in protecting Israel from Gog and
Magog], everyone will realize that He
truly possesses the power to shield
those who trust in Him (*Rashi*). [Thus
they will no longer deny God's om-
nipotence by asking, 'If God is truly
All-Powerful, how could He permit
heathens to kill the martyrs?' They will
realize that although God could have
shielded the martyrs, He wished to
grant them the incomparable privilege
of sanctifying His holy name.]

Ibn Ezra and *Radak* render מָגִנֵּי as *nobles, kings* [who provide their subjects
with physical protection] as in *Psalm
89:19* and *Hosea 4:18*. This description

corresponds with נְדִיבֵי, *nobles.*

Sforno also connects both titles, explaining that these men are
philanthropists who provide shelter for
their neighbors and shield the souls of
their people by teaching them the
proper way to serve God. [Thus they
emulate Abraham.] These men, chosen
by God to fill this role in society, now
gather around Him.

מְאֹד נַעֲלָה — *He is exceedingly exalted.*

According to *Rashi, Radak,* and *Ibn
Ezra*, this describes God, who is no
longer degraded as impotent but
recognized as the Omnipotent Protector
of His faithful.

Sforno interprets this as praise for
Abraham, who fathered a nation which
faithfully adheres to his actions and
beliefs. This feat has never been
duplicated by any other man.

comforted them by offering proof that the Senator had, in fact, undergone a secret circumcision and conversion.

The Rabbis then applied our verse to him, explaining, *the nobles of the nations gathered,
the nation of the God of Abraham* (the converts), *for god's are the shields of the earth;* your
husband deserves many shields from God, because Abraham put his life in danger only after
God promised *I am your shield* (*Genesis* 15:1), but this noble martyr sacrificed his life without
any divine assurance. *He is greatly exalted* — even more exalted than Abraham!

מזמור מח 48

The previous psalm describes the defeat of all the nations hostile to God, which will take place in Messianic times. It concludes with a call to all who were faithful to God to gather together in the Holy Land and in the chosen city of Jerusalem.

Here the Psalmist describes the future glory of this city which now lays in ruins. Its reconstruction will be no mere architectural feat of mortar and stone. Rather, the restoration of the sacred city will signal an era of national renewal. We will be like children returning to their father's home, and God, our father, will invest us with new energy and vitality to lift our souls to immortality (v. 15).

This psalm is the שִׁיר שֶׁל יוֹם, Song of the Day, during the Temple service of the second day of the week, for on the second day of Creation, God separated between the heavenly and earthly components of the universe and ruled over both (Rosh Hashanah 31a).

Furthermore, the Midrash explains that on the second day, division [מַחְלוֹקֶת, schism; strife] was created, when the upper and lower waters were separated against their will, so to speak.

Rabbeinu Bachya explains that this schism was the root of all subsequent strife and defiance in the world. The Talmud (Shabbos 156a) states: 'One who is born on the second day will be bad-tempered, because on that day the waters were divided.' Rashi comments that as a result of his bad temper, he will become 'divided' — i.e., estranged — from other people.

Resisei Layla explains that this division between heaven and earth initiated the eternal strife between the physical and the spiritual. Therefore, it was fitting that the psalm for the second day was composed by the sons of Korach, for he was the instigator of strife against Moses in the Wilderness. (See ArtScroll Genesis 1:7, commentary and footnote).

According to the Zohar, Korach's sons composed the psalm while tottering on the brink of Gehinnom where, had they not repented, they would have descended with their father. [The Talmud (Pesachim 54a) states that the Torah omits the words כִּי טוֹב, that it was good, from the narrative of the second day of Creation because on that day the fire of Gehinnom was created.] Therefore, concludes the Zohar, this psalm is the appropriate daily song for the second day of the week.

1. שִׁיר מִזְמוֹר — *A song with musical accompaniment.*

[Ibn Ezra states that the titles שִׁיר מִזְמוֹר and שִׁיר מִזְמוֹר share the same meaning; therefore, our translation here follows that used for שִׁיר מִזְמוֹר in 30:1. See *commentary* there for futher explanation.]

The *Zohar* (*Acharei Mos*) explains that this apparent redundancy emphasizes the great significance of this psalm. Similarly, *Psalm 92* begins with the repetition שִׁיר לְיוֹם הַשַּׁבָּת and the word שִׁיר, *song*, is repeated in the title of שִׁיר הַשִּׁירִים, *the Song of Songs*, in both cases to indicate their importance.

2. גָּדוֹל ה' וּמְהֻלָּל מְאֹד — *Great is HASHEM and much praised.*

Indeed, HASHEM's greatness is universal and unchanging. During the exile, however, this greatness is not readily apparent; therefore, the very name יהו"ה has been reduced to י"ה [*Eruvin* 18b] (*Eretz HaChaim*).

In the future, however, God's Name will be restored to its former size and greatness, and He will be *much praised* (*Sforno*).

This is especially so in the city of Jerusalem and particulary on the Temple Mount, which is the only place where God's complete name is pronounced properly in its entirety (*Zerah Yaakov*).

Shevet MiYisrael explains that not only will God's name be magnified in this city, but also the city will be enlarged to demonstrate the greatness of the God who dwells there. The *Midrash* says: In the future, the Temple will expand to cover the entire area of Jerusalem and Jerusalem will expand over all of Eretz Yisrael (see *Maharsha*, *Bava Basra* 75b s.v. ירושלים).

בְּעִיר אֱלֹהֵינוּ הַר קָדְשׁוֹ — *In the city of our God, Mount of His Holiness.*

When *the city of our God* is inhabited and built up, God is recognized as גָּדוֹל, *great*. But when it is destroyed and the Temple lays in ruins, and all that remains is the bare *Mount of His Holiness*, then God is *much praised*, i.e.,He is praised even more than previously, because the sanctity the Temple Mount which still remains even while the Temple itself is in ruins, demonstrates the intensity of God's holy spirit, which can never be blotted out or chased away (*Alshich*) [see *Rambam, Beis HaBechirah* 6:16.]

Malbim observes that, generally speaking, awe is best cultivated and maintained at a distance. As one grows closer and more intimate with the object of wonder, the awe steadily diminishes for 'familiarity breeds contempt.' With HASHEM it is not so. The closer we draw to Him — living together in *His city* and constantly visiting *His mount of Holiness*, the more convinced we become that *Great is HASHEM and much praised.*

3. יְפֵה נוֹף — *Fairest of sites.*

This translation of נוֹף follows *Menachem* (in *Rashi*), *Ibn Ezra*, and *Radak* who render נוֹף as *section, area,* as in שְׁלֹשֶׁת הַנָּפֶת, *three districts* (*Joshua* 17:11).

Rav Yoseif Kimchi (quoted by his son, *Radak*) draws our attention to the fact that the globe is divided into seven distinctly different climate zones. Ordinarily, a change of climate has an adverse affect on one's health. However, those who move to Israel suffer no harmful effects. Moreover, if they move into the holy atmosphere of Jerusalem, they feel not the slightest

XLVIII
1-3

*A song with musical accompaniment
by the sons of Korach.*

*² Great is HASHEM and much praised,
in the city of our God,
Mount of His Holiness.*

³ Fairest of sites, joy of all the earth, Mount Zion

trace of discomfort, for the air of this city is the world's finest.

Similarly, the Sages (*Bava Basra* 158b) said in praise of the atmosphere of the Holy Land, 'The very air of the land of Israel makes one wise' (*Sforno*).

Dunash (quoted in *Rashi*) renders נוֹף as a *branch* of a tree, referring to the prominent mountain of the holy city, Mount Olives [which symbolizes the fertility and abundant wealth of Jerusalem.]

Indeed, the נוֹף is not a thin twig, but a very large branch or tree trunk which supports and nourishes many smaller twigs to sprout. So is Jerusalem the fountainhead of the blessings which God showers on the earth. Every tree needs roots, and the roots of Jerusalem emanate from יְרוּשָׁלַיִם שֶׁל מַעְלָה *the celestial Jerusalem*, which is the ultimate source of the blessings of this world (*Yaavetz haDoresh*).

Similarly, *Ramban* in the introduction to his commentary on the Torah cites the Rabbinic tradition that King Solomon successfully cultivated every type of fruit, vegetable and plant in Jerusalem; even exotic and rare spices thrived in his gardens. This accomplishment defies all established rules of agriculture, for different plants normally require extremely diverse climate and soil conditions in order to grow.

Ramban explains that at Creation, God first created the substance of Jerusalem. He then expanded that substance and enlarged it to the dimensions of the world. Thus, all nutrients and forces invested in the earth emanate

from Zion. That the soil of one area is suited to a particular fruit, is an indication that a rich vein of nutrients is branching off from the main trunk in Jerusalem in the direction of that specific country. Solomon knew which location in Jerusalem was the source of each individual vein of fertility; thus he successfully planted all growing organisms on that site [see *Tosafos Rabbeinu Peretz, Pesachim* 8b.]

A number of additional interpretations of נוֹף are offered:

— This is derived from the Greek word *nymph*, meaning *bride*, hence, יָפֶה נוֹף, *a beautiful bride* (*Rashi*).

— This alludes to the הֲנָפָה, *raising up*, of the Omer barley offering on the second day of Passover [to symbolize that the Temple is the source of fertility.] Also, the nations of the world are destined to be *raised up*, (i.e., spiritually elevated) in Jerusalem in the future (*Tanchuma, Pikudei* 8).

— Jerusalem is as sweet and desirable as נוֹפֶת *honey* [see 19:11] of the highest grade, made of the tastiest nectar (*Zohar Chadash*).

— Egypt is the most fertile of all lands and Nof, נֹף (= מֹף, *Memphis*) is the richest of Egypt's cities [see *Jeremiah* 46:19, *Isaiah* 19:13], for it is embellished with 395 Divine adornments. Nevertheless, the beauty of Jerusalem surpasses it, for the Holy City is יָפֶה נוֹף, *fairer than Nof* (*Midrash Ha Ne'elam*).

— All of this is true because the יָפֶה נוֹף of Jerusalem is an all-encompassing fairness. Jerusalem is כְּלִילַת יֹפִי *perfect in beauty* (*Lamentations* 2:15), and all

ד יַרְכְּתֵי צָפוֹן קִרְיַת מֶלֶךְ רָב: אֱלֹהִים
ה בְּאַרְמְנוֹתֶיהָ נוֹדַע לְמִשְׂגָּב: כִּי־הִנֵּה
ו הַמְּלָכִים נוֹעֲדוּ עָבְרוּ יַחְדָּו: הֵמָּה רָאוּ כֵּן
ז תָּמָהוּ נִבְהֲלוּ נֶחְפָּזוּ: רְעָדָה אֲחָזָתַם שָׁם

of the nations recognize this (*Shemos Rabbah* 36:1). [1]

מְשׂוֹשׂ כָּל הָאָרֶץ — *[The] joy of all the earth.*

[Cf. *Lamentations* 2:15: מָשׂוֹשׂ לְכָל הָאָרֶץ, *a cause for joy for the whole earth.*]

What manner of joy did Jerusalem offer? A man arrived in the city downcast and deeply troubled by the burden of sin which he carried. In the Temple he sacrificed a sin-offering or a guilt-offering; this atonement absolved him of his sins. Thus he left cleansed and brimming with joy. Futhermore, the [communal] sacrifices of the Temple were a source of blessing for [Israel and] the entire world (*Rashi*).

The sacred atmosphere of Jerusalem is conducive to producing scholars of the highest caliber, who then go forth to guide the entire world towards truth, which is the epitome of joy (*Sforno*).

[When the Sages first established a system of public Torah education for youngsters, they wanted the central school to be in Jerusalem, for they knew that if the children witnessed the Priests totally immersed in the divine service and sensed the sanctity which envelopes the city, they would advance tremendously in their studies, thus fulfilling the verse [*Isaiah* 2:3]: *from Zion, Torah

goes forth* (*Bava Basra* 21a; *Tosafos* s.v. כִּי מִצִּיוֹן).]

[No melancholy or depressed spirits were tolerated in this city of joy.] The *Midrash* (*Shemos Rabbah* 52:5) relates: Ouíside of Jerusalem there was a large rock, כִּיפָּה שֶׁל חֶשְׁבּוֹנוֹת *The Rock of Calculations.* Whenever a person needed to analyze his financial affairs he would leave the city to make is computations at this rock [lest his account prove unfavorable, thus causing him anguish (*Zerah Ephraim*) which cannot be tolerated in Jerusalem, intended as it is to be '*the joy of all the earth.'*]

הַר צִיּוֹן — *Mount Zion.*

A צִיּוֹן is a *marker* or *monument* used as a memorial for the dead (*II Kings* 23:17). Spelled צִיּוֹן, it refers to the site of God's Sanctuary, a timeless memorial for the preservation of truth for the benefit of mankind. Even after the Temple was destroyed the mountain and its symbolism remain to remind mankind of the presence of the true God (*Hirsch*).

יַרְכְּתֵי צָפוֹן — *By the northern sides* [lit. *The sides of the north.*]

Sforno explains that the Land of Israel and Jerusalem are strategically located in the center of the middle east, between the two great northern land masses of Europe, on one side, and Asia,

---

1. Ten measures of beauty were allotted to the world. Jerusalem took nine and one measure remains for the remainder of the world (*Kiddushin* 49b).

The Sages took great pains to preserve this beauty and place many restrictions on the city to protect its environment (*Bava Kamma* 82b). For example, no garbage dumps were allowed within the city; no large ovens or kilns were permitted, because they produce smoke which blackens the white walls of the city; while the rose gardens which were planted in the days of the early prophets were allowed, other gardens and orchards were prohibited, lest people throw weeds and undesirable plants in the streets and lest the air be polluted by the stench of the manure used as fertilizer.

XLVIII
4-6

by the northern sides, city of the great king.
God, in her palaces is known
as the stronghold.

⁵ *For behold the kings assembled,*
they came together.

⁶ *They saw and were forthwith astounded,*
they were terrified and fled in haste.

---

on the other (hence the description *the sides of the north*). These two continents, the cradles of civilization, derived their cultural and intellectual treasures from the spiritual riches flowing from Jerusalem.

Rashi stresses that the prime gladness emanating from Jerusalem is the joy of atonement obtained through sacrifice. The sin-offerings and the guilt offerings were slaughtered on *the northern side* of the altar.

קִרְיַת מֶלֶךְ רָב — *The city of the great king.*

This refers to the city of David, as in קִרְיַת חָנָה דָוִד, *the city of David's encampment* [Isaiah 29:1], and the city of the Messiah (*Radak*).

4. אֱלֹהִים בְּאַרְמְנוֹתֶיהָ נוֹדַע לְמִשְׂגָּב — *God, in her palaces, is known as the stronghold.*

This fact will only be fully appreciated in the future, when God's presence will be very close to the inhabitants of the city (*Rashi*).

Ordinarily the prowess of a warrior is not known until he leaves the security of his fortress, for only then can he display his courage and strength. With God it is not so. Even when He dwells within the safe haven of the palace, He is still famous as a *stronghold* of might (*Yaavetz haDoresh*).

Others say that אַרְמְנוֹתֶיהָ *her palaces* refers to Jerusalem's two bastions of Jewish faith, i.e., the First and Second Temples (*Dorash Moshe; Chazah Zion*).[The Temple was the *stronghold*

of Jewish might, as we read, *May He dispatch your help from the Sanctuary and support you from Zion* (20:3).]

5. כִּי הִנֵּה הַמְּלָכִים נוֹעֲדוּ — *For behold, the kings assembled.*

The armies of Gog and Magog assemble to attack Jerusalem (*Rashi*).

At that time, they will recognize that God is the *stronghold* (v. 4) of this city [for their mighty assault will be to no avail] (*Radak*).

עָבְרוּ יַחְדָּו — *They came* [lit. *passed over*] *together.*

The *Midrash* (Bereishis Rabbah 93:2) renders עָבְרוּ as *they were angered* [from עֶבְרָה *wrath*] יַחְדָּו *at each other*, referring to the terrible feud between Judah and the ten tribes of Israel, which brought their kings *together* to clash in battle.

6. הֵמָּה רָאוּ כֵּן תָּמָהוּ — *They saw and were forthwith astounded.*

When the kings who attacked Jerusalem witnessed the wondrous feats which God performed in His battle against their armies, they were astounded and terrified (*Radak*).

According to *Midrash Shocher Tov*, this refers to the many potentates who came to *pass over* (v. 5) and tour the ruins of Jerusalem after her destruction. They were amazed and shocked by the utter desolation.

Sforno says that this describes the monarchs who came to visit the holy city in its glory. They were astonished by the wealth of scholarship and

ח חַיִל כַּיּוֹלֵדָה: בְּרוּחַ קָדִים תְּשַׁבֵּר אֳנִיּוֹת
ט תַּרְשִׁישׁ: כַּאֲשֶׁר שָׁמַעְנוּ | כֵּן רָאִינוּ בְּעִיר־
יהוה צְבָאוֹת בְּעִיר אֱלֹהֵינוּ אֱלֹהִים
י יְכוֹנְנֶהָ עַד־עוֹלָם סֶלָה: דִּמִּינוּ אֱלֹהִים

wisdom which they discovered. They began to fear that the brilliant inihabitants of Jerusalem would decide to conquer the world (which they could have done with ease); therefore, *they were terrified and trembling.*

רְעָדָה אֲחָזָתַם שָׁם — *Trembling gripped them there.*

I.e., in the very place where the enemy sought to slaughter multitudes of Jews and to plunder vast treasures, *there* they were gripped with terror before the awesome might of God (*Radak*).

8. בְּרוּחַ קָדִים — *With an east wind.*

This is th wind which is reserved for God's punishments, as seen during the destruction of the Egyptians at the Sea: *And God swept the sea with a strong eastern wind* (Exodus 14:21) and during the downfall of Tyre: *The eastern wind smashed you in the midst of the seas* (Ezekiel 27:26) (*Rashi*).

Ibn Ezra comments that this refers to the mighty storm wind which will stir up turbulence in the sea, causing *convulsions like a woman in birth travail* (v. 7).

תְּשַׁבֵּר אֳנִיּוֹת תַּרְשִׁישׁ — *You smashed the ships of Tarshish.*

[Tarshish is mentioned frequently in Scripture as a flourishing distant seaport from which many valuable and exotic goods were imported to Israel.] As for its exact location, *Rashi* here offers these enigmatic directions: 'They are neighbors of Tyre which is in Africa [and was founded by] a descendant of Edom.'

Some identify it with Tartessus in ancient Spain, beyond the Rock of Gibraltar. *Kesses HaSofer* claims that this identification is without basis because the description of Tarshish in *Ezekiel* 27:12 places it amid countries of Asia Minor. Perhaps it refers to Tarzia in the Balkans. [See comm. to ArtScroll *Gen.* 10:4, and *Jonah* 1:3.]

Radak observes that throughout Scriptures we find Tarshish described as a major seaport which sent out great fleets of ships [throughout the Mediterrannean Sea] as in *Jonah* 1:3 and *Ezekiel* 27:25.

[The prophet (Ezekiel 27:25-26) echoes the Psalmist in predicting that the naval might of Tarshish is doomed. *The ships of Tarshish were your caravans for your wares; you were replenished and heavily laden in the heart of the seas. Your rowers brought you into great waters; the east wind has broken you in the heart of the Seas.*]

Hirsch explains that since תַּרְשִׁישׁ was west of *Eretz Yisrael,* her ships could reach the Holy Land only if they were propelled eastward by a strong wind from the west. Therefore, the Almighty sends an eastern wind against this fleet, driving it westward, away from its destination.

9. [On that day, when Israel will witness the downfall of the enemy as described in *vs.* 5-8, they will pay homage to Hashem:]

כַּאֲשֶׁר שָׁמַעְנוּ — *As we heard.*

We heard from our forefathers the wonders which You performed for them (*Rav Shlomo Atiyah*), and we listened to the prophets who foretold

7 *Trembling gripped them there,*
  convulsions like a woman in birth travail.
8 *With an east wind*
  You smashed the ships of Tarshish.
9 *As we heard, so we saw —*
  in the city of HASHEM of Legions,
in the city of our God —
  may God establish it to eternity, Selah!
10 *We hoped, O God, for Your kindness*

---

the doom of Gog and Magog (*Radak*), and we were well aware of the passage in the Torah [*Deuteronomy* 28:1] which promises: *and God will place you as most high above all the peoples of the earth* (*Sforno*).

כֵּן רָאִינוּ — *So we saw.*
All the prophecies of consolation which the prophets envisioned came true (*Rashi*).[1]

בְּעִיר ה' צְבָאוֹת — *In the city of HASHEM of legions.*
The Almighty is master of the celestial Legions above and the earthly legions below. It is He Who allows the legions of Gog and Magog to assemble against Jerusalem and it is He Who causes their defeat (*Radak*).

בְּעִיר אֱלֹהֵינוּ — *In the city of our God.*
In this war God acts as אֱלֹהִים שֶׁלָּנוּ *our Judge,* to render a verdict in our

favor against our enemies and to destroy them (*Radak*).

10. דִּמִּינוּ אֱלֹהִים חַסְדֶּךָ — *We hoped, O God, for Your kindness.*
This translation follows *Rashi* and *Metzudos,* who relate דִּמִּינוּ to דּוֹם, as in דּוֹם לַה׳, *hope for HASHEM* (*Psalms* 37:7). As *Rashi* explains, the Psalmist now launches into a fervent prayer to God, (yearning to see the fulfillment of the victories described in the preceding verses). He says, 'We have always placed our hopes in Your kindness, awaiting Your salvation which will appear in the midst of Your Sanctuary.'
Others derive this word from דמה *to think, imagine, conceive* (*Menachem; Ibn Ezra; Radak; Sforno*) [for Israel will say in the future: 'the wondrous events which we just witnessed live up to the conception of triumph which we imagined long ago.']

---

1. The *Vilna Gaon* detects here an allusion to the verse in the portion of תּוֹכָחָה *Admonition* in *Deuteronomy* 28:63: *And it shall come to pass, just as* (כַּאֲשֶׁר) *God rejoiced over you to do you good and to increase you, so* (כֵּן) *will He rejoice over you to doom you and to destroy you.*
  Here the Psalmist states: The first part of the aforementioned prophecy which tells of the good reward reserved for the Jews is introduced with the word כַּאֲשֶׁר. Our downtrodden people has not been fortunate enought to *see this,* i.e., the blessing of כַּאֲשֶׁר has remained in the realm of שָׁמַעְנוּ, *we heard,* for we have *heard* of ancient blessings, but not *seen* them in our time.
  However, the second half of the prophecy contains a threat of severe punishment. This harsh warning begins with the work כֵּן. Unfortunately, these tragic sufferings are not mere hearsay; רָאִינוּ, *we have seen* them with our own eyes.

מח
יא־יד

יא חַסְדְּךָ בְּקֶרֶב הֵיכָלֶךָ: כְּשִׁמְךָ | אֱלֹהִים כֵּן
תְּהִלָּתְךָ עַל־קַצְוֵי־אֶרֶץ צֶדֶק מָלְאָה
יב יְמִינֶךָ: יִשְׂמַח | הַר־צִיּוֹן תָּגֵלְנָה בְּנוֹת
יג יְהוּדָה לְמַעַן מִשְׁפָּטֶיךָ: סֹבּוּ צִיּוֹן
יד וְהַקִּיפוּהָ סִפְרוּ מִגְדָּלֶיהָ: שִׁיתוּ לִבְּכֶם |

בְּקֶרֶב הֵיכָלֶךָ — *In the midst of Your Sanctuary.*

Originally דִּמִּינוּ *we imagined* that Your kindness and benevolence would be confined to the limited area of *Your Sanctuary.* But now we see that *Your spirit overflows* to the extent that *Your praise is to the end of the land* (v. 11) [i.e., the land of Israel.] Therefore *Mount Zion will rejoice over the good fortune of the Temple area and the daughters of Judea will be glad* (v. 12), i.e., the other cities of Israel [which are considered Jerusalem's children.] will also have cause for joy (*Abarbanel*).

Others punctuate the verse differently, to read דִּמִּינוּ אֱלֹהִים — *We imagined* (when we witnessed the past destruction of Israel) that You were acting as אֱלֹהִים, *the Dispenser of Strict Justice.*

But now, when we see the final outcome of history, we are convinced that in *Your Sanctuary* above, i.e., in Your heavenly abode, which is the source of all Your thoughts and decisions, You were motivated by pure חֶסֶד, kindness, i.e., Your afflictions were truly for our good (*Otzar Yesharim*).

Thus we also appreciate the destruction which You brought into *the midst of Your Sanctuary* below, i.e., into the Temple. This too was kindness, for You partially vented Your rage on the wood and the stones, rather than unleashing Your full fury on the Children of Israel (*Zerah Yaakov*).

11. כְּשִׁמְךָ אֱלֹהִים כֵּן תְּהִלָּתְךָ — *Like Your Name, O God, so is Your praise.*

The prophets described Your might to Israel and gave You exalted names and titles. We can now testify that Your praiseworthy deeds do indeed match those names and live up to Your reputation. Therefore, even those who were so far removed from belief in You, O God, that they were seen as having gone *to the ends of the earth,* can now proclaim that *righteousness fills Your right hand* (*Radak*).

A king of flesh and blood may be landed as a mighty warrior when he is actually weak. He may be praised as beautiful, when he is ugly. He may be hailed as merciful, when he is actually quite cruel. But the Holy One, Blessed be He, truly surpasses any possible praise, as it says (*Nechemiah 9:5*) *You are exalted above all blessing and praise* (*Tanchyuma Shemos 2*).

12. יִשְׂמַח הַר צִיּוֹן — *May Mount Zion be glad.*

[On the day of victory, when the inhabitants of Zion will rejoice.]

תָּגֵלְנָה בְּנוֹת יְהוּדָה — *May the daughters of Judea rejoice.*

Jerusalem is the 'mother' city, and the cities around her, are like her 'daughters' [who rejoice at their mother's success (*Ibn Ezra*).

לְמַעַן מִשְׁפָּטֶיךָ — *Because of Your judgments.*

This refers to the harsh punishments You meted out to the nations which assaulted Jerusalem (*Ibn Ezra*).

Some say that the *judgments* refer to the destruction of the Temple. This, too, is a cause for rejoicing, inasmuch as God vented His fury primarily on wood and stones, but spared the nation (*Shaarei Chaim*).

תהלים [606]

1-14   ¹¹ *Like Your Name, O God, so is Your praise —*
to the ends of the earth.
Righteousness fills Your right hand.
¹² *May Mount Zion be glad,*
may the daughters of Judah rejoice,
because of Your judgments.
¹³ *Walk about Zion and encircle her,*
count her towers.
¹⁴ *Mark well her ramparts, raise up her palaces,*

The Talmud (*Makkos* 23a) relates that when Rabbi Akiva saw foxes roaming amid the Temple ruins, he laughed for joy. He explained that there were prophecies of both destruction and renewal. When we see that the first promise, of devastation, was completely fulfilled, we can be confident that the second promise, of renewal, will be similarly fulfilled. Thus, Zion may joyfully anticipate reconstruction *because of Your judgments,* since the conclusion of the judgments heralds the dawn of the redemption (*Dorash Moshe*).

13. סֹבּוּ צִיּוֹן וְהַקִּיפוּהָ — *Walk about Zion and encircle her.*

Walk about the inside of the city; *encircle her* from without (*Chazah Zion*).

Rashi maintains that this verse is addressed to those who will be engaged in the reconstruction of Jerusalem. They are bidden to calculate exactly how many soaring towers are necessary for a city of such stature.

Ibn Ezra and *Radak* interpret this as a call to all of the *nations* to gather around Jerusalem [rebuilt] to marvel over her vastness, strength, and beauty.

Zera Yaakov calls our attention to the *Midrash Shocher Tov,* which says that the area of Jerusalem is destined to expand tremendously in the future (see *comm. v.* 2) and that thousand of structures will be added to the city. The Psalmist bids the people to encircle and measure the present small area of Jerusalem and to count its few houses and towers, so that we will properly appreciate its future expansion.

סִפְרוּ מִגְדָּלֶיהָ — *Count her towers.*

Hirsch suggest that counting the towers is part of routine care and maintenance of the fortress. He notes that in *Isaiah* 33:18, the אֶת סֹפֵר הַמִּגְדָּלִים is listed among the officals who administer the operation of the city. [*Rashi'* there refers to our verse.][1]

14. שִׁיתוּ לְבַבְּכֶם — *Mark well* [lit. *put your hearts.*]

The *Midrash* (*Bereishis Rabbah* 48:11) teaches that counting the human heart should ordinarily be spelled with a double 'ב' as לְבַבְכֶם, because it is composed of two parts: — the good and the evil inclinations. However, the hearts of angels are called לְבָּכֶם (*Genesis* 18:5)

---

1. It was said of the renowned *tzaddik* Rabbi Yosef Zundel of Salant that he sought to fulfill this verse whenever he traveled about Jerusalem, by counting the number of houses in the holy city including those of the gentiles. It was also a time-honored custom of the pious to walk all around the outer wall of Jerusalem every Erev Rosh Chodesh (*Tenuas HaMussar* Vol. I, p. 108).

לְחֵילָה פַּסְּגוּ אַרְמְנוֹתֶיהָ לְמַעַן תְּסַפְּרוּ **מח**
טו לְדוֹר אַחֲרוֹן: כִּי זֶה אֱלֹהִים אֱלֹהֵינוּ טו
עוֹלָם וָעֶד הוּא יְנַהֲגֵנוּ עַל־מוּת:

with a single 'ב', because they possess only the good inclination. The Psalmist here addresses the people of the Messianic era; he uses לְבַבְכֶם to teach us that at that time the evil inclination will no longer control the hearts of men. [Thus, men will resemble angels.]

לְחֵילָה — [To] her ramparts.]
In *Lamentations* 2:8, we read of the חֵל וְחוֹמָה, *the rampart and wall*, of the city. The Talmud (*Pesachim* 86a) describes חֵל as a low wall within a חוֹמָה, *principle wall* which is higher (*Rashi, Pesachim* 86a).

The verse in *Lamentations* suggest that originally *HASHEM had resolved to destroy* [only] the outer wall of Zion. Once the destruction was underway, however, He destroyed the low rampart as well (*Lechem Dim'ah*).

[Here the Psalmist stresses that Jerusalem will be reconstructed completely, down to the minutest, most insignificant detail, including the low rampart which is not an essential part of the fortifications.]

Targum renders חֵילָה as אוּבְלוּסְהָא her *vast populace*: Take note of the teeming masses which inhabit this city and undoubtedly exceed the city's normal absorption capacity.

The fact that there is room for everyone in this metropolis defies rational explanation and can only be ascribed to a Divine miracle. The

Mishnah (*Avos* 5:7) relates that one of the ten miracles which transpired in the Temple and Jerusalem was that no man ever said, 'It is too cramped for me to spend the night in Jerusalem' (*Alshich*).

Others render חֵילָה as *her strength*, to indicate, 'Take note of the unique strength of Jerusalem which is from God alone' (*Tefillah L'Moshe*).

פַּסְּגוּ אַרְמְנוֹתֶיהָ — *Raise up her palaces*. פַּסְּגוּ, as in *Deuternomy* 3:27, is a *height*. Therefore פֵּסֵג means *to raise aloft*, i.e., to make eminent (*Hirsch*).

Since the city of Jerusalem would seem to be terribly cramped for space, it is enigmatic how so many massive palaces fit into the city. It therefore appears as if these palaces are *raised up*, i.e., 'floating on thin air' (*Alshich*).

לְמַעַן תְּסַפְּרוּ לְדוֹר אַחֲרוֹן — *That you may recount it to succeeding generations* [lit. *the last generation*.]

The translation follows *Rashi* who interprets the verse as an exhortation to each generation to tell its successors of Jerusalem's glory.

The previous exhortation to scrutinize the wonders of Jerusalem refers mainly to the city of the future. Nevertheless, this obligation is also in force regarding Jerusalem in its original state. The Talmud states (*Succah* 52b), 'Whoever never beheld Jerusalem in her glory, never saw a truly desirable city.'

Therefore, recount to your descen-

*that you may recount it
to succeeding generations,*
¹⁵ *that this is God, our God,
forever and ever,
He will guide us like children.*

dants the beauty which you beheld in Jerusalem of old but which they were not privileged to see, so that they may anticipate the even greater splendor of the rebuilt Jerusalem. For the prophet (Isaiah 54:11-12) foretells, *Behold I will cover your stones with fair colors, and lay your foundations with sapphires. And I will make your windows of rubies and your gates of beryl and all your borders of the choicest stones* (Radak).

15. כִּי זֶה אֱלֹהִים אֱלֹהֵינוּ עוֹלָם וָעֶד — *That this is God, our God, forever and ever.*

What will be related to your descendants down to the last generation? *That this is God,* the Lord Who was with us in the past, in the former Jerusalem. He will never change and will continue to be our God *forever and ever* in the Jerusalem of the future (Sforno).

הוּא יְנַהֲגֵנוּ עַל־מוּת — *He will guide us like children.*

This translation follows *Targum* and *Rashi,* who render this as one word עֲלָמוֹת *youth* or *childhood,* meaning He will guide us with extreme caution and care, as a father who leads his young child.

Or: He will preserve our youthful energy and vitality so that even in old age we will be as vigorous as young children (Meiri).

Menachem exegetically reads the word as עוֹלָמִית, *forever,* i.e., in both עוֹלָמוֹת, *worlds:* This World and the World to Come.'

Ibn Ezra mentions the opinion that the word is related to הֶעְלֵם, *the unseen,* alluding to the fact that God's administration of the world's affairs is hidden from the eye and above human comprehension.

However, according to the correct *Masores* tradition, these are two separate words (Ibn Ezra) which mean עַד מָוֶת *until death* (Radak).

The *Midrash* interprets these words literally, to mean *above death,* i.e., *He leads us to immortatilty.* This will occur in the future, for when Israel beholds God's presence *eye to eye,* they will live forever (Tanchuma, Bamidbar 17). [This may also allude to the authors of this psalm, the sons of Korach, who, through penitence, transcended above a fiery death in Gehinnom.]

In the future, שִׁיתוּ לִבְּכֶם לְחֵילָה (v. 14) Rivet your attention upon God, Who will be in the center of the חוֹלָה *circle* surrounded on all sides by the righteous who dance around Him with עֲלָמוֹת *youthful energy* and sing: 'This is God our God forever and ever: He will lead us into עוֹלָמוֹת — this world and the next!' (Yerushalmi Megillah 2:4).

Solomon, son of David, once said, 'There is a sickening evil which I have seen under the sun, riches hoarded by their owner to his misfortune' (Koheles 5:12). This refers to the wealth of Korach, which led to his unrealistic ambitions and his eventual downfall (Rashi, ibid. and Pesachim 119a).

The sons of Korach, who recognized monetary greed as the root of their father's evil, concluded their series of instructive psalms with a final hymn concerning the relationship between man's material goods and his spiritual and moral mission (Alshich).

They taught that man must utilize all of his material and physical resources to enhance his spiritual existence, so that his soul will survive its brief sojourn on earth and ascend to immortality upon the death of its body.

If, however, man mistakenly regards the acquisition of riches as an absolute good and as the primary aim of life, he then forfeits his aspirations for eternity in both worlds and his existence does not continue beyond the grave (Hirsch).

Therefore, it is customary to recite this psalm after the prayers in the house of mourning (during the seven days of the Shivah period) to emphasize the true meaning of life — and death, for the benefit of those who have just suffered the loss of a relative.

It is thus quite evident why this psalm is placed after the preceding one, which concludes הוּא יְנַהֲגֵנוּ עַל מוּת, He will lead us beyond death — to immortality.

1. לִבְנֵי קֹרַח מִזְמוֹר — *By the sons of Korach, a song.*

In the preceding psalms, the sons of Korach addressed themselves to the chosen people of Israel (*Hirsch*) and spoke of the Jews' exile and redemption. Now they offer a song of universal significance, a lesson to all people who are overwhelmed by the desire to amass riches (*Yaavetz HaDoresh*).

Meiri notes that this psalm is also addressed to Israel in exile. For the exiled Jews who behold the wealth of their oppressors and contrast it with their own wretched penury may grow envious. Therefore, the Psalmist depicts the dismal end of those who exist for the purpose of accumulating riches.

Ibn Yachya adds that this lesson will be of particular significance in the trying period of חֶבְלֵי מָשִׁיחַ, *the travails of Messiah*, when the poverty and oppression of Israel will be particularly desperate and discouraging.

2. שִׁמְעוּ זֹאת כָּל הָעַמִּים — *Hear this all you nations.*

People of all nations err by relying on their money; therefore, all must be admonished (*Rashi*).

Alshich differentiates between two ways of utilizing the ears. שִׁמְעָה, *hearing*, is to hear a voice from afar. הַאֲזָנָה *giving ear*, is to hear a voice at very close range; by drawing quite close to the speaker in order to catch his low, intimate whisper [see *Deuteronomy 32:1; Daas Zekeinim*, ibid.]

Those who have not yet been overcome by the lust for wealth, the ordinary people represented by כָל הָעַמִּים (שִׁמְעוּ) require only a warning from afar concerning this evil. However, those who have already become infected with the passion for wealth, the יֹשְׁבֵי חָלֶד, the

permanent *inhabitants of the decaying earth, require more vigorous advice and admonishment. Therefore, they are encouraged to give ear* הַאֲזִינוּ, i.e., to pay close attention.

הַאֲזִינוּ — *Give ear.*

This reflects the words of the *Midrash*: When a man falls from a high ladder and suffers multiple injuries, the physician must bind each wound individually. However, when a man's sins cause him to plummet from his lofty spiritual peak and to 'bruise' all the 'organs' of his soul, God, the Great Healer of the human spirit does *not* need to treat each wound individually. He tells the sinner 'All I ask of you is one organ: your ear. Let your ear hearken to My advice and be cured, and the rest of you will swiftly regain its health' (*Yalkut Eliezer*).

חָלֶד — *Decaying earth.*

[See *Commentary* to 17:14 and 39:6.]

Rashi relates חָלֶד to חֲלוּדָה, *rust*. It describes our transitory world which can readily *decay* and *rust* away.

[The prophet *Isaiah* (38:11) refers to יֹשְׁבֵי חָדֶל, *the inhabitants of the world which ceases to exist*. The commentators (*Ibn Ezra; Metzudos; Radak*; and *Kara*) all identify that word as synonymous with חָלֶד, since we often find words in which the letters interchange.]

Why are the *inhabitants of decaying earth* likened to the 'weasel' [i.e., the word חָלֶד is related to חוּלְדָה, *weasel*]? This rodent incessantly snatches food and drags it away to hoard in hiding places, without ever wondering, 'For whom am I collecting all of these stores? Who will benefit from this surplus?'

In similar fashion, many men spend their lives busily earning and saving,

For the Conductor, by the sons of Korach,
   a song.
² Hear this all you nations,
   give ear all you dwellers of decaying earth.
³ Even sons of Adam, even sons of man;
   together — rich man, poor man.

---

toiling and hoarding, without ever asking, 'For whom and for what do I slave?' Concerning such people, the Psalmist lamented (39:7), *In darkness only man makes his way, his lustful pursuits are completely futile, he heaps up riches yet he knows not who will gather them in* (Yerushalmi, Shabbos 14:1).

3. בְּנֵי אָדָם — [Even] sons of Adam (Targum).

Amudei Sheish observes that the Psalmist begins his condemnation of material lust by addressing Cain and Abel, the *sons of Adam*, who were the first ones to quarrel over worldly possessions. [See *Genesis* 4:8 and *Tanchuma, ibid.*] Cain said to Abel: 'Let us divide the world. I am the oldest, so I get a double share.' Strife ensued, and Cain killed Abel.

The *Midrash* adds that when the two brothers divided the world, one took the immovable land and the other took the movable objects. The former said, 'You are standing on my land', while the latter said 'What you are wearing is mine!' One said, 'Disrobe!', while the other retorted, 'Fly! (off my land)'...]

According to *Rashi*, בְּנֵי אָדָם refers to the nations descended from Ishmael and the sons of Keturah. They are called sons of *Adam* [i.e. a great man] because their father, Abraham, was described as הָאָדָם הַגָּדוֹל בָּעֲנָקִים, the man who was great among the giants (Joshua 14:15).

בְּנֵי אִישׁ — [Even] sons of man.

Targum identifies these as the sons of Jacob [for Jacob's face is etched upon God's celestial throne, as representative of all humanity. Jacob was called אִישׁ תָּם, *a perfect man* (Genesis 25:27).]

Rashi says that this refers to the sons of Noah who was titled אִישׁ צַדִּיק *a righteous man* (Genesis 6:9). *Amudei Sheish* explains this as a reference to Ham, the son of Noah, who castrated his father to prevent him from fathering any more children who would share in Noah's wealth and estate (Genesis 9:22; Sanhedrin 70a)

Hirsch explains that the *sons of man* are people who derive social and financial advantage through the fact that they can trace their ancestry back to men of distinction. *Sons of Adam* includes the vast majority of humans who know only that Adam was their forbear and who lack any other pedigree. The message of this psalm is of equal importance to both categories of men: Power and wealth are overrated and worshiped not only by those who possess and were born into them, but to the same extent — if not even more so — by those who lack them, and were born without them.

יַחַד עָשִׁיר וְאֶבְיוֹן — Together — rich man, poor man.

Both rich and poor alike are infatuated by money. Concerning the rich, Solomon said, 'A lover of money will never be satisfied with money (Koheles 5:9). The impoverished אֶבְיוֹן is similarly תָּאֵב לְכָל, desirous of everything (Ohr Olam).

The *Targum* renders בְּחַדָא וַכָּאָה וְחַיָּבָא, Together as one — both those (rich) with merits and those (impoverished) with guilt. This alludes to

ד פִּי יְדַבֵּר חָכְמוֹת וְהָגוּת לִבִּי תְבוּנוֹת:
ה אַטֶּה לְמָשָׁל אָזְנִי אֶפְתַּח בְּכִנּוֹר חִידָתִי:
ו לָמָּה אִירָא בִּימֵי רָע עֲוֹן עֲקֵבַי יְסוּבֵּנִי:

the words of *Midrash Shocher Tov* which warn that it is possible that one who is rich in Torah knowledge and one who [in his extreme ignorance] is 'poor' in Torah, may both descend to Gehinnom.

[Doeg and Achitophel were both *rich* in Torah, were heads of Sanhedrin, yet they did not put their knowledge into practice; therefore they were doomed. Others have the talent and opportunity to study Torah but neglect it, remaining *poor* and ignorant. All these men are culpable and they will burn *together*.]

[Realizing the tremendous importance of Torah study, the sons of Korach emphasized its predominance in the verse immmediately following: *My mouth shall speak wisdom* (i.e., Torah).]

4. פִּי יְדַבֵּר חָכְמוֹת — *My mouth shall speak wisdom* [lit. *wise sayings, maxims*].

Wisdom refers to the *understanding* which results from *the meditation of my heart* (Radak).

Contemplation of things Divine causes the Divine Spirit to descend upon the prophet. Then his mouth becomes a sacred instrument of God, as David said of himself (*II Samuel 23:2*): *'The spirit of Hashem spoke through me and His word was on my lips'* (Alshich).

וְהָגוּת לִבִּי תְבוּנוֹת — *And the meditations of my heart are insightful.*

[Insight is a Divine reward which the scholar merits when he exerts himself to share his wisdom with others. Thus, if his *mouth shall speak wisdom* while transmitting his knowledge to others, God will fill his heart with fresh insights and abundant understanding

ensuring him an inexhaustible supply of wisdom to share with his students.]

Tehillos Hashem draws our attention to Rabbi Meir's formula for presenting a popular Torah lecture: The speaker should divide his discourse into three parts: One part אַגָּדָה, *homiletics and moral sayings,* referred to here as: *my mouth shall speak wisdom*; one part הֲלָכָה, *deep legal discussions,* namely: *the meditations of my heart* which *are insightful*; and one part מְשָׁלִים, *parables and wise sayings,* as in the next verse: *I will incline my ear to the parable.* [See *Sanhedrin* 38b.]

5. אַטֶּה לְמָשָׁל אָזְנִי — *I will incline my ear to the parable.*

Indeed, the parable par excellence is nothing less than the Torah itself, which David calls (*I Samuel 24:13*) מְשַׁל הַקַּדְמֹנִי, *the parable of the Ancient One* [i.e., God] (Rashi).

HaRav Gifter explains that a parable is a story designed to help the listener comprehend a deeper truth which would be almost impossible to grasp if it were communicated directly. God's being and His will are totally incomprehensible to the limited, mortal mind of man. The Torah couches these eternal, ineffable truths in human terms, and, as such, the Torah resembles a parable.

[In this composition the Psalmist searches for the meaning of life and of man's mission on earth. Therefore, he turns to God's blueprint for the world, the Holy Torah, for guidance and direction.]

אֶפְתַּח בְּכִנּוֹר חִידָתִי — *I will solve* [lit. *open*] *my riddle with the harp.*

[The ways of God and the complexities of life are often an unfathomable

⁴ *My mouth shall speak wisdom,*
          and the meditations of my heart are insightful.
⁵ *I will incline my ear to the parable,*
          I will solve my riddle with the harp.
⁶ *Why should I fear in days of evil? —*
          The sin I trod upon surrounds me!

mystery. Only he who is blessed with Divine inspiration and enlightenment can solve these riddles. Sacred music is conducive to lifting the soul to the level of transcendental ecstasy which precedes such Divine revelation (*Shabbos* 30b).]

According to *Ya'aros Devash*, these words capture the essence of David's personality. To discover the secret of David's soul, study the workings of the harp: The more vigorously its strings are plucked, the louder its sound and the more resonant its tone. The more God 'plucked' David's heartstrings with pain and affliction, the louder and more beautiful his songs became. עוּרָה כְבוֹדִי עוּרָה הַנֵּבֶל וְכִנּוֹר, *Awake, my soul, awake O lyre and harp!* (57:9). The soul is aroused and stimulated in the very same way as the lyre and harp. (See *Overview* part III).

6. לָמָה אִירָא בִּימֵי רָע — *Why should I fear in days of evil?*

[This verse reveals the *riddle* which deeply troubled the Psalmist and succinctly records the answer which he discovered through the inspiration induced by his harp.

Man is beset with anxiety and self-doubt. He is perplexed and alarmed by an unknown danger which seems to dog his steps. Man, therefore, cries out in anguish, 'What is this dread which robs my soul of its natural serenity and destroys my peace of mind? Every small threat of evil suddenly seems to be magnified a thousand-fold, and I am terrified by my own shadow!']

In particular, man dreads the insecurity of old age, which *Koheles* (12:1) describes as יְמֵי הָרָעָה, *evil days* (*Ibn Ezra*). Old age is frightening because of its attendant infirmity and frail health (*Rashi, Koheles* ad loc.), and because it heralds the approach of death, which is followed by Divine punishment for one's sins (*Taalumos Chochmah, Koheles* ad loc.).

Radak observes that man's entire existence in this temporary world may be described as *days of evil*, for one who immerses himself in the pursuit of worldly goods brings misfortune and evil upon himself. According to *Radak*, the riddle continues: If the honest, thinking man realizes the futility of evil greed, why does he still brood over the acquisition of wealth and persist in hoarding his possessions, which he regards as a symbol of his success and status?

Even more bewildering, adds *Amudei Sheish*, is that when man actually reaches *the evil days* of old age, when all other lusts and cravings have ceased to affect the worn, brittle body, the passion for wealth remains relentless.

עֲוֹן עֲקֵבַי יְסֻבֵּנִי — *The sin I trod upon* [lit. my heels] *surrounds me.*

The cause of dread are the sins which a person considers inconsequential. There are sins which some people consider so minor that they commit them with impunity, as if grinding them underfoot. Therefore they are called עֲבֵרוֹת שֶׁאָדָם דָּשׁ בַּעֲקֵבָיו, *the sins which a person treads upon with his heels*. It is because of such sins that a person will

feel dread when his time of judgment
arrives (Rashi).

[In a single pithy statement, the
Psalmist now offers a solution to the
puzzle of human anxiety and insecurity.

This statement is not addressed to an
inveterate, deliberate evildoer, for the
cáuse of *his* troubled soul is easy to
diagnose. Rather, these words are
dedicated to the purportedly religious
individual who seems to be following
God's *parable*, i.e., the Divine blueprint
for life set down in the Torah. He does
not sin intentionally, yet his life contains countless, unintentional transgressions, which he ignores.

Thus, he is surrounded (יְסוּבֵּנִי) and
imprisoned by the unintentional sins to
which he attached no importance. In
this sense, his offenses, caused by
negligence, were 'crushed underfoot
with his heels' (i.e., עֲוֹן עֲקֵבַי), for the
heel is the most insensitive part of the
foot (*Midrash*; see *footnotes* and *commentary* 19:12, בְּשָׁמְרָם עֵקֶב רָב).]

Despite his external facade of righteousness, this man who treads casually
on 'minor' sins misunderstands the
basic concept of the Jew's responsibility
to his Maker and Master. Our
obedience to the command of God must
be based solely on the fact that each
commandment represents His will. We
have no right to weigh the comparative
value of each command to decide which
one deserves greater adherence and
which deserves less. All must be fulfilled equally, because all represent
God's will.

It is upon the men who serve their
own will and values that God brings the
sadness and anxiety of *evil days*, in
order to awaken them to earnest reflection concerning their careless lapses and
to teach them to be more mindful of
their true duty in life (*Hirsch*).

7. הַבֹּטְחִים עַל חֵילָם — *Those who trust
in their riches* [lit. *strength*].

[Most men do not react properly to
the benign warnings of the *days of evil*.
They pay no heed to the call of God
which is contained in their afflictions, in
their anxiety, and in the stirrings of
their uneasy conscience. God cries out,
'You yearn for security and tranquility;
discover security by surrendering
yourself to the protective shield of My
will!'

[But man remains as insensitive as the
tough, thick skin of the עָקֵב, *heel*. He
strives to still his pangs of insecurity by
building a financial fortress for himself.
His real Temple of worship is the bank,
not the House of Prayer.]

To people such as these, *Targum*
cries out: 'Woe unto those who put
their faith in their possessions!' Of
what avail is your wealth in the face of
death, the Angel of Death who relentlessly makes his rounds and does not
discriminate between the rich and the
poor? (*Meiri*).

[Korach is a perfect example of a man
who trusted in his wealth and grew
over confident and over ambitious.
Korach was the treasurer of Pharoah's
palace and held the keys to all of the
king's vaults. But God warned him,
'Korach, what benefit will you derive
from this wealth? The money is
destined for the use of all Israel; you
shall not enjoy it' (*Bamidbar Rabbah*
18:15).

Korach found the treasure troves full
of gold and silver which had been hidden away by Joseph, who had amassed
all the world's wealth during the years
of the famine. Korach sought to use
these riches to wipe Moses and Aaron
from the face of the earth (*Targum
Yonasan, Numbers* 16:19; see also
Sanhedrin 110a and *Pesachim* 119a).

⁷ *Those who trust in their riches,*
and of their great wealth they boast —
⁸ *But a brother he cannot redeem,*
nor redeem himself;
nor give to God his ransom.

Finally, the *Midrash (Bamidbar Rabbah 22:6)* states: Three wonderful gifts were created in this world, he who merits even one of them is blessed with the greatest fortune of life. Wealth is one of these divine gifts. But when is it a blessing? When this gift comes from heaven by virtue of one's Torah scholarship. However the wealth and power which creatures of flesh and blood seize for themselves are worthless and will not endure—as happened with Korach!

Thus, Korach exemplifies those who trust in חֵילָם, *the strength of their riches.*]

וּבְרֹב עָשְׁרָם יִתְהַלָּלוּ — *And of their great wealth they boast.*

These men slowly sank from bad to worse. At first, they believed in God and His assistance and only placed a portion of *trust in their riches.* But, as their wealth increased, their faith in God diminished, until eventually the mention of the Name vanished from their lips. Then they denied God's assistance and glorified only themselves for their shrewd dealings and sharp business acumen. This is nothing less than total כְּפִירָה, *heresy (Maharam Almosnino).*

Jeremiah warned Israel not to get ensnared in this terrible heresy, crying out *(Jeremiah 9:22,23): Let not the rich man boast in his riches. But let him who boasts, boast in this, that he understands and knows Me (Radak).*

There is another disastrous tendency found in men of wealth. They will sin repeatedly without fear or misgiving, because, *they trust in their riches* and

plan to redeem their corrupted souls by 'bribing' God with *charity which saves from death (Proverbs 10:2,11:4).*

But here their greed backfires, ensnaring them in a trap of their own making.

First they promise enormous sums to charities, and publicly *boast of their great wealth.* But when the time comes to redeem their pledges, their greed is so overpowering that they simply cannot part with their precious wealth. Thus, *(v. 9) [Too] precious is the redemption of their soul, and unattainable forever (Dorash Moshe).*

8. אָח לֹא פָדֹה יִפְדֶּה אִישׁ — *[But] a brother he cannot redeem, nor redeem himself [lit. a man].*

This translation follows *Ibn Ezra* who identifies אִישׁ, *man,* as the subject and אָח, *brother,* as the object. The adverb לֹא, *cannot;* modifies both פָדֹה and יִפְדֶּה. Thus, 'The riches of the affluent man [אִישׁ] are useless for they cannot redeem [פָדֹה] a brother (i.e., his family and loved ones), and neither can the man save himself [יִפְדֶּה אִישׁ] with his wealth.'

This greedy, perverted man is classed with those *whose money is dearer to them than their own lives (Pesachim 25a).* Since the miser would rather die than spend his money to save his own life, he will certainly not give money to redeem a brother *(Kli Chemdah).*

לֹא יִתֵּן לֵאלֹהִים כָּפְרוֹ — *Nor give to God his ransom.*

Even if he would wish to ransom his soul from God, in whose hands rests the power of life and death — he could not,

ט יִתֵּן לֵאלֹהִים כָּפְרוֹ: וְיֵקַר פִּדְיוֹן נַפְשָׁם
י וְחָדַל לְעוֹלָם: וִיחִי־עוֹד לָנֶצַח לֹא יִרְאֶה
יא הַשָּׁחַת: כִּי יִרְאֶה | חֲכָמִים יָמוּתוּ יַחַד
כְּסִיל וָבַעַר יֹאבֵדוּ וְעָזְבוּ לַאֲחֵרִים חֵילָם:

for God does not accept bribes (*Radak*).

[Charity brings atonement only when it accompanies genuine repentance and reflects sincere concern for one's fellow man. It is worthless if given mechanically, as a 'pay-off,' by a remorseless sinner.]

Sifri (*Haazinu* 32) comments that the merits of righteous fathers will not save their wicked sons. Abraham cannot save Ishmael, nor can Isaac save Esau. Furthermore, since *a brother he cannot redeem*, Isaac cannot save Ishmael, nor can Jacob save Esau — even if they offered all the money in the world.

9. וְיֵקַר פִּדְיוֹן נַפְשָׁם — *For precious is the redemption of their soul.*

God very much desires that they liberate their souls from the shackles of lust, for the pure soul is *precious* to Him (*Sforno*). Yet since the soul is so priceless and *precious*, if man should damage it through sin, no amount of money can compensate for the damage (*Sifri*).

וְחָדַל לְעוֹלָם — *And unattainable* [lit. ceased, halted] *forever.*

Not only is *redemption* by means of mere money יֵקַר, *precious*, i.e., difficult to attain, it is truly impossible (*Metzudas David*).

In the event of sincere repentance, however, such *redemption* is not only possible, but it is also יֵקַר, *precious*, to God. This occurs when the penitent experiences such acute remorse over his sins that it becomes חָדַל, *impossible*, for him to return to his former erring ways (*Sforno*). [See *Rambam, Hilchos Teshuvah* 2:2.]

Targum echoes these sentiments: 'If

he will pay the precious ransom [of true penitence], then his disgrace and punishment will be חָדַל, *halted* forever.'

10. וִיחִי־עוֹד לָנֶצַח — *Shall he, then,* [lit. *and he will*] *live for eternity?*

It is *forever* unattainable (*v.* 9) that the sinner *should live on for eternity* (*Radak*), unless he repents; then his soul can and will *live on for eternity* (*Sforno*).

This opportunity to gain immortality is itself the greatest incentive spurring man to repentance, for if he renounces the petty pleasures of sin, *he will live on for eternity* (*Tehillos HaShem*).

לֹא יִרְאֶה הַשָּׁחַת — *And never see the pit?*

[Had Korach repented, he could have lived out his life in dignity and could have gained immortality in God's service. But he was remorseless, and his rebelliousness led to actual heresy: 'There is no Torah from heaven, Moses is no Prophet, Aaron is no High Priest! (*Yerushalmi Sanhedrin* 10:1).

Korach even denied that God was the Creator the world (*Zohar*).

God therefore invented a unique creation especially designed to deal with Korach. The pit inflicted extra punishment on Korach, as the *Midrash* (*Bamidbar Rabbah* 18:19) explains: Korach suffered devastation more than all the other sinners. While all were watching, the fire sprang at him and set him ablaze. The flames enveloped him, wrapping him in a fiery ball; he rolled around helplessly, until he sank into the pit with all his cohorts.]

11. כִּי יִרְאֶה חֲכָמִים יָמוּתוּ — *For he sees that wise men die.*

⁹ *For precious is the redemption of their soul,*
and unattainable forever.
¹⁰ *Shall he, then, live for eternity*
and never see the pit?
¹¹ *For he sees that wise men die;*
Together the foolish and the senseless perish,
and leave their wealth for others.

According to *Rashi* and *Radak*, it is this phenomenon which discourages the wealthy sinner, for when he observes the struggle on the battlefield of life, he notes that death always emerges as the victor. No one escapes death's grasp, not even the righteous and wise. Disheartened, the sinner makes no effort to redeem his own soul from sin or to redeem the body of his brother from mortal danger.

On the other hand, *Hirsch* suggests that the inescapable specter of the grave should be sufficient to shake the sinner from his stupor and arouse him to self-examination. For if even the meritorious [*the wise men*] eventually die, then certainly the sinners will share this fate. Therefore, it is only logical for a person to prepare his soul for death and for Divine judgment.

יַחַד כְּסִיל וָבַעַר יֹאבֵדוּ — *Together the foolish and the senseless perish.*

Wise men merely *die,* i.e., only their bodies fade away. Their souls live on and can expect a glorious future. Not so *the foolish* sinners who *perish* completely, leaving no trace of body or soul (*Radak, Rashi*).

Furthermore, only foolish people *leave their wealth to others,* for their only resources are material ones, which cannot accompany them to the grave. Not so the wise, however, who enrich their souls and intellect; therefore, they 'profit' from their 'earnings' forever, for their spiritual treasure accompanies them into the World to Come (*Yad Yosef*).

כְּסִיל וָבַעַר — *The foolish and the senseless.*

There is a marked difference between these two. The כְּסִיל is not unintelligent; in fact, he may very well have a brilliant mind, full of wisdom. Yet his intelligence is surpassed by his insatiable lusts and desires. The unbridled pursuit of gratification is so detrimental that the כְּסִיל eventually comes to despise moral and ethical wisdom, for he fears it will deprive him of his pleasures. As Solomon said, וּכְסִילִים יִשְׂנְאוּ דָעַת *And fools despise wisdom* (*Proverbs* 1:22; *Malbim, ibid.*).

Hirsch (to *Genesis* 45:17) explains that the כְּסִיל is one who tenaciously adheres to an unjustified point of view. He foolishly insists on his own opinion, regardless of contrary teachings or arguments. The בַּעַר, however, lacks intelligence and resembles the בְּעִיר, *animals,* as we read, *I am senseless* (בַּעַר) *and know nothing, I am like an animal with You* (73:22).

Hirsch also notes that the true root of this word is בָּעַר, *burning,* which describes the life of an animal who is 'ablaze' with Divinely implanted impulses and instinctive desires which cannot be bridled. Similarly, the men described as בַּעַר heed only the sensual 'fires' of their flesh, totally disregarding their minds, which become blank and devoid of sensibility.

וְעָזְבוּ לַאֲחֵרִים חֵילָם — *And* [*they*] *leave their wealth* [lit. *strength*] *for others.*

[This is the most forceful argument against the rich who are intent on

יב   קִרְבָּם בָּתֵּימוֹ | לְעוֹלָם מִשְׁכְּנֹתָם לְדֹר

יג   וָדֹר קָרְאוּ בִשְׁמוֹתָם עֲלֵי אֲדָמוֹת: וְאָדָם

יד   בִּיקָר בַּל־יָלִין נִמְשַׁל כַּבְּהֵמוֹת נִדְמוּ: זֶה

hoarding vast fortunes which they cannot possibly spend. What purpose is there in amassing wealth which will not serve its owner?] [1]

12. קִרְבָּם — [Yet] they imagine [lit. their inner thoughts].

This translation follows *Rashi, Ibn Ezra,* and *Radak.* The verse refers to the men who waste their intellectual endowments devising 'secure', 'indestructible' construction projects which are doomed to eventual decay and obsolescence. Nevertheless, they delude themselves into thinking that *their houses are forever.*

Other commentators transpose the letters so that this word reads קִבְרָם, *their grave,* (Moed Katan 9b). Because the wicked have no merits, they will not arise at the time of resurrection; therefore 'their grave' will remain בָּתֵּימוֹ, *their houses forever* (Ibn Ezra).

מִשְׁכְּנֹתָם לְדֹר וָדֹר — *Their dwellings for generation after generation.*

Their main aspiration was that their

massive construction [for the public] should survive as a *house forever.* Failing this, they wished that at least their private מִשְׁכָּן, *dwelling,* would stay in their own family to perpetuate their illustrious name *from generation to generation* of their descendants and heirs (Divrei Shlomo).

[מִשְׁכָּן may also be translated as *Tabernacle. Harav Gifter* notes that when Korach challenged Moses, he did not stop at mere threats. He actually built his own tabernacle to vie with the one built by Moses and Aaron. Therefore, we find constant reference to מִשְׁכָּן קֹרַח, *the Tabernacle of Korach,* throughout the episode. (see Numbers 16:24,27 and *Pirkei Torah,* ibid.)

Korach imagined that his מִשְׁכָּן would endure for generations, but it did not.]

קָרְאוּ בִשְׁמוֹתָם עֲלֵי אֲדָמוֹת — *They have proclaimed their names* [lit. *with their names*] throughout [lit. *upon*] *the lands.*

[Every man instinctively yearns for immortality. Those who deny the soul's immortality in the World to Come seek

1. The *Talmud* (*Eruvin* 54a) relates: Shmuel said, 'Snatch and eat, snatch and drink, for this temporary world from which we are destined to depart is like a wedding feast.' *Rashi* explains, that a wedding, although a great event, lasts for a short time. Therefore, do not waste this brief opportunity. If you possess money which you can use for your benefit and pleasure, don't save it for tomorrow, lest tomorrow find you in the grave, and your money unspent, fulfilling no purpose. For if God gave this money to you, He wanted you to spend it wisely, to purchase the necessities and amenities which would assist you in His service.

The *Talmud* continues: Rav said to Rav Hamnuna, 'My son, if you have money, enjoy it! For there are no pleasures in the grave and death is all but imminent; it does not delay! Perhaps you are concerned about leaving an estate for your children? Who can assure you that they will keep their portion after your death? [If it is God's will that they be poor, your bequests will be of no avail. If God has determined that they be rich, your efforts are not necessary.] People are like blades of grass. Some wither and die; others sprout to take their place. As the grass grows taller and its nutritional needs become larger, its source of sustenance increases proportionately. Similarly, as children grow and develop, their income grows proportionately. Since God provides, fathers need not leave their children with anything (Rashi).

Finally, the *Talmud* (*Gittin* 47a) relates that when Resh Lakish died, he left only one bushel of spices for his heirs; yet he mourned that he had wasted precious time to acquire a commodity which he would never use. Sadly, he described his wasted efforts with this verse, *And they leave their wealth for others.*

¹² *Yet they imagine that their houses are forever,*
their dwellings for generation after generation;
They have proclaimed their names
throughout the lands.
¹³ *But as for man, in glory he shall not repose,*
he is likened to the silenced animals.

ways to eternalize their names only in
This World.]

The wicked build great metropolises
in their own honor. Tiberius, the
Roman Emperor built טְבֶרְיָא, Tiberias;
Alexander the Great built Alexandria;
Antiochus the Greek built Antioch
(*Bereshis Rabbah* 23:1).

Alshich points out that Scripture
recounts still another attempt at self-
immortalization: *Absalom in his lifetime had taken and erected for himself
the pillar which is in the King's Valley,
for he said, 'I have no son to keep my
name in remembrance,' and he called
the pillar after his own name and it is
called Absalom's Monument unto this
day* (*II Samuel* 18:18).

[The *Talmud* (*Sotah* 11a) states that
Absalom did indeed have children, three
sons and a daughter (*II Samuel* 14:27).
But, because of his violent nature, they
lacked the benefit of sound paternal
guidance; therefore, they amounted to
nothing. Having failed to erect a human
monument of heart and spirit, Absalom
constructed a lifeless shrine of stone *to
proclaim his name throughout the
lands.*]

13. וְאָדָם בִּיקָר בַּל יָלִין — *But as for man
— in glory he shall not repose.*

[The preceding verse emphasized
man's futile struggle to immortalize
himself, *his memory* on earth. Now the
Psalmist demonstrates clearly just how
precarious a foothold man really has in
this world.]

Man refers to the guilty man who is
condemned (*Targum*); he is immediately removed from his *glory.* On the sixth

day of creation, Adam was created. In
the fifth hour of the day he stood on his
feet. In the tenth hour he committed a
sin. In the eleventh hour, he was
judged. In the twelfth (and last) hour of
that day he was driven out of Eden and
never spent a single night of 'repose' in
יְקָר, *the glory*, originally prepared for
him in Eden (*Sanhedrin* 38a).

Ibn Ezra maintains that יְקָר also
refers to money, which man imagines to
be his *glory.* When a man is laid to rest
in the grave, his money will *not repose*
with him there.

In addition, suggests *Radak*, יְקָר
describes the soul which is identified
elsewhere as כָּבוֹד, *glory; honor* [see
16:9, 30:13 and *commentary ibid.*].

נִמְשַׁל כַּבְּהֵמוֹת נִדְמוּ — *He is likened to the
silenced animals.*

Most commentaries derive the word
נִמְשַׁל in our verse from מָשָׁל, *parable,
comparison,* and note that the fate of
the wicked is comparable to that of the
animal after its death.

The man who squanders his life in
pursuit of the useless vanities of This
World will find, to his dismay, that
when he slips into the *repose* of death,
he will be stripped of the soul which he
corrupted. His soul will have become so
overwhelmed by his body that it will
decay along with his moldering flesh.
Thus this man will *not repose* with his
honor i.e., his soul, because he spent his
life *likened to the animals* who are
silenced forever at death, since they
leave no soul.

The introduction to *Sefer Mitzvos
Hagadol* explains that man is composed

דַּרְכָּם כֵּסֶל לָמוֹ וְאַחֲרֵיהֶם | בְּפִיהֶם יִרְצוּ

סֶלָה: כַּצֹּאן | לִשְׁאוֹל שַׁתּוּ מָוֶת יִרְעֵם   טו

טו

of two parts: angel and animal. The challenge of life is to determine which part will vanquish the other. After death, the struggle ends and the two contestants disengage. The animal descends to the grave, and the angel ascends heavenward. Therefore, the כתיב, *traditional spelling*, is נִדְמָה in the singular, for during life the two opponents are joined as one. But the קרי, *traditional pronunciation*, is נִדְמוּ in the plural which alludes to the separation of man's two aspects after death. [See *Minchas Shai* for a lengthy discussion of the קרי and כתיב of this word.]

The *Talmud* (*Sanhedrin* 38b) homiletically translates נִמְשַׁל as *ruled over, conquered* (from מוֹשֵׁל), and נִדְמוּ is rendered as *they appear*. Ordinarily, animals fear humans and accept man's mastery with docility, because man was created in God's image, the image of sovereignty. If however, animals attack men and *rule over* them, this signifies that the men have sinned and thereby distorted their Divine features to the extent that now *they appear* to be *animals* themselves.

נִדְמוּ — *Silenced.*

This translation follows *Rashi*: the soul of the sinner is *silenced* after death; thus he resembles the dead animal, which has no afterlife.

Radak comments that נִדְמוּ may be rendered *cut off* as in נִדְמָה מֶלֶךְ יִשְׂרָאֵל, *The king of Israel is completely cut off* (*Hoshea* 10:15).

Or נִדְמוּ may be related to דּוּמָה,

similar in appearance, in which case this word is a repetition of נִמְשַׁל and means *he is comparable (to the animals).*

Maharam Almosnino suggests that נִדְמוּ describes the animals as creatures of דִּמְיוֹן, *confused, distorted imagination*, unlike man, who was meant to be a creature of שֵׂכֶל, *clear, rational logic*. If man would analyze life with his clear, objective mind, he would embrace faith and reject sin.

[This echoes the words of *Sotah* 5a: No man sins unless he is possessed by a spirit of foolishness.

Sforno (*Genesis* 3:6) explains that the evil inclination is powerless without the aid of the imagination, which distorts reality and magnifies the temptation of sin.] [1]

14. זֶה דַרְכָּם — *This is their way.*

[The wicked do not sin by chance or whim; rather they are convinced that *their way* is the right way. They are so confident of this that they even recommend their way to their descendants who follow them].

כֵּסֶל לָמוֹ — *Folly is theirs.*

They simply cannot travel the proper path of life because their כְּסִילוּת, *foolishness*, accompanies them wherever they go (*Radak*).

Rashi cites the *Talmud* (*Shabbos* 31b) which relates כֵּסֶל to חֵלֶב הַכְּסָלִים, *the fat on the flanks* (*Leviticus* 3:4) over the kidneys. The kidneys are the seat of understanding and sound advice [see *Berachos* 61a, and *Psalms* 7:10, 16:7].

---

1. [Korach too was a victim of his own imagination, which conjured illusions of grandeur and tempted him to stray. The *Midrash* (*Bamidbar Rabbah* 18:8, quoted by *Rashi*) observes that Korach was truly perceptive; if so, what prompted him to embark upon this madness? His eyes deceived him, for he saw in a vision the long line of his illustrious descendants. Therefore, he exclaimed, 'If such prestigious progeny will be descended from me, is it possible that I should sit by quietly?' However, he didn't see clearly; for these illustrious descendants were the offspring of his sons, who repented. Moses, however, knew the truth with prophetic clarity.]

XLIX

14 *This is their way — folly is theirs,*
yet of their destiny their mouths speak soothingly,
Selah!
15 *Like sheep,*
for the Lower World are they destined.
Death shall consume them

Why then do the kidneys of the wicked fail to guide them? The wicked are fully aware that the folly of their ways will ultimately bring them down. But they allow their *fat* [i.e., their lust] to blind their common sense to cover the kidneys, as it were. Therefore, they plunge into sin (*Shabbos* 31b).

וְאַחֲרֵיהֶם בְּפִיהֶם יִרְצוּ סֶלָה — *Yet of their destiny, their mouths speak soothingly, Selah!*

The Talmud (*Shabbos* 31b) continues: Is it possible, perhaps, to attempt to minimize some of their evil by attributing it to the blindness resulting from the כֶּסֶל, fat which numbs their understanding? No! This is impossible, for they themselves constantly *speak of their afterlife* (אַחֲרֵיהֶם) and insist that it is reserved only for those who follow their wicked ways. This proves that their offenses are intentional and deliberate (*Rashi*).

Radak renders: וְאַחֲרֵיהֶם, *and their descendants* [lit., those who follow them], בְּפִיהֶם יִרְצוּ, *give approval* [to their parents] *with their mouths.*

The wicked foster a tradition of evil which they transmit to their children in such glowing terms that the children regard their parents with deep admira-

tion and praise their parents' corrupt craving for wealth.

Meiri offers another interpretation: וְאַחֲרֵיהֶם, *their end,* implies the end of their days, when they see the shadow of death fast approaching. At that time בְּפִיהֶם, *with their mouths,* i.e., with insincere lip service, יִרְצוּ, *they will express a desire* for סֶלָה, *eternity* [see 3:3].

Their wish will be rejected, however, because they have no sincere interest in repentance. The proof is that even if you challenge them on their deathbeds to return their stolen riches to those whom they cheated and robbed, they will refuse, for wealth remains dearer to them than their own souls.[1]

15. כַּצֹּאן לִשְׁאוֹל שַׁתּוּ — *Like sheep, for the Lower World are they destined* [lit. *placed, appointed*].

The wicked are like senseless animals who give no thought to their fate, like unsuspecting sheep, huddled in the slaughter pen (*Rashi*).

Only at the last minute, when death looms before them, do they become alarmed; but then it is too late (*Rabbeinu Yonah, Shaarei Teshuvah* 2:17).

Hirsch, based on *Isaiah* 22:7, defines שַׁתּוּ as a turning of one's steps toward a certain path which, in this verse, was

---

1. *Midrash Halsamari* perceives in this phrase an allusion to Rabba bar bar Chana's statement (*Sanhedrin* 110a): A Bedouin once offered to show me where Korach was swallowed up in the wilderness. He led me to two gaping craters belching forth smoke. When I bent my ear to the ground, I heard Korach's band screaming, 'Moses is true and his Torah is true, and we are liars.' The Bedouin testified [from his personal investigation and observation (*Rashi*)] that these sinners are perpetually roasted over the fires of Gehinnom, but that once every thirty days, they return to where they were swallowed, in order to make their proclamation.
In the light of this, the sons of Korach said: וְאַחֲרֵיהֶם, when in the end they come to their final punishment, בְּפִיהֶם יִרְצוּ, they try to make amends by confessing their guilt with their mouths. They follow this routine סֶלָה, *forever,* but to no avail, for their confession is too late!

not the path originally intended; i.e., the Lower World was certainly not intended to be man's final destination. However, the wicked have rerouted their lives away from heaven and towards Gehinnom.

מָוֶת יִרְעֵם — *Death shall consume them.* This translation follows *Rashi* and *Rabbeinu Yonah* (*Shaarei Teshuvah* 2:17), who explain that the death of the wicked is not like that of the beasts. Beasts die once, but the wicked are consumed by death every day. The soul of the wicked is constantly prey to destruction and deterioration, until it decays, disintegrates, and disappears.

In addition, Rashi translates יִרְעֵם as 'He shatters them' [see 2:9].

Others suggest that this word is related to רֹעֶה, *shepherd.* The shepherd allows his flock to graze in lush meadows to fatten them for the kill, although the sheep fail to realize that with every tempting bite they are moving a bit closer to the butcher's knife.

So too, the wicked wallow in wealth and satiate themselves with luxuries, unaware that none other than the Angel of Death is stuffing them in This World so as to bring them closer to their doom in the next (*Maharam Almosnino*).

So said the prophet (*Hoshea* 4:16) Hashem shall pasture (the wicked) like sheep in a broad meadow. Elsewhere the Psalmist (37:20) reiterates his prophecy of their destruction: *The wicked shall perish, and the foes of HASHEM are like the fattened sheep, they vanish, like smoke they vanish* (*Vidal HaTzorfati*).

וַיִּרְדּוּ בָם יְשָׁרִים לַבֹּקֶר — *And the upright shall dominate them* [lit. *subdue them*] *at daybreak.*

Nowadays [in the dark night of the lonely exile] the wicked are brazenfaced and audacious, their confidence reinforced by their wealth and might.

Now they dare to dominate and oppress the upright. But when the Day of Final Judgment arrives, the righteous will overcome them, as the prophet Malachi (3:21) promises: *And you shall tread upon the wicked, for they shall be ashes under the soles of your feet, on the day when I shall act, so says HASHEM of Legions* (*Radak*).

Rabbeinu Yonah notes that the *Talmud* (*Rosh Hashanah* 17a), derives from the above verse that the wicked descend to Gehinnom for twelve months. After twelve months their bodies are destroyed, and their souls are burned, and they become ashes under the feet of the upright!

לַבֹּקֶר — *At daybreak.*

Rabbeinu Yonah explains that the time of the revival of the dead is compared to morning, when a man wakes from his sleep, as it is written, *And many of them that sleep in the dust of the earth shall awaken* (*Daniel* 12:2).

That day will shine for the righteous like a radiant dawn, as the prophet Malachi (3:20) said, *But unto you who fear My name shall the sun of righteousness arise with healing in its wings.* That very same sun shall set the wicked ablaze like a roaring furnce (*Rashi; Radak*).

[The prophetic statement *And the upright shall dominate them at daybreak* alludes to the episode of Korach. Immediately following Korach's initial assault on Moses, Moses was Divinely inspired and replied בֹּקֶר וְיֹדַע ה' אֶת אֲשֶׁר לוֹ, *At daybreak then HASHEM will make known the man who is His own* (*Numbers* 16:5)].

וְצוּרָם לְבַלּוֹת שְׁאוֹל — *And their form shall erode* [lit. *wear away*] *the Lower World.*

Rashi and Rabbeinu Yonah render

and the upright shall dominate them at daybreak,
And their form shall erode the Lower World
from being a shelter for them.
¹⁶ *But God will redeem my soul from the grip of*
the Lower World,

צורם as צורתם, *their form, essence,* a simile for soul. [*Rabbeinu Yonah* cites *Hoshea* 13:2 as an example of a similar linguistic peculiarity.]

This alludes to the statement of the *Talmud* (*Rosh HaShanah* 17a) that there is a class of the most vicious sinners for whom a twelve month sojourn in Gehinnom does not suffice. This group includes the heretics, apostates, and those who deny the Torah and have no faith in the resurrection of the dead. Their punishment is everlasting. Even after Gehinnom 'wears away' and its fires are extinguished, they will continue to suffer (*Rashi*).

[Gehinnom is designated as a place of re-formation. Those who warped themselves with sin in this world resemble broken metal vessels which are returned to the fiery kiln to be melted down and reshaped. Our verse, however, speaks of sinners who are so hopelessly misshapen that nothing can change them; even after ages in Gehinnom, they still retain צורם, *their* (grotesque) *form.*

Korach is an example of a man condemned to burn forever, as is stated in *Sanhedrin* 110a (see *commentary* to v. 15).]

Hirsch comments on the relationship between the כתיב, *traditional spelling,* and the קרי, *traditional pronunciation,* צורם [lit. *their rock*].

This describes the soul of man, for a rock is a symbol of that which is solid and unchangeable. However, the צור, *soul,* of man earns eternity only if it regards itself as a ציר, *messenger,* of Hashem, an instrument dedicated to Divine service.

It makes no difference to the faithful messenger what powers or possessions the Divine Dispatcher has provided him for the fullfillment of his earthly mission. His only concern is to remain loyal in fulfilling his Divinely assigned task.

מזבל לו — *From being a shelter* [lit. *habitation*] *for them* [lit. *him*].

This alludes to Gehinnom, which will *wear away,* leaving the guilty soul lost, with no place to go (*Rashi*).

According to *Rabbeinu Yonah*, this means that the wicked man has deprived his soul of dwelling in the celestial regions where it originated. This heavenly abode is called זבל קדשך, *Your holy habitation* (*Isaiah* 63:15).

Rabbeinu Yonah continues: Through his sins, the evildoer causes his precious, exalted soul to forsake its sublime habitation and to decay in the depths of the lower world. How hard death is for the sinner who did not, during his lifetime, divorce the lusts of the world from his soul. The Sages said (*Derech Eretz*), 'Is it your desire not to die? Die, so that you do not die'. That is, one who wishes his day of death to lead to eternal life will resolve within himself that since in the end, he is destined to leave the earth and his bodily desires, and in fact to despise them, he will abandon them in his lifetime and make use of the earth only in the service of the exalted God. Then, his day of death will truly lead to eternal life.

אַךְ אֱלֹהִים יִפְדֶּה נַפְשִׁי מִיַּד שְׁאוֹל‪.‬ **16.** — *But God will redeem my soul from the grip of the Lower World.*

The Psalmist has concluded his observations concerning the wicked and

יז מִיַּד שְׁאוֹל כִּי יִקָּחֵנִי סֶלָה: אַל־תִּירָא כִּי־
יח יַעֲשִׁר אִישׁ כִּי־יִרְבֶּה כְּבוֹד בֵּיתוֹ: כִּי לֹא
יט בְמוֹתוֹ יִקַּח הַכֹּל לֹא־יֵרֵד אַחֲרָיו כְּבוֹדוֹ:
יט כִּי־נַפְשׁוֹ בְּחַיָּיו יְבָרֵךְ וְיוֹדֻךָ כִּי־תֵיטִיב

the doomed. He now refers to his own soul with words of encouragement and confidence.

He declares, 'I have not allowed myself to be lulled into lethargy by the comforts and enticements of this world. I have been alert to *incline my ear to the instructive parable;* therefore, I *have solved the riddle* (v. 5). Thus I am certain that God will bring me close to Him, far from *the grip of the Lower World'* (Rashi).

כִּי יִקָּחֵנִי סֶלָה — *For He will take me, Selah.*

When my love for God is so all-consuming that the very letters of His name become indelibly etched in my heart (Ibn Ezra), and when I think of Him incessantly and my yearning soul cleaves to Him, then it is impossible that my spirit should not merge with the Divine Spirit (Rashbam).

Thus I shall never die; rather, my soul will be drawn upwards, until it disappears into the heavenly abode, as we read of the ancient *tzaddik (Genesis 5:24): And Chanoch walked with God, then he was no more, for God had taken him* (Ibn Ezra).

17. אַל־תִּירָא כִּי יַעֲשִׁר אִישׁ — *Fear not when a man grows rich.*

Now the Psalmist turns to the people who are sensible enough to listen to his sage advice. He admonishes them for being dejected and discouraged by the success of the wicked.

He argues, 'Will his riches assure the wicked man a longer, better life? Despite your poverty, you may very well outlive the prosperous! And if you fear that his riches will be an asset in the World to Come, rest assured that he will take nothing with him' (Radak).

According to *Targum,* this verse is addressed specifically to Moses, encouraging him not to be afraid of the wealth and might of Korach.

כִּי־יִרְבֶּה כְּבוֹד בֵּיתוֹ — *When he increases the splendor* [lit. honor] *of his house.*

According to *Divrei Shlomo,* כִּי may be translated as *because,* i.e., you needn't fear the prosperity of the wicked 'because' he only increases the splendor of his earthly house and pays no attention to erecting a 'house' in heaven by means of charitable deeds. When he dies he will thus be left a pauper, and you will be the rich owner of a celestial palace.[1]

18. כִּי לֹא בְמוֹתוֹ יִקַּח הַכֹּל — *For upon his death he will not take anything.*

הַכֹּל is usually translated *all, every-*

---

1. *Yad Yoseif* pursues this thought further, explaining that even if the wicked *do* give charity, death will nonetheless strip them of their possessions. This idea is poignantly illustrated by the Talmudic tale (*Kesubos* 66b-67a) of the daughter of Nakdimon ben Gurion, a man of immense wealth. The Sages once found her scrounging in the dung of the animals belonging to the Arabs, searching for kernels of barley. So tattered were her garments that she had to wrap herself in her long, wild tresses of hair in order to stand in the presence of the Sages. The Sages remembered that her wedding dowry had been one million golden zuzim, and they were astonished at her tragic descent into abject poverty.

She herself explained the cause of the terrible reverse in her family's fortunes: 'The people of Jerusalem have a saying for it, מֶלַח מָמוֹן חֶסֶר, *the salt* (preservative) *of money is depletion* (expenditure for charity).' [She thereby implied that her family had not given enough charity.

for He will take me, Selah!

17 Fear not when a man grows rich,
    when he increases the splendor of his house.
18 For upon his death he will not take anything,
    his splendor will not descend after him;
19 Because himself does he bless in his lifetime;

thing; however, here it means *any-thing*, i.e., when he dies he shall not take *anything* (Radak; Ibn Ezra). [Combined with the negative לא, *not*, *every-thing*, becomes *nothing*.]

Rabbeinu Bachya (Exodus 25:23) records the custom of the devout Jews of medieval France who built their own coffins, using the wood from their dining table. In this way, they signify that, at death, man takes nothing with him; the charity which he gave and the kindness which he displayed to the poor guests at his table are the only remnants of his earthly toil which remain.

לֹא יֵרֵד אַחֲרָיו כְּבוֹדוֹ — *His splendor will not descend after him.*

[The demise of Korach would seem to refute the opening statement of this verse, for when he descended into the bowels of the earth, he and his followers *did* take *everything* with them: *their houses ... all of their possessions* (Numbers 16:32). Even their clothes which were in the hands of the launderers were ripped away, and rolled into the pit (Bamidbar Rabbah 18:13). Even their names which were inscribed in documents, even their needles which had been loaned to others, were swallowed

by the earth (Yerushalmi, Sanhedrin 10:1).

The answer, of course, is that since Korach could not use these possessions in the grave, they were, in effect, lost to him. Moreover, God decreed that these things be swallowed in order to erase Korach's name and honor, not to enhance it. Of Korach we can surely say, *His splendor shall not descend after him.*]

כִּי נַפְשׁוֹ בְּחַיָּיו יְבָרֵךְ **19.** — *Because himself does he bless in his lifetime.*

Rashi explains that the wicked brim with self-confidence until they are confronted with the harsh realities of the grave. Before that grim moment of truth, they lack even the most remote fear of retribution and declare, 'My soul will be at peace.'

There is, however, one peculiarity in the hymn of self-praise which the wicked man sings to himself: it is a solo. Only *he himself* blesses his soul; no one else joins in his hymn, for all others regard him with contempt and derision.

Radak interprets these words as a lament over the golden opportunity of life, which was wasted by the wicked: In his lifetime, man is given the chance

By not 'depleting' its resources for good causes, it doomed itself to lose its fortune.]

The *Talmud* questions the accuracy of this explanation, for Nakdimon ben Gurion was famed for his generosity: 'When he used to step out of his home to go to the House of Study, silk cloth was rolled out before him. After he passed, the poor were free to take the expensive cloth for themselves.'

The *Talmud* concluded with the insight: 'All the charity which he performed was solely for enhancing his own honor! (See *Maharasha*).

This is the lesson the Psalmist teaches here. There is no need to fear that the rich man will take his money with him, for even his charity is worthless because he gave it only to increase the honor of his own house.

כ לֶךְ: תָּבוֹא עַד־דּוֹר אֲבוֹתָיו עַד־נֵצַח לֹא
כא יִרְאוּ־אוֹר: אָדָם בִּיקָר וְלֹא יָבִין נִמְשַׁל
כַּבְּהֵמוֹת נִדְמוּ:

to shower abundant blessings upon his soul, something which only *he himself* can accomplish. This can be achieved by concentrating on the enrichment of his spirit with Torah and *mitzvos* and by neglecting the petty desires of the body.

According to *Targum*, ' this verse describes a man who did take full advantage of the opportunities offered by life: The soul of Moses did bless You during his lifetime, and similarly וְיוֹדֶךָ, *all the righteous praise You*, תֵּיטִיב, *for You do good for those who serve* (לְךָ), You.

וְיוֹדֶךָ כִּי תֵיטִיב לָךְ — *Others will praise you if you improve yourself.*

The Psalmist now addresses himself to the over-confident sinner and offers a suggestion which will help him to achieve universal acclaim: 'Straighten your crooked path, improve your deeds, and then others will also eagerly recite your praises' *(Rashi)*.

20. תָּבֹא עַד דּוֹר אֲבוֹתָיו — *You shall come to the generation of his fathers.*

The Psalmist continues to encourage the wicked man to mend his ways, explaining that he will fully appreciate the benefits of his repentance after his death. Then he will behold the generations of the wicked who are incarcerated in Gehinnom from long ago (i.e., the ancestors, the fathers of the wicked men of today) and who are doomed to darkness for all eternity *(Rashi)*.

According to *Targum*, these words are a promise to the righteous: 'The good reputation of the upright shall ascend to the level of their righteous fathers'.

עַד נֵצַח לֹא יִרְאוּ אוֹר — *To eternity they shall see no light.*

Rabbeinu Yonah (Shaarei Teshuvah 2:18) describes the condemnation of the wicked most vividly: The soul which lusted only for the desires of the body will be severed from its roots, and descend at death to the earth, the place of its lust. But first it *does* ascend to the heights for Justice and Judgment, to witness how it bartered the heavens for the lower world. It resembles a stone flung from a sling, for after rising on high, it falls (in accordance with nature) to the earth.

Both the souls of the righteous and the wicked arise heavenward for Judgment. The souls of the righteous are

Others will praise you if you improve yourself.
20 *You shall come to the generation of his fathers —*
    to eternity they shall see no light.
21 *Man is in glory but understands not,*
    he is likened to the silenced animals.

found to be worthy and are seated beneath the throne of God. The souls of the wicked are driven back to earth. There is no hope for them ever to emerge from the darkness, for, as the Psalmist said, *To eternity they shall see no light.*

21. אָדָם בִּיקָר וְלֹא יָבִין — *Man is in glory but understands not.*

The tragedy of the sinner can be perceived with dreadful clarity. For man, created in the image of God, possesses glorious potential *(Sforno).* His soul which is made of the glorious substance of the heavens, is a splendor *(Radak).* The world in which the soul is placed presents glorious opportunities for spiritual advancement and self-improvement *(Bris Avraham).*

But alas, man, in his obsession with wealth, is oblivious to the glory and *understands it not (Rashi).*

נִמְשַׁל כַּבְּהֵמוֹת נִדְמוּ — *He is likened to the silenced animals.*

The man who neglects his mission can only be likened to the dead animal, the silenced one. For the live animal is above this lowly perversion of humanity. As the prophet said *(Isaiah*

1:3), *The ox knows his owner and the ass, his master's feeding bag; but Israel does not know, My nation does not consider (Bris Avraham).*

According to *Midrash Shocher Tov,* this verse depicts Korach, who basked in glory as head of the Levites. He was a profound scholar and merited the unsurpassed privilege of carrying the אֲרוֹן, Ark of the Covenant *(Bamidbar Rabbah* 8:3).

When Moses inaugurated the Levites for the Temple service, he shaved their heads. In the heavens, God and His ministering angels admired this symbol of purity and cleanliness, regarding it as a semblance of the Divine. Thus was Korach's name derived, for קָרַח literally means *bald.*

But Korach failed to appreciate this symbolic act and was deeply humiliated by his baldness. Therefore, he rebelled.

God announced: 'I sought to endow him with the glory of the heavenly heights, but now he shall sink to the lowest depths! *(Zohar).*

Truly, Korach *was in glory but understood it not.* Therefore he sank into oblivion and *is likened to the silenced animals.*

50 מזמור נ

This psalm describes the intense desire of the Creator to reveal Himself to his beloved Israel. This powerful desire is truly the yearning of a father who wants to envelop his son in his protective embrace. Yet, God cannot indicate His Presence to His children until they, too, demonstrate a sincere desire to draw near to Him (v. 1-7).

For those who have strayed, one means of return is the sacrifice. The word קָרְבָּן derives from קָרוֹב, close. By no means is God's favor won by the physical act of placing the parts of the offering upon the fire of the altar. It is the new awakening of the heart and soul accompanying the sacrifice which clothes the penitent with humility and makes him worthy of God's Presence (v. 8-15).

The Psalmist tells us that the most effective means of drawing close to God is by immersing the mind in His Torah. Rabbi Chaim of Volozhin would say: He who merely observes the commandments establishes a 'servant-master' relationship with God. But he who studies Torah makes himself worthy of being God's son. As we recite in the daily Amidah prayer, הֲשִׁיבֵנוּ אָבִינוּ לְתוֹרָתֶךָ, Return us, our Father, to Your Torah.

Here, too, the student must be sincere and his motives pure. If his inner soul is decayed, his lips polluted with slander, and his eyes made venal with evil, of what value is his Torah?

Finally the Psalmist outlines the reward for each man in accordance with his efforts. Eventually, the gentiles and even the corrupt men of Israel, will perish (v. 16-22). But those who sincerely yearned for God, those who acknowledged and paid tribute to Him, will behold His Presence. He who offers acknowledgement honors Me, preparing the way and I will show him the salvation of God (v. 23).

א מִזְמוֹר לְאָסָף אֵל | אֱלֹהִים יְהוָה דִּבֶּר

וַיִּקְרָא־אָרֶץ מִמִּזְרַח־שֶׁמֶשׁ עַד־מְבֹאוֹ:

ב־ג מִצִּיּוֹן מִכְלַל־יֹפִי אֱלֹהִים הוֹפִיעַ: יָבֹא

1. מִזְמוֹר לְאָסָף — *A song of Assaf.*

[This psalm introduces us to Assaf, one of the ten composers who contributed to the Book of *Tehillim (Bava Basra* 14b). In addition to this work, Assaf wrote eleven more psalms *(73-83)* making him the most prolific psalmist after David himself.

Assaf was the leading Levite musician of his times [*I Chronicles* 16:5,7; 25:1,2,6] and his name is often equated with that of David, [*Nehemiah* 12:46]. Assaf was more than a composer, he was also endowed with the spirit of prophecy [*I Chronicles* 25:2]. Many centuries later we find that when King Chizkiyahu rededicated the Temple he commanded the Levites to praise Hashem *With the words of David and Assaf the Seer* [*II Chronicles* 29:30, see *Tanna d'Bei Eliyahu Chap.* 30].

The Sages differ as to the precise identity of Assaf. Rabbi Yochanan says that Assaf is one of the three sons of Korach who jointly composed many of the psalms. However, since he was a devoted Torah scholar, he merited the privilege of composing songs himself as well as in collaboration with his brothers. Based on a series of verses (*I Chronicles* 6:22-28 citing the lineages of Assaf and Aviassaf) Rav maintains that Assaf could *not* have been one of Korach's sons (*Shir HaShirim Rabbah* 4:4).

אֵל — *Almighty.*

This translation follows *Targum* which renders this title as תְּקִיפָא *powerful.*

[This translation is in consonance with *Sefer Hameonos* who explains that the Name אֵל alludes to God's mercy — not the relatively, mild mercy implied by the Name HASHEM — but rather an intense and powerful compassion which is reserved for the most righteous men who are lost in distress [see *footnote* to 22:2; and *Rashi* to *Exodus* 34:6].

The translation of אֵל as *Almighty* differs from our usual translation. Elsewhere in *Psalms* we render it as *God,* following *Targum* (ad loc.) who translates אֱלָהָא; see also 10:11 and 18:31.

Perhaps the deviation in this verse is because here the Psalmist enumerates three distinctly different names of God. For the sake of complete accuracy *Targum* here emphasizes the unique aspect of the Name אֵל which is best described as תְּקִיפָא, *powerful* of compassion. See also *Ibn Ezra* and *Rashbam.*]

אֱלֹהִים — *God.*

This psalm describes God as He will appear in His role of Supreme Judge in Messianic times, as the Prophet foretells: *When I shall return the captives of Judah and Jerusalem, I will gather all of the nations ... and I will enter into judgment with them* (Joel 4:1,2). The juxtaposition of אֵל to אֱלֹהִים serves to clarify the description of God as 'Judge of all judges, Mightiest of the mighty' (*Radak*).

ה׳ — *HASHEM.*

This describes the divine מִדַּת הָרַחֲמִים, *Attribute of Mercy* and completes the list of God's three primary forms of revelations to mankind: אֵל is the intense and powerful מִדַּת הַחֶסֶד, *Attribute of Almighty Mercy,* reserved for the completely righteous; אֱלֹהִים is the strong מִדַּת הַדִּין, *Attribute of Strict Justice,* which is administered to the wicked; ה׳, HASHEM, is reserved for the person who constantly vacillates

L

1-2

A song of Assaf,
Almighty, God, HASHEM spoke summoning the
earth
from the rising of the sun to its setting.
² Out of Zion, consummation of beauty,
God appeared.

between good and bad. He is judged
with the gentle מִדַּת הָרַחֲמִים *Attribute of
Mercy*, but HASHEM does not
overwhelm him with intense *Almighty
Kindness* (Eretz HaChaim).

Alshich delves yet deeper into the
meaning of these three divine titles. In
creating the world, אֵל, *the Almighty*,
was inspired by a profound desire to do
חֶסֶד, *kindness*, with all souls. Rather
than allowing the souls to bask in unearned celestial bliss, God sought to
provide them with an opportunity to be
challenged and tested so that they could
earn their reward by adhering to rigid
standards of conduct despite earthly
temptation and distraction of sin. At
first the implementation of this plan required that God be exacting in His
evaluation of each soul's performance,
applying His Name of אֱלֹהִים, indicating
the Attribute of Strict Justice. But God
realized that the בֵּינוֹנִי *the average man*
— fallible and temptation-prone — could
not survive such demands and so He
tempered Strict Justice with Mercy.
Thus the *Kindness* of אֵל together with
the *Justice of* אֱלֹהִים fostered the concept of ה', *HASHEM — Mercy*.

דִּבֶּר וַיִּקְרָא אָרֶץ — *Spoke, summoning the
earth.*

God issued a call to all mankind to
enlist in His service. He did this at a
time when the entire human race consisted only of individuals as when He issued commands to Adam and Eve and
later to Noah and his sons, instructing
them in the seven Noahide laws
(Sforno).

And in the future He will once again

call out to mankind. But then He will
judge them for having neglected His
commands. He will summon them from
all the corners of the earth, *from the rising of the sun to its setting*, arousing in
them militant spirits to gather and make
war upon Jerusalem (together with Gog
and Magog) so that He may destroy
them (Radak).

[At that epic moment in history, the
Almighty will exercise great חֶסֶד,
kindness, with the righteous nation of
Israel, and דִּין, *Strict Justice*, with the
wicked nations of the world. Thus, he
will appear as אֵל and אֱלֹהִים at one and
the same time.]

מִמִּזְרַח שֶׁמֶשׁ עַד מְבֹאוֹ — *From the rising
of the sun to its setting.*

All of creation cries out to the wicked
who are spread over the face of the
earth: 'Since you sinned you must be
judged with severity, but let it be
known that this was not God's intention! עוֹלָם חֶסֶד יִבָּנֶה, *the world is built
for kindness'* (89:3).

Even the daily orbit of the sun attests
to this truth, for morning is the time of
special kindness as the Psalmist says
לְהַגִּיד בַּבֹּקֶר חַסְדֶּךָ, *To tell in the morning
of Your kindness* (92:3). Whereas the
dark night is reserved for harsh justice
(Chazah Zion; Eretz Hachaim).

2. מִצִּיוֹן מִכְלַל יֹפִי אֱלֹהִים הוֹפִיעַ — *Out of
Zion, consummation of beauty, God ap-
peared.*

Because the nations of the earth did
not hearken to God's call, He abandoned them and chose the one beautiful
nation who paid heed, Israel (Sforno).

נ   אֱלֹהֵינוּ וְאַל־יֶחֱרַשׁ אֵשׁ־לְפָנָיו תֹּאכֵל
ד   וּסְבִיבָיו נִשְׂעֲרָה מְאֹד: יִקְרָא אֶל־
הַשָּׁמַיִם מֵעָל וְאֶל־הָאָרֶץ לָדִין עַמּוֹ:

[God bestowed *mitzvos* upon men to enlighten their souls that they may reflect the splendor of the divine. All the nations rejected this opportunity, but the obedient people of Zion polished their souls to be the *consummation of beauty;* in them the reflection of *God appeared*.][1]

Rabbeinu Bachya interprets this psalm as a prophecy of the future תְּחִיַּת הַמֵּתִים, *Resuscitation of the Dead.* God originally created the world from Zion, the rock upon which the Holy Ark was later emplaced, and He continued to pour His blessings of life and sustenance down through the channel of Zion. Therefore, it is from this place that all of life is destined to be resurrected. [See 48:3 for complete discussion of Zion as the source of the earth's abundance based on this verse.]

3. יָבֹא אֱלֹהֵינוּ וְאַל יֶחֱרַשׁ — *May our God come and not be silent.*

God has chosen to conceal Himself in This World. He neither appears to administer well-deserved punishment to the wicked, nor bestow rewards upon the deserving righteous ones. He even seems to remain silent in the face of atrocities — such as the wanton murder of His faithful followers (*Rashi*).

But we hope with faith and pray with confidence that this silence will be broken in the future (*Sforno*).

אֵשׁ לְפָנָיו תֹּאכֵל — *A fire consuming* [lit. *will consume*] *before Him.*

In the future a fiery wrath will emanate from Him and consume the wicked who hitherto went unscathed (*Radak*).

וּסְבִיבָיו נִשְׂעֲרָה מְאֹד — *And His surroundings exceedingly turbulent.*

The question arises — Why indeed does God wait for the future to punish the nations while He allows them to tyrranize Israel in her times of exile? Why does He seem to be oblivious to their heinous crimes while at the same time being fearfully accurate and demanding in enforcing the most minute subtleties of the law with regard to Israel?

The answer is that one always pays much closer attention to that which is right before his eyes. God's gaze is fixed on Israel, His beloved people, so even their slightest flaws are readily discernible. Thus *His surroundings* [i.e., Israel which is near Him] *is exceedingly turbulent* [because He exacts judgment upon His near ones]. (*Yaavetz HaDoresh*).

So said the Sages (*Yerushalmi, Shekalim* 5:1): To those who stand close, סְבִיבָיו, *surrounding Him*, God is נִשְׂעֲרָה i.e., He disciplines them scrupulously even for a deviation as minute as a שַׂעֲרָה, *a hair's-breadth.* The Psalmist repeats this principle elsewhere too, saying, וְנוֹרָא עַל כָּל סְבִיבָיו, *He is awesome over all those surrounding Him* (89:8).

The *Yerushalmi* continues: Do not think that God is lax or forgiving towards the enemy nations. Whosoever dares to insinuate that God's justice is lax — let that man's innards be severed and loosened! With the nation God bides His time, waiting for the opportunity to administer final devastating retribution.

The *Mechilta* (*Beshalach* 15:11)

1. History will bear testimony to four divine appearances: God appeared in Egypt to perform miracles for Israel, and at Sinai to transmit the Torah. He is destined to reveal Himself a third time in the War of Gog and Magog and finally in the Epoch of Messiah, as it says, *Out of Zion the consummation of beauty, God appeared* (*Sifri, Parshas Brocho,* 33:2).

תהלים   [634]

L

3-4

³ May our God come and not be silent.
A fire consuming before Him,
and His surroundings exceedingly turbulent.
⁴ He will summon the heavens above and the earth,
that He may avenge His people.

derives from these words how different
the ways of God are from those of man.
A king, in order to be held in awe by the
masses, must keep his distance from
them. Those close to him soon learn that
he is a mere mortal — no better nor
worse than they. Not so with the
Almighty God. The more one knows
Him and aspires to be close to Him —
the greater the awe, to the point where
the most intimate tremble, for *His surroundings are exceedingly turbulent.*

4. יִקְרָא אֶל הַשָּׁמַיִם מֵעָל — *He will
summon the heavens above.*

[Every nation on earth is represented
above in the heavenly *family* by a
spiritual force which is known as its
מַלְאָךְ, *angel,* or שַׂר, *prince.* All relations
which God has with the nation on earth
begin with the שַׂר above, and so the
Talmud teaches that when Hashem
seeks to punish a nation He begins by
afflicting their *angel,* as it says: (*Isaiah
24:21*) *On that day HASHEM will
punish the legions of the high ones on
high* [and afterwards] *the kings of the
earth upon the earth*].

In the time to come, God will initiate
His retribution against the nations by
summoning their *angels* in heaven
(*Rashi; Ibn Ezra*). [See Targum here and
in verse 6 who renders שָׁמַיִם as אַנְגְלֵי,
angels].

Radak notes that in the past God has
also called upon an *angel* to smite a
nation as we read: *And the angel of
HASHEM went out and smote in the
camp of Assyria, one hundred and
eighty five thousand* (*II Kings* 19:35).

Others suggest that we may interpret
these words literally, i.e. that God will

actually call upon the heavens to testify
on behalf of Israel, as the Torah
says:(*Deuteronomy* 31:28) *And I will
call upon heaven and the earth to bear
witness on them* [cf. *Avoda Zara* 3a]
(*Yaavetz HaDoresh*). Both heaven and
earth will declare that even when Israel
was swept into the depths of exile they
continued to fulfill the Torah and its
mitzvos (*Sforno*).

וְאֶל הָאָרֶץ לָדִין עַמּוֹ — *And [to] the earth
that He may avenge* [lit. *to judge*] *His
people.*

The punishment visited upon the
heavenly *angels* will descend to the
earth where the kings and nations will
be afflicted as well. This will fulfill the
prophecy (*Deuteronomy* 32:36,43) כִּי
יָדִין ה' עַמּוֹ .... כִּי דַם עֲבָדָיו יִקּוֹם, *For
HASHEM will judge* [for the sake of] *His
nation ... for He will avenge the blood
of His servants* (*Rashi*).

Radak observes: The peoples of the
earth will actually participate in bringing their own punishment upon
themselves. God will sweep all of them
into a storm of chaos and confusion
which will bring men to slaughter their
own brothers as is predicted by the
prophets [*Ezekiel* 38:21; *Zechariah*
14:13].

Radak also cites the opinion of the
Talmud (*Sanhedrin* 91b) that *the
heavens* refers to the soul and *the earth*
refers to the body. Both will be called to
account on the day of reckoning.

In this vein the *Rokeach* (*Hilchos
Rosh Hashana* 201) notes that הַשָּׁמַיִם,
the heavens is the numerical equivalent
of נְשָׁמָה, *soul* = 395; and לָדִין, *to
avenge,* [which follows the word הָאָרֶץ

ה אִסְפוּ־לִי חֲסִידָי כֹּרְתֵי בְרִיתִי עֲלֵי־זָבַח:
ו וַיַּגִּידוּ שָׁמַיִם צִדְקוֹ כִּי־אֱלֹהִים | שֹׁפֵט
ז הוּא סֶלָה: שִׁמְעָה עַמִּי | וַאֲדַבֵּרָה יִשְׂרָאֵל

the earth], is the equivalent of הַגּוּף *the body* = 94.[1]

5. אִסְפוּ לִי חֲסִידָי — *Gather Me My devout.*

God will call upon the natural forces of heaven and earth (*Rashi*) and He will demand of the gentile nations as well (*Radak*), that they all assist in gathering the scattered exiles of Israel into Jerusalem. Only the children of Israel can be considered God's *devout ones* for they alone struck an eternal pact of allegiance to the Almighty.

כֹּרְתֵי בְרִיתִי עֲלֵי זָבַח — *Sealers of My covenant through sacrifice.*

At Sinai, Israel entered into an eternal covenant with God and commemorated this solemn pact with the offering of שְׁלָמִים, *peace-offerings* (Exodus 24:5). Moses sprinkled half of the sacrificial blood on the altar and half on the people (*Rashi, Radak*). [This ritual was the official ceremony of conversion which accorded the Israelites the status of complete Jews (*Krissus* 9b). The sprinkling of the blood symbolized Israel's willingness to uphold the divine covenant even to the point of sacrificing its own life-blood to do so!]

It must be remembered that when they left the bondage of Egypt, the devout men of Israel endangered themselves by swiftly performing the hazardous covenant of circumcision in order to partake of the Passover lamb. Circumcision is the basis of Israel's special covenant with God (*Radak; Shemos Rabbah* 19:5. See ArtScroll *Bereishis* 17:1-14).

At that time the Children of Israel were truly taking their lives into their hands, for the lamb was the deity of Egypt and to slaughter it was an act of total defiance which was sure to infuriate the Egyptians and provoke bloody vengeance. Moreover, at that very crucial moment when the Jewish people required all the strength they could muster in their own self-defense, they incapacitated themselves instead by performing an operation that would exhaust them — the *Bris Milah!*

Thus, they submitted themselves completely to the protection of God and sealed their Divine Covenant with total surrender and sacrifice (*Alshich*).

Eretz HaChaim observes that the covenant of *Milah*, even today, is still sealed *through sacrifice,* i.e., with a costly feast, which demonstrates how joyous and precious the *Bris Milah* is to Jews [*Shabbos* 130a].

The *Talmud* (*Sanhedrin* 108a) identifies those in history who epitomize the ideals set forth in this verse: *sealers of My covenant* — this refers to Chananya, Mishael, and Azarya who refused to betray their covenant with God by bowing to Nebuchadnezzar's idol and were

---

1. The Roman Emperor Antoninus mentioned to Rabbi Judah the Prince that both the body and the soul can present an argument which will exempt them from future judgment. The body can claim, 'All my sins must be due to the soul for since the soul has departed from me [at death] I repose in the grave like a silent, lifeless rock [which proves that I am completely incapable of any sin when left to myself].' The soul retorts, 'From the moment I left the body I wander aimlessly and helplessly like a bird [and I have done no evil].'

Rabbi Judah replied that the solution to this dilemma may be illustrated with a parable. A king cultivated a splendid orchard and entrusted its safekeeping in the hands of two watchmen — one was crippled and the other was blind. Once, the cripple said to the blind

⁵ *Gather Me My devout ones,*
sealers of My covenant through sacrifice.
⁶ *And the heavens will proclaim His righteousness,*
for God is the Judge, Selah!
⁷ *Pay heed, My people, and I shall speak;*

therefore thrown into the blazing furnace.

עֲלֵי זָבַח — *Through sacrifice.*

This refers to Rabbi Akiva who joyfully sacrificed his life for the sanctification of God's Name.

Targum emphasizes that in everyday life the Jew has the opportunity to renew this covenant daily with sincere prayer which is likened to sacrifice.

וַיַּגִּידוּ שָׁמַיִם צִדְקוֹ — *The heavens will proclaim* [lit. *will relate*] *His righteousness.*

No transient creature whose sojourn in the world is brief can bear true witness to the righteousness of God. For history is in a constant state of flux, and no situation is static or enduring.

Therefore, only the heavens and the celestial legions which exist forever can attest to the past, present, and future, and confirm that God never betrayed His covenant with Israel. These permanent observers of world events are the only ones who can testify that God never failed ultimately to take revenge upon those who oppressed Israel (*Radak*).

כִּי אֱלֹהִים שֹׁפֵט הוּא סֶלָה — *For God is the Judge, Selah.*

The heavens will also testify that even when God smote us harshly in His role of אֱלֹהִים, *the Dispenser of Strict Justice,* He acted with righteousness, and only for our ultimate benefit (*Tehillos Hashem*).

7. שִׁמְעָה עַמִּי וַאֲדַבֵּרָה — *Pay heed, My people and I shall speak.*

Radak explains: After God will condemn the wicked nations and seal their doom, He will turn His attention to Israel and He will not spare them from the rebuke which they deserve for their sinful deeds. God will remove the wicked men of the nation and obliterate them leaving only the righteous, whom He will admonish.

Many prophets foretold these events. Zephaniah (3:11,12) said: *For then I shall remove from your midst your proudly exulting ones. ... And I will leave in your midst an afflicted and poor people.*

Zechariah (13:8,9) predicted: *And it shall come to pass that of all the land, says HASHEM of legions, two parts within it shall be excised and die, and only the third part will be left within it. And I will bring the third part through the fire and will refine them as silver is refined.*

man, 'I see luscious first fruits in the orchard! Come, place me on your shoulders and I will pluck them'. The blind man consented, and the fruits were plucked and eaten by both men.

Soon the royal owner of the orchard arrived and demanded to know what had happened to his fruits. The blind man defended himself, 'Do I have eyes to see them?' And the cripple argued, 'Do I have feet to get them?' What did the clever king do? He placed the cripple on the shoulders of the blind man and judged them both together as one!

Rabbi Judah concluded: Similarly, in the future, God will thrust the soul back into the lifeless body and judge them together, as it says: *He will summon the heavens above* (the soul) *and the earth* (the body), *that He may judge His people* (Sanhedrin 91b).

נ

ח-י

ח וְאָעִידָה בָּךְ אֱלֹהִים אֱלֹהֶיךָ אָנֹכִי: לֹא
עַל־זְבָחֶיךָ אוֹכִיחֶךָ וְעוֹלֹתֶיךָ לְנֶגְדִּי
ט תָמִיד: לֹא־אֶקַּח מִבֵּיתְךָ פָר מִמִּכְלְאֹתֶיךָ
י עַתּוּדִים: כִּי־לִי כָל־חַיְתוֹ־יָעַר בְּהֵמוֹת

יִשְׂרָאֵל וְאָעִידָה בָּךְ — *O Israel, and I shall
bear witness against you.*

My people [עַמִּי] refers to the ordinary people of simple faith and devotion to whom God speaks simply
[וַאֲדַבְּרָה]. *Israel* refers to the elite, the
scholars and the very pious who bear
greater responsibility for the faults of
the people; thus they are treated with
greater severity. God Himself bears
witness against them and their shortcomings [וְאָעִידָה] (*Alshich*).

But, as *Radak* points out, all who survive God's initial purge of the truly
wicked, will be men of basically fine
character who deserve to be admonished
only for relatively minor offenses as
Isaiah (4:3) said: *And it shall come to
pass that he who is left in Zion, and he
who remains in Jerusalem, shall be called 'holy'.*

אֱלֹהִים אֱלֹהֶיךָ אָנֹכִי — *God, your God, am
I.*

God declares to Israel: You have just
seen me appear as אֱלֹהִים, *the Judge,* of
the world, meting out strict, harsh
justice to the nations. Fear not for
yourselves! A special judgment is
reserved for you, because you have
remained faithful and have not abandoned My ways. I am אֱלֹהֶיךָ, *your [per-
sonal] Judge* who will find ways to
remedy your sins without punishment
for the past, but rather by instruction
and warning for the future (*Sforno*).

8. לֹא עַל־זְבָחֶיךָ אוֹכִיחֶךָ — *I shall not
rebuke you for your sacrifices.*

Says God: I am not dismayed if you
neglect to offer up to me zevachim,
sacrifices (*Rashi*), such as the חַטָּאת *sin-
offering* or the אָשָׁם *guilt-offering* (*Ibn
Ezra*). My only concern is for the sins

which you commit [which necessitate
such acts of atonement and ap-
peasement] (*Radak*).

Rabbi Moshe Isserlis points out that
the קָרְבָּן, *sacrifice,* is merely a *means*
towards an end. The root of the word is
קָרַב, *close,* for the sacrifice is a means
for the alienated to draw close to God
once again. How? By entering into קְרָב,
battle [lit. *'close combat'*], with the
forces of evil which the sinner himself
created.

וְעוֹלֹתֶיךָ לְנֶגְדִּי תָמִיד — *[Nor] are your
burnt-offerings My constant concern*
[lit. *before Me always*].

Our translation follows *Rashi* and
Radak who interpret the first word of
the verse — לֹא, *not* — as referring to
both parts of the vers—

Targum however, renders the verse
differently: 'I shall not rebuke you for
the many sacrifices which you failed to
bring throughout your period of exile,
because the burnt-offerings which your
fathers offered up to Me in the past
constantly occupy My attention [and
appease Me].

9. לֹא אֶקַּח מִבֵּיתְךָ פָר — *I take not from
your household any bullock.*

Although the bullock is in *your* possession, it is not truly yours. You must
understand that whatever God claims
from you is His, just as all the world is
His (*Rashi*).

The Psalmist singles out the bullock
for it is the largest of the animals
brought as a sacrifice (*Ibn Ezra; Radak*).

He refers to it in the singular because
a person usually offers up no more than
one at a time of these large and expensive animals (*Chazah Zion*).

תהלים [638]

> Israel, and I shall bear witness against you.
>   God, your God, Am I.
> ⁸ I shall not rebuke you for your sacrifices,
>   nor are your burnt offerings
>   my constant concern.
> ⁹ I take not from your household any bullock,
>   nor from your pens any goats.
> ¹⁰ For Mine is every beast of the forest
>   the Behemoth of a thousand mountains.

ממכלאתיך — [Nor] from your pens.

The מכלה is a כלא, prison, lock-up for the sheep and goats [cf. Habakuk 3:17] (Ibn Ezra; Metzudas Zion).

עתודים — Goats.

The עתודים specified here are representatives of the entire goat family because they are its largest members (Radak).

Nevertheless, in comparison to the bullock the goat is small, so people customarily offer up a few at a time, hence the plural usage, goats (Chazah Zion).

10. כי לי כל חיתו יער — For Mine is every beast of the forest.

Not only the animals which 'seem' to belong to you really belong to Me, but even the animals which belong to no one, the wild beasts of the forest which appear to be totally independent — they, too, are Mine (Radak).

Before the giving of the Torah, when offerings were made voluntarily, all clean animals were fit for Divine sacrifice, as is evidenced by Noah who sacrificed from all the clean species. However, at Sinai when God commanded that sacrifices be offered to Him, He did not demand that Israel offer every beast of the forest — which is Mine. Rather He narrowed the obligation to very few species — the cow family, the sheep family, and the dovefamily

— which shows that the purpose of all sacrifices is for the betterment and atonement of Israel not for the benefit of God (Sforno).

Midrash Tanchuma (Pinchas 12) amplifies this theme: God says: Not to satisfy my appetite did I command you to offer sacrifices, for all that you bring is already Mine ... Ten species of clean animals exist, three are domesticated, seven are not. Did I then, for My sake, burden you to exert yourselves to comb the hills and mountains for the seven inaccessible species? No! I asked you only to offer the three animal species which are readily available — oxen, sheep, and goats.

בהמות בהררי אלף — The Behemoth of [lit. in] a thousand mountains.

Targum and Rashi identify בהמות as the ox that is designated for the feast of the righteous which is destined to take place in the Garden of Eden. From Rashi [based on Tanchuma, Pinchas 12] it seems that although the plural form is used, i.e. בהמות, in truth, this is really only one very huge animal called Behemoth. It grazes upon a thousand lush mountains, every day and strips them bare. Nevertheless, a miracle occurs and immediately, upon every mountain, there sprouts forth a new growth of fresh green grass.[See Akdamus Millin, Artscroll ed. v. 75 for a discussion of Behomoth.]

יא בְּהַרְרֵי־אָלֶף: יָדַעְתִּי כָּל־עוֹף הָרִים וְזִיז

יא־טו

יב שָׂדַי עִמָּדִי: אִם־אֶרְעַב לֹא־אֹמַר לָךְ כִּי־

יג לִי תֵבֵל וּמְלֹאָהּ: הַאוֹכַל בְּשַׂר אַבִּירִים

יד וְדַם עַתּוּדִים אֶשְׁתֶּה: זְבַח לֵאלֹהִים

טו תּוֹדָה וְשַׁלֵּם לְעֶלְיוֹן נְדָרֶיךָ: וּקְרָאֵנִי בְּיוֹם

Rashi also suggests that אָלֶף, *a thousand*, may refer to the number of animals, not mountains, or it may describe the height of one mountain — a formidable one thousand *parsas*.

11. יָדַעְתִּי כָּל עוֹף הָרִים — *I know every bird of the mountains.*

God continues: There are so many different species of birds which fly the skies that it is impossible for man to know them all (*Ibn Ezra*). Also, many are completely inaccessible to man for they live on remote mountains (*Radak*), and yet all of these myriad species are well-known to Me (*Targum*).

וְזִיז שָׂדַי עִמָּדִי — *And what creeps upon fields is with Me.*

I know clearly every reptile, every creeping thing which זִיז, *moves*, from place to place. They are עִמָּדִי, *with me* i.e. within the range of my knowledge (*Rashi*).

According to *Vayikra Rabbah* 22:10, the זִיז is a huge bird with a wingspan so enormous that it blots out the light of the sun. It feeds on the grasses of many fields which taste differently, therefore its flesh contains many flavors. *Targum*, based on *Bava Basra* 73b, also identifies זִיז as a giant bird whose feet are planted on earth [i.e. *my fields*] and whose head pierces the heavens where it sings before God, i.e. עִמָּדִי *with Me*.

Meiri however, in an entirely different interpretation translates זִיז as the *choicest grain* of שָׂדַי, *my fields*. This alludes to the מְנָחוֹת, *meal offerings*, which are brought before God in the Temple.

12. אִם אֶרְעַב לֹא אֹמַר לָךְ — *Were I hungry I would not tell you.*

God says: Even if I possessed the properties of a frail man who becomes hungry, I would never ask to be fed with sacrifices. I lack nothing since the entire world is Mine (*Ibn Ezra; Radak*).

Moses, whose mission it was to live on Mount Sinai for forty days and forty nights in order to receive the Torah, had no need for food and drink throughout that time. If he who was merely God's agent did without food, then surely God himself, whom Moses served, never experiences thirst or hunger (*Tanchuma Pinchas* 12).

כִּי לִי תֵבֵל וּמְלֹאָהּ — *For Mine is the world and its fullness.*

Although God is Master of the world, nevertheless, He desires the sacrifices of Israel and He describes them as רֵיחַ נִיחֹחִי, *My pleasant savor* (*Numbers* 28:2).

Why did God desire that Israel sacrifice two communal lambs every day, one in the morning and one in the afternoon? So that their remembrance and the remembrance of their forefathers should rise up before Him!

So said the Holy One, Blessed be He, to Israel: 'My sons, My beloved ones, am I lacking anything that I need to make demands of you? All that I ask is that you should love each other, honor each other, and respect each other ... (*Tanna D'Bei Eliyahu Rabbah*, 28).

13. הַאוֹכַל בְּשַׂר אַבִּירִים — *Need I eat the flesh of bulls?*

This refers back to the פָּרִים, *bullocks*,

¹¹ *I know every bird of the mountains,*
     and what creeps upon My fields is with Me.
¹² *Were I hungry I would not tell you,*
     for Mine is the world and its fullness.
¹³ *Need I eat the flesh of bulls?*
     Or the blood of goats need I drink?
¹⁴ *Offer God confession —*
     then redeem to the Most High your vows.

and עַתּוּדִים, *goats*, of verse 9. Once again God emphasizes that He does not demand these offerings in order to satisfy His hunger (*Ibn Ezra*).

Although the halachah requires a person to bring sacrifices in specific instances, it is not the flesh which I desire. Rather, My pleasure derives from the fact that you heed My words and fulfill My wish (*Rashi*).

וְדַם עַתּוּדִים אֶשְׁתֶּה — *Or the blood of goats need I drink?*

Targum perceives this phrase as a euphemism for the זְרִיקַת הַדָּם *the sprinkling of the blood* of the sacrifice on the walls of the altar.

14. זֶבַח לֵאלֹהִים תּוֹדָה — *Offer God confession* [lit. *thanks*].

The translation follows *Rashi* who renders תּוֹדָה as *confession* [of sin] rather than in its more common translation of *thanksgiving offering*. Thus: acknowledge your errors and sincerely repent — this is the sacrifice which I truly desire. After you have discharged this primary obligation you can proceed to *redeem to the Most High your vows*, i.e. to offer the animal sacrifices which you pledged. Only then will those sacrifices find favor before Me (*Rashi*).

Offer sacrifice by placing your Evil Inclination before God and this will be reckoned as if you had brought an actual קָרְבָּן תּוֹדָה, *thanksgiving offering* (*Targum*).

Alshich comments: Not only must you thank the Holy One, Blessed be He when He appears as הי, with His *Attribute of Mercy*, but even when He is revealed as אֱלֹהִים in His *Attribute of Strict Justice*, you must acknowledge His kindness. To recognize God's goodness even in the harshest of situations requires a great humbleness of the spirit as it says זִבְחֵי אֱלֹהִים רוּחַ נִשְׁבָּרָה, *The sacrifices of God are the broken spirit* (51:19).

Ibn Yachya concludes that since the קָרְבָּן תּוֹדָה reflects the achievement of deep perception and appreciation of the ways of God and indicates a true humility of the spirit, this sacrifice is preferable to all the other offerings which are presented to God. Small wonder, then, that the Sages tell us that even though all sacrifices will be discontinued in the post-Messianic era, the *thanksgiving offering* will still be brought, and prayers of thanksgiving and acknowledgement of God's mercy will still be recited (*Tanchuma Emor* 14).

וְשַׁלֵּם לְעֶלְיוֹן נְדָרֶיךָ — *And redeem to the Most High your vows.*

Tehillos Hashem explains that this alludes to the vow which every infant makes at the behest of the angel before he is allowed to leave his mother's womb (*Niddah* 30b): Swear that you will be righteous and not wicked!

15. וּקְרָאֵנִי בְּיוֹם צָרָה — *Beseech Me* [lit. *call upon me*] *in day of distress.*

If you have protected and sanctified your speech by fulfilling your vows (v. 14) then God will pay your words close attention and surely listen to your call in the day of distress (*Ibn Ezra*).

It will not be necessary for you to engage in prolonged prayer. The moment you merely *call out* to God, He will respond (*Alshich*).

אֲחַלֶּצְךָ וּתְכַבְּדֵנִי — *I will release you and you will honor Me.*

God says: 'Since you are trustworthy and sincere I am proud to associate with you. I will not give to an angel the privilege of redeeming you on the day of your distress. Instead, I will be honored to do this Myself (*Alshich*).

You honored Me in the past by scrupulously observing My commandments. In response I will honor you now (*Radak*).

After I release you, you will continue to *honor Me* by fulfilling the vows you made (v. 14) in your distress (*Ibn Ezra*), and by offering me praise and acknowledgement (v. 14; *Sforno*).

But, if you present sacrifices that are not accompanied by sincere repentance, they will be not an honor but a true disgrace to Me [God] for then it will that seem you imagine that you can deceive Me and conceal from My vision the secret evil which lies in your heart (*Radak*).

16. וְלָרָשָׁע אָמַר אֱלֹהִים — *But to the wicked, God said.*

In introduction to this verse, *Radak* defines the *wicked* one as a scholar whose outward piety is a mask for a failure to practice what he learns. This form of hypocrisy is dangerous both to the sinner and to those around him.

[There is hope for the man whose evil

is unconcealed; his concerned neighbors and friends have the opportunity to admonish him for his sinful ways. But one who sins in secrecy in order to avoid the criticism of his peers, denies the omnipresence of God who sees everything. He fears only the probing eyes of man. Outwardly he displays devoutness, therefore no one can admonish him (see *Bava Kama* 79b).

Moreover, this pseudo-sage cannot deceive all men indefinitely. Eventually, people will recognize his immorality and will react in one of two ways. Some ignorant people will be influenced to emulate his sins, arguing that if a scholar performs such deeds, they cannot be evil in the eyes of God. Others will be outraged by his conduct and blame his hypocrisy and insincerity on the Torah he has studied.]

God tells these unscrupulous masters of deception to desist from their Torah studies which, in their results, are detrimental!

The Sages (*Sanhedrin* 106b) cite Doeg the Edomite, David's archenemy, as a classic example of the great Torah scholar whose teachings were riddled with hypocrisy. It was he who mercilessly slandered David to Saul and incited the melancholy king to massacre the entire priestly city of Nob. The Holy One, Blessed be He, asked of Doeg: 'When you arrive at the Torah portion of לְשׁוֹן הָרַע, *slanderous talk*, and the portion of רְצִיחָה, *murder*, what lesson can you expound?'

[Another tragic example is Elisha ben Avuya who was reknowned as a brilliant Torah master. Yet, while he seemed to studying diligently he was secretly studying heretical books which he hid in his bosom (*Chagigah* 15b). Finally he shed his masquerade and openly defied the Torah earning the title

L

15-16

 ¹⁵ Beseech Me in day of distress,
I will release you and you will honor Me.
¹⁶ But to the wicked, God said,
'To what purpose do you recount My decrees
while bearing My covenant upon your lips?'

אַחֵר, *the Other One* i.e. the man who changed from his former self.]

מַה לְּךָ לְסַפֵּר חֻקָּי — *To what purpose do you recount My statutes.*

This scholar is well-versed in the vastness and complexity of the Torah. He speaks glibly of the many duties incumbent upon the loyal Jew and prates of his staunch faith. Yet, all of this display of knowledge is nothing but a סִפּוּר, the *recounting* of a tale which he takes lightly. It has no personal effect on him. To this corrupt man, Torah study is merely a pleasant intellectual exercise for the mind *(Hirsch)*.

The חֹק is a *decree* which has no apparent rational reason, such as the law of the Red Heifer or *shatnez*. These unfathomable statutes are designed to provide man with an opportunity to sacrifice his logic and intellect before the will of God and to display his total submission to the will of his Maker. The arrogant, wicked sage does not pay homage to a superior being. He worships only his own intellect. Therefore, the חֹק *decree* is the special target of his scorn, and he never misses an opportunity to *recount* and mock the decrees *(Ibn Yachya; Shevet Mussar)*.

Kesef Mezukak suggests that this verse continues the earlier discussion of sacrifices. Even when guilt stirs the conscience of the wicked man and prods him to offer a sacrifice, he performs this ritual with improper intentions.

The sacrifices are really *not* חֻקִּים, *decrees*; their purpose can be understood. Instead, of allowing his human intelligence to guide his actions, the sinner acted like a mindless, lustful animal, thus forfeiting his privilege of continuing in life. But, the merciful Creator presented man with a means of atonement. He said, 'Slaughter an animal in your place and recognize that such a fate should have been yours, for you have acted like the dumb beast.' It is easy to understand how the renewed awareness brought about by the sacrifice is a forceful means of repentance and ultimate atonement.

But the wicked go through the motions of the sacrificial ritual and remain indifferent and unaffected. They claim that this ancient ceremony is a meaningless decree to be performed without any reason or feelings of contrition. Therefore, God angrily challenges them here, demanding, *To what purpose do you recount* My ritual of sacrifice if you regard it as no more than an empty decree?'

וַתִּשָּׂא בְרִיתִי עֲלֵי פִיךָ — *While bearing* [lit. *you bore*] *My covenant upon your lips.*

The teachings of the Torah do not affect the inner feelings of the wicked scholar. His heart is not in his studies, He bears the covenant of God only *upon his lips*, but his soul is oblivious of it *(Hirsch)*.

In *Sanhedrin* 106b, the Sages declare that Doeg's knowledge was merely 'from the lips outward'. But God rejects this for He desires only the sincerity of the heart (רַחֲמָנָא לִבָּא בָּעֵי). [See 5:6-11 and Psalm 52 for a lengthy discussion of Doeg's shallow, perverted scholarship].

נ

יז-כ

יז עָלֶיךָ-פִּיךָ: וְאַתָּה שָׂנֵאתָ מוּסָר וַתַּשְׁלֵךְ
יח דְּבָרַי אַחֲרֶיךָ: אִם-רָאִיתָ גַּנָּב וַתִּרֶץ עִמּוֹ
יט וְעִם מְנָאֲפִים חֶלְקֶךָ: פִּיךָ שָׁלַחְתָּ בְרָעָה
כ וּלְשׁוֹנְךָ תַּצְמִיד מִרְמָה: תֵּשֵׁב בְּאָחִיךָ

17. וְאַתָּה שָׂנֵאתָ מוּסָר — *For you hate discipline.*

This refers to the study of proper conduct between man and his fellow man (Radak).

The covenant of God (v. 16) places limitations upon man's actions and speech, but you despise this מוּסָר [lit. chain, restraint] because it inhibits your pursuit of gratification (Hirsch).

[This alludes to Doeg, for the Talmud (Sanhedrin 106b) says, 'Doeg did not die until he forgot his Torah learning as it says, הוּא יָמוּת בְּאֵין מוּסָר, *He will die without discipline* (Proverbs 5:23). Although he was a brilliant student of the wisdom of the Torah, Doeg despised the Divine discipline imposed by it, so ultimately he abandoned his Torah studies].

וַתַּשְׁלֵךְ דְּבָרַי אַחֲרֶיךָ — *And you threw My words behind you.*

This refers to all other commands of the Torah [specifically those controlling the relationship between man and God] (Radak).

The rebellion of the wicked who totally reject God did not erupt overnight. Their heresy is the result of a drawn out process of alienation which began even while they were still observing God's commandments. Their very first step towards heresy was taken when they made God's service secondary in their lives and ceased to give God their attention. Once they tossed God's words behind them and treated them as insignificant, they eventually sunk to the point where they hate discipline (Tehillos Hashem).

אִם רָאִיתָ גַּנָּב וַתִּרֶץ עִמּוֹ — *If you saw a thief you sanctioned him.*

The word וַתִּרֶץ derives from רָצוֹן, *approval, sanction.* You agree to join the criminal in his lawless acts (Rashi; Radak).

Even though you are not a thief or an adulterer, nevertheless you approve of these crimes in principle. You rejoice when you see that the Torah's statutes do not subdue the passions of men and you sanction the wanton and licentious conduct of others for it excuses your own lack of discipline (Hirsch).

Targum relates וַתִּרֶץ to רָץ, *running* i.e. you run to join the thief in his crime. *Tehillos Hashem* adds that the man described here, originally set out to make a rendezvous with others for an immoral purpose i.e. *and with adulterers is your lot.* However, on the way he saw an opportunity to profit by joining in a theft. He *runs* to complete the robbery so that he will not miss his rendezvous for adultery.

וְעִם מְנָאֲפִים חֶלְקֶךָ — *And with adulterers is your lot.*

At first the hypocrite sought to justify himself by claiming that he rejected merely decrees that make no sense to him (v. 16). But eventually the true extent of his heresy is revealed when he transgresses even the universally understood prohibitions against theft and adultery. This proves that he is concerned only with satisfying his selfish desires and whims and has no interest in submitting to Divine authority (Ohel Yaakov).

The path of crime begins when a sinner participates in one theft which in itself is a relatively minor wrongdoing. He deludes himself that his career of lawlessness will stop there. He is mistaken, for once a man has forfeited his

L
17-20

¹⁷ *For you hate discipline*
     and you threw My words behind you.
¹⁸ *If you saw a thief you sanctioned him*
     and with adulterers was your lot.
¹⁹ *You dispatched your mouth for evil,*
     and your tongue adheres to deceit.
²⁰ *As you sit — against your brother you speak;*

self-control and submitted to his passions he is no longer his own master. Ultimately, he will surrender even to the lust for adultery, and be doomed. Therefore, we find that in the Ten Commandments the prohibitions against theft and adultery are written together, side by side (*Exodus* 20:13) to emphasize that a minor infraction leads to a major offense (*Alshich*).

19. פִּיךָ שָׁלַחְתָּ בְרָעָה — *You sent forth your mouth for evil.*

You accustomed your mouth to spread slanderous tales about others (*Radak*) and to teach false ideas and beliefs (*Sforno*).

Slander is described as dispatching the words of evil, for the disastrous effects of tale-bearing soar beyond all geographic boundaries and limitations. A man can sit in Jerusalem and spread slander about his enemy in Rome (*Kesef Mezukak*)!

וּלְשׁוֹנְךָ תַּצְמִיד מִרְמָה — *And your tongue adheres to deceit.*

Slander eventually leads to deceit, for when the slanderer is confronted by the man whose reputation he has tainted, he seeks to cover up his actions with lies (*Tehillos Hashem*).

Be'er Avraham explains that the verb roots רבק and חבר describe the joining of two objects which maintain their separate identities even after they are brought together. But צמד refers to a complete merging of two units into one

indivisible whole as in צָמִיד פָּתִיל עָלָיו, *the covering bound tightly upon it* (*Numbers* 19:15). [The slanderer's tale is repeated so often that to utter falsehood becomes the ingrained, habitual behavior of his tongue. This conduct becomes an irrevocable part of his personality].

Since he seeks to corrupt the masses by disseminating evil ideas, this man fears that the intelligent leaders will detect his sinister plot. Therefore, he resorts to treachery and deceit in order to conceal his true intentions (*Sforno*).

Furthermore, he becomes a master at composing and *joining together* false tales (*Rashi*) and he usually *joins together* with other liars and slanderers to share their company (*Radak*).

20. תשב — [*As*] *you sit* [lit. *you will sit*].

The company of slanderers and scoffers is referred to as a session of people who sit, as in מוֹשַׁב לֵצִים, *the session of scorners* (1:1). In such company, you dispatch your words of ridicule and slander (*Ibn Ezra*).

בְּאָחִיךָ תְדַבֵּר — *Against your brother you speak.*

Radak explains that this is a paternal brother. This implies that your motive in disparaging your *father's son* is because you share the same inheritance; thus there is a rivalry between you (*Radak*).

כא תְּדַבֵּר בְּבֶן־אִמְּךָ תִּתֶּן־דֹּפִי: אֵלֶּה עָשִׂיתָ ׀
וְהֶחֱרַשְׁתִּי דִּמִּיתָ הֱיוֹת־אֶהְיֶה כָמוֹךָ
כב אוֹכִיחֲךָ וְאֶעֶרְכָה לְעֵינֶיךָ: בִּינוּ־נָא זֹאת
כג שֹׁכְחֵי אֱלוֹהַּ פֶּן־אֶטְרֹף וְאֵין מַצִּיל: זֹבֵחַ
תּוֹדָה יְכַבְּדָנְנִי וְשָׂם דֶּרֶךְ אַרְאֶנּוּ בְּיֵשַׁע
אֱלֹהִים:

בְּבֶן אִמְּךָ — *Against your mother's son.*
If you permit your tongue to grow accustomed to slander for profit as in your dispute with your paternal brother who is a fellow heir, you will come to slander even those with whom you have no reason to quarrel such as your maternal brother with whom you share no estate (Rashi; Radak).

The Sages stress that there is no innocent slander; any form of gossip corrupts the character and leads to more serious offenses: 'If you have allowed your tongue to grow accustomed to slandering your colleague who is not of your people you will ultimately degrade your fellow Jew' (Devarim Rabbah 6:9).

'If you speak against Esau who is the son of your brother you will eventually sink to the point where you will speak against a son of your own nation who is as distinguished as Moses, the Master of all Prophets' (Tanchuma Pikudei 7).

תִּתֶּן דֹּפִי — *You spread* [lit. *you will give*] *contempt.*
Rashi relates דֹפִי to לַהְדֹּף, *to reject.* The slanderer causes his victim to become a social outcast, a pariah, by heaping disgrace upon him and ruining his reputation.

21. אֵלֶּה עָשִׂיתָ וְהֶחֱרַשְׁתִּי — *These have you done and I kept silent.*
You were guilty of all these crimes, yet I patiently kept silent and ignored your sins (Ibn Ezra; Radak) so as to give you an opportunity to repent of your own accord (Targum).

You perverted your role and mission as a Torah scholar. Instead of guiding the people toward goodness and truth, you set an example of evil — and yet I was merciful and held back punishment (Sforno).

דִּמִּיתָ הֱיוֹת אֶהְיֶה כָמוֹךָ — *You thought I would be like you.*
[The repetition of אֶהְיֶה הֱיוֹת lit. 'it would be, I would be' denotes a complete state of being i.e. 'I would be altogether'].

You misinterpreted my patient silence and deluded yourselves with the false assumption that My silence was proof of My unawareness of your concealed crimes. You compared Me to yourselves and imagined that just as mortals are ignorant of conspiracies, so, too, is God (Ibn Ezra; Sforno).

Radak adds in the name of 'an old scholar': I kept silent despite all the things you have done to anger Me, but for this sin I can no longer keep still. If you imagine that I am a corporeal body like yourself, finite and fallible — this gross misconception is intolerable, and must be refuted!

Targum renders: דִּמִּיתָ, *you harbored illusions of immortality* and imagined that הֱיוֹת, *you would exist* peacefully forever. אֶהְיֶה כָמוֹךָ, *you said in your heart, I will be mighty like You, O God!*

Imrei Yehuda notes that the numerical value of כָמוֹךָ is 86 which is equal to the numerical value of אֱלֹהִים.

אוֹכִיחֲךָ וְאֶעֶרְכָה לְעֵינֶיךָ — *I will rebuke you and indict you* [lit. *prepare it*] *before your eyes.*
God warns: my patience will come to an end and I will rebuke you and set

against your mother's son you spread contempt.
²¹ *These have you done and I kept silent;*
You thought I would be like you —
I will rebuke you
and reveal it before your eyes!
²² *Understand this please,*
you who have forgotten God,
Lest I tear you asunder and
there be none to set you free.

²³ *He who offers confession, honors Me,*
then preparing the way,
I will show him the salvation of God.

forth the case against you. I will then enumerate every one of your concealed sins, clearly demonstrating that I always knew your secrets. Malachi (3:18) foretold the day when hypocrites will be unmasked and their evil revealed, *Then you shall come back and differentiate between the righteous and the wicked, between him that serves HASHEM and him who serves Him not* (Radak).

22. בִּינוּ נָא זֹאת שֹׁכְחֵי אֱלוֹהַּ — *Understand this now, you who are oblivious to God.*

You robbers, adulterers, and slanderers who have erased God from your consciousness, understand the clear rebuke which is addressed to you and return to a new awareness of God (Ibn Ezra; Radak).

This teaches that the person who engages in לְשׁוֹן הָרָע, *slander*, will eventually become so corrupted that he will come to deny the existence of God Himself, for the Psalmist addresses the slanderers as *you who are oblivious to God* (Yerushalmi, Peah 1:1).

פֶּן אֶטְרֹף וְאֵין מַצִּיל — *Lest I tear asunder there is no rescuer.*

In this world I can wait patiently for

you to return (v. 21) but when the day of final judgment arrives, there will be no way to avoid the wrath of My strict justice. If you have not prepared yourself with a *rescuer* i.e., repentance and good deeds, then you are doomed to be *torn asunder* by My righteous fury (Radak; Alshich).

The word טוֹרֵף, *tear asunder*, is often used to describe an attack by a lion from which there is no rescue. However, when the flock is attacked by a wolf and a bear, the shepherd can still save his sheep (Ibn Ezra). [See 7:3 *Lest he tear my soul asunder like a lion, dismembering without rescuer.*]

23. זֹבֵחַ תּוֹדָה יְכַבְּדָנְנִי — *He who offers confession, honors Me.*

The choicest sacrifice is brought by him who repents and acknowledges his errors. This sincere penitent truly honor me (Rashi).

So said Solomon in his wisdom (Proverbs 21:3), *To do righteousness and justice is more acceptable to HASHEM than sacrifice* (Rav Shlomo Alkabetz).

The word תּוֹדָה can also be taken in its literal sense of a *thanksgiving*

sacrifice. If so, the Psalmist declares that God prefers such an expression of sincere appreciation of His goodness far more than all other offerings which come to atone for sin. *Midrash Tanchuma*, (*Tsav* 7) notes that David alludes to this in the peculiar spelling of יְכַבְּדָנְנִי in which the suffixial נ, *nun*, is repeated although grammatically there should be but a single *nun* — יְכַבְּדָנִי. This implies that in God's eyes, a תּוֹדָה, *thanksgiving sacrifice*, honors Him doubly.

וְשָׂם דָּרֶךְ — *Then, preparing the way* [lit. *and set the way.*]

All I ask of the sinner is that he should make the first move towards repentance by acknowledging his shortcomings, then I will immediately respond and prepare the way for him to return to Me completely. [In this interpretation, וְשָׂם דָּרֶךְ, *preparing the way*, refers to God Who eases the path of the penitent] (*Rashi*).

According to *Sforno* the one who prepares the way is not God, but the penitent who struggles to find the path of righteousness which leads to the World to Come.

The Sages say that the title דָּרֶךְ שָׂם, i.e., one who engages in *preparing the way*, befits anyone who exerts himself to make the path of Torah observance easier and smoother for all people (*Vayikra Rabbah* 9:2).

— This is the teacher who faithfully guides his young pupils on the path of Torah.

— This is the merchant who deals honestly and separates the tithes properly from his produce so as to provide his customers with permissible food.

— This is the man who removes the rocks, thorns, and obstacles from the public highway.[1]

אַרְאֶנּוּ בְּיֵשַׁע אֱלֹהִים — *I will show him the salvation of God.*

God declares: On the future day of judgment and reward, I will reveal the good fortune which was always reserved for the righteous, but which had remained concealed until then. At that time I will display the glory of the truly deservant ones who will be granted the eternal bliss of divine illumination (*Radak*).

---

1. The *Midrash* cites as an example of the public benefactor, *who prepares the way* a person who kindles lights to illuminate the streets for passersby. Reish Lakish said: Saul was granted the royal throne only in the merit of his pious grandfather who lit lamps on the dark streets leading to the House of Study. Because of this he was called (*I Chronicles* 8:33) נֵר, *lamp*, and saw the *salvation of God* through his grandson, Saul (*Radal*).

Moed Katan (5a) homiletically reads וְשָׂם (with a שׂ, *shin*), *he who appraises*, i.e., the person who acts intelligently in all situations and can evaluate the benefits or drawbacks of a given action. The *Talmud* cites as an example, a disciple of Rav Yannai who always posed difficult questions during his master's lectures. However, he would raise his challenging queries only during private lectures attended by the close disciples who fully appreciated Rav Yannai's greatness. During public lectures for the unlearned masses, the student would sit in silence lest his question be one which Rav Yannai could not answer. Were that to happen, Rav Yannai's stature would be diminished in the eyes of the unsophisticated audience.

In his monumental work, *Shaarei Teshuvah*, *Rabbeinu Yonah* devotes the entire first section to a comprehensive discussion of the twenty principles of repentance. He quotes frequently from this psalm, which he calls פֶּרֶק הַתְּשׁוּבָה, the Chapter of Repentance, because it is יְסוֹד מוּסָד לְעִקְּרֵי הַתְּשׁוּבָה, 'the basic foundation of all the principles of repentance' (*Shaarei Teshuvah* 1:23).

Indeed, every fiber of David's being was immersed in the spirit of repentance. Our Rabbis teach, 'Whoever wishes to repent should scrutinize the deeds of David' (*Midrash Shocher Tov* 4:4).

David is described as 'the man who made the yoke of repentance sublime' (*Moed Katan* 16b).

By virtue of David's devotion to constant self-improvement, his efforts merited special Divine assistance. God sent the prophet Nathan to inform him of his sin and to guide him on the path of return. [See Overview, chapters 4-5 for a deeper understanding of David's sin and repentance.] David composed this psalm at that time.

Since the theme of this chapter is penitence and purity, it is customary to recite it on the Sabbath when פָּרָשַׁת פָּרָה, the Portion of the Red Heifer is read, in order to remind the congregation to purify itself in anticipation of the Passover festival.

א־ג

1. לַמְנַצֵּחַ מִזְמוֹר לְדָוִד — *For the Conductor, a song of David.*

Indeed, when Nathan came to David a dirge and a lament would have been more suitable *(Alshich)* [for the prophet rebuked David severely and warned him of the harsh punishment he could expect. Nevertheless, even in that moment of wrath, God treated David kindly; therefore, he sang].

Midrash Shocher Tov comments that this psalm illustrates the verse, *Death and life are in the power of the tongue* (Proverbs 18:1), for David merited life in the World to Come because of his tongue, which said to Nathan, *I have sinned against HASHEM* (II *Samuel* 12:13). As soon as Nathan said to David, *HASHEM also has forgiven your sin, you shall not die* (II *Samuel* ibid), David composed this psalm.

Zera Yaakov points out that after the incident with Bath Sheba, רוּחַ הַקֹּדֶשׁ, *the holy spirit*, departed from David. The penitent king composed a מִזְמוֹר, *song*, in order to reach a state of ecstasy, so that the holy spirit could again descend לְדָוִד *unto David* [see comm. to 3:1].

Finally, *Shaarei Chaim* explains that repentance which is spurred by אַהֲבָה, *love* is far superior to that which is motivated by יִרְאָה, *fear* of punishment. David composed this psalm to uplift his spirit to that level of love which is a prerequisite for the *teshuvah* of אַהֲבָה.

2. בְּבוֹא אֵלָיו נָתָן הַנָּבִיא — *When Nathan the prophet came to him.*

[In this phrase, we detect three elements of Divine kindness.]

First, the prophet came *to him* i.e., Nathan came to David privately, when he was alone, and thereby saved him great embarrassment (*Alshich; Toras Chesed*).

Second, God's agent was the distinguished Nathan, rather than an ordinary man. In the Talmud (*Berachos* 10a) we find that when God wanted Isaiah to chastise King Chizkiyahu, the question arose whether the king should go to the prophet (and thus honor him) or whether the prophet should go to the king (and thus honor *him*). Despite David's sin, God still honored him by sending His prophet to the king (*Tehillos Hashem*).

Third, David's sin concerning Bath Sheba is one of the most misunderstood incidents in all of Scripture. Within this puzzling episode lies the mystery of David's נְשָׁמָה, soul . [It is essential to emphasize that David sinned solely for the sake of God (see *v.* 6).] David rejoiced that God had sent a man of penetrating prophetic vision to rebuke him, for an ordinary man would be ignorant of the true nature of the king's sin (*Tehillos Hashem*).

[Indeed, David praised God as מֵרִים רֹאשִׁי, *He who raises up my pride* (3:5), — alluding to the fact that God saved his reputation through the words of the prophet Nathan (*Midrash Shocher Tov, ibid.*).]

כַּאֲשֶׁר־בָּא אֶל בַּת שֶׁבַע — *When he came to Bath Sheba.*

Dorash Moshe emphasizes that, in fact, Nathan did not go to David until after Bath Sheba bore David her first son (II *Samuel* 11:27, 12:2), almost a year after David's sin. Until then, David did *not* repent, because he excused his conduct with a number of 'righteous' rationalizations. However, when Nathan voiced God's displeasure, the king was immediately filled with deep remorse [see *Shaarei Teshuvah* 1:3]. Therefore it is considered as if David repented immediately after his sin,

For the Conductor,
    a song of David.
² When Nathan the prophet came to him,
    when he came to Bath Sheba.
³ Show me favor, according to Your kindness,
    according to Your vast compassion
    erase my transgressions.

although it occurred a year earlier.

In his commentary to *II Samuel* 12:2, *Alshich* explains that since God loved David and had mercy on him, he did not send Nathan to rebuke him until long after the sin. If David had been accused immediately, his life would have been forfeited, because it was ordained in heaven that only death could atone for David's offense. After his son was born, only to become ill and die soon after, the infant's life took the place of his father's.[1]

חָנֵּנִי אֱלֹהִים כְּחַסְדֶּךָ — *Show me favor, according to Your kindness.*

This request appears to be self-contradictory. First David implies that his merits are totally inadequate, for he appeals for God's *favor* and *kindness*. Yet he calls upon אֱלֹהִים *Elokim*, the Divine name which characterizes God as the Enforcer of Strict Justice, rather than upon 'ה *HASHEM*, the Divine name which characterizes God as the Dispenser of Mercy. The fact that David chose to use the former Divine Name would seem to imply that he is righteous enough to withstand the

strictest Divine judgment (*Shevet Mussar, Tehillos Hashem*).

[We can reconcile this apparent contradiction with the explanation that David considers himself only *partially* deservant; therefore, he asks for Divine *kindness* in addition to his own righteous merits. This idea is illustrated by *Midrash Shocher Tov:* David's situation is comparable to that of a wounded man who sought treatment from a physician. The doctor told him, 'I cannot treat your wound, for it is large, and the amount of money in your hand is small.' The wounded man pleaded, 'Take all the money I possess as your payment, and concerning the balance of my bill, show me kindness!']

כְּרֹב רַחֲמֶיךָ מְחֵה פְשָׁעָי — *According to Your vast compassion erase my transgressions.*

Radak notes that the plural form *transgressions* implies that two offenses were involved; the taking of Bath Sheba and the death of Uriah.

Beis Elokim explains the use of the word מְחֵה, *erase.* An intentional transgression adheres to the soul like a

1. The *Midrash* relates that at the time David slew Goliath, Uriah the Hittite had not yet converted to Judaism. David was unsuccessful in his attempt to strip the chain-mail armor from the dead giant so that he could decapitate him, because David couldn't find the knotted end of the metal thread which linked all the chain-mail hooks together. Then Uriah approached David and asked, 'If I show you the knot, will you give me an Israelite woman for a wife?' When David consented, Uriah showed him the knot, which had been tied on Goliath's sole.

God was angry with David for promising a daughter of Israel to a gentile. He decreed that Bath Sheba, the woman who had been preordained to be David's wife, should be Uriah's wife first. [The Sages say (*Sanhedrin* 107a), 'Bath Sheba was designated as David's mate from the six days of Creation, but David took her before the proper time (see *Maharal* and *Toras Chaim, Sanhedrin ibid.*)]

פְּשָׁעָי: °הַרְבֵּה כַּבְּסֵנִי מֵעֲוֹנִי וּמֵחַטָּאתִי

טַהֲרֵנִי: כִּי־פְשָׁעַי אֲנִי אֵדָע וְחַטָּאתִי נֶגְדִּי

תָמִיד: לְךָ לְבַדְּךָ חָטָאתִי וְהָרַע בְּעֵינֶיךָ

clinging substance. It resembles dirt adhering to surface of a fabric which must be thoroughly scraped and *erased* if the soul is to regain its cleanliness.

4. הֶרֶב כַּבְּסֵנִי מֵעֲוֹנִי — *Abundantly cleanse me from my iniquity.*

Sforno explains that David's iniquity was that he did not confess and repent [for almost a year], until Nathan the prophet came to rebuke him. For a man of David's spiritual stature, such a delay was a serious offense.

Radak notes that the word is written (הֶרְבֵּה, *kesiv*), *many,* but is pronounced הֶרֶב *thoroughly; much.* David said 'You have performed *many* kindnesses for me in the past; therefore I ask You to continue Your mercy now by *thoroughly* washing off my iniquity.'

Beis Elokim states that the spiritually defiling 'residue' created by *iniquity* penetrates deeper than that which is created by *transgression.* Transgression is a clear-cut offense which is readily identified. *Iniquity* is more subtle and covert. Therefore it is comparable to dirt so deeply absorbed into a fabric that it can be removed only by repeated, 'thorough' laundering.

וּמֵחַטָּאתִי טַהֲרֵנִי — *And from my sin purify me.*

David accepted responsibility for the deaths of all the other soldiers who died in the battle in which Uriah was killed. Although he had never sought their deaths, David blamed himself for the casualties, considering each death to be his own [unintentional] *sin* (*Sforno*).

Beis Elokim observes that the unintentional *sin* is comparable to dust which clings lightly to the surface of a garment. Brushing or shaking the garment will suffice to *purify* the fabric; no

vigorous scraping or laundering is necessary.

Malbim draws the following distinction between the two forms of transgression: עָוֹן *iniquity* describes an עוות *distortion* of the intellect which causes a person to err and neglect a Torah command. The חֵטְא, *sin,* is an (unintentional) offense, a superficial deed which is comparable to contracting טומאה, *impurity* through contact with an unclean object. Purity is easily regained by immersion in a ritual bath (mikvah).

Atonement for חֵטְא is relatively easy to obtain; all David asks is: *From my sin purify me.* But even after the sin is gone, the spiritual damage remains. The blemish on the soul, the intellectual distortion(עוות), these are deeply ingrained. For this David vigorously pleads, *Abundantly cleanse me of my iniquity.*

5. כִּי פְשָׁעַי אֲנִי אֵדָע — *For my transgressions I recognize.*

I readily acknowledge my wrongdoing and make no attempt to deny or hide it. I am not like Cain, who feigned ignorance of his brother's murder, saying (Genesis 3:9) לֹא יָדַעְתִּי, *I do not know* (*Radak*).

This admission of guilt is in itself a virtue which makes me worthy of forgiveness (*Sforno*).

Alshich notes that David does not use the past or present tense, but the future tense אֲנִי אֵדָע, *I will know.* He suggests: As long as I live this knowledge will be with me and I shall never forget it!

וְחַטָּאתִי נֶגְדִּי תָמִיד — *And my sin is before me always.*

Since my sin fills me with perpetual regret and constant anxiety, it looms

⁴ *Abundantly cleanse me from my iniquity,*
    and from my sin purify me.
⁵ *For my transgressions I recognize,*
    and my sin is before me always.
⁶ *Against You alone did I sin,*
    And evil in Your eyes did I do,

before me incessantly *(Rashi).* Thus, I
am constantly reminded never to repeat
such an error again, even unintentionally *(Sforno).*

In the *Talmud (Yoma* 86b) we find a
difference of opinion. The Rabbis maintain that when a person confesses to a
sin, repents on Yom Kippur, and does
not repeat his offense, it is despicable
for him to confess and repent the same
sin the following Yom Kippur. To do so
is like 'a dog who returns to its vomit'.

Rabbi Eliezer ben Yaakov, however,
claims that repeated confession and
repentance are highly desirable, for
David said, *And my sin is before me
always,* i.e., 'I never feel that it is
washed away and forgotten; it looms
before my eyes constantly' *(Rashi)*
[*Rambam (Hilchos Teshuvah* 2:8)
decides in favor of Rabbi Eliezer.][1]

Alshich comments: every sin creates
an evil spiritual force in heaven which
acts as a קַטֵּיגוֹר, an *'accusing angel'*
which spreads a negative and detrimental influence against the sinner. David
mourns: חֲטָאתִי 'the harmful force of
my own creation' נֶגְדִּי 'works against
me', תָמִיד 'always interfering with my
spiritual growth and enrichment'.

6. לְךָ לְבַדְּךָ חָטָאתִי — *Against You alone
did I sin.*

[As David said to Nathan, 'חָטָאתִי לַה:

I have sinned to HASHEM (II *Samuel*
12:13), for I violated the spirit of the
law, thereby creating a climate of disregard for God's mitzvos (see II *Samuel*
12:4 and *Rashi).* In other respects, I did
not actually transgress, for Bath Sheba
was legally divorced and Uriah was condemned to die because of insubordina-
tion against me, the king (see *Overview
Part IV).*]

Radak provides additional insight
into David's apology: David admitted,
'Since I realized that my actions might
be misinterpreted, I took pains to exercise discretion. My servants, unaware of
my intentions, brought Bath Sheba to
me in secrecy. I sent Joab a secret message, urging him to make Uriah's death
seem to be a chance casualty of war. I
sinned only in the privacy of my heart,
for my intentions were tainted with
lust.'[See *Rashi* and *Maharsha* on *Shabbos* 56 a]. 'Although I harmed no innocent man, I realize that, to You, my
thoughts were offensive; for this, I
readily admit my guilt.'

Therefore, my forgiveness is exclusively in Your hands *(Rashi).* Even
if I wished to ask forgiveness of Uriah
and the other soldiers killed with him, I
could not, for they are all dead *(Sforno).*

וְהָרַע בְּעֵינֶיךָ עָשִׂיתִי — *And evil in Your
eyes did I do.*

---

1. The Torah (*Leviticus* 9:7) relates that when the Tabernacle was dedicated, Moses had to
coax Aaron to enter it to perform the service. *Ramban (ad loc.)* explains that Aaron, God's
consecrated servant, had never committted a sin other than that of participating in the Golden
Calf. The specter of that sin was deeply etched into his consciousness and he constantly saw
the image of the calf before his eyes, preventing him from feeling worthy, just as David said
And my sin is before me always. Therefore, Moses had to allay Aaron's fears to persuade him
that he was indeed worthy of the priesthood.

עָשִׂיתִי לְמַעַן תִּצְדַּק בְּדָבְרֶךָ תִּזְכֶּה
בְשָׁפְטֶךָ: הֵן־בְּעָווֹן חוֹלָלְתִּי וּבְחֵטְא
יֶחֱמַתְנִי אִמִּי: הֵן־אֱמֶת חָפַצְתָּ בַטֻּחוֹת
וּבְסָתֻם חָכְמָה תוֹדִיעֵנִי: תְּחַטְּאֵנִי בְאֵזוֹב

ז

ח

ט

[As Nathan thundered against me, 'Why have you despised the word of HASHEM to do that which is evil in His eyes' (II Samuel 12:9).]

Beis Aharon explains that עֵינֶיךָ, *your eyes*, in our verse does not refer to the eyes *of God*, but to David's eyes, i.e., David confesses that he has misused *Your eyes* — the ones which God provided him along with all the parts of his body.

[See *Overview*, Part II, where it is explained that God endowed David with a unique attribute: יְפֵה עֵינַיִם *beautiful eyes* (I Samuel 16:12), which represented a clarity of vision focused exclusively on God's will and completely unaffected by lust and temptation. David failed his trial with Bath Sheba because desire for her blurred his clear vision.]

לְמַעַן תִּצְדַּק בְּדָבְרֶךָ — *So that You would be justified when You speak.*

Rashi (based on *Sanhedrin* 107b) explains that David had asked God to test his ability to withstand temptation. God told him that he was as yet unprepared for such a trial and would surely fail. After the sin, David addressed God, saying, 'It is clearly revealed and known to You that if I had tried to subdue my lust I could have done so, but I gave in to temptation *purposely so that You would be justified*, lest people say that the servant has bested his Master. For had I passed the test, Your divine prediction would have been proven in-

accurate.' [The commentaries emphasize that, in reality, David *did* fail to conquer his passions; the excuse he offered was a rationalization. See Publisher's Preface to *Levush Mordecai* on *Bava Kama* and *Ha'amek Davar, Numbers* 22:33.]

Radak and *Sforno* interpret these words as David's argument as to why God should accept his repentance: 'You spoke of repentance to Cain and promised, *surely if you improve yourself you will be forgiven* (Genesis 4:7). To Moses You revealed Yourself as, *forgiving iniquity and transgression and sin* (Exodus 34:7). Now I beg You to justify those words by forgiving me!'

תִּזְכֶּה בְשָׁפְטֶךָ — *And be in the right when You judge.*

'Forgive me, so that when You judge, condemn, and punish the wicked who refused to repent their evil ways, they won't be able to protest, "What good would our repentance have done, for You would not have forgiven us anyway?"' (*Rashi*; *Radak*; *Sforno*).

7. הֵן בְּעָווֹן חוֹלָלְתִּי — *Behold, in iniquity was I fashioned.*

Rashi explains: 'I was formed by a male and a female, both creatures of flesh and blood who were full of sin.' [Even the most devout man can have some contact with sin (*Vayikra Rabbah* 14:5). Now I beg You to justify those words by forgiving me!' עָווֹן *iniquity* is written מָלֵא 'full' (with two 'vavs' וֹ), in order to emphasize man's great tendency towards sin.][1]

---

1. [Although the *Talmud* (*Bava Basra* 17a) counts Jesse, the father of David, as one of the rare individuals who were completely innocent of any act of personal sin, nevertheless as a descendant of Adam and Eve, he too had the instinctive human tendency towards passion and error which resulted from their sin in the Garden of Eden (see *Overview, I*). David laments that this basic human weakness was passed on to him at conception although he imputes no sinful *deed* to Jesse.]

So that You would be justified when You speak,
and be in the right when You judge.
⁷ Behold, in iniquity was I fashioned,
and in sin did my mother conceive me.
⁸ Behold, You desire truth
in the concealments,
And in my innermost heart
You revealed to me wisdom.

Beis Elokim explicates, 'From the moment of my birth, I was affected by the Evil Inclination, or it attached itself to me at the moment I left my mother's womb, as Scripture says, לַפֶּתַח חַטָּאת רבֵץ, *Sin rests at the door (Genesis 4:7).*

[At the time of birth, the Evil Inclination displaces the Good Inclination, which does not return until the child reaches maturity *(Piskei Tosafos, Nedarim 62).*]

Maharal emphasizes that David never used these arguments as an excuse to allow himself to sin. Rather after he *did* stumble into sin, he pleaded with God to take into consideration the natural human tendency towards iniquity, and to judge him with understanding and compassion [see *Sforno*].

וּבְחֵטְא יֶחֱמַתְנִי אִמִּי — *And in sin did my mother conceive me.*

Rashi observes יֶחֱמַתְנִי is derived from חוּם, *warmth,* referring to a woman's heat at the time of procreation and conception (see *Genesis* 30:38).

Maharam Arama adds, that by the process of elimination, David attributes *sin* to his mother, because his father, Jesse, was one of the four men in all history who died without any trace of personal sin *(Shabbos* 55b; *Targum Ruth* 4:22; see footnote).

Ibn Ezra comments this alludes to the fact that Eve, the mother of all mankind, did not bear children until after she sinned. [This would appear to be the case according to the order of events set forth in the third and fourth chapters of *Genesis.* However, according to the *Talmud (Sanhedrin* 38a), Eve bore children before the sin.]

8. הֵן אֱמֶת חָפַצְתָּ בַטֻחוֹת — *Behold You desire truth in the concealments.*

The commentaries identify the טֻחוֹת as the kidneys, which are טֻחוֹת, *concealed* [see *Leviticus* 14:43] with protective fat *(Metzudas David; Rashi).* [The kidneys are considered to be the seat of human intellect, as in *Job* 38:36 and *Psalms* 7:10, 16:7.] David said, 'Although I have sinned, O God, nevertheless my true faith in You is still intact deep within the *concealments* of my being. This strong conviction and *truth* is what You *desire.* Therefore, please forgive my sin, which was spurred only by momentary, external temptation and was not an integral part of my inner being.

The most convincing argument which I can offer to prove that I never meant to rebel against You or deny Your sovereignty is that I now regret my sin so bitterly and beseech You to guide me towards the path of truth *(Ibn Ezra; Radak).*

וּבְסָתֻם חָכְמָה תוֹדִיעֵנִי — *And in my innermost heart You revealed to me wisdom.*

Inside the concealed chambers of my heart You have taught me how to [recognize and] confess my sins; such awareness requires great wisdom *(Rashi).*

[As explained previously (v. 6) David's transgressions were violations

וְאֶטְהָר תְּכַבְּסֵנִי וּמִשֶּׁלֶג אַלְבִּין:
י תַּשְׁמִיעֵנִי שָׂשׂוֹן וְשִׂמְחָה תָּגֵלְנָה עֲצָמוֹת
יא דִּכִּיתָ: הַסְתֵּר פָּנֶיךָ מֵחֲטָאָי וְכָל-עֲוֹנֹתַי

of the spirit, not the letter, of the law. On the surface, his actions could be justified; the crime lay concealed in the impure intentions of his innermost heart, deep in his unconscious mind. David himself was hardly aware of these concealed motivations.]

I ask that in the future You grant me the wisdom to recognize the true nature of סְתָם the *innermost*, so that I will not misinterpret them again. [I.e., until Nathan rebuked me, I had felt that my motives for taking Bath Sheba were completely noble and pure] (Radak).

9. תְּחַטְּאֵנִי בְאֵזוֹב וְאֶטְהָר — *Purge me with hyssop and I shall be pure.*

David compared the taint which sin placed on his soul to a leprous spot afflicting the body (Ibn Ezra). Indeed, the Talmud (Sanhedrin 107b) says that for six months, David was actually plagued with leprosy because of his transgressions [cf. Yoma 22b; Tosafos; Rabbeinu Chananel; and Tosafos Yeshanim 22b].

The hyssop [together with the cedar wood] is used to sprinkle the pure waters on the leper during his final process of purification [see Leviticus 14:6] (Rashi; Radak).

Leprosy is a punishment for arrogance; therefore, the man who proudly lifts himself above others like the towering cedar tree is afflicted. But when he modestly lowers himself to the height of the humble hyssop, he is cured (Bamidbar Rabbah 19:3).

David displayed excessive pride and extreme over-confidence when he demanded that God test him (Harav Melamed). Moreover, he acted in a high-handed manner when he exercised his royal perogative to seize Bath Sheba at will to dispose of Uriah. The punishment for this arrogance was leprosy (Tefillah L'Moshe).

תְּכַבְּסֵנִי וּמִשֶּׁלֶג אַלְבִּין — *Cleanse me and I shall be whiter than snow.*

[As the prophet Isaiah (1:18) says concerning the penitent, *Though your sins be as scarlet, they shall be as white as snow.*]

Malbim explains that the most prominent form of leprosy is the בַּהֶרֶת, which is as white as snow (Negaim 1:1). When such a spot erupts on the surface of the skin, it indicates a black, evil character trait which must be cleansed by repentance and 'whitened' like snow. [מְצוּרָע is a contraction of מוֹצִיא רָע, *to remove the evil*]. The halacha is that if the leprosy spreads until it covers the entire body, then the leper is considered as clean, because this shows that this man has mobilized his entire body to sincerely regret his ways. Thus, David declares: מִשֶּׁלֶג, *from the snow* [—colored] growth which covers all of my skin on the outside, אַלְבִּין I shall be whitened — on the inside as well.'

10. תַּשְׁמִיעֵנִי שָׂשׂוֹן וְשִׂמְחָה — *Make me hear joy and gladness.*

Please inform me that I am forgiven (Rashi).

At first, David's soul was shrouded in a dark spirit of mourning because of his sins *It begs for release from this gloom* (Ibn Ezra; Radak).

Malbim adds that the leper is plunged into intensive mourning. He must isolate himself from society and rend his garments. He is obliged to publicly bemoan his uncleanliness and sorrow. Thus, David yearned to return to the normal joys of healthy life.

[The day preceding Yom Kippur is designated as a day of joyous feasting (Rosh Hashonah 9a). Rabbeinu Yonah (Shaarei Teshuvah 4:8) explains that this rejoicing displays genuine gladness at the arrival of this opportunity for

⁹ *Purge me with hyssop and I shall be pure,*
  cleanse me and I shall be whiter than snow.
¹⁰ *Make me hear joy and gladness,*
  may the bones which You crushed, exult.
¹¹ *Hide Your face from my sins,*
  and all my iniquities erase.

atonement, and bears testimony to sincere worry over our guilt and our deep sorrow over our transgressions. Similarly, David seeks this joy of Divine forgiveness.[1]

תָּגֵלְנָה עֲצָמוֹת דִּכִּיתָ — *May the bones which You crushed, exult.*

Solomon taught: *Good tidings make the bones fat (Proverbs 16:30),* but mourning crushes them *(Tefillah L'Moshe).* Moreover, the imprint of each wrongdoing is stamped [i.e., crushed] indelibly on the organ which committed the sin, until the sinner is forgiven *(Eretz HaChaim).*

Radak explains that upon hearing Nathan's accusations, David immediately confessed his sin. Nathan said: *God also has forgiven Your sin; you shall not die (II Samuel 12:13).* However, the prophet told David that his life would be plagued by many miseries and sufferings *(II Samuel 12:10-14).* David never asked to be exempted from these afflictions, for he realized that he deserved them and that they were essential for his repentance. Here he longs for the day when his ultimate atonement will bring him joy and when 'the crushing of his bones' will no longer be necessary.

11. הַסְתֵּר פָּנֶיךָ מֵחֲטָאָי — *Hide Your face from my sins.*

Ibn Ezra maintains that David is speaking euphemistically, as if to say 'Shield my face from Your wrath, which was aroused by my sins'; allow my repentance to erase their unpleasant memory from Your presence *(Radak).*

Alshich (based on his commentary to v.4) interprets: Please disregard the 'accusing angel' which I created, with my sin.

וְכָל עֲוֹנֹתַי מְחֵה — *And all my iniquities erase.*

Alshich explains that in the fourth verse, David spoke in the singular; *my iniquity, my sin* because he was referring to the one great sin of his lifetime, the incident with Bath Sheba. Here, however, he speaks in the plural asking forgiveness for all other *sins* and *iniquities* which he committed. Therefore, David makes no mention here of פֶּשַׁע, *transgression,* for he never committed another intentional offense. [See commentary on v.3, concerning the plural, פְּשָׁעַי, *my transgressions.* This form was used because David was guilty of *two* counts of intentional wrongdoing during this *one* episode: taking Bath Sheba and killing Uriah.]

1. *The Vilna Gaon* says that שִׂמְחָה describes the *gladness* experienced at the beginning of an undertaking, and that שָׂשׂוֹן denotes the *joy* of completion, as we sing in the Sabbath אֵל אָרוֹן hymn — שְׂמֵחִים בְּצֵאתָם וְשָׂשִׂים בְּבוֹאָם 'Glad as they set out and joyous when they return'. Similarly, we sing, שִׂישׂוּ וְשִׂמְחוּ בְּשִׂמְחַת תּוֹרָה 'Rejoice and be glad on Simchas Torah'. On that day, שָׂשׂוֹן precedes שִׂמְחָה because we experience first the joy of ending the Torah reading and then the gladness of beginning the reading anew.

In view of this, we may interpret David's words as '*Make me hear joy,* i.e., the joy of knowing that my atonement is complete, *and gladness,* i.e., allow me to make a fresh, pure beginning in Your service.

יב מְחֵה: לֵב טָהוֹר בְּרָא־לִי אֱלֹהִים וְרוּחַ
יג נָכוֹן חַדֵּשׁ בְּקִרְבִּי: אַל־תַּשְׁלִיכֵנִי מִלְּפָנֶיךָ
יד וְרוּחַ קָדְשְׁךָ אַל־תִּקַּח מִמֶּנִּי: הָשִׁיבָה לִּי
שְׂשׂוֹן יִשְׁעֶךָ וְרוּחַ נְדִיבָה תִסְמְכֵנִי:
טו אֲלַמְּדָה פֹשְׁעִים דְּרָכֶיךָ וְחַטָּאִים אֵלֶיךָ

12. לֵב טָהוֹר בְּרָא לִי אֱלֹהִים — *A pure heart create for me, O God.*

Until now, David was struggling to purify his heart of past sins. Now he calls for Divine assistance to protect his future integrity (*Rashi; Ibn Ezra*). He deserves this aid for 'He who strives to purify himself merits God's assistance' (*Yoma 38a*). Thus fortified against future sins, his heart would resemble a new creation (*Radak*). If the heart is pure, then the entire body (which depends on the heart) will be pure (*Reishis Chochmah*).

[*Rambam* (*Hilchos Teshuvah* 2:4) emphasizes that a fundamental of total repentance is to consider oneself as a newborn creature, totally divorced from the errors of the past: Among the techniques of *teshuvah* are to ... change one's name, as if to say, I am someone else, I am not the man who committed those offences! and he reforms his actions and goes out into exile ... '

We can also understand David's concern for preserving the purity of his heart in light of the *Rambam's* teaching (*Hilchos Melachim* 3:6) that the Torah was especially concerned lest the king's heart be distracted [by women],...for the heart of the king is the collective heart of the entire congregation of Israel (see *Overview* Part IV).]

וְרוּחַ נָכוֹן חַדֵּשׁ בְּקִרְבִּי — *And a steadfast spirit renew within me.*

This refers to an upright spirit (*Metzudas David*) [which does not bend or succumb to temptation].

S'forno renders נָכוֹן as synonymous with מוּכָן, *prepared*, i.e., Grant me an intellect (soul) capable of understanding God's ways and equipped to communicate these truths to others.

13. אַל תַּשְׁלִיכֵנִי מִלְּפָנֶיךָ — *Cast me not away from Your Presence.*

The servant who betrays his master may be forgiven, but never again will he enjoy the confidence of his master or be included in his counsel. David says, Although I have sinned, do not end our intimate relationship, for I am like a creature reborn, endowed with a pure, new heart; I am no longer the same person who offended You! (*Yaavetz HaDoresh*).

וְרוּחַ קָדְשְׁךָ אַל תִּקַּח מִמֶּנִּי — *And Your holy spirit take not from me.*

Ibn Ezra notes that David was endowed with God's holy spirit, as he himself said, רוּחַ ה' דִּבֶּר בִּי וּמִלָּתוֹ עַל לְשׁוֹנִי, *The spirit of HASHEM spoke through me and His word was on my lips* (*II Samuel* 23:2).

Radak adds that it was under the inspiration of this sacred ecstasy that David composed his songs and psalms. When he sinned, this spirit abandoned him. Now he pleads that it should return and never leave him again.

14. הָשִׁיבָה לִּי שְׂשׂוֹן יִשְׁעֶךָ — *Restore to me the joy of Your salvation.*

The Talmud (*Sanhedrin* 107b) infers from this that during the six month period of David's leprosy, the holy spirit abandoned him [as did all the members of the Great Sanhedrin]. He now pleads that the holy spirit be restored (*Rashi*).

Ibn Ezra says that before this incident, David was always happy because

12 *A pure heart create for me, O God,*
and a steadfast spirit renew within me.
13 *Cast me not away from Your Presence,*
And Your Holy Spirit take not from me.
14 *Restore to me the joy of Your salvation.*
and with a generous spirit sustain me.
15 *Then I will teach transgressors Your ways,*
and sinners shall repent to You.

at no other time had he sinned [intentionally] (see *Alshich, v.* 10).

Alshich translates יִשְׁעֶךָ as 'Your victory' explaining that although *II Samuel,* Chapter 2 is devoted to the episode of David and Bath Sheba, the opening verse of the chapter describes David's victory over Ammon [which, it would seem, should have been included in the preceding chapter]. This juxtaposition serves to teach that David's pride concerning his military triumph encouraged his Evil Inclination to sin.

Nevertheless, David now asks God to help him in his future battles and to *restore the joy of 'Your victory'.*

He argues that his only motivation for waging war was to alleviate the misery of his harassed and impoverished subjects [see *Berachos* 3b]. David's warfare was inspired by a רוּחַ נְדִיבָה *a spirit of charity* rather than by a desire for personal glory.

וְרוּחַ נְדִיבָה תִסְמְכֵנִי — *And with a generous spirit sustain me.*

This refers to the holy spirit, which generously suffuses the heart with songs of praise for God *(Radak).*

Rashbam translates רוּחַ נְדִיבָה as 'a ruling spirit' (as in נְדִיבֵי עַמִּים *the rulers of nations,* 47:10); i.e., 'Uphold my resolve to repent by strengthening my intellect so that it may rule over and subdue my passions.'

'Furthermore, let no obstacle arise which would interfere with my repentance' *(Rambam, Hilchos Teshuvah* 6:4).

15. אֲלַמְּדָה פֹשְׁעִים דְּרָכֶיךָ — *[Then] I will teach transgressors Your ways.*

When You will forgive me I will be able to serve as an example for others, who will recognize the efficacy of repentance. Then, they too will be encouraged to mend their ways *(Radak).*

Indeed this is why I requested *a pure heart created for me* (v. 12), because the admonition of a teacher can affect the hearts of his students only if his words come from a pure heart *(Alshich).* [Compare *Berachos* 6b, 'Whoever has a fear of heaven merits that his words be heeded'.]

Rabbeinu Yonah (Shaarei Teshuvah 1:50) lists this as the twentieth and final principle of repentance: 'Turn back as many people as possible from transgression, as Scripture says, *Return and turn back others from all your transgressions (Ezekiel 18:30).* Furthermore, if one does not rebuke others, he himself is punished for their sins. David said in the Psalm of Repentance, *I will teach transgressors Your ways.*

וְחַטָּאִים אֵלֶיךָ יָשׁוּבוּ — *And sinners shall repent to You.*

[The *Talmud (Avodah Zarah* 4b) states that, considering David's lofty level of personal piety, it is inconceivable that he should have sinned as he did, except for the fact that God decreed that his sin should come to pass (see *Rashi.*)]

Maharsha (ad. loc.) and *Alshich* (Ps. 131) explain that God never forces any man to sin; the Sages mean to say

טז יָשׁוּבוּ: הַצִּילֵנִי מִדָּמִים| אֱלֹהִים אֱלֹהֵי
יז תְּשׁוּעָתִי תְּרַנֵּן לְשׁוֹנִי צִדְקָתֶךָ: אֲדֹנָי
יח שְׂפָתַי תִּפְתָּח וּפִי יַגִּיד תְּהִלָּתֶךָ: כִּי| לֹא־
תַחְפֹּץ זֶבַח וְאֶתֵּנָה עוֹלָה לֹא תִרְצֶה:
יט זִבְחֵי אֱלֹהִים רוּחַ נִשְׁבָּרָה לֵב־נִשְׁבָּר

that God usually protects the devout and helps them to subdue their lusts and passions. Here, this customary סִיַּעְתָּא דִשְׁמַיָּא, *Divine assistance* was not granted to David.]

This happened in order that an individual who commits an offense and despairs of repentance can be told, 'Go learn from King David, who repented and was completely forgiven'.]

16. הַצִּילֵנִי מִדָּמִים אֱלֹהִים — *Rescue me from blood-guilt — O God.*

'Let me not die violently by the sword, as a punishment for having caused the death of Uriah' (Rashi).

'I call upon You as אֱלֹהִים, the *Supreme Judge Who has the final authority* to decide whether to condemn or whether to exonerate me' (Radak).

תְּרַנֵּן לְשׁוֹנִי צִדְקָתֶךָ — *Let my tongue sing joyously of Your righteousness.*

Spare me the task of eliminating my enemies through violence so that no *blood-guilt* will taint my hands. In return *my tongue will sing joyously of Your righteousness* and kindness (Chazah Zion).

Fill my mouth with the sweet words of Torah and my tongue *will sing joyously of Your righteousness.* Thus, my tongue, so well occupied, will have no opportunity for spreading words of slander and I will be rescued from blood-guilt (Na'avah Tehillah).

17. אֲדֹנָי שְׂפָתַי תִּפְתָּח — *My Lord, open my lips.*

Open my lips so that I may speak words of Torah (Targum). Forgive me now and provide me with cause to recite Your praises (Rashi). Cleanse me

of sin so that I will be worthy of teaching others Your ways (Sforno).

Return to me Your holy spirit, which, before my sin, stirred my lips to compose Divinely inspired melodies, (Radak).

Ramban (Emunah U'Bitachon, Chapter 5) maintains that שְׂפָתַי is related to שְׂפַת הַנָּהָר the river bank, i.e., the barriers which confine the river in its narrow channel. *Harav Gifter* explains that man is self-centered and limited. His soul is restricted and stifled within the narrow confines of his finite body. But when man stands before the infinity of his Maker, his eternal soul surges until it 'overflows' the 'banks' of his body. For this reason, the Sages (Berachos 4b) decreed that this verse should be recited before a person stands in God's presence to pray.

וּפִי יַגִּיד תְּהִלָּתֶךָ — *That my mouth may declare Your praise.*

[When man, so frail and insignificant, stands before his Maker and contemplates His praises, he should be struck silent with awe. Therefore he must pray for Divine assistance to open his mouth and grant it the ability to declare God's praises.]

18. כִּי לֹא תַחְפֹּץ זֶבַח וְאֶתֵּנָה — *For You desire no offering, else I would give it.*

According to the letter of the law, David did not sin at all (Shabbos 56a), but David, in his piety, considered himself a sinner (Arvei Nachal). Therefore he says, 'If I had committed this crime unintentionally, I could atone for it with a חַטָּאת, *sin offering, but my sin was a* מֵזִיד, an intentional transgression (Rashi; Ibn Ezra). Therefore, all I

¹⁶ *Rescue me from blood-guilt — O God,*
       God of my salvation.
Let my tongue sing joyously of Your righteousness.

¹⁷ *My Lord, open my lips,*
       that my mouth may declare Your praise.

¹⁸ *For You desire no offering, else I would give it,*
       A burnt-offering You do not favor.

¹⁹ *The offerings of God*
       are a broken spirit,
A heart broken and crushed

can offer is a broken heart, subdued in sincere repentance (*Radak*).

עוֹלָה לֹא תִרְצֶה — *A burnt-offering You do not favor.*

Rather You hope that the burning of the sacrificial flesh will inspire the sinner to 'burn out' the animal lusts which corrupt his heart (*Radak*).

19. זִבְחֵי אֱלֹהִים רוּחַ נִשְׁבָּרָה — *The offerings of God are a broken spirit.*

The name אֱלֹהִים appears six times in this psalm, but the name ה׳, *HASHEM* appears not once (*Chazah Zion*). Animal sacrifices are offered to ה׳, the Divine Name indicating God's attribute of Mercy, in order to obtain forgiveness for unintentional errors. But intentional transgressions require that one offer extreme remorse and complete repentance in order to appease אֱלֹהִים, the Divine Name indicating God's Attribute of Strict Justice (*Tanya*).[1]

לֵב נִשְׁבָּר וְנִדְכֶּה — *A heart broken and crushed.*

[See *Commentary* to 34:19: HASHEM is close to those who are broken at heart, and those who are crushed in spirit He saves.]

Rabbeinu Yonah (*Shaarei Teshuvah* 1:33) explains that a *broken heart* connotes a modest and humble spirit; *A crushed heart* connotes the breaking of physical lust, for the heart is the repository of desire. If one breaks his physical urges, he accrues a great advantage for when he is tempted to transgress, he will reason, 'I did not even succumb to my desire for what is permitted, how then shall I stretch forth my hand for what is forbidden?' (*Shaarei Teshuvah* 1:32).

Furthermore, the Psalmist makes an analogy here to the breaking of impure vessels which by rendering them unfit for their precious service, purifies them,

1. The Talmud (*Sotah* 5b) states that Rabbi Joshua ben Levi said: 'How great are those who subdue their spirits, for when the Temple stood, if a person gave a burnt-offering, he gained the merit of only that single burnt-offering. If he donated a meal-offering, he was given credit only for that single meal-offering. But he who sacrifices his pride and subdues his spirit with genuine humility is considered as if he offered every form of sacrifice, for it says *the offerings* [the plural indicates many offerings'] *of God are a broken spirit* [the singular form of רוּחַ, *spirit* indicates that this single act of submission is as precious as many sacrifices]. In addition, this man's prayer is never rejected, as the verse continues, *a heart, broken and crushed, O God, You despise not.*

Maharal (*Nesiv HaTeshuvah*, Chapter 2) explains that קָרְבָּן literally means a *way of drawing near*. Passion and pride separate man from his Maker; when these are removed by means of sincere repentance and genuine submission, man draws as near to God as humanly possible.

כ וְנִדְכֶּה אֱלֹהִים לֹא תִבְזֶה: הֵיטִיבָה
בִרְצוֹנְךָ אֶת־צִיּוֹן תִּבְנֶה חוֹמוֹת יְרוּשָׁלָ͏ִם:
כא אָז תַּחְפֹּץ זִבְחֵי־צֶדֶק עוֹלָה וְכָלִיל אָז
יַעֲלוּ עַל־מִזְבַּחֲךָ פָרִים:

as Scripture commands, (Leviticus
11:35) Whether oven or stove, it shall
be broken in pieces (Shaarei Teshuvah
1:23).

אֱלֹהִים לֹא תִבְזֶה — O God You will
despise not.

You despise the animal sacrifice
when it is not accompanied by a broken
heart, but You do not despise the
broken heart even though it is not accompanied by an animal sacrifice
(Radak).

Rambam (Hilchos Matnos Aniyim
10:5) rules that it is prohibited to display anger or shout at an impoverished
beggar because his spirits have already
been shattered, and Scripture teaches, A
heart broken and crushed, O God, You
despise not [i.e., God is concerned for
the welfare of these unfortunate people,
and will be angered if they are abused.]

20. הֵיטִיבָה בִרְצוֹנְךָ אֶת צִיּוֹן — Benefit
with Your grace unto Zion.

Radak explains that David previously pleaded for the return of the holy
spirit, which had left him when he sinned be returned to him, saying: Restore
unto me the joy of Your salvation, v.
14). The two final verses of this Psalm
are evidence that his request will
ultimately be fulfilled; the verses
foretell the destruction of the First and
Second Temples. The multitude of
sacrifices in them could not avert the
destruction, for the people were debased
with evil and sin.

However, in the Messianic era, God
will delight in the sacrifices of Israel, for
they will all unite to serve God devoted-
ly as one. Concerning that utopian

epoch, the psalmist prays, Benefit with
Your grace unto Zion.

Ibn Yachya perceives in the word
הֵיטִיבָה a request for the return of God's
Presence, which is called טוֹב, good, as
Scripture states, אֲנִי אַעֲבִיר כָּל טוּבִי עַל
פָּנֶיךָ, I will make all My goodness pass
before You (Exodus 33:19).

תִּבְנֶה חוֹמוֹת יְרוּשָׁלַ͏ִם — Build the walls of
Jerusalem.

Ibn Yachya notes that David was
concerned about the building of the
First Temple. He prayed that God
should grant him, or one of his sons, the
privilege of building the Temple and the
walls of the city, and should not deem
him unworthy because of his sins.

The Zohar (Parshas Mishpatim)
observes, How different are the ways of
God from the ways of man. Men first
construct the outer walls of the city for
protection and then they build the
houses inside. But God will first build
the future Beis HaMikdash, called Zion,
and only afterwards build the walls of
Jerusalem.

21. אָז תַּחְפֹּץ זִבְחֵי צֶדֶק — Then You will
desire the sacrifices of righteousness.

Then, in the days of the Messiah,
when the earth shall be full of the
knowledge of Hashem, as the waters
cover the sea (Isaiah 11:9), no man will
sin; therefore, no sin or guilt offerings
will be sacrificed. Only שְׁלָמִים, peace offerings will be donated voluntarily by
the righteous (Metzudas David).

These offerings will be accompanied
by the most desirable of all sacrifices,
the heart broken and crushed (Sforno).

> O God, You will despise not.
> ²⁰ Benefit with Your grace unto Zion,
>   build the walls of Jerusalem.
> ²¹ Then You will desire
>   the sacrifices of righteousness,
>   burnt-offering and whole-offering.
> Then they will offer bullocks
>   upon Your altar.

עולה — *Burnt-offering.*

This refers to the עולַת תָּמִיד, *the daily burnt-offering,* which was offered in the morning and in the afternoon (*Ibn Ezra*).

The prophet Isaiah (56:7) envisions this future era. God promises, *I will bring them to My holy mountain and make them joyful in My House of Prayer; their burnt-offerings and sacrifices shall be favorably accepted upon My altar* (*Abarbanel*).

וְכָלִיל — *And whole-offering.*

According to *Ibn Ezra*, this refers to the meal-offering brought by the priest, which is burned whole. [It is called כָלִיל in *Leviticus* 6:15-16].

Sforno identifies this as the incense offering, which is called כָלִיל in *Deuteronomy* 33:10.

However, *Rashi and Ibn Ezra* (based on *Yoma 26a*) identify כָלִיל as an עוֹלָה,

burnt-offering (see *Baal HaTurim Deuteronomy 3:10*). In *I Samuel* 7:9 we find the term כָלִיל עוֹלָה. Thus, in our verse, עוֹלָה and כָלִיל may be considered synonymous.

אָז יַעֲלוּ עַל מִזְבַּחֲךָ פָּרִים — *Then they will offer bullocks upon Your altar.*

According to *Rabbeinu Yonah* (*Shaarei Teshuvah* 1:4), bullocks symbolize deep repentance. The prophet Hoshea (14:3) said, *we shall render the words of our lips to be as bullocks,* i.e., 'accept our confessions of sin and let them be considered as sin-offerings.' Bullocks are mentioned specifically because the blood of a bullock *sin-offering* was sprinkled on the inner curtain and on the golden altar. [Therefore, the bullock symbolizes repentance which penetrates to the inner core of the man and uproots the very source of the sin].[1]

---

1. *Shaarei Chaim* renders the verse, 'Then the bullocks will [voluntarily] go up upon Your altars. He offers a explanation, based on *Yalkut Shimoni* (*Melachim 214*), which relates the story of Elijah on Mount Carmel. The prophet selected two identical twin bullocks. The one chosen for Elijah's sacrifice eagerly ran after him to be slaughtered on the altar of this righteous person. The other twin, designated for the priests of the idol Baal, refused to budge; all nine hundred and fifty pagan priests could not move an inch.

In the first two Temples, the bullocks did not voluntarily run to the slaughter because the poeple of Israel were not worthy. But in the future, when all of Israel shall be sanctified and purified by repentance, the entire world will be eager to serve them, including 'the bullocks, who will go up [וְיַעֲלוּ] by themselves upon your altar.'

Once again David addresses himself to the most critical moral problem of his generation: the jealous enmity between men which undermines their principles to the point of King they are willing to spread slander and fabricate evil tales in order to destroy their rivals. David cites a painful incident from his personal life which illustrates this theme.

David is forced to flee like a beggar from the blind, jealous wrath of his father-in-law, Saul. Starving and unarmed, David comes to Nob, the city of Priests, in which the Tabernacle was situated, and asks Achimelech the priest to give him bread and a sword. Assuming that David is on a mission in the loyal service of King Saul, the unsuspecting Achimelech supplies the fugitive with his needs.

But, at that time, Doeg the Edomite, the head of Sanhedrin and Saul's closest adviser, was in spiritual retreat at the Tabernacle of God. He reported the transaction to Saul in such a manner as to implicate Achimelech as a conspirator against the insecure king. This treacherous slander incited the despairing King to condemn the entire city of Nob to death, as rebels against the monarchy, a horrible sentence which was eagerly carried out by Doeg himself (I Samuel, Chapters 21-22).

These tragic events moved David to compose this Maskil, (an instructive psalm), to inform the people of the treachery of Doeg and slanderers like him.

1. לַמְנַצֵּחַ — For the Conductor

Maharal (Nesivos Olam, Nesiv Ha-lashon, Chapter 4), comments that David sought to combat the moral degeneration of his time with the songs he composed for the Temple. This idea is based on Midrash Shocher Tov (12:7):

Even children living in the days of Saul, David, and Samuel knew those subtle distinctions of תּוֹרָה שֶׁבְּעַל פֶּה, the Oral Law, which elaborate forty-nine arguments by which a creature may be proven clean and forty-nine other arguments by which it may be proven unclean. Yet despite their intellectual achievments, David's scholarly subjects fell before their enemies in battle because they were corrupted by the vice of tale-bearing (Yerushalmi, Peah 1:1). [See Prefatory Remarks to Psalm 15].

The Evil Inclination tempts a man to sin in the very area in which he excels. Therefore, since David's contemporaries were distinguished in their speech, which were devoted to the study of the Oral Law, their Evil Inclination concentrated his advances on the sins of the mouth. The nation succumbed to the temptation and sinned with its tongue. David sought to atone for this transgression by composing Tehillim, songs of praise designed to purge and purify their twisted tongues.

מַשְׂכִּיל לְדָוִד — A Maskil, by David.

The Maskil is a psalm composed with special intellectual effort to teach an essential lesson. Since the sin of לְשׁוֹן הָרַע, evil speech, is so widespread and tempting and the laws governing speech

are so complex, great שֵׂכֶל, wisdom, is needed to fulfill the teachings of the Torah in this area (Eretz Hachaim).

Chazah David notes the relationship between this psalm and the preceding one. Solomon said, Death and life are in the power of the tongue (Proverbs 18:21). In the previous psalm, David was condemned to die, until he confessed, חָטָאתִי, I have sinned. Immediately, he was forgiven and granted eternal life. This psalm depicts the opposite situation, for Doeg's wicked tongue brought him to eternal damnation.

Chazah David continues:

David was אַדְמוֹנִי, ruddy, i.e., passionate and sensual [see Overview I] and Doeg was אֲדוֹמִי red. The numerical value of דָוִד is fourteen, as is that of the name דּוֹאֵג. These similarities show that essentially David and Doeg were once equals who could be differentiated only by their divergent modes of speech.[1]

Concerning Doeg and his kind, Solomon observed, Permit not your mouth to bring your flesh into guilt (Koheles 5:5).

2. דּוֹאֵג — Doeg.

[The name דּוֹאֵג literally means the worrier, revealing the defect in Doeg's character. Torah study should fill the scholar's heart with complete confidence and faith in God, whose Torah he studies. The scholar who devotes himself to the daily study of the Word of God should feel as serene as a child cradled in his father's arms. Doeg, however, studied Torah without feel-

---

1. Throughout Chronicles, David's name is spelled דָוִיד which has the numerical value of twenty-four, alluding to David's great achievement of setting up twenty-four priestly watches in the Temple. Chida in Rosh David explains that this change of spelling was in response to David's request that even the numerical value of his name not be the same as Doeg's. Homiletically, this is the intent of David's prayer: עֲשֵׂה עִמִּי אוֹת לְטוֹבָה וְיִרְאוּ שֹׂנְאַי וְיֵבֹשׁוּ, Make for me an [extra] אוֹת, letter [lit. sign] for the good, so that my enemies may see and be shamed (86:17).

For the Conductor.
a Maskil, by David,
² Upon the arrival of Doeg the Edomite,
who informed Saul, saying to him,

ings of faith, as an empty cultural or academic pursuit. Selfishly, he used his knowledge as a tool, by which to elevate his own position. He found security in his status rather than in God. Jealous and fearful of rivals, he was tormented by anxiety and worry [see *Ben Yehoyada, Sanhedrin* 106b]. How different was David, whose name is spelled דוד, *lover*, symbolizing his deep trust in, and love of, God.]

Midrash Shocher Tov explains that an entire psalm is dedicated to Doeg because God reveals the evil of the hypocrite in order to make the nature of his deeds understood. Otherwise, the punishment that befalls him would cause men to question God's justice. In this case, Doeg, who was well-known as the Head of Sanhedrin [אַבִּיר הָרֹעִים, *chief of the shepherds (I Samuel* 21:8)], possessed considerable knowledge of the Torah. Therefore, Scripture publicizes the fact that he was a slanderer.

הָאֲדֹמִי — *The Edomite.*

According to *Radak,* Doeg lived in the land of Edom.

Midrash Shocher Tov offers six explanations for this name:

First, Doeg was called *the Edomite* [derived from אָדֹם, *red*] because he was envious of David, who was called אַדְמוֹנִי, *ruddy (I Samuel* 16:12). Nor was Doeg alone in his envy of David: all the members of his clan, the Ziphites, Nabal the Carmelite, and the men of Keilah, were envious of him.

Second, he was called *the Edomite* [related to דָם, *blood*] *because he perverted the truth in order to bring about the shedding of the blood of Nob, city of Priests, which he exterminated*

singlehandedly, as it says: Doeg the Edomite turned, and he fell upon the priests, and he slew that day eighty-five men (I Samuel 22:18).

Third, it was he who called for the shedding of the blood of David, saying to Saul, *'he deserves to die' (I Samuel* 20:31).

Fourth, Doeg the Edomite forbade Saul to shed the blood of Agag, King of Amalek. Because of Doeg's ruling, Saul was judged guilty of the heavenly death penalty for having spared the life of a guilty Amalekite.

Fifth, he was called *the Edomite* because his superior scholarship enabled him to מַאֲדִים, *redden with shame,* the faces of those who argued the law with him. During debates, Doeg would use his superior arguments to reduce his opponent to silence [דוֹמֵם, *silent,* is also related to אֲדוֹמִי].

Sixth, in that he sullied the attainments of David, he was like Edom who disparages Israel. Just as Edom seeks vengeance, so did Doeg seek vengeance against David.

וַיַּגֵּד לְשָׁאוּל — *Who informed Saul.*

Midrash Shocher Tov relates וַיַּגֵּד to the root word אָגַד, *joined, bound;* i.e., when Doeg recounted the episode, he *added* his own opinions and ideas in such a way that Saul was aroused to burning fury.

He said, 'Achimelech has made David king even while you are still living. For, although inquiry may not be made of the Urim V'Tumim on behalf of any man except the king, members of the court, or one upon whom the needs of the public depend; nevertheless, inquiry was made on behalf of David!'

When Doeg said this, a spirit of

malicious envy entered Saul. Achimelech sought to defend himself, saying, *Who amongst all of your servants is so trusted as David, who is the king's son-in-law? Have I only today begun to inquire of God for him? (I Samuel 22:14-15).* 'This was not the first time, for it has long been my custom to inquire on behalf of David!'

[See *Parashas Derachim, Derech HaRabbim* 13 for a discussion of the halachic background of Doeg's argument and Achimelech's justification.]

This explanation infuriated the King even more, and he issued a death sentence against Achimelech (*I Samuel* 22:17). However, Saul's guards, Abner and Amasa, refused to harm the priests.

In desperation, Saul turned to Doeg, and said, 'Why do you stand still? You already smote the priests of Nob with your tongue; rise now and smite them with the sword!' Doeg then single-handedly slaughtered the entire city of Priests.

וַיֹּאמֶר לוֹ — *Saying to him.*

The phrases '*he informed Saul saying to him*' seem to be redundant. In order to understand the purpose of this double wording, *Shaarei Chaim* applies *Rashi's* comment (*Exodus* 19:3) that יַגֵּד means to speak words which arouse the listener, whereas אָמַר means to speak gently and soothingly.

The sly Doeg did not wish to appear as a vicious prosecutor of the priests. Therefore, once he incited Saul's wrath and was confident that his accusations had struck home (וַיַּגֵּד), he cunningly

changed his tone of voice in an insincere 'attempt' to assuage Saul's anger by seeking apologies in defense of the priests (וַיֹּאמֶר). By concluding his inflammatory denunciation with soothing words of conciliation, he hoped to shift the blame for the slaughter from himself to Saul.

Doeg was motivated by the desire to punish and injure everyone who associated with David. As the *Talmud* (*Shabbos* 149b) states, 'Whoever causes his fellow to be punished on his account is barred from entering the presence of God ... for he who is a cause of evil is himself considered evil.' Doeg was jealous primarily because David enjoyed God's intimate closeness (cf. *Sanhedrin* 93b, *Shabbos* 56a) [See *comm. v.* 9, which indicates that Doeg did partially succeed in his ambition to damage David.] [1]

בָּא דָוִד אֶל בֵּית אֲחִימֶלֶךְ — *David came to the house of Achimelech.*

Alshich explains that Doeg happened to be visiting the Tabernacle when David arrived. If David had merely spoken to Achimelech in the Tabernacle itself, in full view of Doeg, the king's trusted confidant, then there could be no suspicion of conspiracy. But Doeg emphasized that the two men had retired to the privacy of Achimelech's personal residence, charging that they spoke of treacherous plots which had to be concealed from Doeg, the supporter of King Saul.

It is hard to understand why Doeg went to such lengths to implicate

1. We can also understand Doeg's mad desire to destroy the priests by noting that the Tabernacle was at the root of Doeg's jealousy. The *Talmud* (*Zevachim* 54b) relates that on the night when David first fled from Saul, Samuel chose David as Saul's successor and gave him a scroll containing secret traditions concerning the construction of the Temple in place of the Tabernacle, 'It was this privilege which kindled Doeg's jealousy', the *Talmud* concludes.

Fittingly, the cause of Doeg's death also emanated from the Tabernacle. 'A fiery shaft sprang out of the Holy of Holies and burned all around him [Doeg]' (*Yerushalmi, Sanhedrin* 10:2).

'David came to the house of Achimelech.'
³ Why do you pride yourself with evil
O mighty warrior?
The kindness of God
is all day long.

Achimelech in this fabricated conspiracy. *Parashas Derachim (Derech Hamelech* 11 and *Derech Harabbim* 13) explains that Doeg bore no particular grudge against Achimelech. Rather his intention was to use Achimelech as a pawn to bring punishment upon David, for if the priests were to suffer because of David's association with them, he would be held liable by God for having been a cause of another's misfortune [see *comm.* to v. 10].

3. מַה תִּתְהַלֵּל בְּרָעָה הַגִּבּוֹר — *Why do you pride yourself with evil, O mighty warrior?*

David cries out to Doeg with the vocative form הַגִּבּוֹר, *O mighty warrior!* 'You are not an ordinary scholar, a mere גִּבּוֹר [i.e., warrior in the battlefield of learning]; you are, in fact, הַגִּבּוֹר *the greatest scholar' (Radak).*

Why then do you, a distinguished and universally acclaimed Torah sage, prefer to be honored for your evil deeds? *(Rashi). Strangely, you continue to boast of the feat of physical might which you performed when you single-handedly massacred the entire city of Nob (Midrash)* [see *comm.* 5:6.]

The Torah in which you excel is called תּוֹרַת חֶסֶד, *the law of kindness (Proverbs* 31:26). Why then do you boast of your cruelty?

David asked Doeg, 'Is a man truly mighty when he sees his fellow at the edge of a pit and pushes him in, when he sees his fellow on top of a roof and pushes him off? On the contrary, a man deserves to be called *a mighty warrior* when his fellow is about to fall into a pit and he grasps his hand to prevent his fall or when he lifts the fallen man from the pit. But when you saw that Saul was angry at me, you persisted in vilifying me' *(Midrash Shocher Tov).*

Had you subdued your Evil Inclination [רָעָה], and refrained from slandering me, then you would truly be considered a mighty גִּבּוֹר, for the Sages said: *Who is mighty? He who conquers his Evil Inclination! (Avos* 4:1). But now that you have so disgracefully surrendered yourself to your own evil inclination, how dare you pride youself as a גִּבּוֹר? *(Os HaBris).*

חֶסֶד אֵל כָּל הַיּוֹם — *The kindness of God is all the day long.*]

Your might and slander were powerless, because God's kindness enveloped me continually. His kindness saved me from Saul again and again and will continue to preserve me in the future *(Radak).*

Furthermore, why do you consider Achimelech's kindness the evidence of complicity? Do you really think that without his aid I would have died of starvation? Don't you realize that a Divine spirit of mercy hovers over Israel all day long, inspiring all Jews to perform acts of kindness? If Achimelech had not helped, many others would certainly have eagerly come to my rescue! *(Rashi).*[1]

[Since Doeg was selfish and cruel, he was truly amazed even by relatively

1. Ironically, the tragedy of Nob came about because David's dearest friend, Jonathan, inadvertently neglected to do kindness with his comrade. The *Talmud (Sanhedrin* 104a) lauds one who provides food for his wayfarers and guests, and emphasizes the terrible harm which can result from missing an opportunity for kindness: If Jonathan had lent David only two loaves

ה לְשׁוֹנֶךָ כְּתַעַר מְלֻטָּשׁ עֹשֵׂה רְמִיָּה: אָהַבְתָּ

ו רָע מִטּוֹב שֶׁקֶר | מִדַּבֵּר צֶדֶק סֶלָה: אָהַבְתָּ

ז כָל־דִּבְרֵי־בָלַע לָשׁוֹן מִרְמָה: גַּם־אֵל

יִתָּצְךָ לָנֶצַח יַחְתְּךָ וְיִסָּחֲךָ מֵאֹהֶל וְשֵׁרֶשְׁךָ

ח מֵאֶרֶץ חַיִּים סֶלָה: וְיִרְאוּ צַדִּיקִים וְיִירָאוּ

minor acts of hospitality; thus, he considered Achimelech's actions to be extraordinary and hence, suspicious.]

Finally, ought a man who practices mercy towards God (so to speak) engage in cruelty? For he who occupies himself with Torah study is considered to be practicing mercy towards God! (*Midrash Shocher Tov*).

The man who recognizes God's mercy should permit his mouth to engage in nothing but the recounting of *the kindness of God all day long* (Ibn Ezra).

6. לְשׁוֹן מִרְמָה — *A tongue of deceit.*

Had Doeg had sincerely sought the welfare of Saul and Achimelech, he would have confronted Achimelech and warned him that if he assisted David he would arouse Saul's wrath. But Doeg preferred to be deceptive; therefore, he allowed Achimelech to help David so that he could later slander him (*Radak*).

Malbim explains that Doeg was ultimately destroyed by his own *deceitful tongue.*

In *II Samuel* (Chapter 1) we read that Saul's Amelekite attendant informed David of the king's death and claimed responsibility for it, expecting that this would earn him David's favor. The truth was that Saul had mortally wounded himself by falling on his own sword. Nevertheless, David slew the Amelekite because he claimed to have harmed the anointed king of God.

Rashi (II Samuel 1:2 and 1:9) quotes

the *Pesikta* which identifies this Amalekite as Doeg the Edomite! After David's attendant stabbed Doeg to death, David said (*II Samuel* 1:16): *The guilt of your blood is upon yourself alone, for your own mouth testified against you, saying, 'I have slain the anointed of HASHEM.'*

Malbim explains David's words thus; Even though your *deceitful tongue* is now lying in regard to the death of Saul (for you only sought to gain my favor by claiming to have avenged me upon my enemy), nevertheless, you shall die because of your earlier crime of slaughtering Achimelech the High Priest, *the anointed of HASHEM.*

7. גַּם אֵל יִתָּצְךָ לָנֶצַח — *Likewise, God will smash you for eternity.*

[Doeg, the war which you wage is not merely a campaign against David; rather you are challenging God Himself who has chosen David.] Furthermore, you dared to massacre God's chosen servants, the priests, in the very House of God (*Radak*).

'You teach a distorted version of God's own Torah in order to justify your wicked deeds. Therefore, *God Himself will smash you!* (*Sforno*).

[The *Mishnah* (*Sanhedrin* 11:1) lists Doeg among the individuals who forfeited their share in the World to Come.]

Midrash Shocher Tov observes that even in this world Doeg was afflicted with leprosy, which is the punishment

of bread [before David set out in flight from Saul] then David would have had no reason to ask Acimelech for food. Nob the city of priests would not have been destroyed, Doeg would not have been ruined, and Saul and his sons [including Jonathan] would not have been slain.

⁴ Treachery does your tongue devise,
   like a sharpened razor working deceit.
⁵ you love evil more than good,
   falsehood more than speaking righteousness,
   Selah.
⁶ You love all devouring words,
   a tongue of deceit.
⁷ Likewise, God will smash you for eternity,
   He will shatter you and tear you from the tent,
   and uproot you from the land of life, Selah.
⁸ The righteous will see it and be frightened,

reserved for slanderers. His leprosy is indicated by the fact that here it says *God will smash you*, just as it says of the leper's house, *He will smash the house* (Lev. 14:45).

יַחְתְּךָ — *He will shatter you.*

This translation follows *Rashi* and *Targum. Radak* renders *He will take you away*, for he maintains that the word is related to חוֹתֶה אֵשׁ, *raking away fiery coals*. His father *Rav Yoseif Kimchi*, also derives חוֹתָה from יַחְתְּךָ, but translates *He will burn you.*

וְיִסָּחֲךָ — *And He will tear you.*

Again the translation is according to *Rashi*, however *Radak* renders *He will destroy you.*

מֵאֹהֶל — *From the tent.*

God will not allow you to dwell in His tent, the Tabernacle (*Targum*), [for your visit to the Tabernacle resulted in the massacre at Nob.] Nor will you have the privilege of studying in the tent of Torah, the Beis Hamidrash (*Sforno*).

Furthermore, your teachings on the Torah will never be taught in the schools of Jewish learning (*Sanhedrin* 106b).

Yalkut Shimoni (I Samuel 131) describes Doeg's last moments: 'Doeg was teaching his students; as they absorbed what he said, he forgot his own wisdom, bit by bit. When his students finally

realized that he was falsifying and distorting the law, they tied ropes to his feet and dragged him away.' [Cf. *Pesikta*'s version of Doeg's death cited in v. 6 above.]

According to the *Talmud*, three angels of destruction accosted Doeg: One caused him to forget his learning; one burned his soul; and one took his ashes and scattered them in every synagogue and house of study (*Sanhedrin* 106b) [see *comm.* to 5:11.]

וְשֵׁרֶשְׁךָ מֵאֶרֶץ חַיִּים סֶלָה — *And He will uproot you from the land of life, Selah.*

Even your roots will be ripped out of the earth so that no remembrance of you will remain. You will not leave any sons who are worthy Torah scholars (*Sanhedrin* 106b). This punishment is fitting because you uprooted the entire family of Achimelech, leaving no infant alive (*Ibn Ezra*).

8. וְיִרְאוּ צַדִּיקִים וְיִירָאוּ — *The righteous will see it and be frightened.*

When they witness the revenge which God will take on behalf of the slain priests, their fear of the Almighty will increase (*Radak*), [compare 40:4 וְיִרְאוּ רַבִּים וְיִירָאוּ.]

At first, the righteous men feared Doeg's slander, for his vicious barbs were aimed at all men of good will. After his downfall, however, righteous

ט וְעָלָיו יִשְׂחָקוּ: הִנֵּה הַגֶּבֶר לֹא יָשִׂים
אֱלֹהִים מָעוּזּוֹ וַיִּבְטַח בְּרֹב עָשְׁרוֹ יָעֹז
י בְּהַוָּתוֹ: וַאֲנִי | כְּזַיִת רַעֲנָן בְּבֵית אֱלֹהִים
יא בָּטַחְתִּי בְחֶסֶד־אֱלֹהִים עוֹלָם וָעֶד: אוֹדְךָ
לְעוֹלָם כִּי עָשִׂיתָ וַאֲקַוֶּה שִׁמְךָ כִי־טוֹב
נֶגֶד חֲסִידֶיךָ:

men laughed in relief (*Sanhedrin* 106a, *Maharsha, ibid.*).

[Throughout the generations *the righteous* Sages were *afraid* and anxious lest one of their students develop into a Doeg-like scholar. The *Talmud* (*Berachos* 17b) relates that when the Rabbis took leave of each other after the lesson they would pray: May our group not resemble Saul's group, from whose ranks there came forth Doeg the Edomite.]

וְעָלָיו יִשְׂחָקוּ — *But [lit. and] they will jeer at him.*

They will laugh when they detect the irony of Doeg's fate. His mouth, which caused the death of so many innocent men, finally confessed his own guilt and sealed his doom when he told David that he had killed Saul (*Malbim*).

9. הִנֵּה הַגֶּבֶר לֹא יָשִׂים אֱלֹהִים מָעוּזּוֹ — *Behold this is the man who did not make God his stronghold.*

This is the proclamation people will make when they see Doeg's ignominious end (*Radak*).

He will serve as an everlasting example of the futility of seeking success through evil (*Ibn Ezra*).

[The man who protects his personal interests by resorting to slander thereby denies that God is a *stronghold* with the ability to ensure the security of those who trust in Him.]

וַיִּבְטַח בְּרֹב עָשְׁרוֹ — *But trusted in his abundance of wealth.*

Doeg was confident that Saul would

reward him handsomely for the zealous loyalty he displayed in annihilating an entire city accused of treason (*Sforno*).

יָעֹז בְּהַוָּתוֹ — *And drew strength from his treachery.*

Doeg sought to strengthen his own postion by finding favor in Saul's eyes when he denounced the *treachery* of Nob (*Metzudas David*).

10. וַאֲנִי כְּזַיִת רַעֲנָן — *But I am like an evergreen olive.*

The leaf of the olive tree remains green and moist throughout the year; it never withers (*Radak*). [See 1:3 where the righteous man is described as one *whose leaf never withers.*]

David said, 'Although I now flee like a fugitive who appears to have no future, I am confident that I will become as productive as the olive tree and that I will sire children and grandchildren who will dwell in the House of God (*Rashi*).

Furthermore, I hope to be a source of enlightenment and illumination for my people, just as kindled olive oil lights up the darkness (*Sforno*). [See *Shemos Rabbah* 36:2].

Alshich notes that the olive, noted for its bitter taste, symbolizes the difficulties and afflictions of life [see *Eruvin* 18b.] The Rabbis [*Menachos* 53b] say, Just as the olive discharges the oil only after being crushed, the Jew extracts the full measure of piety from within himself only after experiencing suffering and affliction (*Shevet*

> *but they will jeer at him:*
> ⁹ *Behold this is the man*
> *who did not make God his stronghold,*
> *But trusted in his abundance of wealth,*
> *drew strength from his treachery.'*
> ¹⁰ *But I am like an evergreen olive*
> *in the House of God,*
> *I trust in the kindness of God*
> *forever and ever.*
> ¹¹ *I will thank You forever when You do it,*
> *and put hope in Your name;*
> *For You are good to Your devout ones.*

M'Yisroel). Here David states that, because of the bitter suffering which he experienced [as a result of Doeg's slander and persecution], *I trust* [that these afflictions will enable me to merit] *the kindness of God forever and ever.*

בְּבֵית אֱלֹהִים — *In the House of God.*

Concerning Doeg, David said earlier (v. 7), *God ... will pluck you from the tent* [i.e., the Tabernacle] *and uproot you from the land of life.* In contrast, David hopes that by virtue of his own complete trust in God, he will deserve to be rooted in the House of God forever (Ibn Ezra; Radak).

Scripture describes the visit of Doeg to the Tabernacle, *And he was detained before HASHEM* (I Samuel 21:8), implying that the House of God was not his true home and source of existence, but that he was merely *detained* there momentarily. David, in contrast, sunk the roots of his being into the holy soil of God's Sanctuary (Malbim).

בָּטַחְתִּי בְחֶסֶד אֱלֹהִים עוֹלָם וָעֶד — *I trust in the kindness of God forever and ever.*

Alshich explains that *the kindness of* אֱלֹהִים, *the Arbiter of Strict Justice,* reforms the sinner and brings him to the World to Come.

Chomas Anoch interprets this verse in light of the *Talmud (Sanhedrin 95a),* which reveals how much God demands of intimate devotees such as David. The Talmud notes that although David was the innocent victim of Doeg's vehemence and Saul's jealousy, David was responsible, in a sense, for having aroused the worst in these men. It was because of David that the city of Nob was massacred, that Saul and his sons were slain in battle, and that Doeg was killed. Any person who is the cause of so much bloodshed, albeit inadvertently, cannot be considered totally guiltless. [*Chamra V'Chaia (Sanhedrin* 102b) says that David should have generously and wholeheartedly forgiven his enemies and thereby spare them from punishment.]

The use of the name אֱלֹהִים, *Dispenser of Strict Justice,* in our verse, indicates that David was to be punished. Nevertheless, David trusted בְּחֶסֶד אֱלֹהִים, *in the 'kindness' of God,* with which His Judgment was tempered. God offered David a choice of punishments, and David finally accepted the punishment that his own descendants would be annihilated. [See *comm.* to 7:1.] This occurred when Ataliah slaughtered the entire royal family, with the exception of the infant

Yoash, who was hidden in the attic above the Holy of Holies in the Temple [see *II Kings* 11:1-2 and Prefatory Remarks, *Psalms* 12.]

In this psalm, David foretells the doom of Doeg and recognizes that ultimately his own descendants will be threatened as a result of this enmity. Therefore, David prays that his offspring will flourish *like an evergreen olive in the House of God*, i.e., in the attic of the Holy of Holies where the last remnant of his seed will be replanted. Also, says David, *I trust in the kindness of God forever and ever* that my progeny will never be completely destroyed.

11. אוֹדְךָ לְעוֹלָם כִּי עָשִׂיתָ—*I will thank You forever when You do it.*

I.e., when You take revenge against my enemies and defend my rights *(Targum; Radak).*

When You help me to become a flourishing olive, thriving in Your House· *(Sforno).*

וַאֲקַוֶּה שִׁמְךָ כִי טוֹב נֶגֶד חֲסִידֶיךָ — *And [I will] put hope in Your Name; You are good to Your devout ones (Targum).*

Radak כִּי טוֹב: *that You are good,* i.e.,'This is what I shall tell those who are devoted to You of Your kindness, and I will hope for the טוֹב, *goodness,* of the World to Come' (see *Sforno*).

53 מזמור נג

$\mathbf{T}$his psalm is almost an exact replica of Psalm 14. Both
compositions speak of the exile and the future redemption.
However, as explained in the Prefatory Remarks to Psalm 14, the
earlier work focuses on the destruction of the First Temple at the
hands of Nebuchadnezzar, whereas this psalm describes the destruction of the Second Temple by Titus (Rashi).

Radak and Meiri explain that this position in the Book of Tehillim
was chosen with great care in order to emphasize its theme.

The founding of the royal house of David met with fierce opposition from those who denied David's right to rule. They resorted to the
most devious and treacherous means to prevent David's ascent to the
throne. In Psalm 52, we read of Doeg's evil machinations and slander.
In Psalm 54, we learn of the Ziphites who mercilessly betrayed David
to Saul. In both cases, God foiled the plots of those who attempted to
disrupt the establishment of David's reign.

Psalm 53 depicts the climax and the conclusion of the Davidean
line, which will occur with the advent of Messiah, who will end the
exile and clear the ruins of the Second Temple by dedicating the
Third. Like his ancestor David, Messiah will suffer persecution at
the hands of sceptics and scoffers, who will refuse to recognize his
sovereignty and will scheme to assassinate him to destroy his
monarchy. Furthermore, throughout Jewish history, we will be
threatened by wicked men, such as Titus, who will attempt to destroy
Israel, the nation of David. However, all of these villains will share
the fate of Doeg and the Ziphites: utter failure and terrible misfortune.

1. מָחֲלַת — Machalas.

Rashi identifies the *Machalas* as a special type of musical instrument. In addition, he relates this word to מַחֲלָה, *malady, affliction*, referring to the downtrodden state of Israel after the destruction of the Second Temple, when the Jews were plagued with countless tragedies.

Meiri, following his customary approach [see 5:1; 22:1], demonstrates how this unique musical accompaniment complements the special theme of this psalm: It is known to those who are well-versed in the science of musicology that certain strings and chords are tuned to give forth a depressing, mourning sound which evokes feelings of anxiety, sorrow and weeping. The *Machalas* instrument had the ability to draw forth such tragic emotions from the depths of the heart.

[This word does not appear in Psalm 14, suggesting that the *malady* and *afflictions* of the second destruction far surpassed those of the first. The First (Babylonian) exile lasted but seventy years, whereas the Second, (Roman) exile has continued for almost two thousand years (see *Yoma* 9b).]

Chazah Zion renders מָחֲלַת as מְחִילָה, *forgiveness*, [thus, this psalm would be related to Psalm 51, which speaks of repentance, atonement and reconciliation with God.] The *degraded man* who denies God's presence sees nothing wrong with sin; therefore, he never seeks *forgiveness*. But the מַשְׂכִּיל [lit. *wise man*] realizes that *from heaven God gazes down upon mankind* (v. 3).

God recounts man's sins and requires those who transgress to seek forgiveness.[1]

מַשְׂכִּיל — A Maskil.

[This word, too, is absent from Psalm 14. As explained in 32:11, the term *Maskil* denotes a psalm composed with special intellectual effort to serve as an instructive essay devoted to heightening Israel's comprehension of God's ways.

After the terrible events of the second destruction and the ensuing exile, Israel felt very alienated from God. It was extremely difficult for the Jews to appreciate the divine plan and purpose which guided their destinies as they wandered aimlessly from persecution to persecution. Groping blindly in the gloom of an apparently endless *galus*, Israel felt abandoned and forlorn. Therefore, this psalm of intensive instruction seeks to help Israel gain an understanding of God's ways in the Second Exile.]

According to *Sforno*, this psalm is a direct continuation of the previous one and represents a diagnosis of the מָחֲלַת מַשְׂכִּיל, [lit. *the malady of the intellectuals*]. This refers to the Torah scholars who have healthy minds but sick hearts; they must improve their character and conduct. Doeg and those who resemble him are prime examples of this 'malady'.

[In truth, *Sforno's* interpretation of this psalm complements that of *Rashi*. The *malady* of the exile will reach its most agonizing proportions when the

---

1. In describing Israel's celebration around the Golden Calf, Scripture says, *And he* [Moses] *saw the calf and the mecholos* (Exodus 32:19).

Rabbeinu Bachya (ibid.) points out that nine different types of musical instruments are mentioned in Scripture. Undoubtedly, many instruments were used to encourage the pagan festivities around the calf, but the Divine Will ordained that Moses should notice only the *mecholos* instrument. This was meant to signify to him that despite the severity of the offense, the nation would merit *mechilah*, forgiveness.

LIII
1-2

For the Conductor upon the Machalas,
      a Maskil of David.
    ² The degraded man says in his heart,
      'There is no God!'
They acted corruptly and despicably
      through iniquity;
Not one does good.

nation of Israel falls under the leadership of irresponsible pseudo-scholars who suffer from a moral and spiritual *malady.*

The *Talmud (Sotah* 49b) states that this problem will plague Israel in the chaotic times preceding the advent of Messiah when there will be no rebuke or discipline, the wisdom of the Sages will fall into ruin, and truth will completely vanish.]

2. אָמַר נָבָל בְּלִבּו — *The degraded man* [or: 'degenerate'] *says in his heart.*

Rashi maintains that the *degraded man* described here is Titus. The *Talmud (Gittin* 56b) relates the story of the atrocities which this Roman general perpetrated: Titus hurled words of blasphemy and curses heavenward. He dragged a prostitute into the Holy of Holies where he performed a lewd act upon an open Torah Scroll. He then grasped his sword and slashed the *Paroches,* the curtain in front of the Holy of Holies. A miracle occurred and blood spurted from the gash. Titus imagined this to be a sign that he had killed God Himself (ח״ו)! [Actually, this blood showed that God's heart was 'bleeding', as it were, because of the destruction, (*Tosafos ibid.*).]. Gloating over his success, Titus then made the *Paroches* into a sack and stuffed it with the precious vessels of the Temple, which he loaded on a ship for display at the time of his triumphant entry into Rome.

According to *Midrash Shocher Tov,* נָבָל in this verse is not an adjective

meaning *degenerate,* but a proper noun referring to *Nabal the Carmelite* [*I Samuel* 25], *a wealthy man so selfish that he refused David's plea to provide food and drink for his hungry troops.*

Norah Tehillos explains that this psalm was purposely placed directly after *Psalm 52* in order to emphasize the stark contrast between Achimelech (*Psalm* 52:2) and Nabal. Achimelech gladly sacrificed his life in order to extend hospitality to David. He generously supplied David with everything he desired. Nabal, however, not only vehemently denied David's request but also insulted him.

Sforno identifies the נָבָל as the insincere scholar whose external piety and wisdom cloak a heart which questions the very existence of God! As the *Talmud (Sanhedrin* 106b) says: 'All of Doeg's Torah knowledge was from the lips outward [i.e., insincere] ... but what God truly desires is the heart!'

אֵין אֱלֹהִים — *There is no God!*

When Titus slashed the *Poroches* and blood flowed, he exulted 'God is dead!' (*Rashi*).

[*Nabal the Carmelite* denied David's authority and his claim to the throne (see *I Sam.* 25:10). Thus he is considered to have denied the authority of God Himself! (*Midrash Shocher Tov*; see Article 12 of *Rambam's 'Thirteen Principles of Faith'* cited in comm. to 2:2).]

הִשְׁחִיתוּ — *They acted corruptly.*

[This term is used to describe lewd

ג עָוֶל אֵין עָשָׂה־טּוֹב: אֱלֹהִים מִשָּׁמַיִם
הִשְׁקִיף עַל־בְּנֵי־אָדָם לִרְאוֹת הֲיֵשׁ
ד מַשְׂכִּיל דֹּרֵשׁ אֶת־אֱלֹהִים: כֻּלּוֹ סָג יַחְדָּו

acts of unchastity, as in *Genesis* 6:12. It alludes to the abominable behavior of Titus and his prostitute in the Holy of Holies. According to *Midrash Shocher Tov*, Nabal the Carmelite was also guilty of such corrupt wanton acts.]

וְהִתְעִיבוּ עָוֶל — *And despicably* [through] *iniquity*.

Their total corruption and depravity rendered them despicable in the eyes of others (*Radak*).

[We often find in Scriptures that *iniquity* is considered *despicable*, as in *Deuteronomy* 25:16 and *Proverbs* 29:27.]

Chazah Zion observes that עָוֶל refers specifically to dishonesty in monetary affairs (see *Lev.* 19:15, 35).

[In the very beginning of the era of the Second Temple, the children of Israel underwent a major transformation: no longer were they plagued by the desire to worship idols (*Yoma* 69b), but by the desire to amass wealth. It is well known that the Second Temple was destroyed as a result of שִׂנְאַת חִנָּם, *unwarranted hatred*. *Yerushalmi Yoma* (1:9) explains: 'Since they loved their money, they came to hate one another!' Thus it was a fitting punishment that the Second Temple was destroyed by Rome, an empire which was particularly notorious for avarice. The *Midrash* (*Shemos Rabbah* 35:5) relates that no wheel moved in Rome unless it was well oiled with money: מִתְרַפֵּס בְּרַצֵּי כָסֶף *submitting to pieces of silver* (68:31) This describes the government of Rome!]

3. אֱלֹהִים — *God.*

The essential difference between this psalm and *Psalm* 14 is the Name used to refer to God. In *Psalm* 14, the name *HASHEM* predominates, while in *Psalm*

53 the designation אֱלֹהִים, *God* occurs throughout (*Hirsch*).

[The moral decay and *malady* (מַחֲלַת) which afflicted the Jewish people during the Second Temple brought about a spiritual degeneration. Only the harsh remedies meted out by אֱלֹהִים, '*the Dispenser of Strict Justice*', could serve as an effective cure for this alarming spiritual disease. After the first destruction, however, the spiritual caliber of the people was such that they still deserved the manifestation of God's Mercy represented by the Name HASHEM.]

מִשָּׁמַיִם הִשְׁקִיף — *From heaven* [God] *gazed down.*

[In general, the term הִשְׁקִיף, *He gazed*, denotes a critical observation for the sake of meting out punishment. [See *Rashi Gen.* 18:16 and *Yerushalmi Maaser Sheni* 5:5. See *Torah Temimah* on *Deut.* 26:15, suggesting that this rule applies only to the Pentateuch and not to other Scriptures such as *Psalms*, as evidenced by *Psalms* 85:12, 102:20, and *Songs* 6:10.]

Dorash Moshe explains that רְאִיָּה *looking*, means enlargement of the span of vision to encompass the broadest possible area, whereas הַשְׁקָפָה, *gazing*, means to reduce the focus of vision in order to scrutinize a single object. Naturally, if a person seeks to find fault with someone he must use הַשְׁקָפָה to study his subject closely.

לִרְאוֹת הֲיֵשׁ מַשְׂכִּיל — *To see if there be one who reflects.*

This refers to a person who ponders the words of the Torah, seeking guidance (*Targum*).

[David exemplified this quality, as it says, וַיְהִי דָוִד לְכָל דְּרָכָיו מַשְׂכִּיל, '*And David was intelligent in all of his ways*'

³ *From heaven God gazed down upon mankind*
to see if there be one who reflects;
one who seeks out God.
⁴ *They are all dross,*
together become depraved;

(*I Samuel* 18:14). He succeeded in following the upright ways of God;
therefore, וַיְהִי עִמּוֹ, *and HASHEM was
with him* (ibid.). It was David's genius
for acting wisely which stirred Saul's
jealousy, *And Saul saw that he was
most intelligent and he stood in fear of
him* (ibid. v. 15).

The conflict between these two men
is a symbol of the larger conflict
between Israel and the nations. Their
hatred is aroused because they see that
Israel has made the wise choice of following God, whereas they have failed to
do so. (See *Prefatory Remarks, Psalm
68.*) The depraved culture of Rome
demanded that the intellectual and
spiritual heritage of Israel be eradicated,
lest the arguments of the Torah uncover
the inherent worthlessness of Roman
thought.]

דֹּרֵשׁ אֶת אֱלֹהִים — [One] *who seeks out
God.*

I.e., one who seeks out God by clinging to the Sages of His Torah, in order
to learn from them the will of the
Almighty. Prior to the destruction of the
Temple, God sought such devoted disciples of the rabbis, but found none in
whose merit the Temple could be
spared. The *Talmud (Shabbos* 119b)
says that Jerusalem was destroyed only
because its inhabitants disgraced Torah
Sages (*Yoseif Tehillos*).

4. כֻּלּוֹ סָג — *They are* [lit. *he is*] *all
dross.*

This translation follows *Rashi* who
sees סָג as cognate with סִיגִים, *im-
purities; dross.*

Ibn Yachya and *Metzudas David*
define סָג as a verb related to נָסוֹג, *to
turn back; retreat* [i.e., since the
destruction, Israel has made no progress
but has remained in a state of perpetual
failure and decline.]

Targum renders: 'They all scatter'
[i.e., the exile has dispersed Israel to
every corner of the earth.]

In Psalm 14, we have a variant
reading, הַכֹּל סָר, *they have all gone
astray. Midrash Shocher Tov* comments: At first they merely *had all gone
astray.* Thus, there was still hope, for
the man who deviates from the path can
be brought back in repentance. Now,
however, everyone has become totally
filled with dross; therefore, the situation is hopeless.

Hirsch explains that they degenerated
to the point that any former spark of
nobility and refinement disppeared. As
a result, they seem to be beyond return,
just as base dross can never be converted into refined metal.[1]

יַחְדָּו נֶאֱלָחוּ — *Together become depraved.*

They are rotten from without [in
their affairs with other men] and from

---

1. *Yoseif Tehillos* observes that in the word סָג we can detect an allusion to the root of one's
spiritual malady, i.e., excessive pride which is known as רוּחַ גַּס, *haughtiness of spirit.* The
Talmud (Sotah 5a) allows the Torah scholar to display a minute trace of pride (נְסוּ) in order
to demonstrate his authority to his community. The *Talmud* prescribes that only 'one-eighth
of an eighth', i.e., one-sixty-fourth of one's pride may be expressed. No more than this minute
fraction of pride can be tolerated. The numerical value of סָג or סָג equals sixty-three, corresponding to the sixty-three parts of pride which must be suppressed [even by one who is
thoroughly familiar with סֵ"ג, the *sixty-three* volumes of the *Talmud.*].

ה נֶאֱלָחוּ אֵין עֹשֵׂה־טוֹב אֵין גַּם־אֶחָד: הֲלֹא
יָדְעוּ פֹּעֲלֵי אָוֶן אֹכְלֵי עַמִּי אָכְלוּ לֶחֶם
ו אֱלֹהִים לֹא קָרָאוּ: שָׁם | פָּחֲדוּ־פַחַד לֹא־
הָיָה פָחַד כִּי־אֱלֹהִים פִּזַּר עַצְמוֹת חֹנָךְ
ז הֱבִשֹׁתָה כִּי־אֱלֹהִים מְאָסָם: מִי יִתֵּן
מִצִּיּוֹן יְשֻׁעוֹת יִשְׂרָאֵל בְּשׁוּב אֱלֹהִים
שְׁבוּת עַמּוֹ יָגֵל יַעֲקֹב יִשְׂמַח יִשְׂרָאֵל:

within [in their inner feelings toward
God] (Midrash Shocher Tov).

אֵין עֹשֵׂה טוֹב אֵין גַּם אֶחָד — *None does
good, not even one.*

There is not a single man among the
legions of Titus who protests this
atrocity (Rashi).

[The historian Josephus makes an attempt to apologize for Titus, claiming
that he actually tried to stop his troops
from burning down the Beis Hamikdash
but could not hold back the wild hordes
who were bent on destruction.

Maharal in *Be'er Hagolah* (באר השני
ד"ה עוד אסף) stresses that, beyond any
doubt, the intentions of Titus were far
more savage and blasphemous than
those of Nebuchadnezzar. The
Babylonian king destroyed the Temple
only as a military action to suppress the
Jewish revolt which flared against him.
Titus, however, sought to vanquish
God Himself by destroying His holy
Sanctuary.

Maharal continues that even if we accept the testimony of Josephus, Titus
will not be vindicated. For the Sages, in
their holy vision, saw that Titus' true
motive for sparing the Temple was his
desire to desecrate it with his
abominable actions while it still stood in
all its glory and grandeur! (see *Netzach
Yisroel*, Chap. 5).]

5. הֲלֹא יָדְעוּ פֹּעֲלֵי אָוֶן — *Do they not
realize* [lit. *know*], *those evildoers?*

If they are not aware of the doom

which faces them for devouring my
people, then someone should forewarn
them of the impending disaster (Rashi).

According to *Sforno*, this incredulous
query is addressed to the corrupt
scholars and judges, who should realize
the impact of their depravity.

אֹכְלֵי עַמִּי אָכְלוּ לֶחֶם — *They who devour
my people [as they would] devour
bread.*

These corrupt sages and magistrates
put a price on their decisions and sold
their rulings in exchange for a bribe.
This is the prime source of their lavish
income. Thus, they unjustly devour the
innocent people so that they can earn
their sustenance and devour bread
(Sforno).

אֱלֹהִים לֹא קָרָאוּ — *They who do not call
upon God.*

[In Psalm 14, the name ה' appears instead of אֱלֹהִים.]

The Sages should lead the people in
prayer, penitence, and Torah study,
calling upon God for salvation. Instead
they lead others into crime (Sforno).

Targum renders this entire verse, All
those men of deceit know full well that
it is I [God] Who supply their bread;
why then do they devour bread and
refuse to call upon My Name by
reciting a blessing?

6. שָׁם פָּחֲדוּ פַחַד לֹא הָיָה פָחַד — *There
they will be stricken with terror, a terror
such as never was.*

LIII
5-7

None does good, not even one.

⁵ Do they not realize, those evil doers? —
They who devour my people
as they would devour bread,
They who do not call upon God.

⁶ They will be stricken with terror;
a terror such as never was.
For God scatters the bones of those encamped
against you.
You shamed them for God has rejected them.

⁷ O, that out of Zion
will come Israel's salvations!
When God returns the captivity of His nation,
Jacob will exult,
Israel will rejoice.

Even the sheer terror experienced by
Belshazzar on the night of his downfall
[see *Daniel* 5:1 and *comm. to* 14:5] cannot compare to the horror which awaits
this enemy (*Rashi*).

At the 'End of Days', the armies
which assemble with Gog and Magog
will panic when they witness that the
host of weapons arrayed against them
includes pestilence and blood, torrential
floods and devastating hailstones
(*Meiri*).

Dorash Moshe interprets this homiletically: The wicked will be terrrified by
the fires of Gehinnom in the future only
because they never had any fear of God
in the past.

כִּי אֱלֹהִים פִּזַּר עַצְמוֹת חֹנָךְ — *For God scat-*

ters the bones of those encamped
against you.

This refers to the armies which will
encamp around Jerusalem and beseige
it (*Radak*).[1]

הֱבִישֹׁתָה כִּי אֱלֹהִים מְאָסָם — *You shamed*
them for God has rejected them.

In Psalm 14, this verse is very brief
and reads: *There they will be stricken*
with terror, for God is with the right-
eous generation. Rashi (ibid.) explains
that even during the exile, God's holy
spirit never departed from the righteous
men of Israel. This refers to Babylon,
where God's presence accompanied
King Yechanyah and his myriad Torah
scholars. However, in the Second
(Roman) Exile, this was not the case.

---

1. [We can also perceive here an allusion to the ignominious fate of Titus. The Talmud (*Gittin*
56b) relates that on his deathbed Titus gave the following instructions: 'After death, cremate
my body and scatter the ashes over the seven seas, so the God of the Jews will not be able
to find me to bring me before His Tribunal of Justice.'

Titus did not succeed in his attempt to escape Divine retribution. Indeed, the very sentence
which he passed upon himself is meticulously fulfilled. Every day his ashes are gathered and
he is judged and condemned to another cremation, and once again his ashes are scattered over
the seven seas (see *comm. to* 21:10).]

Therefore the Psalmist deletes that statement from this psalm and substitutes a description of the humiliation which eventually came upon our persecutors.[1]

7. ישוּעַת יִשְׂרָאֵל — *Israel's salvations.*

In Psalm 14, we read יְשׁוּעַת יִשְׂרָאֵל, *Israel's salvation,* in the singular form because that psalm speaks of one event: the redemption from the First (Babylonian) Exile. However, that redemption was not really a total one, for many people remained in the diaspora and the Second (Roman) Exile was already in the making. The return to Israel at that time was not a final rest, but a mere interlude.

The final redemption of the future will be a complete one, marking the end of all exiles. This redemption will put an end to the countless exiles and expulsions which the Jews have endured throughout history; the culmination of an ever-repeating, vicious cycle. Therefore, it is most appropriately described as *the* (many) *salvations of Israel* (Chazah Zion).

Our nation can merit a swift and early redemption in either of two ways: by virtue of exceptionally meritorious conduct, or by virtue of excessive sufferings, for the intensity of our pain can compensate for the lack of the exile's completion. Thus the Psalmist wishes, *'O that out of Zion would come the salvations* which are not caused by extra suffering but rather may be attributed to the merits *of Israel' (Panim Yofos).*

בְּשׁוּב אֱלֹהִים — *When God returns.*

Here *Israel's salvations* [plural] are many and complete, because they come about at the hands of אֱלֹהִים, indicating God as the *Dispenser of Strict Justice.* If Israel merits salvation by its good deeds, then this salvation will endure forever. However, in Psalm 14 we read בְּשׁוּב ה׳, *When HASHEM returns,* indicating that *God as the Dispenser of Mercy* took pity on them and redeemed them, although they did not deserve it. Such a redemption is incomplete and short-lived, merely ישׁוּעַת יִשְׂרָאֵל an isolated instance of a single salvation of Israel (Midbar Kedemos; Mikdash Me'at).

יָגֵל יַעֲקֹב יִשְׂמַח יִשְׂרָאֵל — *Jacob will exult, Israel will rejoice.*

The name *Jacob* always describes the Jewish masses, the common-folk. However, *Israel* denotes the elite, the scholars and saints who guide the masses [see *comm.* to 14:7.] All of them together will rejoice at the final redemption (Malbim).

---

1. Ultimately, God rejected the proud tyrant Titus and humiliated him. The Talmud (*Gittin* 56b) relates that a great storm threatened Titus' ship as he sped back to Rome from Jerusalem. He roared, 'The God of the Jews has power only over the seas! Let Him challenge me on dry land, where I will surely vanquish him!'

A heavenly voice went forth, 'You wicked villain, I placed a tiny, insignificant creature in this world, the gnat. I will dispatch this weak insect to do battle with you on dry land!'

A gnat flew by, entered Titus' nose, penetrated his skull and pecked at his brain for seven years. The relentless pain was maddening. Once Titus passed by a blacksmith and the sound of the hammer crashing down on the anvil silenced the gnat. Henceforth, Titus had a blacksmith bang before him every day. If the smith was a gentile, he was paid for his work. If the smith was a Jew, Titus would say, 'You deserve no pay! Let it suffice that you have the pleasure of witnessing the humiliation of your enemy.'

This remedy helped for but thirty days. When Titus finally died after seven years of agony, they opened his head, releasing a giant gnat the size of a bird, armed with a sharp beak of copper and nails of iron.

In Psalm 52 we read of Doeg, an individual, who became corrupted because he engaged in slander; in Psalm 54 we learn of an entire community which was ruined because it engaged in talebearing. Psalm 53 was placed between these two compositions because it related to them both. It describes the נָבָל, the degraded man; who blasphemes, There is no God!' Despite his vehement protestations of innocence, the slanderer described in this psalm, personified by the men of Ziph, is no better than the heretical נָבָל, for the Sages said, 'He who slanders is considered as if he denied the existence of God' (Baalei Bris Avraham).

The treachery of the Ziphites surpassed that of Doeg, for the Ziphites, who were of the tribe of Judah, were David's own relatives. Even Saul was amazed that the Ziphites would betray their kinsman to a king from the tribe of Benjamin. But these treacherous men willingly sacrificed their integrity in the hopes of satisfying their greed and ambition by currying favor with King Saul.

David was so depressed by their abominable conduct that he employed special נְגִינֹת, musical instruments, (verse 1) to accompany this psalm, in order to lift his spirits to a level of prophetic ecstasy (Alshich).

לַמְנַצֵּחַ בִּנְגִינֹת מַשְׂכִּיל לְדָוִד: בְּבוֹא
הַזִּיפִים וַיֹּאמְרוּ לְשָׁאוּל הֲלֹא דָוִד
ג מִסְתַּתֵּר עִמָּנוּ: אֱלֹהִים בְּשִׁמְךָ הוֹשִׁיעֵנִי
ד וּבִגְבוּרָתְךָ תְדִינֵנִי: אֱלֹהִים שְׁמַע תְּפִלָּתִי
ה הַאֲזִינָה לְאִמְרֵי־פִי: כִּי זָרִים | קָמוּ עָלַי
וְעָרִיצִים בִּקְשׁוּ נַפְשִׁי לֹא שָׂמוּ אֱלֹהִים

---

1. מַשְׂכִּיל — *A Maskil* [lit. *instruction*].

This psalm of *instruction* teaches a vital lesson. Although David was in mortal danger as a result of the treachery of the Ziphites, he did not despair but prayed for Hashem's mercy in this apparently hopeless situation. This illustrates David's credo (*Berachos* 10a), 'Even when a lethal sword is poised at a person's throat, he should not refrain from beseeching God's mercy' (*Nora Tehillos*).

2. בְּבוֹא הַזִּיפִים — *When the Ziphites came.*

[David and his men escaped from Saul into the wilderness of Ziph. When the Ziphites discovered David's hideaway, they promptly sped to Saul's headquarters in Givah to inform him of David's exact location. They boasted proudly, '*Therefore, O King, according to your heart's desire to descend* (i.e. attack) — *descend; and our responsibility shall be to deliver him (David) into the hands of the King*' (v.20)]

Rabbi Yochanan says: They were called זִיפִים, *Ziphites*, because they *falsified* (מְזַיְּיף) their words (*Sotah* 48b).

Maharsha (ibid.) explains that they lied by claiming that they could easily deliver David into Saul's hands, despite the fact that David was actually far removed from their grasp.

וַיֹּאמְרוּ לְשָׁאוּל — *And [they] said to Saul.*

Solomon said, '*If a ruler pays heed to lies, all his servants will be wicked*' (*Prov.* 29:12). So it was in Israel. When the Ziphites noticed that Saul was influenced by the slander he heard about

David, they also felt encouraged to betray him. Saul was eager to hear evil reports from others; for example, '*Doeg the Edomite came and told Saul* [slanderous reports]' (52:2), and Nabal also mocked David [and supported Saul (53:2).]. Observing this, the Ziphites did not hesitate to slander David to Saul, (*Midrash Shocher Tov*).

הֲלֹא דָוִד מִסְתַּתֵּר עִמָּנוּ — *Is not David in hiding among* [lit. *with*] *us?*

Eretz Hachaim notes that it would seem that they should have said, מִסְתַּתֵּר אֶצְלֵנוּ, *He hides near us*, because עִמָּנוּ, *with us*, implies that David and the Ziphites were hiding together.

He explains that the Ziphites were in fact saying to Saul, 'We tricked David by pretending that we too are your enemies. We purported to hide from you, so that David would feel secure among us.'

3. אֱלֹהִים בְּשִׁמְךָ הוֹשִׁיעֵנִי — *O God, save me by Your Name*

David said to the Holy One, Blessed be He, 'Master of the Universe, when an officer persecutes a man, the man can complain to the prefect. If the prefect persecutes him, he can complain to the Emperor. But if the Emperor persecutes a man, to whom can he complain? Saul is king. To whom shall I complain about him? I can complain only to You!' (*Midrash Shocher Tov*).

וּבִגְבוּרָתְךָ תְדִינֵנִי — *And by Your might vindicate me.*

'Treat me according to the dictates of

LIV
1-5

For the Conductor; with instrumental music,
a Maskil to David
² When the Ziphites came and said to Saul
'Is not David in hiding among us?'
³ O God, by Your Name save me,
and by Your might vindicate me.
⁴ O God, hear my prayer
give ear to the utterances of my mouth.
⁵ For strangers have risen up against me
and powerful men sought my soul.
They have not set God before themselves, Selah.

Your might (the Torah), for You have written therein: *You shall not deliver to his master a slave who escaped his master and came to you* [for refuge] (*Deut.* 23:16). If You display such concern for the slave who only yesterday served idols, then certainly You will care for me and guard me from Saul. For I am a prince, the son of a prince from the royal family of Judah!' (*Midrash Shocher Tov*).

4. אֱלֹהִים שְׁמַע תְּפִלָּתִי — *O God, hear my prayer.*

Radak and *Ibn Ezra* explain that the 'prayer' mentioned here is the inner, unspoken request of the heart.

The *Zohar* (*Parshas Metzora*) teaches that God rejects the prayers of those who spread evil tales. Therefore David asks God to hear his prayers but not those of the Ziphites, who are tainted by slander (*Dorash Moshe*).

הַאֲזִינָה לְאִמְרֵי פִי — *Give ear to the utterances of my mouth.*

'Please pay close attention to my words so that You can respond to my entreaty even before I voice the entire supplication (*Alshich*).

Doeg and the Ziphites came to Saul

and he gave ear to their slander. I shall not go to Saul, but to You. Hear me, give ear unto me (*Midrash Shocher Tov*).

5. כִּי זָרִים קָמוּ עָלַי — *For strangers have risen up against me.*

Ibn Ezra and *Radak* identify these as the alien gentiles; *Metzudas David* maintains that the verse refers to the Ziphites, who estranged themselves from their relative, David, by supporting Saul, who was a stranger to them.

וְעָרִיצִים בִּקְשׁוּ נַפְשִׁי — *And powerful men sought my soul.*

This refers to Doeg and Achitophel. Whereas the Ziphites threatened only my body, they assaulted my soul, as well. Not only did then challenge me with weapons, but they attacked me with arguments from the Torah, claiming that, as a result of my sins, my soul would never merit the World to Come (*Chazah Zion*).

לֹא שָׂמוּ אֱלֹהִים לְנֶגְדָּם — *They have not set God before themselves.*

Their deeds are not inspired by a desire to please God (*Sforno*).

לְנֶגְדָּם סֶלָה: הִנֵּה אֱלֹהִים עֹזֵר לִי אֲדֹנָי ו

בְּסֹמְכֵי נַפְשִׁי: °יָשׁוֹב הָרַע לְשֹׁרְרָי ו־ט ‏ יָשִׁיב קרי‏ ז

בַּאֲמִתְּךָ הַצְמִיתֵם: בִּנְדָבָה אֶזְבְּחָה־לָּךְ ח

אוֹדֶה שִּׁמְךָ יהוה כִּי־טוֹב: כִּי מִכָּל־צָרָה ט

הִצִּילָנִי וּבְאֹיְבַי רָאֲתָה עֵינִי:

They curry favor with Saul because he is the king, ignoring God's promise that Saul will be replaced by a worthier monarch (*Vidal HaTzrofati*).

They fail to consider the warning contained in the Torah (*Deut.* 27:24), *Cursed be he who smites his friend in secret* [through slander]. Instead they rely on Saul's blessing to them: ברוכים אַתֶּם לַה׳, *Blessed be you unto HASHEM* (I *Sam.* 23:21). Obviously, Saul's blessing is useless if they are accursed by God (*Midrash Shocher Tov*).

6. הִנֵּה אֱלֹהִים עֹזֵר לִי — *Behold! God is my helper.*

Therefore, slander cannot harm me (*Radak*).

What was the outcome of the Ziphite's treachery? Saul and his army surrounded David in a trap from which there seemed no possible escape. Suddenly, however, a messenger appeared, summoning Saul to depart immediately to protect the land from a surprise Philistine invasion (I *Sam.* 23:27-28; see footnote to 18:3).

David declares that he recognizes that it was God Himself who rescued him from this death-trap by sending an angel to serve as the messenger (*Maharam Markado*).

אֲדֹנָי בְּסֹמְכֵי נַפְשִׁי — *My Lord is with supporters of my soul.*

David prays for the welfare and success of those who do not slander but support him (*Ibn Ezra*).

[Furthermore, David recognizes that any help he receives from men is actually a manifestation of Hashem's favor.]

7. יָשׁוֹב הָרַע לְשֹׁרְרָי — *May He repay the evil to those who watch for me.*

The word is written (כתיב) יָשׁוֹב, *It* [the evil] *will return*, but it is read (קרי) יָשִׁיב, *He* [God] *will repay*, [i.e., cause to be returned.] David prayed: 'May the evil which they planned recoil upon them (יָשׁוֹב) but let their punishment come in such a way that it is clearly an

⁶ Behold! God is my helper,
  my Lord is with supporters of my soul.
⁷ May He repay the evil to those
  who watch for me.
Because of Your truths cut them down!
⁸ With a free-will offering I will sacrifice to You,
  I will thank Your Name, HASHEM, for it is good.
⁹ For from every distress has He rescued me,
  and upon my foes has my eye looked.

act of divine retribution, for God Himself *will return* (יָשִׁיב) their evil to them' (*Hirsch*).

בַּאֲמִתְּךָ הַצְמִיתֵם — *Because of Your truths cut them down.*

It is true that You decreed that I will survive to replace Saul as king. Therefore, those who wish to interfere with Your solemn decree must be cut down and removed (*Radak*).

8. בִּנְדָבָה אֶזְבְּחָה לָּךְ — *With a free-will offering I will sacrifice to You.*

I cannot bring a קָרְבַּן תּוֹדָה, *a thanksgiving offering,* because that is appropriate where a dangerous situation has been resolved to the satisfaction of all involved. In this case, however, God is saddened because He must destroy those of His creatures who threaten me. Therefore, I will merely sacrifice a *free-will offering* to demonstrate my appreciation for my personal salvation (*Sforno*).

9. כִּי מִכָּל צָרָה הִצִּילָנִי — *For from every distress has He rescued me.*

[God has mercifully saved me from myriad misfortunes of which I will always remain unaware. For this, too, I must render Him thanks.]

וּבְאֹיְבַי רָאֲתָה עֵינִי — *And upon my foes has my eye looked.*

The Sages teach that the person who deserves salvation is granted the privilege of witnessing the downfall of his enemies, as when Israel saw the destruction of Egypt at the Red Sea. But he who is saved by the merits of others does not deserve this privilege. Therefore, Lot, who was saved by virtue of Abraham's merit, was forbidden to look back upon the destruction of Sodom.

David exults that he is privileged to witness his enemies' defeat because this indicates his righteousness (*Nava Tehillah*).

In the preceding Psalms, David recounts his early suffering at the hands of Saul, Doeg, and the Ziphites, malicious adversaries who were bent on his destruction. Nevertheless, the grief they caused David cannnot compare to the suffering inflicted by Achitophel, an intimate friend who later became his archenemy.

As Alshich (v. 13) observes, the pinprick inflicted by a friend is far more painful than the sword wound dealt by an enemy.

Late in David's life he was betrayed by Achitophel, the wisest sage of the realm, the brilliant strategist, the unerring statesman, who had skillfully guided the fortunes of David's monarchy throughout the most crucial period of his reign.

Their strong bond of friendship had been forged not only by political considerations, but also by spiritual communion. For David and Achitophel studied the Word of God together, sharing the secrets of the holy Torah.

How utterly bereft David was when Achitophel abruptly ruined this remarkable relationship by inciting David's son Absalom to launch an assassination plot against his father! Bitterly, David surveys the past and realizes too late, that Achitophel's 'friendship' had never been inspired by love or admiration. A selfish opportunist, he was motivated solely by envy and by a passion to ascend to the throne. Actually, Achitophel planned to depose Absalom in order to seize the crown for himself. [See Prefatory Remarks, Psalms 4 and 5].

Distraught and disillusioned, David flees Jerusalem before his foes. As he sinks into despair, he yearns to abandon the society of all men, for, whom can he now trust? If someone would but give me wings like the dove! I would fly off and find rest! (v. 7). Ultimately, however, David realizes his responsibility to remain at the head of his people, despite his personal anguish. He asks only for peace and for the eradication of chief enemy, Achitophel, who treacherously robbed him of life's most precious treasure: faithful friendship.

א-ב לַמְנַצֵּחַ בִּנְגִינֹת מַשְׂכִּיל לְדָוִד: הַאֲזִינָה

אֱלֹהִים תְּפִלָּתִי וְאַל-תִּתְעַלַּם מִתְּחִנָּתִי:

ג הַקְשִׁיבָה לִּי וַעֲנֵנִי אָרִיד בְּשִׂיחִי

ד וְאָהִימָה: מִקּוֹל אוֹיֵב מִפְּנֵי עָקַת רָשָׁע

ה כִּי-יָמִיטוּ עָלַי אָוֶן וּבְאַף יִשְׂטְמוּנִי: לִבִּי

יָחִיל בְּקִרְבִּי וְאֵימוֹת מָוֶת נָפְלוּ עָלָי:

ו יִרְאָה וָרַעַד יָבֹא בִי וַתְּכַסֵּנִי פַּלָּצוּת:

---

1. לַמְנַצֵּחַ בִּנְגִינֹת — *For the Conductor, with musical instruments.*

David composed this Psalm as he fled from Absalom his son [see 3:1] (*Maharam Markado*). As agony and despair threatened to envelop him, he employed cheerful *musical instruments* to dispel the gloom and to lift himself to the ecstatic level of Divine inspiration (*Alshich*).

2. הַאֲזִינָה אֱלֹהִים תְּפִלָּתִי — *Give ear, O God, to my prayer.*

Rav Yehuda bar Yitzchak taught that David had no greater friend than Achitophel who was the king's counselor (I Chronicles 27:33).

Rav Nachman taught that David was not afraid of any man except Achitophel. Hence David beseeched, *Give ear, O God, to my prayer.* The Holy One, Blessed be He, asked David: 'Haven't you said, "Though an army would besiege me, my heart would not fear"'? (27:3)?

David replied, 'Master of the Universe, give me such enemies of whom I can say, "I pursued my foes and overtook them and returned not until I had annihilated them" (18:38). This Achitophel is not such an enemy, for he is greater than I am!' (*Midrash Shocher Tov*).

וְאַל תִּתְעַלַּם מִתְּחִנָּתִי — *Do not disregard my pleas.*

When David heard that Achitophel was with Absalom and his conspirators, he pleaded (II Samuel 15:31), *Please HASHEM, turn the counsel of Achitophel into foolishness* (*Midrash Shocher Tov*).

3. אָרִיד בְּשִׂיחִי — *I lament as I speak.*

This translation, based on *Genesis* 27:40, follows *Rashi, Ibn Ezra,* and *Radak. Menachem,* however, relates אָרִיד to רָדָה *rule, dominate* as in *Genesis* 1:28 and renders this phrase, *I control* (my fate) *with my words* (of prayer).

וְאָהִימָה — *And I moan.*

This alludes to the description of David's flight (II Samuel 14:30): *And David went up by the ascent of the Mount of Olives and wept as he went up, and he had his head covered and went barefoot, and all the people who were with him covered their heads* [in mourning], *and they ascended, weeping as they went up* (*Maharam Markado*).

4. מִקּוֹל אוֹיֵב — *At the shout* [lit. *voice*] *of the foe.*

Alshich explains that this alludes to the loud curses and threats which Shimi ben Gera hurled at David as the king fled before Absalom (II Samuel 16:5-13).

מִפְּנֵי עָקַת רָשָׁע — *On account of the oppression of the wicked.*

They not only curse me, but also they

For the Conductor,
  with musical instruments, a Maskil by David.
² Give ear, O God, to my prayer,
  do not disregard my pleas.
³ Pay me heed and answer me.
  I lament as I speak, and I moan.
⁴ At the shout of the foe,
  on account of the oppression of the wicked,
for they accuse me of evil and passionately hate me.
⁵ My heart shudders within me,
  and the terrors of death have befallen me.
⁶ Fear and trembling penetrate me,
  and I am overcome with horror.

---

oppress me physically by pursuing me
(Kiflayim L'Tushiya).

כִּי יָמִיטוּ עָלַי אָוֶן — For they accuse me
[lit. they drop on me] of evil.

They claim that I desecrated the holy
Name of God by my sins and that the
scales of justice are tipped against me.
Accordingly, they dropped the balance
of the scales against me and declared me
completely guilty (Eretz Hachaim).

וּבְאַף יִשְׂטְמוּנִי — And passionately hate
me.

The people of Israel once wholeheartedly pledged their allegiance to me
and gladly accepted me as their king,
but today their love has changed to passionate hatred, and they have crowned
my son in my place (Radak).

According to Hirsch, ישטום is related
to סָתוּם, locked up, and refers to hatred
previously concealed in the heart, but
now unleashed in its full fury.

5. לִבִּי יָחִיל בְּקִרְבִּי — My heart shudders
within me.

Even when no immediate danger
looms before my eyes, I am still uneasy.
Anxiety and fear of the unknown

agitate my spirit and give me no rest.
This is a signal of impending doom, as
the Talmud (Megillah 3a) says: Even
though his eyes do not see, his soul
senses calamity (Shaarei Chaim).

וְאֵימוֹת מָוֶת נָפְלוּ עָלַי — And the terrors of
death have befallen me.

Radak observes that the specter of
death loomed over David in particular
when Achitophel advised Absalom: 'Let
me now choose out twelve thousand
men and I will arise and pursue David
this night. And I will come upon him
while he is weary and weak-handed,
and I will make him afraid, and all the
people who are with him shall flee, and I
will smite only the king. I will bring
back all of the people to you and when
all have returned except the one man
whom you seek then all the people will
be in peace.' And this saying pleased
Absalom well and all the elders of Israel
(II Samuel 17:1-4).

6. יִרְאָה וָרַעַד יָבֹא בִי — Fear and
trembling penetrate me.

The vague anxiety of my heart (v. 5)
grows and increases (Shaarei Chaim),
until [mental] fear and [physical] trem-

נה
ז-י״א

ז וָאֹמַר מִי־יִתֶּן־לִּי אֵבֶר כַּיּוֹנָה אָעוּפָה

ח וְאֶשְׁכֹּנָה: הִנֵּה אַרְחִיק נְדֹד אָלִין בַּמִּדְבָּר

ט סֶלָה: אָחִישָׁה מִפְלָט לִי מֵרוּחַ סֹעָה

י מִסָּעַר: בַּלַּע אֲדֹנָי פַּלַּג לְשׁוֹנָם כִּי־רָאִיתִי

יא חָמָס וְרִיב בָּעִיר: יוֹמָם וָלַיְלָה יְסוֹבְבֻהָ

bling become part of my very being (Ibn Ezra).

7. וָאֹמַר — Then I said.

[The terrible anguish within David's heart surges outward, until the bitterness bursts forth from his lips in this powerful plea.]

מִי־יִתֶּן לִי אֵבֶר כַּיּוֹנָה — If someone would but give me wings like the dove!

Ibn Ezra suggests that David is familiar with the dove because it is synonymous with the carrier pigeon, which kings were accustomed to use for sending messages.

The Midrash, (Bereishis Rabbah 39:8) offers the explanation that all other birds, when they are exhausted, stop to rest on a boulder or a tree, but when the dove grows weary, it merely folds one wing to give it rest and continues to fly with the other wing.

'With wings like the dove', says David, 'I would flee from my pursuers and be assured of a successful escape' (Sforno).

וְאֶשְׁכֹּנָה אָעוּפָה — [Then] I would fly off and find rest.

I would fly until I found a secure haven, where I could finally rest from the fear and trembling which overcame me (Radak).

Norah Tehillos notes that David's words seem to be self-contradictory. If he flew, then he would not be at rest; and if he seeks rest, why does he ask to fly? Actually, this statement alludes to the Midrash cited above, which explains that even while the dove flies with one wing, it is at rest with the other.

8. הִנֵּה אַרְחִיק נְדֹד — Behold, I would wander afar.

I would make my way to some distant wilderness where there would be no possibility for my enemies to send spies to discover my whereabouts (Sforno).

אָלִין בַּמִּדְבָּר — And [I would] dwell in the wilderness.

[Rambam (Hilchos Deos 6:1) recommends this as the proper course of action for anyone who feels that civilization is a threat to both his body and his soul: Man's nature is that he is influenced by his environment and the society of people ... Therefore, if a man finds himself in a country whose inhabitants are evil, he must remove himself to a different land where righteous men dwell. If all countries are corrupt, as is the case in our times, then he should live all alone. If he is not allowed to live in isolation, then he must flee to the caves, the badlands, and the wilderness to escape the detrimental influence of the sinners.']

9. אָחִישָׁה מִפְלָט לִי — I would speed myself to shelter.

This alludes to the time when David was trapped by Saul in the wilderness of Maon. Scripture states (I Samuel 23:26), And David made great haste to escape for fear of Saul, for Saul and his men encircled David and his men round about to seize them (Sforno).

מֵרוּחַ סֹעָה — From violent wind.

The word סֹעָה is related to נָסַע, to journey, suggesting that this wind travels great distances (Menachem).

The violent wind uproots mighty

⁷ Then I said, 'If someone would but give me wings
    like the dove! I would fly off and find rest!

⁸ Behold! I would wander afar,
    and dwell in the wilderness, Selah.

⁹ 'I would speed myself to shelter
    from violent wind, from tempest.'

¹⁰ Consume, my Lord, and confuse their tongue,
    for I saw violence and strife in the city.

¹¹ Day and night they encircle it upon its walls,

---

trees and makes them 'travel' to a new
position (Rashi).

This describes David's enemies,
whose passionate hate resembles a
violent storm [for they threaten to uproot him from his throne] (Radak).

10. בֶּלַּע אֲדֹנָי — Consume [lit. swallow
up], my Lord.

['May Achitophel and his henchmen
who spout words of evil treachery
against me be forced to swallow up their
own words!']

פַּלַּג לְשׁוֹנָם — And confuse [lit. divide]
their tongue.

Cast a spirit of dissension and discord
among them, so that they will be split
into many conflicting factions. Let them
be paralyzed by dispute (Radak;
Sforno).

[Indeed, David's wish was immediately fulfilled, for Chushai the
Arkite (who secretly supported David)
offered advice to Absalom which con-
tradicted that of Achitophel. He claimed
that it would be preferable to wait until
a tremendous force of soldiers could be
gathered, so that Absalom's massive
army could overwhelm David's tiny
force. And Absalom and all the men of
Israel said, 'The counsel of Chushai the
Arkite is better than the counsel of
Achitophel'; for HASHEM had ordained
to defeat the good counsel of
Achitophel so that HASHEM might
bring evil upon Absalom (II Samuel
17:14).

Furthermore, the counsel of Achitophel was literally swallowed up when he
strangled himself and died in utter disgrace.]

כִּי רָאִיתִי חָמָס וְרִיב בָּעִיר — For I saw
violence and strife in the city.

'Already I see that they are quarreling
among themselves in the city of
Jerusalem (Radak) concerning how
they should share the spoils' (Sforno).

[The Psalmist stresses that the strife
occurred in the city of Jerusalem, for
such dissension is a radical departure
from the placid nature of this center of
שָׁלוֹם (שָׁלֵם) Peace. Elsewhere, David
himself described Jerusalem as The city
where all of Israel become good friends
(122:3; Yerushalmi, Chagiga 3:6).]

This internal discord assures their
ultimate downfall, for the Sages say
(Bamidbar Rabbah 11:7): Even when
men worship idols, if they act with
peace and brotherhood, they will be
spared the harsh sentence of strict
justice. But if men are embroiled in
feuds, then, even if they are righteous,
they are doomed (Tehillos Hashem).

11. יְסוֹבְבֻהָ עַל חוֹמֹתֶיהָ — Encircle it
upon its walls.

The Psalmist likens the city to a large
circle. Violence and strife are on the cir-
cumference. Thereby, the wicked
protect the inner core of iniquity and
mischief which is at the heart of the city
(Ibn Ezra).

נה

יב-טו

יב עַל־חוֹמֹתֶיהָ וְאָוֶן וְעָמָל בְּקִרְבָּהּ: הַוּוֹת
בְּקִרְבָּהּ וְלֹא־יָמִישׁ מֵרְחֹבָהּ תֹּךְ וּמִרְמָה:
יג כִּי לֹא־אוֹיֵב יְחָרְפֵנִי וְאֶשָּׂא לֹא־מְשַׂנְאִי
יד עָלַי הִגְדִּיל וְאֶסָּתֵר מִמֶּנּוּ: וְאַתָּה אֱנוֹשׁ
טו כְּעֶרְכִּי אַלּוּפִי וּמְיֻדָּעִי: אֲשֶׁר יַחְדָּו נַמְתִּיק

12. הַוּוֹת בְּקִרְבָּהּ — *Treachery is within it.*

[The very essence of the city has become treachery. The lives of her citizens are dedicated to crime and guile.]

וְלֹא יָמִישׁ מֵרְחֹבָהּ — *Never leaving its square.*

It is in the broad, main street of the city that all of Absalom's supporters gather to hatch their plots of *fraud and deception* (Radak).

[They openly engage in malicious conspiracy and make no attempt to conceal their shameful treachery. Similarly, a prophet of another era describes the decline of Jerusalem and laments (*Isaiah* 59:14), *Justice is turned away and righteousness stands far off, for truth has stumbled in her broad avenue and uprightness cannot enter.*]

תֹּךְ — *Fraud.*

This word is synonymous with מִרְמָה *deception*; they are also used together in 10:7. Literally, תֹּךְ (תּוֹךְ) means *inside*, and suggests that the deceitful man uses friendly words to camouflage the malice concealed inside his heart. This describes Absalom and his supporters, who originally disguised themselves as admirers of David, in order to catch him unawares (Radak).

We also find this word used in connection with חָמָס, *violence* (see 72:14), for the ultimate purpose of this masquerade was to facilitate brutal plundering and looting (Rashbam).

13. כִּי לֹא אוֹיֵב יְחָרְפֵנִי וְאֶשָּׂא — *For no foe can revile me that I can endure.*

This translation follows *Rashi* David states that if any other than Achitophel had cursed and betrayed him, he would not have *endured* (i.e., overlooked) such calumny. However, at first David felt compelled to show Achitophel special consideration, despite his rages, for, David venerated him as an extraordinary scholar and teacher (v. 14).

Radak offers a totally different interpretation: David says, 'If any other foe had cursed me, I *would* have gallantly accepted his insults and ignored their vicious intent. But you, Achitophel, were לֹא אוֹיֵב, 'not a foe', but a trusted intimate. Now that you suddenly *revile me*, I am so utterly shocked by your betrayal that I cannot *endure* it.'

לֹא מְשַׂנְאִי עָלַי הִגְדִּיל וְאֶסָּתֵר מִמֶּנּוּ — *No enemy can grow so great against me that I be put in hiding from him.*

The translation follows *Rashi*. 'I would not cower or hide from any enemy, rather I would stand up and fight. Only you, Achitophel, did I avoid out of respect for your Torah scholarship.'

Radak offers a different interpretation: 'With a different enemy, who made his malice known, I would have protected myself or gone into hiding. But you, Achitophel, caught me completely by surprise!'

Alshich paraphrases, 'I could silently bear the curses of Shimi ben Gera, and I could calmly accept the threats of King Saul, who *made himself great against me*. Only your treachery, Achitophel, is too much for me to bear, — for the pin-

תהלים **[694]**

iniquity and mischief are within it.

¹² *Treachery is within it,*
never leaving its square are fraud and deception.

¹³ *For no foe can revile me that I can endure,*
no enemy can grow so great against me
that I be put in hiding from him.

¹⁴ *But you are a man, of my measure,*
my guide, and my intimate friend,

¹⁵ *With whom together we would share*
sweet counsel,

---

prick inflicted by a friend is far more painful than the sword wound dealt by an enemy!'

14. וְאַתָּה אֱנוֹשׁ כְּעֶרְכִּי — *But you are a man of my measure.*

[David now explains why Achitophel differs from all other adversaries.] 'You are a great man whose stature is equal to my own. I always treated you as an equal, despite the fact that I am a king and you are a commoner' (*Radak*).

[*Midrash Shocher Tov* relates עֶרְכִּי to עוֹרֵךְ, *to place in order*, suggesting that Achitophel's academic role was to arrange Torah laws in proper order so as to facilitate David's program of studies.]

Alshich emphasizes that despite Achitophel's academic brilliance, he did not surpass David's scholastic achievements, for David was the greatest sage of his time and and an essential link in the chain of מָסוֹרָה, *Tradition*, which was transmitted from generation to generation. [See Introduction of *Rambam* to *Yad Hachazakah.*]

אַלּוּפִי — *My guide* [lit. *leader*].

'Although you, Achitophel, were only my equal and peer, I treated you as my superior, and as one who had authority over me' (*Radak*).

According to *Targum* and *Midrash Shocher Tov*, this is related to אַלֵּף, *to*

teach, implying, 'You were my mentor and guide in Torah studies.'

וּמְיֻדָּעִי — *And my intimate friend.*

'You were my closest confidante, the one with whom I shared my most intimate secrets' (*Radak*).

15. אֲשֶׁר יַחְדָּו נַמְתִּיק סוֹד — *With whom together we would share sweet counsel* [lit. *secret*].

Together we would delve into the intricacies of the Torah (*Rashi*).

Our relationship was idyllic, a model of sweet comradery and perfect trust (*Sforno*).

Moreover, no plan or counsel seemed *sweet* and acceptable to me until I consulted Achitophel and received his approval (*Radak*).

According to the Rabbis, David was particularly indebted to Achitophel for having instructed him on two occasions. Once, when Achitophel found David alone, engaged in Torah study, He asked, 'David why do you delve into Torah alone? Its wisdom will be revealed to you and endure only if you study, together with friends! Let us therefore take *sweet counsel* together and engage in Torah learning' (*Avos* 6:3; *Rashi* and *Mechzor Vitry*, ibid.; and *Kallah Rabbosi*). [The second instance in which Achitophel offered im-

סוֹד בְּבֵית אֱלֹהִים נְהַלֵּךְ בְּרָגֶשׁ:
טז יַשִּׁימָוֶת | עָלֵימוֹ יֵרְדוּ שְׁאוֹל חַיִּים כִּי־
יז רָעוֹת בִּמְגוּרָם בְּקִרְבָּם אֲנִי אֶל־אֱלֹהִים
יח אֶקְרָא וַיהוה יוֹשִׁיעֵנִי: עֶרֶב וָבֹקֶר

portant guidance to David is described below.]

בְּבֵית אֱלֹהִים נְהַלֵּךְ בְּרָגֶשׁ — *In the House of God we would walk with multitudes.*

The word רָגֶשׁ means *a great assemblage*, as in לָמָּה רָגְשׁוּ גוֹים, *Why do the nations gather?* (2:1). We would walk together to the House of God to study or pray (Rashi; Radak).

When a king goes out, he usually walks alone at the head of the royal procession, with his retinue following behind. However, David accorded Achitophel an unprecedented honor by allowing him to walk beside the king, as his equal. Achitophel 'repaid' this generosity by betraying David (Alshich).

The second significant recommendation which Achitophel made to David occurred when Achitophel found David going to the House of Prayer alone. He asked, 'Don't you realize that *amid a great company of people is the* [divine] *king's glory (Proverbs 24:28)?'* [God's honor is enhanced when a multitude of people pray in unison.]

Others translate רָגֶשׁ as *speed*; accordingly Achitophel said, 'When you go

to pray, go swiftly, like a man hastening after his sovereign.'

According to the variant version propounded by *Rashi (Avos 6:3)*, once Achitophel found David entering the House of Study with an erect, military bearing [suggesting a trace of pride]. He admonished him, 'A person should enter the House of God with רָגֶשׁ *feelings of awe*, so that the fear of heaven might rest upon him when he studies.'[1]

16. יַשִּׁיא מָוֶת עָלֵימוֹ — *May He incite death against them.*

The translation follows *Rashi*, who relates it to הַנָּחָשׁ הִשִּׁיאַנִי, *the serpent incited me (Genesis 3:13).* [Although this phrase is written (כְּתִיב) as one word (יַשִּׁימָוֶת), it is read (קְרִי) as two words (יַשִּׁיא מָוֶת).]

Ibn Ezra and *Radak* render יַשִּׁיא as *command* (see 89:23), which is also related to נָשָׁה, *to demand payment of a debt* (see *Exodus* 22:24), indicating: 'May God command the Angel of Death to demand that this villain pay his debt with his life.'

An alternative interpretation in *Ibn Ezra* defines יַשִּׁיא as *'make them forget'* (see *Genesis* 42:51; *Deuteronomy* 32:18),

1. If one learns one chapter, one halacha, one verse, one expression, or even one letter from his fellowman, he should treat him with esteem. This can be derived from the conduct of David, king of Israel, for he learned from Achitophel only two things, yet he called him his *master,* his *guide* and his *intimate friend.* A logical inference (*kal Va-chomer*) can be drawn: If David, king of Israel, (who learned only two things from Achitophel) called him *master, guide,* and *intimate friend,* then when someone learns from his fellow man one chapter, one halacha, one verse, one expression or even one letter, he has an even greater obligation to treat the teacher with respect (*Avos* 6:3).

Many commentaries puzzle over the 'logic' of this deduction. From David's example we know only that one should honor his teacher after learning *two things* from him. It has not yet been proven that one should accord his teacher respect after learning as little as *one letter* from him.

> in the House of God we would walk
>   with multitudes.
> ¹⁶ May He incite death against them,
>   let them descend to the Lower World, alive,
> for evil is in their dwelling and within them.
> ¹⁷ As for me, upon God shall I call,
>   and HASHEM will save me.

suggesting that the best deterrent against sin is constant fear of the day of death [see *Berachos* 5a.] Thus: Make these men oblivious to the specter of death, so that it should pounce on them suddenly and take them by surprise!

Malbim notes that this wish was soon fulfilled when Achitophel, (whose counsel had never before been rejected), suddenly found his advice ignored; he committed suicide rather than live on in shame.

יֵרְדוּ שְׁאוֹל חַיִּים — *Let them descend to the Lower World, alive.*

Let them die suddenly, without any previous warning. Let them not be sick before they depart; rather allow them to be robust and *alive* when they are abruptly swallowed up (*Radak*).

[This punishment fit Achitophel's crime perfectly, for the most painful aspect of his treachery was not the actual rebellion but the traumatic shock which David suffered at this sudden betrayal by his trusted companion.]

כִּי רָעוֹת בִּמְגוּרָם בְּקִרְבָּם — *For evil is in their dwelling and within them.*

This translation follows *Rashi* and *Targum*. However, *Radak* and *Ibn Ezra* render בִּמְגוּרָם as *their place of assembly*, to signify: The evil plots which are within them (against David) are revealed when they all gather in their place of assembly in Jerusalem.

17. אֲנִי אֶל אֱלֹהִים אֶקְרָא — *As for me, upon God shall I call.*

When danger and suffering threaten me, I am prepared to accept the affliction graciously as just punishment for my sins. I call upon אֱלֹהִים, *the Divine Attribute of Strict Justice*, declaring that I recognize the equity of His verdict against me (*Tehillos Hashem*).

וַה' יוֹשִׁיעֵנִי — *And HASHEM will save me.*

This recognition of God's perfect justice is in itself a great merit, by virtue of which God softens the harsh sentence against me and treats me with

Meiri and Rabbi Chaim of Volozhin in *Ruach Chaim* resolve this problem with the perception that 'one letter' is no trifle, for every letter contains the entirety of the Torah, as each part of God's wisdom is a reflection of and a link to the whole body of sacred knowledge. However, 'one letter' has significance only if it is learned from a truly God-fearing man whose teachings are infused with the spirit of the entire Torah.

Achitophel had no fear of God. His lessons, despite their logic and intellectual appeal, were truly hollow, profane, and secular. The *Tanna* chooses his words with utmost care. From Achitophel, David learned שְׁנֵי דְבָרִים *two ideas*, rather than genuine Torah teachings; the word בִּלְבַד, *only*, implies that these teachings stood alone, totally divorced from the entire body of Torah wisdom. Nevertheless, David showed tremendous gratitude even for Achitophel's limited 'secular' advice. Thus a student should certainly venerate the person who links him to the entire Torah, albeit through the vehicle of a single letter!

וְצָהֳרַיִם אָשִׂיחָה וְאֶהֱמֶה וַיִּשְׁמַע קוֹלִי:

יט   פָּדָה בְשָׁלוֹם נַפְשִׁי מִקְּרָב־לִי כִּי־בְרַבִּים

the compassionate name ה', *the Divine Attribute of Mercy* (Tehillos Hashem).

18. עֶרֶב וָבֹקֶר וְצָהֳרַיִם אָשִׂיחָה וְאֶהֱמֶה — *Evening, morning, and noon* [I] *supplicate and I moan.*

These three periods of prayer correspond to the three times of day when the position of the sun changes most noticeably: in the evening the sun vanishes, at dawn it appears, at noon it reaches its zenith (Radak).

[This serves as an inspiration. First, the sight of the ever-changing sun should teach man not to remain static and stagnant but to strive for self-improvement and self-transformation. Second, the inexorable passage of time and the change of seasons should heighten man's awareness and appreciation of his Creator, who is the Prime Force behind this constant movement, although He Himself never changes.][1]

The *Kuzari* (3:5) describes the significance of the prescribed times of prayer: The three times of daily prayer are the real produce of the day and night; they are the spiritual center of a man's time, while the other hours serve merely as the path which leads to this center. Man eagerly anticipates the approach of this time, for during prayer he resembles the spiritual, celestial beings

and removes himself from mere animal existence.

Prayer sustains the soul, just as food nourishes the body. The blessed influence of one prayer endures until the time of the next, just as the strength derived from the morning meal lasts until dinner. The further the soul is removed from the time of prayer, the more it is darkened by coming into contact with the mundane world.

The great Kabbalist, *Rabbi Menachem Azarya of Pano* makes a calculation that relates David's own prayers to his role as the spiritual heir of Adam [see *Overview*]: *Adam lived to be 930 years of age* (Genesis 5:5). After his sin, he dedicated his life to repentance, engaging in prayer at the three designated times, עֶרֶב וָבֹקֶר וְצָהֳרַיִם *evening, morning, and noon.* These three words have the numerical value of 930. He also engaged in *fasting,* תַּעֲנִית which also has the numerical value of 930.

19. פָּדָה בְשָׁלוֹם נַפְשִׁי — *He redeemed my soul in* [lit. *with*] *peace.*

In the merit of my incessant daily prayer (v. 18), HASHEM redeemed me from Absalom long before the decisive encounter on the battlefield. While peace still reigned, before the hostilities

---

1. From this verse, the Rabbis learn that a person should not pray more than three times a day. The Emperor Antoninus once asked Rabbi Judah the Prince, 'May one pray continually?'

'No', the Rabbi replied, 'for one who acts in this manner will come to treat God's presence with levity.' The Emperor refused to accept this answer [convinced that more frequent prayer was preferable].

The next day, the holy Rabbi arose early and stood before the monarch shouting, 'Hail Caesar!' After a brief interval he approached again, proclaiming, 'A salute to the Emperor!' Next he declared, 'Peace to you, O king!'

The Emperor was very annoyed because these constant salutations seemed ludicrous. He said, 'Rabbi, you are disgracing the royal name!'

Rabbi Judah replied, 'Listen to your own words! You are merely a mortal king of flesh and blood and yet you feel that constant praise to your name is a mockery, rather than an honor. To an even greater extent would constant prayer be a ridiculous show before the Master of the Universe!' (Tanchuma, Mikeitz 9).

> [18] *Evening, morning, and noon I supplicate*
> *and moan — and He hears my voice.*
> [19] *He redeemed my soul in peace from battles*
> *drawing near me,*
> *for the sake of masses who were with me.*

actually began, God had already prepared my victory and salvation (*Alshich*).

Tehillos Hashem suggests that the Psalmist is referring to David's last blessing to Absalom, which proved to be a fatal curse. The *Talmud (Berachos* 64a) states: He who takes leave of his friend should wish him לֵךְ לְשָׁלוֹם, *Go on to peace'* [which implies that he has a long life of accomplishment still ahead of him] and not לֵךְ בְּשָׁלוֹם, *Go with peace'* [which implies that he has already acquired peace and fulfillment and therefore no longer needs to continue his life]. This lesson may be learned from David who said to Absalom, לֵךְ בְּשָׁלוֹם, *go with peace'* (II Samuel 15:9), and Absalom was killed.'

When David bid Absalom farewell, he had no idea of his son's plotplot. David innocently believed that Absalom's purpose in going to Hebron was to offer his annual Nazirite sacrifice to God (II *Samuel* 15:7-8). In truth, Absalom went to Hebron in order to rally his conspirators and begin his revolt against his father. Although David was caught unprepared, God was not! God put into David's mouth the fatal words לֵךְ בְּשָׁלוֹם *Go with peace*, which sealed Absalom's doom. Therefore, David gives thanks here, *He redeemed my soul* [by causing me to say, 'Go בְּשָׁלוֹם] *with peace.'*

מִקְּרָב לִי — *From battles drawing near me.*

The word קְרָב means *battle* (*Radak*). [It also means *close*, *near*, implying fighting at close range in hand-to-hand combat.] God prevented such a fierce battle from *drawing near* to harm me, (*Ibn Ezra*) and redeemed me even before the battle began (*Alshich*).

כִּי בְרַבִּים הָיוּ עִמָּדִי — *For the sake of masses who were with me.*

This translation follows *Rashi*, who explains that David attributes his ultimate victory to the prayers of the masses who petitioned God on his behalf.

[In truth, the *masses* of Israel and their leaders seemed to support Absalom. Nevertheless, the Rabbis note (*Yerushalmi, Sotah* 1:8), that the followers of Absalom grew disillusioned with their leader's arrogance and lack of sympathy. They secretly began to sympathize with David, praying, 'May we fall into the hands of David and not into ours, because if we fall into David's, he will surely have mercy on us, but if he falls into our hands, we will not (be allowed to) show him any mercy!

Perhaps this explains the usage of the word בְּרַבִּים (literally, *within the masses*), rather than simply רַבִּים, *the masses*, because ostensibly the masses were *not* with David. However, 'within them', i.e., deep in their hearts, they prayed secretly for David.]

Our translation, which follows *Rashi*, is supported by *Berachos* 8a, which derives from here that the prayers of the masses are never rejected by God.

Radak, however, was troubled by the fact that the masses were overtly hostile to David, differs with *Rashi* and translates, *from the masses who were against me.*

Midrash Shocher Tov, following the

כ הָיוּ עִמָּדִי: יִשְׁמַע | אֵל | וְיַעֲנֵם וְיֹשֵׁב קֶדֶם
סֶלָה אֲשֶׁר אֵין חֲלִיפוֹת לָמוֹ וְלֹא יָרְאוּ
כא אֱלֹהִים: שָׁלַח יָדָיו בִּשְׁלֹמָיו חִלֵּל בְּרִיתוֹ:
כב חָלְקוּ | מַחְמָאֹת פִּיו וְקְרָב־לִבּוֹ רַכּוּ
כג דְבָרָיו מִשֶּׁמֶן וְהֵמָּה פְּתִחוֹת: הַשְׁלֵךְ עַל־

---

translation of *Rashi*, interprets this verse in a mystical vein, as an allusion to the never-ending battle of daily life. When a person sins, he creates evil forces which literally saturate the atmosphere around him. These detrimental forces seek to harm the sinner who created them, yet God, in His mercy, provides salvation. Every good deed which man performs brings even greater 'masses of angels', i.e., good influences and positive forces, into the world; they overwhelm the evil and *redeem the soul with peace.*

20. יִשְׁמַע אֵל וְיַעֲנֵם — *May God hear and answer them.*

[This plea is a direct continuation of the preceding verse.] According to *Rashi* this verse means: May God hear the prayers of the masses who sympathize with me and answer them. However, *Radak*, who understands the previous verse to mean that the masses were against David, relates וְיַעֲנֵם to עִנּוּי, *suffering*, rather than to עָנָה , *answering*, translating: May God hear me and cause them [the masses] to suffer.

וְיֹשֵׁב קֶדֶם סֶלָה — *He who is enthroned from days of old, Selah.*

Your existence, O God, preceded that of all Your creations, for You are enthroned from the dawn of the world. Since, Your strength undoubtedly surpasses that of any creature, You have the power to humble the wicked (*Radak*).

Targum translates *Selah* as *forever;* thus the word serves to emphasize God's eternal existence [see 3:3].

אֲשֶׁר אֵין חֲלִיפוֹת לָמוֹ — *Against those who ignore their own demise* [lit. *transfer.*]

These are the wicked, who deem themselves immortal and never consider the day of death, when they will be 'transferred' from the living to the dead (*Rashi*).

Neither do they fear that their good fortune may be 'transferred' to bad (*Ibn Ezra*).

Therefore, they stubbornly refuse to repent and 'transform' their ways (*Sforno*).

Radak, however, interprets these words as a continuation of the description of God, *Who is enthroned from days of old.* It is He Who *ignores* the specter of *demise* or *transformation.*

וְלֹא יָרְאוּ אֱלֹהִים — *And fear not God.*

Since good fortune persistently smiles upon these wicked men, they have no fear of אֱלֹהִים, *the Enforcer of Strict Justice.*

21. שָׁלַח יָדָיו בִּשְׁלֹמָיו — *He stretched out* [lit. *sent forth*] *his hands against his peaceful ones.*

This refers to Achitophel, for he attempted to harm David who trusted him implicitly and who desired to live in peace and harmony with him (*Rashi*; *Radak*).

[The term שְׁלֹמָיו fits David perfectly, because he was the quintessence of peace. The *Midrash* (*Bamidbar Rabbah* 11:7) states that the blessing, *And may He give you peace* (*Numbers* 6:26) refers to the kingship of the House of David, which is the epitome of peace.]

LV
20-23

²⁰ May God hear and answer them —
He Who is enthroned from days of old, Selah —
against those who ignore their own demise
and fear not God.
²¹ He stretched out his hands against His peaceful ones,
he profaned his covenant.
²² Smoother than butter were the words of his mouth,
but his heart was at war;
his words were softer than oil,
yet they were curses.
²³ Cast upon HASHEM your burden

חִלֵּל בְּרִיתוֹ — He profaned his covenant.
Achitophel contemptuously broke his pact of friendship with David (Radak).

22. חָלְקוּ מַחֲמָאֹת פִּיו — Smoother than butter were the words of his mouth.
David now contemplates the polished phrases of Achitophel and realizes, in retrospect, that the convincing words of this treacherous counselor were no more than deceitful 'smooth talk' designed to cause David to relax his guard (Radak).

וּקְרָב לִבּוֹ — But his heart was at war [lit. battle].
When Achitophel finally revealed his battle-plan to pursue David immediately with 12,000 men and to capture the weak and exhausted king, his logical, convincing strategy seemed flawless, an operation as 'smooth as butter.' It was universally acclaimed: And the plan found favor in the eyes of Absalom and in the eyes of all the Elders of Israel (II Samuel 17:4).
When David saw that everyone was pleased with Achitophel's strategy, he was terrified. But the Holy One, Blessed be He, said to him, 'Fear not, for I am with you!' (Midrash Shocher Tov).
Words of peace flowed smoothly from his lips, but his heart planned a war (Radak).

רַכּוּ דְבָרָיו מִשָּׁמֶן — His words were softer than oil.
[Butter generally smoothes over the outer surface, whereas oil is used to penetrate into the pores of the skin, to saturate and thoroughly soften it. Achitophel hoped that his reassuring words would be not only smoother than butter, but also softer than oil. Achitophel hoped to penetrate and to soften David's heart so that later he could stab it with a dagger.]

וְהֵמָּה פְתִחוֹת — Yet they were curses.
The translation follows Rashi. However, Targum, Menachem, and Ibn Ezra render this as a sharpened, lethal dagger called פְּתִיחוֹת [literally, open ones] because it is open, unsheathed, and prepared for the kill.

23. הַשְׁלֵךְ עַל ה׳ יְהָבְךָ — Cast upon HASHEM your burden.
Sforno and Alshich explain that whenever David began to suspect that a conspiracy was forming against him, Achitophel would attempt to drive away his misgivings with 'smooth words' of faith. 'Dismiss every fear from your mind;' he would say, 'cast your burden of anxiety upon HASHEM, who will surely protect you.'
Although this credo is very true, Achitophel did not himself believe it; he

[701]   Tehillim

כד יְהֹוָה| יְהָבְךָ וְהוּא יְכַלְכְּלֶךָ לֹא־יִתֵּן
כד לְעוֹלָם מוֹט לַצַּדִּיק: וְאַתָּה אֱלֹהִים|
תּוֹרִדֵם לִבְאֵר שַׁחַת אַנְשֵׁי דָמִים וּמִרְמָה
לֹא־יֶחֱצוּ יְמֵיהֶם וַאֲנִי אֶבְטַח־בָּךְ:

offered this advice only to deceive the
king *(Norah Tehillos).*

According to *Rashi,* the Holy Spirit is
speaking to David at the conclusion of
this doleful and depressing Psalm,
dedicated to David's disillusionment
with man. The hopeful message is clear:
'Even if every man on earth betrays
you, you can always place your trust in
God!'.

Radak adds that David now transmits
this encouraging message to all other
pious men.

Midrash Shocher Tov observes:
When a mortal who has a patron goes to
him for the first time, the patron
receives him; the second time, he also
receives him; the third time, he does not
welcome him personally; and the fourth
time, he cannot spare a moment for him.
Not so the Holy One, Blessed be He;
every time you impose yourself upon
Him, He receives you personally.
Hence, *Cast upon HASHEM your
burden and He will sustain you.*[1]

וְהוּא יְכַלְכְּלֶךָ — *And he will sustain you.*

[The word כַּלְכָּלָה is a repetitious form
of כֹּל, *everything.* It implies that not
only will God supply פַּרְנָסָה, *livelihood,*
i.e., the basic requirements of life, but
He will also generously provide
everything a person needs.]

לֹא יִתֵּן לְעוֹלָם מוֹט לַצַּדִּיק — *He will never
allow faltering of the righteous.*

[Not only does God sustain the body,
He also provides for the soul. Even
when the righteous man is pursued and
harassed, God instills within him the
spiritual fortitude to overcome every
obstacle and to retain his faith.

Thus, David consoles his wounded
soul: 'Although I have been bitterly disappointed by men, I am confident that
God will never disappoint me.']

24. וְאַתָּה אֱלֹהִים תּוֹרִדֵם לִבְאֵר שַׁחַת —
*But You, O God, shall lower them into
the well of destruction.*

[Whereas God invites the righteous
to draw near to Him and to cast their
burdens upon Him, he utterly despises
the wicked and casts them away to the

1. The *Dubno Maggid* illustrates our verse with a parable: A weary tramp was walking on the
road, carrying his heavy pack. A wagon driver passed by and offered him a lift, which was
eagerly accepted. After traveling a while, the wagon driver noticed that his passenger still kept
his heavy load on his shoulders, even though there was plenty of empty space in the wagon.
Upon the driver's inquiry, the considerate tramp explained, 'I appreciate your kindness, but
really it's enough that you are carrying me on your wagon; should I bother you to carry my
load as well?'

'Fool', exclaimed the driver, 'don't you realize that if I am carrying you, I am also carrying
your load?'

So, too, many people spend their entire lives bent under the tremendous burden of providing themselves with a livelihood. Of course, they believe in God, but they are satisfied with
His generosity in providing life and health. How can they bother Him to sustain them finan-
cially as well?

They fail to realize that the Creator who maintains the life of His creatures also provides
their livelihood. Man's sole responsibility is to remember that he himself does not 'make a living' he merely 'takes a living' from God. Therefore, *Cast upon HASHEM your burden and He
will sustain you.*

> *and He will sustain you,*
> *He will never allow*
> *the faltering of the righteous.*
> ²⁴ *But You, O God, shall lower them*
> *into the well of destruction,*
> *men of bloodshed and deceit shall not live out*
> *half their days;*
> *but as for me, I will trust in You.*

place furthest removed from His Presence, the *well of destruction* i.e., Gehinnom.]

Hirsch notes that David does not call it בּוֹר שַׁחַת, *the pit of destruction*, but בְּאֵר שַׁחַת, *the well of destruction*. A pit is a receptacle which passively collects water from an outside source, it symbolizes the followers who only take orders. A well is a source from which waters spring, signifying the leader who initiates schemes and strategies. Achitophel and Doeg were leaders, initiators of evil, rather than mere imitators. Each one resembled a well, constantly spewing forth malice and hate! Eventually, they were both undone by their own devices of destruction.

אַנְשֵׁי דָמִים וּמִרְמָה — *Men of bloodshed and deceit.*

[These men were intent on shedding innocent blood and did not hesitate to use devious means to achieve their ends.]

לֹא יֶחֱצוּ יְמֵיהֶם — [*They*] *shall not live out half their days.*

Rabbi Yochanan said that Doeg and Achitophel never met each other, Doeg lived during the reign of Saul [when David was in his late twenties

(*Maharsha*)] and Achitophel lived during the reign of David.

[David lived to the age of seventy, and he reigned forty years. Absalom and Achitophel rebelled when David was sixty-five.]

These men did not live out even half of a lifetime [a normal lifespan is seventy years, see 90:10] Doeg lived to be no more than thirty-four years old, and Achitophel lived to be no more than thirty-three. [This demonstrates God's kindness to David, for had his adversaries been contemporaries, David could not have survived their combined onslaught (*Sanhedrin* 106b; *Maharsha*).]

וַאֲנִי אֶבְטַח בָּךְ — *But as for me, I will trust in You.*

I trust that You will save me from my enemies (*Sforno*).

Furthermore, I am confident that just as You destroyed the bodies of my enemies in this world, You will consume their souls in the lower world of Gehinnom, *the well of destruction* (*Radak*).

And, although each is doomed to live less than half of a lifetime, I am confident that You will fulfill the number of *my days*, (*Ibn Ezra*) [indeed, David lived a full seventy years] and establish my kingdom firmly for all time.

This volume is part of
THE ARTSCROLL SERIES®
an ongoing project of
translations, commentaries and expositions
on Scripture, Mishnah, Talmud, Halachah,
liturgy, history and the classic Rabbinic writings;
and biographies, and thought.

For a brochure of current publications
visit your local Hebrew bookseller
or contact the publisher:

Mesorah Publications, ltd

4401 Second Avenue
Brooklyn, New York 11232
(718) 921-9000